$24.95

DEATH AND IDENTITY

Third Edition

DEATH AND IDENTITY

Third Edition

Edited by

Robert Fulton, PhD
and
Robert Bendiksen, PhD

The Charles Press, Publishers
Philadelphia

The Charles Press, Publishers
Post Office Box 15715
Philadelphia, PA 19103

Library of Congress Cataloging-in-Publication Data

Death and identity / edited by Robert Fulton and Robert Bendiksen. – 3rd ed.
p. cm.
Includes bibliographical references and index.
ISBN 0-914783-63-7
1. Death – Psychological aspects. 2. Bereavement – Psychological aspects. 3. Grief. I. Fulton, Robert Lester. II. Bendiksen, Robert.
BF789.D4F8 1993
155.9'37– dc20 93-26364
CIP

Printed in the United States of America

ISBN 0-914783-63-7

Copyright Acknowledgments

Chapter 1: "Death and Contemporary Society," by Robert Fulton and Greg Owen. From *Omega* 18(4), pp. 379-395. Copyright ©1987 by Baywood Publishing, Inc. Reprinted with permission.

Chapter 2: "Conceptual Approaches to the Study of Death," by Kathy Charmaz. From *The Social Reality of Death: Death in Contemporary America,* pp. 16-66. Copyright ©1980 by Addison-Wesley Publishing Company, Inc. Reproduced with permission of McGraw-Hill, Inc.

Chapter 3: "Death in the Western World," by Talcott Parsons. From *Encyclopedia of Bioethics* (Warren T. Reich, Editor in Chief), Vol. 1, pp. 255-261. Copyright ©1978 by Georgetown University. Revised version used by permission of The Free Press, a division of Macmillan, Inc.

Chapter 5: "The Mourning of Children," by John Bowlby. From *Attachment and Loss, Vol. III: Loss, Sadness and Depression*, by John Bowlby. Copyright ©1980 by The Tavistock Institute of Human Relations. Reprinted by permission of Basic Books, a division of HarperCollins Publishers.

Chapter 6: "Grief and Mourning," by John S. Stephenson. Reprinted with the permission of The Free Press, a division of Macmillan, Inc., from *Death, Grief and Mourning: Individual and Social Realities*, by John S. Stephenson. Copyright ©1985 by John S. Stephenson.

Chapter 7: "Is Grief Universal? Cultural Variations in the Emotional Reaction to Loss," by Wolfgang Stroebe and Margaret Stroebe. From *Bereavement and Health: The Psychological and Physical Consequences of Partner Loss,* Chap. 3, pp. 26-55. Copyright ©1980 by Cambridge University Press. Reprinted with permission.

Chapter 8: "Death at a Distance: A Study of Family Surviviors," by Greg Owen, Robert Fulton and Eric Markusen. From *Omega* 13(3), pp. 191-225. Copyright ©1982 by Baywood Publishing, Inc. Reprinted with permission.

Chapter 9: "Religion and Bereavement: A Conceptual Framework," by Robert Wuthnow, Kevin Christiano and John Kuzlowski. From *Journal for the Scientific Study of Religion* 19(4), pp. 408-422. Copyright ©1980 by The Scientific Study of Religion, Inc. Reprinted with permission.

Chapter 10: "Business Temporal Norms and Bereavement Behavior," by Lois Pratt. From *American Sociological Review* 46, pp. 317-333. Copyright ©1981 by the American Sociological Association. Reprinted with permisssion.

Chapter 11: "The Funeral in Contemporary Society," by Robert Fulton. From *Dying: Facing the Facts*, Second Edition (Hannelore Wass, Felix M. Berardo and Robert Neimeyer, eds.), pp. 257-277. Copyright ©1988 by Hemisphere Publishing Corporation. Reproduced with permission. All rights reserved.

Chapter 13: "Death-Related Issues in Biomedicine: Euthanasia and AIDS," by Robert H. Blank. From *Life, Death and Public Policy,* by Robert H. Blank. Copyright ©1988 by Northern Illinois University Press. Reprinted with permission.

Chapter 14: "The Hospice in the Context of an Aging Society," by Judith A. Levy. From *Journal of Aging Studies* 3(4), pp. 385-399. Copyright ©1989 by JAI Press, Inc., Greenwich, CT. Reprinted with permission.

Chapter 15: "AIDS: A Sociological Response," by Robert Fulton and Greg Owen. From *AIDS: Principles, Practices and Politics* (Inge B. Corless and Mary Pittman-Lindeman, eds.), pp. 237-249. Copyright ©1988 by Hemisphere Publishing Corporation. Reprinted with permission.

Chapter 16: "Assumptions and Principles Underlying Standards for Care of the Terminally Ill," by the International Work Group on Death, Dying and Bereavement. From *American Journal of Nursing* 79, pp. 296-297. Copyright ©1979 by The American Journal of Nursing Company. Used with permission. All rights reserved.

"Assumptions and Principles of Spiritual Care," by the International Work Group on Death, Dying and Bereavement. From *Death Studies* 14, pp. 75-81. Copyright ©1990 by Hemisphere Publishing Corporation. Reprinted with permission. All rights reserved.

"Assumptions and Principles Regarding Bereavement," by the International Work Group on Death, Dying and Bereavement. Reprinted with permission.

"Assumptions and Principles Concerning Care for Persons Affected by HIV Disease," by the International Work Group on Death, Dying and Bereavement. From *AIDS and Public Policy Journal* 7(1), pp. 28-31, 1992. Reprinted with permission.

Editors

Robert Fulton, PhD
Professor of Sociology
Director of the Center for
Death Education and Research
University of Minnesota
Minneapolis, Minnesota

Robert Bendiksen, PhD
Professor of Sociology
University of Wisconsin-LaCrosse
LaCrosse, Wisconsin

Contributors

Robert Bendiksen, PhD
Professor of Sociology
University of Wisconsin-LaCrosse
LaCrosse, Wisconsin

Robert H. Blank, PhD
Professor of Political Science
University of Canterbury
Christchurch, New Zealand

John Bowlby, MD
Tavistock Clinic and Institute of Human Relations
London, England

Kathy Charmaz, PhD
Professor of Sociology
Sonoma State University
Rohnert Park, California

Kevin Christiano, PhD
Associate Professor of Sociology
University of Notre Dame
Notre Dame, Indiana

Robert Fulton, PhD
Professor of Sociology
Director of the Center for Death Education and Research
University of Minnesota
Minneapolis, Minnesota

Bernard J. Hammes, PhD
Clinical Ethicist
Director of Medical Humanities
Gundersen Medical Foundation, Ltd.
LaCrosse, Wisconsin

John Kuzloski, PhD
Research Scientist
Jackson, Wyoming

Judith A. Levy, PhD
Associate Professor of Human Resources Management
University of Illinois
School of Public Health
Chicago, Illinois

Eric Markusen, PhD
Professor of Sociology
Southwest State University
Marshall, Minnesota

John D. Morgan, PhD
Secretariat, International Work Group on Death, Dying and Bereavement
London, Ontario, Canada

Greg Owen, PhD
Research Scientist
Amherst H. Wilder Foundation
St. Paul, Minnesota

Talcott Parsons, PhD
Former Professor of Sociology
Harvard University
Cambridge, Massachusetts

Lois Pratt, PhD
Professor of Sociology
Jersey City State College
Jersey City, New Jersey

John S. Stephenson, PhD
Family Therapist
Bowdoinham, Maine

Margaret S. Stroebe, PhD
Research Associate in Psychology
University of Tubingen
Tubingen, Germany

Wolfgang Stroebe, PhD
Professor of Psychology
University of Tubingen
Tubingen, Germany

Robert Wuthnow, PhD
Professor of Sociology
Princeton University
Princeton, New Jersey

Contents

Preface

It has been almost three decades since the publication of the first edition of *Death and Identity* and more than fifteen years since the appearance of the second, revised edition. Over this period of time many changes have occurred in the United States concerning the issues associated with human death, as well as in our understanding of and response to those issues. In 1965 the first edition presented the relevant and systematic research on death-related matters that were available at that time from the social and medical sciences. Its purpose was to provide a basis for a better understanding of the impact of death on our collective as well as individual lives. The second, revised edition published in 1976 built on that foundation. It identified and recorded the significant advances in our knowledge of the social and psychological dimensions of loss through death that had taken place over the intervening years. It also gave evidence to the fact that a growing number of lay as well as professional people were beginning to address the public questions evoked by such loss.

The third edition of *Death and Identity*, while it follows the same format as its predecessors, breaks somewhat with the past in that it introduces the reader to the sociological perspective while incorporating a multidisciplinary approach. In the two earlier editions, the book highlighted the work of scholars and researchers from a spectrum of disciplines: psychiatry, anthropology, psychology, history, the humanities and sociology. With this edition, the reader is initially presented with the theoretical views and introduced to the analytical tools and methodological techniques of sociology as they have been applied to death-related phenomena. The reasons for doing so are threefold: first, to bring to the reader's attention the many and varied contributions that sociology has made toward the understanding of the place of death in social life; second, to bring together important contributions from the related social and behavioral sciences that inform the sociological study of death; and third, to offer a pair of "sociological glasses," as it were, through which the reader may view—and, one hopes, comprehend better—the issues and problems that death engenders in modern society. To help realize these goals and locate present social and behavioral science efforts within a historical framework, we have included the chapter, "The Sociology of Death: A Historical Overview: 1875-1985."

The interest of sociologists in death is coextensive with the history of sociology itself. European sociologists of the 19th century, such as Spencer, Masaryk and Durkheim, as well as the American sociologists Small, Vincent, Ross and Sumner demonstrated a variety of death-related concerns in their writings. This attention continued among American sociologists—as shown in the work of Eliot, Waller, Becker, Hill, Burgess and Locke—until interrupted by World War II. Interest was resumed in the late 1950s when a new generation of sociologists was drawn to the subject. Subsequently during the past three decades sociologists have inquired into such topics as attitudes and responses toward death, the process of dying, the dimensions of grief, funeral practices and mourning rites, morbidity and mortality rates and the meaning and impact of death upon occupations and professions that are attendant upon the dying or the dead.

Sociologists, of course, have long been in the forefront of the study of suicide, as evidenced by the pioneering studies of Masaryk and Durkheim, while sociologists such as Marx, Gumplowitz, Bagehot and more recently Elliot, have discussed the role of the state in connection with war and mortality. Unfortunately, for historical reasons, these different efforts have not been theoretically connected or integrated within the discipline and it is only now with the work of Charmaz and others that these separate issues are being brought together under a unified "sociology of death."

Encouragingly, the subfield of sociology is becoming more clearly defined in area and substance. Progress is seen in the work of Pratt, for example, whose contribution to the book is a systematic analysis of the manner in which government agencies and business organizations place time restrictions on the mourning practices of their employees following a bereavement. The emergence of a distinct "sociology of death" is also seen in the research that has been recently conducted concerning the role of government agencies and health-care institutions in the face of the burgeoning AIDS epidemic.

Since the mid-1970s, the field of death studies has undergone consolidation in the integration of its subject matter as well as in its organizational efforts to promote public awareness and the public good. The past fifteen years have seen, for example, the publication of *Death Studies* and *Illness, Crises and Loss* and the emergence of bereavement counseling programs, support groups and grief centers that address specific types of loss—suicide, homicide, accidental death, catastrophic illness, neonatal death and, more recently, AIDS. Such therapeutically oriented programs are now firmly established in hospitals, schools and churches as well as in clinics and private practices throughout the country. They take their place alongside earlier programs such as Widow-to-Widow, The Society of Compassionate Friends, SIDS and Parents without Partners that emerged out of the first wave of interest in death and loss that crested with the publication of Elisabeth Kübler-Ross' book *On Death and Dying* in 1969.

There are now two professional organizations—the Association for Death Education and Counseling (ADEC) and the International Work Group on Death, Dying and Bereavement (IWG)—that address the varied concerns and interests of their members. These organizations provide broad platforms for the continued examination of, and intervention into, different subject areas. The International Work Group, for instance, has published four position papers on the topics of terminal care, bereavement, spiritual care and AIDS. The social policy assumptions and principles enunciated in these documents have received serious attention within health-care institutions. The Association for Death Education and Research, moreover, has been an important forum for both stimulating and disseminating new ideas and insights among its burgeoning membership.

In addition, for more than a decade, Dr. Balfore Mount of the Royal Victoria Hospital in Montreal has sponsored a conference on dying and bereavement that has increasingly attracted an international audience of health-care professionals as the principles and practices of hospice care are disseminated throughout the world. Dr. Jack Morgan of King's College in Ontario also has held an annual international symposium on death-related topics that has generated strong professional support for death education since the early 1980s.

Changes in the issues surrounding death have also been characteristic of the years since the publication of the second edition of *Death and Identity.* The introduction of the hospice philosophy of terminal care and its acceptance by a broad cross-section of medical caregivers and volunteers in the United States—indeed, throughout the world—is one such example; the debate over American funeral practices that took place during the 1970s is another. Inspired principally by Jessica Mitford's book, *The American Way of Death*, published in 1963, an appreciable sector of the American public were aroused to ire by the question of the relevance of the traditional funeral in American society and the controversy over the questionable business practices of funeral directors. The ensuing debate culminated in hearings before a committee of the U.S. Senate and was ostensibly settled when the Federal Trade Commission issued new and more stringent guidelines for funeral practitioners. During this same time period, the American funeral gave way to a variety of changes including the significantly increased adoption of cremation throughout the country as a mode of human disposition.

Today, new challenges confront American society. The discussion of death has taken a compelling turn as the AIDS epidemic and the emerging debate over euthanasia increasingly command the attention of the public. In keeping with these changes and in response to the different problems they present, Hammes, a clinical ethicist, and Bendiksen, a sociological practitioner, have written the chapter "Prolonging Life—Choosing Death: A Clinical Perspective in Medical/Ethical Decision-Making" which serves as an introduction to the section that deals with the multifaceted issues of euthanasia and palliative care in end-stage disease.

The material in this anthology is arranged in four parts: (1) Perspectives on Death; (2) Grief and the Process of Mourning; (3) Bereavement and the Sociological Response to Death; and (4) Public Policies and Private Decisions: Clinical Perspectives on Death and Dying. Introductions written by the editors serve to put into perspective each section of the book as well as to explicate the different contributions.

A collection of this sort will inevitably be incomplete. It would require a volume several times as large to include all of the relevant material currently available. We believe, however, that the chapters selected will reflect the theoretical perspectives and research interests of scholars presently working in the field. There is, however, one important exception. Limitations of space oblige us to omit the discussion of suicide. In contrast to the other substantive areas that are presented in the compendium, suicide has been studied more thoroughly by social scientists than has any other death-related subject and as a result, an extensive literature is extant.

As of this writing, the "cold war" between the Soviet Union and the United States has been declared officially over and the prospect of international conflict, particularly conflict involving nuclear weapons, is as remote as at any time since the world entered the atomic age. While no one chapter of the text specifically addresses the phenomenon of war, war and its consequences always have been important subjects for social science discussion. Its body of literature is thus substantial, but its development has been separate from that of the "sociology of death." Nevertheless, the effect of war on our general attitudes toward death or on our individual conceptions of "selfhood," are important issues to consider, especially as they concern the "baby-boom" generation that grew up under the threat of a nuclear holocaust. In an initial effort to narrow the gap between "war" literature and "death" literature, the issue of war is addressed in several chapters of the book.

The contributions to this compendium—the theoretical discussions as well as the research reports—share the common goal of illuminating the problems that death poses to both society and the individual. We will have realized our purpose if, through bringing these different materials together, the reader arrives at a greater understanding of the unique yet ubiquitous place that death occupies in human life. It is also our hope in preparing this latest edition of *Death and Identity* that we will have served to stimulate the continued study of this ever-challenging subject by scholars and practitioners alike.

We wish to thank the contributors to this volume and their publishers for permission to republish their essays. We also thank Lauren Meltzer, Editor-in-Chief of The Charles Press, for her good counsel and editorial guidance in bringing this book to completion. Mary Drew, Mary Clements and Annique Gilbert provided bibliographic and clerical assistance and their help is gratefully acknowledged. Finally, Marlie Bendiksen and Carlie Goodrich are remembered for the staunch allies and friends that they are, and for their imperturbable patience and the thoughful suggestions they made during the preparation of the book.

Robert Fulton
Robert Bendiksen

I

Perspectives on Death

Introduction

Sixty-thousand years ago, as the archaeological evidence from the gravesite at Shanidar, Iraq demonstrates, our primordial ancestors buried their dead with ceremony. Moreover, among the petrified human remains items of utility were found—such as weapons and combs—indicating that the belief in a continued existence after death (the belief in immortality), is of ancient origin.

Our understanding of modern social life is deepened by the knowledge that, since the time of Shanidar, humankind has defied the finality of mortal death. Human beings, it has long been believed, do not "die"; they merely go somewhere else. Even when a body is destroyed or corrupted, the prehistoric and widely held conviction has been that the "soul" or "spirit" lives on. If we accept the evidence that Shanidar offers, we are compelled to recognize that life after death is one of humanity's oldest beliefs—indeed one of the most significant and influential beliefs in existence.

How did we come to believe in immortality—an idea that is virtually universal and one that predates the theologies of all known religions by thousands of years? One can only speculate, but evidence suggesting that life persists after death exists everywhere. We have only to observe the regular phases of the moon or the cyclical progression of the seasons to appreciate the truth of this observation. To look at a tree in the depth of winter when it is totally bereft of leaves, and to know that it will bloom again in the spring—and to witness that blooming—is to open oneself to the prospect that all of life is a cycle—an eternal return.

In all likelihood, metamorphosis is another reason why humankind has embraced the idea of immortality. That a caterpillar weaves a cocoon from which it will later emerge as a butterfly, not only challenges the idea of the finality of death, but also, metaphorically, introduces the analogous prospect of transcendent transformation. Such intimations of immortality were also believed to be seen by our forebears in the snake's annual shedding of its skin and the deer's yearly loss and regrowth of its antlers.

But we would suggest that there are other more compelling, more human, reasons why men and women came to believe that mortal death is not the end of human existence. One primary reason, we propose, is the fact that all human beings have the capacity to dream. A singular attribute of dreaming is that when one dreams of an individual who has died, the deceased person can appear in the dream—alive and, importantly, whole. An individual, for example, who may have witnessed the physical annihilation of a deceased person can, in a subsequent dream, envision that person not only as alive, but also as once more intact. This psychological manifestation is analogous to the "phantom-limb phenomenon," first described by psychologist Marianne Zimmel, in which a person who has had a finger or limb amputated experiences the physical sensations of still having the missing member. The particular significance of dreaming that the dead are alive and whole cannot be underestimated; it serves not only to contradict perceived reality, but it also provides a persuasive argument for the existence of an "unperceived" reality. Belief in the "living" dead—a dead with whom one can communicate or a dead that desires contact with the living—becomes, as a result, psychologically possible.

There are also other psychological reasons, such as delusions and hallucinations, that have contributed to the rejection of the idea of death's finality. In the first instance, the delusional person believes—despite all tangible evidence to the contrary—that a dead person is alive, while in the second instance the dead are believed to be seen, heard, or their presence sensed. Particularly widows and parents of a dead child have reported such experiences. Hallucinations may occur over a period of years before diminishing in frequency and intensity. A study of widows in England, for example, reported that on average, hallucinatory episodes involving their dead husbands recurred up to 10 years following the death. In a study conducted at the University of Minnesota, it was found that 10 percent of a sample of widows reported having had hallucinatory episodes. In a comparable study of widows in Japan, on the other hand, the proportion who reported such experiences was more than 70 percent. This higher figure, it is suggested, may be accounted for by the fact that the Japanese continue to practice ancestor worship and deliberately attempt to maintain contact with the dead.

Personal revelations of an afterworld, such as the contemporary popular accounts of "near-death experiences" and the reported "transcendental" experiences of psychics and mystics, have also contributed to the idea of an "upper" and "nether" world as well as contributed to the belief in immortality. Further, mind-altering drugs, such as opium, hashish, peyote and alcohol, have been used for thousands of years in religious ceremonies and other rites with the conviction that when under their influence, people could make contact with the spiritual world and that its immaterial nature would be made manifest.

Communication with the dead or with the "spirit world" without the use of drugs has also been widely claimed. History is replete with accounts of persons who have reported having contact with the human dead or with "spirits"—both benign and malevolent. What should be noted, however, is that the different psychological phenomena that have been reported are not in any direct way connected to traditional religious or spiritual beliefs, per se. For instance, the Christian belief in a supreme being who governs the universe and who possesses the power to resurrect the dead represents a tradition of thought that is separate from the personal psychological experiences reported. We would propose that the belief that there is ultimately no death—that in some way, somewhere, human existence continues—originated primarily as a result of the way the human mind fundamentally functions.

On the other hand, theologians have argued that the idea of a supreme being (and by implication, life after death) is "intuitive" to the soul of humankind. Teilhard de Chardin, the late renowned Catholic philosopher contended that humankind's moral growth, as well as humankind itself, has unfolded in an evolutionary sense. Whatever the ultimate truth may be with respect to the genesis of the belief in immortality, it is important to recognize that humankind "defied" death for psychological reasons long before the historical appearance of Moses, Buddha, Jesus or Muhammad, or other spiritual leaders who have contributed so profoundly to the religious beliefs and moral foundations of the world.

The nineteenth-century sociologist Herbert Spencer predicted that with the advance of civilization the world of the living would increasingly separate itself from the world of the dead. The belief in immortality and in the transcendental world of spirits, he argued, would be compelled to retreat before the advances of science and modern society's mastery over nature. Spencer did not believe that such ideas would be wholly abandoned; rather, he asserted that they would be set aside as a special category of knowing and separated from the knowledge of the temporal world and from that which can be empirically known.

This book addresses the different concerns that have arisen in modern society in connection with the developments, scientific advances and other significant changes that have taken place since the time of Spencer. Contemporary social practices, such as the isolation of the elderly and dying, the perfunctory disposal of the dead and the suppression of personal grief, serve to confirm his prescient observations at the same time that they have captured the attention of sociologists.

In the fourth chapter in this section, "The Sociology of Death: A Historical Overview, 1875-1985," the authors describe the efforts of European and American sociologists during the past century to understand the different attitudes that humans entertain toward death, as well the impact that death has upon their lives. The chapter is testimony to the longstanding concern that sociologists have had for the subject of death, and gives evidence as well to their continued endeavors to examine the multifaceted place that death holds in human life.

While European writers such as Spencer addressed such general questions as the changing relationship between the "world of the living" and the "world of the dead," or the general relationship of irreligiosity to such phenomena as suicide, American sociologists were more specific and pragmatic in their interests. Small and Vincent, for example, concerned themselves with the impact of death upon the family, childhood bereavement and widowhood. European sociologists, on the other hand, tended to focus their attention on the impact that death had on the social order or the role of war in relationship to the "meaning" of death itself. Prior to the Second World War, American sociologists, although they shared an overlapping interest in the subject of death with their European colleagues and were generally familiar with their writings, nevertheless employed a more empirical approach to the subject and were more likely to study death's effect on the individual or the family circle.

This chapter traces the development of the "sociology of death" following the Second World War, when a new generation of American sociologists began to respond not only to the traumatic events of the war itself, but also to the changing patterns of morbidity and mortality that were taking place in North America. For various reasons, not the least of which was the war itself, the work of European and American sociologists relative to death grew apart; it is only in the last decade that efforts have been made to restore the common bonds of interest. The intercontinental collaboration of Parkes and Weiss on widowhood and the work of Markusen and his European colleagues on nuclear war give evidence to this development at the same time that it testifies to the commitment that sociology has made to the broadening field of death studies.

Since the 1960s, American society has experienced an overall aging of its population, the geographic mobility of its elderly citizens and a profound change in who, where and by what causes people die. In addition, society has undergone what has been described as a "medicalization"; that is, the growth of an unprecedented nationwide health care system that progressively separates the elderly, the chronically and terminally ill as well as the dead from their families and the community.

These developments have engaged the interest of sociologists as have the issues that are attendant upon their emergence; for example, the psychosocial dynamics of dying, the question of the role of the contemporary funeral in American life or the propriety of public expressions of grief. Finally, the chapter outlines these and other issues that presently command the attention of sociologists at the same time that new issues such as biomedical ethics, euthanasia and AIDS have appeared to challenge their skills and insights.

Kathy Charmaz, in her chapter, "Sociological Approaches to the Study of Death," delineates three major sociological perspectives on death: symbolic-interactionism, structural-functionalism, and Marxism. Each perspective represents a coherent body of ideas that permits a particular kind of question to be asked and a specific issue to be discussed.

From the perspective of symbolic-interactionism, conceptions of death are perceived to be socially constructed. That is, the "meaning" that death has for anyone is a result of the socially inherited ideas and assumptions that have been formed over the lifetime of the society in which one lives. But the life experience, this perspective holds, is not only an individual experience; it is also a symbolic process. Social interaction is perceived to be an interpretive process that depends upon the individual's capacity for reflection. Thus, human beings are not only seen as active participants within their society, but also as being reflective and creative. While humans are heir to a long social tradition with respect to belief and behavior, symbolic-interactionism emphasizes the freedom of individuals to construct their own reality as well as to potentially reconstruct that which has been inherited. Intrinsic to the idea of freedom of the individual is the possibility of human choice, and with it, a degree of indeterminacy in social interaction. Change is therefore always an imminent possibility. But from the social-interactionist perspective, social life, by definition, implies stable social relationships; consequently routinization and habitualization are an integral part of social life as well. A symbolic dialogue is a perpetual dialogue and it is this debate between the habitual and the "new" that gives rise to the historical process out of which change is experienced. Hence Charmaz concludes, "the present gives shape to the future, but does not determine it."

The symbolic-interactionist perspective, Charmaz argues, has been useful in analyzing the conflicting definitions and attitudes that can be found in the modern hospital, particularly as they have related to the dying; and it has also demonstrated its utility, she contends, in clarifying the recent acrimonious discussion in America over funeral practices and the question of what constitutes the appropriate disposition of the dead.

Structural-functionalism offers a different level of analysis for the student of society. The question for the structural-functionalist is not how individuals perceive or experience their own dying or the death of another, but rather, what is the relationship of dying or death to society as a whole. For instance, as Charmaz points out, we have expectations as to what constitutes a timely death, given the success of public health and modern medicine to extend life-expectancy; that is, it is considered inappropriate today for someone to die before old age. This perception, however, reflecting the success of medical science, has taken precedence over the values and beliefs that traditionally have supported religious institutions concerning the time and circumstances surrounding a person's death.

Finally, from the perspective of Marxism, Charmaz raises the issue of social inequality and its implications for the quality of medical care as reflected in individual death rates. She observes, for example, that both lower-income people as well as minority males and females are systematically deprived of optimal health care and are shown to have appreciably higher death rates than their white, middle-class counterparts. Such mortality rates dramatically show the relationship between death and social class and, she argues, would call for more research. Such differential mortality rates reflect, for instance, not only the death from tuberculosis of a young minority child but also testify to the premature and disproportionate deaths during wartime of minority and working-class youth. Charmaz raises still another relevant aspect between death and social class by drawing attention to the deleterious and hazardous conditions of employment to which millions of workers are exposed daily. Again, she observes, this is another area of research that has not been adequately incorporated into the sociology of death, even though harmful substances such as asbestos and toxic chemicals have been recognized and studied since early in the century.

Fulton and Owen, in their chapter, "Death and Contemporary Society," describe how the American experience with death has changed since the beginning of this century and how these changes have in turn transformed our collective attitudes and responses toward mortality. They contrast the life and death experiences of two different age cohorts—those persons born prior to the development of the atomic bomb, who are now over age 65—and those persons who have been born since the advent of the nuclear age and who are designated as the "baby boom" generation. By drawing a portrait of these two generations, and by utilizing examples from contemporary American literature, film and the plastic arts, the authors attempt to describe not only the shift in modern attitudes toward death, but also the nature of that shift. Fulton and Owen agree with the late German historian Franz Borkenau that the shift in the general attitude toward death has been one from death "defied" (that is, the belief that life ultimately triumphs over the grave) to death "denied" (that is, death is kept at a distance or avoided). Borkenau argued that as the belief in immortality disintegrated in the secular, post-Christian era, the modern world would embrace a nihilistic philosophy that would negate the relevance of selfhood. As a consequence, an individual's death would come to have no social significance and thus death in the modern, science-oriented world, would ultimately be "defeated." While Borkenau explained this cultural change in terms of his psychoanalytically based interpretation of history, Fulton and Owen, on the other hand, argue that the basis for the observed attitudinal shift can be found in the scientific discoveries, technical inventions and demographic changes that have occurred since the beginning of the modern era.

Fulton and Owen explore the responses to death as expressed in popular culture as a way of illuminating the social and psychological developments that have served to form its contemporary definition. They argue that the advent of the nuclear bomb, for instance, has not only changed the manner in which war can be conducted but also has transformed the meaning of mortal conflict. Much of popular culture, with its violence and moral malaise, they contend, is a response to the fact that nuclear war promises to end not only an individual human life, but also an entire generation and, potentially, humankind. The prospect of nuclear war, furthermore, challenges the meaning and legitimacy of the traditional male role by threatening a cataclysm that puts women and men equally at peril. The present generation's preoccupation with violence, the use of drugs and search for vicarious death experiences, they argue, is a reflection of the existential angst generated by this calamitous prospect.

The late distinguished sociologist Talcott Parsons, in the third chapter of this section, examines the question first introduced by Spencer more than a century ago, namely, what is the meaning of death and the status of the belief in immortality in the modern world? Parsons observes that despite our familiarity with death, it is not without its problems for us, nor do the problems that death presents remain constant from generation to generation. Consequently, it is necessary, he observes, just as in Spencer's time, to redefine and reanalyze its place in human life. Parsons begins his essay by defining a human being as the synthesized combination of an "organism" and a "personality." As an organism, an individual comes into existence through bisexual reproduction and like all such higher organisms, lives for a variable length of time and dies; barring an accident or fatal illness, this is approximately one hundred years. But a human is not only a living organism; he or she is an organism who uses symbols such as language and who, through the process of socialization, develops a unique personality. The question that Parsons poses is, "does the personality die along with the organism?" He suggests that the evidence is not so clear-cut, as in the case of the organism, even though it can be observed that with aging can come the breakdown of various components of a personality or with the phenomenon of certain mental illnesses, one can speak of the "death" of a personality. Parsons points to the parallel between an individual organism and its connection to the intergenerational chain of existence and a personality which is also imbedded—in parallel fashion—in an ongoing social "matrix." In a sense, both can be said to survive death. Parsons acknowledges, however, that positivistic philosophy denies this formula for immortality and insists that with organic death comes the death of personality. In response, Parsons observes that despite this modern philosophical perspective, people—from the most primitive to the most sophisticated—have and continue to believe in the existence of an individual human "soul" or "personality."

In the western world, science has been the dominant institution that has come to challenge the world view that there exists an individual human soul. Science, Parsons points out, not only brought about a fundamental change in the meaning of death for human societies but also spearheaded the attack on the doctrine of personal salvation, based as it is on the nondemonstrable concept of an "afterlife" outside the framework of "physical time."

With the rise of modern science there emerged the philosophy of scientific materialism that holds that only the physical world is real, essentially unchanging, and hence, eternal. The death of an organism from this perspective, therefore, is seen simply as a return to the inorganic. Such a view completely negates the concept of immortality since the inorganic, by definition, is the very antithesis of life. With the general acceptance of Darwin's evolutionary theory of existence, moreover, death came to be seen as simply a biological event.

Parsons next considers the role that the philosopher Kant had in the ongoing debate regarding "physical reality" and our different conceptions of "transcendental reality," including the belief in life after death. Parsons argues that Kant relativized our conceptions of reality, thus denying the possibility of ever having ultimate, reliable knowledge of what he termed the "absolute," or God. Kant nevertheless contended that as human beings, we bring to social life the belief in immortality as well as the belief in the existence of God. These ideas, Kant conceded, cannot be rationally proved, but he argued that they are indispensable to the well-being of the individual as well as to the good order of humankind. Kant's subsequent work,

Parsons observes, consisted of his efforts to connect the physical, material level of existence with this transcendental or "telic" level. Parsons points out that Kant's skepticism about "absolute" knowing applied equally well to biology and modern science as it did to theology. Hence, there is ultimately no demonstrable knowledge of the "Ding an sich," to quote Kant's memorable phrase, in any field of scientific endeavor. Kant's skepticism, Parsons notes, opened up two possibilities for humankind regarding the question of the survival of human personality after death. One was to challenge the necessity of believing in the idea and the other was to introduce the concept of intellectual freedom. Kant's idea of freedom meant, simply, that the human will was not bound by any set of rules or "apodictic" dogmas—either theological or scientific—but rather was free to embrace or reject any idea or theory including the idea of immortality itself. Parsons sees the opening up of western culture to eastern religious beliefs as one example of Kant's conception of intellectual or cognitive freedom. But as Parsons observes, the question of the meaning of death in the western world, released from apodictic certainty, means simply that each individual is free to decide what life and death are all about. While this leaves the issue of death and its meaning(s) in a "strangely unsatisfactory state," Parsons contends that it is not necessarily a nihilistic one as Borkenau insists. It is Parsons' conviction that this openness with respect to the meaning of death is associated with the "activistic" tradition in western values and thereby allows an individual to treat life as an "adventure" to be explored, rather than a "fate" to be endured.

1

Death in Contemporary American Society

Robert Fulton, PhD
and Greg Owen, PhD

We will discuss how American experiences with death have changed since the beginning of the twentieth century, and show how these changes have served to transform our attitudes and responses toward death. These changes can be observed in the lives of two age groups whose encounters with death have been distinctively different. These two age groups, in fact, reflect a unique point of transition in human existence. The first group was born prior to the advent of the atomic bomb and the second group was born subsequent to the nuclear age. The consequences and implications of this dramatic shift in human experience will be the focus of this chapter.

A PORTRAIT OF TWO GENERATIONS

The first age group is made up of those persons over age 65 who presently constitute our elderly population. They are 25 million in number and make up 11 percent of the population.[1] They constitute the majority of persons who die in the United States each year.[2] When they were born, their life expectancy was approximately 49 years.[3] When this elderly population was young, the majority (53 percent) of persons who died were children under the age of 15, dying primarily of infectious and contagious diseases.[4] Two-thirds of the persons in this age group were reared on farms or in other non-urban environments at a time when 7 out of 10 gainfully employed persons across the country were associated in some way with agriculture.[5]

At the turn of the century, the American family lived primarily in small, rural communities. Family members were obliged to go to the fields, woods, and waters for their sustenance, and to a great extent depended on their own efforts and those of their families and neighbors for basic survival. While they adhered to Judeo-Christian beliefs, they always had cause to wonder where tomorrow's meal would come from, whether a child would be born alive, whether a cow would calf, or whether fire, drought, hail, or other natural calamity would destroy the work of a person, a family, or a whole generation. Illness, dying, and death took place at home, and was observed by child and adult alike. Animals were slaughtered for food. Death was visible, immediate and real. To a great extent, the American family lived in terms of the simple round of life that humankind had known and accepted since the beginning of time: birth, copulation, and death.

By contrast, the generation born after World War II has, for the most part, experienced death at a distance. When the post-World War II generation was born their life expectancy was approximately 67 years. In the majority of instances they were born in hospitals, and the infectious diseases to which they were exposed were no longer likely to be fatal. This "baby boom" generation, unlike their parents and all previous generations, experienced the maximum benefits of an urbanized and technologically advanced society. Modern health care institutions in particular shielded this generation from general exposure to illness and death, just as the commercial meat processing industry removed the slaughtering of animals from the home. Death for this generation has become invisible and abstract. In fact, it is the first generation in history in which the chance of a child reaching adulthood is 4 out of 5 prior to the death of an immediate family member.

Importantly, the post-World War II generation was also the first generation in America in which education was generally accepted as the *summum bonum.* While we have had colleges and universities since the seventeenth century (Harvard was founded in 1636), it is only since World War II that education, particularly higher education, could be considered a public enterprise. Since that time the enrollment in American colleges has more than quadrupled, from less than 3 million students in 1945 to more than 12 million today.[6] But numbers alone can in no way portray the impact that education, particularly secular education has had, and continues to have, upon our society. Above all, mass public education serves to liberalize traditional values and beliefs, and provides a framework for a more secular and humanistic view of life.

Contributing to the impact of secular education on American youth has been the presence and general pervasiveness of television. By 1960, it has been estimated, more than 80 percent of American homes possessed at least one television set.[7] Importantly, it has also been estimated that during their childhood years, the "baby-boom" generation—which could also be described as the first television generation—viewed 10,000 acts of homicide, rape, or other forms of violence and aggression on television.[8]

The experience of death on television for this generation of young adults essentially revolved around three motifs. The first motif was entertainment; shows such as "Tom and Jerry" presented cartoon characters who systematically annihilated one another in an infinite variety of violent ways, only to reappear alive and unscathed in the next frame or after the commercial break, ready for further mayhem. The second motif was that life was brutal and often lethal; young males killed or were killed through the malevolence of others.[9] From "The Untouchables" to "Miami Vice," the tradition of associating violence and death with the young American male has continued uninterrupted. Finally, the third motif or "message" that was conveyed, particularly to those who grew up during the Vietnam War, was that death, when it actually occurred, occurred elsewhere and mostly to foreigners, "gooks," or to people alien in appearance, language, or national ideology. With only rare exceptions (e.g., the Kennedy assassinations, Lee Harvey Oswald's murder) was the death of an average citizen ever presented on television during this period of time. Accident and disaster victims were always shown with their bodies covered. Discrete avoidance of the corpse was the typical practice. "Real" death or "actual" death as depicted on television only happened outside the continental limits of the United States—and it was generally death by violence. Moreover, until the protests and general rioting of college students put an end to the draft, Vietnam was perceived by many as the gauntlet that the young American male was obliged to run if he wished to participate fully as a good citizen. The death of ordinary citizens, meanwhile, receded from view, and for a whole generation of young people, if death was seen at all, it was observed at a distance through the opaque glass of a television screen.

For those who are now elderly, however, the experience with popular fare on national television was a comfortable one in which old values were affirmed and past actions justified. Such programs as "Phil Silvers," "Milton Berle," "Playhouse 90," and "The Ed Sullivan Show" served to entertain the post-World War II adult population, while a political philosophy was presented that served to justify the hard course that had been taken to assure victory over the Axis powers. The atom bomb for this generation was a technological blessing that was fortuitously denied the Nazi scientists. The death of John F. Kennedy; the civil rights disturbances of the 1960s; the images of American cities in flames; the death of Dr. Martin Luther King; the riot at the 1968 Democratic convention in Chicago; and the pale, still face of Robert Kennedy as captured by television cameras in Los Angeles, all served to inform the older generation that disorder and civil disobedience were twin evils related by communist blood. For the younger generation, the same events were essentially all of a piece with America perceived as a society that would sacrifice them ultimately to the bottomless pit of Vietnam and, in the process, commit the country to the vainglorious mission of a communist-free world.

This disparity in perception between generations was probably best summed up by the anti-Vietnam spokesman Jerry Rubin, who warned those under 30 to distrust those over 30. What he captured in that one statement was the important difference in perspective between those old enough to remember the conclusion of the Second World War and those who feared they would never witness the conclusion of a third. A key aspect that distinguishes these two generations is the nuclear bomb and the view taken toward the role that this unique weapon has played, and promises to play, in human history. That is, the older generation saw the bomb as helping to bring to an abrupt end the terrible conflict of World War II. For the younger generation the bomb is not so much a symbol of peace and stability among nations as it is a threat—not only to humankind in general but also as an insurmountable barrier to the future. As Shneidman[10] has so succinctly stated:

> We live in an oxymoronic century...at the same time [that] we have created the most exquisitely sophisticated technological procedures for saving one individual's life, we have also created lethal technological devices...with the capacity of exterminating millions, or expunging cultures, or jeopardizing time itself by not only erasing the present, but also threatening the future...on the one hand marvelous devices for emergency services, kidney dialysis and organ transplantation promise life; on the other hand, megadeath bombs constantly aimed from above the clouds and beneath the waves promise death. No one is safe; there is no place to hide.

As Shneidman observes, the experience with death in contemporary America is a paradoxical one; the mass media also show it to be a collage of fragmented images.

IMAGES OF DEATH IN POPULAR CULTURE

Death's presence in the media is simultaneously everywhere and nowhere; it is at once illusively fantastical and frighteningly real. It is a dramatic front-page headline reporting an assassination attempt on the Pope or a president, or a fanciful new horror novel by Stephen King. It is a 10-second radio commercial for cemetery plots, an anti-nuclear war demonstration, or the latest spoof on death by Woody Allen or the *National Lampoon.* It is "live coverage" of natural calamities and disasters. It is a report of a murder or of the latest act of terrorism. It is an image of children with swollen bellies dying from starvation in Africa, an academic discussion of capital punishment, a documentary on dying cancer or AIDS patients, or the sheet-draped body of a young suicide victim.

While prime-time television features death and violence relentlessly, particularly among the young, it portrays grief and the ruptured lives that death can leave in its wake only superficially. Television news programs also characteristically submerge the human meaning of death while depersonalizing the event further by sandwiching actual reports of loss of life between commercials or other mundane items.

Movies, far more than television, are explicit in showing violent deaths of, and by, young people. Such films as *The Terminator, Silence of the Lambs,* or *Goodfellas* depict in color and slow motion the detailed destruction of human beings that eclipse the meaning of the death itself.

Death and violence also find contemporary expression in other art forms. Francis Bacon, the expressionist, and his colleague, the painter Acconci, both of whom have some of their paintings on display in the New York Museum of Modern Art, feature works that depict in explicit detail acts of mutilation and annihilation.[11] Jacques Tingueley, who might be termed a French "destructionist," is notable for his mechanical constructions that self-destruct as part of their exhibition.[12]

Popular music directed at today's youth also contains a morbid fascination with death. A few years ago, teenagers flocked to rock concerts to hear Alice Cooper sing "I Love the Dead" while he assaulted a female mannequin or beheaded a likeness of himself. Death continues to be a topic of many of today's rock lyrics. Some emphasize death's catastrophic and destructive elements. A survey of themes of death in popular music shows that death is often viewed as interference rather than inevitability, and death as a natural part of human existence is seldom, if ever, projected.[13]

Similarly, violent death is a staple theme of popular fiction. Murder mysteries and espionage thrillers compete to devise ever more titillating and ingenious methods of killing the victim. A notable example of this genre is *Brain,* a novel by Robin Cook, the author of *Coma.* In this recent contribution to the sci-fi, hi-tech horror literature, the author brings the book to a climax with the image of five nude young women floating in large, liquid-filled glass cases. Skull-less and faceless but artificially alive, their brains hooked up to a battery of computers, these "living corpses" are encouraged to participate in "scientific" experiments through the stimulation of the sensual areas of the brain. As a reward for their participation they will experience an orgasm "a hundred times" more powerful than normal.

This necrophilic fantasy is concluded with the corpses pleading repeatedly, "Stimulate me, please."[14]

Death in the world of everyday life, however, differs significantly from death in the media world, both in cause and consequence. Most actual deaths today involve elderly persons who die in hospitals or nursing homes from such ailments as heart disease, cancer, and stroke; by watching television or movies, one is led to believe that a typical death occurs violently and usually among the young.[15]

The experience of dying is often profound and a death can result in inconsolable grief and shattered lives. Personal and social readjustment in the face of such loss can be both painful and difficult. Although these aspects of death have traditionally been a major theme and inspiration for much of the world's great art, literature and music, they are markedly missing from the popular media. More typically, the media treat death casually and impersonally and tend to ignore the human response to it.

What sense can we make out of this fascination with macabre death that has swept popular culture and, like the Pied Piper, captured the attention of American youth?[16] If we consider for a moment the way Hollywood films, for example, characteristically dealt with death prior to World War II compared to the way they do today, we can perhaps notice a certain change in attitudes toward dying and death that has overtaken our society.

Early film classics such as *Frankenstein* and *Dracula* clearly portrayed the traditional polarities within Christian theology—the struggle between good and evil, spirit and flesh, and life and death. Within the dramatic structure of these films, death was understood as the justifiable punishment for those who trespassed against the moral order or as a ritual of purification for those who died championing it.

The tension between these polarities can be seen with great clarity in the traditional western movie. The hero—chaste, courageous and God-fearing—is confronted with evil in the form of cattle-stealing outlaws, land-stealing speculators, or gold-stealing bandits. Without compromise, the hero rights wrong; as an instrument of justice, he restores law and order; and as a servant of God, he affirms the principles of faith. The world in which good struggled against evil, and the spirit vied with the flesh, finds itself today forced to retreat before the advances of what might be termed relativistic secularism.

In the new genre of film entertainment that is presently being offered to contemporary society and is epitomized by the James Bond thriller, the hierarchical world of Christian transtemporalism is no longer described; rather, what is presented is an existential world in which good and evil reside in both friend and foe alike.

Today the image of modern, existential man portrayed on the screen is a rational, intelligent, sexually attractive, materialistic man who is functioning within an environment of which he is not entirely a part. His values are relativistic and pragmatic. His loyalties are to a group, a movement, or a state. Oftentimes he works in the employ of someone as little known to him and possibly as hostile toward him as is his unknown adversary. For a cause that transcends him, the modern hero is expendable, as are those persons with whom he struggles. His claim to life—and it is a life abundant with power, wealth, and sexual pleasures—is made existentially dramatic by the fact that at any given moment he may be obliged to give it up. Carelessness or expediency may cause him to receive a fatal thrust from an enemy or a deadly push from a friend. Life for the contemporary hero is immediate and sensory, while his potential death is irrelevant. In contrast to the traditional theological conception of a free-thinking and independent self and a passive, if not irrelevant, social structure, this modern image of a human being offers a new vision of humankind and the prospect of a new social order.

CHANGING ATTITUDES TOWARD DEATH

Franz Borkenau, the late German historian, was one of the first scholars to recognize that new definitions of the social self and the social order were in the making. He characterized the modern era as post-Christian and argued that with the disintegration of the belief in immortality, modern society was prepared to embrace a nihilistic philosophy of despair and denial. Borkenau believed that modern secularism would ultimately deny the relevance of selfhood so that death, finally, would be "defeated"; in other words, it would have no social consequence. It was Borkenau's conviction that to avoid existential extinction, the individual would find a sense of identity through some temporal absolute such as a racial, social, or national group.[17] The character of James Bond, it would appear, is a realized image of Borkenau's conception of nihilistic man.

It is Borkenau's provocative theory that the shift in our attitudes toward death is traceable to the conflicting attitudes toward death experienced by the unconscious.[18] Briefly, his psychoanalytic view of history holds that humankind is confronted with a self-contradictory experience of death that is rooted deep within the psyche. While the unconscious is convinced of its own immortality, it also finds one of its motive forces, paradoxically, to be the pursuit of death itself. The coexistence of these two incompatible elements within the unconscious provides an inherent contradiction in human existence. Although a person will struggle to resolve the conflict within, the embracing of one motive force inevitably causes its primal opposite to reassert itself. The human psyche is thus caught in a never-ending debate which, Borkenau proposes, is a basic element in shaping the course of human history.[19] Furthermore, Borkenau argues, the conflicting attitudes toward death unconsciously experienced by the individual are also at work within the culture, so that ultimately there emerge periods when the culture can be characterized as "death-denying" in outlook rather than "death-defying."

The attraction of national or social movements such as communism or fascism, wrapped about as they are with semi-divine attributes of absolute value and the promise of "temporal" eternity, tempt an individual to avoid extinction by an act of self-abandonment. This, Borkenau observes, is also the invitation extended to us by traditional theologies. The difference, however, lies in the fact that "death-denying" cultures seek an immortality in this world, in contrast to "death-defiant" Christianity, which promises a life beyond the grave.[20]

A shift in the popular attitude toward death from one orientation to another appears to mark an epoch in historical evolution. In our time, Borkenau believes, we are experiencing just such a shift. Attitudes toward death have changed in modern society, as Borkenau suggests, and we concur with many of his observations regarding the direction of that change. But we question his explanation for these changes, and contend that the reversal noted in our collective responses to death today is the result of shifts and changes within society itself rather than a consequence of unconscious urges or intrapsychic paradoxes that Borkenau presumes bedevil humankind. Medical science discoveries, technological inventions, demographic changes in the population, and other social and cultural factors have served, we believe, to break the historic round of life and to bring contemporary society to its present condition.

Let us review certain of these social factors and examine the impact they have had both upon our personal lives as well as upon our social institutions. One change that was brought about by the impact of industrialization and specialization upon American family life involves the care of the dead.[21] A little over half a century ago, the task of burying the dead was taken over by a paid functionary—the undertaker. Funeral directors, as they are now designated, have existed in America since colonial times, but the ubiquitous extension of their services generally coincides with World War I, when individuals or small families moved to the cities in great numbers.[22] The general absence of relatives, neighbors, and the familiar rural community, as well as the pressure of urban life and the time-bounded constraints of industrial employment, converged in such a way as to cause the American family to look to the funeral director's public rooms to lay out its dead.[23]

By the time of the Second World War, the principle of specialization that had so benefited industrial enterprise had also come to be adopted by the medical profession. The demands of war and the scarcity of medical resources pressed for the establishment of the all-inclusive public hospital. The "house call" by a physician was no longer practical, efficient, or medically indicated. In 1925, for example, hospital bed occupancy totaled 7 million patients; by 1970, the number had risen to more than 32 million—a fivefold increase—during a period of time when the population increase of the United States was only twofold.[24] Today more than two-thirds of all deaths will occur in hospitals, nursing homes, or settings other than the home. The continued enhancement and extension of public health measures and medical services means not only that the mortality rate has been lowered appreciably and that life expectancy has increased, but it has also changed the time and place of death.

With the burgeoning development of nursing home care for the elderly that followed the Korean War, the process of specialized care for certain categories of persons was extended further. Briefly, what is important to note is that in less than 50 years, the responsibility for the care and disposition of the dead human body has been removed from the family; the seriously and chronically ill are hospitalized; and incapacitated or dependent elderly persons are increasingly placed in nursing homes or other life-care centers.

The long-term implications of these isolating and segregating developments can be better understood, however, if we look at other changes that have concurrently taken place in American society during the past half century. The invention of the artificial kidney machine in Seattle, Washington 30 years ago has brought the issue of life and death into distressingly sharp focus for many people today.[25] The criteria that were initially established to select the first kidney patients in effect implied that some persons have a greater claim to life than others. It has always been true, of course, that wealthy persons could afford better medical care than the poor, but it has never been official medical philosophy that a person of wealth or other social attributes had a greater claim to life than any other person. It was, however, established by an anonymous committee of seven, known portentously as the "Life and Death Committee," that one's right to a life-sustaining machine as determined by a recipient-desirability test was in part a function of one's potential or actual contribution to society. While these intervening years have seen the production of large numbers of kidney machines, as well as the development of new and more effective kidney and other transplant techniques, the moral and ethical issues raised by the Seattle kidney machine still remain to be resolved.[26]

An important consequence of organ transplantation has been the change in the definition of death itself.[27] The question of exactly when death occurs is crucial for the practice of transplant surgery. The traditional definition of death, depending as it did on the heart and with it the circulation of the blood, constituted a serious obstacle to the successful development of this new medical procedure. A new definition of death was needed to match the new technology. The concept of brain death introduced by Beecher at Harvard, and now adopted universally, states that death occurs when the brain is dead, whether or not there is a heartbeat.[28] Such a definition permits the maintenance of the circulatory system until the time of removal of the organ without the negative implication that the organ was, or could be, removed from a still-living individual.

In addition to the clinical redefinition of death, the conception of life that has been long held in western society has also undergone a significant change. What is considered "alive" and what is considered "dead" today are no longer the same. Viability has been foreshortened. Historically, life was thought to begin with conception. With the Supreme Court's ruling that a fetus is not "alive" until after 21 weeks of gestation, "life," in a manner of speaking, has had to pull in its belt.[29]

Family relations have also been directly affected by contemporary mortality and the new social patterns that have emerged. The American family has been transformed both in structure and in types of relationships. It is more mobile, socially as well as geographically, than ever before. Today's family can be characterized as more child-oriented than adult-oriented, more democratic than paternalistic, and more individualized than integrated. The young, contemporary family, moreover, is no longer a part of a rural community, but rather is caught up in a fractionated, urban environment. In the modern-day metropolis, many elderly are retired from work and free of parental obligations. They are frequently outside of, or absent from, the main current of family life. The extension of medical services and the advances in medical science research, moreover, make possible not only the prolongation of life, but also cause those who are hospitalized to be further separated from their families. The number of familial and friendship commitments are reduced by such separations, and emotional and social bonds are loosened. Not the least consequence of these developments is the fact that great numbers of the elderly not only live alone but, as studies show, die alone as well.[30]

Changing attitudes toward the funeral as a meaningful rite for the dead, and the criticism and attacks that have been directed toward it in recent years, also reflect these changing circumstances.[31] In a society in which only half of the adult population is church-affiliated and in which the social and spatial mobility of its citizens is among its more remarkable characteristics, the religious, emotional and economic obligations that a funeral imposes on a family have come to be seen by many as both burdensome and inappropriate. Characteristically, the funeral is for that member of the family least functionally relevant to it. As the anthropologist Goody observes, "Funerals [in America] today have so much less work to do."[32] Advocacy of memorial services, with the body absent, and medical donation of the body or its parts, are attempts within the context of contemporary values to resolve the different problems associated with the disposition of the dead. Other attempts to contain or limit the social impact of a death upon the family or community can be seen in the decline in public obituaries, the dramatic rise in immediate disposition or cremation of the body, the increasing formalization of rules governing an employee's time off for bereavement, and the direct implementation of Federal Trade Commission guidelines on the business practices and procedures of funeral directors.[33]

Contemporary attitudes and reactions to dying and death have not been unidimensional, as Borkenau would contend. The developments that led to the isolation and oftentimes abandonment of the dying elderly in the late 1950s and '60s were accompanied by renewed interest in both the euthanasia and hospice movements. The euthanasia movement, reflecting many of the utilitarian values of our secular and pragmatic society, attempted to solve the problems associated with the distress of dying by advocating assistance to those who might choose to hasten their own death rather than face the prospect of pain or indignity. The hospice movement, on the other hand, recently armed with more effective means of pain control, sought to minimize the distress of dying by holistic care of the patient which eschewed both the heroic measures of the modern hospital and the irrevocable alternative of euthanasia.

The hospice concept was given added impetus in the United States in the early 1970s by the work of the Swiss psychiatrist Elisabeth Kübler-Ross. Her advocacy of compassionate care and relief of pain for the dying received wide recognition by the publication of her book, *On Death and Dying*. The book exposed a sensitive nerve in the health care delivery system of the United States. But it did more than that; it crystallized for many not only the problems of the dying patient but also the issues faced by those—especially nurses—whose task it was to deal with a private death in a public setting.[34]

But there is more to Dr. Kübler-Ross's message than palliative care for the dying. She and Dr. Cicely Saunders, the founder of the modern hospice movement, and Mother Teresa of Calcutta, form a feminine trinity representing essential religious and spiritual values that extend beyond their immediate goal of care for the dying. In their compassionate acts of service they recognize an individual's identity and the prospect of immortality. The importance accorded these ideas in the world today is reflected in the acclaim and honor that these three women have received.[35] The significance of their message, however realized in the practice of hospice care, is muted by the somber reality of the nuclear age. A private and dignified death that was once endangered by the anonymity of the public hospital is now threatened by the specter of mass annihilation from cataclysmic nuclear war.

WAR

As we have stated, what distinguishes the two age cohorts of our analysis as much as any other single factor are the profoundly different meanings that the prospect of nuclear war has for them. Death in past wars was given meaning and significance by the moral and spiritual principles explicit in the transcendental theologies of the world. In Borkenau's terms, such victims died in "defiance" of death. Whether their deaths were sacrificed by reason of a great cause or whether they died as an act of atonement, it was believed that they did not die in vain; immortality awaited them. This can be seen in American history with the trauma of the Civil War and the new themes of death, sacrifice and spiritual rebirth that it introduced.[36]

War traditionally has served the societal function of helping to shape and define the male role.[37] The right and privilege to engage in mortal conflict on behalf of the group or society has been reserved, with rare exception, for the young male. This activity, more than any other, has served historically as a central point of departure for male-female relationships. The Congressional Medal of Honor, Arlington Cemetery, the Tomb of the Unknown Soldier, Memorial Day, and other honorific symbols, occasions and places dramatically articulate this close relationship between masculinity and death.[38] For the first time in human history, the prospect of nuclear war threatens this historic connection. Male honor and the traditional perception of masculinity have been based upon acts of bravery or personal displays of courage in the face of a mortal enemy. Nuclear war, on the other hand, promises to be an impersonal conflict. It will be conducted anonymously, in a technically abstract way, with weapons that are indiscriminant. The prospect of such a cataclysm means that the old as well as the young, women as well as men, are equally at peril. In the face of this mortal challenge, and without the capacity or opportunity to respond in a significantly meaningful way, men can come to share the same sense of helplessness and humiliation that has historically been the lot of women and children. This challenge to the validity of a central aspect of the male role cannot help but create ambiguity and tension for the present generation of young men.

Jerald Bachman of the Institute for Social Research at the University of Michigan has asked graduating seniors from 130 high schools across the nation every year since 1975 to share their thoughts and feelings about a broad range of social issues. In response to the question, "How often do you worry about the chance of a nuclear war?" Bachman reported that "concern with the nuclear issue has been substantial, with the most consistent and steadiest increase in concern of any problem that we asked about." Such concern increased from 7.9 percent of the male students in 1975 to 31.2 percent in 1982. Moreover, in 1982 more than a third of all the high school seniors polled agreed with the statement "nuclear or biological annihilation will probably be the fate of all mankind within my lifetime."[39]

Equally significant are recent findings that indicate communication problems between adults and children on nuclear issues. In a study sponsored by Educators for Social Responsibility, researchers interviewed public school students in the Boston area, grades one through nine, and concluded that adults are unaware of the depth of children's concerns about nuclear war. While children revealed an awareness of the world-destroying potential of nuclear weapons and associated nuclear bombs with vivid personal images of death, the teachers of these students warned the investigators that their students knew nothing about nuclear weapons, did not think about the threat of nuclear war, and would have nothing to say about it. The researchers found that the teachers were wrong.[40]

Concern and fear about nuclear weapons and nuclear war are not limited to children and youth in the United States. In a 1982 study, Chivian, Mack and associates administered questionnaires to 300 children between the ages of 10 and 15 in the former Soviet Union. In addition to the written questionnaires, they conducted several dozen personal interviews with the aid of a translator. They found that Soviet children, like their American counterparts, were widely aware of the nuclear threat and that the vast majority believed that a nuclear war could not be survived.[41]

These studies help us to understand the psychosocial situation in which the present generation of young people—especially young men of military age—find themselves. Caught up in a post-World War II society that stresses personal fulfillment, relative values, technical competence, and faith in science with its corollary challenge to the belief in immortality, young men are also confronted with a social system that seriously circumscribes their autonomy, undermines their masculine identity and jeopardizes their sense of the future. The threat of a sudden anonymous death, moreover, is counterpoised against an immediate experience with death that is either denied or distorted. It is within this social context that they express their fears and frustrations in music, drugs, violence and vicarious death experiences. We propose that by such means they seek escape from the existential dilemma of their lives and the impersonal design for their deaths.

This contemporary *zeitgeist* is not unique to American youth. Alexander and Margarete Mitscherlick found in their study of German youth that they suffered from what the authors described as an "inability to mourn."[42] That is, German youth broke the affective links to their immediate past in order to avoid the intolerable emotions associated with the war guilt of their parents. This was not simply a function of their physical and familial privations following the Second World War, the Mitscherlicks concluded, but was primarily the result of the loss of myth and ideological belief in their country.[43]

NOTES

1. U.S. Bureau of the Census. 1991. *Statistical Abstract of the United States,* Washington DC, Table 13, p. 13.
2. M. Lerner. 1981. When, Why and Where People Die. In *Death and Dying: Challenge and Change,* R. Fulton, et al., eds. San Francisco: Boyd & Fraser, p.88.
3. United States Bureau of the Census, 1980, Table 106, p. 72.
4. M. Lerner, loc. cit.
5. A.M. Schlesinger. 1951. The City in American History. In *Reader in Urban Sociology,* P.H. Hatt and A.J. Reiss, eds. New York: Free Press.
6. *1982 Digest of Educational Statistics,* Table 74: Total Enrollment of Institutions of Higher Learning by Level of Enrollment and by State, Fall 1980.
7. *Historical Statistics of the United States: Colonial Times to 1970,* Part 2, U.S. Department of Commerce, Bureau of the Census.
8. There is considerable controversy among researchers concerning the methods of mass media research on violence as well as its definition. Over the 10 years analyzed, however, crime, action-adventure programs, along with children's cartoons had "high" incidence of measured violence. See G. Gerbner et al. (1978), Violence on the Screen, Cultural Indicators: Violence Profile No. 9, *Journal of Communication* 28:3, *passim.*
9. E.S. Shneidman. 1980. *Death: Current Perspectives,* 2nd Ed. Palo Alto, CA: Mayfield Publishing Co.
10. Ibid., p. xviii.
11. G. Jensen, personal communication; Sexuality in Art, *New Art Examiner* (Chicago), 1979.
12. G. Jensen, loc. cit.
13. J.C. Thrush and G.C. Paulson. 1976. The Concept of Death in Popular Music: A Social Psychological Perspective. Paper presented at the Midwest Popular Culture Association Meetings, Bowling Green State University, Bowling Green, OH.
14. R. Cook. 1982. *Brain.* New York: New American Library, p. 288.
15. M. Lerner, op. cit., p. 91.
16. It is of interest to note that this is not the first time in Western history that popular representations of death have reflected dramatic or profound changes in the

condition of human existence. The French historian Ariès reports that in France following the plague of the fourteenth century, bodies were wrapped and quickly hidden from view following death, and public viewing of the body was forsaken. The burial of the body was quickly accomplished. Concomitantly, he reports, an unusual reaction occurred. Death became fascinating. Throughout France, death came to be represented in the form of half-decomposed corpses while the tomb depicted in paintings, woodcuts and sculptures became a chamber of horrors. Moreover, a macabre association between sexuality and death appeared and a perverse eroticism arose. Paradoxically, Ariès comments, this was at a time characterized by the emergence of rationalism, science and faith in progress. It would appear that these gruesome depictions of death have made their reappearance in twentieth-century America, albeit in a technologically different guise. See P. Ariès (1981), *The Hour of Our Death* (New York: Alfred A. Knopf).

17. F. Borkenau. 1965. The Concept of Death. In *Death and Identity*, R. Fulton ed. New York: John Wiley & Sons.
18. Ibid., p. 47.
19. Ibid., p. 52.
20. Ibid., p. 46; T. Parsons (1963), Death in American Society—A Brief Working Paper, *The American Behavioral Scientist* 6:61-65; R. Blauner (1966), Death and Social Structure, *Psychiatry* 29:378-394.
21. R. Habenstein. 1955. *The History of American Funeral Directing*. Milwaukee: Bulfin.
22. Ibid., Chapter 13.
23. V. Pine. 1975. *Caretaker of the Dead*. New York: Irvington Publishers.
24. *Hospital Statistics*. 1977. Chicago: American Hospital Association.
25. R.G. Simmons and J.A. Fulton. 1973. Ethical Issues in Kidney Transplantation. In C.A. Fraser, ed., *Is It Moral to Modify Man?* Springfield, IL: Charles C Thomas.
26. R.G. Simmons et al. (1977), *Gift of Life: The Social and Psychological Impact of Organ Transplantation* (New York: John Wiley & Sons); R.C. Fox (1976), Advanced Medical Technology—Social and Ethical Considerations, *Annual Review of Sociology* 29:231-268.
27. D.C. Maguire. 1973. *Death by Chance: Death by Choice*. New York: Doubleday.
28. Ibid., p. 63.
29. *Roe v. Wade*, 1973. Washington, DC: United States Supreme Court.
30. G. Owen, R. Fulton and E. Markusen. 1982. Death at a Distance. *Omega* 13:191-224.
31. J. Mitford (1963), *The American Way of Death* (New York: Simon & Schuster); R.M. Harmer (1963), *The High Cost of Dying* (New York: Crowell-Collier Press); L. Bowman (1959), *The American Funeral: A Study in Guilt, Extravagance, and Sublimity* (Washington, DC: Public Affairs Press).
32. J. Goody. 1974. Death and the Interpretation of the Culture. In D.E. Stannard, ed., *Death in America*. Philadelphia: University of Pennsylvania Press, p. 7.
33. *The Cremationist of North America* (1983), New York: Cremation Association of North America; L. Pratt (1981), Business Temporal Norms and Bereavement Behavior, *American Sociological Review* 46:317-333; Funeral Industry Practices, Final Staff Report to the Federal Trade Commission and Proposed Trade Regulation Rule (16 CFR Part 453), Bureau of Consumer Protection, June 1978.
34. E. Kübler-Ross (1969), *On Death and Dying* (New York: Macmillan); S.

Stoddard (1978), *The Hospice Movement: A Better Way of Caring for the Dying* (New York: Stein & Day).

35. Notable among a continuing shower of accolades and honors accorded the women are the following: Mother Teresa, Nobel Prize for Peace, 1979; Cicely Saunders, Knighthood and the Templeton Prize for Progress in Religion, 1980; and Elisabeth Kübler-Ross, Teilhard de Chardin Prize.
36. R. Huntington and P. Metcalf. 1979. Celebrations of Death. Cambridge:22 Cambridge University Press, pp. 206-209.
37. A. Toynbee. 1981. Death in War. In *Death and Dying: Challenge and Change,* R. Fulton et al., eds. San Francisco: Boyd & Fraser.
38. W.L. Warner. 1965. *The Living and the Dead: A Study of the Symbolic Life of Americans.* New Haven: Yale University Press, Chapter 8.
39. J. Bachman. 1983. American High School Seniors View the Military: 1976-1982. *Armed Forces and Society* 10:86-94.
40. Cited in M. Yudkin (1984), When Kids Think the Unthinkable, *Psychology Today*, p. 20.
41. E. Chivian, J. Mack, J. Waletzky, C. Lazaroff, R. Doctor and J. Goldenring. 1982. Soviet Children and the Threat of Nuclear War: A Preliminary Study. *American Journal of Orthopsychiatry* 55:484-502.
42. A. Mitscherlick and M. Mitscherlick. 1975. *The Inability to Mourn.* New York: Grove Press.
43. R.J. Lifton (1965), Psychological Effects of the Atomic Bomb in Hiroshima: The Theme of Death, in *Death and Identity*, R. Fulton, ed. (New York: John Wiley & Sons); G. Owen, R. Fulton and E. Markusen, op. cit.; G.H. Pollock (1961), Mourning and Adaptation, *International Journal of Psychoanalysis* 42:341-361.

2

Conceptual Approaches to the Study of Death

Kathy Charmaz, PhD

In the area of death and dying, as in any study of the human condition, concrete circumstances are known and understood by conceptualizing them into a coherent body of ideas. Whatever perspectives are brought to bear on death, whether they are scientific theorizing, philosophical interpretation, or common-sense reasoning, they give shape and meaning to the reality of it. It can readily be discerned that each perspective suggests particular kinds of questions and therefore has its own particular limitations since questions derived from other perspectives are usually omitted.

In this chapter, three sociological perspectives are introduced and analyzed in relation to death. They include discussions of symbolic interactionist, structural-functionalist, and Marxist approaches. Special emphasis will then be given to explicating the assumptions on which symbolic interactionism rests. That discussion will be followed by a presentation of one of its subtypes, the dramaturgical approach. This approach holds much potential for new research about death through the application of the analogy of the theater to social relations. The structural-functional perspective discussed next is explicated to show the complex institutional relationships that need to be addressed in a study of death. Finally, a Marxist perspective is introduced to raise, primarily, a set of provocative issues largely ignored in the past.

SYMBOLIC INTERACTIONIST PERSPECTIVE

The symbolic interactionist position postulates that selves and social structures are constructed through continuous interaction over time. This general perspective and how it relates to the study of death will be explored in the first part of this section. This will be followed by a synthesis of the perspective's basic premises in order to explicate the fundamental assumptions on which it rests. Last, the dramaturgical method will be introduced.

Statement of the Position

Symbolic interactionism is a theoretical perspective in sociology that assumes that society, reality, and selves are *socially created* through interaction processes (see Blumer[1]; Lindesmith, Strauss and Denzin;[2] and Strauss[3]). Hence, what we know, how we define situations in the world, and who we are, are all built through interaction. In the area of death, then, the symbolic interactionist perspective informs us that our conceptions of death, our images of the social world where death takes place, as well as the everyday actions that constitute the process of "dying," are socially constructed. Although death is a biological fact, what it *means* to us results from our socially shaped ideas and assumptions. In short, from this perspective we can understand "death" only in the context of the definitions and assumptions we have attributed to it. For example, death has varied definitions such as loss, transition, or peace depending on the assumptions one has about it. To illustrate, a young woman confided:

> To me, death is loss. It is more than loss of another person, or a relationship; it is loss of a part of my life. I know a lot of people my age believe in reincarnation and see death as some kind of new beginning, but to me death is a loss.

Meanings of death in the symbolic interactionist perspective are assumed to arise out of the individual's experience. In turn, that experience is grounded in interaction. Furthermore, interaction itself is a *symbolic process.* In order to interact with another, a reasonably similar set of symbols from which meanings develop must be shared. In everyday life, our use of symbols emerges out of language and cultural understandings shared between members of a group. The kinds of symbolic meanings created can be exceedingly diverse, since specific meanings arise in different groups. In turn, these meanings shape the experiences shared by members. Such diversity may be observed in responses of members of different ethnic groups. From Kalish and Reynolds'[4] study of death and ethnicity, one may conclude that Mexican Americans give significant meaning to the family as the major source of emotional support and warmth in the face of dying and death. In contrast, Japanese Americans develop meanings of the family as the "locus of control of shame and pride and of self-identity."[5] As a consequence, one's responsibility to one's family and self emphasizes the importance of emotional control in the face of death by members of this group.

Diverse meanings also may be discerned among others who are not linked by ethnicity. For that matter, group members who share certain practices regarding death may hold rather diverse meanings about other aspects of it. For example, members of a memorial society share similar views about keeping funeral expenses low; however, they may hold rather diverse conceptions of death.

Through experience, interpretations may be changed or reaffirmed. For example, some people who until recently did not have any direct interaction with members of the funeral industry held positive views of it. They now avow that they will set up their own plans outlining their personal preferences for their funerals after their initial experience with representatives of the trade since they felt pressured to purchase unwanted services.

Here, the initial encounter causes them to reassess their views and construct a different course of action in light of the experience. In contrast, others become notably more sympathetic toward the funeral industry after their initial encounter. Hence, in the symbolic interactionist perspective, it is assumed that people reinterpret previously accepted views and construct new meanings as they have new experiences that are not accommodated by their former views.

Since the symbolic interactionist position is predicated upon the premise that interaction consists of an interpretative process, it follows that the interactionist viewpoint heavily stresses the human capacity for reflection. This stress on reflection suggests an image of human nature that views human beings as reflective, creative and active. This view of human nature becomes clearer as it is juxtaposed with views of human beings as passive objects who are pushed and pulled by larger social forces over which they have no control.[6] One who adheres to the symbolic interactionist perspective expects conscious, dying persons to be capable of interpreting their worlds and of participating actively in whatever decisions that are made regarding them. Essentially then from this perspective, meaning shapes experience and experience shapes meaning.

Taken to its logical extension, the symbolic interactionist viewpoint emphasizes the *freedom* of the individual to construct reality since reality is not a given but rather a social construction. Thus, implicit in the perspective is the notion that, to a degree, we shape our own destinies. Worlds of death are then created through the interpretations, choices and actions of interactants. To illustrate, simply because some medical practitioners assume that patients do not wish to be informed of the life-threatening nature of their illness does not mean that this belief is necessarily true. Rather, their assumption is a social construction serving to affirm the validity of their own choice not to inform the patient. It is an assumption that bears a closer relationship to the practitioner's comfort than to the patient's. Anxiety and stress exhibited by the patient also affirm the practitioner's belief that "bad news" will result in further psychological distress for the patient. Consequently, certain practitioners choose to avoid the topic.

The emphasis on the range of human *choice*, which is derived from the individual's interpretation of a given situation, leads the symbolic interactionist to assume a certain amount of *indeterminacy* in interaction and events. From this perspective, it is assumed that people may choose to create new modes of action instead of merely following the dictates of the wider culture. Consequently, the ways in which we treat death in this society represent certain types of choices that have become part of institutionalized patterns of handling death. As new meanings about death emerge, new means of handling death will be developed.

As Blumer[7] repeatedly emphasized, the symbolic interactionist perspective is predicated on the assumption that human beings can think and that they have minds and thus do not respond automatically to the environment as in a stimulus-response reaction. Through our capacity for reflective thought, we can take into account and attempt to understand the different perspectives of others. For example, when a young man told his work supervisor that he would need to be absent on the following day, she was careful to reflect on the tone of his voice and facial expressions, rather than simply listening and responding to his statement. By gently inquiring, she discovered that he was scheduled for a biopsy for a particularly lethal type of cancer and that he was very frightened. Through taking his tone and demeanor into account, she was able to gain insight into his perspective and concerns.

The process of taking into account the perspective of another person is a symbolic process rooted in the meanings that participants attribute to ongoing interaction. Specifically, within the content of interaction, we are able to attribute meanings to what the other person is saying and doing. Unfortunately, much of the existing research on death and dying consists of imputing meanings and therefore motivations to other persons on the assumption that these meanings and motivations represent what these persons actually think and feel. Hence, in fundamental ways, meanings about death and dying have unfortunately been *imposed* on those who are studied instead of *elicited* from them.

In the symbolic interactionist perspective, consciousness is linked to the possession of a self. Having a self means that we can act toward ourselves as we act toward others. People who are dying may act toward themselves as devalued objects in the same way that they have treated others who were dying in the past. For example, a dying man instructed an attentive young nursing assistant:

> Oh, don't bother 'bout me. Spend your time with those who need it. There's some here who can use the help and get out of here. I know I ain't goin' no place... I never bothered much with people in the shape I'm in and I don't see why anyone should bother with me.

In this case, the old man viewed himself as someone who no longer merited help. Importantly, he himself assessed and evaluated his own situation. Speaking generally, because we have selves and minds we can carry on conversations with ourselves as we assess ourselves and our situations. Through the conscious activity of the thinking self, people differentiate objects and events in the world and give them meanings, usually in direct relationship to their own construction of action.

Similarly, because we can see ourselves as objects to assess, we can place valuations on ourselves that differ from the definitions that are socially placed upon us by others. Some dying patients, for example, define themselves as being quite a different kind of "object" than others may define them. Under these circumstances, dying patients view themselves as having an identity that supersedes the negative identities that are placed on them at that time by others.

With the emphasis on the dialectical relationship between interpretation and action, one might question how this perspective accounts for the stable relationships that are so often observed. To answer this question, the symbolic interactionist would ask another: How do members *themselves* voluntarily construct their everyday actions in such a way that they become habitualized? Thus, the stability of social structures is not assumed in advance, but is seen as a product of people acting concertedly to produce this stability. Therefore, if a particular social structure appears to be fixed and stable, one must question how the everyday actions of the members are defined, interpreted and acted on to construct the observed stability. To illustrate, by taking for granted that others consider old men (like the one described above) to be of doubtful value, the old man's self-views and his actions contribute to the tendency of staff in the institution to ignore dying patients.

More generally, routine ways of handling dying in the hospital are stable only as long as people (1) actively and continually recreate the actions constituting that "stability" and (2) take for granted views legitimizing it. From the interactionist standpoint, one cannot have fixed and stable social relationships, scenes, organizations, societies, or selves without full, or at least tacit, cooperation of members who create and recreate those stable situations. The actions upon which stability is founded are *constructed actions*; that is, they are performed consciously by human beings. Everyday processes take on stability when they eventually become *routinized* and *unquestioned*. To underscore the point, since the nature of existence is processural, social stability is contingent upon routinized everyday processes that are constructed by human beings to support that stability.

When actions become *habitualized*, the problematic aspects of everyday actions and events become minimized as they are fit into routines. Consequently, little strain is placed upon people as they interpret their realities and construct their actions.[8] Also, when actions become habitualized, the range of interpretations made about them tends to remain limited by members of the group; in fact, "tunnel vision" may set in. But, to make the point again, actions emerge, nevertheless, out of the choices made by individuals. If what is happening is reinterpreted, then new courses of action may be entertained and organized as the individual ceases to take for granted what had been previously assumed. When someone raises questions about the previously accepted ways of doing things, then that person is opening up the possibility of examining ways in which the group can change their ideas and actions. For example, institutionalized ways of handling dying patients are finally now being questioned. Consequently, more ideas about ways to handle the dying process are emerging. From this, new organizational modes can be experimented with and thus conceivably can lead to the evolution of new institutional forms of dealing with dying and death.

Assumptions Underlying the Symbolic Interactionist Perspective

To sharpen the discussion, a clarification of the assumptions underlying the symbolic interactionist perspective follows. An underlying assumption of this perspective is that social reality consists of *process* and *change*. But processes and changes occur within a context; it is assumed that changes emerge out of present interaction as the future unfolds. Hence, the present gives shape to the future, but it does not determine it. Within the symbolic interactionist perspective a certain flexibility or latitude for change is assumed. But even those changes are predicated on the shared understandings that come with a common language and culture. In the past, perhaps, symbolic interactionists have emphasized the underpinnings of their perspective which emphasize *consensus*, that is, agreement, more than those who deal with the development of conflicting definitions of the situation. But in the study of dying, conflicting definitions with their implied conflicting directions of action become especially important to consider.

Shared meanings about death and dying also need to be analyzed. Some of these shared meanings may lead to actions that contradict the "objective" interests of those who believe them. For example, some lonely elderly persons accept the notion that death is something one ultimately handles alone even though they themselves would prefer social support. For example, an elderly widow encouraged her son to send her to a nursing home. Although frightened by the unfamiliar setting and unfamiliar routines, she believed that she had no other alternative but to endure being there until she died. Not only did she think it improper to discuss death, but she also did not wish to burden either staff or relatives with her concerns. She felt that handling her death on her own was her one last task in life. Although she occasionally hinted to staff that she was not as "strong" as she seemed, she did not disclose her feelings when given the rare occasion to do so. Members of the staff felt that her last days were spent in great loneliness and that she had wanted more support, but she could not accept what little they were able to offer her since she saw this as a burden to them. Under this kind of circumstance, individuals set beliefs and actions into motion that are not in their own interests. By accepting the general conceptions of what has to be done, in effect they perpetuate situations that adversely affect them.

The basic premises supporting symbolic interactionism will be presented here in order to explicate the assumptions underlying subsequent analyses throughout the book. In addition, some major differences between the symbolic interactionist perspective and other theoretical approaches will be mentioned later in the chapter. For the present, discussion of the premises below is designed to synthesize the position as previously stated and to highlight fundamental assumptions.

According to Blumer,[9] the symbolic interactionist position rests upon the following three premises:

1. Human beings act toward things on the basis of the meanings that things have for them.
2. The meaning of such things is derived from, or arises out of, the social interaction that one has with one's fellows.
3. These meanings are handled in, and modified through, an interpretative process used by the person in dealing with the things one encounters.

The first premise shows the rational and pragmatic bias of the symbolic interactionist perspective. Meaning is related to *utility* and to the *practical* aspects of experience. Although the premise is simple, it is an important one, and as Blumer states, one that is frequently overlooked by social scientists. Also, the symbolic interactionist position highlights the *rational* side of human nature implied in Blumer's first premise. Rationality is shown in the premise that meaning and action are linked rather than separate. To illustrate, a pediatrician assumes that one has an obligation to do everything medically and surgically possible for a child, as long as there is some hope of saving life or forestalling death. Hence, one may prescribe radical and sometimes mutilating surgical procedures because of a decision that they are justified. Occasionally, however, what seems like a rational course of treatment to the physician appears to be a cruel prolongation of suffering to the parents. In this case, the pediatrician's meanings are tied to beliefs about sound medical practice learned from experience. From the vantage point of meanings, the rationale for treatment makes sense to the physician, although it may seem disturbing or even irrational to the parents.

This illustration shows that meaning and action are rationally linked when seen from the actor's point of view. In other perspectives, such as a psychiatric perspective, rational meanings are believed to be verbalized by the actor, although irrational ones—hidden even from the actor, and thus unconscious—are typically thought to cause action. In contrast, when studying death and dying, the symbolic interactionist assumes that the individual's perspective has a certain rational basis even when meanings remain implicit and unstated. The interactionist will, for example, take a dying person's assessment of the situation and feelings as "real" in and of itself, whereas those espousing other perspectives—notably psychiatric—will attempt to determine meaning by looking beyond what is directly stated.

The second premise is an important distinguishing assumption because it shows how symbolic interactionism differs from other perspectives. In the interactionist perspective, the derivation or source of meaning is an *emergent*, creative process. Blumer[10] shows this part of this assumption is quite different from the two more traditional ways of attributing meaning. One traditional way of attributing meaning is to consider it as emanating from the object itself, as if meaning is intrinsic to the object. Consequently, this view grants an objective character to meaning because it becomes attributed to the object's inherent qualities or characteristics. To illustrate, practitioners often view laboratory procedures as objects with inherent meaning rather than as objects to which they *give* meanings from their shared set of understandings. From an interactionist viewpoint, meanings can be *conferred* only upon objects. To the extent that meanings are shared, people will relate to the object in much the same way. For example, when physicians agree to define certain readings on a lab test in the same way, they draw the same conclusions about their significance. Another more subtle example concerns viewing cremation as an "object." The meaning of cremation does not lie in the act but in what it symbolizes. Its meaning lies in the value and definition people give it vis-à-vis their own lives. For secular, ecologically minded persons, cremation is apt to be given a positive meaning since it does not use the valuable green space taken by cemeteries. In contrast, those who believe in an afterlife or in reincarnation may give it a negative meaning if they believe that it is necessary to have an intact bodily form. In any case, the meaning does not lie in the act of cremating; it lies in the *values* people have concerning the act and their *definitions* of what the act is.

As Blumer[11] notes, the third premise is often misunderstood by sociologists. Blumer emphasizes the interpretative process through which meanings are derived; he says that it is a mistake to view them as merely an application of previously established meanings. According to Blumer, the interpretative process is an internalized social process in which people make "indications" to themselves through communication. Making indications to oneself means, in short, conversing with oneself.

Through the interpretative process, previously held meanings may shift and change. In one case, for example, a man of 85 had always assumed that he would die much sooner than his wife, who was 66. Since he held a view of death as a peaceful transition into another existence, he seemed to accept the inevitability of his own demise. Although his family had thought him to be remarkably accepting of the idea of death, they came to realize that his seeming acceptance had limits. Always having believed that his wife would survive him, he became shaken and distraught when he discovered that her death would occur before his, a discovery he made long after the rest of his family knew about it. Since they wished to "protect" his fragile health, they did not inform him. After her hospitalization she was sent to a convalescent hospital to die, but he was told that she was sent there to recuperate. At first, he could not understand her listless fatigue. Heavily sedated, she seemed more apathetic than he had ever known her to be. Because he could not believe that she, who had been so full of vitality, could give up so easily, he pleaded with her to live and return home with him. But she slipped into a coma and soon died. He saw her death as a travesty, a failure. For him, the failure had two dimensions: her failure to struggle against death and the practitioners' failure to permit her to try. He blamed the staff for keeping her over-sedated and immobilized, which he believed contributed to her weakened condition. In essence, his interpretation of her death was rooted in the context and his experience of it.

Because the symbolic interactionist emphasizes the interpretative process, it is a particularly suitable frame of reference to use when the researcher wishes to learn the effects of experience on meanings or, alternatively, the effects of meanings on experience. In order to obtain a sense of the ways in which meanings shift and change, it is necessary to have access to the social worlds and social experiences in which they are situated. From a research standpoint, there are two major ways of studying the stability and change of meanings as they are interpreted by people in everyday worlds. First, one way to approach the study of meanings of death and dying is to conduct research in a social world where its members confront it. In studying the views of student nurses, for example, one could begin when they are still novices, unfamiliar with what other nurses deem to be appropriate ways of thinking, feeling and acting toward death. Then through continued participation in the medical world, one could make systematic observations leading to assessment of the ways their socialization process alters their stance toward death. Second, many people have similar social experiences such as facing death or feeling intense grief but do not share the same social world. In this case, the other way of tapping the interpretative process of those studied is to complete in-depth interviews at different intervals to assess if, how and when individuals reinterpreted their experiences and subsequently developed new or altered meanings of death. In both approaches, the researcher seeks to discover the *conditions* contributing to the stability or transformation of subjective meanings through individuals' interpretations of their experiences.

These approaches reveal possibilities for studying empirical implications of Blumer's premises. To extend his position, two more premises could be added to form a more explicit statement. They are:

1. Meanings are interpreted through shared language and communication.
2. The mediation of meaning in social interaction is distinguished by a continually emerging processural nature.

The symbolic interactionist position has several notable strengths that are of particular import in the study of death. Obviously, studying death from a point of view that highlights the thoughts and ideas of the interacting individual is very useful. What death means to people cannot be taken for granted. Consequently, much of what follows in this book will open up major questions regarding the meaning of death to members of varied social worlds and interactional contexts. By looking at what real persons think, feel and do as a starting point, the sociologist can better assess changing images of death and ways of dealing with it. In the examples above, meanings of death were situated in experiences that made them directly significant to the actor. But meanings of death may also be derived from those who are not believed to currently face death as well as from those for whom it is imminent. For example, death may mean quite different things to the same person at different points in the life cycle, as well as at different points in the dying process. One woman who saw death as forbidden in middle age redefined it in old age, at which point she saw it as reunification bringing her back together with her deceased husband. (Her views may also reflect the social-historical times in which she developed them. Death as forbidden was a common theme when she was middle-aged; death as reunification is perhaps more widely held now.) Another woman who was dying of cancer at first viewed death as the enemy to struggle against when she was told of her diagnosis. Shortly before her death, it became apparent that she came to view death as a peaceful release from the anguish caused by her pain.

An important implication of the perspective is the kind of research which is congenial to it. For the symbolic interactionist, the natural world is the world of inquiry; exploration, inquiry and observation all take place within it. Consequently, this perspective is particularly useful for small-scale studies in which firsthand data are obtained. Because sociologists have an intimate knowledge of the situation they are studying, this enables them to study hidden aspects of group existence. For example, taken-for-granted but patterned ways of handling interaction with survivors of patients who died in a medical ward may be discovered by the sociologist, although participants are not aware of the patterns. In an area such as death, where so much of social reality remains tacit and unstated, this task is particularly important.

The symbolic interactionist perspective also emphasizes how the social actor makes sense of problematic situations in everyday life. Interactionists are curious about the kinds of ideologies people have that help them make sense of their situations. For purposes of clarification, an ideology is a *shared* set of values and beliefs held by a group, which provides a *justification* for prior actions and a call for future actions. In any case, symbolic interactionists are interested in the ways in which ideologies focus attention on some issues and discourage raising questions about others. For example, some physicians espouse the following ideological beliefs: (1) the physician should be totally responsible for the patient's treatment, (2) the medical aspects of the case are the most significant, and (3) patients who are seriously ill cannot be expected to be fully rational. As a consequence of their ideology, these physicians take the active role in decision making and, hence, do not question the patient's passive role in the treatment process.

Ideological views are also important in the study of the self, a major topic of research for symbolic interactionists. I contend that, in American society, the self is inherently *evaluational*. That is, selves are fundamentally defined through values, often in deceptively simple terms such as a "good person" or a "poor patient." More subtly, the self-images of physicians who believe in the above ideological view are evaluated on their ability to actively intervene with the disease process and thus control it.

For the dying, maintaining a positive sense of self can often become a significant problematic issue. Since selves are socially created and socially maintained, the social identity *conferred upon* the individual typically has profound implications for any personal identity the individual claims. Often, when a person is dying, the self that the person has claimed throughout his life is stripped away by the institutionalized procedural ways in which dying typically is handled in the medical setting (cf. Goffman[12]). For example, in one case a woman dying of burns was virtually abandoned by her husband and those who had known her before the accident. Her last few months were spent in an intensive care ward, where she was given an identity by nurses as someone who was manipulative, emotionally unstable and undesirable to work with. This identity was ascribed to her partially because she was unable to fit her pain into "appropriate" institutional routines. To the irritation of the nurses, she complained of "too much" pain "too often." Whatever she had been before her injury, her social identity in dying was reduced to that of a "whining sniveler." One wonders if she was able to retain any threads of a more positive personal identity from the past, since no visible remnants of her prior existence were available to her in her terminal months—even her face was drastically changed.

Because the self is so central a concern to symbolic interactionists, attention will be given to it throughout the book. Consequently, the self-images of various participants in diverse arenas where death is an issue will be examined.

The Dramaturgical Approach

One approach derived from the general perspective of symbolic interactionism, the dramaturgical approach, holds much promise of illuminating issues concerning death and dying. This approach uses the *metaphor* of the drama to analyze interactional encounters. By invoking this metaphor, these analysts highlight certain dimensions of reality that might otherwise not be brought into view. In particular, dramaturgical analysts highlight the *construction of action* and its *context*. This context includes the temporal and spatial dimensions of the scene in addition to the social staging of action.

Consistent with the general symbolic interactionist approach, those employing the dramaturgical method aim to study meaningful action. As

Burke,[13] the originator of this approach, stresses, it begins with theories of action rather than theories of knowledge. That is, the dramaturgical approach takes as a starting point of analysis the problematic features of the *action* of the individual. Other approaches, including the general symbolic interactionist perspective discussed above, begin with the problematic features of the *knowledge* of the individual. While the dramaturgical analyst asks first, "What does the social actor do?" the symbolic interactionist asks first, "What does the social actor think and know?"

Since the dramaturgical approach focuses squarely on the ongoing construction of action by participating social actors, the analyst must make a close examination of the dialectical relationships between purposes and actions. It is assumed that actors continually make sense of their interactions and the context in which they occur, thus causing purposes and actions to be continually modified and changed.

Rather than inquiring into the definition of the situation as held and verbalized by each individual actor, the dramaturgical analyst emphasizes the definition of the situation that seems apparent in the *event*, that is, the one that is given in the structure of action. Hence, when someone commits suicide, the dramaturgical analyst would look at how family members acted afterwards. The dramaturgical analyst would assess the meaning of the death to the family as it is visible in what they actually do, rather than in what they might say about it to an interviewer.

Quite clearly then, the dramaturgical approach explicitly takes *nonverbal behavior* into account. Taken-for-granted meanings may then become visible. In this way, dramaturgical analysts are often in a position to make distinctions between the actual performance of actors in an event or scene and their later rationalizations or justifications of their performance in that event or scene. For example, in the situation cited above, a case history by a participant observer of the events following a suicide may look very unlike the accounts given by relatives. Their views of their actions might be cast in explanations that not only absolve themselves from any responsibility for the death, but also justify how they handled it.

The suicide of one college student revealed to me by someone who was not directly involved illustrates the point. Before the student's death, she had aroused the concern of her housemates numerous times. After her boyfriend broke off their relationship, she became very depressed. At first, her housemates were sympathetic and tried to talk with her about her problems, which began to multiply. Being uninterested in her classes, she rarely attended them. Later, she quit her part-time job. By greatly diminishing her activities without adding new ones, she spent the days sitting around the house. For a time her housemates tried to distract her from her preoccupations by suggesting outings or attempting to engage her in conversations. But it wasn't long before they started to feel anger toward her; they felt that she wasn't doing anything to help herself. Even the two women who had been especially supportive and solicitous of her began to exclude her. One moved out, saying she couldn't "take it anymore." The other said, "I hate to go into the living room anymore because she's always sitting there waiting to glom on to anyone who will listen to her; she is such a downer." Although the others decided to ask her to leave, no one had the "chutzpah" to make the request. Besides, the pressures they all felt at the end of the semester caused them to attend less to matters at home. One Saturday night when the others were gone, the woman took an overdose of sleeping pills. After her death, her housemates reconstructed their interpretation of what had happened. They emphasized their initial attentiveness and gave the impression that it lasted for a much longer period than it actually had. Further, when questioned about their later exclusion and rejection of her, they claimed that they were trying to encourage her to become "more independent and resourceful."

What is significant here is the ways in which the participants' views changed after the woman's suicide. If a sociologist were to interview the woman's housemates after her suicide, quite a different response would be obtained than the one gained through the eyes of the observer who witnessed how members of the household actually dealt with this woman. After the suicide, their interpretations of what happened were essentially shaped by their need to justify their actions toward their housemate before she killed herself.

Because of their sensitivity to the subtle uses of rationalizations and justifications and other self-absolving statements to explain behavior, dramaturgical analysts have greatly enriched insight into human motivation. These analysts do not accept the social determinist view that social forces motivate the individual to act. They believe that motives are invoked by social actors as a way of explaining or *accounting* for past actions. Dramaturgical analysts assume that much of social life does not necessitate articulating reasons for behavior. In that way, acts may not be consciously defined. But when actions are frustrated or called into question, then the issue of motivation arises. Actions become *problematic* when actors become self-conscious about what they are doing. For example, terminal patients may not be questioned about their requests for painkillers until staff realize that they are on the verge of addiction. Then, they may call these patients' motives into question and seek accounts from them in order to "explain" the questioned behavior.

Consequently, providing explanations for behavior occurs only when taken-for-granted activity is challenged or interrupted. By interpreting prior action, a stated motive answers the question of "why" behind that action.

In short, motives provide a way of rationalizing or justifying actions when an account is defined as necessary. As Brisett and Edgley put it: "Human beings are consciously rationalizing, not consciously rational."[14]

Dramaturgical analysts assume that people first *act*, then, as a *consequence* of action, define meanings. To illustrate, the possibility of suicide arises in the course of action rather than through long premeditation. As a case in point, a woman recounted her suicidal experience as building up during a weekend bout of drinking and taking sedatives. She did not begin the episode with suicide in mind, but as events progressed she decided to seek what for her was later described as rebirth through the "transition of death" by cutting her wrists.

Dramaturgical analysts typically employ more of an objectivist approach to social reality than those who adhere more purely to the symbolic interactionist perspective described above. Behavior is analyzed from the standpoint of the *observer*, who has a close view of the scene, with stress on the observable played roles and the discernible actions taken, rather than on the subjective meanings of participants. In that way, nonverbal aspects of behavior are brought into view as well as verbal ones. Similarly, the analyst pays more attention to the analysis of the event than to the thoughts of various protagonists within it. For example, a researcher studying funeral directors may describe and analyze in detail the observable role played in front of the bereaved without any elucidation of what the participants actually think and feel while playing that role (see Turner and Edgely[15]).

Because dramaturgical analysts often study behavior from the outside, they carefully record those expressions, gestures, body movements and cues that are unwittingly revealed by the actor in the course of action, in addition to those explicitly strategized to elicit a desired effect or response. Since persons often indicate their "real" intentions through such unwitting disclosures, dramaturgical analysts may then impute specific intentions to those observed (see Goffman[16]). For example, a man was discussing the death of a family friend who had developed heart disease in middle age. He no doubt believed that the statements about his friend were sympathetic. Yet, through the glint in his eye, the combined smugness and nonchalance in his voice, and the erect position of his head, he unwittingly gave me the distinct impression that he felt victorious that his friend had died and not he.

Goffman[17] emphasized the actor's *presentation of self.* In this approach, the analyst attempts to identify what and whom is being presented, the ways in which roles are being played, and how both fit into the ongoing scene. Questions one might ask include: Is the presented self consistent with the role played? Is the role a routine performance or an extraordinary one? For who is it routine? The role of announcing death, for example, is routine for a physician, but it results in an extraordinary event for the bereaved.

The significance of the *audience* is now apparent: Any drama must have its audience. But what is the nature of this audience? What kind of reciprocity exist between audience and performer? What relationship does the audience have to the ongoing scenes? In formal relationships such as those found in hospitals, the relationship between audience and performer tends to be more static than in informal, intimate relationships. Currently, however, we are witnessing something of a reversal in audience-performer roles with the dying. While the stage is typically set for dying patients to constitute the audience while various performances are being played out around them and on their bodies, some dying persons are refusing to remain in the audience! Instead, they wish to take the leading role as the *performer* who gives shape and content to the unfolding drama.

Examining the audience raises other questions: Under what circumstances are there different audiences? Is the same performance played to all of them? Quite clearly, audiences differ and performances must be changed accordingly if they are to be taken as credible and real. For example, the exaggerated deference of a funeral director is quite inappropriate with peers, as is any reference to the deceased as a "stiff" or "corpse" to the bereaved. Similarly, hospital staff often shift their performances according to their assessments of the social class background of the clientele. To illustrate, I noticed that in one convalescent hospital the staff were much less careful about their actions in front of the families of Medi-Cal (state-supported) patients than the private patients. In this particular institution, the aides sometimes had coffee and cigarettes in the rooms of patients whom they deemed to be senile or comatose. When the registered nurse was elsewhere, they would occasionally turn up the patient's radio and practice dance steps. When families visited the Medi-Cal patients, the aides would stop dancing, but unless work was immediately pressing, they finished their coffee and cigarettes while conversing with the visitors. The registered nurse who supervised them did not seem to object to this behavior, but if similar behavior was witnessed by the families of private patients, she chastised them heavily and even threatened to fire several of them (see Sudnow[18] for similar incidents).

The way in which the performance is given is then intertwined with whom, where and when it is given. Generally, dramaturgical analysts have paid more attention to *spatial* and *temporal* arrangements than have their symbolic interactionist counterparts. Hence, they study the effects of territorial arrangements on the scene. In particular, they differentiate between public (or frontstage) territories and private (or backstage) regions (see

Goffman[19]). Of course, vast discrepancies are apt to exist between these two arenas of action. For example, nursing homes might be considered the backstage of the medical care system since what goes on within them is largely outside the purview of the public. Or, to use the term more concretely, hospital staff may attempt to put forth one type of impression in the presence of patients and families, but immediately drop it when observed by peers. Similarly, dramaturgical analysts focus on the timing of actions and events. Whether or not the timing of a performance is "correct" affects its credibility with the audience. For example, Shneidman[20] tells of a Greek immigrant who was admitted to the hospital with advanced leukemia. When Shneidman interviewed him, he seemed depressed. The patient disclosed that a young doctor had asked him, "Are you afraid to die?"[21] Shneidman discovered that the doctor had asked the question *before* the patient knew what the term "leukemia" meant. Obviously, the timing of the doctor's performance was wrong although, no doubt, the question was meant to show concern.

In concluding this discussion of the dramaturgical approach, I need to comment on the conception of human nature implied within it. In the foregoing discussion, one might see human nature as opportunistic, self-interested and strategic. However, the value of the method of analysis does not need to be limited to the study of manipulative performances calculated to have the "edge" on other participants. What happens in everyday life is simply more obvious when actors behave strategically. In any case, by using the dramaturgical method, the analyst gains a sense of the ways in which individuals attempt to *control* their situations, interactions and most importantly, themselves.

Both the dramaturgical and symbolic interactionist approaches begin with analyses of the individual. While the dramaturgical analyst emphasizes action, the symbolic interactionist emphasizes intention. Both perspectives lead to an examination of meanings derived from interaction. Although these perspectives have in the past primarily been used to study the self and interaction, they may also provide a framework for analyzing larger social units.

STRUCTURAL-FUNCTIONAL APPROACH

Basic to a structural approach is the question, how death is related to the *society* as a whole. In response to this question, structural-functional theorists would examine the functions of the ways of handling death that serve the wider society. Since they view society as a social system or organism maintained by the balanced *functioning* of its parts, this approach is based on an *equilibrium model.* The emphasis is placed on how society maintains its equilibrium so that *social integration* is preserved. The parts of the social system contributing to the maintenance of the equilibrium are the *social institutions.* If social integration is to be maintained, institutionalized ways of handling death would have to be consistent with the maintenance of the present social structure. From this perspective, the ways in which death is handled would necessarily have the consequence of providing continuity in the ongoing social structure.

Adopting a structural-functional approach leads one to look closely at the institutionalized cultural foundations of contemporary attitudes toward death. In order to understand these attitudes and place them in perspective, one must look at ritual meanings held by members of society. Explication of meanings about death provides some insight into the reciprocal ways in which death and social structure are linked. For example, Illich[22] argues that ritual meanings about "natural" death become institutionalized into the social structure of medicine as well as in the everyday expectations of lay persons. Even though meanings of a "natural" death become transformed by the institution of medicine, according to Illich, they remain significant for the structuring of actual care by paradoxically creating a pool of passive consumers who are subjected to a technologized dying process.

A structural perspective necessitates an analysis of the *development, structure, functions, consequences of* and *interrelationships* between dominant institutions. Then, an analysis must be constructed of the connections between institutional forms and death. Parsons and Lidz[23] invoke this line of reasoning when they explore the effects of awarding secular institutions major value in modern society. They propose that the rise of science has had the consequence of diminishing the significance of death. Values supporting science have taken precedence over those supporting religious institutions, which Parsons and Lidz claim provide the framework for interpreting death. Further, they imply that such interpretations must be consistent with beliefs supporting science if social integration is to be maintained.

A more subtle interplay between science and death perhaps centers on the area of *death expectations.* People hold institutionalized expectations concerning the "appropriate" type of death, that is, a natural death, and the "correct" timing of it (old age). For example, it is neither proper nor natural to die from a fall at age 30. The significance of these expectations may readily be discerned when they are not met. Lifton's[24] observations of the survivors of the atomic bomb on Hiroshima shed some light on the profound disruption that occurred when not only individual death expectations were shattered but also when the survivors, overwhelmed by their experience, did not and could not respond to their situations with anything resembling a "normal" grief response. Instead, they were left numb as their worlds literally collapsed. Although Lifton's intent was to explore the psychiatric implications of such an experience, the careful study of such dramatic disruptions of institutionalized expectations may reveal much about the preexisting social structure.

Another means of making structural patterns more visible is to conduct comparative studies of diverse cultures. By conducting systematic comparisons of the beliefs and norms of another society with our own, the structural-functionalist may make hidden dimensions of culture more visible. For example, Parsons and Lidz[25] compare the abbreviated and privatized contemporary mourning rituals with those in preindustrial societies wherein death caused much greater disruption of social structure. They hypothesize that the modern approach of brief rituals and private grief may be functional for society since structural continuity is maintained if the survivors quickly resume their former roles and tasks.

Since social structural analysis examines values and practices in relationship to the functioning of society, some positions arrived at stand in stark contrast to those taken by other intellectuals and the public alike. For example, Parsons and Lidz[26] take issue with the commonly accepted view that the dominant cultural attitude toward death in American society is death-denying. In contrast, they claim that the ways in which death is treated are consistent with dominant values requiring *activism* of the individual. Hence, they imply that life in American society presupposes active, forward-looking members whose primary task is to fulfill their social roles. Later, Parsons, Fox and Lidz[27] qualify the earlier argument by stating that much of what passes for "denial" actually is a type of apathy perpetuated by both the stoicism of the Protestant Ethos and everyday medical practice.

Having set forth some of the major concerns of a structural-functional approach to the study of death, I will now examine the potential of death for disrupting the equilibrium of social life. Blauner[28] points out that this potential exists in any society although its extent varies with the type of social structure and the significance of the participation within it of those who die. Thus, standardized practices including customs, norms and laws are developed to handle death in ways which *minimize* the potential disruption and foster the *reintegration* of the group. A modern example of such standardized practices consists of the rituals surrounding the death of police officers who are killed on duty. The full participation of an officer's peers as well as other law enforcement officials in the funeral and burial rites serves to reaffirm the solidarity and purposes of the members. Moreover, the scenario of the procession with uniformed members of their respective agencies marching or riding their motorcycles and horses is a concrete symbol not only of their affiliation but also of their strength. As one policeman commented to me, "I think the real function of the procession is to re-establish a sense of order, particularly for the members of the force of the guy who was killed."

Blauner emphasizes that a disruptive consequence of death for ongoing social life is the social vacuum that is created by death. He argues that death creates a gap in the social structure, and possibly in the institutionalized functioning of a particular group. How serious the social vacuum is depends upon the social and symbolic importance of the person or persons who die. One individual in our society whose death created something of a social vacuum was John F. Kennedy. Quite clearly, in smaller groups or societies in which face-to-face interaction between its members is characteristic of the society, the potential disruption caused by death is much greater than in a mass society. Blauner posits that elaborate funeral, burial and mourning rites were developed in these societies to lessen the disruption of the society as a whole. Through these rites, the duties and rights of the survivors were clearly spelled out. Blauner astutely recognized that death in these societies could have devastating effects upon the kinship and community structure since death frequently occurred while the deceased was an integral part of the group. That is, women died in the midst of their child-raising years and men died while involved in their work. In short, mortality had a grave impact upon the society since those who were responsible for the functioning of the society were affected by it.

Blauner's basic thesis is that fundamental determinants of the impact of death are the *age* and *social contributions* of those who die. According to his argument, those who are younger and who are directly contributing to the functioning of the society are going to create larger social vacuums upon their death. It must be noted, however, that social contributions must be given full credit since in some societies the most important social contributions for maintaining the moral beliefs and norms of the group are made by the elders who rule the group. In our society, most elderly people are afforded little opportunity to contribute to others and are not given much respect for their prior contributions. Consequently, they have a different kind of status in the social structure from what is often observed in traditional societies. Blauner's study represents a typical structural-functional approach because it emphasizes the effects of social roles and social functions on society.

Although death occurs at all ages, functional theorists have been particularly concerned with institutional relationships between death and the elderly, since the death rates in industrial societies are increasingly constituted by them. In our society, retirement, without compensatory tasks and status combined with child-raising in early adulthood, results in a situation where elderly persons no longer are an integral part of the functioning of the society. Further, the elderly have become segregated from the rest of the community in retirement apartments, planned communities, mobile home courts, nursing homes and downtown hotels. Consequently, even their presence is less visible to those who are contributing actively to the maintenance of the society. Blauner points out that a way of reducing the impact of mortality is to reduce the real or ideal significance of those who die. In this vein, he cites the classic example provided by Ariès.[29] Historically, Ariès found that French children were not highly valued when infant mortality was high. At the time children were not seen as individuals until they had attained an age after which their chances of survival became more promising. Consequently, their social loss to the family and to the larger society was kept minimal. Thus the *attitude* was *functional* for a society. Not only do they not contribute to the vital functions of the society, but they are also systematically deprived of their individuality and certainly represent a devalued group. In short, according to this argument, deaths of elderly persons would not necessitate any serious disruption and accommodation by the society. In contrast, in a society where the elderly are fully integrated, institutions would have to arise to distribute their functions, to repair the group of their loss, and to treat death as a visible fact of life.

In the structural-functional approach, the individual and the society exist in a delicately *balanced relationship*. Since death could conceivably alter this delicate balance, social mechanisms are developed that are assumed to be *adaptive* for both the society and the individual. Because aging and death are facts of life, functionalist theorists, such as Blauner, raise questions about the adjustment of the society and individual to these facts. Blauner has provided a cogent analysis of how the society adapts to the deaths of members who are most likely to die. Structural-functional theorists also raise questions as to how the individual adapts so that the fragile equilibrium between self and society is maintained. Since death rates are inevitably high in old age, functional theorists assume that both the society and the individual must prepare for it.

In their theory of *disengagement*, Cumming and Henry[30] provide a theoretical explanation of the development of this preparation. Disengagement means that once-active individuals gradually give up their former social roles that contributed to the work of the society. Disengagement is advantageous, according to the theory, to both the society and the individual. Society gives individuals the freedom to withdraw, something structural-functionalist assume individuals desire. Society then benefits because others can assume the vacated social roles. The advantages to the society are clear—the work of the society is carried out and the unpleasant fact of death is minimized. But how is disengagement satisfying for the individual? Cumming and Henry propose that individuals want to withdraw since death can be accepted with greater equanimity once they no longer have deep social ties anchored in adult responsibilities. Because they are motivated to disengage, their life satisfaction is assumed to be based on prior accomplishments and an increasing concern with inner needs. Structural-functionalists assume that older people voluntarily initiate their disengagement during middle age as they become aware of their decreasing life span. Hence, according to the theory, people gradually relinquish social roles and bonds in order to *prepare for death*. By giving up social roles and reducing the number and intensity of social ties, older people become socially and psychologically prepared for death. Relationships are ended or are resolved; detachment and passivity are permitted as it is assumed that these people do not feel pressured to remain involved. Then, what Cumming and Henry imply is that the social situation of the aged is a *satisfactory* arrangement. Since individuals may prepare for death through their gradual withdrawal, the society does not have to concern itself with either heavy social obligations to the aged, nor does the presence of the aged impede the smooth working of that society. Clearly, individuals do not withdraw with the *motive* or *intent* to "help society out"—reasons are varied. They include apathy, lack of money and, most importantly, I think, ill health. The ultimate *function* of disengagement, however, is that it does "help" maintain the current social structural arrangements.

Cumming and Henry view the process of disengagement as a natural process that is irreversible once set into motion. Psychological and social age are merged in this framework into a developmental conception of a linear process that culminates in death. The first major step of the process usually begins with retirement. But gradually, as individuals withdraw, a new equilibrium is established between them and the society. The type of balance between self and society when individuals are disengaged is qualitatively different from that experienced in middle age. By the time illness and dying are experienced, disengaged people are assumed to be able to accept their inevitable fate.

In a framework such as Cumming and Henry have provided, what is typically observable within the society is elevated to a "natural" and "universal" status. That older people are usually forced to disengage and may currently accept the social pressure to play their passive and often segregated roles does not necessarily mean that the disengagement process we discern reflects anything more than the social structuring of economic existence. Further, on a social psychological level, the passivity and withdrawal of older persons may simply be something of a self-fulfilling prophecy that is socially produced. Hochschild[31] insightfully notes that forced economic disengagement itself fosters passivity and loss of emotional intensity, two conditions which, according to Cumming and Henry, are supposed to be criteria of successful psychological disengagement. Thus, Cumming and Henry elevate an economic necessity within a certain type of society into a functional prerequisite of society itself. The disengagement theory raises some intriguing questions for students on death. Does, in fact, disengagement in old age prepare people for their deaths, or does it perhaps so demoralize them that they no longer have much interest in living? Is resignation confused with acceptance? Does death become viewed as an escape, a way out? Do disengaged persons give more conscious thought to coming to terms with their own deaths than people who are more involved? In order to examine these questions fully, one must look at the empirical world of living, thinking beings rather than being satisfied to posit explanations that may make sense theoretically but are not clearly assessed empirically.

In order to study the implications of this theory empirically, two important questions must be asked from two other perspectives. From a symbolic interactionist perspective, one must ask what disengagement subjectively means to the social actor. The investigator must look at how the individual defines involvement and withdrawal and determine what explicit and implicit criteria the person has for both. Then, too, from a Marxian perspective, disengagement must be studied in conjunction with power arrangements. By and large, old people do not yet have much choice about engagement, and their very lack of choice must be made an object of study. Hence, the structural-functional perspective, by focusing on the functions of processes such as disengagement, tends to ignore the subjective feelings and intentions of individuals, which are emphasized by symbolic interactionists. Structural-functionalists also tend to view the current structural arrangements as necessary. This results in an acceptance of the social order as it is, which Marxists call into question. As will become apparent in the next section, a Marxist structural analysis raises a contrasting set of questions to ask of the social order.

A MARXIST PERSPECTIVE

Perhaps because death is something that happens to the individual, sociologists have, for the most part, neglected to study it from a radical structural critique. However, I propose that any serious sociological treatment of death in American society raises radical issues about its structure. From a Marxist perspective, the institutions supporting American society need restructuring to obtain an equitable distribution of wealth and power. A radical analysis of social structure would then go to the roots or foundations of that structure and seek to transform them. Simply because most sociological studies of death and dying are social-psychological in focus does not mean that the issues are limited to the individual or the interaction process. Besides, the ways in which the individual's concerns and arena of interaction fit into the larger social context are of major significance. Although to date there are no Marxist sociologists who study death, there are a number of studies which suggest dimensions of the issues raised by this perspective. In the following analysis, I shall attempt to show how death in American society might be dealt with from the perspective of Marxist humanism (see Fromm[32]; Giddens[33]; Zeitlin[34]).

One of the obvious issues to be addressed in a Marxist approach to death is that of *inequality*. Inequality is apparent in the availability and quality of medical care as well as in differential death rates. For example, Sudnow[35] documents the moral decisions made in a county hospital. These decisions result in practices which systematically deprive lower-income patients (particularly the elder poor) of optimal care, in general, and of lifesaving procedures, in particular. From a statistical point of view, lower-income people, including most minority people, are shown to have substantially higher death rates for each age bracket than middle-class males (see Goldscheider[36]). Similarly, in one of its recent publications, the Department of Health, Education, and Welfare[37] reported that the age-adjusted death rate in 1973 for minority men was one-third more than the corresponding rate for white counterparts, and the rate for minority women was 50 percent more than the rate for white females.

The inequality observed in mortality rates suggests the kinds of relationships between death and a social structure predicted on a class system that sociologists might further study. Marxists assume that the class system divides people into groups having widely discrepant and often mutually exclusive economic interests, whether or not members of these classes actually recognize their interests. When they do not, it is assumed that they have accepted the dominant ideas and values of the society, which are the ideas of the power elite. Marxists then posit a crucial relationship between social structure and those ideas held within a society. With that crucial relationship in mind, a discussion of ideals about death and social structure may begin.

As a starting point, Marxists would assume that neither the process of dying nor the modes of handling death can be separated from the larger social structure in which they take place. Thus, from a Marxist perspective, a major tenet is that "psychological" reactions seemingly caused by intrapsychic processes are actually fostered by larger social processes. In this view, then, it is a mistake to examine only the subjective view of the individual or, for that matter, the psychological processes that professionals observe in dying patients or the bereaved. The thoughts and feelings that are both unstated and directly expressed by people who may in some way confront death are shaped by their experiences within the society and their exposure to the dominant ideologies and institutions within it. For example, the sister of a woman whose husband was dying in a local hospital made the following statement:

> She [her sister] wants to be with him when he dies, whenever it occurs. I think that she's being unrealistic. Most people die alone today. You live alone and you die alone—that's the way it is. Dying is something you have to do on your own.

This woman's statement reflects her ideological view, one shared by many who believe that the living and dying should be separated. It also shows that the excessive individualism characteristic of a competitive economic system, and the ensuing loneliness, carries over to death as well.

One might raise further questions about how death and ideologies are related. As observed earlier, ideologies not only justify past actions but also foster the creation of future actions. Since death is usually conceived of as a unique experience belonging solely to the individual, at first glance there may seem to be no connection with ideologies. But from a Marxist perspective, most of what we "know" about death represents ideological views rather than a "true" picture of reality. In addition, from this perspective dying cannot be separated from living and what living is all about is also shrouded in ideological beliefs. If so, our modes of conceptualizing death, dying and grieving would be intimately related to our ideological conceptions of living and life. And from a Marxist perspective many parallels can be drawn.

Marxists claim that what is taken for granted to be "true" and "real" by a group of people typically reflects an *unexamined ideology.* Many of our assumptions about death and dying then reflect ideological stances. Ideologies are not necessarily false beliefs or myths that totally obfuscate reality, but they do tend to be partial in character and limited in the scope of reality than they accurately portray. For example, the current belief among some practitioners that the patient must pass through the psychological stages of dying, as first outlined by Kübler-Ross,[38] is an ideological perspective. Many terminally ill patients do go through the stages, although those who would acknowledge that the stages reflect their own experience of the dying process might be a much smaller number than Kübler-Ross's followers might expect. Or, like the belief in romantic love in this culture, to the extent that an ideology about death becomes dominant throughout the society, then people become socialized into making attempts to validate the belief in their own everyday reality.

In any case, when a view of reality is taken as "real" and "true," it tends to become *reified*, or treated as a concrete and stable entity. Major interpretations of the dying process have been treated as if they were fixed and stable entities which then take on a universal character. They are treated as "natural," rather than habitual or culturally defined.

As beliefs take on ideological weight, they provide a form for seeing and understanding reality. The framework through which death is usually studied and understood tends to be a psychiatric framework. This framework, like other conceptual frameworks, highlights certain aspects of reality and blinds its user to others. From a Marxian view, our perspectives on death and dying have blinded us from seeing the ways in which they are ideological and when acted out in practical reality, perpetuate certain power interests. For example, ordinary people who believe in giving relatives the maximum amount of medical intervention possible are unlikely to be aware that the stance they take also supports the pharmaceutical, hospital supply and convalescent hospital industry interests.

Furthermore, from a Marxist perspective, it becomes clear that ideologies serve to mask the divergent interests that different sectors of the society have. Since in this perspective it is assumed that different groups often have *mutually exclusive* interests, it follows that many so-called services for the dying and deceased, such as funeral planning or terminal care, may be designed for the economic interests of those providing services rather than the clientele being served.

Ideologies that reflect more widely held cultural values are also played out in the scenarios surrounding death. Beliefs in individualism, self-reliance, privatism and stoicism are ideological and justify the ways in which dying is handled. The ideological view of dying as a private affair, something that *should* be the responsibility of the family, relieves other social institutions, notably health and welfare organizations, from the necessity of providing comprehensive services. This view is consistent with more generally held beliefs that individuals must handle their own affairs. Such beliefs are justified by ideological views that human beings deserve privacy in their problems, and in order to maintain self-respect, they wish to rely on themselves to handle them whenever possible. When it is not possible, failure may be conferred upon those unable to handle their situations. These beliefs give some indication of the ideological power of the Protestant Ethos that is still embedded in the American consciousness (cf. Gorer[39]).

Such ideologies serve to work against the "objective" interests of many individuals. For those who hold these beliefs, feelings of failure are likely to develop when responsibilities cannot be handled by a single-family unit or, likely, a spouse or adult child. The difficulties in taking care of a terminally ill person tend to multiply and spiral as the person's disease sets in. Hence, the stage is set for the ill person to feel guilty for the burdens on intimates, and then, too, intimates are apt to feel overwhelmed and angry. For example, one elderly woman was afraid of going to an institution. Her middle-aged daughter took care of her as she progressively deteriorated. Since there were no community resources for terminal care, the burden of home care fell on the family, primarily her daughter. For a period of time, the daughter attempted to manage both her job and her mother's care. However, with the downhill course of the disease it became impossible, so the daughter took a leave of absence. The care steadily increased to the point that keeping her mother clean and reasonably comfortable took more than the daughter (whose back was literally giving out) could handle. The mother felt guilty for the strain her daughter was under. The daughter began to feel and, occasionally, express anger at her mother for being so unwilling to go to a nursing home. And by that time there were no available slots at any of the nursing homes the family thought were suitable placements. Yet, this family and often others similarly involved still define the situation as "our" problem and attempt to respond to it only in the most individualistic manner, such as seeing the solution solely in terms of personal expression of negative feelings elicited by the situation.

But a personal and private crisis has public consequences and political implications. What is privately felt and experienced could be changed when brought into the public arena. So long as experiences remain "private matters" they will not be given much public attention. Thus, even when discussed in the realm of public policy by practitioners and concerned citizens, the problems are narrowly defined and the solutions stop-gap and partial.

More common, however, is the tendency for practitioners to reaffirm the definition of the problem as a private one, the solutions for which are to be developed individually, case by case. Hence, for the most part, the experiences of the dying person are not seen in the context of larger social meanings.

In the discussion above, I have emphasized how ideologies are related to our current practices concerning death. Now I wish to offer some ideas about how these practices might be related to everyday life. The Marxian conception of social reality holds the position that human beings are basically creative and reflective beings although social systems, most notably those predicated on advanced industrial capitalism, produce alienated beings who cannot control their fates. In this view, the very form that human nature takes in this historical epoch is twisted into a type of being to correspond to the needs of the system. It is believed that human beings are fundamentally shaped by an alienating, dehumanizing social structure that encourages people to lead atomized, fragmented lives. Competition and the quest for personal gain are believed to feed the isolation and alienation that characterizes life in this society. As a result, people do not recognize their common interests with others and are unlikely to feel secure in challenging their existing mode of life. Thus competition and alienation give birth to the kinds of *controlled individualism* that symbolize the American spirit and, subsequently, mitigate against the development of concerted collective action that would radically change both the structure of society, in general, and the experience of dying, in particular.

In many ways, dying in this society dramatically symbolizes an underlying theme of the alienation and powerlessness of its members that is obscured by the appearance of freedom in everyday life. Dying patients are often left alone, abandoned by relatives, forgotten by friends and feared by practitioners. They may be treated as dead or nonpersons while they are sentient. Their feelings and wishes are subjugated to institutional routines, treatment trends and their relatives' decisions. Not only are they usually powerless, but they are also stripped of their selves as they become objects to be manipulated by those who control them. An example from a case history may help. One old man was discharged to a convalescent hospital to die. Nursing aids in the acute hospital had told him that he would be going "home," but his son had not visited in several weeks. Because he had outlived his friends, his life had been mostly limited to his TV in his boarding house room. Other boarders paid little attention to him. After the transfer to the convalescent hospital, he had virtually no contacts with the outside world except for occasional hurried "visits" from his daughter-in-law. Eventually, those also ceased. He had no control over treatment, though at first he complained much. Because he became a source of staff irritation and resentment, they sedated him heavily. By the time he died, he had become a symbol of death itself to the staff.

The powerlessness of this man surely contributed to a loss of self while he was dying. But his experience is not unique. Perhaps then, the treatment of the dying symbolizes the hollowness of life in an alienated society. And the systematic alienation and isolation of the dying patient shows in bold relief the fundamental premises on which existence in American society is based. But if one attempts to control one's life and take responsibility for that control one might, in turn, decrease one's alienation and, simultaneously, foster conditions which may give rise to a more humane social order. Thus, as alienation decreases, the construction of personal meaning would increase in life as well as in death.

Now I will return to more concrete instances which demonstrate how death may be related to power interests. From a Marxist perspective, one can argue that although we hold ideologies espousing the value of individual life in this society, those in power have little respect for the collective life of the society and particularly for those in the lower classes. Hence, working-class youths find themselves being used as cannon fodder during military crises, factory workers are exposed to life-threatening chemicals in their everyday work, and the aged poor suffer a slow starvation from malnutrition. Economic prerogatives taken by the few in power then may supersede the interests of the larger community. Those in power act in their own interests at the expense of those who do not have it, often without their full awareness of the implications of doing so. Even when those who are affected are dimly aware that extreme hazards might affect them, they may not press charges. Factory workers, for example, may be aware that studies indicate that those who work daily in contact with harmful substances have a higher incidence of certain lethal cancer. But if the studies are not conclusive, and if the predictions of disease are made for 20 or 30 years hence, then workers may shrug off the ominous implications of their work because they need to make a living now. Besides, corporation representatives can threaten closure of the plant if working conditions are changed. If other possibilities for work are few, the workers are apt to be controlled by such tactics.

Returning to the issue of risk to which the worker is exposed, Hesslink and Steinman[40] trace the history of one type of harmful substance, asbestos. They show that a wide gap exists between medical discoveries of harmful chemicals and the implementation and acceptance of government rules. In their example of the asbestos industry, they found that dangers associated with its use were suspected as early at 1906! By 1930 the suspected risk had been confirmed, yet not until 1972 were regulations established. Furthermore, to date, the public has only very recently become at all informed about the dangers of the substance.

According to Hesslink and Steinman, several factors may be operative in the delay of information. First, the industrial physicians who are most likely to first encounter indications of danger seem to identify themselves more as management than as physicians. Second, these physicians may be in danger of demotion or harassment when they take stands that undermine the corporation's objectives. Third, corporations sometimes exert censorship over the publications from their medical employees precisely for protection from lawsuits, raised insurance premiums and workers. This suggests that corporate officials knowingly will place their own economic interests over the general welfare of their workers and the public. Fourth, Hesslink and Steinman demonstrate that beyond the private sphere, government bureaucrats take steps to keep information inaccessible to the public. Government agents, like workers, may at times find it preferable to continue exposure to dangerous materials both for the workers and the public alike than to make drastic changes that could affect the general economic situation at the time. Fifth, even if regulations are passed and public information is made available, the government may not enforce regulations or, if enforced, they may be so weak that corporations break them regularly.

The contradictory interests of different groups of people are shown in the asbestos example. Underlying the issue is the fundamental dilemma of whether the public good is worth more than disrupting the present social arrangements. When dilemmas like this are examined, it becomes apparent that the life and well-being of the people are not necessarily the first consideration of those who shape public policy. Another example of such a dilemma arises in the area of earthquake prediction. Some people take the position that it is "dangerous" to inform the populace of these predictions since the economy will be disrupted if predicted locations are evacuated despite the fact that without advance notice thousands may be killed.

Although the intentional acts of individuals to serve their own interests is a major concern of a Marxian theorist, this perspective also reveals how the limited point of view some people have because they occupy a particular position in society can shape their actions within it. Subsequently, an individual's actions may unintentionally cause or perpetuate an undesirable situation, such as more people becoming critically ill from exposure to asbestos. When dealing with complex medical issues involving interpretation of highly sophisticated data, many of those involved see the situation only from their position. Hence, however unintentionally, important aspects of the problem at hand are often overlooked, though the costs of these blunders may be paid in human lives.

This discussion suggests some of the central questions that might be asked from a Marxist framework. The strength of a Marxist humanist approach is that it links the underlying social structural problems with the psychological responses of individuals. In conclusion, the symbolic interactionist, structural-functionalist and Marxist perspectives, when used concomitantly, provide powerful insight into meanings, individual group relations, underlying root causes and sources of order and change. A sociological investigation into death will profit from all three perspectives.

NOTES

1. Herbert Blumer. 1969. Symbolic Interactionism. Englewood Cliffs, NJ: Prentice-Hall.

2. Alfred Lindesmith, Anselm Strauss and Norman Denzin. 1975. *Social Psychology.* Hindsdale, IL: Dryden.
3. Anselm L. Strauss, ed. 1964. *George Herbert Mead: On Social Psychology.* Chicago: University of Chicago Press.
4. Richard A. Kalish and David K. Reynolds. 1976. *Death and Ethnicity.* Los Angeles: University of California Press.
5. Ibid., p. 70.
6. Lindesmith, Strauss and Denzin, loc. cit.
7. Blumer, loc. cit.
8. Ibid.
9. Ibid., p. 3.
10. Ibid.
11. Ibid.
12. Erving Goffman. 1959. *The Presentation of Self in Everyday Life.* Garden City, NY: Doubleday Anchor Books.
13. Kenneth Burke. 1945. *A Grammar of Motives.* Englewood Cliffs, NJ: Prentice-Hall.
14. Dennis Brisett and Charles Edgley, eds. 1975. *Life as Theatre.* Chicago: Aldine, p. 7.
15. Ronny E. Turner and Charles Edgely. 1975. Death as Theater: A Dramaturgical Analysis of the American Funeral. *Sociology and Social Research* 60:377-392.
16. Goffman, loc. cit.
17. Ibid.
18. David Sudnow. 1967. *Passing On.* Englewood Cliffs, NJ: Prentice-Hall.
19. Goffman, loc. cit.
20. Edwin Shneidman. 1973. *Deaths of Man.* New York: Quadrangle Books.
21. Ibid., p. 31.
22. Ivan Illich. 1974. The Political Uses of Natural Death. In Peter Steinfels and Robert M. Teatch, eds., *Death Inside Out.* New York: Harper & Row.
23. Talcott Parsons and Victor Lidz. 1967. Death in American Society. In Edwin W. Schneidman, ed., *Essays in Self-Destruction.* New York: Science House.
24. Robert Jay Lifton. 1968. *Death in Life.* New York: Random House.
25. Parsons and Lidz, loc. cit.
26. Ibid.
27. Talcott Parsons, Renée C. Fox and Victor M. Lidz. 1973. The "Gift of Life" and Its Reciprocation. In Arien Mack, ed., *Death in American Experience.* New York: Schocken Books.
28. Robert Blauner. 1966. Death and Social Structure. *Psychiatry* 29:378-394.
29. Philippe Ariès. 1962. *Centuries of Childhood: A Social History of Family Life.* New York: Knopf.
30. Elaine Cumming and William Henry. 1961. *Growing Old.* New York: Basic Books.
31. Arlie Hochschild. 1975. Disengagement Theory: A Critique and Proposal. *American Sociological Review* 40:553-569.
32. Erich Fromm. 1962. *Marx's Concept of Man.* New York: Frederick Ungar.
33. Anthony Giddens. 1971. *Capitalism and Modern Social Theory.* Cambridge: Cambridge University Press.
34. Irving Zeitlin. 1968. *Ideology and the Development of Sociological Theory.* Englewood Cliffs, NJ: Prentice-Hall.
35. Sudnow, loc. cit.

36. Calvin Goldscheider. 1975. The Social Inequality of Death. In Edwin S. Schneidman, ed., *Death: Current Perspectives.* Palo Alto, CA: Mayfield.
37. Department of Health, Education, and Welfare. 1977. Parameters of Health in the United States. In Howard D. Schwartz and Cary S. Kart, eds., *Dominant Issues in Medical Sociology.* Reading, MA: Addison-Wesley.
38. Elisabeth Kübler-Ross. 1969. *On Death and Dying.* New York: Macmillan.
39. Geoffrey Gorer. 1965. *Death, Grief and Mourning.* Garden City, NY: Doubleday/Anchor Books.
40. George K. Hesslink and Howard K. Steinman. 1976. Social Awareness of Environmental Health Hazards: The Lag Between Medical Discovery, Governmental Regulation and Public Acceptance. Paper presented at the Pacific Sociological Association.

3

Death in the Western World

Talcott Parsons, PhD

That the death of every known human individual has been one of the central facts of life so long as there has been any human awareness of the human condition does not mean that, being so well known, it is not problematical. On the contrary, like history, it has needed to be redefined and newly analyzed, virtually with every generation. However, as has also been the case with history, with the advancement of knowledge later reinterpretations may have some advantages over earlier.

I start from the proposition that if we are to speak of the death of individuals, we need some conceptualization, beyond common sense, of what a human individual or "person" is. First, I do not propose to discuss the meaning of the deaths of members of other species, insects, elephants, or dogs, but only of human individuals. Second, I propose to confine discussion to individual persons and not to examine societies, civilizations, or races in this sense.

ORGANIC DEATH AND DEATH OF A PERSONALITY

Within these limitations I should like to start with the statement that the human individual is a synthesized *combination* of a living organism and a "personality system," conceived and analyzed at the level of "action" in the sense in which I and various others have used that term.[1] In older terminology, an individual is a combination of a "body" and a "mind." The concept of a personality as *analytically* distinguished from an organism is no more mystical than is that of a "culture" as distinguished from the human population (of organisms) who are its "bearers." The primary criterion of personality, as distinguished from the organism, is an organization in terms of symbols and their meaningful relations to each other and to persons. In the process of evolution, personalities should be regarded as emergent from the organic level, as are cultural systems in a different, though related way.

Human individuals, seen in their organic aspect, come into being through bisexual reproduction—and birth—as do all the higher organisms. They then go through a more or less well defined life course and eventually die. The most important single difference among such individual organisms is the duration of their lives, but for each species there is a maximum span: for humans, it is somewhere between 90 and 100 years. In this sense death is universal, the only question being "at what age?" Within these limits the circumstances of both life and death vary enormously.

It seems that these considerations have an immediate bearing on one of the current controversies about death, namely, the frequent allegation that American society—and some say others—attempts to "deny death."[2] Insofar as this is the case (and I am skeptical), the contention has to be in the face of a vast body of biological knowledge. If any biological proposition can be regarded as firmly established, it is that, for sexually reproducing species, the mortality of individual, "phenotypical" organisms is completely normal. Indeed, mortality could not have evolved if it did not have positive survival value *for the species*, unless evolutionary theory is completely wrong. This fact will be a baseline for our whole analysis.

The human individual is not only a living organism but also a special kind of organism who uses symbols, notably linguistic ones. One learns symbolic meaning, communicates with others and with oneself through them as media, and regulates behavior, thought, and feelings in symbolic terms. I call the individual in this aspect an *actor*. Is an actor "born"? Clearly not in the sense in which an organism is. However, part of the development of the human child is a gradual and complicated process, which has sometimes been called *socialization*, whereby the personality becomes formed. The learning of patterns of relation to others, of language, and of structured ways of handling one's own action in relation to the environment is the center of this process.

Does a personality, then, also die? Because the symbiosis between organism and personality is so close, just as no personality in the human sense can be conceived to develop independently of a living child organism, so it is reasonable to believe that no human personality can be conceived as such to survive the death of the same organism, in the organic sense of death. With respect to causation, however, if the personality is an empirical reality, it certainly influences what happens to the organism, the person's "body," as well as vice versa. The extreme case is suicide, which surely can seldom be explained by purely somatic processes, without any "motives" being involved, as often can a death from cancer. But more generally there is every reason to believe that there are "psychic" factors in many deaths, all manner of illnesses, and various other organic events.

It is firmly established that the viability of the individual organism, human and nonhuman, is self-limiting. This, even in the absence of unfavorable environmental conditions, in the course of the "aging" process, there will occur gradual impairment of various organic capacities, until some combination of these impairments proves fatal. Organic death can be staved off by medical measures but cannot be totally prevented. There seems every reason to believe, but there is less clear-cut evidence on this point, that the same is in principle true of the action-personality component of the individual. This means that, with aging, various components of that complex entity lose the necessary capacities to maintain its balances, which eventually will lead to a breakdown. The cases in which there is virtual cessation of personality function without organic death are suggestive in this sense. More generally, if, as I strongly believe, the phenomena of mental illness are real and not merely epiphenomena of organic processes, then it stands to reason that some of them can be severe enough to eventuate in personality death, partly independent of organic death.

We have already noted that at the organic level the human individual does not stand alone but is part of an intergenerational chain of indefinite, though not infinite, durability, most notably the species. The individual organism dies, but if he reproduces, the "line" continues into future generations. This intergenerational continuity is as much a fact of life as are individual births and deaths.

There is a direct parallel on the action side: An individual personality is "generated" in symbiosis with a growing individual human organism and dies with that organism. But the individual personality is embedded in transindividual action systems, at two levels, social systems (most notably, whole societies) and cultural systems. There is a close analogy between these two and the relation between somatoplasm and germ plasm on the organic side, both of which are "carried" by the individual organism. Thus, the sociocultural "matrix" in which the individual personality is embedded is in an important sense the counterpart of the population-species matrix in which the individual organism is embedded.

At the organic level the individual organism dies, but the species continues, "life goes on." Also, the individual personality dies, but the society and cultural system, of which in life one was a part, also "goes on." I strongly suspect that this parallel is more than simple analogy.

What is organic death? It is of course a many-faceted thing, but as

Freud and many others have said, it is in one principal aspect the "return to the inorganic" state. At this level the human body, as that of other organisms, is made up of inorganic materials but *organized* in quite special ways. When that organization breaks down, the constituent materials are no longer part of a living organism but come to be assimilated to the inorganic environment. In a certain sense this insight has been ancient religious lore; witness the Gospel, "Dust thou art, to dust thou shalt return."

Is death of a personality to be simply assimilated to this organic paradigm? Most positivists and materialists would say, yes. This answer, however, has not been accepted by the majority in most human societies and cultures. From such very primitive peoples as the Australian aborigines, especially as their religion was analyzed by Durkheim,[3] to the most sophisticated of the world religions, there have persisted beliefs in the existence of an individual soul which can be conceived both to antedate and to survive the individual organism or body, though the ideas of preexistence and of survival have now always coexisted in any given culture. The literature of cultural anthropology and of comparative religion can supply many instances.[4] The issue of the individuality of this nonorganic component of the human individual, outside its symbiosis with the living organism, is also a basis of variability.

DEATH IN THE CHRISTIAN PARADIGM

Western civilization has had a historical background in which the dominant religious influence has been that of Christianity. Science has in recent times been the major focus of interpretation of the nonorganic component. Let us then try to outline the main Christian patterns of orientation and indicate modifications of the old materialistic-religious dichotomy that seem to be dictated by the emergence of a complex of disciplines dealing with human problems at the level of action.

In collaboration with Renée Fox and Victor Lidz I have presented an analysis of the Christian orientation to death.[5] There is no doubt of the predominance of a duality of levels in the Christian paradigm of the human condition, the levels of the spiritual and the temporal, as one formula states it. There is a striking resemblance between this duality and that in the organic world between species and individual organisms, as well as between the former and that in the action world between individual personality and sociocultural system. The Christian paradigm, however, seems to bracket the human condition within a still broader dichotomy. On the one hand, there is the material temporal world, of which one religious symbol is "dust" as cited earlier. On the other, there is the spiritual world of "eternal life," which is the location of things divine, not human. The individual soul is conceived as in some sense an "emanation" from this second "world."

We attempted,[6] relying heavily on biblical documentation, to interpret this syndrome in terms of Marcel Mauss's paradigm of the gift and its reciprocation.[7] Seen in this way, the life of the individual is a gift from God, and like other gifts it creates expectations of reciprocation. Living "in the faith" is part of the reciprocation but, more important for us, dying in the faith completes the cycle. It is surely notable that our ordinary language is permeated with references to giving in the connection. Thus, a woman is said to *give* birth to a child and we often say that in dying a person "*gives* up the ghost."

The language of giving also permeates the transcendental (i.e., beyond ordinary experience) level of symbolism in the Christian context. Thus, Mary, like any other woman, *gave* birth to Jesus. God also *gave* his "only begotten son" for the redemption of humankind. Finally, Jesus, in the Crucifixion and thus the Eucharist, *gave* his blood for the same purpose. By the doctrine of reciprocation mankind assumes, it may be said, three principal obligations, namely to "accept" the human condition as ordained by divine will (i.e., the gift of life), to live in the faith, and to die in the faith. If these conditions are fulfilled, salvation is the reward.

One further point should be stressed: the way in which the symbiosis of the organic and the action level of the human condition is symbolized in this Christian complex (that is, through the sacralization of the family, which is the primary social organization having to do with human reproduction, birth and death, health and illness, and their relations). The focus here is the Holy Family, with even the Trinity having certain family-like characteristics: witness God the Father and God the Son. It may further be noted that the two most important Christian seasonal festivals "celebrate" the birth of Jesus—Christmas—and commemorate his death—namely, Easter, though with the doctrine of resurrection, commemoration also becomes celebration.

Christianity, in its Catholic form, has institutionalized a special duality in the human societies and cultures in which it has existed; namely, in medieval terms, that between church and state. These institutional complexes have very closely corresponded to the duality, within the individual between soul and body, with the church having custody, as it were, of the soul. A major change, however, occurred with the Protestant Reformation. This particular version of Christian dualism was "collapsed" in that the sacraments no longer mediated (for Protestants) between God and humanity; no priesthood held the "power of the keys"; and withdrawal from the "world" into monasteries was abolished.

The primary consequence of this collapsing was not, as it has often been interpreted, so much the secularization of the religious component of society as it was the sacralization of secular society, making it the forum for the religious life, notably, though by no means exclusively, through work in a "calling" (as Weber held).[8]

Though Calvin, in his doctrine of predestination, attempted to remove salvation altogether from human control, this doctrine could not survive the cooling of the "effervescence" of the Reformation itself. Thus, later versions of Protestantism all accepted some version of the bearing of the individual's moral or attitudinal (faith) merit on salvation. Such control as there was, however, was no longer vested in an ecclesiastical organization but was left to the individual, thus immensely increasing one's religious and moral responsibility.

The Reformation as such did not fundamentally alter the meaning of death in human societies. The collapse of the Catholic version of duality, however, put great pressure on the received doctrine of salvation. Hence, the promise of a *personal* afterlife in "heaven," especially if this were conceived to be "eternal," which must be taken to mean altogether outside the framework of time, became increasingly difficult to accept. The doctrine of eternal punishment in some kind of "hell" has proved even more difficult to uphold.

The conception of a "higher" level of reality, a "supernatural" world, did not in any immediate sense give way; yet, it became increasingly hard to "visualize" it by simple extrapolation from this-worldly experience. Indeed, a fundamental challenge did emerge as part of the penumbra of the rise of modern science, which by the eighteenth century had produced a philosophy of scientific "materialism." The primary form of this was a "monism" of the physical world. There was, at that time, little "scientific" analysis of the world of action, or even of the organic world, and there was a tendency to regard the physical universe as unchanging and hence eternal. Death then was simple, namely, in Freud's formula, the "return to the inorganic" state, which implies a complete negation of the conception of "eternal life" since the physical, inorganic world is by definition the antithesis of life in any sense.[9]

DEATH IN THE SCIENTIFIC PARADIGM

The development of science has over time changed these matters. The sciences of organic life underwent their first great efflorescence in the nineteenth century and have gone much further in the present one. Moreover, a conception of evolutionary change came to be at the very center of biological thought, crystallizing in the work of Darwin.[10] This development laid the foundation for the view of the biological normality of death.

A second and more recent development was the maturing of what we have been calling the sciences of *action*. These of course have deep roots in humanistic tradition, but only in recent times can a cluster of generalizing sciences be said to have branched off from the humanistic "trunk." Indeed, these disciplines may well not yet have had their "Darwin," though I am inclined to think that the Durkheim-Weber-Freud combination comes close to filling such a role. It seems that a conception of evolutionary change, articulating with the organic theory, has also become an integral part of this scientific movement.

There is also a parallel in that not only has this development of the action disciplines produced a useful conception of the human personality as analytically distinguished from the organism but also it has created an intellectual framework within which the mortality of this personality can be understood to be normal. Moreover, this personality, as entity, can be seen to develop, live, and die within a matrix that is analogous to the physico-organic species matrix of the individual organism. Seen in terms of the nature of societies and cultures, the death of individual persons is presumably just as normal as is that of individual organisms. Of course, again, this action matrix is conceived as evolving, in a sense parallel to organic evolution.

Not least important of the developments of science, finally, was the altered conception of the physical universe in recent times. First, there occurred the relativization of our knowledge of the physical world to the conditions of human observation of it, most saliently put in the ways in which Einstein's theory of relativity modified the previous assumptions of the absolute, empirical givenness of physical nature in Newtonian tradition.[11] Second, evolutionary ideas were extended to the physical cosmos. If one adds the physical to the organic and the action field one comes to the conclusion that for modern people the *whole* of empirical reality is in certain senses conceived to be relative to a human perspective and to be involved in evolutionary changes.

There is a parallel problem of relativization on the other side of the bracketing framework of the human condition. In the philosophical wake of Christian theology, as it were, there has been an energetic search for the conceptualization of the "metaphysical" *absolute*. In the context of the present analysis it seems that this can be likened to the search for the equally absolute, universal laws of physical nature. This quest, too, has been subjected to severe strain as a result of the altered conception of the human condition since the Reformation and has tended to break down in a comparable sense.

PERSONAL IMMORTALITY AND THE TRANSCENDENTAL

Coming late in the crucial eighteenth century, the work of Immanuel Kant seems to me to have been the turning point away from *both* physical absolutism and metaphysical absolutism.[12] Thus, Kant fundamentally accepted the reality of the physical universe, as humanly known, but at the same time in a sense relativized our knowledge of it to the categories of the understanding, which are grounded not in our direct "experience" of physical reality but in something "transcending" this. At the same time, Kant relativized our conceptions of transcendental reality—the existence of which, note, he by no means denied—Kant was no materialist—to something closer to the human condition. Indeed, it may be suggested that, for "substantive" propositions about the absolute, Kant substituted a "procedural" conception.

Kant introduced the conception that what "pure" and "practical" reason can accomplish is to provide *formal*, as distinguished from *substantive*, categorization for human orientation in the relevant problem areas. For the empirical world it was above all the categories of the understanding and for the practical world (in his special sense) it was the categorical imperative which produced the formal structures.

That Kant's formalism in this sense is related to the use of procedural norms and considerations by others is indicated by his own explicit discussion of different kinds of *laws* in these connections. Thus, he held the categories of understanding to be essential to establishing laws for the physical world; whereas in his definition of the categorical imperative he specifically referred to a maxim as having to have the force of "the principle of a general act of *legislation* [Gesetzgebung]."[13] Surely, if procedural norms figure prominently anywhere in modern societies, it is in their legal systems.

It is further essential to realize that Kant did not leave the empirical and practical orders in a simple, yawning dichotomy relative to each other. In *The Critique of Judgment*,[14] the role he assigned to "aesthetic judgment," as he called it, is explicitly that of *mediating*, from the human point of view, between the necessities of the empirical world and the freedom of the world of morality. It is notable that in this connection he spoke of both the "purposiveness" (*Zweckmassigkeit*) of nature and of individual self-interest, indeed pleasure (*Lust*—the same word used by Freud),[15] as well as of judgment as the mode of synthesizing the two.

Though Kant denied the possibility of reliable knowledge of the absolute, he insisted that, in all three of the spheres analyzed in his critiques, human orientation depends on a *transcendental* component, which is more than the simply "given" experience of either the "external" reality in question, of the source of human freedom, or, indeed, in the case of *The Critique of Judgment*, of the individual's own "subjectivity."

In his combination of relativizing and of yet insisting on the indispensability of recognizing a transcendental component of human orientation to the human condition, Kant explicitly included the belief in personal immortality, in the sense of eternal life, in his list, along with belief in the existence of God, beliefs that he maintained could not rationally be proved. Of course, this completely vitiated the fundamentalist (Catholic or Protestant) view of the meaning of death and, along with it, that of life.

At the same time, by contrast with scientific materialism, it is crucial in this connection that Kant did not collapse the difference of levels between the physical and what we may perhaps call the "telic" (i.e., purposeful) realm. He was, in this sense, neither a materialist nor an idealist but recognized the indispensability of both references and attempted to connect them with each other. Yet the way in which he proceeded to do so entailed complex redefinitions of received views throughout.

With respect to the bearing of Kant's philosophy and its influence through subsequent culture on the problem of the meaning of death, there are two primary, interconnected contexts to consider. The first concerns the intermediate zone *between* the realm of the material and that of the transcendental, in Kant's sense, which he tried in a tentative but very significant way to bridge in *The Critique of Judgment.* The second concerns above all the boundary relations between the sphere of action and that aspect of the transcendental realm that Kant attempted to categorize in *The Critique of Practical Reason.*

With reference to the former context, we previously outlined the immense process of development, including differentiation, of the corpus of scientific knowledge, which has occurred roughly since Kant's time. The salient events of that development, from the present point of view, have been the development of biological knowledge and that of systematic, theoretical knowledge in the field of human action, as distinguished from the humanistic tradition. Within each of these spheres, then, there has appeared a crucial line of differentiation. In the organic this is the differentiation between the individual, phenotypical organism and the trans-generational, organic system (prototypically the species). The parallel differentiation within the action sphere is that between the individual as personality and the sociocultural matrix in which one is embedded. The two components of individuality meet in a special symbiosis to constitute a "person." This whole differentiated structure of the human condition may be said to have evolved, on our cultural system, since Kant wrote; nevertheless, it is congruent with, and in part anticipated and influenced by, the Kantian framework.

NEITHER PROOF NOR DISPROOF

In certain respects the structure of the reality postulated between the two Kantian boundaries may be said to be symmetrical, coming to focus on the human individual. But there is one respect in which it is profoundly asymmetrical. This we may state in cybernetic terms; namely, in certain respects organic life can "control" components of the physical world and, in turn, human action systems can in a similar sense control the organic, in the first instance the human body. However, the source of organic energy is physical and that of personality, organic. From this point of view, the transcendental structure of "reason" in Kant's "practical" references is the apex of the cybernetic hierarchy, so far as it involves the human condition. Kant's "relativism," then, may be interpreted to mean that he saw no reason to postulate an "absolute" reality that is humanly knowable, in either direction, but restricted his postulation to what we have called "procedural" forms.

It seems unnecessary to dwell on the problem of the meaning of purely organic death, which is adequately defined as "return to the inorganic state," except for one major point. Some materialists still maintain that this is the only important meaning of death for human beings in modern societies. The proponents of this view, however, can scarcely claim to have the field to themselves[16] since the other direction of the cybernetic series must clearly be taken into account. Their view of the ultimate fate of the individual human being as organism—in an *analytical* sense—may well be correct, but we have argued all along that this creature is not *only* an organism but also a personality. What of *this* fate?

Certainly, incorporation in a "great chain of being," in Lovejoy's sense,[17] in either or both of these aspects can give meaning to a temporally limited life and then to the termination of that life, long after the individual's death. One may surmise that the prominence of ancestral cults is especially marked in societies in which cultural status and social status have tended to be fused. In modern societies, however, they have come to be largely differentiated, especially through the externalization of cultural outputs in writing and printing and in works of art. Neither Kant nor Max Weber was, to my knowledge, one of my biological ancestors, yet I can consider both to have been cultural ancestors in whose line I feel honored to stand. To me, their lives, though limited in temporal duration, were profoundly meaningful; without them my own life would have been greatly impoverished.

I have argued that it was a primary contribution of Kant in his analysis of the relation of the human knower to "external reality," which for him was in the first instance that of the physical world, to refuse to reduce the relation to a simple "mirroring" of that reality in human consciousness, a view which would have erased an essential boundary between the human and the nonhuman worlds. If Kant was right in this position, it seems to me that there are parallels to his fundamental distinction between the sensory and the categorical (i.e., command of one's conscience) components of human empirical knowledge on two levels. The first of these levels is the distinction between the phenotypical aspect of the higher organisms and the genotypical aspect, which is primarily visible only at the level of aggregates, notably the species. The second is the distinction between the human personality, in the action sense, and the larger action systems in which one is embedded, namely the social and cultural systems. With respect to the duality of components and the relations of these components to each other, it seems to me that there is a striking isomorphism. In all three cases the one component—sensory, phenotypical, individual—is temporally limited in its existence, whereas the other component, which is necessary to give the former meaning, is, in Kant's own term, "transcendental" by comparison. Surely such considerations have some bearing on the problem of the meaning of individual death in the human case.

If we accept Kant's fundamental position, which in essentials I do, then his skepticism about absolutes must apply on *both* sides of the fundamental dichotomy. Modern biology certainly must be classed as knowledge of the empirical world in his sense. Hence, the strictures he applied to physical knowledge must apply to it as well and, indeed, to our scientific knowledge of human action. In his famous terminology, there is no demonstrable knowledge of the *Ding an sich* (i.e., thing in itself) in *any* scientific field.

We have continually stressed that, precisely in empirical terms, organic death is completely normal. We have, and according to Kant presumably can have, no knowledge of the survival of any organic entity after death except through the process of organic reproduction, through which the genetic heritage does indeed survive. Kant, however, would equally deny that such survival can be excluded on empirical grounds. This circumstance has an obvious bearing on the Christian doctrine of resurrection of the body. *If* resurrection is meant in a literal, biological sense—and I am aware that this is by no means universally accepted—then the implication is clearly that this phenomenon can never be proved but it can be speculated about and it can be a matter of faith. If, however, it is maintained as dogma, with the implication that it can be either scientifically or philosophically proved, the answer must be negative.

When we turn to the action-personality component of the personality, for partly obverse reasons much the same implications seem to be indicated. Just as there is no *Ding an sich* that is knowable in the empirical realm, there is none in the metaphysical realm. Clearly, the "eternal life" of the individual soul belongs in this category, and the existence of such entities cannot be intellectually proved. However, Kant would insist that they cannot be *disproved* either. Thus, like resurrected bodies, they can be speculated about and believed in as matters of *faith*, which is different.

Among the victims of Kant's skepticism, or as we have called it relativization, is belief in the cognitive *necessity* of belief in survival of human individuality after death. We have stressed that this skepticism applies to the survival of both of the two components of the human individual with which this analysis began and hence obviously to their combination, without dissolution of that combination. These strictures apply with special cogency to the Christian conception of the entry into eternal life, if (as well stated earlier) by this is meant literally timelessness rather than indefinite duration.

All this needs to be seen in the context of what we have called Kant's procedural position. His skepticism both closed and opened doors. It of course undermined the traditional specificities of received, to say nothing of enforced, beliefs. By the same token, by contrast with scientific materialism, it opened the door not merely to *one* alternative to received Christian dogma but to a multiplicity of them.

The grounding of this door opening process lies in Kant's conception of *freedom* as the central feature of what he called "practical reason."[18] In essence, the human "will," as he called it, can no more be bound by a set of metaphysical dogmas than can humans' active intellect be bound by alleged inherent necessities of the empirical, relevant *Ding an sich*. This doctrine of freedom, among other things, opens the door to Western receptivity to other, notably Oriental, religious traditions. Thus, Buddhist tradition, on the whole by contrast with Christian, stresses not the theme of individuality except for *this* terrestrial life but rather the desirability of absorption, after death, into an impersonal, eternal matrix (as opposed to a personal eternal life). The recent vogue of Oriental religion in Western circles suggests that this possibility has become meaningful here.

OPENNESS ABOUT THE MEANING OF DEATH

It has been common to interpret the constraints on absolute human freedom, which Kant dealt with under the heading of *transcendental* matters, as creations of the "human mind" in something like an empirical sense. Thus, at least secondary interpreters of the work of Claude Lévi-Strauss[19] and of Noam Chomsky[20] often use this phraseology in speaking of the structure of culture, on the one hand, and the deep structures of language, on the other. In my opinion this phrasing is open to serious misinterpretation in that "mind" may be held to mean the structure of the human personality, or of some related collective entity, in an *empirical* sense. Clearly, nothing could be further from the Kantian position. Both the human personality and human collectivities—and presumably languages—are empirical objects, "phenomena" in Kant's sense. They cannot possibly be used to ground transcendental ordering in *any* of these contexts.

We would like to state the matter differently. The transcendental framework of human "consciousness," in Kant's sense, is part of the *human* condition but it is not an *object* of human knowledge. It is, rather, in Kant's favorite phrase, an *a priori* set of conditions of human knowledge and orientation more generally. Nevertheless, it constitutes a set of constraints, perhaps in a sense close to Durkheim's,[21] on what can be humanly *meaningful.* Thus, the categories of the understanding are by no means "arbitrary conventions" with which scientists operate in trying to establish cognitively intelligible order in the phenomena they study but which they can alter at will. Similarly, Kant would hold that the categorical imperative is not an arbitrary, culture-bound convention of *one* possible ethical position but is grounded in the human condition itself. I think it is good Kantian doctrine that, only with recognition of the binding qualities of these conditions of meaningfulness, is the basic freedom of the human will itself a meaningful concept. This is a very different position indeed from the contention that the basic organization accessible to human experience is "imposed" by the empirical "human mind."

The developments in science that we have sketched in this essay have elaborated the system of constraints on human freedom, with which Kant dealt as transcendental. In one sense, any person is "free" to deny death—for instance, to "pretend" that a deceased love object is still alive—but this is not meaningful behavior; indeed, it may be in a strict sense pathological. In general, I would class the normality of death, on both the above levels, among the constraints that have been derived from the *combination* of transcendental and empirical factors and which it has thus become "irrational" to "deny."

Kant's sphere of freedom includes the freedom to speculate and to believe. In particular, this is the freedom to symbolize and to mythologize, to construct "representations," individual or collective, that fill the gaps left open by the indeterminacies of both our empirical knowledge and our grasp of transcendental or telic reality. One thing that Kant did was to deprive beliefs in both these areas of the apodictic (i.e., absolute) certainty that had been claimed for them in the received cultural tradition.

This leaves us in the position that the problem of the meaning of death in Western tradition has, from a position of relative closure defined by the Christian syndrome, been opened up in its recent phase. Above all, there is a new freedom, for individuals and sociocultural movements, to try their hand at innovative definitions and conceptions. At the same time, the "viability" of these innovations is subject to the transcendental, as well as the empirical, constraints of the human condition, with which we have been concerned.

It is perhaps relevant, in interpreting the human phenomenon more generally, to refer to the statement of the late Arthur D. Nock, one of the most distinguished students of religion of his generation, that, to his (very extensive) knowledge, no religion had *ever* claimed to be able to "beat death."[22]

This open, in a sense "individualistic," situation with respect to the meaning of death—and of course the life of the individual—is of a piece with the general situation in the modern world, which has seen a pervasive undermining of older certainties and authorities in favor of a variety of enhanced freedoms and autonomics.[23] Perhaps one need only mention the institutionalization of political democracy and of intellectual freedom, especially in the academic world, and also some of the newer freedoms in the realm of more personal conduct. These have by no means become universal, and there are many pessimists about their future. They have certainly encountered formidable resistance, especially on the part of groups that contend their acceptance means the end of all meaningful order in human life. I, for one, however, cannot see that they are so dangerous that it is likely that in our time, or that of our children's children, this main trend will be reversed.

It may be noted that one of Kant's principal emphases in this connection was on the pattern of *universalism*.[24] Not only was the category of causality, for example, to be regarded as of universal relevance in the empirical world, but also the categorical imperative was formulated in parallel terms. If a single keynote of the main trend of the development of modern civilization could be selected, I think it would be the trend toward cultural universalism. The interpretation of this principle involves many complexities. Yet it seems to be an essential conclusion that its universalizability is one of the central conditions of freedom.

This leaves the problem of the meaning of death in Western civilization in what, to many, must appear to be a strangely unsatisfactory state. It seems to come down to the proposition that the meaning of death is that, in the human condition, it cannot have any apodictically certain meaning without abridgment of the essential human freedom of thought, experience, and imagination. Within limits, its meaning, as it is thought about, experienced for the case of others, and anticipated for oneself, must be autonomously interpreted. Is this, however, pure negativism or nihilism?

I think not: This openness is not the same as declaring death, and of course with it individual life, to be meaningless. If this were the case, the human condition as a whole would have to be negatively valued, as indeed it has been in some quarters for many centuries. Kant's views of the purposiveness of nature and its connection with human pleasure, however, seem to indicate that positive acceptance of being human, with all its uncertainties and limitations, is not in the least incompatible with acceptance of both cognitive and attitudinal openness, which in one aspect is uncertainty, about many of the most essential features of the state of being human.

So far as Western society is concerned, I think the tolerability of this relatively open definition of the situation is associated with the "activistic" strain in our values, the attitude that human life is a challenging undertaking that in some respects may be treated as an adventure—by contrast with a view that treats human life as a matter of passively enduring an externally imposed fate. Even though Western religion has sometimes stressed our extreme dependency on God, and indeed the sinfulness of asserting independence, on the whole the activistic strain has been dominant. If this is the case, it seems that humans can face their death and those of others in the spirit that, whatever this unknown future may portend, they can enter upon it with good courage.

PERVASIVE DENIAL VS. THE INEVITABILITY OF DEATH

So far as it is accessible to cognitive understanding at all, the meaning of death for individual human beings must be approached in the framework of the human condition as a whole. It must include both the relevant scientific and philosophical understanding and must attempt to synthesize them. Finally, it must, as clearly as possible, recognize and take account of the limits of our scientific as well as our philosophical understanding.

We have contended that the development of modern science has so changed the picture as to require revision of many of the received features of Christian tradition, both Catholic and Protestant. This development of science took place in three great stages marked by the synthesis of physical science in the seventeenth century, that of biological science in the nineteenth, and that of the action sciences in the nineteenth to twentieth.

The most important generalizations seem to be the following. First, the human individual constitutes a unique symbiotic synthesis of two main components, a living organism and a living personality. Second, both components seem to be *inherently* limited in duration of life, and we have no knowledge which indicates that their symbiosis can be in any radical sense dissociated. Third, the individualized entity *both* is embedded in and derives in some sense from a transgenerational matrix which, seen in relation to individual mortality, has indefinite but not infinite durability.

From this point of view, death, or the limited temporal duration of the individual life course, must be regarded as one of the facts of life that is as inexorable as the need to eat and breathe in order to live. In this sense, death is completely normal, to the point that its "denial" must be regarded as pathological. Moreover, this normality includes the consideration that, from an evolutionary point of view, which we have contended is basic to *all* modern science, death must be regarded as having high survival value, organically at least to the species, actionwise to the future of the sociocultural system. These scientific considerations are not trivial, or conventional, or culture-bound but are *fundamental.*

There is a parallel set of considerations on the philosophical side. For purposes of elucidating this aspect of the problem complex I have used Kant's framework as presented in his three critiques. On the one hand, this orientation is critical in that it challenges the contention that absolute knowledge is demonstrable in *any* of the three aspects of the human condition. Thus, any conception like that of the ontological essence of nature, the idea of God, or the notion of the eternal life of the human soul are categorized as *Ding an sich,* which in principle are not demonstrable by rational cognitive procedures.

At the same time, Kant insisted, and I follow him here, on the cognitive necessity of assuming a transcendental component, a set of categories in each of the three realms, that is not reducible to the status of humanly available inputs from either the empirical or the absolute telic (purposeful) references of the human condition. We have interpreted this to mean that human orientation must be relativized to the human condition, not treated as dogmatically fixed in the nature of things.

The consequence of this relativization that we have particularly emphasized is that it creates a new openness for orientations, which humans are free to exploit by speculation and to commit themselves in faith but with reference to which they cannot claim what Kant called apodictic certainty. At the same time, we again insist with Kant that this openness must be qualified by the continuing subjection of human life to the constraints of the transcendental aspects of the human condition, which presumably cannot be altered by human action.

If this is a correct account of the situation, it is not surprising that there is a great deal of bafflement, anxiety, and indeed downright confusion in contemporary attitudes and opinions in this area. I think that in its broad lines what I have presented is indeed an accurate diagnosis of the situation, but it would certainly be too much to claim that such an orientation is fully institutionalized.

It can be said to be most firmly established at philosophical levels and those of rather abstract scientific theory. Even there, however, there is still much controversy and anything like full consensus seems to be far off. Yet I still maintain that the development, say, from the medieval Catholic synthesis, is the *main line.* The grounds for this belief rest on the conviction that no equally basic alternative is available in the main cultural tradition and that this broad orientation is the most congenial to "reasonable people" in our situation. So far as fundamentals are concerned, I am afraid that, within the limitations of this essay, it will be necessary to leave it at that.

It may help, however, to mitigate the impression of extreme abstractness if in closing I very briefly discuss three empirical points. First, though scientific evidence has established the fact of the inevitability of death with increasing clarity, this does not mean that the *experience* of death by human populations may not change with changing circumstances. Thus, Victor Lidz and I have distinguished between inevitable death and "adventitious" death—that is "premature" relative to the full life span and in principle preventable by human action.[25] Within the last century and a half or so, this latter category of deaths has decreased enormously. The proportion of persons in modern populations over 65 has thus increased greatly, as has the expectancy of life at birth to 72 in 1975 in the United States. This clearly means that a greatly increased proportion of modern humans live out a full life course. Perhaps precisely because of this change, premature deaths from diseases, wars, accidents, or natural disasters like earthquakes have become more, rather than less, disturbing events than they were previously.

Moreover, persons who live to a ripe old age will experience an inevitably larger number of deaths of persons important to them. These will be in decreasing number to the deaths of persons younger than themselves, notably their own children, but increasingly those of their parents and whole ranges of persons of an older generation such as teachers, senior occupational associates, and public figures. (During this writing, for example, I learned of the death of Mao Tse-tung, certainly a figure of worldwide significance.) Quite clearly, these demographic changes have a strong effect on the balance of experience and expectation of the deaths of significant others and on anticipation of one's own death.

Second, one of the centrally important aspects of a process of change in orientation of the sort described should be the appearance of signs of the differentiation of attitudes and conceptions in the relevant area. As Fox, Lidz, and I[26] have pointed out, there has indeed been such a process of differentiation, which seems not yet to be completed, with respect to both ends of the life cycle. With respect to the beginning, there is the controversy over abortion. However this controversy may eventually be resolved, it seems unlikely that public attitudes will go back to the traditional positions of either no abortions in any circumstances or only abortions that are strictly necessary to save the life of the mother. The interesting feature of this controversy is that it has entailed attempts to specify the point at which the life of a human *person*, as distinct from the human *organism* at conception, begins.

Concomitant with this has been an attempt at redefinition of death. So far the most important approach has been to draw a line *within* the organic sector between what has been called "brain death," in which irreversible changes have taken place, destroying the functioning of the central nervous system, and what has been called "metabolic death," in which above all heartbeat and respiration have ceased. The problem has been highlighted by the capacity of "artificial" measures, say, mechanical respirators, to keep persons "alive" for long periods despite the fact that brain function has irreversibly ceased. The point of major interest here is the connection of brain function with the personality level of individuality. Hence, an organism that continues to "live" at *only* the metabolic level may be said to be dead as a person. We would expect still further elaborations of these themes in the future.

Third, we may make a few remarks about the significance for our problem of Freud's most mature theoretical statement.[27] It will be remembered that in his last major theoretical work, Freud rather drastically revised his views on the nature of anxiety, coming to focus on the expectation of the loss of an "object." By "object" Freud meant a human individual standing in an emotionally significant relation to the person of reference. To the child, of course, the parents become "lost objects" as the child grows up in that their significance to that growing child is inevitably "lost." The ultimate loss of a concrete human person as object (of cathexis, Freud said) is the death of that person. To have "grown away" from one's parents is one thing but to experience their actual death is another. Freud's own account of the impact on him of his father's death is a particularly relevant case in point.[28]

Equally clearly, an individual's own death, in anticipation, can be subsumed under the category of object loss, particularly in view of Freud's theory of narcissism,[29] by which he meant the individual's cathexis of his own self as a love object.

Anxiety, however, is neither the actual experience of object loss nor is it, according to Freud, the fear of it. It is an anticipatory orientation in which the actor's own emotional security is particularly involved. It is a field of rather free play of fantasy as to what might be the consequences of an anticipated or merely possible event.

Given the hypothesis, to which I subscribed, that in our scientifically oriented civilization there is widespread acceptance of death—meant as the antithesis of its denial—I see no reason why this should eliminate or even substantially reduce *anxiety* about death, both that of others and one's own. Indeed, in speaking earlier about the impact of demographic changes in the incidence of death, I suggested that in certain circumstances the level of anxiety may be expected to increase rather than the reverse.

It seems that the frequent assertions that our society is characterized by pervasive denial of death may often be interpreted as calling attention to widespread anxiety about death, which I submit is *not* the same thing. There can be no doubt that in most cases death is, in experience and in anticipation, a traumatic event. Fantasies, in such circumstances, are often marked by unrealism. But the prevalence of such phenomena does not constitute a distortion of the basic cultural framework within which we moderns orient ourselves to the meaning of death.

Indeed, in my opinion, this and the two preceding illustrations serve to enhance the importance of clarification at the theoretical and philosophical levels, to which the bulk of this essay has been devoted. Clarification is essential if we are to understand such problems as the shifts in attitudes toward various age groups in modern society, particularly older persons, the relatively sudden eruption of dissatisfaction with traditional modes of conceptualizing the beginning and the termination of human lives, and allegations about the pervasive denial of death, which is often interpreted as a kind of failure of "intestinal fortitude." However important recent movements for increasing expression of emotional interests and the like, ours remains a culture to which its cognitive framework is of paramount significance. It is as a contribution to the understanding of this framework and its meaning, in an area that is emotionally highly sensitive, that I would like this essay to be evaluated.

NOTES

1. Talcott Parsons. 1977. *Social Systems and the Evolution of Action Theory*. New York: Free Press.
2. See Peter Berger and Richard Liban (1960), Kulturelle Wertstruktur und Bestattungspraktiken in den Vereinigten Staaten, *Kölner Zeitschrift für Soziologie und Social Psychologie*, no. 2; and Robert Fulton in collaboration with Robert Bendiksen, eds. (1976), *Death and Identity*, 2nd Ed. (Philadelphia: The Charles Press), especially the articles by Robert J. Lifton, The Sense of Immortality: On Death and the Continuity of Life, and by Erik Lindemann, Symptomatology and Management of Acute Grief.
3. Emile Durkheim. 1961. *The Elementary Forms of the Religious Life*, trans. J.W. Swain. New York: Free Press (first published in French in 1912).
4. See Robert N. Bellah (1961), Religious Evolution, *American Sociological Review*, pp. 358-374; reprinted in idem, *Beyond Belief: Essays on Religion in a Post-Industrial World*. New York: Harper & Row, 1970.

5. Talcott Parsons, Renée C. Fox and Victor M. Lidz. 1972. The "Gift of Life" and Its Reciprocation. *Social Research* 39:367-415.
6. Ibid.
7. Marcel Mauss. 1954. *The Gift: Forms and Functions of Exchange in Archaic Societies.* New York: Free Press (first published in French in 1925).
8. Max Weber. 1930. *The Protestant Ethic and the Spirit of Capitalism,* trans. T. Parsons. New York: Scribner's (first published in German in 1904-05).
9. Sigmund Freud. 1955. *Beyond the Pleasure Principle,* in vol. 18 of *The Standard Edition of the Complete Psychological Works of Sigmund Freud.* London: Hogarth Press and the Institute of Psychoanalysis (first published in German in 1920).
10. Charles Darwin. 1859. *On the Origin of Species by Means of Natural Selection, or The Preservation of Favored Races in the Struggle for Life.* London: Murray.
11. See Alfred N. Whitehead (1925), *Science and the Modern World* (New York: Macmillan).
12. Immanuel Kant (1929), *The Critique of Pure Reason,* trans. N.K. Smith (New York: Macmillan); idem, *The Critique of Practical Reason,* trans. L.W. Beck (Chicago: University of Chicago Press, 1950); and *The Critique of Judgment,* trans. J.C. Meredith (Oxford: Clarendon, 1964). Originally published in German in 1781, 1788 and 1790, respectively.
13. Kant, *Critique of Practical Reason,* loc. cit.
14. Kant, *Critique of Judgment,* loc. cit.
15. Freud, *Beyond the Pleasure Principle,* loc. cit.
16. For a discussion of this view see the Introduction to William McLaughin and Robert N. Bellah, eds. (1969), *Religion in America* (Boston: Houghton Mifflin).
17. Arthur O. Lovejoy. 1961. *The Great Chain of Being: A Study in the History of an Idea.* Cambridge, MA: Harvard University Press (first published in 1936).
18. Kant, *Critique of Practical Reason,* loc. cit.
19. Claude Lévi-Strauss. 1963. *Structural Anthropology.* New York: Basic Books.
20. Noam Chomsky. 1957. *Syntactic Structures.* The Hague: Mouton.
21. Emile Durkheim. 1974. *Sociology and Philosophy,* trans. D.F. Pocock. New York: Free Press.
22. Arthur D. Nock. 1961. *Conversion: The Old and the New in Religion from Alexander the Great to Augustine of Hippo.* New York: Oxford University Press (first published in 1933).
23. See Bellah, Religious Evolution, loc. cit.
24. Kant, *Critique of Practical Reason,* loc. cit.
25. See Talcott Parsons and Victor M. Lidz (1967), Death in American Society, in Edwin Schneidman, ed., *Essays in Self-Destruction* (New York: Science House).
26. Parsons, Fox and Lidz, *The "Gift of Life,"* loc. cit.
27. Sigmund Freud. 1959. *Inhibitions, Symptoms, and Anxiety,* vol. 20 of *The Standard Edition of the Complete Psychological Works of Sigmund Freud.* London: Hogarth Press and the Institute of Psychoanalysis (first published in German in 1926).
28. See Sigmund Freud. 1954. *The Origins of Psychoanalysis: Letters to Wilhelm Fliess, Drafts and Notes, 1887-1902* (New York: Basic Books).
29. Freud, *Inhibitions, Symptoms, and Anxiety,* loc. cit.

4

The Sociology of Death: A Historical Overview, 1875-1985

Greg Owen, PhD
Eric Markusen, PhD
and Robert Fulton, PhD

> We all believe we know what death is because it is a familiar event and one that arouses intense emotion. It seems both ridiculous and sacrilegious to question the value of this intimate knowledge and to wish to apply reason to a subject where only the heart is competent.
>
> Robert Hertz, "A Contribution to the Study of the Collective Representation of Death," 1907

INTRODUCTION

It is only recently in the history of Western thought that the phenomenon of death has become a focal point for scientific inquiry. While death is imminent in life and a part of the continuous transition through which all living organisms grow and decay, there has been little to recommend it as a subject for scientific investigation. Its properties of ultimate mystery and finality, its resistance to human control and its absolute and universal occurrence have all contributed to the scientists' neglect of the topic. Recently, however, the scientific and academic literature devoted to death and death-related topics has burgeoned. At the same time, an increase in interest in the sociology of death has occurred. This chapter will outline the history of this interest, propose an explanation for the current growth of death-related literature, and offer a prospectus for future sociological inquiry.

The history of sociological interest in death is coextensive with the history of sociology itself. European sociologists of the nineteenth century, early American sociologists, as well as the "interwar" sociologists (from 1930 to 1945) all demonstrated a regard for the subject. The following brief sketches are intended to provide a historical framework within which present sociological efforts may be located.

EUROPEAN SOCIOLOGISTS: 1875-1920

Herbert Spencer (1876)

In the first volume of *The Principles of Sociology*[1] Spencer traced the relationship of the world of the living to the world of the dead and argued that the advance of civilization brings about increasing separation of the two spheres. The world of the dead, Spencer speculated, was originally a mirror image of the world of the living. While early beliefs held that the spirits of the deceased have qualities similar to those of the living, increasing evidence about the physical world required modification of such beliefs. In Spencer's words:

> The second self, originally conceived as equally substantial with the first, grows step by step less substantial: now it is semi-solid, now it is aeriform, now it is ethereal. And this stage finally reached, is one in which there cease to be ascribed any of the properties by which we know existence: there remains only the assertion of an existence that is wholly undefined.[2]

Belief in the spirit world and the continued existence of those deceased is not wholly abandoned, however. It is merely removed from the realm of what can be known in an ordinary or empirical way. It is made compatible with science by removing it from the sphere of events that science can aspire to know.

Spencer believed, moreover, that it was the similarity and immediacy of the world of the dead that led to early embalming practices. With immediate resurrection and a life-like world of the dead, "the aim is, or was, to keep the flesh in a state of integrity against the time of resuscitation...we must conclude that embalming was adopted simply as a more effectual method of achieving the same end."[3]

Finally, Spencer hypothesized that as the distance between the world of the dead and the world of the living increases, the propitiation to, and veneration of, the deceased decreases in strength and significance.

Thomas G. Masaryk (1881)

Among the first sociological treatises related to death was Masaryk's *Suicide and the Meaning of Civilization* (*Der Selbstmord als sociale Massenerscheinung der modernen Civilisation*).[4] In this work he attempted to arrive at a social explanation of suicide some 16 years prior to Durkheim's famous monograph. Unlike Durkheim, however, Masaryk did not wholly dismiss environmental causes of suicide (e.g., climate, the seasons, etc.), but he did place great emphasis on the importance of moral decay in explaining suicide rates. Masaryk believed that modern man was more self-reflective than primitive man and as a consequence called into question the meaning of the moral order. He contended "that the morbid suicide tendency gradually increases among all people who have progressed in their development; the social mass phenomena of suicide is the fruit of progress, of education, of civilization."[5] Furthermore, he believed that the decline of Christianity was the major precipitating factor in spiraling suicide rates. He concluded, "The contemporary social mass phenomenon of suicide results from the collapse of a unified world-view that has consistently given Christianity its value among the masses in all civilized countries.... Suicides are the bloody sacrifices of the civilizing process, the sacrifices of the 'Kulturkampf.'"[6]

The theme of moral decay and irreligiosity as a primary conditioning factor in modern orientations toward life and death is one that will be observed to recur in the work of subsequent writers.

Emile Durkheim (1897)

Durkheim is undoubtedly the most readily identified European sociologist connected with the fact of death in social life. Both in *Suicide*[7] and *The Elementary Forms of the Religious Life*,[8] he demonstrated an interest in human orientations and reactions toward death that death itself engenders.

In *Suicide*, Durkheim attempted to identify the qualities of social relationships that result in varying orientations toward suicide. He proposed that individual dispositions toward suicide cannot be explained as a function of climate, biology or psychology, but must be conceived as resulting from prevailing conditions within the social structure. For Durkheim, the nature of one's integration into social life had an important effect on how an individual viewed the dispensability of life.

Less well known of his essays related to death, but equally relevant to our contemporary concerns, were Durkheim's observations on mourning. While mourning is often conceptualized as a natural human reaction to loss, for Durkheim it was a requirement of group life:

> Mourning is not a natural movement of private feelings wounded by a cruel loss; it is a duty imposed by the group. One weeps, not simply because he is sad, but because he is forced to weep. It is a ritual attitude which he is forced to adopt out of respect for custom, but which is, in a large measure, independent of his affective state.[9]

This is consistent with Durkheim's basic assumption that emotional states and attitudes are representations of collective life and that society is the origin of such mental states. For Durkheim,

> one initial fact is constant: mourning is not the spontaneous expression of individual emotion. If the relations weep, lament, mutilate themselves, it is not because they feel themselves personally affected by the death of their kinsman. Of course, it may be that in certain particular cases, the chagrin expressed is really felt. But it is more generally the case that there is no connection between the sentiments felt and the gestures made by the actors in the rite.[10]

Robert Hertz (1907)

Durkheim's student, Hertz, shared his teacher's interest in the phenomena of death. In his study, "The Collective Representation of Death,"[11] he challenged any interpretation of death that regarded it merely as a physical event.

Death, for Hertz, always presented a dilemma for society. The difficulty was not for the individual survivor who may be suffering from grief, but for the life principle of the collective itself. He suggested that beliefs in a spirit world resulted from, among other things, the need for the collective to assert its dominance over the powers that it cannot control. He wrote,

> Because it believes in itself a healthy society cannot admit that an individual who was part of its own substance, and on whom it has set its mark, shall be lost forever. The last word must remain with life: the deceased will rise from the grip of death and will return, in one form or another, to the peace of human association. This release and this reintegration constitute, as we have seen, one of the most solemn actions of collective life in the least advanced societies we can find.[12]

Hertz suggested that resurrection is the promise that every religious system implicitly offers to its members. For the collective consciousness, death is only a *temporary* exclusion of the individual from human society. The continuity of life, both for the individual and for the collective, is rooted in a set of beliefs that specifies and explains the relationship of human existence to what is ultimately unknown and unknowable. He observed, "In the final analysis, death as a social phenomenon consists in a dual and painful process of mental disintegration and synthesis. It is only when this process is completed that society, its peace recovered, can triumph over death."[13]

Arnold van Gennep (1909)

Van Gennep examined the nature of ritualized behavior in promoting and maintaining social forms. In *Rites of Passage*[14] he assigned the greatest importance to the rituals associated with death (rites of incorporation) because he found that funeral rites that had as their express purpose the passage of the deceased into the world of the dead were characteristically the most elaborate. He believed rites of reintegration, that is, those actions taken in support of the survivors, were of less importance than other behaviors following a death because reintegration was less problematical for the community. A belief system that provided specific information about the future following death minimized the issue of social continuity.

Max Weber (1915)

Weber did not write extensively on the problems that death poses for social life. He did, however, identify the value conflicts that were to become so important for the modern physician in a technologically advanced system of medical care. As was true in much of Weber's writings, he foreshadowed the future difficulties of a transformed and rapidly changing social order. In a noted essay, "Science as a Vocation," he offered the following observation:

> The general 'presupposition' of the medical enterprise is stated trivially in the assertion that medical science has the task of maintaining life as such and diminishing suffering as such to the greatest possible degree...Whether life is worthwhile living, and when, is not asked by medicine. Natural science gives us the answer to the question of what we must do if we wish to master life technically. It leaves quite aside, or assumes for its purposes, whether we should and do wish to master life technically and whether it ultimately makes sense to do so.[15]

Weber also discussed the meaning of death in the context of war. In a 1915 article entitled "Religious Rejections of the World and Their Directions," he wrote:

> Since death is a fate that comes to everyone, nobody can ever say why it

> comes precisely to him and why it comes just when it does. As the values of culture increasingly unfold and are sublimated to immeasurable heights, such ordinary death marks an end where only a beginning seems to make sense. Death on the field of battle differs from this merely unavoidable dying in that war, and in this massiveness *only* in war, the individual can *believe* that he knows he is dying 'for' something. The why and the wherefore of his facing death can, as a rule, be so indubitable to him that the problem of the 'meaning' of death does not even occur to him. At least there may be no presuppositions for the emergence of the problem in its universal significance, which is the form in which religions of salvation are impelled to be concerned with the meaning of death. Only those who perish 'in their calling' are in the same situation as the soldier who faces death on the battlefield.[16]

Thus Weber saw that the meaning of death is troublesome when individuals are not engaged in some inspired activity—an activity personally conceived of as one's duty or "calling." It is devotion or inspiration in human activities that removes the sting from death.

AMERICAN SOCIOLOGISTS: 1890-1930

American sociological interest in the subject of death around the turn of the century reflected many of the currents of thought of the European masters. Additionally, it can be observed that the conservative inclinations reflected in the writings of Spencer, Masaryk and Durkheim, as exemplified by their attachment to the traditional moral order, were readily taken up by American ministers and ministers' sons, for whom sociology was a second vocation. While the American sociological literature on death during the period 1890 to 1930 is relatively sparse, it is nonetheless important in the development of a sociology of death.

Albion W. Small and George Vincent (1894)

Although neither Small nor Vincent treated the subject of death at length, their contributions deserve recognition in light of the ideas and insights they provided a later generation of sociologists.

In Small and Vincent's *An Introduction to the Study of Society*[17] they noted the difficulty that a rural family experienced in facing the death of a child. In so doing, they called attention to the importance of social supports involving consolation and aid for the bereaved family. Elsewhere, they addressed the problem of childhood bereavement following the death of a parent and anticipated much of the future psychological literature on the mental health of children in the aftermath of such an event. They observed,

> In the normal family, parents live until children are mature enough and

> sufficiently equipped for independent existence. The death of either parent or both before such a point has been reached produces a manifestly pathological condition. Remarriage and the adoption or guardianship of orphans are means for restoring or replacing the complete family relations, but except in rare cases such expedients fail to secure normal results.[18]

Small and Vincent also addressed the problem of widowhood and noted, along with van Gennep and Sumner, the serious impact of economic hardship following the death of a husband. They suggested that economic security is often the support that makes the difference between good and poor emotional health of the widow following such a crisis.

Edward Allsworth Ross (1901)

Although Ross's contribution to the sociology of death is relatively limited, his observations offer us a partial explanation of the contemporary changes in self-imposed standards of moral behavior. Ross suggested that the world of the dead had a significant impact on the world of the living, especially when ancestors are thought of as living on and taking an interest in the life of their kinfolk. He wrote,

> When loved ones gone are thought of as looking down upon this life with their former interest and concern, we have a powerful motive to do only that which will please them. With us today, in non-religious as well as in religious circles, the influence of this thought in fostering family piety and strengthening family bonds is certainly very great...[19]

Later, however, Ross noted that this belief seemed to be in decline and predicted that it would eventually lead to the loss of one of the most effective social control mechanisms in the realm of personal conduct.

William Graham Sumner (1910)

Sumner's four-volume treatise, *The Science of Society* (with Keller),[20] although not published until 1927, was drafted in rough form prior to Sumner's death in 1910. It is therefore appropriate to include him in the group of early American sociologists who expressed an interest in the topic of death.

Sumner was the most prolific of early American sociologists concerned with death, as shown by his extensive treatment of such diverse topics as ghost fear, the shock of death, mortuary practices, mourning rituals, infanticide, widowhood, war and the right to life. No fewer than 250 pages of his four-volume classic were devoted to the subject of death and death-related topics. While it is impossible in this brief survey to discuss all of the rich material he presented, only a few of his trenchant observations can be mentioned.

Sumner argued, for example, that the right to life is not a natural right at all, but one that is granted by society. He reasoned, "When the presumption that life shall not be taken from anybody has won general concurrence, society is conceding to all a right to life. Then if life is to be taken it shall be in the interest of a superior and societal expediency only."[21] He observed, further, that the right to life will vary as the support for it within society grows or diminishes. Life is "sacred" only so far as the "might" of society supports it. "The very sacredness of life," Sumner concluded, "is a societal product."[22] It should be observed that the current battles being fought at both poles of the age spectrum in American society today concerning abortion and euthanasia are contemporary reminders of the social variability of life's "sacredness" observed by Sumner. Sumner also discussed extensively the problems of widowhood and showed how widows stand in sharp contrast to conditions imposed on the widower:

> The death of the wife is an incidental matter, as it appears, compared to that of the husbands; and the provisions as to the behavior and destiny of the survivor leave the man, for the most part, out of account. Almost never is he forced to accompany his wife to the spirit world; he mourns but little; he is not much limited in the matter of a second marriage. His lot, in short, is not materially changed by the event."[23]

Correspondingly, Sumner found that the majority of anthropological accounts of the widow illustrated the horrible lot that awaited her. Additionally, Sumner discussed what he termed "foeticide" in primitive populations and the functions that such mechanical or drug-induced miscarriages have for those who employ them:

> It would appear that foeticide is carried on as a very obvious expedient for the easement of life, meaning generally the individual life of the woman, not the corporate existence. In by far the greater number of cases, not the remotest concern for the society's welfare enters the mind of anybody.

The practice is highly deleterious to health and in general is to be encountered mainly under conditions of isolation from societal competition. It is held to be directly accountable for certain cases of race-decline in numbers and strength, and appears as an expedient that is highly anti-social....[24]

AMERICAN SOCIOLOGISTS: 1930-1945

The period 1930 to 1945 for the sociology of death is most readily characterized by the Bereavement and Family Crisis literature which focused attention on the impact of death within the family unit. While other currents of thought remained active, this literature predominated. Unlike previous concerns that centered on transformations occurring in the spirit world, ghost fear, the resurrection of the corpse or upon the irreligiosity of the growing industrial society, there was now concern with preserving or rebuilding the foundation of American social structure: the family. Among the family sociologists who contributed to the sociology of death literature during this time were Eliot,[25] Nimkoff,[26] Waller,[27] Fulcomer,[28] Burgess and Locke,[29] and Hill.[30] The literature reflects a concern for the separation and loss experienced by the family during wartime, and a desire to stabilize the family unit in the face of bereavement.

Eliot, recognized as the pioneer sociologist in the area of death, contributed articles to a wide range of professional journals in the 1930s focussing on the problem of familial adjustment to bereavement. In "Bereavement as a Problem for Family Research and Technique"[31] he described the topic as "a new field for research," and one which required the special skills of the social scientist. In that paper, first presented to the American Sociological Society in 1929, he inquired whether the time had not yet come, "for a mental hygiene of grief." He went on to suggest that there has been

> a spontaneous unwillingness to face reality, and a corresponding accumulation of rituals, stereotyped attitudes and practices, euphemisms, jokes, and so on, as a buffer between the individual and the stark reality. These customs are changing rapidly, but we do not know from actual personal evidence what practices, new or old, are comforting or under what circumstances they cause conflict.[32]

Eliot proposed to collect facts and evidence about bereavement through a network of interested scholars in order "to test the values of traditional routes through the Valley of the Shadow of Death."[33] His call for attention to the problem of death and survivorship was answered by interwar family sociologists. In 1934, when Nimkoff wrote *Marriage and the Family*, he noted that

> Death is responsible for nearly three out of four broken homes in the United States, yet some students of family disorganization do not give special consideration to bereavement on the ground that death is inevitable, whereas separation and divorce are not...but bereavement is as truly a disorganizing experience as divorce for it terminates the marital relationship and calls for radical readjustments in behavior.[34]

Later years saw a widespread discussion of the problems engendered by death in the many articles by Eliot in which he continued to call for a social-psychology of bereavement. Family textbooks by Waller and Hill,[35] Burgess and Locke,[36] and later, Hill,[37] all took cognizance of what Waller called the "crisis of family dismemberment." Research and theory expanded during this period to include an examination of stages of grief (Waller), post-bereavement patterns (Burgess and Locke), succession of roles (Waller), problems of remarriage (Waller), group participation in mourning (Waller), and the impact of psychological perceptions of the deceased as they affect family activities (Burgess and Locke).

Significantly, however, bereavement received attention primarily as a result of the sheer number of deaths during wartime. It did not appear that death *per se* was becoming more problematic than it had been previously, for it was still discussed in naturalistic terms which emphasized the tragic nature of death without the expression of outrage or surprise at its distinctiveness or its impact on personal lives or public institutions.

The preceding discussion, however, in no way exhausts the sociological material on death during this time period. In fact, a major component appears to be missing if the literature on war and conflict is to be included. Even prior to this period—in the work of Marx, Bagehot, Ratzenhofer, Gumplowicz and Mannheim—a sociology of war was taking shape. And while the contemporary sociology of death has not usually incorporated such materials, there is no logical reason to exclude them. This is especially true when we consider the massive dimensions of death during wartime. In the interwar period, discussions on war and its effects appeared in the work of Bossard, Waller, Hill, Gruenberg, Speier and Sorokin. Large-scale studies, such as Stouffer's *The American Soldier*,[38] failed, however, to exploit the unparalleled opportunity to investigate the many important questions concerning a soldier's perceptions and attitudes toward death and dying. Interest, however, has focused on the horror of the Nazi death camp experience and its profound consequences for those who survived. With the appearance of Eliot's *Twentieth Century Book of the Dead*[39] in 1972, a broader picture of the holocaust of war was presented. It would seem, however, that the dimensions of such horror can only be examined in retrospect and at a distance.

It would seem, too, that no contemporary sociology of death could be complete without a careful examination of a society's readiness and willingness to go to war or an investigation of the social conditions and values that produce such willingness. If, as Freud and Weber have suggested, the meaning of life and its significance take on new dimensions during wartime, such research might provide useful insights into basic value shifts that occur when war looms large in the lives and consciousness of a people.

While Eliot's legacy can be seen in the bereavement literature associated with the family sociologists of the '30s and '50s, his call for a social psychology of death and bereavement and for research into the problems associated with loss remained essentially unanswered. His student, Becker,[40] after completing a master's thesis on bereavement and publishing monographs on ghost fear and bereavement, turned his attention elsewhere. Becker left it to his student, Fulcomer,[41] to investigate the responses to loss through death of 73 bereaved families. His dissertation went unpublished, however, and the sociology of death entered a period of relative dormancy. Elsewhere, in other academic and scientific circles, death, dying and related topics were attracting the interest of scholars and researchers alike. These activities were to form the milieu within which the sociology of death developed following World War II. Psychiatry, medicine, theology, anthropology and psychology were all to contribute to the form that the sociology of death was eventually to assume.

A CONTEMPORARY SOCIOLOGY OF DEATH: 1945-1985

Defining the Discipline

It was not until 1958, with the appearance of Faunce and Fulton's article "The Sociology of Death: A Neglected Area of Research,"[42] that a contemporary sociology of death was called for. Death was conceptualized as a primary focus of a vast cultural complex around which revolved an array of beliefs and practices, rich in variety and awaiting sociological investigation. As a subdiscipline, the sociology of death assumed the task of investigating, empirically, the individual and collective responses to death, as well as the human orientations toward mortality that particular social and cultural systems engender.

Importantly, the appearance of Parsons' working paper, "Death in American Society" in 1963,[43] helped lend legitimacy to the proposed sociological examination of death and death-related issues called for earlier by Faunce and Fulton.[44] Parson's article,[45] in addition to calling attention to the new discipline, explored the tenor of contemporary attitudes and behaviors in relation to death. He regarded these as responses to a world in which death, like other natural phenomena, had been brought under secular and temporal control. He saw these temporal and secular developments as the basic cause of the so-called taboo of death and its denial rather than the result of fear and anxiety as postulated by Feifel and others during this period.

Parsons' paper was followed in 1966 by Blauner's perceptive article "Death and Social Structure,"[46] which expanded the discussion on death to include the important role of demography in determining the manner in which a society responds to death or is able to confront the loss of its different members. He observed that in advanced, technological societies like the U.S. where dying persons are cared for by specialized caregivers in segregated public institutions, the impact of contemporary death on the larger society is muted. So much so, in fact, that experience with death is minimized and the private reaction to loss is diffused. Blauner predicted the possible disappearance of the funeral as a natural consequence of these contemporary trends.

Also during this period, Fulton conducted two national studies of attitudes toward death, funerals and funeral directors. The first, a survey of the American clergy, served to document the emerging conflict in values between the sacerdotal and secular roles of these two functionaries.[47] The changing character of the significance of death in contemporary American society was further illustrated in Fulton's second study[48] where it was shown that dying, over and above death and its aftermath, appeared to be the issue of greater concern to the American public.

Investigation into the sociology of death was further stimulated in 1965 by the publication of Fulton's *Death and Identity*,[49] an interdisciplinary collection of readings which integrated the theoretical perspectives and research findings on the subject to that date. The topic as a legitimate subject for sociological consideration received added support with the appearance of Nettler's review essay, "Death and Dying," which appeared in the journal *Social Problems* in 1967.[50] Nettler raised the question of whether or not citizens reared in secular, nontraditional environments cannot also have a meaningful life and death philosophy. Riley's "Death: Death and Bereavement" in the *International Encyclopedia of the Social Sciences*[51] also helped delineate the significant issues associated with death and dying as well as call the subject to the attention of the social science community. Also at this time, Glaser and Strauss investigated the social institution of the hospital as it related to the care of the dying patient. Their research, reported in their publications, *Awareness of Dying*[52] and *Time for Dying*,[53] took up the many interpersonal issues associated with the manner in which knowledge of a person's dying is shared with the staff, the family and the patient.

Sudnow contributed to the sociological dialogue on death with the publication of his monograph *Passing On*,[54] an observational study of the differential care accorded lower and middle class patients in public and private hospitals. In doing so, he recorded the invidious distinctions that are made in the emergency care provided people by virtue of their differences in age, social status and presumed moral character. Brim and his colleagues in 1970 added to the body of death literature with the publication of *The Dying Patient*.[55] It served to bring into focus as well as enlarge upon the problems associated with contemporary dying in public institutions articulated earlier by Glaser and Strauss. The first textbook, however, in which death was taken as the central focus was Vernon's *The Sociology of Death: An Analysis of Death-Related Behavior.*[56]

Simmons and her colleagues explored the practical and ethical issues associated with the transplantation of human organs. Thus, they continued to build on the work of Fox, who in 1959 published *Experiment Perilous*, a sociological account of the first efforts to transplant human kidneys.[57]

Later in the decade, Marshall[58] investigated the retirement village and interpreted it as an important socializing agent in the contemporary culture both for the gradual disengagement of the residents from the larger society and as a preparation for their eventual deaths.

In 1976, Pine co-edited the anthology *Acute Grief and the Funeral*[59] which examined from a variety of perspectives the connection between the ritualized, public responses to death and the personal reactions to loss. The funeral, it was concluded, was not simply an effort on the part of society to discuss or deny death as it was an attempt to restore the community's equilibrium that death disturbs. Funeral rituals, it was observed, not only serve to incorporate the deceased into the world of the dead, but they also facilitate the reintegration of grieving survivors into the world of the living. In so doing, death ceremonies and observances give meaning to life as they realize two central goals of society—temporal continuity and spiritual immortality.

In 1977, Fulton published *Death, Grief and Bereavement: A Bibliography, 1845-1975*[60] to acquaint scholars with the scientific research and discussion that had taken place on the subject of death since the middle of the last century. "Interest in the topic has been notable," he observed, "particularly in the past few years." By actual count, he reported, more books and articles had been written on the subject of death and dying over the preceding decade (1965-1975) than during the previous 130 years. In 1978, Fulton in collaboration with Markusen, Owen and Scheiber edited *Death and Dying: Challenge and Change*,[61] a book prepared to accompany a nation-wide newspaper course on death funded by the National Endowment for the Humanities and coordinated by Fulton. The 15-week series, entitled Courses by Newspaper, involved the participation of over 415 newspapers with a combined readership of 12 million. In addition, more than 300 colleges and universities across the United States offered the course in conjunction with the newspaper series. It was reported that more than 12,000 college students enrolled in the course which featured the thoughts and research of prominent scholars from across the social science disciplines.

In 1980 Fox[62] edited a special edition of *The Annals*, the official publication of the Academy of Political and Social Science, in order to explain as well as highlight the new-found prominence that the subject of death was experiencing in certain Western societies—especially in the United States. Fox attributed the "crescendo" of interest in American society, in part, to emergent social, cultural and historical developments and called on her colleagues from medicine, philosophy and the social sciences to join in analyzing and interpreting the phenomenon.

Charmaz[63] in 1980 published the first distinctly sociological analysis of death taking a symbolic interactionist perspective. It was her thesis that the "meanings" surrounding the experience of death, as well as death-related rituals and behavior, could be better explained within a sociological context. Although Charmaz recognizes the contributions to the subject offered by other disciplines, such as Marxism, psychoanalysis and philosophy, to the understanding of the impact of death on society, her main objective was to demonstrate the value of the traditional concepts of sociology in explicating the phenomena of death, grief and bereavement.

In 1981, Fulton published *Death, Grief and Bereavement II: A Bibliography, 1975-1980*[64] as a supplement to the earlier bibliography in response to the dramatic growth in the literature that had occurred over the previous five years. The bibliography also included a guide to doctoral dissertations in sociology on death and dying from 1970 to 1978 (compiled by Santora) which served to provide a stimulus to the subject as the field prepared to consolidate its growth with its new-found focus on death education. In 1983 DeSpelder and Strickland's textbook, *The Last Dance: Encountering Death and Dying*,[65] provided a comprehensive survey of the subject of death and related issues to that date.

Death and Social Class

As Parsons, Blauner and Fulton discussed the effects that demographic changes were having on a contemporary America insulated from the occurrence of death, demographers were examining variations in mortality rates as a function of social class. It was becoming evident that social class not only had consequences for the medical care and treatment one might receive, but also figured into the equation of life expectancy regardless of health. In 1967, Antonovsky,[66] for example, published an international review of mortality studies and demonstrated that higher social classes enjoyed an increased life expectancy, a finding that Kephart[67] had earlier anticipated. In his 1950 study of American cemeteries Kephart showed that social class is reflected and maintained after death by the manner in which the dead are buried.

Occupations and Professions

Significant impetus for the study of death-related occupations came from Hughes and his graduate students at the University of Chicago during the 1950s and '60s. In Hughes' course on occupations and professions several students were stimulated to study the funeral director and the meaning and significance of the contemporary funeral. Under Hughes' guidance, Habenstein completed a master's thesis on the cremation movement and published his doctoral dissertation on the history of American funeral directing.[68] Shortly thereafter, in collaboration with Lamers, he published *Funeral Customs the World Over.* At this time Bowman undertook an analysis of five different funerals which served as the basis for his critical analysis of the funeral director and the funeral in contemporary social life. His book, *The American Funeral: A Study in Guilt, Extravagance and Sublimity,*[69] combined the perspective of van Gennep with the methods of contemporary sociology to produce the first scholarly critique of traditional mortuary practices in America—a critique that was to serve later as the basis for the more popular exposés that appeared. Pine and Phillips in 1970[70] offered an analysis of funeral expenditures in which they conjectured that the survivor's purchase of a funeral may serve as felicitous vehicle for the discharge of guilt. Platt,[71] in her 1981 *American Sociological Review* article, took a functionalist perspective of business temporal norms and bereavement behavior and observed the significant control that American business, as well as governmental agencies, were beginning to exert on the public funeral and the private expressions of grief and mourning rituals—a development anticipated decades earlier by Sumner and other American sociologists. Earlier, Pine had systematically examined the role of the funeral director as a unique occupational type in his book, *Caretaker of the Dead: The American Funeral Director.*[72] He also was the first sociologist to analyze the role of the funeral director in the aftermath of disasters.[73]

Widowhood and Bereavement

The study of the impact of bereavement upon survivors flourished in sociology with researchers such as Volkart,[74] Marris,[75] Berardo,[76] Lopata[77] and others. Lopata showed, for example, that bereavement for widows differs as a function of social class. She found that the middle-class widow appeared to have a more difficult period of adjustment than her working-class counterpart. It was Lopata's observation that companionate relationships leave the middle-class widow more grievously exposed to the problems of survivorship. Lopata has continued her work by exploring the particular problems associated with the African-American widow in the urban environment.[78] Glick and Weiss' monograph, *The First Year of Bereavement*,[79] illustrates the value of cumulative sociological research first called for by Eliot over 40 years ago. Their collaboration with the English psychiatrist Parkes testifies to the importance of the topic as well as to the desirability and fruitfulness of interdisciplinary cooperation.

Rosenblatt[80] summed up the grief experiences of diarists from the nineteenth century in his book, *Bitter, Bitter Tears*. He applied contemporary theories of grief to the reported reactions to bereavement and loss documented by the diarists. In doing so he deepened our understanding of death's aftermath. Parkes and Weiss[81] researched the reactions of widows and widowers. In their book *Recovery From Bereavement* they distinguished between those survivors who got "used to the loss" and those who got "over the loss." They also proposed treatment strategies for those who display problematic reactions.

Since the 1960s, sociologists have also refined their observations regarding the nature of grief. Today, different kinds of grief are delineated by the profession: "normal" grief, "maladaptive" grief, "pathological" grief, "anticipatory" grief and "convalescent" grief. Sociologists are now able to observe grief in terms of a specific situation or with respect to its associational content. Grief is better understood in terms of who the griever is, in relation to the deceased, as well as grief itself in light of the nature of the loss (Folta and Deck[82]). Anthropologists have greatly enhanced the discipline's understanding in this regard. Spiro,[83] for example, in his work among the Ifaluk, has shown that wives do not necessarily grieve for their husbands. According to his observations, a wife was not expected to grieve for her husband because it was believed that her ties were with the male members of her maternal family. That is, she would be expected to grieve for her father, her brothers or her sons, but not for her husband. This is something that needs to be understood, especially considering the new contexts in which dying occurs, and the new relationships that form at the time of one's illness or dying. Particularly is this so today with the prospect of the hospice movements, home care and other palliative care programs. These programs will involve many persons in situations that could result in what has been termed a "surrogate" griever. Grief is to be understood, then, not only in terms of the inner dynamics of the survivor, but also in a situational sense, in terms of a social role.

Finally, a caveat. Time and space limitations lead us to omit from consideration the sociological literature on suicide. In contrast to other substantive areas which have been examined, suicide has been studied more extensively by sociologists than any other death-related subject. Consequently as a field of study with its own literature it has tended, historically, to be complete unto itself while its students, by and large, have not displayed an interest in the broader issues of the sociology of death.

PROSPECTUS

Given what has been presented regarding the general level of interest as well as the breadth of activity in the area of death and death education, the subject of death, we would conclude, has established itself within the discipline of sociology.

When we discuss the sociology of death, however, we must be sensitive to the transitional character of the subject matter. We must also be alert to the fact that concepts and definitions associated with death have changed significantly since the time of Eliot. For instance, just two decades ago, death was something easily determined by the absence of vital signs. Today, organ transplants have frequently made it necessary to perform confirming procedures, usually an electroencephalogram (EEG), to be certain that a person is dead.

Most importantly, in addition to the controversy surrounding the clinical definition of death, the conception of life itself has also changed. In contrast to the 1960s view of when life began the conception of life today has contracted; who is considered alive and who is considered dead today is not the same as it was. Viability in contemporary American society has been foreshortened. Formerly, life began with conception. The Supreme Court has ruled, however, that one is not alive until after 21 weeks of gestation. As a consequence life, in a manner of speaking, has been obliged to "pull in its belt." Thus, with respect to birth as well as death, American attitudes have undergone dramatic change.

Thirty years ago it would have been difficult to anticipate that organ transplantation would have the significance for our society that it now has. The search for donatable organs has led to the development of organ donor programs with sophisticated psychological testing programs for matching related donors and the adoption of the Uniform Anatomical Gift Act. While the full implications and consequences of these developments cannot be fully discussed here, it is worth noting that such legislation may potentially take from the family survivors the right of decision with respect to the deceased's body—a right that has been integral to family life since time immemorial.

What, then, is the task of the sociologist in the light of these changes and developments as they relate to a sociology of death? Clearly, more research needs to be initiated with respect to contemporary controversies surrounding dying within institutions. The former president of the American Medical Association, Dr. Malcom C. Todd, felt constrained to assure the audience at his inaugural address that while their organization would continue to hold to the time-honored principle of respect for life, it would attempt to mitigate the problems created by medicine's new-found ability to extend life. He acknowledged the need for new medical guidelines for patients with fatal illnesses who wished to terminate their life-supporting therapies and proposed that in such cases a committee composed of the patient, the physician, and members of the patient's family be formed to make the final decision. On first view the reasonableness of his proposal seems readily apparent. Moreover, it is consistent with the opinions of a growing number of people across the country who, under the catchphrase "death with dignity," call for a more rational approach to the problems associated with prolonged dying. But a word of caution. Reynolds and Fulton undertook a study which simulated the decision-making process associated with this complex, emotionally charged issue.[84] Posing a hypothetical situation of a middle-aged woman, fatally ill with cancer, who increasingly experiences excruciating pain, the subjects in a study were asked (1) should the physician cease to administer drugs that keep the woman alive and, if so, (2) when should the drugs be withdrawn? The study showed dramatically that group decisions favored withholding the life-preserving drugs more often and at a much earlier point in time than did individual decisions. While we need to know much more before we can speak authoritatively about the behavior of decision-making groups in real-life contexts, the study strongly suggested that utilization of such groups may encourage a systematic bias in the types of decisions reached and that they may be more extreme than the current social norms. There would appear to be little justification, therefore, for the assumption that the "rights of the individual" will be automatically protected by such groups, for it is often these very "rights" that undergo reexamination.

Additionally, more work needs to be done in the area of separation and loss from causes other than death. Bendiksen and Fulton,[85] in examining the causal relationship between childhood bereavement and later behavior disorders, found that separation due to divorce appeared to have a greater and more lasting, deleterious effect upon the child, even into adulthood, than loss due to a death. While the topic of divorce has been addressed previously in the family literature, the long-term effects of such separation have not been fully explored. When we reflect that fewer and fewer children experience loss through death as compared to children who experience the loss of a parent through divorce, it appears that in this instance the burgeoning interest in children and death needs to be complemented by attention to the implications of children and divorce.

Finally, much more needs to be known and understood regarding the manner in which contemporary American youth view themselves in a world that has seen the development of a neutron bomb and where nuclear carnage, despite the dismemberment of the Soviet Union and reduction of tensions between the United States and Russia, is still a possibility. We need to know much more clearly than we do at the present time what the relationship is between this aseptic Damoclean sword and the rising rates of suicide that are found among the young. More needs to be learned about the relationships between delinquency, violence and the preoccupation with death that we find in the mass media and contemporary music. Lifton, in his several works,[86] has coined the expression "psychic numbing" to interpret the post-cataclysmic behavior of the survivors of Hiroshima and Nagasaki. Could it be that in the world of death-rock, punk-rock and doomsday prophecy as well as in the recent proliferation of films vividly depicting homicide, suicide and human mutilation, we are observing a form of "anticipatory numbing," a preparation for a holocaust which for many appears to be not too distant? Additionally, the prospect of a clouded, truncated future may have profound repercussions in a growing movement toward self-seekingness, narcissism and moment-to-moment gratification. Denied a future—either religious or worldly—contemporary youth seek the pleasures of the tentative moment.

In this light, then, the recent phenomenal response to Moody's book *Life After Life*[87] takes on even greater significance for people who, frequently despairing of close relationships with relatives and friends of this world, hope to establish them in the next. In this regard, too, it should be of interest to sociologists to observe whether or not this revived interest in life after life may provide for modern youth an enticement to remove themselves—through suicide—from their troubled earthly environment. These and other issues and concerns await the skills and insights of sociologists.

NOTES

1. Herbert Spencer. 1910. *The Principles of Sociology,* Vol. I. New York: D. Appleton & Co. (first published in 1876).
2. Ibid., p. 183.
3. Ibid., p. 165.
4. Thomas G. Masaryk. 1970. *Suicide and the Meaning of Civilization.* Chicago: University of Chicago Press (first published in 1881).
5. Ibid., p. 144.
6. Ibid., p. 169.
7. Emile Durkheim. 1951. *Suicide* (translated by J. Spaulding and G. Simpson). Glencoe, IL: The Free Press (first published in 1897).
8. Emile Durkheim. 1954. *The Elementary Forms of the Religious Life* (translated by J.W. Swain). Glencoe, IL: The Free Press (first published in 1915).
9. Ibid., p. 445.

10. Ibid., pp. 442-443.
11. Robert Hertz. 1960. The Collective Representation of Death. In *Death and the Right Hand* (translated by R. and C. Needham). Glencoe, IL: The Free Press (first published in 1907).
12. Ibid., p. 78.
13. Ibid., p. 86.
14. Arnold van Gennep. 1909. *Les Rites de Passage.* Paris: Librairie Critique.
15. Max Weber. 1947. Science as a Vocation (p. 144). In *From Max Weber: Essays in Sociology* (translated by H. Gerth and G.W. Mills). New York: Oxford University Press (first published in 1915).
16. Max Weber. 1947. *Religious Rejections of the World and Their Directions,* ibid., p. 335.
17. Albion W. Small and George E. Vincent. 1894. *An Introduction to the Study of Society.* New York: American Book Company, p. 110.
18. Ibid., p. 279.
19. Edward Allsworth Ross. 1959. *Social Control* (p. 59). Boston: Beacon Press (first published in 1901).
20. William Graham Sumner and Albert Gallaway Keller. 1927. *The Science of Society.* New Haven, CT: Yale University Press.
21. Ibid., Vol. I, p. 608.
22. Ibid., Vol. I, p. 610.
23. Ibid., Vol. III, p. 1841.
24. Ibid., Vol. III, p. 1892.
25. Thomas D. Eliot. 1930a: The Adjustive Behavior of Bereaved Families: A New Field for Research. *Social Forces* 8:543-549. 1930b: Bereavement as a Problem for Family Research and Technique. *The Family* 11:114-115. 1932: The Bereaved Family. *Annals of the American Academy of Political and Social Sciences* 160:184-190. 1933: A Step Toward the Social Psychology of Bereavement. *Journal of Abnormal and Social Psychology* 27:380-390. 1938: Bereavement as a Field of Social Research. *Bulletin of the Society for Social Research* 17:4. 1943: Of the Shadow of Death. *Annals of the American Academy of Political and Social Sciences* 229:87-99. 1946: War Bereavements and Their Recovery. *Marriage and Family Living* 8. 1947: *Attitudes Toward Euthanasia* 15:131-134. 1955: Bereavement: Inevitable But Not Insurmountable. In H. Becker and R. Hill, eds., *Family, Marriage and Parenthood.* Boston: Heath.
26. Meyer F. Nimkoff. 1947. *Marriage and Family.* Boston: Cambridge Riverside Press, pp. 613-619.
27. Willard Waller. 1940: *War and the Family.* New York: Dryden Press; 1951: *The Family: A Dynamic Interpretation* (revised by Reubin Hill). New York: Dryden Press (first published in 1938).
28. David Martin Fulcomer. 1942. The Adjustive Behavior of Some Recently Bereaved Spouses. Unpublished Ph.D. dissertation, Northwestern University.
29. Ernest W. Burgess and Harvey Locke. 1953. *The Family,* 2nd Ed. New York: American Book Company, Chapter 21.
30. Reubin Hill. 1949: *Families Under Stress.* New York: Harper; 1951: Bereavement: A Crisis of Family Dismemberment. In *The Family: A Dynamic Interpretation.* New York: Dryden Press; 1958: Social Stresses on the Family. *Social Casework* 39:139-150.
31. Eliot, 1930b, loc. cit.
32. Ibid., p. 115.

33. Eliot, 1943, op. cit., p. 115.
34. Nimkoff, op. cit., p. 612.
35. Waller, 1951, loc. cit.
36. Burgess and Locke, loc. cit.
37. Hill, 1949, loc. cit.
38. Samuel A. Stouffer et al. 1949. *The American Soldier*. Princeton, NJ: Princeton University Press.
39. Gil Elliot. 1972. *Twentieth Century Book of the Dead*. New York: Scribner.
40. Howard P. Becker. 1933: The Sorrow of Bereavement. *Journal of Abnormal and Social Psychology* 27:391-410; Howard P. Becker and David K. Bruner. 1931: Attitudes Toward Death and the Dead and Some Possible Causes of Ghost Fear. *Mental Hygiene* 15:828-837.
41. Fulcomer, loc. cit.
42. William Faunce and Robert Fulton. 1958. The Sociology of Death: A Neglected Area of Research. *Social Forces* 36:205-209.
43. Talcott Parsons. 1963. Death in American Society: A Brief Working Paper. *The American Behavioral Scientist* 6:61-65.
44. Faunce and Fulton, op. cit.
45. Parsons, loc. cit.
46. Robert Blauner. 1966. Death and Social Structure. *Psychiatry* 29:378-394.
47. Robert Fulton. 1961. The Clergyman and the Funeral Director: A Study in Role Conflict. *Social Forces* 39:205-209.
48. Robert Fulton. 1963. *The Sacred and the Secular: Attitudes of the American Public Toward Death*. Milwaukee: Bulfin.
49. Robert Fulton. 1965. *Death and Identity*, 1st Ed. New York: Wiley.
50. Gwynn Nettler. 1967. Review Essay: On Death and Dying. *Social Problems* 14:335-344.
51. John W. Riley, Jr. 1968. Death: Death and Bereavement. *International Encyclopedia of the Social Sciences* 4:19-26.
52. Barney G. Glaser and Anselm L. Strauss. 1965. *Awareness of Dying*. Chicago: Aldine.
53. Barney G. Glaser and Anselm L. Strauss. 1968. *Time for Dying*. Chicago: Aldine.
54. David Sudnow. 1967. *Passing On: The Social Organization of Dying*. Englewood Cliffs, NJ: Prentice-Hall.
55. Orville G. Brim, Jr., et al. (eds.). 1970. *The Dying Patient*. New York: Russell Sage.
56. Glenn M. Vernon. 1970. *Sociology of Death: An Analysis of Death-Related Behavior*. New York: Ronald Press.
57. Roberta G. Simmons et al. 1972. The Prospective Organ Transplant Donor: Problems and Prospects of Medical Innovation. *Omega* 3:331-339; Renée C. Fox. 1959. *Experiment Perilous*. Glencoe, IL: The Free Press.
58. Victor W. Marshall. 1975. Socialization for Impending Death in a Retirement Village. *American Journal of Sociology* 80:1124-1144.
59. Vanderlyn Pine et al. 1976. *Acute Grief and the Funeral*. Springfield, IL: Charles C Thomas.
60. Robert Fulton. 1977. *Death, Grief and Bereavement: A Bibliography, 1845-1975*. New York: Arno Press.
61. Robert Fulton, Eric Markusen, Greg Owen and Jane Sheiber, eds., 1978. *Death and Dying: Challenge and Change*. San Francisco: Boyd & Fraser.

62. Renée C. Fox, ed., 1980. The Social Meaning of Death. *Annals of the Academy of Political and Social Science* 447:1-99.
63. Kathy Charmaz. 1980. *The Social Reality of Death: Death in Contemporary America.* Reading, MA: Addison-Wesley.
64. Robert Fulton with Margaret Reed. 1981. *Death, Grief and Bereavement: A Bibliography, 1975-1980.* New York: Arno Press.
65. Lynne Ann DeSpelder and Albert Lee Strickland. 1983. *The Last Dance: Encountering Death and Dying.* Mountain View, CA: Mayfield.
66. Aaron Antonovsky. 1967. Social Class Life Expectancy and Overall Mortality. *Milbank Memorial Fund Quarterly* 45:31-73.
67. William M. Kephart. 1950. Status After Death. *American Sociological Review* 15:643-653.
68. Robert W. Habenstein. 1955. *The History of American Funeral Directing.* Milwaukee: Bulfin; R.W. Habenstein and W.M. Lamers. 1963. *Funeral Customs the World Over.* Milwaukee: Bulfin.
69. Leroy Bowman. 1959. *The American Funeral.* Washington, DC: Public Affairs Press.
70. Vanderlyn R. Pine and Derek Phillips. 1970. The Cost of Dying: A Sociological Analysis of Funeral Expenditures. *Social Problems* 17:405-417.
71. Lois Platt. 1981. Business Temporal Norms and Bereavement Behavior. *American Sociological Review* 46:317-333.
72. Vanderlyn R. Pine. 1975. *Caretaker of the Dead: The American Funeral Director.* New York: Irvington.
73. Vanderlyn R. Pine. 1974. Grief Work and Dirty Work: The Aftermath of an Aircrash. *Omega* 5:281-286.
74. Edmund H. Volkart and Stanley T. Michael. Bereavement and Mental Health. In A.H. Leighton, ed., *Explorations in Social Psychiatry.* New York: Basic Books.
75. Peter Marris. 1958: *Widows and Their Families.* London: Routledge & Kegan Paul; 1974: *Loss and Change.* New York: Pantheon Books.
76. Felix Berardo. 1968. Widowhood Status in the United States: Perspectives on a Neglected Aspect of the Family Life Cycle. *The Family Coordinator* 17:191-203.
77. Helena Z. Lopata. 1969: Loneliness: Forms and Components. *Social Problems* 17:248-262; 1970: The Social Involvement of American Widows. *American Behavioral Scientist* 14:41-58; 1971: Living Arrangements of American Urban Widows. *Sociological Focus* 5:41-61; 1972a: Social Relations of Widows in Urbanizing Societies. *Sociological Quarterly* 13:259-272; 1972b: *Widowhood in an American City.* Morristown, NJ: Learning Corporation.
78. Lopata, 1972b, loc. cit.
79. Ira O. Glick et al. 1974. *The First Year of Bereavement.* New York: Wiley.
80. Paul C. Rosenblatt. 1983. *Bitter, Bitter Tears.* Minneapolis: University of Minnesota Press.
81. Colin Murray Parkes and Robert S. Weiss. 1983. *Recovery from Bereavement.* New York: Basic Books.
82. Jeannette F. Folta and Edith Deck. 1972. Social Reconstruction after Death. *Tribuna Medica* 10 (October).
83. M. Spiro. 1949. *Ifaluk: A South Sea Culture.* New Haven, CT: Human Relations Area File.
84. Robert Fulton and Paul D. Reynolds. 1973. Decisions for Death: Simulation of

a Societal Consensus. Unpublished paper, Center for Death Education and Research, University of Minnesota.

85. Robert Bendiksen and Robert Fulton. 1975. Death and the Child: An Anterospective Test of the Childhood Bereavement and Later Behavior Disorder Hypothesis. *Omega* 6:45-59.
86. Robert J. Lifton. 1967: *Death in Life: Survivors of Hiroshima.* New York: Random House; 1973: The Sense of Immortality: On Death and the Continuity of Life. *American Journal of Psychoanalysis* 33:3-15; 1975a: On Death and the Continuity of Life: A Psychohistorical Perspective. *Omega* 6:143-197; 1975b: with Eric Olson. *Living and Dying.* New York: Bantam Books.
87. Raymond Moody. 1976. *Life After Life.* New York: Bantam Books.

II

Grief and the Process of Mourning

Introduction

On Thanksgiving eve, 1942, less than a year after the Japanese attack on Pearl Harbor, fire engulfed the Coconut Grove nightclub in Boston, Massachusetts, resulting in the deaths of over 500 young men and women. The Coconut Grove fire was a singular event for two reasons: first, it took a greater toll of human life by fire than had ever occurred within the continental limits of the United States and second, it made the far-distant disaster of Pearl Harbor, coming as it did before the era of television, an immediate reality for all Americans. The fire, as with all similar disasters—with their vivid images and tragic accounts—was imprinted indelibly on the minds of those old enough to remember it.

It was Erich Lindemann, a physician at Massachusetts General Hospital in Boston, however, who brought the profound emotional consequences of that catastrophic fire to our attention. Coming from a background in psychiatry, with an interest in the emotional reactions of patients to body disfigurement and plastic surgery, Lindemann was struck by the similarity of responses between his patients' reactions to facial disfigurement or loss of a body part and the reactions of the survivors of the fire to the loss of their spouses, sweethearts and friends. He found that all of the 101 survivors he interviewed experienced a uniform reaction that included: (1) sensations of somatic distress, such as tightness in the throat, choking and shortness of breath; (2) intense preoccupation with the image of the deceased; (3) strong feelings of guilt; (4) a loss of warmth toward others with a tendency to respond with irritability and anger; and (5) disoriented behavior patterns.

The duration of the grief reaction and the manner in which a person adjusted to loss, Lindemann reported, depended upon the successful outcome of what he termed "grief work." Lindemann observed considerable resistance, however, on the part of some survivors to experience the distress and anguish of their bereavement. These survivors instead chose to avoid the intense pain associated with their grief and to avoid the expression of emotion necessary for it. Lindemann described such behavior as a "morbid grief reaction" in contrast to those behaviors and reactions he identified as "normal grief." A "morbid grief reaction," as Lindemann and others have subsequently documented, can run the gamut of response from such psychosomatic conditions as asthma, ulcerative colitis and rheumatoid arthritis to antisocial behavior and possibly to psychoses. Lindemann's systematic investigation of the grief reactions of the survivors of the Coconut Grove fire inaugurated the scientific study of bereavement at the same time that it defined for a generation of scholars and clinicians the symptomatology of grief.

Freud, of course, had long since advanced his theory on the difference between depression associated with "normal grief" and the mental disorder of melancholia. Theologians, moreover, had discussed for millennia dying and death within the parameters of their different cosmologies, but there was little systematic, clinical understanding of the human reaction to loss. Anthropologists had long reported on the exotic mourning rites and funeral practices of pre-literate societies, but with rare exception, medical and social scientists tended to ignore the subject of grief. The social-psychological crisis of bereavement was not a recognized subject of scientific research until the mid-point of the twentieth century when Feifel published *The Meaning of Death* in 1959. Grief, once a private concern, became in the 1960s an issue for professional as well as public discourse.

This is not to say, however, that individually or collectively, we have not attended to the fact of death or the sorrow of bereavement throughout history. To the contrary, the sacred as well as profane literature in western society is replete with references to the meaning and significance of dying and death, as well as to the tragedy of loss. In John 11:35, we read, for example, that "Jesus wept" upon hearing of the death of his friend, Lazarus. Shakespeare has Othello cry, "My particular grief is of so flood-gate and o'er bearing nature that it engluts and swallows other sorrows." And in Macbeth, he instructs us to "Give sorrow words; the grief that does not speak whispers the o'er fraught heart and bids it break." "Light cares speak, the huge are dumb," states Daniel, while Victor Hugo observed that "It is the peculiarity of grief to bring out the childish side of man." And, again, it is Shakespeare who wisely reminds us that "everyone can master a grief but he that has it." Despite these memorable observations on the experience of grief, to say nothing of the *ars moriendi* (art of dying) literature that described western societies' collective response to dying and death during the past several centuries, the clinical understanding of bereavement was poorly understood. It is only recently that we have come to comprehend, more fully, the potential physiological, psychological and sociological consequences of loss.

Perhaps no contemporary scholar has contributed more to our newfound understanding of grief than did the late John Bowlby, the author of the first essay in this section, "The Mourning of Children." In his sociologically sensitive analysis, the English psychiatrist discusses the different considerations relevant to telling a child about death. As part of his monumental, three-volume work, *Attachment and Loss*, the chapter is a summary of his lifetime research (and that of others) concerning children's ideas about death, differences of children's mourning from that of adults, the risk of psychiatric disorder among bereaved children, and the conditions responsible for differences in the outcome of mourning. Bowlby completes his review of the research literature by concluding that environmental factors (i.e., family and social relationships) have been seriously overlooked in explaining a child's reaction to loss. It is his opinion that the evidence presently available does not support the traditional theoretical standpoint of psychoanalysis that contends that the vagaries of personality development explain most of the differential outcomes associated with childhood loss.

John Stephenson, in his essay "Grief and Mourning," defines grief as "that state of mental and physical pain which is experienced when the loss of a significant object, person or part of the self is realized." Employing this definition, he distinguishes between the psychological process whereby the individual acknowledges loss and the social reality within which the loss is perceived. In recognizing that grief is an intensely personal emotional experience that takes place within a social context, Stephenson provides the reader with both a psychological and sociological perspective with which to view grief and the mourning process.

Under the heading, "The Psychological Dynamics of Grief," Stephenson offers a typology of grief as well as a discussion of the grieving process itself. While he believes grief is intrinsically idiosyncratic, and following Bowlby, believes that it is the expression of a particular amalgam of anxiety, anger and despair, Stephenson nevertheless believes that there are three general stages through which the individual moves in coming to terms with grief. They are: (1) reaction, (2) disorganization and reorganization, and (3) reorientation and recovery. He concludes with a discussion of those factors that are believed to influence the course and outcome of the tri-stage process. In another section of his essay entitled "The Social Process of Mourning," Stephenson considers the social context within which a death occurs and from his sociological perspective, reviews the different prescribed patterns of social interaction that society imposes upon the individuals when they confront a loss.

Is grief universal? This is the issue that psychologists Wolfgang Stroebe and Margaret S. Stroebe address in their contribution to this volume, "Is Grief Universal? Cultural Variations in the Emotional Reaction to Loss." The inter-cultural study of grief, they observe, has been fraught with difficulties. On the one hand, psychologists typically have lacked the skills or opportunity to conduct cross-cultural research while on the other hand, anthropologists traditionally have been interested in public mourning rites rather than personal reactions to loss. In order to break through this methodological impasse, the authors first reviewed the basic assumptions of emotion theory which range from James and Lange, who held that emotions were physiologically driven, to Averill and Hochschild, who believed that emotions were fundamental reflections of culture. After reviewing the various theories, they are moved to conclude that in all likelihood, an emotional experience is the product of both cultural norms and distinct bodily reactions.

To press their analysis further, the Stroebes chose the uniquely human act of crying, examining its presence or absence, as well as its type and timing across different cultures. It was their conclusion that crying is a frequent response to loss through death in both western and nonwestern cultures. While differences were found in those situations in which crying was considered appropriate or even obligatory, the Stroebes nevertheless were able to report that crying behavior occurs consistently among peoples of different cultures.

The Stroebes also examined, cross-culturally, the presence of symptoms of grief such as a self-inflicted injury, horror at the corpse or fear of the ghost. They were able to conclude that there seems to be a "core" response to loss through death, even though beliefs about death and the afterlife, as well as expressions of grief, may vary from culture to culture.

The Stroebes next analyzed the phases of grief, examining patterns of behavior from the abbreviated mourning rituals of the Navajo to the protracted ceremonies of the Kota of southern India. They concluded that "grief is channeled in all cultures along specified lines." In fact, they observed that burial of the dead and mourning are among the few universal human practices that can be identified, even though the manner of those practices may differ diametrically from one another.

In response to the question, "Is grief universal?" the Stroebes do not reply with a simple yes or no, but observe that, on the one hand, the available evidence supports the view that grief seems to be universally felt, while on the other, there is evidence from certain parts of the world that overt signs of grief or the trauma of loss are short-lived.

The Stroebes observe that one consequence of our increased longevity today, as well as the manner in which we turn over our dying and our dead to others for care, is that we are less prepared when death occurs than are those societies where death is a more frequent and intimate experience. They point out that there is much discussion about death in America, and they question whether or not Americans do in fact deny death—an observation that has long been held against the society by scholars and social critics alike. Death education in America, the authors contend, does in fact occur even though it is primarily obtained from sources other than the immediate death experience. The authors conclude with a discussion of grief from losses other than death (such as divorce, retirement or a change of residence), underscoring the importance that the rupture of habitual patterns of behavior has upon a person's emotions.

5

The Mourning of Children

John Bowlby, MD

WHEN AND WHAT A CHILD IS TOLD

Adults are usually present when a near relative dies; if they are not they are likely to be given the news promptly. By contrast, children in Western societies are unlikely to be present at the time of death; not infrequently information about it reaches them only much later, and even then often in a misleading form. In view of that it is hardly surprising that children's responses are apt to be out of keeping with what has happened.

When a child's parent dies it almost always rests with the surviving parent to inform the child. This is an extremely painful task. A majority do it promptly but the younger the child the more likely is the parent to delay; and in a significant minority this delay is of weeks or even months. As a stopgap the child may be told that the father has gone on a trip or perhaps been transferred to another hospital. Of the Boston widows studied by Glick[1] some 70 percent told the children immediately but nearly one in three delayed. Two of them asked a relative to do it for them.

The reports show that in the cultures studied the surviving parent is extremely likely to tell the child that the father has gone to heaven or been taken to heaven. For those who are devout this information accords with the parent's own belief. For many others, however, it does not, so that from the start a discrepancy exists between what the child is told and what the parent believes. This creates difficulties. Unless told otherwise a young child will naturally assume that heaven is no different from other distant places and that return is merely a matter of time. A little girl of four, who like others had been told her father had gone to heaven, was angry a few months later and cried bitterly because he did not come to her birthday party.[2] Other children persist in asking mother where heaven is, what people do there, what they wear or what they eat, all of them questions a disbeliever finds embarrassing.

Another common account, resorted to especially after the deaths of old persons such as a grandparent, is to say that he or she has gone to sleep. Admittedly, this is a well-known figure of speech. Yet a young child has little knowledge of figures of speech and inevitably takes most of such sayings literally. Small wonder, therefore, if falling asleep thenceforward becomes a dangerous activity.

The two crucial items of information which sooner or later a child needs to know are first that the dead parent will never return and secondly that the body is buried in the ground or burned to ashes. For the surviving parent to give such information is extremely difficult because of the deep concern to shield one's child from awareness of death and the pain of mourning that every parent in this situation has, and also, no doubt, because to speak about these things brings home their reality too nakedly. Information regarding disposal of the body is usually postponed sometimes a year or two.[3] Among all the families studied only a small minority of the children attended the funeral, for example, in Marris's London study 11 out of 94. Subsequently children were either not taken to the grave or, if they were, might not be informed of the reason. In a family described by Becker and Margolin the children visited the cemetery with father, placed flowers on the grave and witnessed relatives crying without anyone mentioning their mother's death and burial. The children, moreover, refrained from asking why they and others were there.

Not only is the information given to children often tardy and misleading but every researcher notes also how eager many a surviving parent is to ensure that one's child does not see how distressed one is. Becker and Margolin tell of one mother who avoided talking to the children about how she felt for fear she would cry and not be able to stop. This, she thought, would be too upsetting for them. By contrast, she cried a great deal during interviews and also described how she cried for long hours alone after the children were asleep at night. During the interviews she recognized that a main difficulty was that she could not bear to face the intensity of her children's feelings. Thus, so far from assisting the children to express feeling, a proportion of parents make it almost impossible for them to do so. The difficulty created is vividly illustrated in an account by Palgi[4] of a small boy whose mother chided him for not shedding tears over his father's death. "How can I cry," he retorted, "when I have never seen your tears?"

Children are quick to read the signs. When a parent is afraid of feelings the children will hide their own. When a parent prefers silence, the children, sooner or later, will cease their enquiries. Several observers note how eager many of the children were to learn more about how and why their parent had died and what had happened subsequently, and how their enquiries were met with evasion or silence. Two examples of parents who made their reluctance explicit are given by Kliman.[5] In the first, two boys aged 7 and 9 who had lost their father wanted to know more about him and also pressed their mother to show them some old movie films of him. When she found this too painful, they taught themselves to operate the projector and ran through the films repeatedly on their own. In the second a father had lost both his wife and his son in a fire and blamed himself for not having done more to save them. Unable to bear talking about the event, he made his two young daughters promise that they would never mention their mother again in his presence.

What the proportion of parents in our culture who show reluctance to share information and feeling with their children may be we have no means at present of knowing. A reading of the various reports, however, shows that it is common in both Britain and America. Not only does this finding go far to explain the frequency with which children are said to deny the reality of a parent's death but it may explain also why the theory that a child's ego is too weak and undeveloped to bear the pain of mourning should have become so widely accepted. Indeed the evidence so far presented suggests that, irrespective of what the capacity of children may be, not infrequently the adults surrounding a child are themselves unable to bear the pain of mourning—perhaps that of their own mourning, certainly that of their child's, and especially that of mourning together.

Helping the Surviving Parent to Help the Children

Those who have worked in this field and especially the clinicians are clear that nothing but confusion and pathology results when news of a parent's death is withheld from children, or glossed over, and when expression of feeling is discouraged either implicitly or explicitly. Much effort has therefore been given to finding means to help the surviving parent to help the children.

The first task undoubtedly is to provide the surviving parent with a supportive relationship within which one feels free to reflect on the blow that has fallen and how and why it came about, and to express all those tempestuous urges and feelings that is so necessary if mourning is to take a healthy course. Once a parent has surmounted this hurdle, it becomes less hard to include the children in the mourning process. Modeling one's behavior, perhaps unwittingly, on that of a counselor, one can share with the children such facts as are known and answer their questions as truthfully as one is able. Together they can express their shared sorrow and distress, and also their shared anger and yearning. Often in such circumstances a parent finds that a schoolchild or adolescent has a much greater capacity to face the truth both about the past and their sadly changed future than, perhaps misled by relatives or friends, had hitherto supposed. Only, indeed when one is given true information, and the sympathy and support to bear it, can a child or adolescent be expected to respond to the loss with any degree of realism. This raises the question of how realistic about death children of different ages are capable of being.

CHILDREN'S IDEAS ABOUT DEATH

There has been much controversy concerning how children of different ages think about death. Issues debated include their ideas regarding the nature of death, its causes and what happens afterwards. Since comprehensive reviews of the literature are to be found in Anthony[6] and Furman,[7] together with their own empirical records, we need not dwell long on the controversies.

Study of the literature shows that many divergences of opinion have arisen because a number of workers have confined their attention to the special case of human death or of the even more special case of parent death. Other disagreements can be traced to some of the earlier investigators[8] having failed to realize the extent to which children's ideas about death are derived from the cultural traditions of their families and schoolmates. As a result, notions such that children must be at least 6 years old or even adolescent before they can conceive of death as being irreversible, or that young children inevitably attribute every death to a human or quasi-human agency, gained currency. Once the cultural biases are recognized, however, and the very special problems connected with the death of a parent allowed for, the picture that emerges is radically changed.

In the ordinary course of life even very young children meet with examples of death—a dead beetle, a dead mouse, a dead bird. The phenomenon is puzzling. Contrary to all previous experience with the animal, the dead creature is immobile and fails to respond to anything done to it. As a rule this arouses curiosity. What has happened? Is the creature asleep? How can we prod it into activity? In such circumstances no child is left for long without some explanation being given either by an adult or by another child; and it is from these explanations that children develop their own ideas.

In different families and different cultural settings the explanations given a child vary over an enormous range. At one extreme are ideas of universal reincarnation and of divine purpose, at another ideas of the irreversibility of death and the role of natural causes. Between these extremes lies a wide array of beliefs, including many in which a distinction is made between the death of what are regarded as higher forms of life and lower forms. As a result of distinctions and qualifications of varying sorts being introduced the sets of beliefs about life and death held by adults in western societies contain as a rule many areas of uncertainty, ambiguity and inconsistency. No wonder, therefore, that the beliefs of children vary widely too. Usually they differ from those of the adults around them only by being stated more baldly, by metaphors having been construed too literally, and by ambiguities and inconsistencies being dwelt upon instead of being glossed over.

In their various publications Robert and Erna Furman present evidence to show that even a young child has no more difficulty in conceiving of death as irreversible and as due to natural causes than has an adult and that whether or not he does so turns on what he is told. If a child no more than 2 is told that the dead beetle or the dead bird will never come alive again and that sooner or later death comes to all living creatures he may be incredulous at first but is likely to accept his parent's word. If he is told, too, that when an animal or a person well known dies it is natural to feel sad and to wish we could bring him alive again, he will hardly be surprised since it conforms with his experience and shows that his sorrows are understood. When parents adopt such practices, the Furmans point out, the way is prepared in some degree for helping a child mourn the death of a close relative, even that of a parent, should such a tragic blow fall. Only when a surviving parent genuinely believes in religious or philosophical ideas about death and an afterlife, the evidence suggest, is it useful to introduce them to children: with honest help from the surviving parent a child will be able to make something of them and so be able to share in the family mourning. In other circumstances the complexity of these ideas and the difficulty of distinguishing between bodily and spiritual death leave a child puzzled and confused while a gulf of misunderstanding may open between the child and the surviving parent.

WHEN CONDITIONS ARE FAVORABLE

When adults are observant and sympathetic and other conditions are favorable, children barely 4 years old are found to yearn for a lost parent, to hope and at times to believe that the parent may yet return, and to feel sad and angry when it becomes clear that it will never be so. Many children, it is known, insist on retaining an item of clothing or some other possession of the dead parent, and especially value photographs. So far from forgetting, children given encouragement and help have no difficulty in recalling the dead parent and, as they get older, are eager to hear more about the parent in order to confirm and amplify the picture they have retained, though perhaps reluctant to revise it adversely should they learn unfavorable things about their parent. Among the 17 children aged between 3.9 and 14.3 studied by Kliman,[9] overt and prolonged yearning for the lost parent was recorded in 10.

As with an adult who yearns for a lost spouse, the yearning of a child for a lost parent is especially intense and painful whenever life proves more than usually hard. This was described vividly by a teenage girl who a few months earlier had lost her father suddenly from an accident: "When I was little I remember how I used to cry for Mummy and Daddy to come, but I always had hope. Now when I want to cry for Daddy I know there isn't any hope."

As an initial response to the news of their loss some children weep copiously, others hardly at all. Judging by Kliman's findings, there seems a clear tendency for initial weeping to increase with age. In children under 5 it was little in evidence, in children over 10 often prolonged. Reviewing the accounts given by widowed mothers of their children's initial reactions Marris[10] is impressed by their extreme variety. There were children who cried hysterically for weeks, others especially some of the younger ones who seemed hardly to react. Others again became withdrawn and unsociable. Furman reports repeated and prolonged sobbing in some children who remained inconsolable, whereas for others tears brought relief. Without far more detailed studies than are yet available, however, we are in no position to evaluate these findings. Not only is it necessary to have records of a reasonable number of children at each age-level but exact particulars are necessary both of the children's family relationships and also of the circumstances of the death, including what information was given to the child and how the surviving parent responded. Such data are likely to take many years to collect.

As in the case of adults, some bereaved children have on occasion vivid images of their dead parent linked, clearly, with the hopes and expectations of their returning. Kliman,[11] for example, reports the case of a 6-year-old girl who, with her sister two years older, had witnessed her mother's sudden death from an intracranial hemorrhage. Before getting up in the morning this child frequently had the experience of her mother sitting on her bed talking quietly to her, much as she had when she was alive. Other episodes described in the literature, usually given as examples of children denying the reality of death, may also be explicable in terms of a child having had such an experience. Furman,[12] for example, describes how Bess, aged 3 1/2, who was thought to have been "well aware of the finality of her mother's death," announced one evening to her father, "Mummy called and said she'd have dinner with us," evidently believing it to be true.[13] On one occasion a male cousin of 22, of whom both grandmother and Wendy were fond, came to call. Without thinking, grandmother exclaimed, "Wendy, look who's here!" Wendy looked, and then turned pale; instantly grandmother knew what Wendy was thinking.[14]

Thus the evidence so far available suggests strongly that, when conditions are favorable, the mourning of children no less than of adults is commonly characterized by persisting memories and images of the dead person and by repeated recurrences of yearning and sadness, especially at family reunions and anniversaries or when a current relationship seems to be going wrong.

This conclusion is of great practical importance, especially when a bereaved child is expected to make a new relationship. So far from its being a prerequisite for the success of the new relationship that the memory of the earlier one should fade, the evidence is that the more distinct the two relationships can be kept the better the new one is likely to prosper. This may be testing for any new parent-figure, for the inevitable comparisons may be painful. Yet only when both the surviving parent and/or the new parent-figure are sensitive to the child's persisting loyalties and to the tendency to resent any change which seems to threaten the past relationship is the child likely to accommodate in a stable way to the new faces and the new ways.[15]

Other features of childhood mourning which have great practical implications are the anxiety and anger which a bereavement habitually brings.

As regards anxiety, it is hardly surprising that children who have suffered one major loss should fear lest they suffer another. This will make them especially sensitive to any separation from whoever may be mothering them and also to any event or remark that seems to them to point to another loss. As a result they are likely often to be anxious and clinging in situations that appear to an adult to be innocuous, and more prone to seek comfort by resorting to some old familiar toy or blanket than might be expected at the age they are.

Similar considerations apply to anger, for there can be no doubt that some young children who lose a parent are made extremely angry by it. An example[16] from English literature is of Richard Steele, of *Spectator* fame, who lost his father when he was 4 and who recalled how he had beaten on the coffin in a blind rage. In similar vein a student teacher described how she had reacted at the age of 5 when told that her father had been killed in the war. "I shouted at God all night. I just couldn't believe that he had let them kill my father. I loathed him for it." How frequent these outbursts are we have no means of knowing. Often no doubt they go unobserved and unrecorded, especially when the anger aroused is expressed in indirect ways. An example of this is the grumbling resentment shown by Kathy many months after her father's death which was channeled into her repeated complaints about people who don't keep their promises. Clearly, had Kathy not had a mother who, guided by the therapist, was attuned to the situation and was able to discover the origin of Kathy's complaints, it would have been easy to have dismissed the child as inherently unreasonable and possessed simply of a bad temper.

How prone children are spontaneously to blame themselves for a loss is difficult to know. What, however, is certain is that a child makes a ready scapegoat and it is very easy for a distraught widow or widower to lay blame. In some cases, perhaps, a parent does this but once in a sudden brief outburst; in other cases it may be done in a far more systematic and persistent way. In either case it is likely that the child so blamed will take the matter to heart and thereafter be prone to self-reproach and depression.[17] Such influences seem likely to be responsible for a large majority of cases in which a bereaved child develops a morbid sense of guilt; they have undoubtedly been given far too little weight in traditional theorizing.

Nevertheless, there are certain circumstances surrounding a parent's death which can lead rather easily to children reaching the conclusion that they are to blame, at least in part. Examples are when a child who has been suffering from an infectious illness has infected a parent, and when a child has been in a predicament and a parent, attempting rescue, has lost his life. In such cases only open discussion between the child and his surviving parent, or an appropriate substitute, will enable the child to see the event and one's share in it in a proper perspective.

I question whether there is good evidence that identification with the lost person plays the key role in healthy mourning that traditional theorizing has given it. Much of the evidence at present explained in these terms can be understood far better, I believe, in terms of a persistent, though perhaps disguised, striving to recover the lost person. Other phenomena hitherto presented as evidence of identification can also be explained in other ways. For example, bereaved children's fear that they may also die is found often to be a consequence of their being unclear about the causes of death and as a result supposing that whatever caused their parent's death might well cause their own too, or that, because their parent died as a young man or woman, the same fate was likely to be their's also.

There are, it is true, many cases on record where a child is clearly identifying with a dead parent. Wendy at times treated her father in the same way as her mother had treated him with remarks such as, "Anything interesting happen at the office today?" Other children play at being a teacher, or take great pains over painting, evidently influenced by the fact that the dead father was a teacher or the dead mother a painter. But these examples do little more than show that a child whose parent is dead is no less disposed to emulate him or her than before the death. Whereas the examples demonstrate clearly how real and important the relationship with the parent continues to be even after the death, they provide no evidence of substance that after a loss identification plays either a larger part or a more profound one in a child's life than it does when the parent is alive.

Thus I believe that in regard to identificatory processes, as in so much else, what occurs during childhood mourning is no different in principle to what occurs during the mourning of adults. Furthermore, the part played by identification in the disordered mourning of children seems also to be no different in principle to the part it plays in the disordered mourning of adults.

Mourning in Older Children and Adolescents

If we are right in our conclusion that young children in their fourth and fifth years mourn in ways very similar to adults, we would confidently expect that older children and adolescents would do so too; and all the evidence available supports that conclusion. Contrary opinions have arisen, I believe, only because the experience of clinicians is so often confined to children whose loss and mourning have taken place in unfavorable circumstances.

Yet there is reason to believe that there are also true differences between the mourning of children and the mourning of adults, and it is time now to consider what they may be.

DIFFERENCES BETWEEN CHILDREN'S AND ADULTS' MOURNING

The course taken by the mourning of adults is, we have seen, deeply influenced by the conditions that obtain at the time of the death and during the months and years after it. During childhood the power of these conditions to influence the course of mourning is probably even greater than it is in adults. We start by considering the effects of these conditions.

We noted repeatedly how immensely valuable it is for a bereaved adult to have available some person on whom one can lean and who is willing to give comfort and aid. Here as elsewhere what is important for an adult is even more important for a child. For, whereas most adults have learned that they can survive without the more or less continuous presence of an attachment figure, children have no such experience. For this reason, it is clearly more devastating still for children than it is for an adult should they find themselves alone in a strange world, a situation that can all too easily arise should children have the misfortune to lose both parents or should the surviving parent decide for some reason that they be cared for elsewhere.

Many differences arise from the fact that children are even less their own master than is a grown-up. For example, whereas an adult is likely either to be present at the time of a death or else to be given prompt and detailed information about it, in most cases children are entirely dependent for their information on the decision of their surviving relatives; and they are in no position to institute enquiries as adults would should they be kept in the dark.

In a similar way, children are at even greater disadvantage than are adults should relatives or other companions prove unsympathetic to their yearning, sorrow and anxiety. For, whereas adults can, if they wish, seek further for understanding and comfort should first exchanges prove unhelpful, children are rarely in a position to do so. Thus some at least of the differences between the mourning of children and the mourning of adults are due to children's lives being even less within their control than are that of grown-ups.

Other problems arise from a child having even less knowledge and understanding of issues of life and death than has an adult. In consequence one is more apt to make false inferences from the information one receives and also to misunderstand the significance of events observed and remarks overheard. Figures of speech in particular are apt to mislead. As a result it is necessary for the adults caring for a bereaved child to give even more opportunity to discuss what has happened and its far-reaching implications than it is with an adult. In the great majority of cases in which children are described as having failed totally to respond to news of a parent's death, it seems more than likely that both the information given and the opportunity to discuss its significance were so inadequate that the child had failed to grasp the nature of what had happened.

Yet not all the differences between childhood and adult mourning are due to circumstances. Some stem from a child's tendency to live more in the present than does an adult and from the relative difficulty a young child has in recalling past events. Few people grieve continuously. Even adults whose mourning is progressing healthily forget their grief briefly when some more immediate interest catches hold of them. For a child such occasions are likely to be more frequent than for adults, and the periods during which they are consciously occupied with their loss to be correspondingly more transient. As a result their moods are more changeable and more easily misunderstood. Furthermore, because of these same characteristics, young children are readily distracted, at least for the moment, which makes it easy for those caring for them to deceive themselves that they are not missing their parents.

If this analysis of the differences in the circumstances and psychology of a bereaved child and of a bereaved adult is well based, it is not difficult to see how the idea has developed that a child's ego is too weak to sustain the pain of mourning.

BEHAVIOR OF SURVIVING PARENTS TO THEIR BEREAVED CHILDREN

It is inevitable that when one's parent dies the survivor's treatment of the children should change. Not only is the survivor likely to be in a distressed and emotional state but he or she now has sole responsibility for the children instead of sharing it, and now has to fill two roles, which in most families have been clearly differentiated, instead of the single familiar one.

The death of a child's parent is always untimely and often sudden. Not only is one likely to be young or in early middle-age, but the cause is much more likely to be an accident or suicide than in later life. Sudden illness also is not uncommon. Thus for all the survivors, whether of the child's, the parent's or the grandparent's generation, the death is likely to come as a shock and to shatter every plan and every hope of the future. As a result just when a child needs most the patience and understanding of the adults around, those adults are likely to be least fit to give it to him.

Elsewhere we have considered some of the problems facing widows and widowers with young children and the limited and often very unsatisfactory arrangements from among which they have to choose, one of which is to send the children elsewhere. Here we are concerned only with the behavior of the surviving parent when he or she continues to care for the children at home. Since the behavior of widows and widowers toward their children is likely to differ, and in any case we know much more about that of widows, it is useful to consider the two situations separately.

A widow caring for her children is likely to be both sad and anxious. Preoccupied with her sorrows and the practical problems confronting her, it is far from easy for her to give the children as much time as she gave them formerly and all too easy for her to become impatient and angry when they claim attention and become whiny when they do not get it. A marked tendency to feel angry with their children was reported by about one in five of the widows interviewed by Glick and his colleagues.[18] Becker and Margolin[19] describe the mother of two small girls, of 3 and 6, who could not bear the older one's whining and frequently hit her for it.

An opposite kind of reaction, which is also common, is for a widowed mother to seek comfort for herself from the children. In the Kliman[20] study no less than 7 of the 18 children "began an unprecedented custom of frequently sharing a bed with the surviving parent. This usually began quickly after the death and tended to persist."[21] It is also easy for a lonely widow to burden an older child or adolescent with confidences and responsibilities which it is not easy for him to bear. In other cases she may require a child, usually a younger one, to become a replica either of his dead father or else, if an older child has died, of the dead child. Constant anxiety about the children's health and visits to the doctor as much to obtain his support as for the children's treatment occur commonly.

Not only is a widowed mother liable to be anxious about the children's health but she is likely also to worry about her own, with special reference to what would happen to the children were she to get ill or die too. Sometimes, as Glick[22] reports, a mother will express such anxieties aloud and within earshot of the children. In the light of these findings it is not difficult to see why some bereaved children are apprehensive, refuse to attend school and become diagnosed as "school phobic."

Anxious and emotionally liable herself and without the moderating influence of a second opinion, a widow's modes of discipline are likely to be either over-strict or over-lax, and rather frequently to swing from one extreme to the other. Problems with their children were reported as being of major concern by half of the widows with children who were studied by Glick in Boston.

Our knowledge of changes in the behavior of widowed fathers toward their bereaved children is extremely scanty. No doubt those of them who care for the children mainly themselves are prone to changes in behavior similar to those of widows. Especially when the children are female and/or adolescent are widowed fathers apt to make excessive demands on them for company and comfort.

Should the children be young, however, their care is likely to be principally in other hands, in which case a widowed father may see much less of them than formerly. As a result he may well be unaware of how they feel or what their problems are. Bedell[23] for example, enquired of 34 widowers how they thought their children had been since they lost their mother and what changes they had noticed in them. Few of the fathers had noticed any changes and even then only small ones. In the light of what we know about children's responses to loss of mother, these replies strongly suggest that the fathers were out of touch and poorly informed.

From this brief review we conclude that a substantial proportion of the special difficulties which children experience after loss of a parent are a direct result of the effect that the loss has had on the surviving parent's behavior toward them. Nevertheless there are, fortunately, many other surviving parents who, despite their burdens, are able to maintain relationships with their children intact and to help them mourn the dead parent in such a way that they come through undamaged. That others fail, however, can hardly surprise us.

INCREASED RISK OF PSYCHIATRIC DISORDER

Before describing the great variety of forms that childhood mourning can take when conditions are unfavorable, we pause to consider some of the evidence that shows that children who lose a parent by death are more likely than others to become psychiatric casualties. This view, which has for long been implicit in much psychoanalytic writing, has been advanced explicitly by a number of research workers for at least three decades. Although it has been the subject of much controversy, the more rigorous studies of recent years have shown at least some of the original claims to be valid.

The evidence derives from several sources:

- Studies that show that individuals who have lost a parent by death when children are more likely than others to suffer periods of extreme emotional distress during early adult life.
- Studies that show an increased incidence of childhood bereavement among children and adolescents referred to a child psychiatric clinic.
- Studies that show an increased incidence of childhood bereavement among adults referred to a psychiatric service.

It has been found, furthermore, that loss of a parent by death during childhood influences the symptomatology of any psychiatric disorder from which a person may subsequently suffer.

Since published studies are numerous, and statistical pitfalls many, discussion is limited to a few only of the better-planned examples.

It should be borne in mind that in addition to the studies considered in this chapter and which deal with differential incidence of parent *death* during childhood in psychiatric casualties and controls, there are many more that have the related but broader aim of studying the differential incidence of loss of a parent during childhood *irrespective of the cause of loss.* Since the findings of these other studies are of no less significance for psychiatry than those considered here, their omission (for reasons of consistency) is in many ways regrettable.

Follow-up of Bereaved Children into Adult Life

So far as is known there has been only one study which has attempted to follow a group of bereaved children into their thirties and to compare them with children not bereaved. This is a study undertaken by Bendiksen and Fulton[24] which takes as its initial sample all the ninth-grade students in the Minnesota schools in 1954. At that time certain basic data were obtained on 11,329 15-year-olds in connection with research on the Minnesota Multiphasic Personality Inventory (MMPI). Eighteen years later, in 1972 when they were aged 33, three sub-samples totaling just over 800 individuals were selected for follow-up.

The three sub-samples were selected according to the state of the child's family in 1954, namely whether intact, broken due to death of a parent, or broken due to separation or divorce. The sexes were roughly equal. The plan was to contact all these individuals and to invite them to complete a questionnaire, which covered a fairly wide range of social and psychological information, including marital status, family relations, experience of death, personal problems and health. Despite the high overall wastage rate, discussed below, and the limitations of a postal questionnaire, certain significant differences in regard to health and emotional experiences were found.

The three groups did not differ significantly in regard to sex of subject, educational attainment, community size and similar variables, though there was a slight tendency for those from intact families to be currently married, to have a college degree and a better employment record. The main difference between the groups, however, was in their reports of having experienced extreme emotional distress and major illness, in regard to both of which subjects from intact families had fared better than had those from either of the other groups. Table 1 shows some results.

In interpreting these findings it is well to bear in mind not only that the overall wastage rate was high but that it differed markedly among the sub-samples, which is of interest in its own right. Thus, of the total of 809 in the original sample only 401 could be traced, and of them only 256 completed the questionnaire. At each stage the losses were significantly greater for those from broken families than for those whose families had been intact. Table 2 gives the particulars.

That individuals whose homes had been broken during childhood are more difficult to trace than those from intact families suggests that as a group they are more mobile; while the fact that even when traced fewer of them are willing to complete a questionnaire is suggestive in itself. All in all it seems likely that the differences found between the groups in respect of major illnesses and extreme emotional distress are underestimates of the true position. Further studies with much more complete coverage are obviously desirable.

Table 1.

Incidence of Problems Reported 18 Years Later (for Three Groups whose Family Structures Differed When They Were 15 Years Old)

Problems Reported 18 Years Later	*Family Structure When Aged 15* Percentage Intact	Percentage Bereaved	Divorced/ Separated	*p* for difference between intact and bereaved
Major Illness	8.8	17.1	19.6	<0.08
Extreme emotional distress	19.9	35.5	34.8	<0.05
Arrests/ convictions	2.2	5.6	2.2	NS
Divorce	8.8	7.1	10.9	NS
Size of sub-sample	138	72	46	

Table 2.

Follow-up Reactions to Questionnaire

Subsample	Number Selected for Follow-up	Number Completing Question-naire	Percent Wastage
Intact Family	324	138	57
Bereaved	264	72	73
Parents separated/ divorced	221	46	79
	809	256	—

Incidence of Childhood Bereavement among Child Psychiatric Patients

In a study of over 700 children attending a clinic at the Maudsley Hospital in South London, Rutter[25] found that 11.6 percent had lost a parent by death. This proportion was about two and a half times greater than was to be expected among children of the same age-range in the population from which they were drawn. Bereavements were disproportionately prevalent especially during the third and fourth years of childhood. The death rates for fathers and for mothers were raised by approximately the same ratio; and the ages at which the loss had occurred were similar in the cases of those who had lost a mother and of those who had lost a father.

There was a significant correlation between the sex of the referred child and the sex of the dead parent, the girls having more often lost a mother and the boys a father.

The symptoms and problems presented by the children were equally likely to take the form of neurotic illnesses or neurotic disorders as that of anti-social or delinquent behavior. The date of onset of these symptoms and problems, in relation to the death of the parent, also ranged widely. In some cases the onset had preceded the death, and may perhaps have been a response to the parent having been fatally ill. In other cases they had developed soon after the death. In about one-third, however, the interval had been as long as five years or more.

This long delay before the onset of symptoms leads Rutter to conclude that factors consequent upon the death were probably as important or more so than the death itself. In this connection he points to such hazards as the breakup of the home, frequent changes of caregiver, changes in family roles, the effects of bereavement on the surviving parent, and the arrival of a step-parent (which had occurred in two-fifths of the cases). As we see in the following chapters, there is good evidence that these factors are indeed of much importance in accounting for children's responses. Nevertheless, there is reason to question another of Rutter's conclusions, admittedly tentative, that pathological forms of mourning play only a minor role. For in his discussions of the problem[26] he does not consider the possibility of there being individuals who, though managing to carry on without overt disturbance during childhood and adolescence, are none the less made vulnerable by an early bereavement and thereby more prone than others to react to further loss with a depressive disorder. The most likely conclusion, I believe, and one to which the evidence to be presented points, is that the majority of pathological outcomes are a product of the interaction of adverse conditions following bereavement with the mourning processes set in train by it.

Incidence of Childhood Bereavement among Adult Psychiatric Patients

Several studies showing an increased incidence of childhood bereavement in the histories of psychiatric patients when compared to the general population were published between 1955 and 1965. One by Felix Brown[27] linking childhood bereavement and depressive disorders was particularly influential. Subsequently, however, although some of the further studies confirmed the early finding others did not; and the ensuing controversy was still unsettled in the late 1960s (e.g. Granville-Grossman).[28] Nevertheless, more recent studies, notably by John Birtchnell, a psychiatrist,[29] and George Brown, a sociologist,[30] have not only confirmed certain, though not all, of the original findings but have also shed light on how the controversy arose.

To measure the incidence of parent loss in a group of psychiatric casualties and to compare it with the incidence of such loss in an appropriate group of mentally healthy individuals is a much more complex task than might be supposed. The biggest single problem has been to specify and find a valid comparison group. Not only have the ages of those in the patient and comparison groups to be equated, because death rates in most countries have decreased over time (except during war), but groups that happen to be easily available, for example patients attending other departments of a hospital, may contain many individuals who suffer from concealed psychiatric disorders. The same, it is now realized, may occur also in a representative sample (allowing for age and sex) drawn from the general population from which the group of patients is drawn. Failure to take these and other factors into account, it is now clear, explains why a number of studies have reported no significant differences between groups.

A study which, although it fails to ensure that the control group was free of psychiatric casualties, none the less reports differences statistically significant, though small, is one undertaken in northeast Scotland by Birtchnell.[31] In this large project the incidence of childhood bereavement was measured in over 5000 patients referred to the psychiatric services who were aged 20 and over and were suffering from neuroses, non-organic psychoses and addictions, and also in a control group of over 3000 individuals drawn from the lists of general practitioners in the same area. Since the ages of the patients in the different diagnostic categories differed, for each comparison a different control group suitably matched for age and sex was used. Principal findings were that:

1. It is only for parent deaths that had occurred before the patient's tenth birthday that significant differences between the patient and the control groups were found.

2. An increased incidence of childhood bereavement is found more often among female patients than male.
3. An increased incidence is especially evident in depressive conditions and in alcoholism.
4. When loss of each parent is considered separately it is found that (a) the incidence of loss of mother before the tenth birthday is significantly increased in depressed patients, both male and female, and also in female alcoholics; (b) loss of father before the tenth birthday is significantly increased in both depressed and alcoholic female patients but is not significantly increased in the case of male patients.

In none of the patient groups in this study is the incidence of childhood bereavement greater than double what it is in the controls, and in most groups it is much less. True, in selecting his controls Birtchnell took no steps to exclude individuals who, though not referred to the psychiatric services, may none the less have been in poor mental health and that, had he done so, differences are likely to have been greater. Even so, such evidence as we have suggests that childhood bereavement plays a causal role in only a small minority of cases of mental illness. The value of the work done lies, I believe, in having provided a point of entry for research into parent-child relationships and their influence on mental health which can be pursued in future at a much more sophisticated level.

CONDITIONS RESPONSIBLE FOR DIFFERENCES IN OUTCOME

It will already be clear that, in my view, the variables that influence the course that mourning takes during childhood and adolescence are similar in kind to those that influence it during adult life. They fall into three classes:

1. The causes and circumstances of the loss, with special reference to where and what a child is told and what opportunities are later given him to enquire about what has happened.
2. The family relationships after the loss, with special reference to whether he remains with the surviving parent and, if so, how the patterns of relationship are changed as a result of the loss.
3. The patterns of relationship within the family prior to the loss, with special reference to the patterns obtaining between the parents themselves and between each of them and the bereaved child.

Some of the evidence that supports this theoretical position has already been referred to. It derives from studies of two main types:

1. Studies that compare the experiences of a group of individuals who have developed well despite a childhood bereavement with those of a group who have failed to do so; information is usually obtained during a special research interview or a routine clinical one.
2. Studies that describe the experiences of one or a few individual children or adolescents whose problems are thought to stem from the death of a parent; most of the information is obtained during therapy, though some comes from parents and others.

The strengths and weaknesses of these two types of study tend to be the opposite of one another.

Studies of the first type, which take the form of surveys, include fairly large samples of subjects and give useful information, mostly of a rather general kind, about the individual's experience after the loss but are usually weak on psychopathological detail. Studies of the latter type, the therapeutic, do much to supplement this deficiency but can be gravely misleading when treated in isolation. In the case of surveys the information is commonly obtained many years after the events; whereas in the case of therapeutic studies of children and adolescents the time interval is usually much shorter. Both types of study have the drawback that they rely heavily on information from a single source, the bereaved individual himself.

EVIDENCE FROM SURVEYS

Among all those who have surveyed different groups of individuals who have lost a parent during childhood there is now substantial agreement in regard to the enormous importance of a child's experience after the loss. Individuals who later develop a psychiatric disorder, it is found, are far more likely than are those who do not to have received deficient parental care following the loss. Discontinuities of care, including being cared for in unloving foster homes or institutions and of being moved from one "home" to another, have been the lot of many. Alternatively, should a child have remained in the home, he or she is likely to have had to take a parental role prematurely instead of being cared for. By contrast, those who have developed well despite having lost a parent during childhood are likely to have received continuous and stable parental care during the years following their loss. Among findings that support these conclusions are those of Rutter,[32] of Adam,[33] and of Birtchnell.[34] Among other studies that report closely similar findings is a well-designed one by Hilgard.[35]

Hilgard, who had for many years been interested in the role of parent loss during the childhoods of psychiatric patients, with special reference to anniversary reactions, decided to compare the experiences to which her patients had been exposed following their loss with those of adults who had also lost a parent during childhood but were not patients. With this in view she undertook a community survey and from it identified 100 individuals aged between 19 and 49 who had lost a parent before the age of 19 and who were not at the time under psychiatric care. Of this initial sample, 65 made themselves available for structured interviews lasting 1 or 2 hours. Women outnumbered men by nearly three to one (partly because they were more numerous in the initial hundred and partly because they were more available for interview). Of the women, 29 had lost father and 19 had lost mother; of the men, 13 had lost father and 4 mother.

After interview a sub-sample was identified made up of all those who were deemed to be "reasonably well adjusted" in terms of the following criteria; they were living in an intact home, their marriage appeared to be satisfactory, relationships with their children seemed adequate, and their scores on a brief test of social adaptation were confirmatory. Among 29 women who had lost father 14 met these criteria.

The picture of family life before and after father's death which emerged from the accounts they gave was as follows. Before the loss the parents had provided a stable home in which each had had a well-defined role. After the loss mother had kept the home intact but had usually had to work very hard to do so. Not only was support given to the family by its social network, but mother also had proved capable of making the best use of it. "Strong," "responsible," "hardworking" were the adjectives most used to describe her; "affectionate" less often.

Should a parent have died after an illness, the children were likely to have been told of the outlook and prepared in advance for what lay in store. By these means, Hilgard writes, "a dying parent may convey to his child an acceptance of this complete separation and in so doing may help the child to accept it also." Furthermore, after a father had died mothers were likely to have shared their grief with the children; and it seemed as though this had been of special help to daughters. These family patterns, in which the children had been taken into the parents' confidence, had contributed, Hilgard believes, to the striking absence of guilt about the parent's death that characterized these individuals and that contrasted sharply with what she found in her group of psychiatric patients who also had lost a parent during childhood.

In addition to Hilgard's sub-sample of individuals who were deemed to be "reasonably well adjusted" was a complementary sub-sample of individuals who had failed to meet her criteria (a group analogous to the "community cases" in George Brown's study but not necessarily presenting with diagnosable illness). For members of the second sub-sample the behavior of the surviving parent had been very different to what it had been for members of the well-adjusted sub-sample. In most cases the surviving parent had made strong demands on the children for emotional support; or, to put it in the terminology used in this work, the survivor had inverted the parent-child relationship by seeking to make the child the caregiver. This pattern was especially common among children whose fathers had died.

In the total sample of 65 persons interviewed, there were 13 men who had lost father. In three cases mother had remarried, leaving 10 families in which the son had continued to live with his widowed mother. In no less than nine of these cases, the mothers had "manifested an emotional dependency on their children, particularly the sons." Some felt they had been made into substitute husbands. They had either stayed single until mother had died or else had married but later had divorced and returned to stay with mother. In one case mother had threatened to commit suicide when her son announced his plans to marry. Despite these pressures which had made satisfactory marriages extremely difficult, and possibly even because of them, a number of these sons had been very successful in their work. Some of the girls who had remained living with widowed mothers had also been put under strong emotional pressure to stay home to care for mother.

One of the women whose mother had died young described how, because her mother had died aged 25, she had confidently expected that she also would die at that age. She had therefore postponed her marriage until after the fateful year; but she had nonetheless chosen for her wedding day the same date as her mother's. When interviewed she was about 45 and had been married for 20 years, apparently happily.

In reviewing her findings Hilgard expresses concern about members of the less well-adjusted sub-sample. Although living in the community and passing as mentally healthy, it was evident that for a number their lives had been restricted and their mental health impaired by the pathogenic pressures to which they had been subjected. Clearly some had suffered much more than others, and no doubt some of the sons who had postponed marriage had none the less married successfully later. Nevertheless, her study strongly supports the view that the effect that a parent's death has on a child is powerfully influenced by the pattern of family relationships to which the child is exposed after it.

Certainly all the studies which have reported the childhood experiences of those who subsequently become psychiatric casualties point to the same conclusion. An example is a study by Arthur and Kemme[36] of 83 children and adolescents, aged between 4 1/2 and 17 years, who had been referred to a children's psychiatric hospital in Ann Arbor, Michigan with a variety of emotional and behavioral problems, all of which, having either developed or become greatly exacerbated following the death of a parent, could be regarded as attributable at least in part to the loss. Sixty were boys, of whom 40 had lost father and 20 mother; 23 were girls, of whom 14 had lost father and 9 mother.

Although the details given by Arthur and Kemme are rather sparse, it is evident that the conditions affecting these children and adolescents prior to the loss and/or surrounding it and/or after it had been extremely adverse in a high proportion of cases; and in many of them it was possible to see, at least in outline, how the conditions to which the child had been, or was still being subjected, were contributing to the problems complained of. Among the adverse conditions prominent in this series of cases were parents who had quarreled or separated, and parents who had threatened to abandon the children, children who had experienced several earlier separations, and children who had been made to feel responsible for making the parent ill. After the death many of the children had been given little or no information about it; and subsequently many also had experienced extremely unstable relationships. Of the 83 parental deaths, 10 had been due to suicide.

In the great majority of the cases reported psychological disturbance had been present before the death, often long before it. Nevertheless, in most of them it was evident that bereavement had increased any existing disturbances. As in the case of adults, therefore, the experience of loss is found to interact with the psychological consequences of both previous and subsequent adverse experiences to produce the particular clinical picture seen.

As might be expected, some of the commonest ways in which children and adolescents respond to the loss of a parent include becoming chronically sad or anxious, or some mixture of the two; and many develop elusive somatic symptoms. In the Michigan series over a quarter appeared sad at the time of referral, 16 of the 83 were showing intense separation anxiety and 19 were experiencing acute night-terrors. About a quarter were excessively clinging during the day and/or were insisting at night on sleeping with the surviving parent, or a sibling.

Yet, although many appeared obviously sad and anxious, many others did not. On the contrary, 29 children—about one-third—were overactive and in greater or less degree aggressive. Some engaged in unprovoked violence toward peers or adults or inexplicable destruction of property.

In many of the cases an explanation of children's sadness, anxiety or anger could be found without difficulty in the way they were construing the cause of their parent's death and/or the situation in which they now found themselves. Seventeen were construing the death in terms of their having been abandoned. As one boy put it: "My father left me and I'm very angry with him." Double that number, namely 40 percent, were attributing the cause of death either to themselves or to the surviving parent. Several made plain why they did so. One boy, for example, had been warned by his mother that he would be the death of her. Another supposed that his mother had committed suicide because he had been so naughty. Most of those who were blaming the surviving parent had witnessed violent quarrels between their parents in which one had attacked the other physically.

Many of the younger children disbelieved that death was final and were expecting that they would soon be reunited with their parent, either here or "up in heaven"; some of the older children contemplated suicide with the explicit intention of joining the missing parent. Thirteen had either threatened suicide or attempted it.

EVIDENCE FROM THERAPEUTIC STUDIES

Throughout the last 50 years reports have been published in the psychoanalytic journals of the treatment of adult patients whose present difficulties have been thought to be due at least in part to the loss of a parent, from the death or other cause, during the patient's childhood. Since in all these cases the loss had occurred many years earlier, it is hardly surprising that the reports give little or no information about the conditions that had preceded or succeeded the loss. During the past two decades, however, accounts have multiplied of the treatment of adolescents and children whose loss had occurred comparatively recently; and in many of them a fair amount of detail is given both about the circumstances of the loss itself and about the patterns of family interaction that obtained before and after it.

Those skeptical of the scientific status of material obtained during the course of therapy should note that in hardly one of the cases to be described are the theoretical biases of the authors the same as my own. On the contrary, the majority subscribe more or less explicitly to the theoretical standpoint that has long been dominant among psychoanalysts which, until recently, has given scant weight to the influence of environmental factors and has explained almost all differences in personality development by reference to some phase of development in which the individual is thought to be fixated. When applied to differential outcomes following loss this viewpoint results in the widespread assertions:

- that, owing to their psychological immaturity, children and even adolescents cannot mourn;
- that the emotional problems that follow parental loss can be understood as due to an arrest of development either at the phase thought

to have been reached at the time of the loss,[37] or at some earlier phase.[38]

There is extensive literature based on these premises.[39] Readers interested to probe further are referred to a review of the literature by Miller[40] and another most comprehensive one by Furman in the final chapter of her book.[41]

I believe that the evidence at present available does not support the traditional theories. A principal difficulty with some of them is that, were they to be correct, we should expect the development of every child or adolescent who lost a parent to be impaired, which we know is not the case. It is of much significance, moreover, that the closer in time to the loss that a patient, adolescent or child, has been studied and the larger the number of cases that a clinician has seen the more likely is he not only to describe environmental factors but to implicate them when explaining outcome. Among the many who now lay emphasis on environmental factors, especially the influence of the surviving parent, are the clinicians R.A. Furman,[42] E. Furman,[43] Kliman,[44] Becker and Margolin,[45] and Anthony,[46] and also the social scientists Gorer,[47] Glick[48] and Palgi.[49] The position of other clinicians seems inconsistent with the evidence they present. An example is Wolfenstein[50] who, despite adhering strongly to traditional theory, reports evidence that seems equally strongly to implicate family relationships. Nagera[51] avoids taking sides by embracing both viewpoints impartially. Thus, in a discussion of the origin of children's beliefs that a dead father will return, he writes: "In some cases this happens under the direct influence of mothers who hide the truth from the child to spare it pain, *in other cases phantasies of an identical nature are the child's spontaneous production*" (italics original).

In my analysis, I repeatedly draw attention to the role of environmental variables, both those that the clinicians concerned refer to as having, in their opinion, been of consequence and also others that a reading of the case report has suggested to me may have been operative as well.

NOTES

1. I.O. Glick, R.S. Weiss and C.M. Parkes. 1974. *The First Year of Bereavement.* New York: Wiley Interscience.
2. H. Nagera. 1970. Children's Reactions to the Death of Important Objects: A Developmental Approach. *Psychoanalytic Study of Children* 25:360-400.
3. D. Becker and F. Margolin. 1967. How Surviving Parents Handled their Young Children's Adaptation to the Crisis of Loss. *American Journal of Orthopsychiatry* 37:753-757.
4. P. Palgi. 1973. The Socio-Cultural Expressions and Implications of Death,

Mourning and Bereavement Arising Out of the War Situation in Israel. *Israel Annals of Psychiatry* 2:301-329.

5. G. Kliman. 1965. *Psychological Emergencies of Childhood.* New York: Grune & Stratton.
6. S. Anthony. 1971. *The Discovery of Death in Childhood and After.* London: Penguin.
7. E. Furman. 1974. *A Child's Parent Dies: Studies in Childhood Bereavement.* New Haven: Yale University Press.
8. M. Nagy. 1948. The Child's Theories Concerning Death. *Journal of Genetic Psychology* 73:3-27.
9. Kliman, loc. cit.
10. P. Marris. 1958. *Widows and Their Families.* London: Routledge & Kegan Paul.
11. Kliman, loc. cit.
12. E. Furman, loc. cit.
13. Fortunately Bess's father knew how to respond. Gently he replied, "When we miss Mummy so very much we'd like to think that she is not really dead. I guess it will be a sad dinner for both of us." Ibid., pp. 24-25.
14. Wendy's misinterpretation, born of hopes and expectations, has an almost exact parallel in the experience of a middle-aged widow whose husband had died suddenly of a heart attack in the street. Seven months after his death, a police constable came to her flat and informed her that her husband had had a minor accident and had been taken to the hospital. At once she thought to herself how right she had been all the time in thinking that her husband was still alive and that she had only been dreaming that he was dead. A moment later, however, as her doubts grew, she enquired of the constable whom he was looking for; it proved to be her neighbor next door.
15. Furman, op. cit., pp. 26, 68.
16. M.E. Mitchell. 1966. *The Child's Attitude Toward Death.* New York: Schocken Books.
17. C.S. Moss. 1960. Brief Successful Psychotherapy of a Chronic Phobic Reaction. *Journal of Abnormal and Social Psychology* 60:266-70.
18. Glick, et al., loc. cit.
19. Becker and Margolin, loc. cit.
20. Kliman, loc. cit.
21. Ibid., p. 78.
22. Glick et al., loc. cit.
23. J. Bedell. 1973. The Maternal Orphan: Paternal Perceptions of Mother Loss. Presented at Foundation of Thanatology Symposium on Bereavement, New York. Quoted by B. Raphael, Care-Eliciting Behaviour of Bereaved Children and their Families. Paper presented at Section on Child Psychiatry, Australian and New Zealand College of Psychiatrists.
24. R. Bendiksen and R. Fulton. 1975. Death and the Child: An Anterospective Test of the Childhood Bereavement and Later Behavior Disorder Hypothesis. *Omega* 6:45-59.
25. M. Rutter. 1966. *Children of Sick Parents.* London: Oxford University Press.
26. Ibid.
27. F. Brown. 1961. Depression and Childhood Bereavement. *Journal of Mental Science* 107:754-777.
28. K.L. Granville-Grossman. 1968. The Early Environment of Affective Disorders,

in A. Coppen and A. Walk, eds., *Recent Developments of Affective Disorders.* London: Headley Bros.

29. J. Birtchnell. 1972. Early Parent Death and Psychiatric Diagnosis. *Social Psychiatry* 7:202-210.
30. G.W. Brown, T. Harris and J.R. Copeland. 1977: Depression and Loss. *British Journal of Psychiatry* 130:1-18; 1978: Social Origins of Depression: A Reply. *Psychological Medicine* 8:577-588.
31. Birtchnell, loc. cit.
32. Rutter, loc. cit.
33. K.S. Adam. 1973. Childhood Parental Loss, Suicidal Ideation and Suicidal Behavior, in E.J. Anthony and C. Koupernik, eds., *The Child in His Family: The Impact of Disease and Death.* New York: John Wiley.
34. J. Birtchnell. 1971: Early Death in Relation to Sibship Size and Composition in Psychiatric Patients and General Population Controls. *Acta Psychiatrica Scandinavica* 47:250-70. In this study Birtchnell showed that, when a sample of early bereaved psychiatric patients was compared with a sample of general population controls, they showed an over-representation of older siblings who were of the same sex as the parent lost and who also had younger siblings to be cared for. 1975: Psychiatric Breakdown Following Recent Parent Death. *British Journal of Medical Psychology* 48:379-390.
35. J.R. Hilgard, M.F. Newman and F. Fisk. 1960. Strength of Adult Ego Following Childhood Bereavement. *American Journal of Orthopsychiatry* 30:788-798.
36. B. Arthur and M.L. Kemme. 1964. Bereavement in Childhood. *Journal of Child Psychology and Psychiatry* 5:37-49.
37. J. Fleming and S. Altschul. 1963. Activation of Mourning and Growth by Psychoanalysis. *International Journal of Psychoanalysis* 44:419-431.
38. M. Klein. 1948. *Contributions to Psycho-Analysis 1921-1945.* London: Hogarth (reprinted in *Love, Guilt and Reparation and Other Papers, 1921-1946*).
39. J. Bowlby. 1960. Grief and Mourning in Infancy and Early Childhood. *Psychoanalytic Study of Children* 15:9-52.
40. J.B.M. Miller. 1971. Children's Reaction to the Death of a Parent: A Review of the Psychoanalytic Literature. *Journal of the American Psychoanalytic Association* 19:697-719.
41. Furman, op. cit., pp. 267-293.
42. R.A. Furman. 1968. Additional Remarks on Mourning and the Young Child. *Bulletin of the Philadelphia Association for Psychoanalysis* 18:51-64.
43. Furman, loc. cit.
44. Kliman, loc. cit.
45. Becker and Margolin, loc. cit.
46. E.J. Anthony. 1973. A Working Model for Family Studies, in E.J. Anthony and C. Koupernik, eds., *The Child in His Family: The Impact of Disease and Death.* New York: John Wiley.
47. G. Gorer. 1965. *Death, Grief and Mourning in Contemporary Britain.* London: Tavistock.
48. Glick et al., loc. cit.
49. Palgi, loc. cit.
50. M. Wolfenstein. 1966: How Is Mourning Possible? *Psychoanalytic Study of Children* 21:93-123; 1969: Loss, Rage and Repetition, *Psychoanalytic Study of Children* 24:432-460.
51. Nagera, loc. cit.

6

Grief and Mourning

John S. Stephenson, PhD

Grief can be described as an overwhelming and acute sense of loss and despair. The entire personality is helplessly engulfed in strong, sometimes frightening feelings. Individuals can feel out of control as monstrous waves of emotions sweep over them. Tossed about on this emotional sea, the familiar and secure landmarks of life are no longer in their usual places; the old meanings do not apply, and people may see themselves as victims of forces beyond their control.

This description of grief underscores the powerful feelings involved as the individual becomes aware of a significant loss. *Grief is that state of mental and physical pain that is experienced when the loss of a significant object, person, or part of the self is realized.* The realization of the loss is important because the individual who decides that a particular loss is not of any personal significance will not grieve over that loss. There is, then, a psychological process in which an individual has to acknowledge or "own" the loss. This is a realization not just that the death has occurred, but that it is of personal significance. For example, reading a headline in the paper stating that three women have died in a car accident will not necessarily produce a grief reaction. However, grief will ensue when it is learned that a person significant to the reader had been among the three killed.

To a certain degree, who or what we consider to be personally significant is culturally defined. For example, in the contemporary United States, people are generally expected to grieve over the loss of a biological offspring. The further the individual is from the nuclear family, the less the amount of grief displayed. Volkart and Michael describe primitive tribes in which the care of newborns is shared among may people.[1] As a result, when a baby dies rather than causing a few people intense loss, the grief is felt by many but less intensely. Grief is a function of the intensity of the relationship, and the nature of relationships is strongly influenced by the culture within which they exist.

From the sociologist's point of view, the individual's reality is socially defined: we grieve over those losses that are socially appropriate to grieve over. Psychologists, on the other hand, tend to argue that grief is an intensely personal process, and that without considering the internal psychological dynamics of the individual we cannot arrive at an understanding of grief. The question of the relative importance of psychological and sociological factors in the grief reaction is not one that we can settle here. For our purposes, we shall examine what both the psychological and sociological perspectives have to offer us in terms of developing our understanding of the grief process. While grieving is an intensely personal emotional experience, it takes place within a social reality that defines appropriate grieving behavior as well as the significance of the loss itself. We will first consider grief as a psychological process. Later in this chapter, taking a sociological perspective, we will consider the process of mourning—the behavior in a social context that manifests an acknowledgment of loss.

THE PSYCHOLOGICAL DYNAMICS OF GRIEF

In the earlier definition of grief, two aspects were stressed—the mental and physical pain experienced and the loss of something or someone of significance. First we will discuss the types of losses that an individual may experience and then we will examine the emotional processes of experiencing and resolving grief.

Loss of a Significant Person

The death of someone who is significant to the griever—a member of the immediate family, close friend, lover or mentor—is one of the most common losses that evokes grief. An infant will grieve over the loss of its nurturing biological mother because the infant is aware that many emotional and physical needs are no longer being met by a mother. However, the severity of grief does not necessarily depend on some form of social interaction between two persons. Individuals may grieve over the loss of someone with whom they had only a brief, cursory relationship. A person may grieve deeply over the loss of someone with whom they have not actually interacted, but with whom they strongly identified. The determining factor is not necessarily the proximity of the individuals or the social significance of the relationship, but rather the importance that the griever assigns to the lost person.

Another example of grief over the loss of a "non-intimate other" is the death of a famous personality or leader. In these cases, people who do not actually know a celebrity, but who strongly identify with him, will grieve over the death. The assassinations of President Kennedy and John Lennon produced grief among many people who had never had personal contact with them. The grievers—of whom there were a great many—identified with these famous men and interpreted their deaths as personal losses—perhaps not so much as a loss of individuals, but more as symbols of values held dear to the grievers.

These examples underscore the importance of individual decisions regarding the significance of another person in one's life. While it may be difficult to think of a child as "deciding" that his mother is important, there is an inner process of discrimination that takes place. As children grow in awareness, they become aware of the importance of a mother. The process of assigning a value to something, even something as obvious as a child's nurturing mother, requires the child to decide to assign importance to the mother. Likewise, the young teenager decides to idolize a popular singer, assigning importance to that person even though the two people have never known one another. Often teenagers fantasize that their idol is the only person capable of understanding them, or able to meet their emotional needs. In both cases, the loss of the significant other will elicit a grief reaction.

Separation from a significant person can produce reactions similar to those experienced at times of loss through death. Bowlby's extensive studies of attachment and loss have contributed significant insights into the process of integrating the experience of loss into our lives.[2] Working first with young children and then validating his findings through clinical work with children and adults, Bowlby shows how separation can lead to intensive grief reactions in individuals. A temporary estrangement of an infatuated lover also can be so devastating as to produce a grieving reaction.

To summarize, our first category of loss involves the loss of a significant person. This loss is determined as significant or not by the individual griever. Even temporary loss, when the attachment is seen as vital, may precipitate grieving.

The Loss of a Love Object

The second category of loss is the loss of an object in which the griever has placed special significance—anything that a person decides is important to his life. A toy (be it a teddy bear or a yacht), material goods that signify success, pets, and symbolically linked objects such as national flags are important objects to different people. As much as people may grieve over the loss of an individual, so can they grieve over the loss of an object. A miser will feel the loss of money as deeply as a lover will feel the loss of a sweetheart. Generally, most people do not involve themselves as deeply with objects as they do with people. However, the loss and concomitant grief process may occur and should be appreciated in the context of what the lost object means to the grieving individual.

Loss of a Part of the Self

The third category of loss involves losing something that is central to the individual's being, such as a part of the body, the ability to do tasks, physical or mental capabilities, or roles that the individual is used to performing. Activities or accomplishments external to the self may become ego-extensions of the individual, and as a result the person may grieve when a loss of part of the self takes place. For example, elderly persons may feel sorrow in having to accept the loss of an ability that was a significant part of their life. To give up driving, for example, may mean the loss of the individual's autonomy, and symbolize the encroaching debilitation of old age. The loss of a limb or an organ, such as the eyes, may be seen as a significant loss, perhaps jeopardizing the major means of self-expression that the individual has developed. The loss of attractiveness, perhaps through disfigurement or aging, can produce grief reactions. In American society where personal attractiveness is considered very important, the loss of beauty may be seen as a tragic event by the victim.

The loss of one's role is another form of loss of self which may foster a grief reaction. The loss of the role of mother, for example, may produce a grieving in some women as part of the "empty nest syndrome," the time when children are no longer dependent upon the mother. The woman's sense of self can be intimately involved with her role as a mother, and the loss of that role may provoke a grief reaction. Geoffrey Gorer, writing about his research among the grieving in England, states that he found the greatest amount of grief among parents whose children were grown and who had placed a great deal of meaning upon their roles as parents.[3] The greater the importance of the parenting role, the greater the grief that was felt. It may also be that because parents of adult children are most likely to be beyond their childbearing years, the possibility of them reestablishing themselves in the parent role would be remote. Thus some adult parents not only lose their loved ones, but are thus forced to give up other meaningful activities as well.

I have delineated these three types of losses in order to demonstrate that grief need not be solely a product of the death of a significant other.

More research is needed in the field of loss and loss management. For example, we need to know how the little losses that we have all had in our lives which entail a "giving up" prepare us for dealing with the larger losses of significant persons in our lives. In considering grief in the context of this chapter, we will limit ourselves to the larger losses that are experienced through the death of a significant person.

A TYPOLOGY OF GRIEF

Appropriate and Inappropriate Loss

An important aspect of the degree of significance assigned to the loss lies in the extent to which the death is viewed as an appropriate death. The term "appropriate death" has been used extensively by Avery Weisman.[4] His concern is more with a sense of the appropriateness of the death for the dying person, while ours focuses upon the appropriateness of the death for the griever. Both uses of the term are similar in that the meaning of the event (death) is judged in terms of its purposefulness, meaningfulness and acceptability. Weisman warns that one person's acceptable death may be unacceptable to another; this holds for the griever as well as the dying. Typically, the death of one's 90-year-old grandfather is seen as more appropriate that the death of one's 30-year-old spouse. As people age, the appropriateness of their deaths becomes more accepted, because everyone must die. Inappropriate death, on the other hand, is an unexpected or unjustifiable occurrence. The injustice along with the shock of the loss will precipitate stronger grief reactions than are found in appropriate deaths, as the survivor must struggle with the inappropriateness of the loss as well as the loss itself.

Fulton refers to these two types of grief as "high grief" and "low grief" situations.[5] Unfortunately, he tends to pursue a social definition of high grief (death of a child) and low grief (death of an elderly relative) as indicating the amount of grief to be expected. However, the appropriateness of the death must be considered from the perspective of the griever. For example, while the rest of the family may see the death of an elderly member as appropriate in the larger scheme of things, the surviving spouse may feel a great deal of rage because she may have always expected to be the first to die. Therefore, to the surviving spouse, the death of the other spouse will be seen as unfair and inappropriate. Only by understanding the meaning of the death to the griever can we come to understand the meaning of the grief.

During the grieving process, to be discussed later in this chapter, the individual may be faced with two distinctly different problems. Both these problems involve the meanings that the griever places upon the death. The death may represent the loss of a loved one upon whom the individual placed a great deal of importance. The death may also represent a dramatic reminder of the reality of death in the griever's own life. A well-known researcher in this field disclosed during an interview with me that at the death of his parents he found his grief involving not only the loss of people, but also the realization that he was, chronologically, next in line in his family to die. This internal turmoil, which we shall call *existential grief* may absorb the individual as much as the grief felt over the loss of the loved person, which we shall refer to as *reactive grief.*

Existential Grief

At the onslaught of grief, the individual usually feels a great sense of disorganization. The way in which the survivor meaningfully interacted with the world in the past no longer makes sense, often suddenly calling into doubt the meaning of all of life. People are thrown back on their own inner convictions as to the meaning of existence. For some, their image of the world may be frightening or inadequately developed. Relationships with others may superficially meet these personal inadequacies. Some persons may seek to escape from their internal fears by establishing a relationship with someone else who, in a sense, makes life worth living. In other words, the meaning of life is found in another person. When the relationship is terminated, the person must again face his own internal doubts and fears. For the person who finds meaning in life exclusively through another, the loss of the relationship with that person may force the individual to confront his own internal doubts and fears. The lost relationship may have served as the individual's defense against death. To one who has repressed fear of death, or who has not satisfactorily resolved or defended against the issues surrounding existential mortality, the experience of a significant death may reawaken dormant death anxieties. Infatuated romantic lovers may experience a transcendence of worldly reality that seems to diminish death by its very intensity. The loss of such a loved one may cast the survivor into the depths of his own despair, not only over the lost love, but also because of the grim actuality of death as a fact of life. The fear of death, which is rooted in the primary images described by Lifton, now returns to haunt the person.[6]

The roots of the issues in existential grief can usually be found in childhood. Early in life the infant must confront the reality of the world external to the self. There is a need to be able to interact successfully with the environment. Erikson describes this early interaction as providing for the child the basis for a sense of trust or mistrust of the world.[7] Lifton adds that the individual has a need to develop a sense of connection with the external world. This is a "fundamental issue in human life."[8] Most typically, this initial connection is made with the mother. The infant develops a sense of trust for rewarding connections with the environment. The child learns of separation (individuality) from the environment, and develops a sense of being connected with the environment by interacting with objects in the environment in rewarding ways. In forming these early relationships with the external world, the infant invests emotional energy in those objects and experiences that give physical and emotional substance. Internally, the infant builds images that represent external experiences.

Robert Jay Lifton sees the issue of developing a sense of integrity—a sense of personal wholeness—as a part of the early psychological development of the child. Pointing to Melanie Klein's studies, Lifton argues that the polar opposite of integration, which is disintegration, is rooted in the infant's fear of annihilation. Lifton states that:

> there is from the beginning some sense of the organism's being threatened with dissolution, disintegration. The terms of this negative image or fear are at first entirely physiological, having to do with physical intactness or deterioration; but over the course of time, integrity, without losing its physiological reference, comes to assume primarily ethical-psychological dimensions.[9]

So from early in our existence we have known images of life and death, and one form of our aliveness lies in organizing ourselves in order to deal satisfactorily with those things external to ourselves.

The relationship of Lifton's argument to our discussion of grieving lies in the vital importance of our own sense of organization, our purpose, confidence and wholeness. When this is lacking or incomplete, the individual will seek ways of defending against the reality of death. When a death occurs that is so close as to threaten the person's defenses, or when death takes away the individual who was the person's meaning in life (a defense against meaninglessness), then the person experiences existential grieving that is rooted in primary issues involving the reality of death itself.

As Lifton has shown, early in life children must grapple with the reality of death that they experience in rudimentary images of separation, disintegration and stasis (inactivity).[10] These images also have polar extremes that are a part of the infant's consciousness as well. These are images of connection, integrity and movement. The struggle to master the polar realities of life and death engage us all, probably on a repressed unconscious level, all of our lives. An encounter with an actual death, especially the loss of a loved one, may force us again to encounter our own death, "the terror we carry around in our secret heart."[11] In existential grieving the person's words and feelings connote an inward, rather than outward, orientation (which characterizes reactive grief): "Why was I born, if only to suffer so?" is an expression of existential grief, while, "My life is so empty without my lover," is an example of reactive grieving.

Almost all grievings involve elements of both reactive and existential grief. While individuals grieve over the loss, they generally realize that what is being experienced is a part of life, and that all life, even one's own, ultimately involves death. The underlying motive behind the immature vow to "never love again" is an attempt to avoid one's humanness. Being human means being open to hurt, and this vulnerability reminds us of our mortality. But if people never love, they never feel pain (that is, they never experience their mortality). However, the fallacy in this kind of thinking is that one forfeits humanness in the process of rejecting love, and death still exists, even if love is denied.

Reactive Grief

While existential grief focuses upon the mortality of the griever, reactive grief is concerned with the loss that the death represents to the person. This type of grieving is most evident in those who lose someone who is their significant other. For example, elderly widows and widowers who have lost spouses with whom they have spent the majority of their lives often experience a great deal of reactive grief. The death of an elderly spouse in a world of few meaningful relationships may cause a loss from which one may never recover. The advancing years, with their accompanying loss of energy, may cause the survivor to be ill-equipped to complete the reorganization of life so necessary to the satisfactory resolution of loss. Bereft of the primary other person in the world, the older widow and widower may never resolve the extensive grief in their lives.[12]

Past unresolved grief may also be triggered by a recent loss. This may be especially powerful if there has been a lack of resolution over a previous loss. The severity and the extent of reactive grief that the person experiences will depend upon several factors: the degree to which the person was dependent upon the former relationship; the individual's perceived ability to establish new relationships that could meet the needs that are now unfulfilled; and finally, the griever's social reality which will influence their method of grieving because it establishes acceptable modes of conduct concerning grieving and reestablishing relationships in order to meet the needs once satisfied by the deceased.

In order to understand fully the grieving person, we must become aware of the degree to which his grief is reactive or existential. Both types of grief require distinct and separate ways of resolving the emotional crisis brought about by the experience of the death of a significant person. This is often referred to as "grief work" and may involve having to establish new meanings in life, resolving or repressing issues surrounding one's own mortality, or developing new relationships to meet one's needs. In the following section we will explore this process in more detail.

THE GRIEVING PROCESS

In discussing the grieving process it is impossible to account for the entire range of possible idiosyncratic manifestations of grief. While we can speak of three general phases in the process, it is difficult to account for all individual responses to grief. As Bowlby states, "Grief, I believe, is *a peculiar amalgam* of anxiety, anger and despair following the experience of what is feared to be irretrievable loss" (italics added).[13] In this definition Bowlby argues for the inclusion of those factors that combine in unique ways within each individual, a process that makes grief a very personal process. The following descriptions of the phases of the grief process should be interpreted as presenting general stages through which the individuals pass in their own unique way of working through the bereavement. The phases are not delineated by any particular entry or exit criteria, but as representative of that point in the grieving process when the characteristics described are most prevalent.

While we may speak of the general process of doing grief work, it is important to be aware that the process can also be seen as a series of repeated experiences of grief. Rosenblatt points out that often the bereaved will put aside grief work for a while, only to be reminded of it by reencountering the reality of the loss. "If it is granted that there are fresh reminders, that losses cannot be worked all of a piece, it becomes possible that normal involves repeated surges of grief."[14] A person may manifest a denial of the loss in one aspect of life while appearing to have resolved the issues of grief in another. An example of this would be a woman who assumes many of the duties previously performed by her late husband (acceptance of the loss), but still keeps all of his clothes hanging in the closet just as they were the day he died (denial). The following phases, then, are general categories wherein the predominant characteristics are those described under each phase. As C.S. Lewis wrote:

> Grief is like a long valley, a winding valley where any bend may reveal a totally new landscape. As I've already noted, not every bend does. Sometimes a surprise is the opposite one; you are presented with exactly the same sort of country you thought you had left behind miles ago. This is when you wonder whether the valley isn't a circular trench. But it isn't. There are partial recurrences, but the sequence doesn't repeat.[15]

Phase One: Reaction

> The intellect is stunned by the shock and but gropingly gathers the meaning of the words. The power to realize their full import is mercifully wanting. The mind has a dim sense of vast loss—that is all. It will take mind and memory months and possibly years to gather the details and thus learn and know the whole extent of the loss.
>
> Samuel Clemens, *Autobiography*

The initial phase of grief is generally described as a shocking blow, a loss that stuns people to the very essence of their being. Numbness sets in; one doesn't feel, one just "does." A grieving parent told me, "It is as if I'm in a daze and I can only manage to dumbly put one foot in front of the other." People in this early stage tend to do those things that need to be done, such as making funeral arrangements and notifying others; and they usually handle these tasks in matter-of-fact ways. They continue to function on an intellectual level, but they often strongly repress their true feelings.

> I just don't want to go on. There are times when I'm suspended.... I think that the normal reaction after 6 months is that so many little things come up. There is such a gap between just knowing and really feeling all this.[16]

This tendency to have feelings be numbed may be a life-preserving way of adapting to an emergency situation; in a disaster or accident this reaction may allow the individual to survive immediate danger. Instead of dissolving into a state of incapacitated grief, a person becomes emotionally numb, as if in a state of shock, and this allows a him to focus on the tasks necessary to save his life. Such was the case of a young boy involved in a private plane crash that took the life of his father. He was able to save himself by putting into action what his father had taught him about survival; by suppressing his grief he could concentrate on saving himself. In a less dramatic example, occasionally a family member who plays the role of a nurturing parent for others may put aside his own grieving in order to minister to the needs of others. However positive this setting-aside method may be, if numbing becomes a permanent state, it will inhibit the resolution of grief.

The early part of the first phase of grief is usually characterized by a state of bewilderment; the individual tries to assign some meaning to what has occurred. The more inappropriate and unexpected the loss, the greater the challenge to make sense out of the event. This attempt to understand the news of an inappropriate death may have two motives. One is to understand the news itself, the other is involved with the existential issues provoked by the loss. In the first case, the survivor's bewilderment is caused by the realization that the loss has occurred: "I can't believe she's dead. I talked with her just yesterday." In the second case, the bewilderment centers on existential grief; "What kind of a world is it that allows innocent babies to die?" Or, "My wife had immediate acceptance. But me! I said to God, why such a hurt? Why such a pain? Why did you call?"[17]

As the reality of the loss begins to be accepted into a person's understanding, there is often a great urge to recover the lost object. This may be an involuntary or unconscious action, but either way it is a very common theme in this initial stage of grief. The person may cry out in sorrow. Bowlby argues that there is a biological basis for such behavior.[18] When animal infants lose their mothers, their crying sounds will often bring about the mother's return. However, in case of death, no amount of crying will bring about the return of the lost loved object. Human beings, Bowlby maintains, are also moved to cry out in order to regain the lost object.

We are all aware of the building tension, perhaps the attempt to suppress the welling up of feelings, and the final resignation and giving in to the release of tension that results in tears. The power of crying to aid in the recovering process of the lost object is not merely a lower animal adaptive function. In the case of loss through death, the cries may produce solace from others (a positive function in itself), but they cannot regain the loss by bringing the deceased back to life. Averill, in a lengthy discussion of this issue, points out that a psychobiological basis for the grief reaction exists. While the grief process is influenced by both the social environment and one's unique life experiences, research has shown that there is "a stereotype set of psychological physiological reactions of biological origin"—most notable in the mother-offspring dyad—that we know as "grieving."[19] The strong desire to restore things to the way they were before, and the need to cry out in sorrow are basic to the grief process.

Anger also can be seen during this first stage. Often of the more common forms of loss, a "small or large dash of aggression will be fruitful in bringing about a satisfactory solution to separation."[20] As with the crying behavior described earlier, we can see how this urge to action might be functional in common threats of loss, but these efforts are to no avail in bringing back the dead. In death loss, obviously, this anger will not produce the desired result of restoring the lost relationship, but it may occur anyway: "Tumor…an unknown virus…fibrosis…I wanted to hammer that tumor out."[21]

To their own bewilderment and perhaps guilt, bereaved persons may find themselves reproaching the dead for having deserted them (the dead are the perpetrators of this evil deed). Anger and disrespect for the dead are generally not approved of in our society, but are acceptable behaviors in some societies where the dead are openly reproached for having died.

This is an effort to undo the wrong that has occurred, to reestablish the former relationship.[22] Sometimes people see God as the cause of the pain that is felt, and later the individual may feel anxious and guilty for having cursed God.

> Then they told me the little one was gone...God hates me!
>
> After I lost my son, sometimes I would get up and walk out of the church. I think it was resentment of God, really. [23]

A hospital chaplain described this process to me, saying that he would not reprove the griever for this initial outburst, because he understood the deeper need to find any cause for the loss. He reconciled this with his reverence for God by stating that, "God is big enough to handle and understand this anger."

The anger bereaved persons feel may take other forms as they attempt to regain control of life. The assignation of blame may serve many purposes. Often an attempt will be made to assign blame to anyone or anything. It may provide protection against guilt by assigning the cause of death to someone or something else. By finding fault or assigning blame, the griever may be able to relieve himself of any fears of responsibility for the death.[24] This is often a difficult problem for parents who lose a child. In our culture parents have a great deal of responsibility for their children, therefore a child's death can often evoke a great deal of guilt for them.

Blaming may provide revenge; a sense of restitution can be achieved if it seems that a wrong has been corrected. The bereaved seek to restore things to the way they were and at the same time give vent to the anger that is a part of their grief. This explanation of the root motivations behind anger and blame provides an irrational yet understandable context for the urge to strike out, to do something in response to the loss felt.

In this initial stage of the grieving process, after the first shock wave has passed, the most common activities involve crying and aggressive, angry efforts that are motivated by a desire to restore the lost loved person to the bereaved. Even though the deceased person is gone, the needs persist on the part of the bereaved. The griever cries out for the lost loved one, feels a desire to "do something" about the loss to somehow correct this terrible event. But these efforts are in vain.

Another form of anger may be a show of hostility toward those who try to comfort the bereaved. The hostility has its roots in the aggressive urge to reestablish contact with the lost person. The comforter is attempting to help the bereaved to accept the loss, which, at this point, is exactly what the bereaved does not want to do. Accepting the grief by working it through means accepting the loss as well. For example, one grieving parent stated, "I keep a photograph of the (stillborn) baby on the mantle. I don't plan on ever getting over it."[25] Many a well-intentioned friend has been shocked by the anger with which an offer of support was met. The consoler is unaware that the grieving individual may feel a need to regain the loss and may not want to accept the death of the lost person (however unrealistic that might appear to the observer). In effect, the bereaved person is saying, "Do not ask me to give up my grief—it is all that I have left."

Literature often serves to describe the emotions and motivations of people better than case histories. Illustrative of the initial phase of grief, Edgar Allan Poe, in his poem "The Raven," lyrically describes his efforts to accept the loss of his loved one.[26] So strong is his urge to regain her that upon answering what he thinks to be a knock at his door and finding no one there, and "Doubting, dreaming dreams no mortal ever dared to dream before," he calls out to his dead love. His irrational hope is that somehow, in some inexplicable way (and one that is terrifying in its implications), Lenore has returned to him. But there is nothing there, save an echo of his own words, "Merely this and nothing more."

As Poe encounters Death in the form of the raven, he initially tries to deny its impact by stating that death, too, will pass quickly through his life. The raven encompasses the reality of death into one word and replies, "Nevermore." Poe then decides to confront the visitor in an intellectual manner, by reasoning what this "grim, ungainly, ghastly, gaunt, and ominous" bird could mean by his curious uttering of the answer "nevermore." But even this fails, for he suddenly realizes that he is resting his head upon a pillow that reminds him of Lenore and his loss. Suddenly overwhelmed with grief, he begs for release from sorrow. Again the bird replies, "Nevermore." The urge to recover the lost object wells up in him once more, and Poe asks Death if he will at least be reunited in heaven with his lost love. To this also the bird replies, "Nevermore." Now shrieking in anger, the poet orders Death to leave and to "take thy beak from out of my heart." Again, relentlessly, the reply is, "Nevermore." Finally, realizing his efforts are in vain, Poe resigns himself to what he perceives as an eternity of sorrows. For Death, in the form of the raven, "never flitting, still is sitting, *still* is sitting," perched in the narrator's personal world, and the shadow of death, which is sorrow, covers his soul. In resignation to his fate, the poet admits that the shadow of his sorrow shall never be lifted from his soul.

In the poem, Poe describes the strong and quick mood shifts that can be a part of early grief; one moment rational, the next angry, suddenly despairing, as the narrator attempts to come to grips with his loss. But every effort to control or mitigate the pain of loss is fruitless. Poe, with the use of almost maddening and repetitious understatement, sums up in one word the stoic and uncompromising reality of death. The efforts to resolve the pain fail and the narrator resigns himself to what he perceives as neverending sorrow. The second phase of grief now begins.

Phase Two: Disorganization and Reorganization

As the attempts to recover what has been lost fail, the disappointment mounts. Deep, sometimes incapacitating despair sets in. No longer do the grievers try to focus their efforts to "find" the lost person. The realization that the person has died leaves them with no place to focus their thoughts. Lindemann describes this feeling as "a painful lack of capacity to initiate and maintain organized patterns of activity."[27] This characterization implies that the grief process itself somehow imposes this lack of organization. We should be aware that in actuality the griever still has the mental ability to organize activities, but the old methods of organization *just don't make sense anymore.* So, rather than the ability to organize life being somehow taken away by grief, we would argue that the grieving person ceases activity because the usual reasons for activity have lost their meaning. In view of the circumstances, this cessation of activity may be a logical decision. With the loss of a loved person, a great many of the bereaved's former activities are no longer rewarding in the same way. The individual often stops normal habits because now, with the disruptive event of death, actions and the motives for them must be rethought. A process of internal reorganization must commence. Deciding to stop many activities certainly makes sense in view of the situational context. To continue former patterns of activity as if this new event had not occurred would be, in a sense, reality-denying behavior.

> I supported that child. I took that child to school the first day. I took that child to the doctor. Now what the hell do I do?[28]

Lindemann points out that if some pre-loss activities persist out of habit, or if one finds oneself ceasing to do those things that were formerly routine activities, one may begin to realize how many of those activities had meaning, at least in part, in the now lost relationship.[29] This new lack of meaning in life may lead to a strong, if temporary, dependency on others who, in their willingness to help the bereaved, say, in effect, "I will make sense out of your world for you."

During the second phase of grief the individual may appear to be in a state of disorganization. As Bowlby points out, before people can rebuild their lives, they must dismantle old mental constructs.[30] While externally it may appear difficult, if not impossible, to focus one's own activities, important internal adjustments to loss may be taking place. The former frame of reference that had guided the individual's behavior no longer applies. Before grievers can reorient themselves to the changed external world the old image of the world must be dismantled and a new one constructed. This is the primary work going on during the second phase. Marris describes the reorganization process as "painful, because it begins in such helplessness and uncertainty."[31] Those experiencing grief may feel a loss of a sense of personal integrity or personal wholeness. The one who supplied so much meaning to life and around whom so many of the person's activities were focused, now has been lost to death.

> I had been so used to buying four items, and for a while I would actually forget, you know, and get four things, and I would just keep the other for myself.[32]

C.S. Lewis, writing about the loss of his wife, says, "Did you ever know, dear, how much you took away with you when you left? You have stripped me even of my past, even of the things we never shared."[33] That vital sense of internal integrity, perhaps never consciously realized before, is now useless.

In their study of the first year of bereavement, Glick, Weiss and Parkes found that some widows described their loss as the loss of an actual part of themselves, so deep was their grief.[34] In a sense, this description is apt. They have lost a great deal of the symbolic organization they had developed—a symbolic organization that gave meaning to their world. Since so much meaning was based upon the spouse, his dying destroyed their inner world. Often this grieving expresses itself by an obsessional attempt to relive the past. This reviewing of the old patterns of symbolic organization is a way of dismantling the old world and preparing a new one that accommodates life without the deceased. In other words, the death event forces the individual to reorganize his life around a new reality. To deny this reality only lengthens the grieving process, or it may lead to forms of inappropriate behavior.

The desolation and despair that the survivor feels are deeply rooted in primary images of disorganization and disintegration. A person who reports a fear of being destroyed by grief is closer to the truth than we might think at first. The inner symbolic organization no longer works because it is no longer an adequate image of the relationship between the person and the world. Because the individual's image of the world can no longer be applied to reality, the bereaved person cannot use it as a basis for action.

Erich Lindemann, in his important study, "Symptomatology and Management of Acute Grief," presents his findings from studying over 100 grieving persons.[35] He describes the bereaved as often avoiding those who would console them, because these meetings would release a flood of feelings of desolation and distress. The bereaved may feel a sense of unreality and a lack of emotional closeness with others. Sometimes there will be a preoccupation with the deceased, as the formerly accurate internal symbolization of the world,not yet completely dismissed, reasserts itself. There may be also a fear of forgetting the lost person if the grief process is completed. Giving up grief may also be resisted because of feelings of guilt. To grieve is to pay a debt. The loss itself may also be seen as a punishment, and to grieve is to accept that punishment, to "serve out the sentence" in a sense.

Sometimes individuals may remain deeply involved in grief, seeming to make no progress because they find a certain amount of satisfaction (secondary gain) in grieving. The person suffers well and to finish grieving would mean giving up the tragic role, which while painful, may be a role that the person is adept at and therefore gives them a great amount of reinforcement and satisfaction.

During grieving, one's state of disorganization and lack of a sense of personal integrity are shattered further by the lack of experience with these new and overwhelming feelings. One feeling that many are afraid to share openly is fear. C.S. Lewis, describing his bereavement over the loss of his wife, said, "No one ever told me grief felt so much like fear."[36] Often this is fear that the loss of inner integrity and the onslaught of terrifying emotions that accompanies loss of a loved one mean that one might actually be losing one's mind.

> I've been numb from my toes to my head and I can hardly breathe at night.... I have weird reactions, fantasies...I'm scared. I have been a person I don't know.[37]

The bereaved person must learn that the frightening thoughts and feelings that are experienced during normal grief are to be expected, and that they make sense in the context of loss of a dearly loved person.

Phase Three: Reorientation and Recovery

In the final phase of grief, the loss has taken on different meanings for the griever. The memory of the lost person no longer elicits strong grieving reactions. The griever may sense a resolution of previously felt strong feelings. The lost person may be referred to in reminiscences which may entail feelings of pleasure as well as sadness. As grievers reorganize their symbolic world, the dead person may be given a new image, and the griever may state that the lost person is now in a particular place, such as "heaven," which is a more concrete description of the new status of the deceased.

The dead person is now understood differently than before. The deceased, at least in the mind of the griever, is now in a timeless state. He is no longer associated with the time-bound world, but takes on a new identity in the mind of the griever. This is a necessary step if grievers are to reorganize their understanding of the world so that it is congruent with reality. The new identity assigned to the dead person removes him from the everyday world, thus allowing the griever to adapt to life without the deceased. The ceremonies that surround death are, in part, social affirmations of the changed status of the dead person.

The new symbolic world of the griever may be formed in part from meanings and values connected to the deceased. I visited the home of a deceased test pilot, whose memory was an active part of the family's shared images. There were many mementos, pictures and awards around the house that had been won by the late father and the teenage children spoke openly and matter-of-factly about their father. They continued to take an active part in leadership roles in school and athletics and the son eventually became an Air Force pilot himself. Even after their father's death, the values he had stood for continued to have an influence on his children's development.

As the deceased is put into a new perspective by the survivors, new meanings are taken on regarding the lost person's life. The griever attempts to make sense of the loss and incorporates these new meanings as a part of changed images of the world. A child may decide to become a doctor to find a cure for the disease that killed a loved one. Someone else may decide that the deceased person died for a cause that must be carried on. The image of the deceased takes on new meanings as the griever becomes oriented to a world without the loved one. As Marris observes, "The grief is mastered, not by ceasing to care for the dead, but by abstracting what was fundamentally important in the relationship and rehabilitating it."[38]

> I held her a long time after she died and nobody made me budge. I stayed in that room with her about 40 or 50 minutes after she died and it was really neat. But my little girl did have a message. She has a message for me, she has a message for everybody here: the only thing when the chips are down that really matters is kindness. That's the only thing that really matters. You can spell it any way you want. Some people say love, some say compassion but when you act it out, what is it, it's kindness."[39]

In the statement above the parent acknowledges that a loss has occurred. The father was able to give meaning to the loss because there was something that the little girl had left behind—a lesson—that the only thing that mattered was kindness, a message that gave meaning to the child's life and death. After a death, as individuals begin to interact with their surroundings, they begin to implement a new perspective on the world. This reorganized view may develop almost immediately following death, or it may take much longer. An older child may begin to take on some aspects of a deceased parent's role soon after the parent's death. (This may or may not be appropriate; nonetheless, it is an attempt to build an image of the world without the dead parent.) Aging widows and widowers may choose never to rebuild their lives, but to spend the rest of their days almost totally immersed in memories.

The successful resolution of grief is accomplished when the grievers are able to reintegrate themselves in the external world. This new inner symbolization of life will contain elements of the individual's past experiences and a reorientation toward life without the lost loved one. The person is no longer influenced by overwhelming feelings of despair. Feelings of grief are no longer as uncontrollable as they were before. Individuals regain a sense of personal integration and connection and can now redirect and take charge of their life. Life begins to move forward again, and the individual regains the ability to interact openly with others. Bertha Simos sums up the resolution of the grief process in this manner:

> The task of mourning is completed when a personality reorganization takes place, through which the old self and the new self now without that which has been lost, are integrated. This is different from the attempt at retrieval of the loss that characterizes the first phase of grief. That which has been lost is now retained in memory. A sense of identity, an new stability, a hopeful and positive interest in the present and future mark the end of grief and mourning. The search for new avenues of gratification leads to restitution for the loss through new relationships, new interests, new values, and new goals. With restitution comes a restoration of the sense of self-esteem damaged by the loss. The new self is enriched by the memories of that which has been lost as well as by the growth through suffering and the mastery of grief. Healthy grieving should end with new avenues for creative living.[40]

Factors Affecting Successful Grief Work

Throughout our discussion of grief, we have implied different factors that can affect the grief process. The griever's death fears and anxieties may exacerbate their grieving; existential grief can present more of a problem than the loss itself. The intensity of the lost relationship will be a factor in reactive grieving, as will the availability of other love objects that will serve to support the griever and provide for the needs once met by the deceased.

The degree to which the death may be perceived by the griever as preventable can be a factor that can interfere in the grief process[41] in that it may produce feelings of guilt. Anger at a needless death—one easily avoided by stronger laws or better medical care—may affect the ease with which people can resolve their grief. Also, the basic personality and emotional makeup of the survivor will affect his ability to cope with the crisis. Past losses and the individual's experiences in resolving them can provide valuable information on how the individual will cope with the current loss. Conversely, if a person has experienced many recent losses, he may be in a weakened emotional state. This has been noted among the elderly, who often lose a number of important people within a short period of time. Because grieving also takes a physical toll, the health of grievers may affect their ability to cope with the loss and regain their former state of emotional composure.

As we mentioned earlier, the degree to which the death is seen as appropriate will greatly affect an individual's grief reaction. Appropriate losses, though painful, may be seen as "right." However, inappropriate death not only destroys the relationship, but also one's sense of the meaning of existence itself.

THE SOCIAL PROCESS OF MOURNING

We will now shift our perspective from concern with the internal dynamics of grief to the social world in which the act occurs. One sociological perspective defines emotions as products of the social reality in which people exist. According to this perspective, society tells us what kind of thought and behavior is acceptable. This is a result of socially proscribed patterns of interaction, as well as socially reinforced ways of feeling. The sociological perspective differs from the psychological perspective in that it does not emphasize internal feelings. Emile Durkheim, one of the founders of sociology, believed that "mourning is not a natural movement of private feelings wounded by a cruel loss; it is a duty imposed by the group."[42]

This sociological position immediately raises questions concerning the biological basis for grief. Rather than debating this issue here, we will assume that the interplay of both the individual's psyche and the social environment will affect feelings and behaviors. The development of personality is affected not only by external experiences, but also by the individual's ability to internalize the experiences. As such, attitudes toward death and feelings involved in acknowledging loss (grief) are a product of both social and psychological processes. Mourning—the social experience of grief—permits the individual to experience external validation for one's feelings. When examining mourning, we will focus on the effect and importance of mourning for the individual griever. When we consider social rituals surrounding death, we will examine the significance of mourning for the larger society.

The social environment provides us with a stage upon which to express our inner selves. Our lives and ways of looking at the world may be enhanced or constrained by our environment. Some investigators, following Freud and Marx, believed that individuals are constrained by the social environment. Others argue that we tend to limit our vision and that our potential as individuals is more self-constrained than socially repressed. In fact, a good deal of the current wave of popular psychology argues that we tend to limit our own abilities more than they are limited by the social environment. This kind of "bootstrap psychology" focuses upon the individual taking responsibility for his life and therefore, that we bring about the changes that we desire. While accepting responsibility may be an important part of change, this perspective often implies a naive and potentially dangerous approach to the social environment. In our discussion of the mourning process, we will examine both the positive and negative aspects of the social environment as well as its influence on those who are grieving.

The Repression of Feeling in American Society

It is necessary at this point to examine the social contexts that exist in America in order to understand the reality within which individuals experience grief and to appreciate how the social environment can facilitate or discourage the grieving process. Also, the judgments regarding what is considered acceptable and appropriate mourning influence the ease with which individuals are able to mourn. In the extreme, it can be argued that negative social influences on the mourner may promote exceptional grief reactions.

A useful concept to discuss here is *labeling*,[43] a process in which individuals are placed in specific categories determined by their behavior. Deviation implies a digression from the norms of society. What are the norms of American society concerning emotional behaviors such as mourning? Thomas Scheff argues that industrial mass society predominantly denies the value of "the unalienated individual, passionately engaged , and in intimate contact with at least one other person."[44] Scheff, on the other hand, describes industrial societies as modeled after Martin Buber's I-it relationship, wherein the person is emotionally isolated from society, others and even from himself. On a societal level, these values are epitomized in the bureaucratic organization as opposed to a more humanistic and communal form of organization.

Those of us who live in a bureaucratized and industrialized society find that norms and values are influenced by, and also, in turn, influence social organization. Spontaneously expressed feelings are not approved of in bureaucratic society, that instead prefers predictability, control and efficiency. Scheff notes that "the ideal person for such servitude is reliably obedient, predictable and orderly."[45] The need to control children's feelings is one of the major centers of conflict in the socialization of children. Sadness and anger, the two earliest emotions expressed by the child, are objects of parental control. These two emotions, so basic to the grief process, are suppressed through socialization. This goes beyond the immediate family, as society reacts negatively to "spoiled brats" and "cry babies." Important also is the fact that the social world in which we live does not take an interest in the child's inner state—the source of emotions—but instead punitively socializes children to suppress their feelings and to comply with society's norms. Scheff's description of the results of this process is worth quoting directly:

> The first consequence is usually an adult whose emotions are so severely repressed that he seems to others and even to himself to be virtually emotionless. Although the personality of this adult is well-suited for human contact in which hierarchy, order and predictability are emphasized, he is likely to be quite rigid in most areas and lacking in spontaneity and creativity. Like the bureaucracy he is apt to serve, he is suited for short-term efficiency in using means to an end, but is unlikely to be innovative, creative, or responsive to changing conditions.

A second consequence of the punitive socialization of emotions is likely to be an individual who's as intolerant of emotions in others as his parents were of his own emotions as a child.[46]

In describing Tomkin's work on the socialization of crying in children, Scheff points out how emotions are suppressed and given a negative connotation through socialization.[47] Another consequence of socialization described by Scheff is that those who display their feelings openly are labeled as deviant.

In sum, American society does not approve of mourning except within the rigid confines of a funeral. Any other display of emotion or indication of one's emotional state (such as wearing black mourning band on the arm), is no longer normatively accepted behavior. After a death, the survivor is expected to return to the workday world quickly and after that time not to burden others with open displays of grieving. The bureaucratic world has little tolerance for feelings.

What is of interest to us about this are the ramifications of such a social reality upon the individual. The result of this kind of normative order is to encourage denial and suppression of the griever's feelings. Grief is something to be mastered, rather than experienced. At the funeral for the late President Kennedy, his widow was admired for her stoicism. Triumph over one's feelings, suffering in silence, and refusal to be overcome by emotions are seen as admirable traits in American society. To deviate from the norm is to invite social disapproval and to be labeled as "weak," a "bleeding heart," or perhaps even "crazy." This final label of "crazy" is worth further comment. I was told by one person that he feared his own strong emotions at a time of grieving. Because strong emotions are not acceptable in American culture, many who experience them are often fearful when they occur. This applies to positive as well as negative emotions. Often a chief cause of the reluctance to enter fully into sexual interactions is the fear of losing control. Likewise, those who experience the overwhelming emotion associated with grief and who have been socialized to suppress (and hence not experience) the strong emotions of anger and sorrow, may feel that they are losing their mind. In a society of unresponsive people who are preoccupied with control, the fear of unsuppressible feelings may contribute to morbid grief reactions. A lack of familiarity with the possible range of human emotions may place the individual in a precarious position when confronting a significant loss, to say nothing of impoverishing life in general.

It is generally accepted that the initial phase of grief may last as long as several weeks or even months, during which time the individual is often overwhelmed with feelings. When one must return to work before the grief process is complete, a great deal of effort must be expended by the individual to maintain a facade of nonemotionality. It may be necessary for the person to deny feelings in order to continue to function in the world of work. Something of one's humanness must be sacrificed in order to bring home the paycheck. This imposition of behaviors on the mourner may be a product of the bureaucratic form of organization.[48] In a bureaucracy, death is not known. As Marris points out, in a bureaucracy there is always a replacement available to step in and fill the vacancy. While returning to work may be a sign of reintegration for some, when it is imposed upon the individual before he is ready, it may do much more harm than good.

Usually our society demands a brief mourning period. The individual, forced to act in a way contrary to his emotions, is caught on the horns of a dilemma. If one takes the time to work through the grief, one may have to sacrifice a form of livelihood. If one returns to the public world, it may be at the expense of one's emotions. Marris has observed that until the "thread of continuity is reestablished, the individual cannot authentically interact with the world." The process of reconnecting with the world in positive ways is "itself the only deeply meaningful activity in which the bereaved can be engaged."[49]

Other societies, and even our own at one time, have recognized the personal needs of the mourner, and have provided a context in which the mourner could express grief. Phillippe Ariès has described the purposes of the seclusion of the family in mourning during ancient times.[50] First, the person was allowed to do nothing but grieve. This custom, still a part of Orthodox Jewish tradition, does not leave room for denial, an act that occurs so easily in contemporary grieving patterns. Second, the seclusion of a family for a specific period of time prevents the family from mourning "too quickly" and thereby not fully resolving their grief.[51] Taking a historical view of mourning customs, Ariès states:

> If one were to draw a "mourning curve," there would first be a peak stage of frank violent spontaneity until somewhere around the 13th century, then a long phase of ritualization until the 18th century and then in the 19th century a period of impassion, self-indulgent grief, dramatic demonstration and funeral mythology.... In the mid-20th century the ancient necessity for mourning—more or less spontaneous or enforced depending on the century—has been succeeded by its prohibition. During the course of one generation the situation has been reversed: what had always been required by individual conscience or social obligation is now forbidden; what had always been forbidden is now required. It is no longer correct to display one's grief, nor even to feel any.[52]

The rise of bureaucracy and technology have combined to devalue the individual in favor of the larger organization. Today it would appear that to the extent the individual allows himself to become an extension of the bureaucratic organization, he must sacrifice some unique humanness. While in everyday life it may feel rewarding to be a part of an organization, in times of overwhelming loss the personal need to mourn is often subjugated to the demands of bureaucratic society. A bureaucracy is not concerned with an individual's feelings, but with his ability to do the assigned job. Rational thinking must take priority. While one may be rewarded financially, emotionally the person may become impoverished. As Benoliel points out, "The process [of grief work] cannot be hurried beyond the individual's capacity to assimilate the change into one's definition of reality."[53] To rush this process in order to meet social demands may foster more severe reactions at a later date.

Thus far we have seen that the value that society places on individual death will affect the ways of acceptable mourning available to its members. Where loss of the individual is considered important, the society will provide a means of acknowledging the loss, such as a state funeral. In mass societies such as the contemporary United States, where individual death (except of significant leaders) is not usually an important national or community event, a social recognition of loss is almost nonexistent.

In American society there is a lack of ritual in interacting with one who is mourning. "I don't know what to say," is the most common statement one hears in response to another's bereavement. As an example of this avoidance mechanism, Vernon describes a study in which he asked people how they would respond if they met someone who had lost a loved one through death since their last meeting.[54] Only 25 percent of the respondents said that they would mention the death, while 64 percent stated that they would either wait for the other party to mention the loss or would prefer that no mention be made of the loss at all. Another 10 percent stated that they just didn't feel prepared to answer the question. This preference for avoiding the subject by the majority of people interviewed is an example of the lack of socially acceptable behavior when interacting with one in mourning. From the mourner's point of view, the situation is most likely to be similar to Glaser and Strauss's mutual pretense theory, as an unauthentic interaction drama is played out. In this type of interaction, the mourner receives no validation or reinforcement for the grief he is feeling. In fact, the mourner is being encouraged to deny that he is grieving at all.

Vernon went on to ask his respondents how they would like to be treated if they were in mourning themselves. While 38 percent stated that they would prefer to be left alone, another 38 percent stated they would prefer some form of interaction with others concerning their mourning. Interestingly, over 22 percent had no opinion as to how they would prefer to be treated during mourning. One thing that stands out is the desire of a large portion of the sample for some form of social validation for their feelings; another is the large proportion of people who had no idea of how to act or how they think they would like to be treated during mourning.

The lack of customary mourning behavior can leave the mourner with an even greater sense of personal disorganization than was felt previously. This points out the attractiveness of denying one's need to mourn in order to become accepted back into society. Gorer speaks to this point as well and contrasts various kinds of nonnormative behavior with that of the Orthodox Jewish community.[55] Within that group, mourning is rigidly proscribed. Initially, the individual must do nothing for seven days but grieve. After that period of time, the men must not shave or cut their hair for one month, and twice daily for the next 11 months someone must go to the temple and say prayers (Kaddish) for the deceased. Then a grave marker is erected and the mourning ends. The group, in this case as in many traditional societies, provides a format within which the survivors may mourn. It provides for acceptable mourning behaviors within a social context.

Even though the individual may express extreme behaviors during mourning, as in some primitive tribes, it is taking place within a social context.[56] The people may inflict wounds upon themselves, scream and tear out their hair and act out other behaviors that would be considered harmful, if not pathological, in our society. But they do so within a defined social context that controls the behaviors and will guide the individual back to the normal patterns of social interaction upon completion of the mourning ritual. When the mourning behavior is ended, the individual reaches a closure to the loss and is ready to reintegrate into the mainstream of society. In contemporary American society, oftentimes people do not feel a sense of resolution to the loss because of the lack of recognition of mourning by the social group and disapproval of the open display of strong feelings.

Anger, a normal emotion in grief, is often expressed in a social context. Rosenblatt points out the need a society has either to channel the anger of mourning into socially acceptable or nonthreatening behaviors or to isolate the mourner in order to protect other members of society from harm. In the contemporary United States, there are no specialists who direct the mourner's anger, as in other societies where designated group members such as priests prescribe ritual behaviors for the mourners. In America, mourners are left to their own devices. A lack of a socially defined and safe means of releasing anger during mourning may contribute to the violence so prevalent in current American society. In other words, much of today's violence may be caused by the enormous amount of unreleased anger reactions that stem from loss.

Another by-product of the lack of normative patterns of interaction with those in mourning is the social isolation that results from this avoidance. At a point in time when people are most in need of social support from others they are often deprived of it.[57] Mourning behavior involves those outside immediate family only during the funeral. Many grieving people report a great sense of loneliness after the funeral, when others return to their usual routines.

EXCEPTIONAL AND ANTICIPATORY GRIEF

The acceptance of loss facilitated by the grief process enables a person to interact again with the external world in gratifying ways and to continue a meaningful existence. In this section we will examine two special cases of grief: exceptional grief, wherein the individual does not successfully complete the grieving process, and anticipatory grief, which means knowing that a loss will take place some time in the future.

Defining Exceptional Grief

Perhaps one of the most difficult issues to grapple with in studying grief involves the question of successful and unsuccessful grieving. Bowlby acknowledges the complexity of this issue and agrees with Lindemann's view that pathological responses to loss are best seen as "exaggerations and caricatures of the normal process."[58] Siggins argues that when the process of grieving is "abnormally delayed, protracted, or intense," we are witnessing a morbid reaction.[59] DeVaul and Zisook state that unresolved grief involves the absence of a prolonged enough grief process.[60] They cite three clinical symptoms of exceptional grief: (1) painful response when the deceased is mentioned, (2) realization of unresolved grief by the individual, and (3) unaccountable depression or the emergence of medical symptoms on the anniversary of the loss.

Welu has addressed the issue of criteria for pathological grief and offers the following tentative guidelines: (1) self-destructive behavior (suicide attempts, excessive use of alcohol and drugs), (2) suicidal thoughts or feelings, (3) physiological problems, (4) social withdrawal, (5) depressive states with obvious clinical symptoms, (6) hospitalization for psychiatric symptoms, and (7) the taking of psychotherapeutic drugs.[61]

Siggins states that a noticeable exaggeration of any of the typical reactions to the grief process may signal a morbid reaction.[62] More specifically, she speaks of the *persistent* experience of an emotion usually associated with grief, a lack of progress in the grieving process, indeed, what could almost be termed a determination on the part of the griever not to give up the lost object, and distortions of the grieving process described by Lindemann (outlined in some detail later in this chapter).

This brief review of the existing literature points out the imprecise and subjective nature of psychological diagnosis. Anthropological studies describe a great many grieving reactions that are contained in the descriptions of pathological behavior given above, but are considered normal (typical, expected) behaviors in different cultures.[63] Nevertheless, it is probably safe to assume that a lack of recognition of a significant loss, an extreme reaction far in excess of normative cultural expectations, and a lack of movement through the grief process can be considered to indicate difficulty in resolving the loss, and this we label exceptional grief.

Erich Lindemann conducted the pioneering work that described distortions of the typical phases of grief resolution. In his study, Lindemann describes several manifestations of unsuccessful grief work.[64] Since Lindemann's work was published in 1944 others have contributed to both the symptomatic and theoretical perspectives of unresolved bereavement. The following is a compilation of typical manifestations of unresolved grief.

Denial

Probably one of the most common forms of an exceptional grief reaction is denial. When an individual does not allow himself to grieve, the feelings and images involving the loss are repressed. The factors that influence the individual's decision to repress his grief may be external or internal in origin. Internal processes that inhibit open grieving may be based on the desire to be strong for others who are grieving, or perhaps on earlier resolutions not to express feelings of sorrow due to a traumatic experience.

An example of such a resolution is a young man who told me of a boyhood experience in which he was forced by his father to skin and clean his pet rabbit who had died, because, said the father, "we don't waste food in this house." The experience was so traumatic for the young boy that as an adult he often denies his feelings of sadness and grief. Robert Jay Lifton uses the term "psychic numbing" to describe the inability of an individual to incorporate meaningfully the information (death) into his symbolic framework. "Psychic numbing refers to an incapacity to feel or to confront certain kinds of experiences, due to the blocking or absences of inner forms or imagery that can connect with such experience."[65] Lifton states that the impact of death, when judged to be intolerable in its destructiveness of all meaning in life, is severed from all thinking and feeling:

> To say that emotion is lost while cognition is retained is more or less true, but does not really capture what the mind is experiencing. What is more basic is the self's being severed from its own history; from its grounding in such psychic forms as caring for others, communal involvement, and other ultimate values.[66]

By numbing oneself to what are perceived as shattering events, the individual manages to preserve his integrity; a sense of personal organization. But the cost of this numbing is exceedingly high. Denying the emotional impact of the loss of a loved person impairs the individual's vitality. The very things that mean life, such as spontaneity, open and emotionally satisfying relationships and a sense of wholeness, must be sacrificed in order for the individual to numb himself to the awful reality of death. Thus the person stops feeling in order to survive. Ironically, the flattened emotions that result contribute to the characterization of that person as a member of the living dead.

Lifton, in his studies of Hiroshima victims, described their numbness as so powerful that it became a permanent part of their personalities.[67] In that particular situation, the nuclear holocaust had so traumatized the entire community as to make the recovery process difficult to achieve. In the case of an individual griever, the person may be intellectually aware of not functioning as a complete person, or the social environment may react to one's denial of emotional involvement in the loss in ways that encourage the individual to seek help with resolving grief.

Barry presents case material of individuals who had not fully acknowledged their grief.[68] One patient sought treatment for psychosomatic ailments, another because of difficulties in social interactions, and the third because of persistent dysphoria. All of these cases involved individuals who denied the emotional impact of their loss through death of a significant other and reported having no feelings about the loss. The awareness that they were not functioning in appropriate ways had led them to seek professional help. However, few of them were aware that the locus of their problem lay in a morbid reaction to grief. In the following case history, the man who presented himself for therapy complained of dysphoric feelings, although he was a noted success in his chosen profession, was surrounded by luxurious possessions and would generally be considered a "success" by standards of contemporary American society. Barry describes the interaction that took place during his initial interview:

> His demeanor was one of aloof arrogance and he seemed determined to keep others at a distance. When asked how it was that he grew up in an orphanage, he replied impatiently that it was because his parents had both died when he was six years old. He resisted answering questions about what happened to his parents, saying that "all that ancient history couldn't have anything to do with the way I feel now." The question was pressed. He finally answered in a matter of fact tone that his father had become psychotic, had shot and killed the mother and had then committed suicide. I was completely taken aback and asked lamely, "Who told you about this?" He glared at me. "Nobody had to tell me; I was in the room when it happened."
>
> Out of my shock and sympathy I said with deep feeling, "You poor guy." At this he literally catapulted out of his chair on to the floor, sobbing convulsively, and I found myself sitting on the floor beside him, holding him in my arms. In the next half hour he alternately wept uncontrollably and apologized for his childishness. Later he told me that after his parents' death, the surviving relatives had been so shocked and horrified at this terrible scandal that they could not seem to bear to be around him. After numerous shiftings from one home to another he was finally placed in the orphanage. This is where he had chosen to begin his story.

He had never allowed himself to weep, grieve, or even think about his loss before.[69]

The delay of grief reaction may last a lifetime, or only a few moments until the mind can incorporate the information that a loss has taken place. In cases of natural disasters such as floods or tornadoes, this numbing may last only until it is "safe" for the individual to release his feelings. Often there are release mechanisms that serve to trigger the suppressed grief. For example, discovering an object that is strongly linked to the image of the dead person, or hearing certain music may trigger the release of pent-up feelings.

Anniversary Reactions

Another source of renewed grief may be the anniversary date of the loss. Bornstein and Clayton, in a study of 92 widows and widowers, report that 67 percent described a grieving reaction on the anniversary of the death of their spouse.[70] Anniversary reactions may also serve to release feelings that were denied at the time of loss, such as anger at being deserted. Anniversary reactions may also take place when the griever reaches the age at which the person died. Lindemann, among others, speaks of the survivors' belief that they would live to be no older than the deceased and reports that they can experience emotional turmoil during the year that matched the age of the deceased person.[71] Thinking that they are fated to die at the same age as the deceased, these people may feel a sense of impending doom or manifest somatic complaints at the anniversary of the death of the significant person. Anniversary reactions usually refer to some chronological factor that exacerbates an unresolved grief. It is quite possible that the recurrence of social situations that were an important part of the relationship may also trigger a grief reaction. The return to a memory-laden place, or a social gathering that was important to the dyad may foster the same kinds of grief reactions as those linked to an important date.

Ambivalent Reactions

Inability to resolve grief may also be due to ambivalent reactions to the death of a loved one. If the individual had both love and hate feelings for the other person when he was alive, then those feelings will often continue after death. This causes the grieving process to become confused, as the individual is both sad and glad that the other is dead. Often, feelings of hatred for the loved one are unacceptable to the survivor, and so they must be denied. Feelings of sadness are also mixed with unacceptable feelings of satisfaction ("He finally got what he deserved") or anger ("She left me all alone"). Guilt may now become a part of the grief and the survivor may seek some form of self-punishment for these unacceptable feelings. Verwoerdt speaks of this process as hostile identification, that may manifest itself as an unhealthy identification with the deceased in that the survivor assumes symptoms of the deceased's illness.[72]

Identifying with the Deceased

The griever manifests the symptoms of problems that are the same as those of the deceased prior to death. This may be an attempt on the survivors' part to keep the deceased with them. Instead of successfully completing the grieving process, they keep the lost one "alive" by acquiring the symptoms that the deceased person manifested prior to death or by developing a problem that was a significant part of the character of the deceased person. DeVaul and Zisook describe a patient who never drank alcohol but after the death of her alcoholic husband became an alcoholic.[73] The acquisition of symptoms belonging to the last illness of the deceased was noted also by Lindemann.[74] Psychosomatically caused diseases such as asthma, rheumatoid arthritis and colitis may also be aggravated by suppressed grief.

Lindemann listed several other distortions of behavior that manifest themselves in cases of unresolved grief. One is a display of overactivity without a sense of loss; a person's psychic numbing process is replaced with a hysteric "sense of well-being and zest."[75] Alterations in relationships with friends and relatives occur as the individual continues to defend against emotional involvement with the external world. Furious hostility against specific persons is a way of venting any pent-up anger that may be a normal part of the grieving process. This anger, Lindemann points out, may often be directed against hospital staff and doctors. We should also be aware, however, that "furious hostility" may not always be a morbid grief reaction, but may be appropriate anger at incompetent or inconsiderate care of the deceased. Many societies provide through ritualistic behavior a means for the venting of anger in socially acceptable ways. When there is no way of releasing this anger, it may take the form of extreme anger at someone who can be blamed as a cause of the death.

A state of denial that reaches a point where the individual becomes psychically numbed to the trauma of the loss is described by Lindemann as a state of affect *resembling wooden pictures*. The person appears to be totally without feelings. As a result of the repression of strong feelings around the loss, the individual fears the manifestation of any emotions and thus suppresses all displays of affect. Lindemann also noted that a *lasting loss of patterns of social interaction* may occur; unable to reorganize their symbolic world, the survivors cannot any longer interact meaningfully with those who were a part of their world prior to the loss. It is the inability to work through the grief process that causes this inability to interact. The survivor, stuck in the second phase of grief, is unable to reconnect with the external world. Occasionally, when the guilt and need for self-punishment are unresolved, the survivors will engage in behaviors that are detrimental to their own social and economic existence. For example, individuals manifesting this morbid grief reaction may start spending money with reckless abandon. In extreme cases, this morbid grief reaction takes the form of *agitated depression* and this may lead to suicide.

Mummification

Another more morbid grief reaction described by Gorer is mummification.[76] In this case the griever preserves a part of the house and the objects contained in it exactly as it was at the time of death, as if expecting the deceased to return at any moment. Rituals may develop around the daily activities that are involved in keeping things as they were—laying out clothes for the deceased to wear, displaying fresh flowers and cleaning and caretaking of the area—activities that can take on a sacred air. Gorer contends that these rituals of unresolved grief develop as maladaptations in a ritualless society. The lack of grieving rituals, especially those that are religious, leave people to their own devices. The morbid reaction of mummification may be an unhealthy attempt to create personal forms of mourning ritual.

In the above descriptions we see examples of the grieving process going awry; of people getting stuck at some particular phase of the grief process. There are two factors in this process that have been touched upon but need further clarification. First, the social environment may do much to facilitate or stunt the grief process and thereby improve or obstruct the chances of a successful resolution. Many societies provide for the grief process by imposing behaviors upon mourners and provide rituals for the acting-out of grief. Conversely, societies may also act in such ways as to encourage the individual not to complete grief work successfully. Two examples of this in the contemporary United States are the emphasis upon grief as a private experience and the reinforcement of denial by the current mourning customs that serve to mask the reality of the loss. The second factor to be taken into account is the psychological makeup of the individual. Individuals who are just able to cope with daily living may find the experience of grief too much of a burden for their fragile psyches. Obviously, the psychological well-being of individuals at the time of the onslaught of grief is going to be a factor in their ability to cope adequately with the grieving process.

Pseudo-Resolution: A Special Case of Exceptional Grief

Albert and Barbara Cain present us with some startling case histories involving families who sought to replace one dead child with another.[77]

Their study included cases of disturbed children whose parents conceived the child with the specific intention of replacing their other child who had died. As one might suspect, the parents had suffered severe grief reactions at the time of the death of their child. At the time when their despair was at its greatest intensity the idea of having another child to replace the dead one appeared to offer a possible resolution.

For the parents who choose to do this, the idealized image of the dead child came to dominate the life of the replacement child. The replacement "was born into a world of mourning, of apathetic withdrawn parents; a world focused on the past and literally worshiping the image of the dead."[78] The new children found themselves in a world where they were constantly compared to a hyper-idealized image of the dead child—a perfect ghost. While living children were unable to achieve recognition for their own uniqueness, they also lived in a world where they feared for their own well-being. Normal parental concerns over the health and safety of their child were magnified to phobic proportions because the parents feared losing this child, as they had their earlier one. The children, presented at a child guidance center for evaluation, all showed signs of fearfulness and vulnerability. All were convinced that they would die as children, and some even exhibited physical symptoms similar to those present in the dead child. The children had internalized the parents' derogatory comparisons of them with their dead sibling, and saw themselves as never measuring up to the deceased sibling.

The parents in this situation had, on the surface, manifested a successful grieving process, but in fact were exhibiting a pseudo-resolution. While appearing to move through the third phase of the grieving process by having another child, in fact they were creating a new version of the old world. What appeared to be progress was really an attempt to use the future to hold on to the past. Again we see the importance of the symbolic meanings placed upon behaviors by the individual. The Cains point out that the reinvestment of emotional energies in new objects may have negative consequences if the grief has not been adequately resolved. For example, bereaved parents who continue to work as volunteers in the wards where their children died may often be tragically trapped in the grieving process.

The pseudo-resolution of grief may be fostered in a society that is uncomfortable with grief and seeks to resolve the process as soon as possible. It is noteworthy that several of the parents in the Cain study reported that their doctors suggested that they have another child, even though they themselves had decided not to have any more. In these cases, society was offering a way out of the grieving process that in reality turned out to be an unhealthy way of coping with grief.

While this manifestation of pseudo-resolution is not a common one, the hyper-idealization of the deceased is a common theme in grief work. The clinical example of "replacing" a child is a morbid reaction for those grieving a lost child. It is useful, however, in pointing out how vulnerable the griever is to derailment and how powerful the external world is in imposing itself upon the disorganized symbolic world of the griever.

Anticipatory Grief

As modern medicine becomes more exact, it is becoming more commonplace for people to know of impending death. Since death can be anticipated, grief may commence before a death has occurred. Anticipatory grief, a term first used by Lindemann, refers to *the emotional reaction that occurs before an expected loss.* While retaining many of the characteristics of the typical grief reaction after a loss, anticipatory grief has some unique characteristics that are worthy of discussion.

As was evident in our exploration of the grief process, there are many factors that determine the nature of the grief reaction: the individual's personality (including emotional well-being), the nature of the relationship, the appropriate/inappropriate nature of the loss, and the social reality in which the loss takes place. In anticipatory grief all of these factors are present, but the nature of their relationship to anticipatory grief differs from that of a typical grief reaction. In this section, we will examine anticipatory grief in terms of the model of the grieving process provided and consider the differences and similarities that exist in both typical and anticipatory grief.

Like typical grief, the initial phase of anticipatory grief involves the reaction to the news of the impending loss. When the person's physical status is diagnosed as "terminal," those involved with the patient may experience the shock of impending loss and yet it may be tempered with hope. This is one of the subtle differences that makes anticipatory grief unique. While the descriptions of usual grief speak of the depths of desolation felt by the grievers, anticipatory grief may seem to be more like an emotional roller coaster, depending on the type of illness involved. Experiences of physical degeneration, a worsening of symptoms, or more heroic medical measures may be interspersed with remissions, good days, and seeming progress toward health.

Doris Lund, in her story of her son's fight against leukemia, describes both the shock and the hope of entering anticipatory grief:

> A tremendous splash split the world. The bolt entered the top of my skull as I got the message. Eric had leukemia. It was something happening right this minute in his bones. We'd been struck. It was ours. Our first goal, then, was

> remission. I didn't know exactly just what a remission was. But I'd read enough to know it was a good period of time, maybe lasting for weeks or months, when the disease was under control and retreated for awhile. In remission you could live your life again.[79]

This roller coaster effect inhibits the grieving process by aiding in what might be considered denial. This is an interesting point that warrants further scrutiny. One cannot deny what has not yet occurred. In other words, the loss is anticipated, but because it has not yet occurred there is a chance, however small, that it might not occur at all. While individuals are integrating the anticipated loss into awareness, they are also becoming aware that the loss is not a *fait accompli*. The reality of the situation is that the death is expected, but exactly when it will take place is not known. This indefinite nature of the information complicates the grieving process, as it discourages the acceptance of the impending loss.

As a result, the social context within which one is existing has an influence on anticipatory grief. American culture rejects a fatalistic approach to life and many aspects of life are seen as solvable problems in American society. Does one move the family to a foreign country to try a new cure? Will the family be impoverished while trying exotic new treatments? Should experimental drugs be tried? If death itself is seen as problematic, then often others feel responsible or guilty for not having tried everything to save the patient's life.

As with the typical grief reaction, sadness and anger are present in the initial stage of anticipatory grief. The anger may be directed at the patient who is deserting the griever. Also, it may take the form of impatience at the suffering one must endure. Like the pragmatic death-as-a-problem definition in American society, so, too, suffering has been defined as a waste of time; a needless imposition on one's life. Many anticipatory grief reactions may include a number of ambivalent feelings: sorrow over the possible loss, anger, impatience (a wish that it would end) and thoughts as to how one will live on after the death. Some of these thoughts may naturally cause feelings of guilt in the griever.

The second phase of grief, disorganization and reorganization, is the phase the person will most typically stay in during anticipatory grief. Although the old symbolic patterns of organization still must be maintained, they are not going to last. Becker claims that although we delude ourselves into assuming that a bad thing will not last forever, that death will not touch us, the diagnosis of terminality brings us back face-to-face with the reality of death, a reality that we have sought to deny.[80] Limitless time now becomes limited and perhaps this is the basis for all anticipatory grief. But unlike the typical griever, the anticipatory griever does not totally abandon the old symbolic constructs and build a new image of the world as long as the dying person lives. Sometimes this ambiguous status is too much for a person to maintain and so he continues to resolve the grief, even though the dying person is still alive. Lindemann describes a pattern of resolved anticipatory grief following World War II: some returning soldiers found that their wives had never expected them to survive the war and once they returned, their wives, having successfully grieved, no longer loved them.[81]

Glick and his colleagues cautioned against encouraging the grief process among those experiencing anticipatory grief, arguing that mourning can only be done by withdrawing from the terminal person.[82] This, in turn, may lead to feelings of guilt at a later time. Also, it is entirely appropriate for the individual to remain in a state of non-resolution, for, in fact, the entire matter has not yet resolved itself in death.

The person experiencing anticipatory grief may find that he is caught between meeting his needs, such as finding new love objects, and remaining faithful to the dying. During anticipatory grief one may feel that time spent away from the dying person is somehow "stolen." Since the time left is limited, shouldn't as much time as possible be spent with the patient? How much time can be taken away from other obligations, other roles? Again we find ourselves facing questions to which there are, in our society, no cut-and-dried answers.

Successful anticipatory grieving does not mean moving ahead to readjustment and recovery. Successful anticipatory grieving means being aware of the disorganization that is taking place and having to live with it. Within the confines of current American social reality, this is a difficult position to be in. Our society favors problem-solving, progress and a mastery over the world. To be involved in anticipatory grief means to acknowledge and live with death, to acknowledge one's inability to be the master of one's fate. Understandably, Americans feel ill-equipped to deal with such a traumatic situation.

Although the prolonged period of anticipatory grief may be a very difficult experience for someone to go through, there are some beneficial aspects that should be noted. Because the loss has not yet occurred, the anticipatory grief period may provide an opportunity for resolution of past interpersonal issues and a reorientation can be begun with the approval of the dying person.[83] There are cases where divorce and marriage have taken place with the understanding and blessing of the spouse who was dying. A man who was permanently hospitalized could thus be sure that his wife and child would be taken care of and presumably he could draw some relief from this. While this case may illustrate a particularly heroic form of action, other people may find that preparatory grieving provides the time needed to resolve the questions of existential grief. Both existential and reactive grief may be worked through on a partial basis as the individual uses the time of anticipatory grief to prepare to deal with the expected loss.

Rando interviewed parents whose children had died from cancer and suggested that there is an optimum length of anticipatory grief (6 to 18 months). A shorter period did not give parents enough time to prepare for the loss and a longer period had a debilitating effect. The longer the illness, the greater the anger and the number of atypical responses found among the sample in her study.[84]

Just as typical grief can be physically debilitating, so is anticipatory grief. The constant emergencies and the inexorable disintegration of life of a loved one understandably can take their toll. A long-term anticipatory grieving period may exacerbate the negative aspects of the situation. It may also affect other relationships that some may tend to ignore because of the nearness of the impending loss.

One issue in the existing literature concerns whether or not anticipatory grief allows the individual to adjust better to a loss when it does occur. Clayton reports that having experienced anticipatory grief did not lead her respondents to a more satisfactory resolution after the death, but that a possible correlation existed between those experiencing anticipatory grief and post-death depression.[85] However, it should be noted that those experiencing depression symptoms prior to death may have been depressed prior to anticipatory grief and hence the outcome may not be the result of anticipatory grief, but a personality trait unrelated to the crisis itself. Others have reported that anticipatory grief aids in the resolution of the grief. Glick, Weiss and Parkes report that anticipation of the husband's death among a sample of widows is "one of the most important determinants of the adequacy of recovery."[86] They agree with Clayton's findings, stating the widows in their sample who were most upset by their husband's illness tended to be the most upset at his death. Still, 94 percent of those who anticipated their husband's deaths moved toward reorganization, as compared to only 77 percent of those who had not anticipated the death. Glick and his colleagues do not attribute the successful reorganization among those who had anticipated their loss to successful anticipatory grieving or to an ability to free themselves from the old relationships, but see the process of recovery from anticipated and unanticipated loss as being different from each other:

> In the anticipated death, there has been a period preceding the death during which the wife and husband together gradually have given up hope as they were progressively failed by therapies and regimes. The death, when it came, was traumatic, but its cause was understood. But when the death happened unexpectedly there might be no such sense of the death having resulted from what had become a familiar, if hated, process. Now the widow might not know what to feel.[87]

Our theoretical perspective would predict that those experiencing anticipatory grief would be better able to reorganize their lives following the loss. The partial grieving could allow a preparation for the inevitable collapse of the old symbolic organization. While the intensity of the grief may not be determined by having anticipated the loss, the eventual reorganization and resolution should benefit if the time of anticipatory grief is used to begin tentatively the reorganization of the individual's symbolic construct. Clinical researchers speak of the guilt and ambivalence present during anticipatory grief. These studies, although focusing on the pathological, indicate that during anticipatory grief an individual is beginning the process of integrating the expected loss into symbolic organization. This would indicate that anticipatory grief may serve to prepare the individual for the loss in some ways. This is not meant to ameliorate or lessen the burden of anticipatory grief. The stress, both physical and emotional, of a long grieving over an expected loss may take a terrible toll on an individual. However, it is important to realize that vital processes may be at work during that time, which may be beneficial in the final resolution and acceptance of the loss.

One of the emotions present at the end of anticipatory grief—the time of death—is a feeling of relief. In a sense, the anticipated loss can be anticlimactic. Something inevitable yet so long-battled, perhaps denied to some degree and most often experienced through sadness and despair, has finally occurred. One victim of such a struggle against inexorable death experienced a tremendous surge of energy that lasted for more than a day after the loss finally took place. This was followed by an extended period of grieving. This tremendous release of energy, so bound up during months of anticipatory grief, describes the very nature of the anticipatory grief process, as it binds the individual through sorrow to an event that has yet to occur.

Although exceptional and anticipatory grief are two very different aspects of grief, they share similar characteristics. Both involve the person who has not completed the grieving process. In exceptional reactions, we see that the individual becomes fixated at some point in the grieving process and that this inhibits the successful resolution of the loss. In anticipatory grief, the individual is in a state of emotional limbo, unable to resolve the loss because it has not yet occurred and at the same time, unable to avoid the authoritative diagnosis that the death will occur. While therapeutic intervention may be used to aid the exceptional griever to continue to move through the grieving process, this would not be beneficial to the person in anticipatory grief, as it might lead to a premature withdrawal from the dying person.

The Mid-Life Crisis: A Form of Anticipatory Grief

Recent literature has focused on the concept of a mid-life crisis, that point at which one must come to grips with the finiteness of life.[88] Some years ago, Elliott Jaques described the role of death in the mid-life crisis. Jaques contends that this crisis arises out of the knowledge that one has reached a point where growing-up ceases and growing old begins. The individual becomes aware that life is no longer an infinitude of opportunities. Rather, the realization is that one has made one's bed and now must sleep in it.

Death lies ahead. No longer is it easily avoided, no longer is it so far off in the future that it can be ignored. Now, as family and friends die, the realization that one cannot go on forever is an issue to be reckoned with. The reality of the distinct and unavoidable fact of one's own death demands to be acknowledged. And in acknowledging death, perhaps for the first time, the reality of death means accepting the reality of one's life. No longer is life infinite, no longer can one start all over; the reality of what one has made out of life must be accepted and lived with. This may mean dealing with some truths about oneself that have been denied in the past.

The following is an example of mid-life crisis. I treated a couple in therapy whose marriage of many years (their children were grown and married) was suddenly in crisis due to the husband's announcement of his deep marital unhappiness. When pressed, he admitted he had almost always been unhappy in the relationship. His recent awareness of his loss of youth and the inevitability of old age made the situation now seem desperate. What had been a familiar misery had been answered by telling himself that "some day things will get better." Now time was running out, and he was realizing that his time was not infinite, that in fact he soon would be growing old.

I have known of other cases that involved the sudden rejection of a lifestyle of many years in an attempt to recapture youth through owning more youthful clothes, cars and having younger lovers. In the contemporary United States, this is much more acceptable behavior for men than for women. At the base of this behavior is perhaps a sudden realization and reaction to death. Sometimes, as above, some make an effort to avoid aging and death by trying to "become young" again. Others become depressed, which clinically may be seen as a reaction to loss; a loss of youth, of opportunities, of endless life.

Working through this particular form of anticipatory grief can, as do most grieving processes, serve as a growing experience. The person can learn to accept the realities of his life and become more comfortable with himself. This may entail the rejection of some now unrealistic goals. It may mean a reassessment of one's life, as the internal reorganization demands a new perspective. Additionally, this new realization of the finiteness of life can lead to a new respect for the days that are left and the desire to place higher value on each remaining day.

The adaptational value of anticipatory grief has not been researched in great depth. Information concerning the process and possible outcomes of anticipatory grief could aid in better preparing people to work through the experience of expected loss in such ways as to benefit the total grieving process and its final resolution.

The lack of a social structure within which mourning can take place and the grief process successfully worked through can contribute to a sense of helplessness. Overwhelmed by grief, struggling to reorganize their thinking, mourners find that the social world offers no direction, no recognition of their plight. There are few predetermined behaviors that help promote grief work. Mourning behavior norms may provide a structure within which the grief-stricken can own up to their feelings and acknowledge the loss. The lack of such social structures within contemporary American society forces individuals to cope alone as best they can with grief.

NOTES

1. Edmund H. Volkart and Stanley T. Michael. 1957. Bereavement and Mental Health, in Alexander H. Leighton et al., eds., *Explorations in Social Psychiatry.* New York: Basic Books.
2. John Bowlby. 1969, 1973, 1980: *Attachment and Loss,* Vols. I-III. New York: Basic Books; 1961: The Process of Mourning. *The International Journal of Psychoanalysis* 42:331.
3. Geoffrey Gorer. 1965. *Death, Grief and Mourning.* Garden City, NY: Doubleday, pp. 121-122.
4. Avery D. Weisman. 1972. *On Dying and Denying.* New York: Behavioral Publications.
5. Robert Fulton. 1970. Death, Grief, and Social Recuperation. *Omega* 1:27.
6. Robert Jay Lifton. 1976: The Sense of Immortality: On Death and the Continuity of Life, in Robert Fulton, ed., *Death and Identity,* 2nd Ed. Bowie, MD: The Charles Press; 1979: *The Broken Connection.* New York: Simon & Schuster.
7. Erik Erikson. 1950: *Childhood and Society.* New York: Norton; 1968: *Identity: Youth and Crisis.* New York: Norton.
8. Lifton, 1979, op. cit., p. 54.
9. Lifton, 1976, op. cit., p. 27.
10. Ibid.
11. Ernest Becker. 1973. *The Denial of Death.* New York: The Free Press.
12. Gorer, loc. cit.
13. Bowlby, 1961, op. cit., p. 331.
14. Paul C. Rosenblatt. 1983. *Bitter, Bitter Tears.* Minneapolis: University of Minnesota Press, p. 155.
15. C.S. Lewis. 1976. *A Grief Observed.* New York: Bantam, p. 69.
16. J. Fischoff and N. O'Brien. 1976. After the Child Dies. *The Journal of Pediatrics* 88:142.

17. Ibid., p. 142.
18. Bowlby, op. cit., pp. 328-331.
19. James R. Averill. 1968. Grief: Its Nature and Significance. *Psychological Bulletin* 70:721-748.
20. Bowlby, op. cit., p. 333.
21. Fischoff and O'Brien, op. cit., p. 141.
22. Bowlby, ibid.
23. Fischoff and O'Brien, op. cit., pp. 141-142.
24. Erich Lindemann. Symptomatology and Management of Acute Grief. In Robert Fulton, 1976, op. cit., p. 212.
25. Jane Rowe et al. 1978. Follow-up of Families who Experience a Perinatal Death. *Pediatrics* 62:167.
26. Edgar Allan Poe. 1902. The Raven, in *The Complete Works of Edgar Allan Poe.* New York: Crowell.
27. Lindemann, op. cit., p. 212.
28. Fischoff and O'Brien, op. cit., p. 142.
29. Lindemann, op. cit., p. 212.
30. Bowlby, op. cit., p. 336.
31. Peter Marris. 1958. *Widows and Their Families.* London: Routledge & Kegan Paul, p. 88.
32. Fischoff and O'Brien, op. cit., pp. 141-142.
33. Lewis, op. cit., pp. 70-71.
34. Ira O. Glick, Robert S. Weiss and C. Murray Parkes. 1974. *The First Year of Bereavement.* New York: Wiley.
35. Lindemann, op. cit., pp. 210-221.
36. Lewis, op. cit., p. 1.
37. Fischoff and O'Brien, op. cit., p. 141.
38. Marris, op. cit., p. 34.
39. Fischoff and O'Brien, op. cit., p. 146.
40. Bertha Simos. 1979. *A Time to Grieve.* New York: Family Services, p. 45.
41. Margaret S. Miles and Alice S. Demi. 1983. Toward the Development of a Theory of Bereavement Guilt. *Omega* 14:299-314.
42. Emile Durkheim. 1961. *The Elementary Forms of the Religious Life.* New York: Collier, p. 443.
43. Howard Becker. 1963. *The Outsiders.* New York: The Free Press.
44. Thomas J. Scheff. 1975. Labeling, Emotion, and Individual Change, in *Labeling Madness*. Englewood Cliffs, NJ: Prentice-Hall.
45. Ibid.
46. Ibid., p. 83.
47. Ibid., pp. 82-84.
48. Lois Pratt. 1981. Business Temporal Norms and Bereavement Behavior. *American Sociological Review* 46:317-333.
49. Marris, op. cit., p. 92.
50. Philippe Ariès. 1974. The Reversal of Death. *American Quarterly* 26:536-560.
51. Ibid.
52. Ibid., p. 548.
53. Jeanne Quint Benoliel. 1971. Assessments of Loss and Grief. *Journal of Thanatology* 1:189.
54. Glenn M. Vernon. 1970. *The Sociology of Death*. New York: The Ronald Press.

55. Gorer, op. cit., pp. 76-80. See also Maurice Lamm. 1969. *The Jewish Way in Death and Mourning*. New York: Jonathan David.
56. Paul N. Rosenblatt et al. 1976. *Grief and Mourning in Cross-Cultural Perspective.* New Haven: HRAF Press.
57. Beverly Raphael. 1983. *The Anatomy of Bereavement.* New York: Basic Books, p. 47.
58. Bowlby, op. cit., p. 332.
59. Lorraine D. Siggins. 1966. Mourning: A Critical Survey of the Literature. *International Journal of Psychoanalysis* 47:268.
60. Richard A. DeVaul and Sidney Zisook. 1976. Unresolved Grief. *Postgraduate Medicine* 59:267.
61. Thomas C. Welu. 1975. Presenting Pathological Bereavement, in Bernard Schoenberg et al., eds., *Bereavement: Its Psychosocial Aspects.* New York: Columbia University Press.
62. Siggins, op. cit.
63. Durkheim, op. cit., pp. 442-449; Rosenblatt, op. cit.
64. Lindemann, op. cit., pp. 215-221.
65. Lifton, 1976, op. cit., p. 21.
66. Lifton, 1979, op. cit., p. 175.
67. Ibid.
68. Maurice J. Barry. 1973. The Prolonged Grief Reaction. *Mayo Clinic Proceedings* 48:329-335.
69. Ibid., p. 335.
70. Philipp E. Bornstein and Paula Clayton. 1972. The Anniversary Reaction. *Diseases of the Nervous System* 33:443-456.
71. Lindemann, op. cit., pp. 215-219.
72. Adrian Verwoerdt. 1976. *Clinical Geropsychiatry*. Baltimore: Williams & Wilkins, p. 75.
73. DeVaul and Zisook, op. cit.
74. Lindemann, op. cit., p. 216.
75. Ibid.
76. Gorer, op. cit., pp. 85-87.
77. Albert Cain and Barbara Cain. 1964. On Replacing a Dead Child. *Journal of the American Academy of Child Psychiatry* 3:443-456.
78. Ibid. p. 445.
79. Doris Lund. 1974. *Eric.* New York: Dell, pp. 11-12.
80. Becker, op. cit., pp. 47-66.
81. Lindemann, op. cit., pp. 220-221.
82. Glick et al., op. cit., p. 294.
83. Kathy Charmaz. 1980. *The Social Reality of Death*. Reading, MA: Addison-Wesley, p. 286.
84. Therese A. Rando. 1983. An Investigation of Grief and Adaptation in Parents Whose Children Have Died from Cancer. *Journal of Pediatric Psychology* 8:3-20.
85. Paula J. Clayton et al. 1973. Anticipatory Grief and Widowhood. *British Journal of Psychiatry* 122:47-51.
86. Glick et al., op. cit., p. 256.
87. Ibid.
88. Elliott Jaques. 1965. Death and the Mid-Life Crisis. *International Journal of Psychoanalysis* 46:502-514.

7

Is Grief Universal? Cultural Variations in the Emotional Reaction to Loss

Wolfgang Stroebe, PhD and Margaret S. Stroebe, PhD

INTRODUCTION

This chapter explores the relationship between culture and grief, investigates whether the core of grief symptoms common to Western cultures can be demonstrated interculturally and discusses the implications of cultural patterning of grief for the theoretical analysis of this emotion. Since psychologists typically lack the inclination or skills to conduct observational studies of a great variety of different cultures, we will base our analysis of cultural variations in grief reactions on ethnographic data collected by anthropologists. This is problematic because emotional components of responses to death, of central interest to psychologists, are not directly the subject matter of anthropologists, who focus on public rituals or mourning customs.[1]

Can we draw any inferences about private grief experiences from such public display of mourning behavior? The answer to this question depends to some extent on the theory of emotion on which one's understanding of grief is based. If we conceive of emotional experience as the subjective reflection of a bodily state, then grief as the physiologically driven emotional response to loss can be clearly distinguished from the norm-governed public display of emotions involved in mourning. If, on the other hand, one accepts that the emotional experience is itself shaped by social norms, that both grief and mourning are socially constituted response patterns,[2] then the study of mourning rituals may well provide valuable information on the nature of the grief experience in a given culture. To clarify this issue and to further our understanding of the nature of emotional responses, we begin our discussion of the cultural relativity of grief with a brief review of some of the basic assumptions of emotion theory.

THE ROLE OF CULTURAL FACTORS IN EMOTION

There are two potential avenues by which cultural factors may shape emotional experience, namely through *appraisal processes* and through *feeling rules*. Ekman[3] argued that the emotional reactions to most events are learned, and learned in such a fashion that the elicitors will often vary with culture. For example, the appraisal of a given situation as joyful or embarrassing is largely determined by cultural factors. Cultural factors may be less important, however, in linking grief to loss experiences. There is evidence from primate research[4] and observational studies of children[5] to suggest that grief is a characteristic response of many species to the loss of an attachment figure and may thus be fairly independent of learning processes. The biological basis of grief has been convincingly argued by Averill[6] and by Bowlby.[7] Human beings, like many other primates, are group-living and require a social form of existence for survival.[8] If separation from the group cannot be avoided (as in the case of the death of a partner) the relevant reactions for returning to it may nevertheless run their course, even if this causes acute psychological and physiological distress.[9]

This would limit the cultural influence on the emotional reaction to loss to one avenue, namely to the shaping of the emotional experience itself. There is a great deal of disagreement among emotion theorists, however, as to whether the emotional experience resulting from the appraisal is merely a reflection of cultural norms or "feeling rules"[10] or patterned by the bodily reactions elicited by the emotional event. Theories of emotion can be placed on a continuum according to the degree to which they conceive of emotions as physiologically driven or shaped by culture. At one extreme we have the proprioceptive-feedback theories of James,[11] Lange,[12] Izard,[13] and Tomkins,[14] who understand emotions as determined by bodily states. The other extreme is represented by the social constructivist approaches of Averill[15] and Hochschild,[16] for whom emotions are culturally constituted.

The Proprioceptive-Feedback Theory of James and Lange

The best-known version of a proprioceptive-feedback theory is that of James,[17] considered so similar to Lange's[18] approach that the two are usually referred to as the James-Lange theory. The basic tenet of this theory has been aptly formulated by James[19] in his widely quoted statement:

> Bodily changes follow directly the perception of the exciting fact, and that our feelings of the same changes as they occur is the emotion. Common sense says we lose our fortune, are sorry, and weep; we meet a bear, are frightened, and run; we are insulted by a rival, are angry, and strike. The hypothesis here to be defended says that this order of sequence is incorrect, that the one mental state is not immediately induced by the other and that the bodily manifestations must first be interposed between. The more rational statement is that we feel sorry because we cry; angry, because we strike; afraid because we tremble; and not that we cry, strike, or tremble, because we are sorry, angry or fearful, as the case may be.[20]

Thus, James argued that our subjective emotional experience is patterned by the feedback from the activity of our bodily organs. The two sources of bodily information he considered are expressive behavior and autonomic or visceral action.

According to this theory, the quality of the experience of grief is determined by the feedback from the physiological changes that take place in grieving. Grief is the subjective reflection of the feedback from changes in the state of various bodily systems such as the facial muscles, "the weeping, with its profuse secretion of tears, its swollen reddened face, red eyes, and augmented secretion from the nasal mucous membrane," the "weakness of the entire voluntary motor apparatus," the contraction of the "vasomotor apparatus," the contraction of the smaller vessels of the lung (which Lange claimed were responsible for the breathlessness typical in grief) and many other changes "which are so indefinitely numerous and subtle that the entire organism may be called a sounding board."[21]

Although James[22] explicitly considered expressive behavior as one of the sources of bodily information, most textbook descriptions of the James-Lange theory misrepresent it as a theory that construes emotion solely in terms of feedback from viscera and the autonomous nervous system. Expressive behavior is not even mentioned as a source of bodily information in some of the most widely read accounts.[23] Since cultural factors have little effect on autonomic and visceral action, there is no place in such a theory for cultural influences on emotional experience. Thus, little variability should be expected across cultures in the symptomatology of emotions.

If one consults James[24] directly, it becomes obvious, however, that cultural factors could influence emotional experience in his version of the proprioceptive-feedback theory. James not only assumed that facial feedback was one of the sources of bodily information that patterned our emotional experience, but he also suggested that one could block feelings by enacting expressive patterns which were in conflict with the emotions one was experiencing at the moment:

> If we wish to conquer undesirable emotional tendencies in ourselves, we must assiduously, and in the first instance coldbloodedly, go through the outward movements of those contrary dispositions which we prefer to cultivate. The reward of persistency will infallibly come, in the fading out of the sullenness or depression, and the advent of real cheerfulness and kindliness in their stead.[25]

Since facial and other outward expressions of emotions are frequently affected by social norms, the assumption that voluntary control of facial expressions can shape the emotional experience suggests one mechanism by which cultural norms can influence emotional experience.

Most of the critics of the proprioceptive-feedback theory completely disregarded James's discussion of the role of facial expression in emotion. Thus, Cannon's[26] devastating attack on the James-Lange theory is exclusively aimed at disproving the role of feedback from viscera and the autonomous nervous system. Cannon[27] argued that if the assumption that our emotions are merely the experiential reflection of certain physiological changes in viscera and the autonomous nervous system were correct, it would follow that different emotions should be associated with different patterns of physiological changes. Furthermore, it should be possible by inducing such reactions (e.g., with epinephrine injections) to create emotional experiences in the individual. Cannon[28] and later Schacter[29] discussed evidence that seemed to demonstrate that neither of these assumptions of the James-Lange theory could be maintained. It was neither possible to distinguish differential patterns of physiological changes associated with different emotions, nor did the induction of arousal through the injection of epinephrine cause emotional experiences.[30] The majority of individuals who had been given epinephrine injections reported feelings of arousal but not emotion.

The Cognition-Arousal Theory

To accommodate these findings, Schacter developed a *cognition-arousal theory* of emotion that conceives of emotions as patterned by cognitions rather than by bodily reactions. The bodily reactions, in this case general physiological arousal, merely constitute the clay from which the emotions are molded. According to this theory, an emotional state is the result of the interaction between two components: an unspecific physiological arousal and a cognition about the arousing situation. Since an emotion is only experienced if the arousal is labeled in terms of the emotionally relevant cognition, Schacter implicitly assumed a third component to be necessary for an emotional experience, that is, the attribution of the arousal as caused by the situation.

Schacter and Singer[31] tested this theory in an ingenious experiment that demonstrated that individuals who had unwittingly been aroused by the injection of what they believed to be a vitamin, but which was in fact epinephrine, experienced different emotions depending on situational cues manipulated by the experimenters. Thus signs were more marked than those of subjects who had been injected with a placebo solution. Although later attempts to replicate these findings have met with little success,[32] Schacter's theory is still the dominant theory of emotion in social psychology as well as sociology.

According to this theory, the experience of grief would result whenever unspecific physiological arousal is attributed to a loss or some other grief-arousing event. By "interpreting" the arousal as *caused by* the loss, the individual feels grief. One limitation of Schacter's theory is that although it is left to individuals to shape their emotional experience, the processes by which individuals learn what they should experience in different situations are not spelled out. Emotional syndromes consist of a differentiated set of responses and it is difficult to understand how different individuals with independent interpretations could consistently mold their arousal into the same complex pattern. One way this consensus could be accounted for in terms of a cognition-arousal theory is to assume that culture patterns emotional experiences by providing individuals with culture-specific *feeling rules*, that is, guidelines about how arousal should be interpreted in various situations. Thus, cultural norms would be the source of both grief and mourning.

The Social Constructivist Approach

This solution has been adopted by the social constructivist approach.[33] According to this perspective, the way that individuals interpret their arousal and what they feel is guided or even determined by cultural norms or feeling rules. These feeling rules are social norms that prescribe certain emotions as appropriate for a given social situation.[34] Similarly, Averill[35] defined emotions as transitory social roles and emphasized that in order to count as a social role, the emotional response must be meaningful in terms of social expectations and that the individuals must attempt to conform their behavior to those expectations. In terms of this approach, grief is a complex syndrome of emotional responses, which is constituted by social norms and rules and incorporates bodily reactions as well as expressive and instrumental actions. If it is accepted, however, that emotional experiences are culturally constituted, it must be assumed that different cultures impose different rules. According to this perspective, therefore, a great deal of variation across cultures has to be expected in the symptomatology of emotional syndromes such as grief.

The Concept of "Emotion Work"

The assumption that emotional experiences are influenced or governed by social norms has implications which go beyond the attributional rules incorporated in Schachter's cognition-arousal theory. Since deviant behavior is negatively sanctioned by society, individuals must be able to control emotional experiences to avoid sanctions and to bring their emotions in line with societal expectations. Hochschild[36] uses the concept of *emotion work* to refer to attempts by individuals to arouse the emotions they think they should feel in a given situation or to suppress emotions they think are inappropriate. From her descriptions of various techniques of emotion work, it becomes evident that Hochschild[37] considers bodily feedback part of the emotional experience and also accepts that there is some interplay between cognition and physiological reactions. She distinguished three techniques:

> One is cognitive: the attempts to change images, ideas, or thoughts in the service of changing the feelings associated with them. A second is bodily: the attempt to change somatic or other physical symptoms of emotion (e.g., trying to breathe slower, trying not to shake). Third, there is expressive emotion work: trying to change expressive gestures in the service of changing inner feeling (e.g., trying to smile, or to cry). This differs from simple display in that it is directed toward change in feeling.[38]

By incorporating these assumptions into the social constructivist approach Hochschild seems to accept that emotions are to some extent patterned by bodily reactions (otherwise it would make little sense to work on them). She thus narrows the gap between her position and that of William James[39] who, as we mentioned earlier, believed that emotions could be controlled through the control of one's facial expression.

Conclusions and Implications

Despite significant discrepancies between the various theories of emotion, all except the simplified version of the proprioceptive-feedback theory allow for some influence of societal norms on the emotion experiences. Thus, only this oversimplified position, which seems to have mainly served the function of a target for social constructivist attacks, would maintain that mourning and grief are completely independent response systems. According to the theory actually espoused by James[40] emotions are shaped by feedback from facial as well as visceral reactions to the emotion-arousing event. Thus, going through the full display of sadness and despair which is required during mourning is likely to evoke some form of emotional experience consistent with this expressive display.

Let us hasten to add, however, that the research on the influence of voluntary facial movements on emotions is less than conclusive. Thus, Tourangeau and Ellsworth,[41] who had subjects watch a film eliciting sadness or no emotion, while holding their facial muscles in the position characteristic of fear or sadness, or in an effortful but nonemotional grimace, did not find any effect of these voluntary facial expressions on emotional experience. However, the fact that the short-term role-playing engaged in by these subjects was insufficient to influence emotional experience does not rule out the possibility that the long-term display of emotions during mourning, which involves posture as well as facial expression, has some impact on altering the mourners' emotions. Furthermore, Laird,[42] a supporter of the facial feedback hypothesis, contrasted the results of ten studies which demonstrated that manipulated facial expression does produce corresponding emotional experience with "Tourangeau and Ellsworth's sole published failure to demonstrate this relation."[43] He also argues that six other studies, using a different but theoretically consistent paradigm, also observed facial feedback effects. However, other researchers in the area of emotion[44] find this evidence less than conclusive.

To the social constructivist both mourning and grief are culturally constituted response patterns or transitory roles which mainly differ in the level of involvement. Thus, from a social constructivist perspective, the study of mourning rituals should provide valid information about the emotional experiences of the mourners. Although social constructivists are somewhat vague about the exact nature of the contribution of bodily reactions to the emotional experience, Hochschild's discussion of emotion work indicates that she accepts that emotional experiences are shaped by both distinct bodily reactions as well as social norms. This position, which avoids complete cultural relativity while allowing for some variation across cultures in emotional symptomatology, seems eminently plausible to us. It appears also to be consistent with the findings of cultural variation in grief symptoms as well as in the duration of grief.

CROSS-CULTURAL VARIATIONS IN SYMPTOMATOLOGY: THE CASE OF CRYING

In view of the limitations of ethnographic descriptions of grief reactions, we will adopt the strategy of examining in detail one symptom, crying, which combines a number of characteristics to make it ideally suited to our purpose. (1) Crying out of sadness is a uniquely human experience: though animals may shed tears because of irritants to the eyes, they never do from sorrow. (2) Crying is considered a normal symptom of grief in the West, provided that its expression is not too extreme or prolonged. (3) The fact that crying is the universal response of babies and small children to unpleasant or painful experiences tends to indicate that crying during bereavement expresses authentic feelings or attempts to communicate socially that such feelings are being experienced. (4) There is evidence to suggest that the link between facial expression of emotion and emotional experience is stable across cultures: studies using facial photographs depicting various emotions have shown that emotional expressions can be correctly identified in all the cultures studied. Thus, Izard[45] reported data from a study of 12 different nations or cultures, which indicated cross-cultural agreement in the categorization of pictures reflecting these basic emotions. Similar results were found by Ekman and Friesen[46] in a study of children and adults in New Guinea, who did not speak English and lived far away from any white settlements. This evidence has been considered strong support for a genetic link between emotional experience and facial expression of emotions.[47]

The Presence of Crying in Other Cultures

Rosenblatt, Walsh and Jackson[48] examined the occurrence of crying among bereaved persons in different cultures, as described in the ethnographic literature on 78 societies. They found reports of crying after bereavement in all but one of the cultures that could be rated on crying after loss (73 societies). In most of the cultures crying was judged to be a frequent response. Rosenblatt and co-workers[49] regarded this as strong evidence that people from cultures very dissimilar to our own respond in a similar way emotionally to what we find here.

But does the fact that crying was absent in one culture imply that this emotional response does not occur universally? Rosenblatt[50] examined this particular culture (the Balinese) in somewhat more detail and at first hand.

They argued that lack of crying when bereaved was in line with Balinese emotional responses in other situations: The investigators observed that sometimes, when recounting tragic events, relaters even laughed or smiled. They interpreted this in terms of an effort to control the emotional response and suggested that the Balinese were fearful that they would cry if they did not force the opposite expression. Rosenblatt related this to religious beliefs which encourage calmness, and to the belief that communication with the gods is impeded if such equanimity is not maintained (personal communication).

Along similar lines the Norwegian anthropologist Wikan,[51] who has done extensive field work in Bali, argued that the assumption that the Balinese do not cry is misleading and built "on the mistaken assumption that the public domain constitutes the whole of a people's culture."[52] She argued that the pressure in Balinese culture against any expression of grief is partly due to the "belief that emotions exert a direct influence on health through their effect on spiritual and bodily resistance to illness and afflictions of every kind."[53] To protect one's health and welfare one must cultivate "good" emotions and attitudes that will strengthen one's spirit and body.

Thus, even though the Balinese tend to suppress the overt expression of grief, there is some evidence that this is due, for cultural reasons, to a stoic suppression of this behavior, rather than to lack of emotional feeling. According to this interpretation, the presence of smiling and laughter during grief in the Balinese is not evidence for the absence of feelings of sorrow, but rather represents a desperate attempt to control them. A similar phenomenon, practiced for a different reason, has been observed among the Japanese, who may smile at strangers or acquaintances during bereavement, not to control their own emotion, but in order not to burden others with their grief.[54]

Occasionally accounts can be found of an absence of crying, or indeed of any emotional expression of grief, following certain types of bereavement (though not of others), which would be the cause of acute grief in the West. For example, Johnson[55] observed that the Yoruba of Nigeria apparently unfeelingly disposed of their dead babies by throwing them into the bush. However, this "barbaric" or "unthinkable" response to loss, in our terms, becomes very understandable when the significance of the death for these bereaved parents is known: Their dead baby, if buried, would be considered as deeply offending the earth shrines who bring fertility and ward off death.[56]

If these analyses are correct, then we have no instances so far of any peoples who respond to loss of a close person with emotional indifference. We return to the discussion of possible exceptions to the universality of grief in the general discussion later. So far we have found evidence to support the position that crying and emotional upset seem to be universal even though overt expression may be tailored to cultural norms and values.

Types and Occasions of Crying in Other Cultures

Rosenblatt's[57] ingenious study was, by the constraints of the data, limited to a secondary analysis of only the occurrence and frequency of crying. If one looks more closely at the crying behavior, then a different impression about the universality of crying during bereavement emerges, for, just as there are individual differences in crying behavior within our own culture, so are there differences not only in the frequency but also in the type and timing of crying in and between other cultures.

To illustrate, reports of crying at funerals come in from all over the world: It seems to be a usual time for people to cry. But here the similarity between cultures ends. In the West crying from grief is typically spontaneous. Those close to the deceased person tend to be overcome with grief and to shed tears, sob, or even cry out loud. This is permissible behavior and evokes sympathy rather than censure from others. But it is not required by custom. In certain other societies, on the other hand, crying is not merely tolerated but required at certain moments. At other times it is strictly forbidden, when weeping and wailing and tears can be seen to stop as soon as they started. Such ceremonial or ritual crying has been the subject of much anthropological investigation. While psychologists, due to the absence of further evidence, might tend to discount such information as irrelevant to the emotion of grief, such analyses have been central to anthropology. For examples of such ceremonial weeping and interpretations regarding the emotion of grief one needs to look at anthropological or ethnographic accounts more closely.

A classic example is recorded in *The Andaman Islanders* by Radcliffe-Brown,[58] who analyzed ritual weeping and who based his whole theory of social integration on the ritual expression of sentiments, taking the Andaman Islanders as an example. Radcliffe-Brown recorded the occasions on which the Andamese "sits down and wails and howls and the tears stream down his or her face."[59] The occasions for such displays include specific times after death. For example, at the end of the period of mourning there is communal weeping, indulged in by friends of mourners who have not themselves mourned.

The pattern of ritualistic weeping among the Andamese contrasts with that among the Bara of Madagascar. Huntington and Metcalfe[60] reported that the Bara wail ritually only at funerals, and at only two specific times during the ceremony: While the body is lying in the women's hut before burial, and just before the secondary burial of the exhumed bodies. During preparations for burial and exhumation weeping is strictly prohibited. Different again is the pattern among the Thonga of South Africa. Junod[61] described the funeral procedure after the burial and prayer as follows: "The wailing begins. The women get on their feet and shout loudly, throwing themselves on the ground. The wife of the deceased cries more than anyone else."[62]

Mandelbaum[63] gave a detailed account of funeral practices among the Kota people, who live in a remote part of India. As in the above examples, public weeping occurs at specific times. Mandelbaum describes how the Dry Funeral begins. This ceremony is a second funeral held once each year, or every two years, for all those who have died since the previous Dry Funeral. Mandelbaum[64] gives a compelling account of weeping behavior at the commencement of this ceremony:

> Bereaved women stop in their tracks. A rush of sorrow suffuses them; they sit down where they are, cover their heads with their shoulder cloths, and wail and sob through much of that day and the next. Men of a bereaved household have much to do in preparation for the ceremony and do not drop everything to mourn aloud as do the bereaved women. But even they stop from time to time to weep. Most grief-stricken of all are the widows and widowers.[65]

A final example of ritualistic weeping comes from Papua New Guinea. Among the Huli people keening begins when someone dies. Scores of women gather, as the news spreads, to join in. They gather at the *duguanda*, which literally means "crying house," where the body lies, and weep freely, bewailing their loss. Frankel and Smith[66] describe the crying as intense and continuous. It reaches a pitch of anguish at the interment the following day. After the funeral those women closest to the deceased may return to the duguanda, sometimes remaining there for weeks and crying intermittently. Only women are permitted to do this. As Frankel and Smith[67] note, "In contrast to this intimacy of shared grief available to women, a weeping man seems a comparatively solitary figure. His fellows will try to distract him, jollying him along, and seeming to suffer some discomfort at his display of grief."[68]

Sex Differences in Crying Behavior in Other Cultures

The above and other anthropological accounts show that, as in the West, it is more often the women than the men who cry following death. Rosenblatt's[69] analysis of the ethnographic literature supports this; of 60 societies which could be rated for sex differences in crying during bereavement, 32 were judged to have similar crying frequencies for males and females. In all of the remaining 28, adult females had a greater crying frequency than men. It seems that there is a culturally determined inclination of men in certain societies to suppress tears. This does not necessarily mean either that men experience less emotion of grief or that the sex difference is completely culturally determined: Bindra[70] reported that men experience watery eyes significantly more often than women, whereas women were significantly more prone to have flowing tears. Further, Bindra suggests that greater amounts of lacrimal fluid released by young women may make it more difficult for them to suppress the flow of tears.

The Interpretation of Ritualistic Crying

The above examples clearly show that, even though crying may occur in practically all societies, very different patterns of weeping following a death can be found. How can this be interpreted? One central issue here is whether the ritualistic crying that has so frequently been documented by anthropologists is actually indicative of grief, that is, of an emotional reaction of sadness. The impression from these accounts is hardly one of the spontaneous expression of feeling that we expect in the West. In contrast to the uncontrollable overflowing of tears that bereaved people here are prone to, crying in these other cultures often appears mandatory, and the individual appears to be in complete control of the production of tears. Are they really sad or are they indifferent?

Anthropologists have offered several interpretations of ritualistic crying. Their accounts reflect implicit theories of emotions which could be placed somewhere between the positions of James and Hochschild. They typically assume some kind of interaction between ritual crying and emotional experience. Thus, Durkheim[71] concluded from his early study of funeral rites of Aboriginal Australians that ritualistic weeping is experienced by the mourners with an emotional reaction of sorrow. Emotional feelings of sadness were not, however, thought to lead to participation in the funeral rite in the first place. Durkheim[72] believed that the emotional reaction of grief actually developed and was intensified by participation: "Sorrow, like joy, becomes exalted and amplified when leaping from mind to mind, and therefore expresses itself outwardly in the form of exuberant and violent movements."[73] Thus the obligatory display is thought to lead to an emotion of grief. And by sharing the sorrow of others, commitment to them and to the group as a whole is confirmed. Radcliffe-Brown[74] argued in a similar way that the sentiment of sorrow was not the cause of ritualistic behavior such as communal weeping: Mourners came to feel emotion through participation. But there is an important difference between the two theories.

Radcliffe-Brown did not interpret the emotional response as one of sorrow at this point, but as one of a feeling of attachment between persons. He argued that it was the purpose of the rite to affirm the existence of a social bond between two or more persons.[75]

Other accounts of ritualistic weeping are at odds with either of these two interpretations. Henry[76] and Rosenblatt,[77] who reported the former study by Henry, have no trouble in accepting the notion that feelings of grief similar to those in the West are observed. Henry[78] described the death of a baby among the Kaingang of South America:

> I was awakened several hours before dawn by the frantic keening of Waikome. One by one, others joined her, and I knew then that the baby was dead. As I watched, the emotion gradually grew more intense.... There was no play-acting here, no singling out of those whom relationship obliged to weep from those who could just look on. Those who were not affected kept aloof and performed their daily tasks.[79]

So which, if any, of these interpretations is correct? As they are not really contradictory, they could all be valid, the differences being either due to the perspective taken or to differences in the cultures studied. Thus, Durkheim's suggestion that ritual crying will intensify existing emotions would be quite consistent with our theoretical perspective. Furthermore, as crying also signals to others that an individual experiences grief, it could increase the feeling of attachment within a cultural group. Finally, the mourning rituals of the Kaingang may differ from those of the cultures studied by Durkheim and Radcliffe-Brown. If there were no normative prescriptions regulating crying, it is quite possible that those Kaingang who cried did so because they were overcome by feelings of grief.

Unfortunately, it is very difficult to evaluate the validity of these interpretations given only the data presented by these authors. For example, one has no way of knowing from the anthropological accounts whether the Andamese or Thonga either feel sorrow during ritual weeping, or whether their grief may have caused them to weep privately or at other times which were not the subject of observation. At the other extreme, the account by Henry[80] of the Kaingang clearly attributes an emotional response of grief as occurring during ritual wailing. This may be a correct interpretation, but it is also possibly a purely subjective and unwarranted interpretation on the part of one observer.

Attribution theorists[81] have made it clear that when there are strong norms to behave in a certain way, personal attributions cannot be made. Thus, when mourning customs are strongly prescribed, no one can tell whether the individuals are play acting or whether they are feeling grief. We would argue, however, that the existence of cultural norms which regulate crying during mourning can also be used as evidence for the universality of grief. Norms are not ends in themselves, but typically develop for some reason. If there never had been any crying during mourning in a given society, it would seem pointless for norms regulating crying to develop.

Conclusions

The evidence presented above does indicate that crying is a frequent response to loss through death by some people in both Western and non-Western cultures. We have no reports of an absence of crying through indifference to the death of a close relative or friend in other cultures. The examples given above show differences in the occasions after a death on which crying is appropriate, tolerated, or even required, and in the type of crying that is exhibited publicly. But it is also remarkable how consistently, despite cultural differences, crying behavior occurs among bereaved persons.

SYMPTOMS OF GRIEF PARTICULAR TO NON-WESTERN CULTURES

In reading accounts of bereavement in other cultures, whether preliterate or literate, past or contemporary, one becomes aware, not only of responses general to cultures and of responses which typify only Western cultures, but also of the possibility of finding symptoms with which we are unfamiliar in the West.

Self-Infliction of Injury

One of the most obvious of these is self-infliction of injury, documented so vividly by Durkheim[82] for Australian tribal peoples. Durkheim cites an account made by an ethnographer called Stanbridge:

> Everywhere...we find this same frenzy for beating one's self, lacerating one's self and burning one's self. In central Victoria, when death visits a tribe there is great weeping and lamentation amongst the women, the elder portion of who lacerate their temples with their nails. The parents of the deceased lacerate themselves fearfully, especially if it be an only son whose loss they deplore. The father beats and cuts his head with a tomahawk until he utters bitter groans, the mother sits by the fire and burns her breasts and abdomen with a small firestick. Sometimes the burns thus inflicted are so severe as to cause death.[83]

It is striking how widespread various practices of cutting or mutilation of the body are, or have been, during mourning, even though not apparent in Western cultures today: Self-infliction of injury is recorded in the Old Testament (Jeremiah, Amos, Isaiah) and in ancient Greece, Assyria, Armenia, and Rome. It has been described for Africans, Abyssinians, Liberians, Native North Americans, Turks, Polynesians, and Australian tribes, among others.[84] Despite variations, the basic pattern is very similar across the different groups, the world over and throughout time.

The significance of self-mutilation has been a matter of much debate.[85] Are these acts of anger and aggression turned inward (just another way of blaming oneself and showing remorse), or are they to keep off the spirit of the dead and derive from fear and dread of vengeance from above? Do they relate to inner emotions at all? Durkheim's opinion was that such rituals have the function of strengthening social bonds and confirming group solidarity though, as Huntington and Metcalfe[86] query: "How can he claim that the violent, destructive, unplanned-for and negative behavior surrounding a death fulfills this sociologically Pollyanna-like function?"[87]

Cawte[88] maintained not only that self-infliction of injury still occurred among Australian Aborigines but that this was motivated by fear of blame, which compounded "true" feelings of grief:

> A variant of reactive depression is common-place aboriginal grief. After misfortunes ranging from trivial injury to the death of a dog, a group of natives is seen sitting in a ring wailing and lamenting. After a serious loss or a death, self-infliction of injury is still routine, and bears little resemblance to the attempted suicide common in modern western culture. In all this formal expression of grief, the recognizable motivation is fear of blame. When society attributes misfortune to evil-wishing by some person, extreme scrupulosity in mourning is necessary to disavow personal blame. The motive of wishing to avoid being blamed for the incident compounds whatever true grief may be felt.[89]

If the interpretation of self-infliction of injuries as aggression toward the self is correct, then parallels can certainly be found in Western cultures. In this case, the overt expression would be the cultural variant, whereas the underlying emotional feeling (self-blame, anger, remorse, etc.) would be similar across cultures. Again, the emotional concomitants of the observed behavior need further investigation before firm conclusions can be made.

Horror at the Corpse and Fear of the Ghost

Two further symptoms of grief in non-Western cultures are readily found in the literature. Anthropologists have focused on horror at the corpse (accompanied at times by a feeling of contamination) and fear of the ghost as being the dominant feelings of survivors. They (notably Wilhelm Wundt) have been criticized by Malinowski[90] for assuming this "half-truth," and the point is well taken:

> The emotions are extremely complex and even contradictory; the dominant elements, love of the dead and loathing of the corpse, passionate attachment to the personality still lingering about the body and a shattering fear of the gruesome thing that has been left over, these two elements seem to mingle and play into each other.[91]

Nevertheless, these feelings seem to be specific to certain non-Western cultures, with many of the reports coming from earlier times. The Hopi, for example, are afraid of the dead[92] and, like the Kotas and many other peoples, believe that death brings pollution:

> The sovereign desire is to dismiss the body and the event. The urge is to dispatch the spirit to another realm where it will not challenge the Hopi ideals of good, harmonious, happy existence in *this* world and where, as a being of another and well-known kind, it can be methodically controlled by the ritual apparatus of the Hopi culture.[93]

Further accounts of fear of the ghost of a deceased person abound, for example, among the Native American Maya[94] and Navajo.[95] These are in contrast with accounts from the West, where fear of the corpse or ghost are not acknowledged among symptoms of grief. They would, in fact, probably be considered pathological here if overt or verbalized. On the other hand, until recently death was a relatively taboo topic and dissociation from the corpse was almost complete: Few Westerners, in comparison with those from other cultures, have actually seen a corpse.[96] Further, in the West, even if people typically show no fear of the ghost or spirit of the deceased, great respect is felt toward them; no evil should be spoken of the departed, they are memorialized and prayed for.

Conclusions

Certain symptoms of grief with which we are unfamiliar do appear in certain other cultures. It is interesting to note that those described above appear not idiosyncratically for just one single non-Western culture, but for a number of cultures, as if here, too, one is observing a "core" response to bereavement. It is also notable that the manifestations of these symptoms can often be tied closely to beliefs about death and the afterlife. Finally, while the expression of grief may vary across cultures (due, for example, to these different beliefs), similarities in core responses (e.g., self-injury, with aggression toward the self) can be drawn between the non-Western symptoms described above and those found in Western cultures.

PHASES OF GRIEF IN CROSS-CULTURAL PERSPECTIVE

Bereaved people in Western cultures move through a succession of reactions to loss over the course of the weeks and months following a death. The "typical" sequence of phases among the bereaved in Western cultures can be summarized as follows. The numbness and shock of the first few hours or days is replaced by yearning, pining, and searching for the deceased. When the futility of attempts to recover the beloved person is realized, and this may take many weeks, despair and depression set in. This is a time of great desolation and feelings of hopelessness, when life seems hardly worth living at times. It is only very gradually that the bereaved adjust to life without the loved person and restitution and recovery begin to take place. In fact, bereavement researchers[97] have come to realize that the whole process of adaptation to life without the deceased may take very much longer than the calendar year that is typically regarded as the acceptable time for "getting over" a loss. Further, although symptoms may recede and greater proportions of each day be spent in equilibrium and even enjoyment, at later periods, too, it is possible for bouts of utter despair or yearning to recur.

Information from other cultures provides fascinating contrasts with the pattern of recovery outlined above. In some, not only are mourning practices rigidly and stringently laid down but the timing for inherent feelings of grief of the bereaved are also prescribed. In the following sections examples of very short phases of grief as well as of extended phases will be discussed.

Abbreviated Phases of Grief

One of the most extreme examples of abbreviated responses to loss occurs among the Navajo, which clearly demonstrates the "interplay between various psychodynamic mechanisms and cultural influences," as Miller and Schoenfeld,[98] who studied this tribe, phrased it. A traditional pattern of mourning is followed not only by those who adhere to traditional religious beliefs but also by many Native Americans who are members of the Christian churches which have been founded on this reservation. The accepted pattern of mourning among the Navajo is limited to a period of only four days. During this period, and this period alone, is expression of grief and discussion of the deceased condoned. Even then, an excessive show of emotion is frowned upon by the community. When the four days have passed, the bereaved are expected to return to normal everyday life, not to grieve, and neither to speak of the deceased nor discuss their loss. Underlying this is the fear of the power of the spirit of the dead person and the belief that this can do the living harm.

It certainly looks from this account as though the Navajo recover from loss without the long and harrowing months of grief that are to be endured elsewhere. For these people, normal functioning is resumed at a time when bereaved people in the West have hardly realized the impact of their loss and would scarcely be in a frame of mind to do routine chores, let alone take up a full working and social life as if nothing had happened. Miller and Schoenfeld[99] are, however, of the opinion that there is a high price to pay for this apparently easy transition through bereavement, at least among the Navajo. They argue that there is a direct causal link between prohibition of mourning and grieving and the occurrence of pathological grief reactions (notably of depression) among these people.

The Navajo are not alone in the brevity of their reactions to loss. Similarly abbreviated responses have been recorded for a number of other cultures.[100] The pattern found among the Navajo is, for example, not unlike that of another Native American tribe, the Maya; for here, too, at least in ancient times, the period of mourning and apparent grieving lasted a matter of days rather than months. Steele[101] reported that this was a time at which the community sanctioned the display of intense feelings of loss and despair during the first four days of bereavement, as exemplified in profuse crying. But social pressure was brought to bear on the bereaved to delimit the mourning period and curtail overt expressions of grief beyond this time. The bereaved were encouraged by others to turn their thoughts and activities away from the deceased. Again, mourning rituals served the important purpose of "providing a safe separation of the spirit from the earth and the speeding of it on its journey to the other world, where the soul or spirit would be of no danger to the living."[102] A widow would become "unclean" on the death of her husband, and remain so as long as the tie to the deceased remained. Pressure was therefore strong for the rituals to be completed and the widow's time of uncleanliness to be over.

A final example of abbreviated grief is worth considering because of the contrast with the above examples and with phases in the West. The Samoans, whose key value is reciprocity, were reported by Ablon[103] to recover rapidly and comparatively painlessly from loss of loved ones, even when, as Ablon observed, this followed a sudden and disastrous fire. Some five years after this catastrophic event Ablon questioned the bereaved retrospectively on their grief experiences, using items derived from Lindemann's[104] account of grief in the West. While, not surprisingly, little active grief was elicited, due to the time interval since the catastrophe, what was remarkable was the Samoans' reactions to Lindemann's items. Ablon was repeatedly told the Samoans "do not have these things" and that there was no widespread depression among bereaved persons. The implication of this is that Samoans, in contrast to the Navajo, do not suffer the risk of pathological grief due to the shortness of the grieving period.

Protracted Phases of Grief

Far more protracted are the phases of readjustment among the Kota of south India. These people still, to a large extent, follow the ancient forms of funeral rites of their culture, which required two funeral ceremonies, the so-called Green and Dry Funerals. Interestingly, the terms "green" and "dry" are analogous to a cut plant. The first funeral, held shortly after the death when the body is cremated, is called "green" because the loss is new in the minds of the bereaved and a fresh experience to them. The second ceremony usually takes place at annual intervals and is a large and extended ceremony (lasting eleven days) for all those who have died since the previous one. It is termed "dry" because by then the loss is dried up, withered, or sere. Thus, these terms seem analogous, too, to psychological reactions of severance from the deceased.

Certainly, the Dry Funeral marks the ending of the sanctioning of grief. The ceremony provides ample opportunity for the venting of sorrow, which, Mandelbaum[105] suggests, may help the bereaved to overcome their grief. After a first phase in which the deceased are individually memorialized, and one during which a second cremation is enacted (when low voices and pervasive sadness characterize the atmosphere) there is an abrupt ending of the mood of somberness. When the morning star is sighted by those at the funeral place, dancing and feasting suddenly begin, and the widowed perform a number of rituals each of which bring them back more closely to normal social life. When night falls a pot is ceremoniously broken, the mourners return quickly to their village, and the widowed have sexual intercourse, preferably with a sibling of the dead spouse. This signifies a further normalization in social relationships of the widowed. Mandelbaum,[106] in detailing such roles and prescriptions for behavior among the Kota, emphasized how they served an important function in bringing the bereaved through their shock and sorrow and back to a normal status in the society. Although the bereaved are encouraged to let their grief have overt expression, the period for indulging this is limited far more specifically and stringently than is normal practice in the West.

That the Kota Indians grieve for their dead is evident to Mandelbaum,[107] who describes the widowed as shocked and disoriented by loss, as being bewildered and withdrawn from others. Personal sorrow is felt though its expression is culturally stereotyped and clearly prescribed across time, as are the newly widowed role requirements. There are, then, both notable similarities and notable differences with Western cultures in the phases through which the grief-stricken Kota pass.

Like Mandelbaum,[108] Mathison[109] also related favorable adjustment to loss of a loved one to the more structured ritualized role of the widowed in non-Western cultures. The role provided for widows in the Trobiand Islands, for example, was regarded as serving as an "effective emotional release." Mathison described the first phase of grief among these islanders as encompassing the several days of funeral rites, during which the widow is expected to howl loudly with grief and shave her head. Following this stage, she enters a cage built into her home, and remains in the dark there for a period of 6 months to 2 years, in order to avoid her husband's ghost from finding her. Maladaptive as this may seem to us, she is never left alone, and at the end of the prescribed period she can anticipate a ceremonial cleansing, being attired in a colorful grass skirt, and being free again to remarry, which, we are told, very often happens. Mathison[110] comments on this healthy situation as follows:

> The widow has the comfort of a highly structured period of mourning in which she knows exactly what response society expects of her. She is given a socially accepted way to express grief openly. Though she has lost one role, she is supplied with another very formal role to play out for a definite period of time. She can then look forward to assuming the role of wife again with the approval of her kinsmen and peers.[111]

Among the most highly prescribed sequences of mourning rituals are those of Orthodox Jews. The length of time traditionally permitted for completion of mourning is a calendar year, after which the bereaved are expected to return to a more normal social life. Jewish customs have been described as highly supportive for the bereaved, as they detail in almost every particular just how the bereaved person should behave. In line with this clear prescription, Gorer[112] found that the Orthodox Jewish community in Britain stood alone as one which knew how to console a bereaved person on first contact after loss. The mourner is greeted with a standard phrase expressing condolence and this demands no reply; after it has been spoken the conversation proceeds normally.

Pollock[113] goes so far as to suggest that each of the several stages of mourning prescribed by the Jewish religion can be related to one of the psychological phases through which healthy grieving progresses. It is certainly true to say that the bereaved are assisted both by the family and the community to face loss. Strict laws and rituals exist not only for the bereaved but also for their comforters, the latter role being frequently praised in the Torah. Thus, for example, the 7 days of mourning after the burial, called the "Shiva," is a time when the family is united the mourners generally being gathered in one dwelling, namely, "the House of Shiva." This is a period of lamentation and weeping, when friends come to express concern, share their sorrow and give companionship. The bereaved are encouraged to talk of their loss and are offered comfort. This process of grieving is considered beneficial.[114] The following period, called the "Sheloshim," which covers the 30 days after burial, provides a transition for mourners to return to more active involvement in community affairs. The end of this period marks the end of ritual mourning. Finally, the "Unveiling" at the end of 30 days is a commemorative service and the formal dedication of the stone to the deceased. This service indicates that the soul of the deceased has been redeemed and it signifies the official closure of the mourning period.[115] However, this does not mean that the loved one will be forgotten. The expression of grief is encouraged on anniversaries and on certain holidays, and it is considered normal to dwell on and to relate memories of the departed at times of joy and sadness. The community continues to support the bereaved at these times, although excessive grief is frowned upon.

Conclusions

Given only these few examples, it is evident that there are substantial differences in the rules laid down by cultures as to how long the deceased should be grieved over and how long mourning should last. Grief is channeled in all cultures along specified lines. Anthropologists have frequently observed that among the few universal practices pertaining across all cultures are those which dispose of the deceased and prescribe mourning behavior for the survivors. But what is sanctioned or prohibited in one culture may differ diametrically from what is or is not permitted in another.

That the individual emotional response of grief to loss is influenced and also, to some extent, ritualized by mourning rites is generally accepted by the social anthropologists who have provided most of the information. We have no way of knowing, however, whether a Navajo or a Samoan widow who, after four days of mourning and grieving apparently puts her loss behind her and returns to normal daily routine life, actually succeeds in grieving no more. What one can say, quite unequivocally, is that the phases of mourning and the overt expression of grief across the duration of bereavement are not universal.

CULTURAL VARIABLES AND DIFFERENCES IN THE DURATION OF GRIEF

It becomes evident from the preceding examples of differences in the duration of grief, that factors such as attitudes toward death, religious beliefs, or persisting ties or bonding with the deceased are generally employed in explanation of differences in the duration of grief. These variables all have to do with the meaning that the loss has for bereaved persons in a particular culture. However, as follows from some of the theoretical approaches described at the beginning of the chapter, others have focused on the possibility that the performance of prescribed bereavement rituals themselves have an impact on the duration and course that grief will take. A third group of variables reflects cultural difference in social support during bereavement. Clearly, these three types of explanation are neither mutually exclusive nor are they contradictory. Because researchers have tended to focus on the one or the other type of cultural variable, they are considered separately below.

The Personal Meaning of Loss

In Western cultures the bond that is felt with the deceased person by their bereaved is not relinquished easily or quickly. Understanding the process through which it is considered necessary to go to sever this tie has been given a place of central importance by theorists in the field, notably, Freud,[116] Lindemann[117] and Bowlby.[118] The period of searching for the deceased is understood in terms of attempts to recover the lost object and retain the tie; constant talking of the deceased, recalling joint experiences, hearing her voice or movement around the house, preparing things unwittingly (setting the table for two), treasuring possessions and photos, are all seen as indications of a fundamental desire not to relinquish the bond with the lost person.

Natural though this bonding seems to us, it is by no means universally found, and systematic differences in patterns of grief can be related to cultural differences in the personal meaning of loss. This is illustrated by contrasting two very different cultural groups, the Hopi and the Japanese. Among the Hopi of Arizona the funeral ceremony, in contrast with other ceremonies which are held with great elaboration, is a small and meager affair, conducted and forgotten as quickly as possible. The reason for this is that the Hopi dislike and are afraid of death and the dead. After the burial service the survivors try to forget the deceased and carry on life as usual. This, too, is in accordance with their general beliefs about the afterworld. Many rituals are performed for the express purpose of breaking off contact between mortals and spirits.

In this context their strong desire to forget the deceased as individuals becomes understandable. They in fact express no desire whatsoever to recall the memory of a deceased person for any reason at all. Certainly, no occasion is given for singing the praises or recounting the contribution of the deceased person to the society: "The sovereign desire is to dismiss the body and the event."[119]

Quite different is the meaning of loss and its impact on personal adjustment of survivors that is found in Japan. Both in Shintoism, the indigenous religion of the country, and in Buddhism, which is also widely practiced, the deceased become ancestors. In the Shinto religion the deceased become *Kami-sama*. *Kami* means god, or divine. As Yamamoto[120] explained, the significance for the bereaved of the belief that the deceased become ancestors is that they can maintain contact with the departed person: "The ancestor remains accessible, the mourner can talk to the ancestor, he can offer goodies such as food or even cigars, altogether the ancestor is revered, fed, watered, and remains with the bereaved."[121] Contact with the deceased in this way is facilitated by the presence in practically all homes of an altar, where the ancestor is worshipped (or, more accurately, revered).

Yamamoto[122] attributed the relatively easy acceptance of loss among the Japanese widows, as compared with those in Western cultures, to the belief in an afterlife for the deceased, and to the cultivation of the sense of their continued presence as ancestors.

These two examples illustrate that identification mechanisms are closely bound to a society's beliefs about the meaning of life and death, and the nature of the afterlife. But these are not the only mechanisms underlying cultural differences in the meaning of loss. For not only is the tie to the deceased closely related to these beliefs, but also to the extent of dependency on the deceased and the availability of others after death as replacements. Volkart and Michael[123] cite an example of the Ifaluk, a Micronesian culture among whom the immediate family is less central in the upbringing of children than is typically found elsewhere. Grief for family members is keenly felt, but of short duration, ending usually with the funeral. Likewise, in contrast to societies such as the traditional Japanese described above, where veneration of the deceased is expected of the widowed, are those which provide for any early replacement of loss and continuity of the role of wife. Among the Ubena tribes in Africa, where the widowed are provided with new mates on the death of their husbands, grief, though genuinely felt, is also short-lived.[124]

It is evident from research in the West that the trauma of loss or separation is greater, the more the attachment or dependency toward the lost person.[125] What becomes evident from the cross-cultural variations described above is that the cultural norms with regard to patterns of attachment strongly affect the emotional response following death.

The Impact of Bereavement Rituals

Just as more attention has been paid to the description of mourning customs and funeral rites than to the cross-cultural patterning of the emotion of grief, so have theoretical analyses been directed toward explaining the social function of these customs rather than looking at their potential benefit for, or adverse effect on, the individual. Funeral rites have been interpreted as serving the social function of strengthening group solidarity,[126] as reflecting and shaping social values,[127] as "rites of passage" by incorporating individuals into the group and its culturally defined roles and statuses,[128] as ensuring continued social cohesion,[129] and as social bonding.[130]

In contrast, early interpretations of grief[131] disregarded completely the potential impact of mourning rites and other social influences on the course of grief. With his critique of this intrapersonal perspective and his analysis of the role that society plays in assisting the bereaved through their grief, Gorer[132] was largely responsible for a shift in interest of researchers in the field to a more interpersonal approach. Since then, the role that rituals play in dealing with grief has been emphasized by a number of researchers in the area of bereavement (e.g., Marris;[133] Firth;[134] Eisenbruch;[135] Mandelbaum;[136] Volkart and Michael[137]). Most of these accounts claim that adherence to rituals moderates the bereavement reaction in a positive way, and many take the example of the United States as a culture which has become deritualized and which leaves bereaved persons helpless as to what to do following loss. This was argued by Mandelbaum[138] in his chapter "The Social Uses of Funeral Rites." It is supported, too, by the study by Aguilar and Wood,[139] who claimed that Mexican funeral rites lead to good bereavement outcomes, and who criticized the impact of North American culture on Mexican patterns.

Salzberger[140] similarly criticized the ideological and ritual deficits in the West, and pointed to the negative consequences for bereaved persons. Gorer[141] drew attention to the fact that the majority of bereaved persons in Britain suffered long-lasting grief and depression because of the lack of secular rituals to help them and reincorporate them into society.

Pollock,[142] as noted above, argued that Orthodox Jewish mourning rites follow the "natural" grief process, that "cultural mechanisms ... were probably derived from the awareness of intrapsychic needs of the individuals, singly and collectively, and the necessity for achieved social-psychic equilibrium through institutional regulations."[143] It would be useful to know whether Jewish persons who adhere to these traditional stages adjust better to bereavement than those who do not.

That extreme brevity of rituals could also have negative effects on coping with grief was suggested by Miller and Schoenfeld.[144] In their study of the mourning rite of the Navajo, which limits mourning to a period of four days only, Miller and Schoenfeld[145] argue that there is a direct causal link between the prohibition of mourning and an increase in the incidence of postbereavement depression among these people. Unfortunately, the evidence presented to support this suggestion is rather inconclusive.

Finally, a recent proponent of the view that bereavement practices affect recovery from grief, Eisenbruch,[146] has made a comparative analysis of bereavement practices of diverse ethnic and cultural groups in the United States. Eisenbruch argued that, while adapting partly to Western patterns, at the same time these groups adhere to the bereavement procedures of their own culture and that such a "deep cultural code" has implications not only for the course of grief, but for diagnoses of pathological grief and health care of the bereaved from different cultural origins. Again, little empirical data is available to support these plausible arguments.

In summary, then, although there is little empirical evidence there seems to be substantial agreement that following culturally prescribed rituals aids recovery from bereavement. The absence of rites and rituals has been causally linked by many observes to increased distress, depression, and to poor ultimate grief outcome.

The Role of Social Support

Others have explained cultural differences in grief responses, in symptomatology and outcomes, in terms of cultural differences in support systems. Melanie Klein[147] was the first to draw attention to the role played by family and friends in promoting recovery after loss, a theme which was taken up by Gorer.[148] Lopata,[149] in a more detailed analysis, later argued that grief is more rapidly resolved in those societies where there is family or community support (or both), taking historical changes within the United States as evidence, rather than present-day, cross-cultural comparisons. Ablon[150] considered patterns of social support in Samoa, comparing them with those in the United States and also concluded that grief is more rapidly resolved in cultures where there is family or community support for the bereaved.

These writers see social support as a buffer to the stress of bereavement. More detailed indications about precisely how social support helps the bereaved have been given by a few. Ramsay[151] pointed to the importance of reviewing of death events in a social setting and the grief-work facilitation available in some cultures. Similarly Parkes and Weiss[152] emphasized that encouragement of the overt expression of grief, which varies between cultures, goes some way to counteract delayed or avoided grief response.

However, some (e.g., Amir and Sharon;[153] Lopata[154]) have also emphasized the negative effect that intended social support can have on bereavement recovery. In some cultures role expectations, social control, or pressure from the support group toward normalcy may be a hindrance to the resolution of grief. This is a point which Lopata[155] argued convincingly. Working with the widowed in Chicago, she reported how undue pressure is frequently put on the widowed by informal support groups to normalcy regarding the behavior and timing of emotions. This can lead to much distress on the part of widowed persons if, for example, they feel unable to initiate social contact, conform to expectations, or follow the proffered advice.

Implications of Cross-Cultural Differences

What is the significance of these cross-cultural differences in bereavement patterns for the theoretical analysis of the health consequences of partner loss? One way of viewing bereavement customs and beliefs in different societies is that they represent different attempts at providing solutions to the putative problems (mental and physical health detriments) brought about by bereavement. One would predict that those societies with clearly defined customs or clear-cut beliefs about particular deficits would evince lower symptomatology and fewer problems with regard to that specific aspect of loss.

Examples in support of this interpretation are not hard to find among the above descriptions (although, as we noted, the psychological implications are drawn inferentially). Thus, the Buddhist or Shinto custom of ancestor reverence alleviates loss of the companionship for the deceased by maintaining contact with the departed relative as an "ancestor." Survivors accordingly reported a continued sense of the presence of the deceased and comparatively few problems with longing and loneliness. Or, the loss of a sexual partner is substituted among Kota Indians, on return to normal social life, by sexual intercourse with the deceased spouse's sibling, a provision which would be expected to ameliorate this deficit. Further, the dry funeral of this culture could be interpreted as a way of providing "closure" to grieving, a permission to the bereaved to stop grieving, which is lacking in Western cultures and may be related to chronic grief among the latter.

On a general level, it can be surmised that order or structure in one's life is lost when someone around whom one's daily activities revolved is taken away and that the very existence of such cultural norms concerning behavior following bereavement provides new orienting structure and a substitute, at least temporarily, for previous patterns of activity which have been disrupted by the death event.

INSTANCES OF THE APPARENT ABSENCE OF GRIEF: DO THEY WEAKEN THE CASE FOR UNIVERSALITY?

While practically all scientific investigations that we have found support the position that grief over the loss of a close person is universally felt, a few isolated accounts of reactions in certain cultures seem to indicate an absence of grief through apparent indifference to a death. Very different types of examples come to mind. One thinks of reports of Iranian women, who are said in some cases to be happily proud when their children die "in the name of Allah." Different again is the behavior of the Irish at a wake, a "mourning" ceremony which is anything but a subdued, harrowing occasion and is little marked by displays of the emotion of grief. These examples do not seriously challenge the claim for the universality of grief in the form we have argued, since we have stressed the cultural patterning of the emotion. Thus, as Flesch[156] describes it, the "traditional Irish wake and funeral required strict adherence to an established pattern, down to the actual words and wailing which followed the corpse to the grave."[157] With regard to reports of Iranian women, it would be consistent with our earlier discussion if the fact that one's son is considered to have died a "heroic death" for a "worthwhile cause" should soften the blow of the loss and that at times pride might outweigh feelings of grief. However the absence of expressions of grief could also be the result of social pressure against the public display of grief which might be believed to undermine the war effort.

There is one account in the literature, however, which is sufficiently detailed to challenge the claim for the universality of grief, the description of the Ik, given by Colin Turnbull[158] in his monograph *The Mountain People.* According to Turnbull, the Ik simply abandon their dead by the roadside as if no affection had been felt and no grief experienced on their loss: "I had seen no evidence of family life.... I had seen no sign of love.... I had seen things that made me want to cry, though as yet I had not cried but I had never seen an Ik anywhere near tears or sorrow."[159] However, there seems to be serious doubt among anthropologists about the validity of the description of the Ik given by Turnbull.[160] For example, Barth[161] called Turnbull's account "poor anthropology in method, in data, and in reasoning...deeply misleading to the public it sets out to inform."[162]

There are good reasons for arguing that grief is in a sense innate: As we noted at the beginning of this chapter, there are many species that show attachment behavior to other members of their species and considerable distress on death or separation. In certain cases cultural beliefs or norms "override" the natural grief. Thus we would argue that it is not indifference to the death which leads to an absence of overt grief but conformity to culturally determined patterns, whatever these in a particular culture might be.

GENERAL CONCLUSIONS

The answer to the question "Is grief universal?" cannot be a simple yes or no. On the one hand, we have argued that the available evidence supports the view that people in very diverse societies do experience feelings of sadness and despondency on the loss of a person to whom they were close. There are neither reports of indifference being the typical response to death of a friend or relative, nor ones of joy or happiness predominating. As far as can be said on the basis of nonexhaustive data, then, grief seems to be universally felt.

On the other hand, manifestations of grief in different cultures are extremely varied: Whereas in the West despair and depression and many other symptoms of grief last for months and even years, in certain parts of the world any overt sign of grief ceases after a matter of days and there is every indication that the trauma of loss is overcome in the space of a very short time. It appears that symptoms and phases of grief are modified very considerably by cultural factors, and, while no specific empirical examinations exist to test this more closely, systematic variations across cultural groups in social support and social norms, in funeral rites and in the meaning assigned to loss, can be linked with differences in the emotional reaction to loss. These cultural variants do, then, appear to have a moderating influence on the symptoms and phases of grief. We have suggested that these different cultural prescriptions may represent attempts of particular societies to come to terms with the deficits arising through a death of those persons who survive.

NOTES

1. E. Durkheim. 1976: *The Elementary Forms of the Religious Life.* London: Allen & Unwin (first published in 1915); R. Huntington and P. Metcalfe. 1979: *Celebrations of Death: The Anthropology of Mortuary Ritual.* Cambridge University Press; A.R. Radcliffe-Brown. 1964: *The Andaman Islanders.* New York: Free Press (first published in 1922).
2. J.R. Averill. 1982. *Anger and Aggression.* New York: Springer Verlag.
3. P. Ekman. 1971. Universal and Cultural Differences in Facial Expressions of Emotion. In D. Levin, ed., *Nebraska Symposium on Motivation.* Lincoln: University of Nebraska Press.
4. S. Mineka and S.J. Suomi. 1978: Social Separation in Monkeys. *Psychological Bulletin* 85:376-400; M. Reite, R. Short, C. Seiler and J.D. Pauley. 1981: Attachment, Loss, and Depression. *Journal of Child Psychology and Psychiatry* 22:141-169.

5. J. Bowlby. 1979. *The Making and Breaking of Affectional Bonds.* London: Tavistock.
6. J. Averill. 1968: Grief: Its Nature and Significance. *Psychological Bulletin* 70:721-728; 1979: The Functions of Grief, in C.E. Izard, ed., *Emotions in Personality and Psychopathology.* New York: Plenum.
7. J. Bowlby. 1960: Grief and Mourning in Infancy and Early Childhood. *Psychoanalytic Study of the Child* 15:9-52; 1961: Processes of Mourning. *International Journal of Psychoanalysis* 42:317-340; 1971: *Attachment and Loss,* Vol. 1: *Attachment.* Harmondsworth, England: Pelican Books.
8. Averill, 1968, loc. cit.
9. Averill, 1979, loc. cit.
10. A.R. Hochschild. 1979. Emotion Work, Feeling Rules, and Social Structure. *American Journal of Sociology* 85:551-575.
11. W. James. 1950. The Principles of Psychology, Vol. 2. New York: Dover (first published in 1890).
12. C.G. Lange. 1922. *The Emotions.* Baltimore: Williams & Wilkins (first published in 1885).
13. C.E. Izard. 1971: *Patterns of Emotions: A New Analysis of Anxiety and Depression.* New York: Academic Press; 1977: *Human Emotions.* New York: Plenum.
14. S.S. Tomkins. 1962. *Affect, Imagery, Consciousness,* Vol. 1. *The Positive Affects.* New York: Springer; 1963: *Affect Imagery, Consciousness,* Vol. 2. *The Negative Affects.* New York: Springer.
15. Averill, 1982, loc. cit.
16. Hochschild, 1979, loc. cit.
17. James, 1950, loc. cit.
18. Lange, 1922, loc. cit.
19. James, 1950, loc. cit.
20. Ibid., pp. 449-450.
21. James, op. cit., p. 450.
22. Ibid.
23. S. Schacter. 1964. The Interaction of Cognitive and Physiological Determinants of Emotional State, in L. Berkowitz, ed., *Advances of Experimental Social Psychology,* Vol. 1. New York: Academic Press.
24. James, loc. cit.
25. Ibid., p. 463.
26. W.B. Cannon. 1929. *Bodily Changes in Pain, Hunger, Fear, and Rage.* New York: Appleton.
27. Ibid.
28. Ibid.
29. Schacter, loc. cit.
30. H. Cantril and W.A. Hunt. 1932: Emotional Effects Produced by the Injection of Adrenalin. *American Journal of Psychology* 44:300-307; C. Landis and W.A. Hunt. 1932: Adrenaline and Avoidance Learning. *Psychological Review* 39:467-485; G. Maranon. 1924: Contribution a l'etude de l'action emotive de l'adrenaline. *Revue francaise d'Endocrinologie* 2:301-325.
31. S. Schacter and J.E. Singer. 1962. Cognitive, Social, and Physiological Determinants of Emotional State. *Psychological Review* 69:379-399.
32. G. Erdman and W. Janke. 1978: Interaction Between Physiological and Cognitive Determinants of Emotions: Experimental Studies of Schachter's Theory of

Emotion. *Biological Psychology* 6:61-74; C. Maslach. 1978. The Emotional Consequences of Arousal Without Reason, in C.E. Izard, ed., *Emotions in Personality and Psychopathology*. New York: Plenum.

33. Averill, 1982, loc. cit; Hochschild, loc. cit.
34. Ibid.
35. Averill, 1982, loc. cit.
36. Hochschild, loc. cit.
37. Ibid.
38. Ibid., p. 562.
39. James, loc. cit.
40. Ibid.
41. R. Tourangeau and P.C. Ellsworth. 1979. The Role of Facial Response in the Experience of Emotion. *Journal of Personality and Social Psychology* 37:519-531.
42. J.D. Laird. 1984. The Real Role of Facial Response in the Experience of Emotion: A Reply to Tourangeau and Ellsworth, and Others. *Journal of Personality and Social Psychology* 47:909-917.
43. Ibid., p. 909.
44. H. Leventhal. 1984. A Perceptual-Motor Theory of Emotion, in L. Berkowitz, ed., *Advances in Experimental Social Psychology*, Vol. 17. New York: Academic Press.
45. Izard, loc. cit.
46. P. Ekman and W.V. Friesen. 1971. Constants Across Cultures in the Face and Emotion. *Journal of Personality and Social Psychology* 17:124-129.
47. Izard, loc. cit.
48. P.C. Rosenblatt, R.P. Walsh and D.A. Jackson. 1976. *Grief and Mourning in Cross-Cultural Perspective*. New Haven, CT: HRAF Press.
49. Ibid.
50. Ibid.
51. U. Wikan. 1986. The Role of Emotions in Balinese Popular Health Care. Unpublished manuscript, Ethnographic Museum of the University of Oslo.
52. Ibid., p. 6.
53. Ibid., p. 9.
54. Izard, loc. cit.
55. S. Johnson. 1921. *The History of the Yorubas. Lagos: Christian Missionary Society* (cited in M. Eisenbruch. 1984: Cross-Cultural Aspects of Bereavement. I: A Conceptual Framework for Comparative Analysis. *Culture, Medicine, and Psychiatry* 8:283-309).
56. Ibid.
57. Rosenblatt, Walsh and Jackson, loc. cit.
58. Radcliffe-Brown, loc. cit.
59. Ibid., p. 117.
60. Huntington and Metcalfe, loc. cit.
61. H.A. Junod. 1927. *The Life of a South African Tribe.* London: Macmillan (reported in P.C. Rosenblatt. 1981. Grief in Crosscultural and Historical Perspective, in P.K. Pegg and E. Metze, eds., *Death and Dying*. London: Pitman).
62. Rosenblatt, Ibid., p. 143.
63. D.G. Mandelbaum. 1959. Social Uses of Funeral Rites, in H. Feifel, ed., *The Meaning of Death*. New York: McGraw-Hill.
64. Ibid.

65. Ibid., p. 193.
66. S. Frankel and D. Smith. 1982. Conjugal Bereavement Among the Huli People of Papua, New Guinea. *British Journal of Psychiatry* 141:302-305.
67. Ibid.
68. Ibid., p. 303.
69. Rosenblatt, Walsh and Jackson, loc. cit.
70. D. Bindra. 1972. Weeping: A Problem of Many Facets. *Bulletin of the British Psychological Society* 25:281-284.
71. Durkheim, loc. cit.
72. Ibid.
73. Ibid., p. 400.
74. Radcliffe-Brown, loc. cit.
75. Ibid.
76. T. Henry. 1964. *Jungle People.* New York: Vintage (first published in 1941).
77. Rosenblatt, loc. cit.
78. Henry, loc. cit.
79. Ibid., p. 66.
80. Ibid.
81. D.J. Bem. 1972. Self-Perception Theory, in L. Berkowitz, ed., *Advances in Experimental Social Psychology,* Vol. 6. New York: Academic Press; H.H. Kelley. 1973. The Processes of Causal Attribution. *American Psychologist* 28:107-128.
82. Durkheim, loc. cit.
83. Ibid., p. 392.
84. J.G. Frazer. 1911. *The Dying God. The Golden Bough, Part III.* (3rd Ed.). London: Macmillan; J.G. Frazer. 1914. *Adonis, Attis, Osiris. The Golden Bough, Part IV* (Vol. 1; 3rd Ed.). London: Macmillan; 1923: *Folk-Lore in the Old Testament.* New York: Tudor Publishing Company; G. Pollock. 1972. On Mourning and Anniversaries: The Relationship of Culturally Constituted Defense Systems to Intra-Psychic Adaptive Processes. *Israel Annals of Psychiatry* 10:9-40.
85. Huntington and Metcalfe, loc. cit.
86. Ibid.
87. Ibid., p. 31.
88. J.E. Cawte. 1964. Australian Ethno-Psychiatry in the Field: A Sampling in North Kimberly. *Medical Journal of Australia* 1:467-472.
89. Ibid., p. 470.
90. B. Malinowski. 1982. *Magic, Science, and Religion.* London: Souvenir Press.
91. Ibid., p. 48.
92. Mandelbaum, loc. cit.
93. Ibid., p. 203.
94. R.L. Steele. 1977. Dying, Death, and Bereavement Among the Maya Indians of Meso-America: A Study of Anthropological Psychology. *American Psychologist* 32:1060-1068.
95. S.I. Miller and L. Schoenfeld. 1973. Grief in the Navajo: Psychodynamics and Culture. *International Journal of Social Psychiatry* 19:187-191.
96. J. Mitford. 1963. *The American Way of Death.* New York: Simon & Schuster.
97. C.M. Parkes and R.S. Weiss. 1983. *Recovery from Bereavement.* New York: Basic Books; Rosenblatt, loc. cit.
98. Miller and Schoenfeld, op. cit.
99. Ibid.

100. Mandelbaum, loc. cit.; Steele, loc. cit.; E.H. Volkart and S.T. Michael. 1957. Bereavement and Mental Health, in A.H. Leighton, J.A. Clausen and R.N. Wilson, eds., *Explorations in Social Psychiatry.* New York: Basic Books.
101. Steele, loc. cit.
102. Ibid., p. 1065.
103. J. Ablon. 1971. Bereavement in a Samoan Community. *British Journal of Medical Psychology* 44:329-337.
104. E. Lindemann. 1944. Symptomatology and Management of Acute Grief. *American Journal of Psychiatry* 101:141-148.
105. Mandelbaum, loc. cit.
106. Ibid.
107. Ibid.
108. Ibid.
109. J. Mathison. 1970. A Cross-Cultural View of Widowhood. *Omega* 1:201-218.
110. Ibid.
111. Ibid., p. 209.
112. G.D. Gorer. 1965. *Death, Grief and Mourning.* New York: Doubleday.
113. Pollock, loc. cit.
114. H.S. Goldberg. 1981. Funeral and Bereavement Rituals of Kota Indians and Orthodox Jews. *Omega* 12:117-128.
115. Ibid.
116. S. Freud. 1917. Trauer und Melancholic. *Internationale Zeitschrift Arztliche Psychoanalyse* 4:288-301.
117. Lindemann, loc. cit.
118. J. Bowlby. 1981. *Attachment and Loss,* Vol. 3: *Loss, Sadness and Depression.* Harmondsworth, England: Penguin Books.
119. Mandelbaum, op. cit., p. 203.
120. J. Yamamoto. 1970. Cultural Factors in Loneliness, Death, and Separation. *Medical Times* 98:177-183.
121. Ibid., p. 181.
122. Ibid.
123. Volkart and Michael, loc. cit.
124. A.T. Culwick and G.M. Culwick. 1935. *Ubena of the Rivers.* London: Allen & Unwin.
125. Bowlby, 1971, 1981, loc. cit.
126. Mandelbaum, loc. cit.
127. C. Geertz. 1973. *The Interpretation of Cultures.* New York: Basic Books.
128. A. van Gennep. 1977. *The Rites of Passage.* London: Routledge & Kegan Paul (first published in 1909).
129. Malinowski, loc. cit.
130. Radcliffe-Brown, loc. cit.
131. Freud, loc. cit.; Lindemann, loc. cit.
132. Gorer, loc. cit.
133. P. Marris. 1958. *Widows and Their Families.* London: Routledge & Kegan Paul.
134. R. Firth. 1961. *Elements of Social Organization.* London: Tavistock.
135. M. Eisenbruch. 1984b. Cross-Cultural Aspects of Bereavement. II: Ethnic and Cultural Variations in the Development of Bereavement Practices. *Culture, Medicine and Psychiatry* 8:315-347.
136. Mandelbaum, loc. cit.
137. Volkart and Michael, loc. cit.

138. Mandelbaum, loc. cit.
139. I. Aguilar and V. Wood. 1976. Therapy Through a Death Ritual. *Social Work* 21:49-54.
140. R.C. Salzberger. 1975. Death: Beliefs, Activities, and Reactions of the Bereaved—Some Psychological and Anthropological Observations. *The Human Context* 7:103-116.
141. Gorer, loc. cit.
142. Pollock, loc. cit.
143. Ibid., p. 38.
144. Miller and Schoenfeld, loc. cit.
145. Ibid.
146. Eisenbruch, 1984b, loc. cit.
147. M. Klein. 1940. Mourning and Its Relation to Manic-Depressive Status. *International Journal of Psychoanalysis* 21:125-153.
148. Gorer, loc. cit.
149. H.Z. Lopata. 1979. *Women as Widows: Support Systems.* New York: Elsevier.
150. Ablon, loc. cit.
151. R.W. Ramsay. 1979. Bereavement: A Behavioral Treatment of Pathological Grief, in P.O. Sjoden, S. Bates and W.S. Dorkens III, eds., *Trends in Behavior Therapy.* New York: Academic Press.
152. Parkes and Weiss, loc. cit.
153. Y. Amir and I. Sharon. 1982. Factors in the Adjustment of War Widows in Israel, in C.D. Spielberger, I.G. Sarason and N.A. Milgrim, eds., *Stress and Anxiety,* Vol. 8. Washington, DC: Hemisphere.
154. H.Z. Lopata. 1975. On Widowhood: Grief Work and Identity Reconstruction. *Journal of Geriatric Psychiatrics* 8:41-55; 1979, loc. cit.
155. Ibid.
156. R. Flesch. 1969. The Condolence Call, in A.H. Kutscher, ed., *Death and Bereavement.* Springfield, IL: Charles C Thomas.
157. Ibid., p. 237.
158. C. Turnbull. 1972. *The Mountain People.* New York: Simon & Schuster.
159. Ibid., pp. 129-130.
160. Ibid.
161. F. Barth. 1974. On Responsibility and Humanity: Calling a Colleague to Account. *Current Anthropology* 15:99-102.
162. Ibid., p. 100.

III

Bereavement and the Response to Death

Introduction

Death, like birth, puberty and marriage, is a most significant event for individuals, families and society. The responses and reactions engendered by death have a sociological as well as a personal immediacy. Like most profound events, death is universally recognized, marked by ritual and ceremony and socially defined in role expectations.

The sociological role of bereavement is often confused with the psychosocial processes of grief and mourning. As we observed in the previous section, *grief* refers to a personal change in one's emotional attachments and sense of self-worth and identity, while the *mourning* process involves the *work* of recovery from loss. *Bereavement* focuses attention on the sociological dimensions of loss in marriage and family roles, religious beliefs and practices and business norms, without necessarily addressing the emotional impact of the loss itself upon the survivors.

The authors in this section analyze bereavement and the sociological response to death from various institutional and organizational perspectives. Owen, Fulton and Markusen studied 558 bereaved family members in Minneapolis and St. Paul, Minnesota. Wuthnow and his colleagues have written a set of research propositions on religion and bereavement and Pratt examines how business norms "shape" bereavement behavior. Finally, Fulton explores sociological dimensions of the funeral in contemporary society.

The chapter by Greg Owen, Robert Fulton and Eric Markusen, "Death at a Distance: A Study of Family Survivors," reports on the social-psychological adjustment to loss through death of 558 bereaved persons in the metropolitan area of Minneapolis/St. Paul. Mailed questionnaires were sent to a sample of bereaved families in the Twin Cities, and personal interviews were conducted. The questionnaire included demographic questions about the respondents, their religiosity, the nature and circumstances of the death, funeralization, post-death relationships, memories and perceptions of the deceased and post-death adjustments.

The data in the study were analyzed by comparing the responses of (1) parents whose child had died, (2) widows and widowers whose spouse had died, and (3) adult sons and daughters whose elderly parent had died. The study showed that the impact on parents of the death of their child included major grief symptoms that last longer than 6 months and that cause parents to struggle with the meaning of the death of their child. Widows and widowers, in contrast, vary in their responses to the death of their spouse depending on many factors associated with the survivor and the death. Adult children, on the other hand, respond to the death of their parent in ways that reflect their age and gender. Those under 45 years old appear more attached to their parent and report greater grief reactions than those over 45. In cross-gender relationships (son-mother and daughter-father) the findings indicated more often appear to retain their bond from younger years as expressed in the grief displayed in these types of adult losses.

The significance of the Owen, Fulton and Markusen study is in the internal comparisons they conducted among the three types of bereaved families. Samples of 500 respondents are not often recruited, nor have bereavement studies often employed multiple methods of data gathering. A more refined analysis of the data would have been desirable, but the authors have documented important variables in family bereavement.

The association of religion and bereavement is conceptualized in a set of 48 propositions by Robert Wuthnow, Kevin Christiano and John Kuzloski in their chapter, "Religion and Bereavement: A Conceptual Framework." The propositions are organized under three major topics: "Religion as a Source of Meaning," "Religion as a Source of Belonging" and "Funerary Rites." The first topic includes propositions on religious belief (belief in God, belief in life after death and theodicies); moral obligations (service to God, service to others and service to self); and religious/peak experiences. The second set of propositions addresses religious participation, vicarious participation and charitable services for the bereaved, while the third set of propositions focuses on the rites associated with death.

Religion as a social institution has a role to play in bereavement, even though only approximately half of adult Americans report church membership. As Wuthnow and his colleagues remind us, research in the sociology of religion has found that religion is salient for older persons who are more often bereaved; religious organizations provide a social support network; religion is a source of subjective meaning; and religious commitment affects how people respond to stress and crises like bereavement. The chapter, however, does not take account of the diversity of religious customs among and within faith groups. The emphasis a faith group or denomination places on personal or collective responses may well intervene in Wuthnow's propositions. Similarly, the function of religion in the spiritual aspects of well-being are known to be affected by the intrinsic (e.g., meditation) or extrinsic (e.g., church attendance) manifestations of religiosity.

Lois Pratt in her chapter, "Business Temporal Norms and Bereavement Behavior," takes a historical look at how business norms regarding bereavement practices for employees have become more specific in definition and less generous in benefits. The corporate response to personal loss has been to control the use of time-off through precise measurement and limitation of time in a standardized policy that adapts business time to personal time. Pratt concludes that "The trend over the past three decades to limit paid bereavement leave to 3 days is consistent with and gives further impetus to the trend in this century to shorten the formal mourning period." The aspects of bereavement that have been affected include role eligibility (immediate family); role obligations (minimal for friends and other relatives); site of mourning (excluded from workplace); funerary rites and rituals (brief, simple, private); mourning practices (simple, not ostentatious); and timing of mourning (3 days for immediate family members).

The final chapter in this section, "The Funeral in Contemporary Society" by Robert Fulton, discusses the meaning of this dramaturgic celebration of death and its significance for the community and bereaved individuals and families. The funeral, according to Fulton, is a "rite of passage" that not only marks the completion of a life, but also reaffirms the social character of human existence. Changes in the structure of American family life, as well as in business norms, have wrought changes in the role of the bereaved person. It would seem that the modern funeral ceremony, if it is to be effective in aiding the bereaved to cope with their loss and grief, must be responsive to these new social facts. A ceremony that no longer appropriately symbolizes the understood meaning of death, or fails to dramatize correctly the changes that have overtaken the living and the dead, can create confusion and strain for the bereaved.

Social strain and anomie (i.e., "normlessness") in connection with mourning and burial rites reflect the cultural change, social conflicts, structural dissolutions and attempted reintegrations that are characteristic of our changing world. Simply stated, the meaning of a prayer today is lost upon a person who holds no religious beliefs. So too, a ceremony that invites all to mourn a death presents serious difficulties for the person who has come to believe that grief is private and personal. Fulton and Pratt document changes in the expectations and ritual practices at funerals and memorial services. Increasingly, a funeral that attempts to represent relationships, ideas or values that the individual or family no longer believes to hold true may thwart and frustrate the mourner rather than achieve its intended end. Yet for others who seek to express the meaning of a lost life in sacred, or even secular, rituals, it may mean that they are left unfulfilled in their bereavement.

8

Death at a Distance: A Study of Family Bereavement

Greg Owen, PhD
Robert Fulton, PhD
and Eric Markusen, PhD

INTRODUCTION

This chapter reports a study of the social-psychological adjustment to loss through death of 558 bereaved persons. The participants lived in the Minneapolis/St. Paul metropolitan area at the time of the death of a family member. This exploratory study was undertaken to add to our knowledge and understanding of the impact of loss through death on survivors and to discover how and in what ways people react to loss, as well as learn how and in what ways they are aided and abetted in their recovery from it. In addition, we were also interested in the role that mortuary customs, rites and other ceremonies play in a survivor's response to death.

It is our hope that the study will contribute toward a greater understanding of the nature of our personal and public reaction to loss through death, as well as further our knowledge of the social and psychological functions of the public and private acts that we share in response to the death of another.

RELEVANT LITERATURE

Bereavement has been an intermittent topic of scientific inquiry since the beginning of the twentieth century. In 1913, Freud postulated a relationship between grief and severe depression and discussed the meaning and significance of this association for the survivor. In *Mourning and Melancholia* he wrote:

> Although grief involves grave departures from the normal attitude to life, it never occurs to us to regard it as a morbid condition and hand the mourner over to medical treatment. We rest assured that after a lapse of time it will be overcome, and we look upon any interference with it as inadvisable or even harmful.[1]

Later, however, he notes:

> Where there is a disposition to obsessional neurosis the conflict of *ambivalence* casts a pathological shade on the grief, forcing it to express itself in the form of self-reproaches, to the effect that the mourner himself is to blame for the loss of the loved one, i.e., desired it.[2]

In 1932 Eliot, an American sociologist, called upon his colleagues to develop a general social-psychology of bereavement.[3] It was his hope to generate a wealth of bereavement data through the active collaboration of a network of concerned scholars. Except for the work of his own students—Becker and Fulcomer[4]—his request went unheeded.

It is important to note that at this time the terms bereavement and grief were often used interchangeably. Grief was the natural result of bereavement. If one were bereaved, one grieved. Today we are careful to separate loss through death—bereavement—from the grief response that it may engender. In 1944 Lindemann proposed in his classic paper, "The Symptomatology and Management of Acute Grief," that the absence of grief itself was a pathology and indicative of a deep-rooted emotional crisis in the survivor.[5]

During the past 20 years research on bereavement has intensified. Gorer,[6] Parkes,[7] Glick,[8] Volkart,[9] Kraus and Lillenfeld,[10] Lopata[11] and others have each contributed important empirical observations describing the human response to loss. Their work, however, focused primarily on the widow or widower. The present study is an attempt to help fill the gap in the literature by considering not only the response of the surviving spouse to death, but also the bereavement response of parents following the death of a child as well as that of an adult child following the death of an aged parent.

BACKGROUND AND PROCEDURE

The material presented is part of an ongoing study of bereavement conducted by the Center for Death Education and Research at the University of Minnesota. A questionnaire/interview schedule was prepared that included questions concerning personal information about the respondents, their religiosity, the nature and circumstances of the death, funeralization, post-death relationships, memories and perceptions of the deceased, and post-death adjustment.

A stratified list of names of survivors according to the age of the deceased at time of death was drawn up from the obituary columns of the two major newspapers serving the Minneapolis/St. Paul area—the *Minneapolis Star* and the *Minneapolis Tribune*—for the period of time between January 1, 1971 and May 31, 1973.[12]

From these files the names and addresses of 1838 immediate survivors were compiled. In order to be assured a representation of persons from ethnic or religious minorities as well as a sample of persons who would have held a "nontraditional" funeral, local funeral directors who served such groups or offered such services were requested to submit lists of names. Six funeral homes provided us with lists totaling 350 names. Further, in order to make a comparison in the adjustment behavior of persons who availed themselves of post-bereavement programs such as Widow-to-Widow or Theo, names were solicited from those organizations as well. Fifty-nine names were received from two such organizations. In total 2237 names of survivors were compiled and mailed the questionnaire.

To probe the issue of loss as deeply as our resources would permit, every third name was also selected for a home interview. Such a procedure has two major advantages: it permits the researcher to check on the representatives and reliability of the mailed responses at the same time that it allows a more careful and extensive examination of the survivor's responses. Previous research suggests that such a procedure serves as an important check on the content and consistency of the responses in this emotionally charged area.[13]

In all, we were able to solicit the cooperation of 571 bereaved persons representing 436 persons who returned a mailed questionnaire and 135 who permitted themselves to be personally interviewed.[14] An analysis of the responses showed that there were no significant differences between the two groups, so for purposes of analysis their responses were combined.

The problems associated with a study of this kind are many and complex. We think it will be appreciated by the reader that the delicate and sensitive area of loss evokes strong emotions, among them fear and anger. This was amply demonstrated by the study in a number of ways; a great many of the questionnaires were returned unanswered or with a highly critical letter. Some persons wrote or phoned a complaint to university officials or members of the state legislature. Other persons were apparently less critical of the study but, nevertheless, were unable to carry through with their intentions to participate and either canceled their appointments with an interviewer (sometimes repeatedly) or returned the questionnaire only partially completed.

In sharp contrast to these reactions to the study, however, many respondents among the interviewed group were very receptive to the study, as well as to the interviewer—sometimes embarrassingly so. For instance, the respondents often would insist that the interviewer remain long past the allotted time for the interview. In more than a few instances, respondents attempted to continue contact with the interviewer by letters and phone calls to the Center. On several occasions, the interviewer was invited to take part in social engagements in the home of respondents, and in one instance, an interviewer was even invited to Thanksgiving dinner. The desire for human contact and the need to express pent-up emotions was dramatically portrayed over and over again by the respondents, and their behavior told us, poignantly, of the need for a greater understanding and awareness of the impact of death upon our lives.

DEMOGRAPHIC PROFILE

The 558 respondents in the sample are briefly described below:

Sex:	Seventy-two percent of the bereaved respondents were female.
Race:	Ninety-seven percent of the respondents were white.
Age:	Sixty-six percent of the respondents were over 50 years of age.
Religion:	Thirty-three percent of the respondents were Lutheran, 27 percent were Catholic, other Protestant faiths made up 30 percent of the sample and 5 percent of the sample was Jewish. Less than 2 percent of the sample reported no religious belief.
Occupation:	The categories housewife, retired or unemployed made up approximately half of the sample (52 percent); 17 percent of the sample reported professional or managerial

occupations; clerical employment was reported in 13 percent of the cases, and the remaining 18 percent reported being employed in skilled, semi-skilled or other occupations.

Education: Twenty-four percent of the sample reported having had less than a high school education, 26 percent reported high school graduation, 19.6 percent reported some college, while 14.6 percent reported college graduation or post-college training. Technical school or other formal training was reported by the remaining 15 percent of the sample.

Marital Status: Fifty-nine percent reported their current marital status as widow, 16 percent reported their status as widower, 19 percent were married, 2 percent were single, and 5 percent reported some other status.

Living Arrangements: Forty-seven percent of the sample lived alone, 26 percent lived with their children, 25 percent lived with a spouse and children, 6 percent lived with a spouse, 3 percent lived with a relative other than a spouse or children, 1 percent lived with friends, and 1 percent reported other kinds of living arrangements.

Housing Arrangements: Eighty percent of the respondents lived in a house, compared to 15 percent who lived in an apartment. The remainder lived in nursing homes, trailer homes or other accommodations.

Religiosity: More than one quarter (26 percent) of the sample reported being "very religious," while about two-thirds (62 percent) reported being "somewhat religious" in outlook. On the other hand, 3 percent reported being "somewhat non-religious" and 2 percent of the respondents reported being "definitely non-religious."

Beliefs:	The findings on religiosity are in response to the question on "ideas about God prior to death." More than 7 out of 10 of the respondents (72 percent) reported a belief in a divine God. Another 10 percent believed in a power greater than themselves (God or Nature), while 4 percent reported a belief in the religion of humanity. Six percent reported not being sure of what they believed, while less than 6 percent reported no belief in God or a Supreme Being.	
Church Attendance:	The majority of the respondents attended church services once a week or more (55 percent). Another 17 percent reported attendance about once or twice a month, while 12 percent reported going to church mainly on important occasions. Ten percent reported almost never going to church, while 4 percent of the sample reported never attending church.	
Income:	Under $4000	18 percent
	$4000 to 6999	21
	$7000 to 9999	15
	$10,000 to 12,999	12
	$13,000 to 17,999	11
	$18,000 to 22,000	5
	Greater than $22,000	8
	No answer	10
	Total	100 percent

Income reported in the sample generally followed the income pattern for the community as a whole. The median income for Hennepin County was reported to be $10,000 by the 1970 Census Data.

THE SIGNIFICANCE OF RELATIONSHIPS

An analysis of the data demonstrated the theoretical importance of separating the sample on the basis of the respondent's relationship to the deceased. One of the most significant findings to come out of the preliminary analysis was that the data could be understood most meaningfully if the sample were divided into three groups:[15] (1) parents responding to the death of a child; (2) a widow or widower responding to the death of a spouse; and (3) an "adult" son or daughter responding to the death of an elderly parent. The data were grouped in terms of these marital and social bonds and analyzed in the light of the consequences that a death had for these three distinct types of survivors.

Personal Data

While a demographic profile of the entire sample permits us to see in rough outline the characteristics of the respondents, at the same time it obscures the nature of the relationship and the subtleties of the responses contained in the body of information gathered. The following discussion delineates the demographic characteristics of the respondents into the three designated groups—spouse, parent and adult son or daughter. When the sample of 558 respondents is divided on the basis of how they are related to the deceased, different patterns emerge. We see confirmed, as expected, that the most frequently reported relationship in which a death occurs is that of husband and wife where the husband was the predecessor. Moreover, this rupture in the relationship occurs when the wife is, approximately, in her sixth decade of life.

The study showed that (as is found in the state as a whole) denominational proportions generally remained constant for all three groups. The exception occurred among the adult children with 15 percent reporting membership in the Jewish faith. Age and sex differences were reflected again in the educational achievement of the respondents, with the parent and adult son or daughter groups reporting appreciably more formal education than the spouse group. While occupation was not as clearly consistent with education as we might have expected, we did observe that the parent and adult child groups typically reported higher incomes than did the spouse group. Finally, we saw in current living arrangements an important factor that in all probability bears heavily upon the sum of responses reported in the study; namely, the proportion of the spouse group who reported living alone in comparison to the parent and adult child groups. This finding in and of itself is important and cannot help but color both the immediate response to a death or the long-term consequences that loss and separation have for the surviving spouse.

The Context of Death

The experience of bereavement for a parent, a spouse and an adult child varies according to a wide range of factors associated with the death.

Differences in age, sex, cause of death, circumstances of dying, religious beliefs and ceremonialization will combine in a way that individualizes the survivors' bereavement. For the sample of spouses, it was the surviving wife in the majority of instances who experienced the death of her husband, while conversely, parents in the sample, in two out of three instances, suffered the death of a male child. It was also observed that while the wife characteristically lost her husband in the sixth decade of her life, an adult son or daughter reported most frequently attending the funeral of a widowed mother. The parents in the sample, on the other hand, were typically confronted with the death of a teenage child.

Another important aspect of the reaction and response to loss is the cause of death itself. For the spouses as well as for the adult sons or daughters the cause of death of their deceased relative was generally attributed to heart disease, cancer, stroke, or other degenerative diseases associated with old age. For the parents, on the other hand, accidental death was the most common cause of death of a child.

The manner in which the survivor learns about a death is also important for an understanding of the responses and adjustment to loss. The spouse group reported most frequently that a doctor reported the death, the adult child group reported that it was a relative, while the parent group reported that a police officer or coroner most often informed them of the death of the child.

Regarding funeralization, it was observed that the highest percentage holding a traditional funeral was the spouse group (72.6 percent), while the adult child group reported holding a traditional funeral less than 50 percent of the time. In addition, the adult child group reported selecting cremation as the method of disposition in 28 percent of the cases. This is more than five times and eight times greater than what was reported for the other two groups, respectively, and approximately six times greater than the cremation rate for the state as a whole. With the question, "Did you have the body of the deceased viewed?" there is a declining order of affirmative responses with the spouse group reporting "yes" in 85.5 percent of the cases; the parent group, 77 percent; and adult child group, 53.8 percent. While the adult son or daughter group contained a disproportionate numbers of Jews—who traditionally do not view—the trend remained the same even when they were removed from the sample. In addition, the adult child group reported fewer post-death observances.

Finally, the findings showed that the respondents in general were fundamentally religious, but that the adult child group was somewhat less religious than the others. Interestingly, while few people reported a change in their religious beliefs following a death, it was the parent group who most often experienced a diminution of their faith when a death occurred.

The Response to Death

An important dimension of loss and its resolution is the response that a survivor exhibits following a death. The three groups of survivors were compared in terms of their emotional and behavioral reactions to bereavement. The responses showed that the pattern of post-death adjustment followed the configuration of responses observed thus far: adult sons and daughters reported the fewest adjustment problems among the three groups as determined by the established categories.

It was also observed that while the overwhelming majority of respondents reported no marked hostility toward others—either inside or outside the family following the death—an appreciable percentage of the respondents did express hostile feelings. In cases outside of the family, the physician was most often designated as the individual toward whom hostile sentiments were expressed. While the number of cases we are dealing with is relatively small, it is nevertheless interesting that in the entire sample of 558 persons, only one respondent named the funeral director as an object of hostility.

We observed further that the adult child group reported the smallest increase in the "consumption of tranquilizers" or "barbiturates" as well as the smallest increase in the "consumption of alcohol." They also fell short of the other groups in the reporting of "insomnia" and "headaches." They reported, moreover, the least "preoccupation with the memory of the deceased" and less "anger" or "hostility" toward others than did the other two groups. Additionally, they were the lowest of the three groups in the reporting of "other" physical complaints.

These findings are complemented by the information obtained in the second set of responses concerning the "worthwhileness of life," "interest in others" and "dissatisfaction with one's life." The responses again indicated that the adult child group appeared to have the least difficulty in post-death adjustment. This is reinforced by the further observation regarding their general emotional state. They reported being the least "depressed" and "unhappy" of the three groups while also having the least sense of being "punished" by the loss.

When the respondents were asked to describe their feelings since the death of the deceased, generally the responses of the three groups were consistent with the overall reactions reported. For instance, the adult child group did not report feeling "cut-off" or "isolated" from others as did the other two groups and neither did they report, as frequently, a "feeling of being alone." Perhaps the general difference in reaction to the respective deaths can be seen with the responses to the statement, "I enjoy my family more." It might be interpreted that the relatively low response of the adult sons and daughters to these questions was indicative of the relative impact that the death of the elderly parent occasioned. This pattern of response was observed again with the question on general health, where it was seen that the adult child group reported "poorer health" following the death less frequently than did the other two groups.

In the preceding discussion we have focused on a description of the three groups using percentage comparisons based on the numerical counting of observations. The nature of the subject matter, however, demands a more detailed account of the bereavement responses and for that purpose we turn to the following case accounts.

CASE ACCOUNTS

The Responses of Parents to the Death of a Child

The death of persons between the ages of one and fourteen account for less than 5 percent of all deaths in the United States today. Such deaths are unusual, out of the ordinary and seldom anticipated. Their occurrence leaves parents in a state of shock and disbelief with many reporting feelings of being "cheated," "helpless," and "angry." In this study, parents frequently reported grief symptoms of major proportions that lasted longer than 6 months. Also, parents appeared to have the greatest difficulty in resolving such a loss. The meanings that a child's death may have for a parent are illustrated in the following case excerpts:

Case 1

A 33-year-old mother of five children responded to the questionnaire 5 months following the death of her 15-year-old son. The boy drowned accidentally while swimming with friends. The mother said she continues to feel hostility toward "the kids he went swimming with because they promised he would stay out of the water." She said that the death is "painful," "sometimes unbearable," and that she feels "cheated" and "helpless." A traditional funeral was held for her son with a public viewing. She felt that the viewing was important "because we wanted to be with him and see him as long as we could." After 5 months she reported the following behaviors and feelings: "insomnia," "preoccupation with the memory of the deceased," feelings of "depression" and "unhappiness," feelings that "the deceased is alive and present," "inability to concentrate attention," and weekly visits to the cemetery. At the same time, she said that "family closeness has increased," that she feels "more warmth toward others," that she is "more helpful and considerate than before" and has "a desire to be with others often."

When asked to describe those things that were most difficult for her following the death, she wrote:

> ...trying to comfort my only son about his brother—and looking at other boys his age. Also, making meals when nobody is hungry and taking the children somewhere while one is still missing. To live a normal life like before it happened and talk about his plans for the coming year. Nothing is easier.

When asked what things had helped her adjust to her bereavement she said: "I have my husband and children and friends and relatives to be with me and it makes it easier. We all feel the loss and share it."

While it is clear that there are many aspects of this loss that are still painful and difficult for this mother, there are also indications of normal resolution. The support and continued help of her family and friends is perceived as important and beneficial in coping with the death of her son. The mother's responses show that the child was dearly loved and his death had great significance for her life and the life of her family.

Case 2

We may compare this experience with the responses of a 32-year-old mother of 6 girls who experienced the death of her youngest daughter approximately 8 months before the interview. The child died of pneumonia at age 2, after being hospitalized many times previously for a variety of illnesses. The parents chose to have a public funeral service with a private viewing of the body. The mother wrote that the body should be viewed because it "helps other children to realize the death and is helpful to other members of the family from out of town. It may erase guilt and it is important to say a final farewell."

The mother reported a large number of grief symptoms including feelings of "guilt" and "helplessness," "insomnia," "weight gain," a "decreased interest in others," a feeling that "she was to blame for what happened," feelings of "depression" and "unhappiness" most of the time, "loneliness," "vivid depiction of the deceased," "auditory hallucinations" of an infant crying and "general disorganization."

She said, however, that she was "very-well adjusted" to her loss and that she was aided by her belief in God and life after death. Reading the Bible was a comfort to her and "the mere fact that I have six other children to care for and not much time for thinking of past days." When asked which experiences she found most difficult following the death, she listed the following:

1. Removing already wrapped Christmas presents from the closet and disposing of clothing and toys.
2. To be around small children.
3. To organize my work and daily tasks.
4. To hear my 4-year-old "talk" to her in heaven.
5. To organize my thinking.

We see in these responses a continued disorientation and distress in the mother when thinking about her deceased child. While it is impossible to isolate any single variable as the cause of this difficulty, the importance of this child in a family of six other daughters was undeniably great.

Case 3

A 34-year-old attorney responded to the death of his 11-year-old son following hospitalization for a bone marrow malignancy. The father's symptoms of "insomnia" and "vivid depiction of the deceased" were not unusual for parents in the sample. For this father, the death had significant meanings that he discussed in the questionnaire:

> He was a beautiful child and taught me and many other adults some great lessons about love and courage…I think the most important thing is just to be able to accept without regret and to look back on the good and not to blame anyone or ask why.

The Responses of Husbands and Wives to the Death of a Spouse

The death of a husband or wife is seldom without meaning to the surviving partner. There are no easy generalizations that can apply to all cases of such deaths. A careful study of circumstances is necessary in order to perceive correctly the meaning that a surviving spouse attaches to the death of the marital partner. The following case histories profile a variety of experiences that can be associated with this type of bereavement.

Case 1

A wife responded to the death of her 34-year-old husband in the following way: she found that her 15-year-old daughter was very helpful in providing her with emotional and physical support. She commented, "She has become like a right hand and very protective." Her 7-year-old son, however, grew very fearful at the prospect of his mother leaving the house for any reason. The husband, who had been a traveling salesman, was away much of the time and this separation and absence from his father took on a new and fearful meaning for the child following his death. His mother could not be allowed to be absent in the same way.

The wife's symptomatology was not out of the ordinary. It included "insomnia," "weight loss," "feelings of isolation" and "confusion." Six months following the death, however, she considered herself "very well-adjusted" and listed the following items helpful in her adjustment:

1. Open communication in family.
2. Not being afraid to ask for help from those who hold out a hand; it gets easier.
3. Having faith that if you try, things will get better.
4. Keeping busy so you don't have time to feel sorry for yourself.
5. Children to care for and about.
6. Having lost my father at an early age.

The significance of kinship can come into sharp focus following the death of a spouse and distinct battle lines may be drawn between families as reported in the following case.

Case 2

A 38-year-old truck driver and beer salesman responded to the death of his 35-year-old wife. He returned the questionnaire approximately 6 months after his wife's death and stated that she had spent almost a third of the preceding year in the hospital. He now lives with his four children and shows no symptoms of prolonged or unusual grief. In fact, he said that he has become "more sensitive to others" and feels that he is "more considerate and helpful than before." When asked if he felt any marked hostility toward anyone following the death, he wrote: "[I] hate my mother-in-law." When asked to explain he added: "My mother-in-law blamed me." The respondent indicated that a traditional funeral service was held and that his wife's body was viewed. He wrote: "It should be viewed to let people pay their last respects."

He indicated that he had begun to feel better than before and had gained the weight back that he lost during his wife's illness. When asked what had helped him adjust to the bereavement and what he might recommend to others, he wrote: "Look around you at the other people you have seen who have the same or worse troubles than you." The sense of a comparative justice (or "distributive justice" as it is called by Homans) in weighing one's fortune following death is clearly important to this man in coping with his loss.[16]

Case 3

A 33-year-old high school administrator related his experiences following the death of his 33-year-old wife after she suffered a ruptured aneurysm. The respondent was left with two children and by the time he had returned the questionnaire (8 months after the death), he had hired a housekeeper to assist him in the management of his home. He stated that a public funeral service was held for his deceased wife together with a public reviewal. This to him seemed like "a fine tribute to a well-liked and loved person." He noted some tension between himself and his wife's family, however and wrote: "They feel uncomfortable at times and so do I. I communicate with my wife's mother OK, but it is not the same."

He reported many ordinary grief symptoms including "insomnia," "headaches," "increased consumption of alcohol," "tobacco" and "tranquilizers" as well as "a sense of having vividly seen his wife in his imagination" and "a wish to change many parts of his life." He talked with both his minister and a psychiatrist following the death and when asked how the death had affected his life in a *negative* manner, he listed the following:

1. Loss of security aspect of home
2. Loss of sounding board for problems and successes
3. Loss of feelings of love for someone
4. Loss of meaningful sex life
5. Need for somewhat aggressive sexual behavior

There is, however, an indication that some progress toward resolution of the death has been made. He wrote: "I am now more open to others and their lifestyles and more understanding of another's problems. I am more open to relationships with other women and have more freedom to do things. The problem is that I need a reason to do them." For him the most difficult experience following the death occurred when "a friend of my wife came to visit and did not know. She asked me where Jeanne was." When asked for advice for others in similar circumstances he stated: "You must be at peace with the memory of your loss and not live in self-guilt; [you] must understand death as a part of life."

The Responses of Adult Children to the Death of an Aged Parent

A significant feature of the modern world is the extension of life expectancy. It is not out of the ordinary for men and women in the United States to live well past their sixtieth birthday; indeed most do. When this fact is considered in conjunction with contemporary family patterns involving the emotional and physical disengagement of adult children from their elderly parents, we have the elements of a peculiarly modern form of bereavement.

Two important variables that come into focus in an examination of the grief responses of the adult child are age and sex. Typically, a younger surviving child is responding to the death of a younger parent. In such a case, it is usual for the parent-child bond to involve a greater amount of interaction and represent a wider array of meanings than in the case of the older child (45 and older) and the elderly parent (over age 75). In addition to this, we have noted that the termination of cross-sex parent-child bonds by death (e.g., a son and his mother or a daughter and her father) are more likely to produce a grief reaction similar to a "normal" grief response than would be the case for same sex kin (e.g., son and father or daughter and mother). While there were, of course, exceptions to both of the above generalizations, a pattern was observed from the interviews. The following cases are illustrative:

Case 1

A 25-year-old married woman with two small sons responded to the questionnaire approximately 8 months following the death of her 63-year-old father. He died in a hospital while suffering from intestinal difficulties for over a year. The funeral was a small gathering of about 25 people with only the daughter viewing the body. She did not have an open reviewal because it was her father's "last request" that this should not be done. Following the funeral she stated that she "lost respect for an uncle who lived 20 miles away and couldn't manage to get to the funeral of his only brother." She noted, however, that "[the brother's family] called to find out how much was inherited. The brother wanted everything although they were never close."

When asked if she were reluctant to think of the deceased, she responded, "No. He lived a beautiful life." She acknowledged, however, that it was difficult to "go through his things without thinking of him." She wondered, "Why me?" She also stated that she wanted to change many aspects of her life: "I won't rely on material things."

The daughter felt "very well-adjusted" to the death and partially accounted for this adjustment by the fact that "he was just so sick, I thank God He took him." She said that her "Church, husband and friends" were most helpful and that the experience had brought her own family closer together.

Case 2

A 22-year-old married male construction worker responded to the questionnaire one year following the death of his 50-year-old mother. His mother died a slow death from cancer and was hospitalized one month prior to her death. A traditional funeral service was held with a public viewing and burial. Approximately 75 people were in attendance. The son felt that viewing was an important part of the service. He wrote, "People that haven't seen her should be allowed to—like relatives who haven't seen her for a long time." The son displayed only one grief symptom in his responses a year following the death—"vivid depiction of the deceased in his imagination." There was evidence that he had already achieved a good deal of resolution. He noted that he "enjoyed being around people more" now and he "felt confident in giving orders." When left to care for his younger brothers, he found that they now had a greater respect for him. He stated that family closeness had increased and he was not reluctant to think of the deceased. "I grew up without a father so I relied on her [his mother] a great deal. We loved each other very much."

These two cases of younger, cross-sex bereavements stand out in sharp contrast to the following cases of older, same-sex bereavements.

Case 3

The respondent, a 45-year-old male construction worker, had the primary responsibility of attending to the death of his 79-year-old father after a long bout with emphysema. His father had planned in advance that his body should be cremated with no service of any kind and the son complied with his wishes. The interviewer wrote, "[The respondent] and one brother took 'the last ride' with his father from the funeral home to the crematorium. At one point he looked into the furnace which he regretted for a time. Later he distributed the ashes in a nearby lake, taking the ride alone with his father's ashes."

At another point in the interview, after the respondent had denied experiencing any of the ordinary grief symptoms, the interviewer asked him what had helped him adjust to his loss. He responded by saying: "There was no adjustment required. After all, my father's body is just so much meat. I don't consider myself bereaved." When the interviewer asked him why he had chosen not to view the body, he said that he would have, "had the person been especially close, like a wife or a child."

Case 4

A 62-year-old single woman was interviewed concerning the death of her 94-year-old mother a year following its occurrence. Her mother had been confined to a nursing home because of senility for a year and a half prior to the death. Death was by "natural causes" and was neither sudden nor unexpected. While the daughter acknowledged that she and her brother viewed the body, they decided not to have a public viewing or service. She noted that the body should not be publicly viewed because "it's an intrusion on the privacy of the individual and the family."

The daughter denied any symptoms of grief. She stated clearly, "It hasn't affected my outlook on life at all." When asked what situations she found difficult following the death, she replied, "There weren't any difficult situations." Additional responses in our sample shed light on a number of other contemporary issues regarding the care and treatment of the elderly as well as responses to their dying and their deaths.

Case 5

A 42-year-old banker was interviewed following the death of his 81-year-old mother after she had developed pneumonia, 5 months following nursing home confinement. He acknowledged no symptoms of grief to the interviewer, but did note that he felt angry with his mother's physician. He felt that the doctor had gone to "extreme efforts to maintain her life after she developed pneumonia. When intravenous feeding was not effective (her hand swelled up), the doctor would not accept assurance that there would be no malpractice suit."

Case 6

A 51-year-old life insurance agent who responded to the questionnaire 18 months after the death of his 79-year-old mother, stated that the death "hasn't made any significant difference." When asked what he would recommend to others in similar circumstances, he wrote: "Recognition and better use of the life insurance man in counseling survivors (i.e., Social Security, pensions, fringe benefits, equities, profit-sharing plans). Their expertise far surpasses that of most lawyers, but they are often overlooked."

Case 7

A 58-year-old lawyer experienced the loss of his 87-year-old father. When he was interviewed 6 months following the death, there was no evidence that he was suffering any of the ordinary grief symptoms. Both he and his father were members of a memorial society and disposition of the body was by cremation. The respondent indicated that his father was nearly blind, had been declining in health and he could not think of any way in which the death had affected his life or the life of his family. He felt it was most important to "work out details in advance to spare the survivors. You should join a memorial society." The anticipation of the death was clearly seen when the respondent was asked what had helped him adjust to his loss. He responded that "There really wasn't any adjustment necessary, after all, he was 87 and we all have to go sometime."

It is apparent that many of the responses to death in the sample of adult children are very different from the responses reported by the sample of spouses and parents. We have observed that increased longevity of the aged parent brings with it *increased anticipation* of death for many adult children. We have noted also that for a significant number of respondents in this group there is little or no evidence of what could be termed a "normal" grief response.

CONCLUSION

In the study we have examined the emotional and social responses of three groups of bereaved persons. We found that the responses of the adult children differed in significant ways from the response of both the bereaved spouses and the bereaved parents. These differences were analyzed for content in both the mailed questionnaire and in the interview forms. We conclude that:

1. For some adult-children the death of an aged parent appears as an event with limited emotional significance. Two persons in the sample (both sons responding to the deaths of their fathers) indicated that they did not consider themselves bereaved at all. Circumstances that are associated with this pattern include: (a) advanced age of parent, (b) institutionalization of parent, (c) loss of functioning of parent, (d) substantial disengagement from social interaction with parent and (e) same sex of surviving child as parent.
2. Mortuary behaviors associated with this muted or absent grief response typically involve limited ceremonialization. Death in these cases was anticipated long before its occurrence. For the cases described, there is evidence of immediate disposition of the body (occasionally without the survivor viewing the body) followed by private burial or cremation. In at least two cases there was no formal recognition of the death. This differs significantly from the responses

of the spouse and parent groups, both of whom usually chose public ceremonies and viewed the body unless it was severely mutilated or disfigured.

DISCUSSION

We have observed that the constellation of feelings and behaviors precipitated in some adult children by the death of an elderly parent was frequently characterized by diminished or absent grief followed by limited post-death activities. While the number of adult children in the study was few and the number of persons who displayed the behavior and reported the muted feelings that were discussed was even fewer, it is our opinion that we are witness to a development in interpersonal relationships that promises to grow more pronounced in the years ahead. Like the tip of an iceberg, the responses of the adult children suggest the magnitude of the changes that lie hidden below the surface of social practices. While the tip in no way tells us of the iceberg's actual proportions, nor of its potential, it does inform us of the iceberg's presence. It is in like manner that we view the responses of the bereaved adult children.

In the following discussion we will attempt to substantiate our estimation of the significance of these observations by examining certain contemporary trends and social developments that appear relevant for our findings. In particular, we will focus on changes in the nature and function of the nuclear family, the changing status and role of the elderly, the institutionalization of the dying and the changing conceptions of life and death that are presently manifest in American society. It is within the context of such changes that our findings display their full meaning. Finally, we will propose some theoretical implications that are suggested by the results of the survey.

Changes in the character of American culture have been so rapid, complex and far-reaching that any analysis must of necessity be selective and incomplete. There can be little doubt, however, that change in the larger society is affected by, as well as reflects, change in the nature and function of the family and its members. The muted psychological and social aftermath of the death of elderly parents, that were reported in the study, appear to reflect features of family life that are characteristic of our time.

It is important to recognize that the mature adult child need not experience the grief reaction or the profound sense of loss that has been documented in the case of the parent or spouse following a death. In modern society, the elderly are often defined differently than are other age groups. They "have had their life." It is only "normal" and "natural" that they die. Death brings "peace to a troubled mind" and "freedom from pain" to a person racked with cancer. Furthermore, the modern industrial world has a strong work ethic. Personal worth for men (and increasingly for women) is calculated in terms of one's economic value to the community. The principles of economy, efficiency and utility bear heavily upon an age group that is not only retired from employment but is also increasingly dependent upon younger wage-earners for support and sustenance. This attitude is reflected in the increased concern that is expressed about the level of taxation associated with social security payments, medicare and other programs of support specifically designed for the elderly.

In this connection, too, we must take note of the fact that while the elderly are the primary consumers of health services, no sector of the economy has reflected a greater increase in growth or cost in the past few years than the field of medical care. That this is occurring in a period of increased taxation merely adds to the burden of the wage-earner while it aggravates the problems of our dependent and elderly population. Moreover, the decline of direct familial support of the elderly and the emergence of professional care in institutional settings, funded frequently by third-party payees, merely serves to complicate matters further. Social ties and familial bonds are loosened by such developments and give impetus and support to the behaviors that have been reported. When we reflect also on the centrifugal force that occupation plays on the extended family by increasingly requiring that the wage-earner become geographically mobile in order to progress within the hierarchy of an organization, we not only have a society consisting of families separated by age and occupation, but a society in which many families are segregated by time and distance as well.

On the other hand, the remarkable success of medical science over the past several decades, together with the public health programs and other technologies that have contributed so greatly to our general health and overall longevity, make it increasingly difficult not to turn our elderly relative over to the health care establishment when they are sick. Belief in the health care institution on the one hand and the propriety of doing the utmost for an ill relative on the other serves the paradoxical function of expressing concern while it diminishes contact.

The findings presented in the study suggest that the death of an elderly person is frequently anticipated long before its actual occurrence. In the process, affectional relationships are strained as family members face the immediate and prospective problems associated with the eventual death. The phenomenon that accounts for this process of emotional diminishment is anticipatory grief. It is illustrated in the following case of a physician's wife who lost her husband to cancer of the abdomen.

> A physician experimented on himself while in medical school. He ingested some radioactive fats as part of his work toward a Ph.D. thesis on carcinogenic substances. Two and a half years later, as he was about to graduate, he became ill and his cancer was subsequently discovered. A university medical team decided to film his dying for educational purposes, recording those events that occurred between him and his wife as well as videotaping a series of interviews with a psychiatrist who was both a colleague and friend. Over the four to five month period that the interviews were conducted the wife's appearance changed dramatically. Initially, she wore her long hair severely pulled back, dark horn-rimmed glasses, long skirts and "sensible" shoes. By the end of the interviews, however, she had become "Vogue-like" in appearance—the opposite of the image she first presented the viewer. Neither she nor the psychiatrist acknowledged this change, nor were they conscious of talking about her husband in the *past tense* (even though he was present at the interview). Neither she nor the psychiatrist displayed an awareness of the mental shift that had occurred in them both.

We would argue that anticipatory grief played a very important part in the dramatic changes that were observed in the wife's behavior, as well as in her physical appearance. One is left to ask how she thought of herself, or what others, who knew the couple, thought of her behavior or appearance at the time of her husband's death.

The question is relevant given the fact that in other comparable cases the spouse's life is complicated further by what is being increasingly observed: physicians, nurses and paramedical personnel becoming more involved in the lives of their patients. In a seminar held at Wayne State University, one of the authors was present when a nurse exclaimed with great emotion that "if family survivors couldn't behave the way they should following a death, they should stay away from the hospital and from the funeral!" To repeat: it can happen that by the time the death of the patient occurs, the staff will experience the loss of the patient more deeply than expected. On the other hand, a confused family member, not understanding her lack of affect or unable to cry or express grief, will attempt to brave it out and assume the role of host or hostess. Thus, it can happen that a survivor's behavior will be judged by the staff as heartless.

This phenomenon gives rise to the potential for role discrepancy and role reversal on the part of the caregiver and the survivor. The caregiver grieves but is not bereaved, while the bereft survivor may be beyond or incapable of experiencing grief. As a result, the professional caregiver not only has the potential of complicating the dying process, but the situation also has the capacity of casting in an unfavorable light the muted responses of the survivor. There can be misunderstandings between caregiver and surviving kin regarding post-death behaviors and reactions to loss. The data showed less ceremonialization, higher cremation rates and a decreased frequency of reviewal of the body on the part of the adult children, as well as a diminished likelihood that they would later acknowledge or memorialize the death. The reasons offered by the respondents for these reactions included not only economic factors but philosophical and aesthetic considerations also. Moreover, some respondents felt that such ceremonies would be inappropriate or empty gestures considering the small number of people who would be affected in any way by the death. Additionally, a portion of the respondents reported being repulsed by traditional funeral practices and found the preparation and viewing of the dead body to be "barbaric," "primitive," "pagan," "disgusting" or "sick."

It is important to observe that the emotions expressed with regard to traditional funeral practices, and particularly viewing rites, stand in sharp contrast to the noticeable lack of affect reported by these respondents in connection with the death itself. It is reasonable to propose that the negative responses reported in the study could be generated, in part, by embarrassment that emanates from the appearance that an elderly person, often emaciated by long illness, frequently presents at the time of death. Many middle-class Americans live sheltered aseptic lives and attempt to protect themselves from "offensive" smells, "unsightly" views and "unpleasant" experiences and may find, in the wrinkled visage of death, a sight too disturbing to behold.

We offer this explanation as one among many that could explain why an appreciable number of adult children chose not to view the body of the deceased. While the majority of all respondents reported that the body of their family member was viewed, it is important, we believe, to explore this controversial issue further, particularly when it is apparent from our analysis that the tenor and thrust of the reasons for not viewing displayed such wide variability.

Among the parent group, for example, disfigurement and mutilation were the primary considerations for those who chose not to have the body of their child viewed. The parents of children who were burned, drowned, or mutilated often felt that viewing might spoil the memory of the deceased. Some parents were reluctant to have other persons view the body for fear that they would do so only out of morbid curiosity. Those parents wished to protect their own privacy and the privacy of their child. On the other hand, a small number of parents, as in the adult child group, characterized the practice of viewing as "primitive," "barbaric" and "grotesque." Others wished to avoid what they characterized as "unnecessary pain." Finally, a few parents of newborns were encouraged by others not to view the body of their child for fear of aggravating their anguish.

For surviving husbands and wives who chose not to have the body of their spouse viewed, the primary consideration was a wish to remember the deceased alive and well and a feeling that viewing "leaves an emotionally bad impression" or a "haunting memory." As in the other cases, a few felt that the practice was "barbaric," "uncivilized," "artificial" and "pagan" or that the body meant "nothing" after death. Others in this group did not view because of "bodily disfigurement" or "severe illness." Some felt the cosmetology required would be a "waste of money." Still others reported they did not view out of "respect" for the wishes of the deceased but felt regretful that the body could not be viewed. Finally, a few felt that "reviewal would only increase the sorrow of survivors," or "help people to cling to the unreality of the death."

For the adult children who chose not to have the body of their elderly parent viewed, most characterized the practice, as noted earlier, in ways that connoted greater feeling about the practice than the other two groups. The adult child group more often cited religious or philosophical reasons rather than the personal or practical considerations that were noted among the responses of the parents and spouses. The following statements characterize the tone of the adult child's responses to the practice of viewing: "pagan," "ghoulish," "depressing," "useless," "morbid," "ridiculously expensive" or "unclean." A few noted that they had viewed the body of someone close in their youth and felt emotionally scarred by the experience. Some felt viewing to be an invasion of privacy or else felt that doing so would ruin their memories. One man respected his mother's wishes not to view but noted "the body should be viewed unless there is some disfigurement." Another made the interesting observation that the survivor is "a victim of many forces and at such times funeral directors and rabbis seem to fear emotional outbreaks and want to avoid these for their own reasons." Finally, some in this group did not view because it would have interfered with their plans for immediate cremation.

In addition, we would suggest that many survivors who are ultimately responsible for the disposition of the deceased and other post-death activities may be hesitant out of concern for the negative judgments that others may pass regarding the limited emotional response that they display. Traditionally, when a death occurs within a family, the cultural directive is to mourn. Failure to do so has not only been defined as pathological by psychologists and debated by anthropologists, but as has been observed, can also generate emotional outbursts from professional caregivers. It may well be that what has been observed in the study regarding the abandonment of funeralization and other commemorative or memorial services by adult children is an attempt to avoid social criticism or the stigma of "a death in the family."

The following remarks, however, serve to characterize the range and substance of the feelings and beliefs of those respondents of all three groups who reported that the body of the deceased had been viewed and who expressed their belief that the practice of viewing was proper.

A wife wrote:	I felt good about him—he looked good. I long ago wondered why people wanted to view the body—but it's different when it's your own loved one.
A mother stated:	When you can't view the body, you're left with a cold, empty feeling. It gives you more time to prepare for his being gone forever—much better for the mourners.
A mother commented:	I thought it would hurt people who loved him if I didn't permit viewing.
A wife stated:	I followed general practice—this is something one should do. My last image of him in the casket was a better memory than seeing him just after death in the hospital.
A husband observed:	I had a warm natural feeling about being with friends during this time.
A son responded to the death of his mother:	If a person dies from natural causes and is not disfigured, she should be viewed. It helped me to see her look natural—to face the fact of her death.
A wife wrote:	He had been looking so poorly—now he was at peace.
A mother commented:	Our family decision was to have the body viewed—I just wanted to be with him a bit longer. Many people attended the visitation.
A husband wrote:	It helps you to realize that the person is really dead.

The findings of the study demonstrate that grief is neither a unitary concept nor an unvarying experience. On the contrary, the perspective on grief that emerges is that of a highly complex, multi-dimensional phenomenon that varies widely according to social as well as psychological attributes. An individual grief reaction represents the interaction of psychological, physiological and social factors. Our study underscores the significance that these factors play in the determination of a particular grief response. First, it can be observed that social processes exercise an important role in determining the nature of the grief precipitated. Societal processes such as the change in the nature of the nuclear family, the change in status and role of the elderly and the institutionalization of the dying, serve to influence both the meaning and character of interpersonal relationships. Second, we have observed that the nature of the relationship severed by death is an important determinate of the grief response. Just as every relationship has a unique meaning for each of the participants, so too does the grief occasioned by the rupture of each relationship have a unique quality. Its significance and importance, however, are affected and circumscribed by relevant social and cultural forces. Third, the study focused on the functions of ritual and ceremony as collective responses to the profound life event of death. And it was observed that as the character of the grief experienced generally reflects the nature of the relationship, so too the character of the grief experienced influences the manner of the funeral ceremony.

Additionally, we have come to see that ceremonies and rituals such as the funeral may be differentially perceived and received in the death/grief constellation. The study, moreover, indicates that the distinction between "pathological" and "normal" grief may not be as clearly delineated or as readily determined as has been thought. Both Freud and Lindemann, for example, believed that the absence of grief indicated an "abnormal" condition while the literature on the topic generally takes for granted that the affectional bond among kin, when ruptured, results in grief. The observations that the anthropologist Spiro[17] made among the Ifaluk more than 40 years ago, however, argue strongly in favor of the conclusion that the response to loss is culturally learned and not genetically determined. In other words, humankind does not "naturally" grieve any more than it "naturally" laughs or cries. These activities, like walking, talking, eating and sleeping, are to an important degree products of our social experiences and cultural conditioning. Spiro reported that the immediate survivors displayed grief and distress only until the conclusion of the funeral. Then they behaved "as if they had suffered no loss at all." Their grief, Spiro reported, "seemed to disappear as if by magic."

Among the Trobriand Islanders, bereavement reactions are considerably different from our own. In that society, who is bereaved depends upon one's degree of relationship to the deceased's mother. Thus, it is believed that maternal kin, regardless of the degree of relationship, are more affected by the death than any of the paternal relatives or even the spouse. Thus, a wife may grieve at the death of her husband, but this is primarily obligatory and ceremonial. It is not recognized as spontaneous and she is not considered to be bereaved in the same sense as are her husband's maternal kin.

The changing meanings of life and death, as well as the contemporary development of new and complex interpersonal relationships, may require a more subtle and complex typology of grief than has seemed necessary in the past. The difference between "high-grief" and "low-grief" potential deaths, the phenomenon of anticipatory grief, the role of the surrogate griever and the experience of "griefless bereavement" are psychological and sociological phenomena that call for further study.

Clinically, the preliminary findings of the study suggest that attention needs to be focused in several directions. Further study of the changing nuclear family from the perspective of its death-related behavior is strongly recommended. Death is both a crisis of family dismemberment and a crisis of personal identity. It is well known that crises can serve to tighten the cohesion and reinforce the social and affectional ties of a family or group. We also know that crises can overburden personal and familial resources and precipitate serious social and emotional disturbances.

Within the family system, the death of one member will affect survivors differently. The nature of the prior relationship, involvement during the dying trajectory, physical and emotional proximity are only some of the variables that affect individual responses to death and which enhance or handicap a family's ability to cope with a loss. Some members may experience their grief in an anticipatory manner prior to the death; others may feel little sense of loss at any time, while others may be deeply and acutely affected by the bereavement. The heterogeneity of responses has the potential to complicate communication among family members brought together by the death. Some may resent the apparent coldness and grieflessness of others, while those who have already disengaged themselves emotionally from the deceased may feel guilty for their failure to display an "appropriate" response. Peers of the elderly deceased may resent the apparent casualness with which the younger survivors—even the children of the deceased—dispose of the deceased's remains or effects. While feelings such as these are seldom expressed or acknowledged, their existence may serve to widen the generation gap, while increasing the potential for conscious feelings of guilt, resentment and hostility.

Death and dying are increasingly the experience of the aged. The findings of the study suggest that more attention needs to be paid to the intergenerational dynamics within a family. There are observable trends in modern society that function to isolate and disengage the elderly from their families. The muting of affect and the delimiting of ceremony reported in the study appear to be manifestations of such disengagement. To the extent that the elderly are socially removed, the personal, familial and societal impact of their deaths are diminished with the result that there is a lessened desire to commemorate their passing. Such a situation may have dysfunctional consequences both for the elderly and for their "griefless" survivors. For the elderly sick, the personal implications of anticipatory grief may be a form of social death, in the sense that they are increasingly "dead to the world" of their previous relationships. At the time of their actual deaths, they may be mourned more by elderly friends or by the professional hospital staff than by their own sons or daughters.

Moreover, the lack of emotional and minimal ceremony following the death of an aged parent and grandparent may have latent dysfunctional consequences for grandchildren. The young grandchild witnessing a grief-limited ceremony and other muted patterns of post-death behavior may well conclude that the elderly are not very consequential. A child may have seen a parent show more emotion during an argument or following the death of a family pet than at the funeral of the grandparent. A child may wonder if one's own passing would evoke the same response. While these considerations are both speculative and subtle, they, nevertheless, merit our attention.

Finally, at the sociocultural level of analysis, the findings of the study raise questions regarding the function of ceremonies in modern society. The limited ceremonialization following the death of a socially disengaged, elderly person may "make sense" at the personal level. Funerals are for the living and when the living are not seriously upset or disrupted by the passing of a family member the need for a traditional funeral may be diminished. Funerals, however, have other functions in addition to facilitating the resolution of grief among individual survivors. As social ceremonies that bring together a relatively large group of family members and friends, funerals are important socialization experiences that help to transmit important values of the culture from generation to generation. The impulse to exclude children from funerals as well as to eliminate funerals from society may have unintended consequences. In addition to cutting children off from direct experiences with expressions of love, concern and support at the time of a family loss, the delimiting of contemporary funerary customs may also deprive a child of the opportunity to learn about one of life's basic facts—death. Also, the social worth and intrinsic value of the elderly may be implicitly denied by the failure to ceremonialize their deaths. Children and the elderly are increasingly separated from each other in today's world; if this separation is extended at death, we can expect yet a further widening of the generation gap. The long-range personal and social implications inherent in these potential developments require serious study.

NOTES

1. S. Freud. 1959. Mourning and Melancholia. In *The Collected Papers of Sigmund Freud,* Vol. 4. New York: Basic Books (originally published in 1917).
2. Ibid.
3. T.D. Eliot. 1962. The Bereaved Family. *The Annals of the American Academy of Political and Social Sciences* 160:84-90.
4. H.P. Becker. 1926. A Social-Psychological Study of Bereavement. Masters thesis, Northwestern University; D. Fulcomer. 1942. The Adjustive Behavior of Some Recently Bereaved Spouses: A Psycho-Sociological Study. Doctoral dissertation, Northwestern University.
5. E. Lindemann. 1944. Symptomatology and Management of Acute Grief. *American Journal of Psychiatry* 101:141-148.
6. G. Gorer. 1965. *Death, Grief, and Mourning.* New York: Doubleday.
7. C.M. Parkes. 1973. *Bereavement: Studies of Grief and Adult Life.* New York: International Universities Press.
8. I.O. Glick et al. 1974. *The First Year of Bereavement.* New York: John Wiley & Sons.
9. E.H. Volkart and S.T. Michael. 1957. Bereavement and Mental Health, in A.H. Leighton et al., ed., *Explorations in Social Psychology.* New York: Basic Books.
10. A.S. Kraus and A.M. Lillenfeld. 1959. Some Epidemiologic Aspects of the High Mortality Rate in the Young Widowed Group. *Journal of Chronic Disease* 10:207-217.
11. H.Z. Lopata. 1972. *Widowhood in an American City.* Morristown, NJ: General Learning Corporation.
12. We are aware that this procedure introduces a bias into our study given the discrepancy between the actual number of deaths annually and their actual reportage, but the refusal of the State Department of Vital Statistics to permit us access to the death certificates (despite several requests by the director of the Center) left us no other course. The Department's refusal was based on the grounds that it might be left open to criticism if such information reached the hands of unwanted solicitors (i.e., cemetery salesmen). We might add in this regard that on several occasions the subjects challenged the interviewers as having ulterior motives for the survey.
13. R. Fulton. 1964. *The Sacred and the Secular.* Milwaukee: Bulfin.
14. These figures represent the total sample size. However, 13 respondents were related to the deceased in a way that was not typical of others in the sample (e.g., niece, brother-in-law, aunt, etc.). These respondents were dropped from the analysis resulting in a total sample size of 558.
15. G. Owen, R. Fulton and K. Krohn. 1976. Death, Grief and Meaning. Paper presented at the Midwest Sociological Society Meetings, St. Louis.
16. G.C. Homans. 1961. *Social Behavior: Its Elementary Forms.* New York: Harcourt, Brace & World.
17. M. Spiro. 1949. Ifaluk: A South Sea Culture. Unpublished manuscript, National Research Council. New Haven, CT: HRAF Press.

9

Religion and Bereavement: A Conceptual Framework

Robert Wuthnow, PhD
Kevin Christiano, PhD and
John Kuzloski, PhD

INTRODUCTION

Religion has long been regarded as a relevant factor in understanding bereavement.[1] A few studies have examined this relationship.[2] But the kind of extensive research applied to other correlates of religious commitment has yet to be applied to the study of bereavement.

Apart from the results of a few highly limited studies, the basis for making judgments about the relationship between religion and bereavement is restricted to that which can be inferred indirectly from research focusing on related problems. From this material and from the theoretical literature it can be inferred with reasonable confidence that religion is likely to have an important bearing on the manner in which bereaved persons cope with their bereavement. The following, in particular, point to the likelihood of such a relationship.

First, research has found that religious commitment (except measures affected by declining physical health) is particularly salient among older persons; that is, among those most likely to be confronted with bereavement.[3] Indeed, religion in one form or another appears to be a dimension of life that is virtually universal in this age group.

Second, research has demonstrated that religious organizations function, along with family and community, as significant social support systems for many of their members. Religious organizations perform this function by providing friendship ties,[4] by reinforcing localistic loyalties[5] and by serving as "family surrogates."[6]

Third, religion has been conceptualized in the theoretical literature as a source of subjective meaning, a framework that helps to make reality understandable.[7] Empirical evidence has shown positive relationships between religiosity and feelings of purpose in life and well-being.[8]

Finally, research has generally (although not consistently) shown religious commitment to be higher among persons in crisis situations and among persons confronted with subjective stress or anxiety (reviewed in Argyle and Beit-Hallahmi[9]).

In addition to whatever impressionistic notions may be held, these pieces of evidence indicate that religion is likely to have a bearing on coping with bereavement. But they suggest only the likelihood of a relationship, not the nature of content of that relationship. It cannot be presumed that the relationship necessarily is positive. Nor is it at all clear how different beliefs, experiences and practices may be associated with bereavement. We are, therefore, in the curious situation of having strong reason to suspect that religion is an important factor to understand if ways of facilitating adjustment among the bereaved are to be found, but research thus far has failed to reveal the main dimensions of this factor.

The available empirical and theoretical literature does, however, afford some clues about the kinds of religious factors that warrant attention. As the foregoing suggests, some of the likely effects of religion on bereavement derive from the fact that religious orientations seem to provide meaning, while others stem from the support or sense of belonging that religion may provide. The distinction between meaning and belonging is, in fact, one that has been employed usefully in other studies of religion (e.g., Greeley,[10] Roof[11]).

RELIGION AS A SOURCE OF MEANING

In the comparative study of modern religion, problems of bereavement, illness and existential anxiety—in short, "problems of suffering"—have occupied a central position at least as far as theoretical discussion has been concerned. These problems are said to raise "religious questions" in that they confront the believer with questions about the meaningfulness of existence. Geertz[12] writes in his celebrated essay on the definition of religion: "As a religious problem, the problem of suffering is, paradoxically, not how to avoid suffering but how to suffer, how to make of physical pain, personal loss, worldly defect, or the helpless contemplation of others' agony something bearable, supportable—something, as we say, sufferable." Religions attempt to make bereavement "sufferable" by locating it within a symbolic context, an interpretive framework, in which suffering becomes understandable and bearable.

Religious Belief

At the level of belief, religions attempt to create a conception of existence—a *nomos*, to use Peter Berger's[13] term—in which death is incorporated as a meaningful element. In the Judeo-Christian tradition the beliefs functioning most directly to incorporate death within a framework of meaningful events include conceptions of God, an afterlife and explanations of evil (theodicies).

Belief in God

As with any widely shared belief, there is considerable variation in the beliefs about God that people hold and these variations must be compared in order to determine their relationships with bereavement. Much research has been devoted to this problem (reviewed in Roof[14]), resulting in a number of conceptual distinctions and empirical measures. Two such distinctions appear particularly relevant.

The first distinguishes belief in God according to degrees of certainty about God's existence. Studies employing this distinction have demonstrated that certainty is significantly associated with a variety of other attitudes and values. As a result, measures of certainty of belief in God have become one of the most commonly employed empirical items in quantitative research on religious commitment.

The second variable concerns differences in images of God. A distinction that appears particularly promising is that between intimate (or personal) and remote images of God; that is, images positing immediate and direct cognizance of an influence over the individual on the part of a divine being versus images positing only indirect or generalized influences.[15]

It may be hypothesized that certainty of God's existence and intimacy of imagery about God will be positively associated with perceptions of divine comfort and guidance among the bereaved (except perhaps among those imbued with a wrathful image of God) and these perceptions, in turn, will be positively associated with a sense of meaning, purpose and well-being. To the extent that psychological and emotional well-being constitute significant dimensions of overall health—a concept gaining increasing acceptance among health practitioners—these perceptions may also be associated positively with physical reductions in stress and with enhanced physical functioning.

Although no research has examined the entire nexus of these relationships, research addressing particular aspects of the hypothesized relationships suggests that they should be evident among the bereaved in the form predicted. For example, some research among members of a mainline Protestant denomination indicates that certainty of belief and intimacy of imagery about God are positively associated with perceptions of God's comfort and guidance.[16] For another example, Hochschild[17] found that many of the elderly widows in her study regarded God as a personal "Heavenly Father" whose presence was intimate and protective. This imagery of God appeared to provide strength, comfort and meaning in the face of loneliness and grief (cf. Glick et al.[18]). Well-being, more particularly, appears likely to be enhanced among the bereaved insofar as personal imagery about God counteracts feelings of desperation or anomie stemming from the loss of a loved one or the additional responsibilities that bereavement imposes on a surviving spouse. To the extent that God is perceived as a personally caring being, feelings of vulnerability of the kind often noted among survivors of tragedies (e.g., Erikson[19]) may also be inhibited.

These assertions can be formalized as a set of hypotheses:

H1: Certainty of belief in God will be positively associated with perceptions of divine comfort and guidance.

H2: Personal or intimate imagery of God will be associated positively with perceptions of divine comfort and guidance.

H3: Perceptions of divine comfort and guidance will be negatively associated with feelings of anomie and vulnerability among the bereaved.

H4: Perceptions of divine comfort and guidance will be positively associated with a sense of meaning, purpose and well-being among the bereaved.

H5: Certainty of belief in God and personal imagery about God will be positively associated with one another.

It is also worth noting that these relationships may function differently for widows and widowers. Hochschild's[20] research suggests that God may function, as it were, as a surrogate authority figure and more particularly as a surrogate spouse among widows. However, the masculinity of conventional imagery about the nature of God makes it more likely that this imagery will serve as a surrogate spouse for women than for men. Thus, an additional hypothesis might be:

H6: Personal or intimate imagery of God will be more common among widows than among widowers.

Belief in Life After Death

Belief in life after death has also been widely regarded as having an important connection with bereavement, not simply because it denies the finality of death (which may be of either positive or negative import), but because it has traditionally involved a conception of reward which compensates for the trials and anguish of the present life and, in certain interpretations, holds forth the possibility of a spiritual reunion between the bereaved and the deceased. The traditional conception of an afterlife, therefore, provides meaning to the bereaved by devaluing the circumstances of the present world. This devaluation pertains both to perceptions of the fate of the deceased and to fears about one's own death (which are likely to be exacerbated by bereavement). The following hypotheses are suggested:

H7: Belief in the existence of an afterlife will be associated with positive feelings about the fate of the deceased.
H8: Belief in the existence of an afterlife will be negatively associated with anxieties about one's own death.

While it seems likely that the traditional imagery of life after death may play an important role in coping with bereavement among the minority who adhere to this imagery, it also appears likely that other religious imagery about the meaning of death may be more widespread and, consequently, more significant to the manner in which a majority of Americans cope with bereavement (cf. Grof and Halifax[21]).

Parsons has suggested a useful conceptualization of American imagery about death.[22] Parsons' approach stresses what he calls "gift of life" imagery inherent in the Judeo-Christian tradition. Following the work of Mauss,[23] Parsons suggests that gift relationships, in general, serve as an important source of self-worth by dramatizing a relationship between individuals and some entity other than themselves. A means of imputing worth to the experience of bereavement, therefore, is to conceive of death as a kind of gift relationship. In Judeo-Christian imagery, such a relationship derives naturally from the belief that life is initially a gift from God. Death, in turn, can be conceived of as a final return of this gift to God; in short as a reciprocation. Parsons suggests that the plausibility of this idea has been enhanced by the fact that most people can now expect to live to old age.

The main secular alternative to this gift imagery, Parsons argues, is to structure death as a kind of defeat for those who in some way were responsible for the well-being of the deceased, such as the attending physicians, the bereaved survivor or the deceased (cf. Krupp and Kligfeld[24]). The main options for expressing this sense of defeat appear to be anger and denial and since anger directed either at the deceased or at the bereaved is likely to be difficult for the bereaved to express, denial is likely to be the most common mode of coping with bereavement, as many have suggested (e.g., Berger and Lieban[25]).

Parsons' formulation has not been tested empirically, but it poses a set of hypotheses worthy of exploration:

H9: Anxieties about death will be negatively associated with measures of overall well-being among the bereaved.

H10: Belief that life is a gift from God will be associated positively with belief that death represents a return to God of the life that God has given.

H11: Conceiving of death as an act of reciprocation to God will be negatively associated with anxieties about death (including anger and denial).

H12: Since the "reciprocation" conception of death represents a *final* act of fulfillment in relation to one's obligations to God, this conception is more likely to be held among older people than among younger people.

Theodicies

In Max Weber's[26] classic discussion of theodicies (explanations of evil), death constitutes an anomaly, an event having no intrinsic meaning or value, but which must be explained if a religious framework is to impose meaning on the totality of human existence. In the Judeo-Christian tradition, the theodicy problem essentially takes the form of explaining how a righteous and all-merciful God can allow death, grief, pain and tragedy to occur.

The particular value of this conception of theodicies for the study of religion and bereavement is that it focuses attention specifically on those elements of religious belief concerned with death. Alternative explanations of suffering are, in Weber's view, decisive factors in telling believers how they are to approach death and what they must do in order to live meaningfully in the face of death. In addition to such generic beliefs as images of God and images of life after death, therefore, theodicies are likely to have an important bearing on the manner in which individuals cope with bereavement.

The empirical study of theodicies is still in an embryonic phase, but previous research has shed enough light on the problem to suggest that theodicies pertaining to the understanding of death are likely to take the following forms:

a. Explanations that blame God or question the mercy of God.
b. Explanations that blame the self for suffering and grief, defining them as punishments for wrong-doing.
c. Explanations that place suffering and tragedies beyond the realm of human comprehension, while affirming the ability of God to turn these events to good purposes.
d. Explanations that regard suffering primarily as a matter of definition or as an attitude of mind.
e. Explanations that deny any meaning or reality to suffering, regarding death instead in fatalistic, coincidental or strictly causal terms.

In short, evil can be attributed, respectively, to God, the self, life, the mind, or the imagination.

The tendency to question or to blame God in the aftermath of bereavement appears to be a relatively common occurrence even among the religiously committed. In such instances, bereavement not only poses the usual problems associated with mourning and adjustment, but also raises doubts for the believer about the adequacy of one's convictions about God and, therewith, about the meaning and purpose of life. Such questioning may fulfill a therapeutic function insofar as it allows the bereaved to objectify and express anger, but it may also contribute to a sense of religious guilt or uncertainty that inhibits a longer-range sense of well-being. Theodicies that blame the self (that is, regard bereavement as punishment for wrong-doing) may also lead to a sense of guilt or failure that must be resolved if long-term adjustment is to take place.

In contrast, theodicies asserting an inscrutable God who is nonetheless purposeful and merciful appear more likely to generate feelings of comfort and guidance of the kind discussed earlier. On occasion, theodicies of this kind also impose an interesting cost-benefit calculus upon the bereaved. Holding fast to the idea that God is able to bring good of even the worst situation, the believer is likely in fact to perceive such benefits. Among them may be an increased understanding of God's love, greater concern for the problems of others, new insights about oneself and particularly in evangelical contexts, the idea that may inspire others to become believers.

The theodicy that regards bereavement chiefly as a matter of mind appears most conducive to taking responsibility for one's own attitudes and feelings. However, it may also generate what has come to be called "survivor guilt" in cases where this responsibility proves too great a burden to be fulfilled successfully. Finally, the fatalistic conception of death appears most likely to discourage the open expression of grief and other emotions associated with bereavement.

These observations must be taken in the spirit of illustration rather than comprehensiveness, but they suggest hypotheses of the following kind:

H13: Questioning or blaming God will be positively associated with the ability to express anger arising in response to bereavement.
H14: Questioning or blaming God will be negatively associated with a sense of well-being among those for whom this questioning raises doubts about the purpose of life.
H15: Blaming oneself for the death of a loved one will be negatively associated with a sense of well-being.
H16: Asserting the ability of God to bring good from evil will be positively associated with a sense of well-being.
H17: Perceptions of divine benefits from bereavement (such as greater understanding of God's love) will be positively associated with a sense of well-being.
H18: Fatalistic conceptions of death will be negatively associated with the ability to express grief or anger in response to bereavement.

Moral Obligations

Whereas religious belief concerns basic assumptions about the nature of reality, moral obligations refer to the concrete responsibilities and loyalties held to be proper and legitimate. The link between moral obligations and bereavement is that coping with bereavement involves a problem of meaning and to a significant degree meaning appears to depend on a sense of attachment or obligation. This sense of attachment may be to God, but it is also likely to involve attachments of a more immediate and tangible kind. Research based on open-ended questions with respondents in the San Francisco Bay Area, for example, showed that the main commitments mentioned as significant sources of meaning in life were service to God, service to one's family and work and personal development.[27]

Service to God

Statements such as "doing God's will," "obeying God's commandments," "telling others about God" and "preparing myself to meet God" were elicited frequently in the Bay Area research. In contrast to beliefs about God, commitments to God may serve as sources of meaning for the bereaved by specifying duties to be fulfilled. The obligation to fulfill these duties, in effect, provides a reason for living. It can be hypothesized:

H19: A perceived obligation to be of service to God will be positively associated with a sense of well-being among the bereaved.

H20: A perceived obligation to be of service to God will be positively associated with measures of belief in God.

Service to Others

The Bay Area research also showed that obligations to others, such as "making my husband happy," "being a good mother," "providing for my family" and "making the world a better place to live," were frequently listed among the activities giving greatest meaning to life. Most of these activities involved commitments to family and work. With the loss of a loved one, therefore, it appears likely that meaning may be enhanced by the presence of other moral obligations; for example, to children, friends, work, church, or community. This hypothesis may be stated as follows:

H21: The greater the strength, number or variety of perceived obligations to help or to serve others, the greater the likelihood of a sense of well-being among the bereaved.

Service to Self

The other set of obligations identified in the Bay Area study as significant sources of meaning consisted of activities such as "discovering who I really am," "being happy," "doing the things I want to" and "developing myself." Such activities appear to be regarded, not simply as diversions, but as moral obligations that must be fulfilled. It can be hypothesized that these attachments also provide meaning to the bereaved:

H22: The greater the strength, number, or variety of perceived obligations to pursue personal interests and self development, the greater the likelihood of a sense of well-being among the bereaved.

There is also some merit to the idea that moral obligations are more likely to reinforce a sense of well-being if they can in fact be fulfilled, than if they cannot. It is worth considering, therefore, that the three kinds of obligations specified above differ in terms of the personal resources required for their fulfillment. Service to God may require no more than time to engage in prayer. Service to others, in contrast, requires the time, energy and good health, as well as the presence of significant others, to serve. Service to self is also likely to require good health, energy and perhaps financial resources. To the extent that one's companion was regarded as a significant means of achieving personal happiness, service to self may be particularly frustrated by the experience of bereavement. It is worth observing, further, that the resources necessary to fulfill the last two kinds of obligations are likely to diminish with age. The following hypotheses can be stated:

H23: Well-being among the bereaved will be positively associated with the degree to which resources are regarded as being available for the fulfillment of moral obligations.

H24: Resources for the fulfillment of moral obligations will diminish with increasing age.

H25: Well-being among the bereaved will diminish with age particularly among persons whose moral obligations require greater resources to be fulfilled.

H26: With increasing age there is likely to be a shift toward moral obligations that can be fulfilled with more restricted resources.

Religious/Peak Experience

Conceptualizations by Maslow,[28] Laski[29] and James,[30]and empirical investigations by Greeley[31] and Wuthnow,[32] indicate the importance of religious, or more generally "peak," experiences as sources of personal meaning. Although negative ("nadir") experiences such as bereavement have received less attention than peak experiences (see Kalish and Reynolds[33]), research by Wuthnow[34] suggests that experiences of grief and tragedy are frequently conducive to positive experiences, particularly experiences with religious content. It can be hypothesized, therefore, that religious experiences may play an important role in the process of adjusting to bereavement.

Research has examined effects associated with differences in the intensity, frequency, explicitness, content and range of peak experiences. This research suggests that range, content and intensity are all positively associated with a variety of other variables, including strength of religious commitment, absence of anxiety about material possessions and social status and ethical relativism. In general, there appears to be empirical support for Maslow's[35] claim that persons having peak experiences tend to be relatively more flexible, open and "self-actualized." The following hypotheses warrant investigation:

H27: The expression of feelings such as grief or depression in response to bereavement will be positively associated with the expression of positive feelings such as those included in descriptions of peak experiences; in other words, the propensity to express feelings may include both negative and positively valued experiences.

H28: Peak experiences will be positively associated with a sense of well-being among the bereaved.

H29: Peak experiences having religious content will also be associated indirectly with a sense of well-being insofar as they reinforce comforting religious beliefs.

RELIGION AS A SOURCE OF BELONGING

Research has consistently demonstrated the contribution of social support systems to the physical and emotional well-being of the aging and the bereaved (e.g., Caplan,[36] Morgan[37]). Among other indications of this contribution, married persons and persons living with family members tend to experience fewer health problems than widowed persons and persons living alone. More broadly, it is a well-established generalization in the social sciences that integration into cohesive social networks is negatively correlated with anomic feelings and their behavioral consequences.

Religious Participation

Along with the family and the local community, religious organizations appear to function as a major locus of social involvement for a large minority, if not for a majority, of the American public. Lenski's[38] study of the Detroit area found that one in three Protestants and more than two in three Jews reported that nearly all of their friends were of the same religion as their own. A study[39] among Protestants found that 60 percent spent at least one evening a week in church activities and that 42 percent regarded religious participation as the major source of satisfaction in life. The study also found that 85 percent had experienced close fellowship with other Christians (other than family), that 32 percent said this fellowship had had a lasting impact on their lives and that 39 percent had felt support from church members during a time of grief or tragedy.

Interpretations of findings such as these vary. One view is that religious organizations currently foster superficial, audience-like participation—however widespread that participation may be (e.g., Berger[40]). A different view is that, at least for certain groups, the communal support found in religious organizations has come to be a stronger basis of commitment than doctrines or teachings (e.g., Greeley[41]). It is an empirical question, therefore, to determine the extent to which people not only participate in religious organizations, but derive meaning and support from their participation. This is particularly true for the elderly and for the bereaved.

The following hypotheses appear worthy of examination:

H30: The greater the frequency of participation (formal and informal) in religious activities, the greater the likelihood of physical and emotional manifestations of well-being.

H31: The greater the frequency of participation (formal and informal) in religious activities, the greater the likelihood of establishing interpersonal networks in which problems and anxieties associated with bereavement can be expressed.

H32: The greater the frequency of participation (formal and informal) in religious activities, the greater the plausibility of religious beliefs concerning the meaning of life.

Two additional hypotheses are necessary. Since the foregoing (H30 and H31) are rooted in assumptions about the general effects of social participation, rather than any particular effects of religious participation, it is conceivable that other forms of social involvement may function as effectively as religious involvement as sources of social support. Thus, it appears likely that the effects of religious involvement may be more critical to those oriented primarily toward religion than to those oriented otherwise. Thus:

H33: The greater the salience of religion, the stronger the relationships between religious participation and a sense of well-being.

It is also the case that religious traditions themselves vary in terms of the amount of emphasis they place on religious participation. It follows from hypothesis H33, therefore, that:

H34: The more a religious organization emphasizes participation, the stronger the relationships will be between participation and well-being.

Vicarious Participation

Research among the aging demonstrates that religious participation declines with increasing age, just as involvements in general tend to become more restricted. It has been concluded, accordingly, that religious participation may not be a significant source of meaning or support among the elderly. However, studies of this kind have seldom included questions about vicarious forms of religious participation—religious radio and television programs, letter writing, Bible reading, prayer (for an exception, see Blazer and Palmore[42]). Thus, the following hypothesis also appears worthy of examination:

H35: As age increases, religious participation may be increasingly substituted for by vicarious religious participation.

Charitable Services for the Bereaved

A dimension of religious belonging that warrants particular examination because of its policy implications is the extent to which bereaved persons receive help, information and other charitable services from the religious organizations to which they belong. Studies of the elderly, and of the bereaved elderly in particular, point to the need for services such as transportation to medical or shopping facilities, meals, home maintenance and nursing and for information about the availability of such services.[43]

While existing evidence points to the likelihood that religious organizations provide needed charitable services for the bereaved, this evidence needs to be expanded in at least three directions. First, evidence needs to be obtained from the recipients of charitable activities, rather than the donors, to determine how much assistance is actually received from religious organizations and how this assistance compares with, overlaps, or substitutes for assistance received from other sources. Second, the kinds of people that are served or not served by religious organizations need to be determined so that more effective efforts can be made to meet the needs of bereaved persons who are not being served. Third, more specific evidence is needed to determine the kinds of assistance being provided—and desired but not provided effectively—by religious organizations.

The following hypotheses may be put forth for empirical test:

H36: The greater the frequency of participation (formal and informal) in religious activities, the greater the likelihood of receiving information and services from religious sources.

H37: The greater the frequency of participation (formal and informal) in religious activities, the greater the likelihood of desiring information and assistance from religious sources rather than from other sources.

H38: Informal sources of assistance will be greater in small religious organizations than in large religious organizations.

H39: Formal sources of assistance will be greater in large religious organizations than in small religious organizations.

H40: Assistance (formal and informal) will be greater, other things being equal, where older people make up a significant proportion of the members of a religious organization.

There is one other way in which charitable services may function among the bereaved. As argued above, moral obligations to serve others may provide an important source of meaning to the bereaved. Insofar as religious organizations emphasize charitable service, they may provide opportunities for these moral obligations to be discharged (e.g., through teaching classes, helping with visitation, doing maintenance or secretarial work, etc.). Therefore:

H41: The greater the frequency of participation (formal and informal) in religious activities, the greater the likelihood of being able to *provide* charitable services to others, which in turn provide meaning and purpose.

FUNERARY RITES

In addition to the above, the relationships between religion, funerary rites and coping with bereavement warrant attention in this context. Although many have studied funeral practices in the United States (e.g., Habenstein and Lamers,[44] Bowman,[45] Mitford[46]), research of a systematic or quantitative nature dealing specifically with the religious aspect of funerals has been too limited to provide a clear indication of the relevant variables. Hence, only a tentative conceptual framework can be suggested.

In the first place, lacking more detailed information, it would appear useful to know the extent to which funerals, in fact, include a religious dimension and whether the inclusion or exclusion of this dimension influences either the immediate response to the funeral or the longer term success with which bereavement is dealt. Since next of kin, in the typical case, are solely or largely responsible for arranging the funeral ceremony, it seems likely that the extent to which a religious dimension is included will be influenced greatly by the extent to which the bereaved themselves are religiously oriented. Under the circumstances, it appears further that the presence of a religious dimension will facilitate the communication of religious meanings and comforts to the bereaved, thereby contributing positively to the successful resolution of the grieving process. These expectations may be formalized as follows:

H42: The greater the degree of religious commitment on the part of the bereaved, the greater the likelihood of religious elements being included in the funeral or burial ceremony.

H43: The greater the extent to which funeral or burial ceremonies include a religious dimension, the greater the likelihood that the bereaved will experience feelings of comfort.

H44: The relationship between religious elements in the funeral ceremony and feelings of comfort will vary directly with the general salience of religious commitment to the bereaved.

Second, it appears warranted, chiefly on the basis of the theoretical literature, to suggest that the nature of participation in the funeral ceremony on the part of relatives, friends and members of the religious organization and community to which the bereaved belongs will have an effect on the resolution of the grieving process. In principle, the funeral and burial services provide a legitimate occasion for acquaintances to acknowledge the new role that the bereaved has come to occupy. Having acknowledged this role, subsequent interaction with the bereaved can take place without embarrassment and in a more openly supportive manner. In short, the funeral rite functions as a "realignment process," to borrow Goffman's[47] term, which reintegrates the bereaved member into a network of supportive relationships.

In the literature on funerary rites, however, the effectiveness of the ritual itself is assumed to be dependent upon—indeed, a reflection of—the degree of pre-existing solidarity within the larger community of acquaintances of which the bereaved and the deceased are members. Participation in the rite, according to Durkheim,[48] depends less on the private feelings of these acquaintances than on their sense of communal obligation. Thus, participation in the rite is merely an extension of prior social relationships. Moreover, the rite leads naturally to ongoing supportive interaction. Where prior sentiments of collective solidarity are weak, therefore, the funerary rite is likely to be less effective in assisting the bereaved through the grieving process.

Insofar as religion is concerned, these considerations suggest that the more general relationships that are established among the members of religious organizations are likely to contribute to the extent to which acquaintances take part in the funeral service and the extent to which this participation promotes subsequent supportive interaction. In light of the so-called let-down period which appears to be a common occurrence after the funeral itself is over, the latter would appear to be of particular importance to the successful resolution of the longer-term grieving process. The foregoing may be summarized as follows:

H45: The greater the religious participation of the bereaved, the greater the likelihood of religious acquaintances attending funerary services.

H46: The greater the attendance of religious acquaintances at funerary services, the greater the likelihood of subsequent supportive interaction with these acquaintances.

H47: The greater the religious participation of the bereaved, the stronger the relationship between attendance at funerary services and subsequent support.

H48: The more cohesive the religious organization of which the bereaved is a member, the stronger the relationship between attendance at funerary services and subsequent support.

FURTHER CONSIDERATIONS

Two specifications need to be added to the foregoing. First, the relationships postulated between religion and bereavement are likely to vary by religious tradition. Some religious traditions attach considerably more credence to some of the beliefs discussed in the foregoing sections than do others. Religious traditions also vary in the kinds of social support provided and in the nature of funerary rites prescribed (see Kübler-Ross,[49] Williams,[50] Greeley[51]).

Second, the relationships postulated are also likely to differ with different dimensions of well-being. Although previous research has frequently found positive relationships between, for example, measures of emotional and physical, or between measures of social and emotional, well-being, these relationships are often of only moderate strength and have not, for the most part, been examined in conjunction with religious variables. While it may well prove that religious variables are associated with all dimensions of well-being, it may just as likely be the case that religious commitment serves to enhance one dimension of well-being in the face of deterioration on other dimensions.

NOTES

1. E. Lindemann. 1944. Symptomatology and Management of Acute Grief. *Journal of Psychiatry* 101:141-148.
2. R.S. Cavan, E.W. Burgess, R.J. Havinghurst and H. Goldhamer. 1949. *Personal Adjustment in Old Age.* Chicago: Science Research Associates; C.M. Parkes. 1972. *Bereavement: Studies of Grief in Adult Life.* New York: International Universities Press; J.N. Edwards and D.L. Klemmack. 1973. Correlates of Life Satisfaction: A Reexamination. *Journal of Gerontology* 28:497:502.
3. R. Wuthnow. 1976a. Recent Patterns of Secularization: A Problem of Generations? *American Sociological Review* 41:850-867; W.C. Roof. 1978a. Social Correlates of Religious Involvement: Review of Recent Survey Research in the United States. *Annual Reviews of the Social Sciences of Religion* 2:53-70.
4. G. Lenski. 1961. *The Religious Factor.* Garden City, NY: Doubleday.

5. W.C. Roof. 1978b. *Community and Commitment: Religious Plausibility in a Liberal Protestant Church.* New York: Elsevier.
6. C.Y. Glock, B. Ringer and E.R. Babbie. 1967. *To Comfort and To Challenge.* Berkeley: University of California Press.
7. R.N. Bellah. 1970. *Beyond Belief.* New York: Harper & Row; C. Geertz. 1973. *The Interpretation of Cultures.* New York: Harper & Row; A.M. Greeley. 1972. *The Denominational Society.* Chicago: Scott, Foresman.
8. G. Gurin, J. Veroof and S. Field. 1960. *Americans View Their Mental Health.* Ann Arbor: University of Michigan Press, p. 245; C.K. Hadaway and W.C. Roof. 1978. Religious Commitment and the Quality of Life in American Society. *Review of Religious Research* 19:295-307.
9. M. Argyle and B. Beit-Hallahmi. 1975. *The Social Psychology of Religion.* London: Routledge & Kegan Paul, pp. 52-57.
10. Greeley, loc. cit.
11. Roof, 1978b, loc. cit.
12. Geertz, op. cit., p. 104.
13. P.L. Berger. 1969. *The Sacred Canopy.* Garden City, NY: Doubleday, pp. 19-20.
14. W.C. Roof. 1979. Concepts and Indicators of Religious Commitment: A Critical Review, in R. Wuthnow, ed., *The Religious Dimension: New Directions in Quantitative Research.* New York: Academic Press.
15. T. Piazza and C.Y. Glock. 1979. Images of God and Their Social Meanings, in R. Wuthnow, ed., *The Religious Dimension: New Directions in Quantitative Research.* New York: Academic Press.
16. R. Wuthnow. 1979. *Religious Belief and Experience.* New York: Office for Research and Planning, Lutheran Church in America.
17. A.R. Hochschild. 1978. *The Unexpected Community: Portrait of an Old-Age Subculture.* Berkeley: University of California Press.
18. I.O. Glick et al. 1974. *The First Year of Bereavement.* New York: John Wiley.
19. K.T. Erikson. 1976. *Everything in Its Path.* New York: Simon & Schuster.
20. Hochschild, loc. cit.
21. S. Grof and J. Halifax. 1977. *The Human Encounter with Death.* New York: E.P. Dutton.
22. T. Parsons, R.C. Fox and W.M. Lidz. 1972. The "Gift of Life" and Its Reciprocation. *Social Research* 39:367-415; T. Parsons. 1978. *Action Theory and the Human Condition.* New York: Free Press.
23. M. Mauss. 1967. *The Gift.* New York: W.W. Norton.
24. G.R. Krupp and B. Kligfeld. 1962. The Bereavement Reaction: A Cross-Cultural Evaluation. *Journal of Religion and Health* 1:222-246.
25. P. Berger and R. Lieban. 1960. Kulturelle Wertstruktur und Bestattungspraktiken in den Vereinigten Staaten. *Kölner Zeitschrift für Soziologie und Sozialpsychologie* 2.
26. M. Weber. 1960. *The Sociology of Religion.* Boston: Beacon Press.
27. R. Wuthnow. 1976b. *The Consciousness Reformation.* Berkeley: University of California Press.
28. A. Maslow. 1962. *Toward a Psychology of Being.* Princeton, NJ: D. van Nostrand; 1970. *Religions, Values, and Peak-Experiences.* New York: Viking.
29. M. Laski. 1961. *Ecstasy: A Study of Some Secular and Religious Experiences.* London: The Cresset Press.
30. W. James. 1958. *The Varieties of Religious Experience.* New York: New American Library.

31. A.M. Greeley. 1975. *The Sociology of the Paranormal: A Reconnaissance.* Beverly Hills, CA: Sage.
32. R. Wuthnow. 1978. Peak Experiences: Some Empirical Tests. *Journal of Humanistic Psychology* 18:59-75.
33. R.A. Kalish and D.K. Reynolds. 1973. Phenomenological Reality and Post-Death Contact. *Journal for the Scientific Study of Religion* 12:209-221.
34. Wuthnow, 1979, loc. cit.
35. Maslow, 1962, loc. cit.
36. G. Caplan. 1976. The Family as a Support System, in G. Caplan and A. Killelie, eds., *Support Systems and Mutual Help.* New York: Grune & Stratton.
37. L.A. Morgan. 1976. A Re-examination of Widowhood and Morale. *Journal of Gerontology* 31:687-695.
38. G. Lenski, 1961, op. cit., pp. 36-42.
39. Wuthnow, 1979, loc. cit.
40. P.L. Berger. 1977. *Facing Up to Modernity.* New York: Basic Books.
41. A.M. Greeley. 1976. *The American Catholic: A Social Portrait.* New York: Basic Books.
42. D. Blazer and E. Palmore. 1976. Religion and Aging in a Longitudinal Panel. *The Gerontologist* 16:82-85.
43. Parkes, loc. cit.
44. R.W. Habenstein and W.M. Lamers. 1960. *Funeral Customs the World Over.* Milwaukee: Bulfin.
45. L. Bowman. 1959. *The American Funeral: A Study in Guilt, Extravagance, and Sublimity.* Washington, DC: Public Affairs Press.
46. J. Mitford. 1963. *The American Way of Death.* New York: Simon & Schuster.
47. E. Goffman. 1959. *The Presentation of Self in Everyday Life.* Garden City, NY: Doubleday.
48. E. Durkheim. 1917. *The Elementary Forms of the Religious Life.* New York: Free Press.
49. E. Kübler-Ross, ed. 1975. *Death: The Final Stage of Growth.* Englewood Cliffs, NJ: Prentice-Hall.
50. M.D. Williams. 1974. *Community in a Black Pentecostal Church.* Pittsburgh: University of Pittsburgh Press.
51. Greeley, 1976, loc. cit.

10

Business Temporal Norms and Bereavement Behavior

Lois Pratt, PhD

The development of modern commerce and industry gave rise to distinctive time concepts and norms governing use of time, which include precise measurement, scheduling, punctuality, standardization, pricing and efficient use of time. It is problematic how extensively the temporal norms of business have come to dominate various aspects of social life. This chapter focuses on bereavement. It examines the process in which business came to cast the situation of the bereaved worker in a temporal framework: "time off." This gave emphasis to time prescriptions as a basis for organizing death work and extended business time conventions to bereavement practices and funerary rituals. As bereavement practices have been brought increasingly into consistency with the business temporal code, bereavement has taken on the meanings of the business system, reflecting and reinforcing a social order based on businesslike management of time.

By tracing changes in procedures used by business when an employee experiences the death of a family member, I examine here the process of shaping bereavement practices in accordance with business temporal patterns. This examination is a specific test of the general hypothesis that the time pattern established by the major economic units in industrialized society tends to control the timing of less dominant activities.[1]

I propose not simply that the work schedule established by commerce and industry preempts time and forces other activities, such as mourning and funerary rituals, to be scheduled in residual time, but that, in addition, business may influence bereavement practices by regulating the bereaved directly. Since almost all of the nearly two million deaths occurring each year in the United States must be mourned by one or more employed persons, business has a stake in prescribing who is eligible to assume the bereaved role and the period of time bereaved persons are permitted to be relieved of work responsibilities. As in the case of illness, a key element in the role prescription for bereavement is that the affected person is temporarily exempted from normal duties.[2]

In establishing rules to govern the bereavement situation, business may influence the collective meanings, norms and ritual forms of mourning by applying the time concepts and norms for the use of time that were developed to facilitate industrial production and exchange. These time conventions include an emphasis on time as a basis for organizing activity, precise measurement and pricing of time, placing value on punctuality and increasing productivity through sequence planning and scheduling. The expected outcome is that the patterning of bereavement is brought into consistency with the temporal pattern of business.

Using historical, survey and other data, this chapter pursues two principal objectives. The first objective is to determine whether modern business has regulated workers' bereavement and whether it has applied some version of the time norms that govern its work operations. Determining this involves documenting any changes in business policies and procedures for managing the bereavement situation and assessing whether the policy changes were based on temporal considerations and reflect basic temporal norms of modern business. The second objective is to determine whether the time norms of business have penetrated American cultural patterns for conducting funerals and bereavement. This involves tracing whether there has been a configural sequence of change over time[3]—an interplay between changing business bereavement procedures and changing funeral and bereavement customs during the same period of time.

The possibility of such a relationship between the structure of the economic system and societal death customs is suggested by evidence indicating that nineteenth century industrial expansion fostered prolonged funeral pomp—lying in state, public processions, floral display, tomb sculpture, ornamented caskets, garden cemeteries and elaborate mourning clothes—as well as protracted bereavement.[4] The possibility that secular activities may shape bereavement customs is underscored by the fact that mourning practices have not been regulated rigidly or uniformly by religion. Only Jewish law prescribed a precisely graduated mourning process—the first 3 days after death, 7 days, 30 days and 12 months—with prescribed activities for each stage.[5] Catholic Canon Law made no mention of mourning time periods or duties other than the desirability of praying for the dead.[6] The Puritan religion, in rejecting even prayers for the dead, prescribed neither time norms nor duties for the bereaved.[7] There may, in fact, be a variety of historical circumstances in which the economic system has shaped bereavement practice.

THE TEMPORAL ORDER OF BUSINESS

Outlining the major features of the temporal organization of modern business will establish a basis for determining whether or not bereavement policies and procedures have been shaped in accordance with business time conventions and whether or not business temporal norms have infiltrated societal bereavement customs.

From the late Middle Ages onward time was increasingly harnessed for secular purposes. The Christian Church had organized the calendar into a fixed round of holy days and imbued days with particular supernatural meanings, thereby ordering time in terms of supernatural events and purposes. With the growth of commerce and industry, time came increasingly to be ordered around important dates of civic and commercial life and the time schedule of business came to dominate the daily, weekly and yearly patterning of societal life.[8]

A fundamental feature of the time orientation of modern business has been the rational and detailed organization of time.[9] The clock made possible precise measurement and the division of time into units of standard length. The Church in the fourteenth century had demonstrated the potential of the clock for ordering human life by scheduling and disciplining life within the monastery, using the belfry clock to symbolize the individual's subordination to higher authority.[10]

In the twentieth century time was refined into smaller units by business. Work tasks were broken down into elementary components, each was timed by stopwatch and the precise amount of time was specified for performing each element of the task. The various sequences of tasks and processes were synchronized and coordinated by detailed time schedules. A key measure of the worker's effectiveness then became one's ability to keep the production line flowing by following the prescribed movements within the prescribed time allotments and rhythms.[11]

The units of industrial time were standardized. As in the Middle Ages, when certain spans of time took on sacred significance—for example, the 7 days to create the world and the 3 days between the death and resurrection of Christ—certain time durations and business acquired special significance both functional and symbolic—in particular, the 8-hour day, 5-day workweek, 2-week vacation and day off.

The standardized workday and workweek became the basis for

compensation for work performed. Time was converted into monetary terms and derived enhanced and precise value thereby. Time in industrial society is valued for what can be derived, produced, or earned from it.[12] Precise measurement and detailed scheduling of time heightens awareness of time passage, focuses attention on alternative uses and encourages productive use and husbanding of time.[13]

This regard for time as scarce and valuable, which is essential for economic development and business productivity, has been extended to the use and valuation of time in other spheres of activity.[14] There is a straining to raise the yield on time devoted to other activities into parity with the yield on working time and a tendency to measure the importance of an activity or relationship by how much time is allocated to it.[15]

The time conventions of business, however, neither fully encompass all aspects of existence nor completely dominate the ordering and experiencing of the activities they do regulate. Much of business life itself does not conform to these time principles: corporate managers do not have fully accurate inventories of workers' time; work processes are not always efficiently coordinated, with resulting "wasted" time; and some jobs are left without rigid time constraints. Basic aspects of our time reckoning system are not fully secularized. We take the birth of Jesus Christ as the standard reference point for reckoning historical time, rather than, say, the founding of the nation state. We retain the 7-day week terminating in a day of rest rather than a system of cycles designed to suit the rhythms of urban industrial society.[16] Nor do business time conventions permeate and dominate all areas of life outside the workplace. Thus, it is problematic how extensively business temporal patterns dominate particular aspects of contemporary life, which temporal norms have been applied and what has been the historical timing of the process.

PROCEDURES AND EVIDENCE

Business Bereavement Policies and Procedures

The first objective is to document changes, if any, in the policies and procedures of American business for handling the situation when a worker experiences a loss by death. Several sources provided relevant information. A series of studies conducted between 1940 and 1973 by the Conference Board (formerly called the National Industrial Conference Board)[17] on business personnel practices provide data on time-off practices, including bereavement leave. Questionnaires were administered to national samples of companies representing the major types of business.

The Bureau of Labor Statistics has sampled companies in its files and reported on time not worked, including bereavement leave, in manufacturing and nonmanufacturing companies employing 1000 or more workers (excluding government, railroads and airlines).[18]

The author and graduate students interviewed the personnel officer and employees of 40 large companies in New Jersey to obtain detailed descriptive accounts of cases of workers' bereavement. The companies were selected from various business directories to include major firms in banking, insurance, public utilities, transportation, several types of manufacturing and retailing. Employee respondents were asked to volunteer for interview on the basis of their familiarity with a bereavement episode, either their own or another worker's. The interview covered all actions taken officially and informally within the company regarding the bereaved worker, the deceased family member, the family, other workers, the union and managers, from the time the worker learned of the death through the days following the worker's return to duty. A total of 156 different bereavements were described, ranging from 3 to 10 in the various companies.

In addition to documenting changes in business bereavement policies and practices, it was necessary to interpret whether or not those changes were based on temporal considerations and reflected business temporal considerations. One source was the studies conducted by the Conference Board of changing objectives and organization of the personnel function. Between 1962 and 1965 senior personnel executives in 249 companies representing the major industrial groupings were surveyed.[19] In 1975 comparable data were obtained from 653 companies.[20] Other sources were the management training texts prepared at different dates under the auspices of the American Management Association, Conference Board and Chamber of Commerce.

Mourning and Funerary Practices

The second major objective is to determine whether there has been a change over time in funerary and mourning practices which corporate policies may have helped to shape. Evidence of changes in normative patterns of mourning and funerary usage was sought in various editions of etiquette books.[21]

Data on changes in funerary practices were obtained from surveys of funeral directors conducted by the National Funeral Directors Association.[22] In 1967 the entire membership of that association and the Jewish Funeral Directors Association were asked in a mailed questionnaire to report on the types of funeral services they provided, the services requested by clients and changes during the preceding five years. In 1970 a national sample of National Funeral Directors Association members were again surveyed. Evidence of change is based on funeral directors' retrospective reports in 1967 of changes in practices and on comparisons between funeral directors' descriptions of practices in the 1967 and 1970 surveys. Evidence of contemporary public attitudes toward funeral service and disposition practices was obtained from a national mail survey conducted by the Casket Manufacturers Association.[23]

The evidence on changes in mourning and funerary practices does not, of course, demonstrate the extent of influence of business bereavement policies. First, gaps in the data make it impossible to track precisely the time sequence of changes in death customs in relation to changes in business bereavement policies. Second, business policies are only one of the social forces that have been affecting mourning and funerary practices. But insofar as the changes in mourning customs and funeral rituals have been consistent in direction and content and have proceeded in temporal sequence with changes in business bereavement procedures, we have evidence suggesting a configural sequence of change over time in which corporate policies have been an active element, both responding to and helping to shape bereavement customs.

Organization of the Analysis

We have found it useful to distinguish between two aspects of business bereavement policy. We examine, first, the norms that are to govern the situation when a worker is bereaved and, second, the definitions of which deaths are covered by the norms.

BUSINESS TEMPORAL CONVENTIONS AND BEREAVEMENT POLICY

Bereavement as a Corporate Policy Issue

Since the early 1960s there has been a trend toward more systematic planning and control of the future of the business organization through personnel planning.[24] The rationale is that corporate profitability depends on effective human performance. In particular, a properly designed benefits structure is seen as a cost-effective system of stimulating high productivity.

As a result, personnel policy making has been centralized and top management has become increasingly involved in formulating benefits policy. In the 1950s, the personnel function was handed over by chief executives to senior personnel officers, but in the 1970s the key management figure in personnel matters was most often the president. Over half (56 percent) of the presidents and a third of the board chairmen in companies surveyed in 1975 participated in formulating benefits policies. There has also been a trend toward having personnel staff units on the corporate level (rather than at the plant level), with many more staff specialists, led by "vice presidents." Increasingly, the personnel staff deals with long-term future effectiveness of the company and serves as a primary agency of overall corporate planning and control.

Bereavement leave, having been absorbed into the corporate benefits program, has become subject to strategic planning by top management. Corporations have tended increasingly to formulate formal policies recognizing employees' right to paid time off when a family member dies. The policies and provisions for implementing them are incorporated in agreements with unions and in personnel procedure manuals. In 1953, 13 percent of companies sampled from the files of the Bureau of Labor Statistics were found to have agreements with provisions for paid funeral leave and this increased to 67 percent of companies in 1975. The increase was especially sharp among manufacturing companies—those most likely to have union agreements.

Other studies, which asked firms whether they provided paid bereavement leave to workers, regardless of whether they had a union agreement to do so, reveal that the increase has been even greater than the above figures suggest. By 1973 at least 90 percent of companies officially granted paid leave for bereavement.[25]

By authorizing bereavement leave as a right rather than a privilege granted at the discretion of management, these policies, agreements and procedures have made it legitimate for workers who experience a loss to declare officially their bereaved status and take leave from the workplace. In a 1970 sample of bereaved next-of-kin, it was found that 92 percent said it was very easy to get off work during the funeral week.[26]

Temporal Construction of Bereavement

These business policies have framed the issue of workers' bereavement almost exclusively in temporal terms: "time off."[27] Five or fewer of the 40 corporations studied in depth had established as company policy any of these other possible responses to a worker's bereavement: attendance by a company representative or coworkers at the funeral or visitation (viewing); flowers for the funeral or a donation to medical research; expression of sympathy from the company by card or letter; transportation of the body from afar (an airline); use of a company car to attend the funeral ; or a cash donation to the bereaved worker. About a third of the companies communicated within the firm the news of a family member's death by formal means—bulletin board, memo or house organ.

This temporal interpretation of bereavement by corporations is consistent with bereavement customs throughout the world. Cross-cultural studies have shown that bereavement norms usually prescribe the period of mourning as well as the conduct for the mourning period.[28] Corporate construction of bereavement is distinguished by interpreting it exclusively in temporal terms and, as will be documented, by applying distinctive temporal norms.

Monetary Expression of Bereavement Time

During the past three decades, corporations' arrangements for workers' bereavement have increasingly tended to render bereavement time in monetary terms. Bereavement leave has become one element in the "fringe benefits" package that includes pensions, insurance and paid time off for vacations, holidays and "personal reasons." "Personal" time off includes bereavement, along with jury duty, sickness, military duty, voting and court appearances.[29]

Before World War II fringe benefits were rare among worker demands. The government's wartime economic policy of limiting wage increases caused unions to direct their demands toward nonwage benefits, which were permitted by the War Labor Board. After World War II, continued prosperity fostered a higher standard of living and workers, seeking greater security and social benefits, continued to press for enhanced fringe benefits[30] and for increased time off in particular.

The costs of time-off benefits have increased accordingly. All paid time off—including holidays, vacations and time off for personal reasons (bereavement, etc.)—represented 7 percent of total payroll costs in 1957 compared to 12 percent in 1975.[31] Figured in dollars, all time off payments cost $311 per employee per year in 1957 compared to $1137 in 1975.

The costs of personal time off (for bereavement, etc.) constitute a small share of total time-off benefits and bereavement leave is a tiny element in the total costs of time off. Considering time off for all personal obligations combined, the costs represented 0.2 percent of total payroll in 1957 and 0.4 percent in 1975. The costs of bereavement leave are not calculated separately in these studies. However, it is estimated that it costs a fraction of a cent (several mills) per hour per employee.[32]

Although bereavement leave is a minor cost item in the overall benefits structure, it is handled the same way as all benefits—within a cost framework. An American Management Association publication, *Negotiating Fringe Benefits*,[33] recommended that "Employers should attempt to price this item as accurately as possible so as to include it in their estimate of the settlement costs."

Negotiation between companies and unions for paid time off has invested bereavement with monetary meaning and value. It represents time that has been formally costed by both management and unions. This reinforces other established practices that render bereavement in monetary terms. For example, the bereaved family is expected to express the magnitude of its loss through its expenditure on the funeral.[34] Life insurance is an established mechanism by which people give monetary expression of their love and concern for the welfare of their heirs after death and in recognition of which their heirs credit them with proportionate "economic immortality."[35]

Corporate Control of Time

By the 1960s corporations had asserted control over bereavement leave by applying techniques that were developed to control employees on the job: formal rules promulgated in written form, processing through vertical channels, written records and monitoring of compliance. *Employer's Handbook for Labor Negotiations* advised management that "Leaves should be kept under the exclusive control of the company."[36] And the first step in achieving control is to specify the provisions, limitations and procedures governing bereavement leave. The National Industrial Conference Board advised that personnel manuals should cover the following:

- Degree of relationship
- Definition of immediate family
- If death occurs during employee's vacation
- If a holiday occurs during the absence
- Maximum time granted
- Notifying the personnel office[37]

The formal vertical channels are used in processing a worker's application for bereavement leave. *Managing the Employee Benefits Program* prescribed that managers authorized to sign employee time cards should control the allowed hours and approve payment for personnel absence.[38] Leaves are processed formally. According to *Employer's Handbook for Labor Negotiations*: "All leaves should be in writing. Set forth the reason for the leave, the date and time on which the leave is to commence, the date and time the employee must return to work and possible penalties for overstaying the leave."[39] Auditors encourage the practice of filing a written permission in the employee's personnel file to verify the legitimacy of an absence.

Management has instituted procedures to detect workers' violations of bereavement leave provisions. Collins warns that

> More grandmothers are purported to die on the opening day of the baseball season than on any other day of the year. The vast majority of employees are honest, but the few who abuse a privilege set an unfavorable example for the others. The problem in the area of pay continuance is thus one of developing adequate controls.[40]

Some companies require an obituary notice to prove a death occurred. A very few stipulate a death certificate but invoke the role only if the employee has had a suspicious number of deaths.[41] *Employer's Handbook for Labor Negotiations*[42] advised that "An employee who gives a false reason for leave should be disciplined."

Precise Measurement and Limitations of Time

There has been a trend in corporate bereavement leave provisions toward increasingly specific and limited time allowances. Keeping in mind that before 1960 only a minority of companies allowed paid leave for bereavement to the general workforce, the tendency in the early policies was to keep open the amount of time allowed, retaining managerial discretion to decide each case. In fact, a 1953 survey found that 13 percent of the companies with leave provisions stipulated that the amount of paid leave was at the company's discretion.[43] Policies generally provided for "time necessary," "reasonable time," "varies depending on the individual case" or "no fixed policy."

Thus, in 1943, 30 percent of the companies with paid funeral leave provisions fixed the time allowance, compared to 82 percent in 1963 and 1973. An increasing proportion of companies have set paid leave at 3 days: one-fifth of companies in 1953 compared to nearly three-fifths in 1973. This provision is likely to become even more widespread because it is propounded in publications of management associations: "many companies today consider the 3 days' pay to be inviolate."[44]

The boundaries of the leave are also specified. It is now standard policy that leave begins after the death occurs, not in the terminal phase of dying. Many policies specify that the paid time off must be taken concurrently with the funeral and on consecutive days.[45] While the 3-day time allowance fixes an end point on the leave, a few companies give even more detailed specifications for calculating the termination date. As recommended in an American Management Association publication: "it is usually expected that when a death occurs on a Saturday the employee should return to work on a Tuesday following the normal time for the funeral."[46]

Some corporations do not allow extension of leave for bereavement and those that do typically prescribe that the time off be taken without pay or that it be deducted from sick leave or vacation. Any such extension requires approval.

Bereavement is thus framed as a distinctive event in time and space. This reinforces the bereaved person's mourning responsibilities during the 3 days at home and calls for decisive termination of the mourning and return to full performance of duties at the workplace when the 3 days are spent.

Standardization of Temporal Policy

Over the past three decades business has tended increasingly to standardize bereavement leave by establishing uniform provisions for all classes of workers. In the past, salaried workers were paid for time off during bereavement, but hourly wage workers were not. In 1940, 95 percent of companies provided this benefit to salaried employees compared to 5 percent to wage employees. As late as 1967 an American Management Association report on employee benefits stated: "The basic policy has been that hourly paid employees are paid only for time worked and weekly paid employees continue to receive pay during period of unavoidable absence."[47] This differential was rooted in the hierarchical pattern of organization. White-collar personnel, who were exempted from overtime pay, received these benefits to assure that they retained an edge over subordinates.

There has been a sweeping trend to grant bereavement leave to hourly workers. By 1954, 27 percent of companies had covered hourly workers; by 1963, 63 percent; and by 1973, 90 percent. There has also been a trend toward standardizing the leave provisions for all classes of workers. In the past, those companies that did extend paid time off for bereavement to wage workers tended to apply different rules to hourly and salaried employees, generally restricting wage workers to a fixed number of days, usually 3 days and allowing greater flexibility and discretion for salaried workers. Salaried workers' provisions have been brought into line with the more restrictive provisions that were being applied to wage workers. In 1943, 70 percent of firms had flexible or open-ended arrangements for salaried workers, compared to 46 percent in 1954 and only 18 percent in 1973.[48]

The standardization of benefits for salaried and hourly workers began when unions negotiated bereavement leave benefits for blue-collar workers, the terms of which precisely delimited and regulated the leave. Next, the flexible provisions that had covered salaried workers were replaced by the more restrictive terms that had been arranged in blue-collar agreements. This reflects the tendency of business, especially large corporations, to seek administrative economies and control by applying the same set of rules to all personnel in the organization.[49]

Adaptation of Business Time to Personal Time

Bereavement leave occupies a special position within the business temporal order. It represents a deviant situation in the sense that a company cannot control the timing of an individual worker's bereavement or the overall quantity and spacing of worker bereavements during the year and also in the sense that bereavement arises from an individual worker's personal life situation rather than from corporate or societal events. Time off from work for bereavement thus represents an adaptation of business affairs to the timing of the individual's life situation.

It is significant, therefore, that bereavement leave is almost the only form of time off for a personal and private need that is provided universally in American business. The primary emphasis in time off practices is to arrange predictable and standardized days off and to observe societal events rather than the worker's personal events.

Most companies do not provide paid leave for illness in the family and the practice has been declining in the same period in which time off for death in the family has become firmly established. Family illness leave for office employees was provided by 67 percent of firms in 1954 but by only 38 percent in 1973; it was provided to hourly workers by very few companies in 1954 or 1973. Paid marriage leave also declined for office employees: from 55 percent of companies in 1954 to 25 percent in 1973. Paid time off to see a doctor or dentist increased slightly during the 20 years. Table 1 shows the percentages of companies providing paid time off for various purposes, compares hourly and salaried workers and shows changes from 1954 to 1973.

It is not only that bereavement leave, in contrast to other forms of personal leave, is granted by more firms, but also that it is granted more uniformly to all classes of workers. While bereavement leave benefits were equalized for blue-collar and white-collar workers by 1973, this did not occur for other forms of personal time off. Fewer firms allow blue-collar workers to have paid time off for medical and dental appointments, marriage and illness in the family, than grant these benefits to white-collar workers.

In contrast to personal and private needs for time off, some, but not all, of the worker's civic and societal responsibilities have been accorded time off by an increasing proportion of companies Paid time off for jury duty is granted by almost all firms and to hourly as well as salaried employees. (A worker is either paid full wages on top of jury fees or paid the difference between usual wages and the fees given by the courts.) A substantial proportion of firms also grant paid time off for summer military duty, voting and appearance in court as a witness; but more firms allow

Table 1.

Percent of Companies Providing Paid Time Off for Various Purposes to Hourly and Salaried Employees: 1954 and 1973

	Hourly		Salaried	
	1954	1973	1954	1973
Death in family	27	90	86	96
Jury duty	34	90	76	38
Illness in family	7	5	67	38
Medical/dental appt.	9	22	68	73
Marriage	6	5	55	25
Summer vacation		68		81
Trial witness		38		66
Voting time		37		51

Sources: National Industrial Conference Board, 1954; Conference Board, 1974

white-collar than blue-collar workers to be paid for time taken to perform these duties.

Very few firms give personal holidays. The employee's birthday was a paid holiday in only 1 percent of companies in 1954. In 1973 about 9 percent gave birthday holidays to office employees and about 18 percent to hourly employees. A floating holiday, which permits the employee to choose the date, was given by about 13 percent of firms in 1973, up from 4 percent in 1963.[50]

In contrast, vacation and fixed holidays have increased. The vacation is now universally provided. This is personal time off in the sense that the worker may do what he wishes in this time, but vacations are prescheduled, nationally synchronized and have been institutionalized on the grounds that this time off serves to refresh the employee for the next year of work. The number of fixed paid holidays has increased from an average of 6 to 7 in 1956 to 8 in 1963 and 9 in 1973. A third of companies had 10 holidays or more in 1973, up from a fifth in 1963.[51] Six specific days are virtually universal business holidays: Christmas, Thanksgiving, New Year's, Independence, Labor and Memorial Day. The total number of days off now exceeds that found in early decades of this century, although it falls short of the number prevailing prior to the fifteenth century in Europe when the Church established a fixed round of holy days.

This business calendar of synchronized holidays tends to bring standardization to the corporate and national temporal order and the holidays chosen symbolize societal unity and order. The pattern is reflected in the costs of various benefits. The average cost per employee per year in 1977 for vacations was $636 and for holidays it was $405, while all forms of personal leave cost only $48 per employee per year.[52]

Viewed in the context of business' overall pattern of paid leaves, bereavement leave has been accorded a special standing. Paid leave is universally provided for bereavement but not for the other unpredictable and personal events in the worker's life. This reinforces the legitimacy of bereavement and points up the bereaved worker's obligation to assume the role and attend to the death duties. By sending the worker home to deal with this most personal of life events, these policies also sharply segregate the time and place for work from the time and place for personal life.[53]

IMPLICATIONS OF BUSINESS TIME POLICY FOR BEREAVEMENT PRACTICES

Implications for Duration of Mourning

The trend over the past 3 decades to limit paid bereavement leave to 3 days is consistent with and gives further impetus to the trend during this century to shorten the formal mourning period. In 1927 Emily Post reported that the prescribed period of formal mourning for a widow was three years, but by 1950 she reported that 2 years was considered extreme and even more than 6 months was rare. Gorer[54] found in Great Britain that fewer than a fifth of bereaved persons in his sample gave up any leisure activities after the funeral and in the minority who gave up diversions the period was for only a week or so.

There are indications that it is coming to be normatively prescribed that the mourning period be brief. According to Fulton,[55] there is an "expectation of stoical acceptance of death. The expression of grief or sympathy for a death is limited to time and place. The dramaturgy of death moves inexorably to a conclusion—often only 3 days. Within a week one is expected to be back on the job." Kutscher[56] reported that in a sample of 125 widows and widowers over 90 percent viewed work as "good for" the bereaved; hence about half would encourage the bereaved to resume work within a week and three-fourths recommended a return within 2 weeks. Recent etiquette books prescribe brief mourning. Amy Vanderbilt[57] advised that the bereaved family should "pursue, or try to pursue, our usual social course within a week or so after a funeral."

Implications for Funerary Ritual

A national survey of funeral directors in 1967, which asked respondents to report changes in their practices during the previous 5 years, showed a decrease in the proportion of full traditional funerals.[58] It was calculated that 9 out of 10 funerals were traditional "complete" funerals in 1967. A re-survey in 1970 revealed that the proportion had dropped further to 7 out of 10 funerals. In nonmetropolitan areas 52 percent of funeral directors still conducted only traditional funerals in 1970, but in large urban areas only 8 percent of the funeral directors did so. One out of five funeral directors reported that families were specifically requesting brief funerals.

There has been some erosion of each step in the funeral. Between 1967 and 1970 funeral directors reported an increase in the number of funerals with no viewing or visitation; dispatching the body directly from the funeral service without a committal service; dispatching the body directly from the hospital for immediate disposition without a funeral service; and donation of the body to science without a viewing, funeral or committal service and sometimes without a memorial service after disposition. Disposal by cremation increased (doubled between 1960 and 1976 to 7 percent of deaths).[59] With direct cremation the body is taken from the place of death directly to the crematory and the whole procedure can be carried out within 24 hours.

These data do not indicate the extent of influence by business policies. However, the data do indicate that the timing and direction of the trends in funerary ritual are consistent with the timing and direction of business bereavement provisions, thus making it plausible to infer an interplay between business policies and the changes in funeral ritual.

REGULATING ELIGIBILITY FOR TIME OFF

Business regulates access to bereavement leave by specifying the categories of persons whose deaths the worker may have paid time off to mourn. Even in 1954 only 6 percent of the firms failed to specify the relationship for which paid leave was authorized and in 1972 all companies with provisions for paid bereavement leave did so specify.[60]

The corporate definitions restrict bereavement leave to deaths of family members. Practically all include spouse, child and parent and a majority include siblings. This was true in 1954 as well as in 1972. Since 1954 there has been a tendency to extend the eligible relationships to include parents-in-law—from less than half of agreements in 1954 to three-fourths in 1972. Siblings-in-law were included in only 6 percent of 1954 agreements and while the proportion has increased in subsequent years, this relationship category was included in fewer than half of the 1972 agreements. The family is defined in bereavement leave agreements as a narrow nuclear unit of spouse, parents and children, plus the spouse's parents.

Grandparents, grandchildren, brothers- and sisters-in-law, aunts and uncles and even relatives residing with the employee are excluded from the provisions of a majority of agreements; and in those agreements that do include these relatives, less time is allowed. An American Management Association publication recommended that for relatives other than immediate family one day should be granted for funeral attendance.[61]

Friends are universally excluded from the formal provisions of bereavement leave agreements. In interviews with workers and personnel officers in 40 corporations, respondents in one-fifth of these firms reported instances in which a worker was allowed time to attend the funeral of a friend who was a coworker; but in almost all cases the worker was paid for the time only if he was designated to attend the funeral as a representative of the work unit.

IMPLICATIONS OF LEAVE ELIGIBILITY RULES FOR BEREAVEMENT PRACTICES

Business policies authorize longer leave for immediate family than for more distant family members, disallow paid leave beyond a fixed circle of close relatives and provide the same leave for all members defined as immediate family. We will examine how these two aspects of leave eligibility bear on which deaths are formally mourned, the number of people participating, the amount of time spent on funerals and the nature of the rituals.

Delimitating the Circle of Bereaved

Exclusion of certain relationship categories (friends and distant relatives) from the contractual definition and limitation of time off for deaths of certain relatives to the day of the funeral or funeral attendance only may tend to reduce overall participation in mourning duties and funerary rituals. Although employed persons are not obliged to confine their bereavement duties to the contractual time allowances, they may be deterred by the regulations from taking unpaid leave or requesting extended or unauthorized leave; and without a leave, it may be awkward or impossible to meet the time requirements of funeral rites and bereavement duties.

The 1967 and 1970 surveys of funeral directors and a 1966 survey of Protestant clergy all found evidence that the number of adults attending funerals had, indeed, decreased during the 1960s.[62]

Corporate policy appears to be leading rather than following social usage in excluding friends and distant relatives. Etiquette books continue to insist that relatives and friends have extensive duties to perform.

> At this time it is of immeasurable help if a very good friend is willing to take charge of the funeral arrangements...Immediately on hearing of the death, intimate friends of the deceased should go to the house of mourning and ask whether they can be of service. There are countless ways in which they can be helpful, from assisting with such material needs of the family as food and child care, to sending telegrams, making phone calls and answering the door.[63]

Assigning higher temporal value to deaths in the immediate family than to deaths of lesser kin invests the nuclear unit with a conspicuous primacy in death work and this may foster more private, simple and abbreviated funerals. Specifying the immediate family in the contractual definition reinforces the family's obligations. Not only is the worker who sustains a family loss permitted to stop work, but she may be expected to do so by coworkers and family, for the definition officially ascribes to that worker the role of bereaved person.

This pattern is consistent with and lends support to the long-term trend, described by Ariès,[64] for the nuclear family to take over the role of mourning from the collectivity and, more specifically, with the established American legal tradition of imposing a real obligation on survivors to care for the dead and to focus on the immediate family as the responsible agent. In practically every state in the United States, the duty falls upon the surviving spouse; if the deceased had no spouse, then upon the nearest kin of sufficient age and possessed of enough money to defray the expenses, in this order: first—father, mother, son, daughter; second—grandparents, grandchild, sibling; third—great grandparents, aunts and uncles, nephews and nieces; fourth—great aunts and uncles, first cousins; fifth—first cousins once removed; and sixth—second cousins.[65] While the corporate definition of the bereaved does reinforce the legal emphasis on the duty of the immediate family it also tends to restrict death work to that unit.

By regulating the manpower of death work, these provisions would be expected to influence the type and amount of funerary ritual. Funerals would be arranged by and for nuclear families. Hence we might expect a trend away from elaborate public ritual and toward simplified private rites.

The national surveys of funeral directors in 1967 and 1970[66] revealed an increase in the proportion of funeral directors who had calls for private viewings, private funerals, private committals and funerals with no viewing and immediate disposal, with either a memorial service following disposal or no memorial service. In 1967, fewer than 2 in 10 funeral directors reported requests for no viewing and a private funeral, but by 1970, 8 in 10 funeral directors had such requests. Private rituals not only narrow the participation in the event, but also eliminate the public procession.

In a survey of Protestant clergy,[67] a majority of the ministers reported that even their church funeral tended increasingly to focus on the family and to leave others in the congregation as passive onlookers. The vast majority (8 in 10) gave a sermon or address that was directed toward the bereaved family. Only a fifth reported that the congregation sang a hymn and half reported the congregation said the Lord's Prayer in unison.

Surveys of the public in the 1970s substantiate the favorable sentiment toward private rituals. A 1974 opinion survey by the American Casket Manufacturers Association[68] found that only 9 percent of the sample thought that funerals should "be large and involve many friends and family." Fifty-four percent felt that "funerals should be small and private."

Homogenizing Mourning for Family Deaths

By fixing bereavement leave at a standard three days for the death of a spouse, child, parent, parent-in-law and sibling, the leave policies serve to equate all relationships within the family. This may have the effect of homogenizing mourning practices for all these family relationships.

This contrasts with traditional patterns of differentiated mourning. In addition to the legal provisions that ranked degrees of kinship as a basis for assigning responsibility, etiquette books show that the prescribed mourning period differed depending on the relationship of the deceased to the mourner, as well as the age and sex of the bereaved person. According to Emily Post in 1927, a man formally mourned the death of his wife for 1 year, his father for 6 months, his brother for 3 months or more, and his child either for the 6 months prescribed for the death of a father or the full year required for a wife.

This differentiated pattern of mourning was enforced by prescribing that the bereaved wear special clothing that identified the mourner's relationship to the deceased. In 1927 a widow was expected to wear deep mourning with crepe veil for a year, plain black the second year and "second mourning" (which permitted black, white, gray and mauve) for the third year. And "Widowers—especially if they are elderly—often go into black clothes and wear very dark gray mixtures with a deep black band on the hat and of course black accessories."[69] Mourning clothes requirements were decreasingly severe for deaths of parents, siblings and grandparents.

While only the affluent would have subscribed fully to these complex and costly prescriptions, it is likely that a large part of the population would have been guided by the basic principle, which was to distinguish the particular loss being mourned by wearing some symbolic form of dress for a specific time.

Subsequent editions of etiquette manuals reveal a trend toward prescribing similar mourning practices regardless of which family member had died. This came about through shortening all mourning and reducing the insignia that had enforced differentiated mourning. By the 1960s the prescribed period was 6 months to a year for any member of the immediate family—spouse, parent or child—and 3 to 6 months for sibling or grandparent.

The influence of business in eroding the costuming customs is evident in the etiquette books. Even in 1927, Post[70] reported on men's mourning clothes, as follows: "The necessities of business and professional affairs, which make withdrawal into seclusion impossible, have also made it entirely correct for a man to go into mourning by the simple expedient of putting a black band on his hat and on the left sleeve of his clothes." By 1950,[71] she noted, "There is an objection to even a sleeve band on business clothes: the implied bid for sympathy, which most men want to avoid."

Post began in 1950 to report the influence of business on women's mourning behavior: "Since mourning is the outward evidence of a personal frame of mind which has no place in the impersonal world of business, mourning which attracts attention is as unsuitable in an office as a black uniform would be on a soldier."[72]

With the virtual elimination of visible signs of mourning for employed people and with the reduction of mourning time for all degrees of kinship, a trend was developing toward equating deaths of all inner-family members for bereavement purposes. Business dress and demeanor codes had been instrumental in generating the trend toward homogenized bereavement practices within the nuclear family and bereavement leave policies of business have given further impetus to the trend.

BEREAVEMENT AS REFLECTION OF THE SOCIAL ORDER

We have examined changes during three decades in business policies and procedures for handling workers' bereavement, changes that represent a tendency to apply the time norms that govern work operations to the bereavement situation. This process included absorbing bereavement leave into the corporate benefits program: framing the bereavement issue in temporal terms; pricing leave time; measuring and limiting leave time precisely; standardizing time for all personnel; asserting company control over terms and eligibility and monitoring compliance; handling by formal procedures, such as written records and vertical channels; and segregating officially the time and place for mourning from the time and place for working.

These business procedures are converging with other social forces to reshape American bereavement customs. One of the other forces, the widespread employment of women, has transformed women from stewards of the traditional pattern of protracted mourning into carriers of the bereavement norms prescribed by business. The tendency for deaths to take place within hospitals has added urgency to death rituals, for hospitals insist that the body be removed promptly after death. Increased longevity means that most people who die are elderly and have long since become disengaged from work, community and relatives. Since they leave no "unfinished business" with the living, the survivors are able to dispatch them quickly.[73] The consumer movement has helped to erode the demand for elaborate funerals by focusing attention on funeral costs.

The bereaved role that is emerging under the influence of corporate policies and these other social forces is taking this form:

1. *Role eligibility.* A narrow category of persons are eligible and obligated to mourn a given death. A clear distinction is made between the directly involved inner core of family members and friends and relatives who are not formally recognized as bereaved.
2. *Role obligations.* Persons who are formally defined as bereaved because of their relationship to the deceased are given time off from regular work and are expected to arrange all the rituals and disposition. Relatives and friends cannot be counted on to give time and attention to the family and are expected to attend no more than one event—the visitation or funeral.
3. *Site.* Mourning activity is excluded from the workplace. The bereaved are expected to leave the work site immediately at the onset of their bereavement, to conduct their mourning in private and to resume full work responsibilities when the prescribed bereavement period is spent. One does not grieve in the workplace.
4. *Rituals.* Funerary rites are brief, simple and private.
5. *Mourning practices.* Brief mourning is prescribed and the duration is the same for all family deaths. One is expected to resume normal activities after the formal bereavement period. One does not display any visible insignia of woe, especially at work or other public places.
6. *Timing.* The bereaved must conform to the time framework prescribed by business. The onset, duration and termination of mourning are prescribed precisely and events are tightly scheduled.

Time prescriptions are a principal basis for organizing the behavior of the bereaved. The emerging behavioral code calls for brief duration, definitive beginning and closure, precise measurement and scheduling of time, punctuality and standardization of timing for all bereavements. These time prescriptions are modeled after and express the underlying principles of the business temporal order.

The business temporal symbols that are coming to be attached to bereavement are carried through in the physical forms of bereavement practices. The brief duration and definitive closure of bereavement time has its counterpart in cremation—a quick form of disposal—and in the practice of unobtrusive mourning, which facilitates abrupt severance of ties with the dead and immediate reintegration of the bereaved into the workplace. This contrasts with the temporal and spatial analogue in the previous century. When bereavement was prolonged in time, the predominant mode of disposition was earth burial in individually marked graves, representing a commitment of the living to maintain the grave and to preserve the memory of the deceased;[74] and distinctive mourning garb emphasized the duty of the bereaved to prolong ties with the dead.

The efficient organization of time that characterizes the emerging pattern of bereavement is carried through in the use of physical space. The modern high-rise mausoleum represents efficient use of space and as a physical replica of the corporate office building—a large-scale filing cabinet—the mausoleum symbolizes orderliness and standardization. In the past, lavish expenditure of time in mourning the dead was expressed spatially in sprawling garden cemeteries—a vast allocation of land to an economically nonproductive purpose and modelled after a spacious residential suburb.

As bereavement practices have been patterned increasingly according to business temporal norms, taking on the shape and meanings of the business system, bereavement has come to reflect and reinforce a view of the social order as efficient, under control and based on businesslike management of time.

NOTES

1. Amos H. Hawley. 1950. *Human Ecology.* New York: Ronald Press.
2. J.D. Robson. 1970. Sick Role and Bereavement Role: Toward a Theoretical Synthesis of Two Ideal Types, in Glenn M. Vernon, ed., *Sociology of Death.* New York: Ronald Press.
3. Max Heirich. 1964. The Use of Time in the Study of Social Change. *American Sociological Review* 29:386-397.
4. Ann Douglas. 1975. Heaven Our Home: Consolation Literature in the Northern United States, 1830-1880, in David E. Stannard, ed., *Death In America.*

Philadelphia: University of Pennsylvania Press; Stanley French. 1975. The Cemetery as Cultural Institution: The Establishment of Mount Auburn and the "Rural Cemetery" Movement, in David E. Stannard, ed., *Death In America.* Philadelphia: University of Pennsylvania Press; Robert W. Habenstein and William M. Lamers. 1975. *The History of American Funeral Directing.* Milwaukee: National Funeral Directors Association.

5. Maurice Lamm. 1969. *The Jewish Way in Death and Mourning.* New York: Jonathan David Publishers.
6. T. Lincoln Bouscaren and Adam C. Ellis. 1946. *Canon Law. A Text and Commentary.* Milwaukee: Bruce Publishing Company.
7. David E. Stannard. 1977. *The Puritan Way of Death.* New York: Oxford University Press; Charles O. Jackson. 1977. American Attitudes to Death. *Journal of American Studies* 2:297-312.
8. Rudol Rezsohazy. 1972. The Concept of Social Time: Its Role in Development. *International Social Science Journal* 24:26-36.
9. Michel Foucault. 1977. *Discipline and Punishment.* New York: Pantheon.
10. Richard Glasser. 1972. *Time in French Life and Thought.* Manchester, England: University of Manchester Press.
11. Daniel J. Boorstin. 1973. *The Americans: The Democratic Experience.* New York: Random House.
12. Max Weber. 1958. *The Protestant Ethic and the Spirit of Capitalism.* New York: Scribners (originally published in 1904).
13. Wilbert E. Moore. 1963. *Man, Time and Society.* New York: John Wiley.
14. Jack Goody. 1968. Time: Social Organization. In *International Encyclopedia of the Social Science,* Vol. 16. New York: Macmillan.
15. Staffan B. Linder. 1970. *The Harried Leisure Class.* New York: Columbia University Press; Barry Schwartz. 1975. *Queuing and Waiting.* Chicago: University of Chicago Press.
16. Eviatar Zerubavel. 1977. The French Republican Calendar: A Case Study in the Sociology of Time. *American Sociological Review* 42:868-877.
17. National Insurance Conference Board. 1940: *Personnel Practices in Factory and Office*; 1943: *Personnel Practices in Factory and Office*; 1948: *Studies in Personnel Policy*; 1954: *Personnel Practices in Factory and Office*; 1965: *Time Off with Pay.* New York: National Industrial Conference Board.
18. U.S. Department of Labor, Bureau of Labor Statistics. 1954: *Labor-Management Contract Provisions*; 1954: *Prevalence and Characteristics of Collective Bargaining Clauses.* Washington, DC: U.S. Government Printing Office; 1970: *Characteristics of Agreements Covering 5,000 Workers or More.* Washington, DC: U.S. Government Printing Office; 1977: *Characteristics of Major Collective Bargaining Agreements, July 1, 1975.* Washington, DC: U.S. Government Printing Office.
19. Allen R. Janger. 1966. *Personnel Administration: Changing Scope and Organization.* New York: National Industrial Conference Board.
20. Allen R. Janger. 1977. *The Personnel Function: Changing Objectives and Organization.* New York: The Conference Board.
21. Emily Post. 1927, 1940, 1950, 1955, 1968. *Etiquette: The Blue Book of Social Usage.* New York: Funk & Wagnalls; 1975. *The New Emily Post's Etiquette.* New York: Funk & Wagnalls; Amy Vanderbilt. 1972. *Etiquette.* New York: Doubleday; Eleanor Roosevelt. 1962. *Eleanor Roosevelt's Book of Common Sense*

Etiquette. New York: Macmillan; Millicent Fenwick. 1948. *Vogue's Book of Etiquette.* New York: Simon & Schuster.
22. Robert Fulton. 1971. A Compilation of Studies of Attitudes Toward Death, Funerals, Funeral Directors; The Funeral and the Funeral Director: A Contemporary Analysis. In Howard C. Raether, ed., *Successful Funeral Service Practice.* Englewood Cliffs, NJ: Prentice-Hall.
23. Roger D. Blackwell and W. Wayne Talarzyk. 1974. *American Attitudes Toward Death and Funerals.* Columbus, OH: Casket Manufacturers Association of America.
24. Janger, loc. cit.
25. Conference Board, loc. cit.
26. Baheej Khleif. 1976. The Sociology of the Mortuary: Relation, Sex, Age, and Kinship Variables, in Vanderlyn R. Pine et al., eds., *Acute Grief and the Funeral.* Springfield, IL: Charles C Thomas.
27. Geneva Seybold. 1961. *Personnel Procedure Manuals.* New York: National Industrial Conference Board.
28. Jean Mathison. 1970. A Cross-Cultural View of Widowhood. *Omega* 1:201-218; Paul C. Rosenblatt, Patricia Walsh and Douglas A. Jackson. 1976. *Grief and Mourning in Cross-Cultural Perspective.* New Haven, CT: HRAF Press.
29. Noel A. Levin. 1973. *Negotiating Fringe Benefits.* New York: American Management Association.
30. Donna Allen. 1969. *Fringe Benefits: Wages of Social Obligation.* Ithaca, NY: New York State School of Labor Relations.
31. Chamber of Commerce of the United States. 1958: *Fringe Benefits, 1957.* Washington, DC: Chamber of Commerce of the United States; 1976: *Employee Benefits, 1975.* Washington, DC: Chamber of Commerce of the United States.
32. Levin, loc. cit.
33. Levin, op. cit., p. 32.
34. Leroy Bowman. 1959. *The American Funeral.* Washington, DC: Public Affairs Press.
35. Viviana A. Zelizer. 1978. Human Values and the Market: The Case of Life Insurance and Death in 19th-Century America. *American Journal of Sociology* 84:591-610.
36. Richard J. Fritz and Arthur M. Stringari. 1964. *Employer's Handbook for Labor Negotiations.* Detroit: Management Labor Relations Service.
37. Seybold, loc. cit.
38. Robert M. McCaffery. 1972. *Managing the Employee Benefits Program.* New York: American Management Association.
39. Fritz and Stringari, op. cit., p. 257.
40. Robert O. Collins. 1967. Other Fringe Benefits, in Arthur J. Deric, ed., *The Total Approach to Employee Benefits.* New York: American Management Association.
41. Levin, loc. cit.
42. Fritz and Stringari, loc. cit.
43. U.S. Department of Labor, 1954, loc. cit.
44. McCaffery, op. cit., p. 125.
45. John Shea. 1972. Holidays, Vacations, Accidents, Sickness, Long-Term Disability and Other Time Off the Job, in Joseph Famularo, ed., *Handbook of Modern Personnel Administration.* New York: McGraw-Hill; Noel A. Levin. 1973. *Negotiating Fringe Benefits.* New York: American Management Association.
46. McCaffery, op. cit. p. 125.

47. Collins, op. cit., pp. 112-113.
48. National Industrial Conference Board. 1943, 1954. *Personnel Practices in Factory and Office.* New York: National Industrial Conference Board; Conference Board. 1974. *Profile of Employee Benefits.* New York: Conference Board.
49. Phelps Tracy and Koya Azumi. 1976. Determinants of Administrative Control: A Test of a Theory with Japanese Factories. *American Sociological Review* 41:80-94.
50. National Industrial Conference Board. 1954. *Personnel Practices in Factory and Office*; 1965: *Time Off with Pay.* New York: National Industrial Conference Board; Conference Board. 1974. *Profile of Employee Benefits.* New York: Conference Board.
51. National Industrial Conference Board, loc. cit.
52. Chamber of Commerce of the United States. 1978. *Employee Benefits, 1977.* Washington, DC: Chamber of Commerce of the United States.
53. Eviatar Zerubavel. 1979. Private Time and Public Time: The Temporal Structure of Social Accessibility and Professional Commitments. *Social Forces* 58:38-57.
54. Geoffrey Gorer. 1965. *Death, Grief, and Mourning.* Garden City, NY: Doubleday.
55. Robert Fulton. 1965. The Sacred and the Secular: Attitudes of the American Public Toward Death, Funerals, and Funeral Directors, in Robert Fulton, ed., *Death and Identity*, 1st Ed. New York: John Wiley.
56. Austin H. Kutscher. 1979. Bereavement, in Peter I. Rose, ed., *Socialization and the Life Cycle.* New York: St. Martin's Press.
57. Amy Vanderbilt. 1972. *Etiquette.* New York: Doubleday, p. 192.
58. Robert Fulton. 1971. A Compilation of Studies of Attitudes Toward Death, Funerals, Funeral Directors; 1971. The Funeral and the Funeral Director: A Contemporary Analysis, in Howard C. Raether, ed., *Successful Funeral Service Practice.* Englewood Cliffs, NJ: Prentice-Hall.
59. Consumer Reports. 1977. *Funerals: Consumers' Last Rights.* New York: W.W. Norton.
60. U.S. Department of Labor. 1954. *Labor-Management Contract Provisions, 1954: Prevalence and Characteristics of Collective Bargaining Clauses.* Washington, DC: U.S. Government Printing Office; Conference Board. 1972. Family Members Whose Death Qualifies Employee for Paid Bereavement Leave. (Mimeograph.)
61. McCaffery, loc. cit.
62. Fulton, loc. cit.; Paul E. Irion. 1966. *The Funeral: Vestige or Value?* Nashville: Parthenon Press.
63. Post, op. cit., pp. 503, 508.
64. Phillippe Ariès. 1981. *The Hour of Our Death.* New York: Alfred A. Knopf.
65. Erwin H. Greenberg. 1976. The Legal Aspects of Death, in V.R. Pine, A.H. Kutscher, D. Peretz, et al., eds., *Acute Grief and the Funeral.* Springfield, IL: Charles C Thomas.
66. Fulton, loc. cit.
67. Irion, loc. cit.
68. Blackwell and Talarzyk, loc. cit.
69. Emily Post. 1927. *Etiquette: The Blue Book of Social Usage.* New York: Funk and Wagnalls, p. 412.
70. Post, op. cit., p. 412.
71. Post, 1950, p. 292

72. Post, op. cit., pp. 292-293.
73. Robert Blauner. 1966. Death and Social Structure. *Psychiatry* 29:378-394.
74. Glenn M. Vernon. 1970. *Sociology of Death*. New York: Ronald Press.

11

The Funeral in Contemporary Society

Robert Fulton, PhD

THE DRAMATURGY OF DEATH

Burial of the dead is an ancient practice among humans. From paleolithic times to the present, human beings have responded to the death of their fellow humans with solemnity and ceremony. Not only has the event of death evoked a religious awe, but also its threat to the survival of communal life has also engendered fear, while its disruption of family life has aroused sorrow. The vehicle through which these reactions to death have been expressed has been the funeral. The funeral has traditionally served as a ceremony acknowledging death, a religious rite, an occasion to reassure and reestablish the social group, a commemoration of a life and a ritual of disposal.

The dramaturgical celebration of death and its significance for the individual and society have long attracted the interest of scholars. Several authors[1] have emphasized the function of ritualized behavior in promoting and maintaining the emotional well-being of the individual as well as the social cohesion and structural integration of the group.

Malinowski,[2] for instance, viewed ceremonies associated with death as a part of the sacralizing institution of religion which bestowed upon individuals the gift of mental integrity, a function, he believed, that was also fulfilled with regard to the whole group. He saw funerary customs as powerful counteracts to the centrifugal forces of fear, dismay and demoralization. He believed they possessed the potential for providing the most powerful means of reintegrating a group's weakened solidarity and reestablishing their shaken morale.

Radcliffe-Brown[3] and Durkheim[4] emphasized the role of ritualized behavior in promoting and maintaining social forms. Durkheim, for example, spoke of ceremony as being a collective expression of sentiment and interpreted certain attitudes and rituals as "objectified sentiments." On the other hand, van Gennep[5] assigned the greatest importance to the rituals associated with death because he found that funeral rites which had as their express purpose the incorporation of the deceased into the "world of the dead" were characteristically the most extensively elaborate.

More recently, Mandelbaum[6] has examined death rites in five widely separated cultures. His research has not only contributed new insights into our understanding of the role of death rituals, but it also permitted us to comprehend more clearly their place and meaning in our changing world. Mandelbaum concluded that funeral ceremonies serve "manifest" as well as "latent" functions. Manifest functions are those activities associated with mortuary rites that are most readily apparent, such as: the disposal of the body; assistance to the bereaved; public acknowledgment of the death and declarations and demonstrations of the groups' continued viability. Mandelbaum characterized latent functions, on the other hand, as funeral customs that include the economic and reciprocal social obligations that are remembered and reenacted at the time of a death. The role taken by participants in a funeral not only reflects their position in society but also reaffirms the social order. Other latent functions identified by Mandelbaum, were the obligations and restrictions placed upon all members of the deceased's family with regard to such things as dress, demeanor, food and social intercourse. Such observances, he noted, serve to identify as well as to demonstrate family cohesion. Still another latent function of the funeral he identified was the acknowledgment and affirmation of the extended kinship system in which members of the larger family console the survivors and frequently share in the expenses of the ceremony.

Mandelbaum argued that participation in the funeral ceremony, the procession, the partaking of food and other social exchanges, as well as the mourning and keening, all contributed to the sense of being a part of a larger social whole, just as the order of precedence in the conduct of the ceremony reminded one that there is structure and order in the social system. Finally, Mandelbaum concurs with van Gennep that the funeral is a "rite of passage." Because, Mandelbaum notes, it not only reaffirms the belief in the immortal character of human existence, but it also marks the end of life and the separation of the dead from the living.

CEREMONY: FUNCTIONAL AND DYSFUNCTIONAL

The question for us, however, is whether or not the funeral (as described by Mandelbaum and others and based, as their analyses have been, on non-Western or preindustrial societies) is relevant for a modern nation state. Is the funeral a functional ceremony in the urban, industrial world of today? Does it meet the needs of contemporary men and women? These are not new questions; yet they are still being asked. Indeed, they still need to be asked—perhaps now more than at any time in our history.

Ritual can be dysfunctional. Geertz[7] cites the case of a funeral in Java in which the insistence on traditional practices served to disrupt, rather than restore, the sense of community. He reports that traditional rites, which were suited to an agricultural village and folk milieu, caused much dissension and confusion among villagers when practiced in town, where the economic, social and political orientations were different from those of the village.

Mandelbaum,[8] too, provides the example of the Kota, where, typically, the traditional funeral ceremony actually aggravated the sorrow of the mourner and provoked social discord. At one stage of the Kota funeral—what is termed the "dry funeral"—there is a juncture when all Kotas who are present at the ceremony come forward one by one to give a parting bow of respect to the relics of the deceased. This has become a time of great tension and conflict. Mandelbaum describes the situation as follows:

> Around this gesture of social unity, violent quarrels often rage. When kinsmen of a deceased Kota are fervent supporters of one of the two opposing factions in Kota society, they may try to prevent a person of the other faction from making this gesture of respect and solidarity. This is tantamount to declaring that those of the other faction are not Kotas at all—a declaration which neither side will quietly accept. Thus a ritual action which symbolizes concord has frequently triggered a good deal of discord. Yet among the Kotas, as in other societies, neutral people try to bring about a compromise—the ceremony is somehow completed with as much show of social unity as can be managed—especially for funerals of the great men of the tribe (p. 213).

In this instance, however, Kota mourning ceremonies appear to be "rituals of rebellion" rather than an illustration of ritually inspired discord and disunity per se.[9]

There is still a further point to consider: the level of social organization. We have come to learn that what may be an operative and functional ritual at one level of social life—for example, the community—may not be functional for or congruent with human aims and purposes at another level of social life—for example, the nation.

Let me illustrate. In 1969, the Minister of Defense for Kenya, Mr. Tom Mboya, was assassinated. His death resulted in the subsequent deaths of more than a dozen fellow citizens among the Luo and Kikuyu tribes of that nation and the destruction of hundreds of thousands of dollars worth of property. The English journal, *The Economist*, reported at the time that never in the history of Nairobi had there been such disturbance and loss of life as that which followed the memorial service that was held in his honor.

In Kenya, it is a family obligation to see that the deceased is returned to his village and buried on his father's land with only members of the tribal community in attendance. Mr. Mboya was killed by a member of the Kikuyu tribe. The Kikuyu were excluded from taking part in his funeral—not only by virtue of the fact that they had been held responsible for his death but, also, because it is traditional for the tribes to exclude all but their own from funeral ceremonies. There was the possibility, therefore, that if Jomo Kenyatta, the prime minister of Kenya, died, there would be civil strife in Kenya—strife of such magnitude that the national aspirations of Kenya could well have been threatened. Mr. Kenyatta came from the Kikuyu tribe. It was highly possible that his mourners would exclude the Luo (who represent the second strongest political party as well as the second largest tribal group in Kenya) from participation in the ceremonies. Indeed, they may have held the Luo responsible for the death itself. If the national state of Kenya survived President Kenyatta's death, it would only be because the Kikuyu and the Luo recognized that the state had to take precedence over tribal traditions and ambitions.*

By way of contrast, America's experience with death in recent years at the national state level has been a study in the functional qualities of the funeral. The sudden and unexpected assassinations of President John F. Kennedy, Senator Robert Kennedy and Dr. Martin Luther King came as successive shocks to the body politic and were sorely felt. To review the events following the assassination of President Kennedy is to recall a period of social and political turmoil unparalleled since the assassination of President Lincoln a century ago. At that time, the country bordered on panic as rumors of conspiracy and intrigue swept through the Capital and across the nation. The attempted assassination of other members of Lincoln's cabinet

* In 1978 Prime Minister Kenyatta died a natural death. His funeral took place amid great mourning but without incident. This was mainly due to the fact that extraordinary efforts were taken to make his funeral as public and as symbolic of the nation as possible. The British government intervened directly. Through its Colonial Office it not only took charge of all the funeral arrangements but it also went so far as to provide the use of Winston Churchhill's funeral coach in order to dramatize the international significance of the event (*The Economist*, August 9, 1969, p. 240).

gave substance to those fears and placed the country on a war emergency alert.

A sequel to that episode was reenacted in the hours and days following President Kennedy's death. At the same time that the nation was plunged into grief and mourned his death, the country was alive to reports and rumors of conspiracies both from the political left and right. The assassination of Lee Harvey Oswald, President Kennedy's alleged assassin, by Jack Ruby, before a nationwide television audience, only aggravated the fears of the nation as it compounded the tragedy.

The state funeral that was held for President Kennedy was the most widely viewed ceremony in history. It is estimated that one-half billion people throughout the world watched the funeral proceedings on television.[10] In attendance—in addition to President Kennedy's immediate family, personal friends and colleagues—were dignitaries from all branches of the government, representatives from the various political parties and the heads of state (or their personal representatives) of ninety nonbelligerent countries.

President Kennedy's funeral served to declare not only that he was dead but also that order had been restored to the country and that the nation was secure in its relations with most other nations of the world.

The funeral of President Kennedy was followed in numbing succession by the funerals of Dr. Martin Luther King and Senator Robert Kennedy. As with President Kennedy's assassination, their violent deaths threatened to cause social and political disruption throughout the nation. The murder of Dr. King, in particular, as one of the countries most celebrated and revered leaders in the peaceful attempt to integrate white and black America, was little short of cataclysmic in its import. It precipitated racial disturbances across the country, resulting in the deaths of more than a score of citizens—both black and white—as well as the destruction of hundreds of millions of dollars worth of property.[11] His death removed the strongest voice of moderation from our racially antagonistic society. Despite this fact, however, and the fact that his assassin was a white man, his funeral included many prominent white political and social leaders. In effect, his funeral gave testimony to the nation as well as to the world that the followers of Dr. King were determined to remain true to his philosophy of nonviolence and to his dream of a racially-mixed nation free of prejudice and discrimination. With his funeral Dr. King's survivors saw an opportunity to bind the wound that his death had inflicted upon the body politic.

Death evokes powerful emotions within us that need to be vented or calmed. This was made evident with the assassinations of President Kennedy, Dr. King and Senator Robert Kennedy. The country grieved their deaths; the nation mourned openly not only as solitary citizens but also as a community. As a society, it observed public as well as private expressions of grief; it participated in three funerals to which the whole world paid heed.

Public evidence of the private reactions to President Kennedy's death is available. Thirty-nine surveys[12] were conducted following his assassination. While the studies were manifestly different in design and intent, certain common reactions were discernible. These reactions are best shown by a study undertaken by the National Opinion Research Center in Chicago[13] which polled a representative national sample of 1400 adults within a week of the assassination. The study showed the following:

1. Preoccupation with the death was almost total.
2. Nine out of ten people reported experiencing one or more physical symptoms such as headache, upset stomach, tiredness, dizziness or loss of appetite.
3. Two-thirds of the respondents felt very nervous and tense during the four days.
4. A majority of the respondents confessed to feeling dazed and numb.
5. Most people—men and women—cried at some period during this time.
6. The event was compared most often to the death of a parent, close friend or relative.
7. There was a tendency to react to the assassination in terms of personal grief and loss rather than in terms of political or ideological concern or anxiety about the future.

As the researchers reported, the reactions of the American people during the four days following the death of President Kennedy followed a well-defined pattern of grief; the funeral of the president channeled that grief and gave it poignant expression. The study supports the conclusion that the funeral of President Kennedy was functional in that it served the formal needs of our society and, at the same time, provided a vehicle for the expression of private as well as public grief.

The value of public rites for the dead was seen most recently following the Challenger space shuttle disaster in January, 1986 in which the entire crew, including the first teacher in space, was killed. Witnessed on national television, the sudden, unexpected explosion of the space shuttle shocked the nation at the same time that it wrenched the emotions of millions of eager and excited school children. Studies conducted following the disaster[14] found essentially the same emotional reactions that were engendered by President Kennedy's assassination, that is: almost half of the respondents reported "crying" or "feeling like crying"; "felt better after talking to other"; and those who informed others about the disaster reported "stronger emotional reactions" than those who did not. There was virtually no difference in the cognitive or emotional responses of the boys or girls to the disaster. Importantly, the nation was able to incorporate effectively the findings and recommendations of the Kennedy studies in dealing with the grief reactions of children and, from all accounts was successful, to a large degree, in palliating the emotional impact of the disaster.

Mortuary rituals, then, are a functional or a dysfunctional set of activities depending upon place and circumstance. In the case of Kenya, the funeral of President Kenyatta had the potential to do the state profound injury, given Kikuyu philosophy and tribal tradition. But for the United States, I would contend, the state funeral for President Kennedy and the funerals of Senator Robert Kennedy, Dr. King and the national as well as local ceremonies arranged for the crew of the Challenger were beneficial with respect to the emotional and social needs of the American public.

But what of the role of ritual or memorialization for the average American? What can be said about the funeral for the ordinary man and woman (or child) who dies an "ordinary" death? Is it also beneficial? The question is more than academic in view of the fact that criticism of the funeral and the funeral director has been both strident and far reaching over the past three decades. The funeral has been charged with being pagan in origin and ostentatious in practice, while the funeral director has been characterized as one who exploits the dead at the expense of the living.[15]

FUNERAL PRACTICES AND ATTITUDES

Over the past 25 years, I have conducted three nationwide surveys[16] dealing with the issues surrounding mortality in the United States. Permit me to highlight the major findings.

The first study,[17] conducted in 1959, surveyed the attitudes of clergymen toward funerals and funeral directors in the United States. It showed that clerical criticism of the funeral director and of funeral practices was both widespread and intensive. Among the different reasons the clergy gave for their negative appraisal, two stand out. First, the funeral director was charged with dramatizing the presence of the body while ignoring the spiritual dimension of death and, second, the funeral director was accused of taking undue advantage of the bereaved. A third factor was left unstated but was, nevertheless, implicit in the clergy's criticism; the profession conflates American funeral customs with those of other cultures and religions. Specifically, the study showed that the Protestant clergy, more so than their Catholic colleagues, were troubled by contemporary funeral practices and by the emerging prominence of the funeral director in the overall conduct of the funeral. Some clergy were rankled by the funeral profession's designation of a funeral establishment as a "chapel" and for what they perceived as encroachment on their role. These developments have led some members of the clergy to label the contemporary funeral as pagan and to describe the expenses associated with it as conspicuous waste. It has also led some of them to the active promotion of what is termed the "simplified" funeral, to advocate cremation or to recommend that monies usually spent on elaborate display be donated to public charities or scientific research.

The second study,[18] conducted in 1962, surveyed the attitudes of the American public toward death, funerals and funeral directors. Included in the study was a cross-section of those persons who were members of the funeral reform or memorial society movement. As with the clergy study, the survey showed that negative and critical attitudes toward contemporary funeral rites and practices are held by segments of the public. The survey showed, however, that these attitudes were not shared equally; rather, criticism of the contemporary funeral varied by religious affiliation, education, occupation and income as well as by geographical region. It was found that a majority of those surveyed were favorably disposed toward the funeral director and present-day funeral practices. They saw the funeral director as a professional person or one who combined a professional service with a business function while they viewed the funeral as providing a meaningful emotional experience for the survivors.

Members of memorial societies, however, expressed views strongly divergent from those of the general public. They believed the funeral director primarily conducted a business and offered the public no professional service whatsoever. The majority of members expressed an unfavorable opinion of funeral directors and funeral costs. In addition, a majority of respondents did not believe that the purposes of the funeral were, in fact, served by contemporary ceremonies. Only 25 percent of the memorial society respondents believed that the funeral served the emotional needs of the family in any way, while 16 percent perceived the traditional funeral as performing no useful function at all. Consistent with these findings, the study further showed that the memorial society members were the strongest advocates for cremation, for the donation of the body to medical programs and scientific research and for recommending that the ritual and ceremony of the funeral be greatly simplified or abandoned.

Of interest is the social profile of the average memorial society member. The study showed that members of memorial societies generally reported higher educational and professional attainment than did nonmembers. They also reported an average annual income twice that of the average American family. On the other hand, they reported being the least religious—or the least religiously affiliated—of those interviewed.

As a whole, the study showed that favorable responses toward funeral directors and funerals varied with religious affiliation. Religious affiliation, or its absence, was the pivotal factor around which the various attitudes expressed revolved. Simply stated, Catholics most often reported being favorably disposed toward the funeral and the funeral director, followed by Protestants, Jews, nonaffiliated respondents and Unitarians. The order was reversed with respect to critical attitudes. The Unitarians were the most critical, followed by Jews, nonaffiliated, Protestants and Catholics. Regionally, the most favorable attitudes toward the funeral and the funeral director were expressed by residents from central sections of the country, while the least favorable views were expressed by respondents residing along the Atlantic and Pacific coasts.

The third study[19] was sought to determine the character of contemporary funeral practices in the United States. A questionnaire was prepared and mailed to the 1967 membership of the National Funeral Directors Association as well as to the membership of the Jewish Funeral Directors Association. In all, 14,144 questionnaires were mailed. One out of every four (24.6 percent) of the funeral directors polled returned the questionnaire for a total of 3474 replies.

In many important aspects, the results of the third study complemented the findings of the previous two. The 1967 study, however, went beyond confirmation. It showed that the funeral in contemporary America represents different things to different people. While what might be called the "traditional" funeral (a public service with a public viewing and a public committal service) is almost totally characteristic of the great central portion of the United States and the predominant mode of behavior everywhere else, it is nevertheless subject to modification and change. New rituals and practices for disposing of the dead, as well as coping with death, are emerging. Emergent variability is a fact in funeral dramaturgy as it is a fact throughout all of society. Change is at work not only in the mode of disposal of the dead but also in every sphere of funeralization as well—from the type of funeral establishment constructed to the emotional climate in which the funeral is conducted to the meaning imputed to death itself.

In order to grasp the significance and implications of the findings of the third study they must be placed within the larger context of American life and ideology. A funeral does not take place in a vacuum. Rather, these three studies can be understood to mirror, albeit in a microcosmic way, what society as a whole has been experiencing by way of a shift in its religious beliefs and values—as they relate to death and dying—since the time of the first World War.

AMERICAN IDEOLOGY

First, let us consider the basic religious tenets of the majority of Americans who are heir to the Judeo-Christian tradition. According to this doctrine, human beings are creatures of God and have been formed in His image. Due to our fall from grace, however, we are born in sin and therefore spiritually flawed. Death is the consequence of that sin and a necessary experience for each one of us if we are to be restored to our prior state of grace. In American society, the funeral has been an instrument of this theology and its ritual has served to dramatize such beliefs for the living at the same time that it effected a liturgy for the dead.

This sacerdotal perception of human life, however, is not shared by everyone. The idea entertained today by a great number of Americans is that death is not the "wages of sin" nor need it be even as certain as taxes. Also it is no longer an unquestioned belief, on the part of many, that life is necessarily a gift from God. The papal encyclical *Humanae vitae*,[20] promulgated in 1968 and restating the Church's opposition to birth control, created a storm of protest and debate in the country that has had almost no precedent. Protests, petitions and pronouncements by clergy and laity, alike, of many different faiths and persuasions, questioned or openly opposed the papal edict. The same year, moreover, saw the first successful heart transplant in the United States, the continued progress toward kidney and other organ transplants and increased speculation regarding the unlimited possibilities of medical technology to extend life. The religious, moral and legal arguments surrounding such practices and prospects and their future implications are only now beginning to take definite form. One thing appears increasingly clear; humankind persists in its refusal to accept the inevitability of death and with death, as with life, seeks to be the final judge.

DEMOGRAPHIC FACTORS

A second point to consider is the demographic aspects of life and death. This year approximately 1 percent of the United States' population, or more than 2 million persons, will die.[21] Over 70 percent of these deaths will occur among persons 65 years of age or older.[22] In excess of 80 percent of these deaths, moreover, will now take place outside the home either in hospital, hospice or nursing home. The number of persons over the age of 65 is now over 31 million or 12 percent of the population.[23] In contrast, 27.5 million, or approximately one-quarter of the population, are children under 15 years of age.[24] Children, however, account for only 4 percent of all deaths.[25] This is a dramatic reversal in mortality statistics as compared to the 1920s when the mortality rate was highest for children.[26] As a matter of fact, contemporary American youth can be called the first "death-free" generation in the history of the world. That is, statistically, a family in the United States has only a one-in-twenty chance of having a death occur among its immediate members within a 20-year span. The implications of these statistics cannot be overlooked. Our conception of death and our expectations as to who will die, as well as our view of what constitutes an appropriate response to a death, are colored by these basic demographic facts.

INFLATION

A third factor that must be considered among the myriad of social and cultural changes that could be mentioned is the detrimental impact that inflation can have on the private household economies of millions of American families. Over 10 million families are headed by a widow who, in the majority of cases, lives on a fixed income consisting of social security or other retirement benefits.[27] Regardless of the provisions made beforehand, death expenses cannot help but be a source of anxiety and concern. Such concern, moreover, is deepened by a fourth factor—the changing character of the American home.

FAMILY

Over the past several generations, the structure of the average American family has changed from a large, extended family to a small, nuclear group. As a consequence it is more mobile—socially as well as geographically—than ever before. It is child-oriented rather than adult-oriented; it is more individualized than integrated. The young, contemporary family is less a part of a rural community or a neighborhood-enclosed group than before, while, increasingly, it tends toward being separated and disengaged in an anonymous urban environment. As it has been pointed out, death is increasingly an experience of the aged, most of whom are retired from work, free of parental obligations and frequently outside of, or absent from, the main current of family life. The extension of medical service and the advances in medical science research, moreover, make possible not only the prolonging of life of the elderly but often cause those hospitalized to be further separated from their families. Familial and friendship commitments are loosened by such separations and emotional and societal bonds are weakened. Not the least consequence of this development is the fact that great numbers of the elderly must not only live alone but, as research shows, they die alone as well.[28] The disengagement of the aged from society prior to their deaths means that their dying has little effect on the round of life.

As I have noted, the death of a leader such as President Kennedy, Senator Robert Kennedy or Dr. King can seriously disrupt the functioning of a modern society. The vacuum left by their deaths in the social and political life of the United States was enormously wrenching. For the common man or woman and for the average family, it is the death of someone either in the middle productive years of life or someone young and unfulfilled that will have a comparable effect upon the familial or social group. Because the elderly are less relevant to the functional working of modern society, their deaths do not compel the same degree of attention. Like the late General MacArthur's "old soldier," they do not die but rather "fade away."

CHANGE IN VALUES

The belief that the funeral is a meaningful rite for the dead has been seriously challenged in the United States in recent years. In a society in which only half of the population is church-affiliated and the social and spatial mobility of its citizens is one of its more remarkable characteristics, the religious, emotional and economic obligations that a funeral has traditionally imposed upon a family are seen by many, today, as inappropriate. Increasingly, the funeral is for that member of the family who is least functionally relevant to it. In a society that is predisposed toward that which is young and healthy as well as that which is practical and economical, an elaborate funeral for an elderly relative strikes the average citizens where they are most sensitive. Advocacy of memorial services with the body absent and the promotion of cremation as a form of human disposition are contemporary attempts to resolve these vexing issues.

THE FUNERAL AS A PIACULAR RITE

What of the funeral, then, in the face of these trends and developments? Sixty thousand years ago, as archaeological discoveries at Shanidar, Iraq have shown, humans buried their dead with ceremony.[29] They did so, given the evidence, because they believed in an afterlife. We must ask ourselves: are paleolithic funeral practices still relevant and functional for contemporary humans?

While burial or entombment of the dead is not universal, it is practiced in many different societies and has served to signify the belief in immortality, the belief that there is a spiritual state that we assume after mortal death. The funeral, it has been believed since time immemorial, is the ritual by which this transition is accomplished.

The funeral, however, is not like other rituals or ceremonies, such as

Thanksgiving or Christmas, that are festive or joyous, or those that mark cyclical or progressive events like New Year's Day or birthdays. The funeral is—to use an anthropological term—a *piacular rite*, that is, it is a ceremony that attempts to atone—or make amends for—a presumed wrongdoing. Piacular rites are those that deal with those aspects of social life that are stigmatized or result in defilement. They are ceremonies intended to remove the onerous blemish that has been cast upon the individual or group by a wrongful act of commission or omission. To die, as already mentioned, is perceived within the Christian tradition as punishment for human sin. By definition a human corpse is evidence of that sin and is thus spiritually unclean. Religious authority for this view can be found in the Old Testament (Leviticus 21:1) where it states that the Lord said to Moses, "Speak to the priests, the sons of Aaron and say to them that none of them shall defile himself for the dead among his people," and further, the Lord commands the chief priest "not to approach a corpse even that of his father or mother for fear of defiling himself" (Leviticus 21:11).

It was the anthropologist van Gennep[30] who observed that funeral rites were the most extensive and elaborate of all human ceremonies—that is, the most costly. I would argue that the reason for the tradition of inordinate expense associated with the funeral has to do with the fact that its main function is expiatory. But the funeral is also, by definition, obligatory. That is, by the fact that we die and by our cultural and/or religious interpretation of death, the funeral is imposed upon the community. Simply, we have no control over our deaths, yet at the same time we believe that to die is evidence of human culpability. Thus, on the one hand, the excessiveness of the funeral reflects the desire to be exonerated from sin and to free the "spirit" from corrupting flesh, while our aversion to the corpse, on the other hand, reflects our fear of religious defilement. Herein lies the paradox: the historic impulse to conduct an elaborate and ostentatious ceremony for the disposition of a human body that at the same time is perceived with fear and dread.

This paradox can also be observed in the place we assign funerals in society as well as in the form and manner that they assume. While the funeral is indeed an ancient and time-honored ceremony that is observed around the world, it also demonstrates a wide variety of forms. Despite the funeral's long history it is actually a most volatile ceremony. This is due to the fact that it is highly subjective in its individual configuration. This can be readily seen in the United States where a wide variety of funeral options, or what might be called "customized" funerals, are available. This historic volatility can also be seen in the dramatic changes that have taken place with respect to the funeral since World War II with the virtual disappearance of such "traditional" funeral practices as the wearing of "widows' weeds";

the black hatband, tie and arm band; the black hearse; and the funeral wreath on the door of the home of the deceased. Additionally, cremation is becoming, in certain regions of the United States, an increasingly preferred mode of disposition. Mourner participation in the funeral has also greatly increased, with friends and relatives contributing poetry reading, songs, musical offerings and eulogies to the ceremony and, even in some instances, designing a complete service that may or may not contain a religious component.

Nor is the volatility and variability of funeral practices limited to the United States. Anthropologists have long observed that among different aboriginal groups, as far removed from each other as North America and South Africa, funeral practices are subject to wide variation and change, even among groups who are in close proximity to each other and who share the same cultural heritage.[31] This, I would argue, is due to the fact that the funeral is the least regarded of all public ceremonies even though it is one of the most necessary (as far as the disposition of the body is concerned) and the most costly. It is also because it allows the idiosyncratic or personal element to be expressed. That is, individual survivors are typically allowed to introduce personal components into the funeral which promotes the instability or change that has been observed. Because the funeral fundamentally represents the negative side of mortal life and is an obligation, reluctantly assumed, it is like no other ceremony in social life. Social etiquette, historically moreover, has generally required the avoidance of any discussion of death, including the problems of widowhood, grief and mourning, the cemetery, or the functions of the embalmer or mortician, except as he may be the object of macabre humor or public censure. As a result the public recognition of these changes has been rarely reported or their implications for social life clearly understood.

Today, the belief in immortality and with it the piacular obligations of the funeral are contrary to the philosophical and ideological beliefs of a large segment of the American public. Many people do not believe in a "life after death," nor do they believe that it is necessary or felicitous to consume the resources of the living for the doubtful benefit they may have for the dead. For some, the most desirable procedure is also the simplest—one that involves as little material expense as possible. For a growing number of people, this means immediate disposition of the body with no public ceremony.[32]

But, as it has been noted, social scientists have recognized that there are important aspects of the funeral other than the expression of a belief in immortality or the dramaturgical incorporation of the dead into an afterlife. I think it is important for us to consider these aspects and their place and function in contemporary society.

THE FUNERAL AS A RITE OF INTEGRATION AND SEPARATION

As well as being a rite of incorporation the funeral is also a rite of separation and integration. The funerals of President Kennedy, Dr. King and Senator Kennedy, as well as that of Mr. Mboya, demonstrated this tripartite character of the funeral. The dramaturgy of those funerals expressed the belief that the world will go on, that we, the survivors, will continue to live, that the social order prevails and that society will continue to believe in the justice and mercy of God. But the funeral is also a drama that tells us that we have lost someone through death. As such, it focuses attention upon the survivors and to the degree that it does so, it is a rite of separation as well.

Psychologically, the loss of a significant person by death is a crisis situation for the survivor. Medical and behavioral science experts have taught us in recent years that such loss evokes powerful emotions that need to be given proper expression.[33]

Several authors[34] inform us, moreover, that the acceptance of separation or permanent loss of a significant other is an exceedingly difficult task to achieve; many persons never do recover from permanent loss or ever wholly accept, or indeed ever admit to, the death of a loved one. "How do we get people to accept permanent loss?" is the question.

Two leading British psychiatrists, John Bowlby and C. Murray Parkes,[35] have pointed out that a major element in acute grief is the denial that a death has occurred. As they describe it:

> There is a restless searching for the lost person, a constant wandering from room to room as if seeking for the loved individual, often calling his or her name. The necessary tasks and rituals, whether they are religious or not, which surround death, serve, however, to bring home gradually to the bereaved person the reality of the loss they have sustained and the knowledge that life will never be quite the same again. Drawing the blinds, viewing the body, attending the funeral service, lowering the coffin into the grave all serve to emphasize the finality and the absoluteness of death and make denial more difficult.

The ritual of the funeral, when it is responsive to the psychological needs of the survivors, can aid in the ventilation of profound emotions and help facilitate the normal dissolution of grief. Viewing the dead potentially allows this dissolution to take place.

It is true, as critics charge, that there are elements of disguise in the cosmetic preparation of the body for the funeral. But such "prettifying" of the corpse is no more the basis of the funeral ceremony than the use of cosmetics or a veil is the basis for a wedding. I am led to propose that the masking of the ravages of an illness or injury is functional to the extent that it assists the grieving survivors to move, psychologically, from shocked denial to acceptance of the death. As Emily Dickinson would have us remember, "The truth must dazzle gradually, else every man be blinded."

The events leading up to the actual interment or cremation of the body are those in which the survivors are invited to gather together, acknowledge the death, share in the grief, participate in the mourning rites and witness the final disposition of the body. The funeral must be understood in terms of this dramaturgical denouement: the deceased has been removed forever from the living community.

IS THE FUNERAL BENEFICIAL?

The question before us still is: If the funeral is a rite of integration and separation, is it beneficial? The answer to that question is a contingent one. Ultimately, it is one that depends upon the individual survivor and the circumstances surrounding a death. For some survivors, the loss of an elderly relative is an occasion for the barest acknowledgment of death and the most expeditious disposal of the body. In such an instance of what could be described as a "low-grief" death, loss can be slight and grief muted. The sudden, unexpected death of a child or of a young husband, on the other hand, may be perceived as premature, unjust, or denied and resented by the survivors. Such a death could be termed a "high-grief" loss. The social and emotional needs of family, friends and community in such instances are infinitely greater and the potential problems of the survivors more extensive than in the case of what has been termed a "low-grief" loss. On the other hand "no grief" may be felt by a relative who is privately relieved or pleased at a death while "improper grief" may be experienced by a person who is not allowed to mourn publicly (the companion of a homosexual man who has died of AIDS but who is not allowed by the deceased's family to attend the funeral is a case in point). Care has to be taken, therefore, not to define too narrowly what funeral rites or behaviors are appropriate for the bereaved. Insensitivity and inadequate social acknowledgment of the intensity or absence of grief and the social expectations of the bereaved can only serve to aggravate their difficulties. For instance, when members of the clergy perceive the funeral as a rite of passage only and describe death as a joyful spiritual victory to be celebrated, they ignore the fact that a death may represent the separation of a husband from a wife or a father from a daughter and as with any irrevocable separation, the survivor may experience a profound sense of loss. Reaction to human loss should never be readily dismissed or denigrated. I am sure that this is the intended insight in the New Testament when in John 11:35 we read that "Jesus wept" upon hearing of the death of his friend Lazarus.

Mourning is the intersection of grief (a psychological drama) and bereavement (a social fact) where loss through death finds expression. The successful orchestration of this public process facilitates healing at the same time that it allows for the expression of private grief. The funeral thus provides the setting in which both private sorrow and public loss can be both expressed and shared. It is Fulcomer's[36] conclusion, based on his case studies of 72 bereaved subjects, that there is a definite indication that the bereaved person's responses are positively affected if she realizes or believes that other persons are also mourning. In other words, "Sorrows tend to be diminished by the knowledge that another sorrows with us."[37] Likewise, it is the conclusion of Glick, Weiss and Parkes,[38] following their recent four-year case analysis of 68 bereaved persons, that even though the survivor frequently experienced mixed feelings, the tasks and activities associated with the ceremonies of leave-taking met profound human needs. It was their observation, however, that many survivors found it difficult to view the corpse. But as they and Elisabeth Kübler-Ross[39] and others have observed, viewing is a way for many to confront the death of their loved one. Glick[40] quotes one widow who remarked, "I didn't believe he was dead until I saw him in the casket."

Loss through death can be a crisis situation. Studies show, however, that survivors display a wide range of responses and demonstrate varying capacities to adjust to death. Prolonged maladjustment, however, as characterized by mental and physical ailments as well as the increased consumption of alcohol and sedatives, is all too common. Findings from a study at the University of Minnesota[41] and the studies of Mole[42] and Glick[43] on the other hand, show that apart from family and friends relatively few health care persons are in contact with a survivor following a death. The Minnesota study shows, for example, that only 15 percent of the survivors out of a sample of 558 widows and widowers reported professional health care contact or support following the death of their spouse. Yet the evidence strongly suggests that many persons are in need of much more than the good will and concern of their closest family members or friends.

The funeral, as a rite of separation and integration, requires of funeral directors that they, too, be cognizant of and sensitive to the social and emotional needs of the families they serve. They must believe—as must the survivors—that the funeral they conduct and in which they participate, is something more than a commercial transaction.

In this connection, it is important to note that, in addition to this author's own previously cited work, both the study by Binger and his colleagues[44] at Langley-Porter Institute and the Harvard Bereavement Study conducted by Glick and coworkers[45] found that the funeral director played a valuable social role in the discharge of his responsibilities. Binger and coworkers reported, for instance, that 15 of the 20 families interviewed "expressed positive feelings toward the mortician or funeral director." They observed that "experience with grief reactions makes them skilled in offering solace to grieving families" (p. 417).

Since the first draft of this chapter was written in 1978, there has appeared an increasing amount of research to support the contention of Binger, Glick and others that bereaved individuals typically find their interaction with funeral directors to be a supportive and helpful experience. Khleif's[46] study of some general populations and the studies of widows and widowers by Winn,[47] Carey [48]and Lieberman and Borman,[49] as well as the studies of bereaved parents by Cook[50] and Anglim,[51] show that the majority of respondents rated their funeral directors as "somewhat" or "very helpful and supportive." Two studies of the widowed, moreover, found that the majority of respondents described their spouse's funeral as helpful to their adjustment.[52]

I think the different studies now available show that the contemporary funeral can be functional to the extent that it recognizes the separation and integration issues associated with death. I would argue, given our newly found understanding of the social and psychological dimension of loss and grief, that we should put greater emphasis upon the funeral as a rite of separation and integration and less emphasis upon the funeral as a rite of incorporation. To do so is not only to recognize the social and personal values to be derived from such an approach to the funeral, but also it is to recognize the decreasing relevance of the funeral as a piacular rite. I would think that in appreciating this subtle but nevertheless significant shift in emphasis, we will do ourselves and our fellow citizens a considerable service.

Of course, citizens must not only be competently and adequately served, but they must also be protected from malpractice. They must have freedom of choice. Ultimately, one's relationship with the funeral director will need to be based on trust.

There is increasing scholarly evidence today that can support social custom in the belief that a funeral is a ceremony of value for the mourner, just as competent funeral directors can be—and are—of assistance to the bereaved.

American society is experiencing rapid social change, particularly with regard to attitudes toward death and death practices. We are presently in the process of defining and redefining grief, bereavement and loss, to say nothing of the meaning of death itself. Comparable issues face us with respect to the elderly and the dying. The role of the funeral director is an emergent one.

It would be beneficial if the funeral director were seen as a potential participant in a community's mental health network. This view would not only support those practices which historically have served human needs, but it would also strengthen the mental health movement within the funeral service play a positive part in helping with the multiple burdens of bereavement. Perhaps, most of all, by treating funeral service personnel as one would normally treat other professional and paraprofessional health caregivers, trust in the good intentions of others is expressed. To do so might be to remove, finally, the admonition *caveat emptor* (let the buyer beware) that has for so long been held over the funeral director's head. I would hope to see that warning replaced by the historic medical directive *primum non nocere* (above all, do no harm)—an admonition to which we might all pay more heed.

The dramaturgy of death compels the recognition that a death has occurred. In a society where there is a strong tendency for many to respond to the death of another by turning away, the funeral is a vehicle through which recovery from the crisis of bereavement can be initiated. The funeral, importantly, is also a ceremony that recognizes the integral worth and dignity of a human being. It is not only a sociological statement that a death has occurred, it also proclaims that a life has been lived.

CONCLUSION

What of the future of the funeral? The funeral, as well as every other social practice invented by human beings, is subject to change. Mourning rites and funeral customs have not been carved in concrete nor do they exist in a vacuum. They are contained, rather, within a cultural context which they serve to delineate as well as define. American funeral customs and practices have continued to evolve, since colonial days, as a result of both internal and external social forces. In the last two decades, however, we have not only observed appreciable changes within traditional funeral practices—the white pall of the Catholic funeral mass and the emergence of the humanistic funeral—but we have also witnessed extensive public criticism of funeral practices from without. Such criticism lead, in the late 1970s, to the direct intervention of the government. The Federal Trade Commission ultimately effected legislation that required funeral directors to abide by rules of conduct and business procedures that more closely protected the public's interest. Change can also be observed in the public's behavior as well. In San Francisco, Los Angeles, New York and other major cities across the United States, upwards of 25 percent of the deaths annually go unreported in the obituary columns of the daily newspaper.[53]

But of more immediate significance is the contemporary scenario for the disposition of the dead that is now practiced in almost one-sixth of all deaths in San Diego County, California. It is as follows: upon the declaration of a patient's death, the body is removed to the hospital morgue; an organization called Telephase is notified; the body is picked up at the morgue and enclosed in a rubberized bag; it is then transported in an unmarked station wagon to a crematorium where it is cremated and the ashes are placed in a cardboard or plastic container for storage, dispersal or delivery to a designated recipient; the legal survivor is later billed. Similar practices are now appearing in other cities across the country in which the body of the deceased is disposed of by means of cremation and in which there is no memorial service or public or religious observances of any kind.

Cremation with or without memorialization, as an alternate form of disposition, is on the increase across the country. While the practice still varies considerably—from approximately 13 percent of all deaths in Minnesota to over 40 percent of all deaths on the Pacific coast—there is little doubt that with the Catholic church conditionally lifting its ban on cremation that the practice will continue to gain in public acceptance.

But another more serendipitous factor may come into play—AIDS. While AIDS is not contagious in the normal course of human interaction, it may, nevertheless, by reason of the fear that it is generating among the American public, result in mandatory changes not only in our funeral customs but in many other social customs as well. Only time will tell whether AIDS will have the same relative impact on contemporary society and on the funeral that the plague did during the successive centuries that it ravaged the populations of Europe.

Talcott Parsons,[54] the late distinguished American sociologist, believed that the emergent changes that have been observed in contemporary funeral practices are the result of the convergence of the social, industrial and medical trends that have characterized the United States since the turn of the century. Advocacy of change in funeral practices, he argued, was natural and to be expected in a society that strives to achieve order, practicality, efficiency and economy in all facets of life. Robert Blauner,[55] another American sociologist, is even more direct in his analysis. He argues that the dramatic changes that have occurred in society, particularly the profound demographic shifts, have resulted in a situation in which the majority of persons who die are those who, for the most part, are no longer central to the stream of life. Their deaths have little consequence for the social order. Under such circumstances, Blauner contends, we should expect the American funeral not only to continue to change significantly—to be diminished—but eventually to "wither away."

There is some evidence to support Blauner's contention that funeral customs, as presently practiced in the United States, could, rather than just change, "wither away." A study of 558 bereaved persons conducted by the

Center for Death Education and Research at the University of Minnesota showed that the death of an elderly parent is appreciably less disruptive emotionally, less debilitating and socially less significant than is the death of either a spouse or a child. To be sure, adult children of the study (average age of 48) did mourn the loss of their parent—in some instances profoundly—but as a group the responses of the adult children were markedly different from the other two groups. The study showed, for instance, that, compared to the bereaved parents and spouses, a significant proportion of the adult children reported the least amount of change in regard to such post-death measures of adjustment as crying, depression, anorexia, insomnia, smoking, drinking and hallucinations. They also reported the least amount of illness following their bereavement. Additionally, the surviving adult children not only reported being the least affected of the three groups on the different behavioral and physiological measures employed, but were also found to be the least socially expressive of their respective losses. That is, they were least likely to conduct traditional funeral rites, least likely to view the body and least likely to observe the anniversary of their parent's death compared to the other two groups.

The study showed further that of the three groups, the adult children were least "affected by memories of the death of the deceased" and least likely to be "preoccupied with that memory." Finally, the adult children were least likely "to be more appreciative of life" following the death of their parents, to be "helpful toward others," to "enjoy life or their families more," or to be "warm toward other persons." On the other hand, the adult children reported more personal guilt and more hostility toward others following the death than did the other two groups of survivors.[56]

The constellation of feelings and behaviors demonstrated by the adult children of the study following the death of an elderly parent was characterized by "diminished" or "transitory" grief followed by limited post-death activities. While the sample of adult children in the study is admittedly small, we may be witness to a potential for diminished interpersonal relationships that promises to grow more pronounced in the years ahead. Like the tip of an iceberg, the responses of the adult children suggest the magnitude of the changes that lie hidden below the surface of social intercourse. Although the tip in no way tells us of the iceberg's actual proportions, it does inform us of the iceberg's presence.

It is important to recognize that the mature adult child need not experience the grief reaction or the profound sense of loss that characterized the responses of the parents and spouses in the Minnesota study. In modern society, the elderly are oftentimes defined differently from other age groups. They "have had their life." It is only "normal" and "natural" that they die.

Minimal rites acknowledging the death of a socially disengaged, elderly person may make sense at the personal level. Funerals, it is said, are for the living and if the living are not seriously affected by the death of a family member, the need for traditional rites of passage may be little felt. A funeral, however, has traditionally had other functions aside from disposing of a corpse or publicly acknowledging a death. As a social ceremony, it serves to bring together the community. As it does so, it provides a socializing experience for the participants, particularly the young. As such, it serves as an important vehicle of cultural transmission. The contemporary movement to preclude funerals from society or to exclude children from funerals can have unintended consequences. In addition to cutting children off from direct expressions of love, concern and support at this time of family crisis, it may deprive them also of the opportunity to learn about life's most basic fact—death. The social meaning and intrinsic value of human life itself, moreover, may be implicitly denied by the failure to acknowledge our mortality.

NOTES

1. A. van Gennep. 1961. *The Rites of Passage* (M.B. Vizedom and G.L. Caffee, trans.). Chicago: University of Chicago Press; A.R. Radcliffe-Brown. 1952. Taboo, in *Structure and Function in Primitive Society.* London: Cohen & West; E.E. Evans-Pritchard. 1965. *Theories of Primitive Religion.* Oxford: Clarendon Press; R. Hertz. 1960. *Death and the Right Hand* (R. Needham, trans.) Glencoe, IL: The Free Press; J. Goody. 1962. *Death, Property and the Ancestors: A Study of the Mortuary Customs of the Lo Dagaa of West Africa.* Palo Alto, CA: Stanford University Press; J. Goody. 1962. Religion and Ritual: The Definitional Problem. *British Journal of Sociology* 12:142-164; D. Mandelbaum. 1959. Social Uses of Funeral Rites. In H. Feifel, ed., *The Meaning of Death.* New York: McGraw-Hill; R.W. Habenstein and W.M. Lamers. 1963. *Funeral Customs the World Over.* Milwaukee: Bulfin; B.S. Puckle. 1926. *Funeral Customs: Their Origin and Development.* London: Laurie; E. Bendann. 1930. *Death Customs: An Analytical Study of Burial Rites.* New York: Knopf.
2. B. Malinowski. 1954. Death and the Reintegration of the Group. In B. Malinowski, ed., *Magic, Science, and Religion and Other Essays.* New York: Doubleday.
3. Radcliffe-Brown, op. cit.
4. E. Durkheim. 1954. *The Elementary Forms of the Religious Life* (J. Swaine, trans.). London: Allen & Unwin.
5. A. van Gennep. 1961. *The Rites of Passage* (M.B. Vizedom and G.L. Caffee, trans.). Chicago: University of Chicago Press.
6. Mandelbaum, 1959, op. cit.
7. C. Geertz. 1957. Ritual and Social Change: A Javanese Example. *American Anthropologist* 59:32-54.
8. Mandelbaum, 1959, op. cit.

9. M. Gluckman. 1962. Rituals of Rebellion in South-East Africa. In M. Gluckman, ed., *Essays on the Ritual of Social Relations.* New York: Humanities Press.
10. Kennedy is Laid to Rest on an Open Slope in Arlington National Cemetery. 1963 (November 26). *The New York Times*, p. 2.
11. They Came to Mourn. 1968 (April 19). *Time*, pp. 18-19.
12. Bureau of Social Science Research. 1966. *Studies of Kennedy's Assassination.* Washington, DC: Bureau of Science Research.
13. P.B. Sheatsley and J.J. Feldman. 1964. The Assassination of President Kennedy: A Preliminary Report on Public Relations and Behavior. *Public Opinion Quarterly* 28:189-215.
14. R.W. Kuby and T. Peluso. 1990. Emotional Response as a Cause of Interpersonal News Diffusion: The Case of the Space Shuttle Tragedy. *Journal of Broadcasting and Electronic Media* 34(1):69-76; M.M. Brabeck and K. Weisgerber. 1988. Responses to the Challenger Tragedy: Subtle and Significant Gender Differences. *Sex-Roles* 19:9-10.
15. J. Mitford. 1963. *The American Way of Death.* New York: Simon & Schuster.
16. R. Fulton. 1961. The Clergyman and the Funeral Director: A Study in Role Conflict. *Social Forces* 39:317-323; 1965: The Sacred and the Secular. In R. Fulton, ed., *Death and Identity*, 2nd Ed. New York: Wiley; 1971: *A Compilation of Studies of Attitudes Toward Death, Funerals and Funeral Directors.* Minneapolis: University of Minnesota; Center for Death Education and Research. 1971: Contemporary Funeral Practices. In H.C. Raether, ed., *Successful Funeral Service Practice.* New York: Prentice-Hall.
17. Fulton, 1961, op. cit.
18. Center for Death Education and Research, op. cit.
19. Fulton, 1971, op. cit.
20. Humanae Vitae. 1968 (July 30). *The New York Times*, pp. 1, 20.
21. U.S. Bureau of the Census. 1990. *Census of Population, CPH-L-74.* Washington, DC: U.S. Government Printing Office.
22. *Monthly Vital Statistics Report*, U.S. Bureau of the Census (Vol. 34[3]), 1985.
23. Ibid.
24. Ibid.
25. U.S. Bureau of the Census, 1990, op. cit.
26. U.S. Bureau of the Census. 1960. *Historical Statistics of the University States, Colonial Times to 1957.* Washington, DC: U.S. Government Printing Office.
27. F. Berardo. 1968. Widowhood Status in the United States: Perspectives on a Neglected Aspect of the Family Life Cycle. *The Family Coordinator* 17:191-203.
28. R. Fulton and V. Gupta. 1974. Psychological Adjustment to Loss. Unpublished manuscript, Center for Death Education and Research, University of Minnesota, Minneapolis.
29. R.S. Solecki. 1971. *Shanidar.* New York: Knopf.
30. Van Gennep, 1961, op. cit.
31. A.L. Kroeber. 1927. Disposal of the Dead. *American Anthropologist* 29:308-315.
32. Fulton, 1971, loc. cit.
33. A. Ciocco. 1940. On the Mortality in Husbands and Wives. *Human Biology* 12:508-531; P. Cox and J.R. Ford. 1964. The Mortality of Widows Shortly After Widowhood. *The Lancet* 1:163-164; J.F. Frederick. 1961. The Physiology of Grief. *Dodge Magazine* 63:8-10; T.H. Holmes and R.H. Rahe. 1967. The Social Readjustment Rating Scale. *Journal of Psychosomatic Research* 11:213-218; A. Kraus and A. Lillenfeld. 1959. Some Epidemiologic Aspects of the High

Mortality Rate in the Young Widowed Group. *Journal of Chronic Diseases* 10:207-217; C.M. Parkes. 1965. Bereavement and Mental Illness (Part I): A Clinical Study of the Grief of Bereaved Psychiatric Patients. *British Journal of Medical Psychology* 38:1-12; C.M. Parkes. 1964. Effects of Bereavement on Physical and Mental Health—A Study of the Medical Records of Widows. *British Medical Journal* 2:274-279; R. Rahe, J. McKean and R.J Arthur. 1967. A Longitudinal Study of Life-Change and Illness Patterns. *Journal of Psychosomatic Research* 10:365; R. Rahe, M. Meyer, et al. 1964. Social Stress and Illness Onset. *Journal of Psychosomatic Research* 8:35-43; D.W. Rees and S. Lutkins. 1967. Mortality of Bereavement. *British Medical Journal* 4:13-26; G. Stern et al. 1961. Alterations in Physiological Measures During Experimentally Induced Attitudes. *Journal of Psychosomatic Research* 5:73-82; G. Wretmark. 1959. A Study of Grief Reactions. *Acta Psychiatrica Neurologica Scandinavica* (Suppl. 136): 292; R. Fulton, ed., 1973. *Bibliography on Death, Grief and Bereavement (1945-1973)*, 3rd Ed. Minneapolis: Center for Death Education and Research, University of Minnesota.

34. E. Lindemann. 1944. Symptomatology and Management of Acute Grief. *American Journal of Psychiatry* 101:141-148; A. Weisman. 1972. *On Dying and Denying*. New York: Behavioral Publications; E. Kübler-Ross. 1969. *On Death and Dying*. New York: Macmillan; J. Bowlby. 1963. Childhood Mourning and Its Implications for Psychiatry. *Journal of the American Psychoanalytic Association* 11:500-541; J. Bowlby. 1953. Some Pathological Processes Engendered by Early Mother-Child Separation. *British Journal of Psychiatry* 99:265-272; M. Young et al. 1963. The Mortality of Widowers. *The Lancet* 2:254-256.
35. J. Bowlby and C.M. Parkes. 1970. In E.J. Anthony and C. Koupernik, eds., *The Child in His Family*. New York: Wiley.
36. D.M. Fulcomer. 1942. The Adjustive Behavior of Some Recently Bereaved Spouses: A Psychosociological Study. Unpublished doctoral dissertation, Northwestern University, Evanston, IL.
37. A.F. Shand. 1914. *The Foundations of Character*. London: MacMillan.
38. I.O. Glick, R.S. Weiss and C.M. Parkes. 1974. *The First Year of Bereavement*. New York: Wiley.
39. Kübler-Ross, 1969, op. cit,
40. Glick, Weiss and Parkes, op. cit., p. 110.
41. Fulton and Gupta, 1974, op. cit.
42. R.L. Mole. 1974. Next of Kin: A Study of Bereavement, Grief and Mourning. Unpublished doctoral dissertation, Howard University, Washington, D.C.
43. Glick, Weiss and Parkes, loc. cit.
44. C.M. Binger et al. 1969. Childhood Leukemia: Emotional Impact on Patient and Family. *New England Journal of Medicine* 208:414-418.
45. Glick, Weiss and Parkes, loc. cit.
46. B. Khleif. 1975. The Sociology of the Mortuary: Attitudes to the Funeral, Funeral Director and Funeral Arrangements. In O. Margolis et al., eds., *Grief and the Meaning of the Funeral*. New York: MSS Information.
47. R.L. Winn. 1981. Perceptions of the Funeral Service and Post-Bereavement Adjustment in Widowed Individuals. *National Reporter* 4:1-8.
48. R.G. Carey. 1979. Weathering Widowhood: Problems and Adjustment of the Widowed During the First Year. *National Reporter* 2:1-5.
49. M.A. Lieberman and L.D. Borman. 1982. Widows View the Helpfulness of the Funeral Service. *National Reporter* 4:1-2.

50. J.A. Cook. 1981: Children's Funerals and Their Effect on Familiar Grief Adjustment. *National Reporter* 4:1-2; 1983: A Death in the Family: Parental Bereavement in the First Year. *Suicide and Life-Threatening Behavior* 13:42-61.
51. M.A. Anglim. 1976. Reintegration of the Family After the Death of a Child. In I. Martinson, ed., *Home Care for the Dying Child: Professional and Family Perspectives.* New York: Appleton-Century-Crofts.
52. Winn, 1981, op. cit.; Lieberman and Borman, 1982, op. cit.
53. J. McReavy. 1980. *N.F.D.A. Paid Obituary Notice Survey.* Milwaukee: National Funeral Directors Association.
54. T. Parsons. 1963. Death in American Society: A Brief Working Paper. *The American Behavioral Scientist* 6:61-65.
55. R. Blauner. 1966. Death and Social Structure. *Psychiatry* 29:378-394.
56. G. Owen, R. Fulton and E. Markusen. 1982. Death at a Distance: A Study of Family Survivors. *Omega* 13:191-226.

IV

Public Policies and Private Decisions

Introduction

Dying patients and bereaved families as well as health care professionals are affected increasingly by public policies and private decisions regarding dying and death. To understand the new dynamics of social interaction, social organization and social policy and to provide a clinical sociological perspective for these issues, the resources of both academic sociologists *of* death and sociological practitioners *in* health care are essential.

Major changes are taking place particularly in medical-ethical decision-making regarding matters of life and death. New "stake-holders" in the care and treatment of dying patients and the bereaved now include hospital policy makers, ethics committees and federal regulators, along with patients and their physicians. These key players are called upon to address such diverse topics as: new definitions of death; living wills; palliative care and hospice programs; physician-assisted suicide and euthanasia; ethical decision-making in medical research; HIV/AIDS research and treatment protocols; patient access to medical care; as well as the spiritual and psychosocial care of the dying and the bereaved.

Dialogue among physicians and others, as they confront medical-ethical issues, increasingly includes not only medical concerns in treating a disease, but also the psychosocial context of the patient and family. When a clinical ethicist is in attendance during "rounds" or "care conferences," ethical questions are framed in terms of the value of patient autonomy, beneficence and justice. These discussions, for example, might include the option of hospice or palliative care when the emphasis is on pain control and comfort care for end-stage cancer patients. Other physicians whose patients are on kidney dialysis might convene the hospital ethics committee for advice about terminating treatment at the request of the patient, which will result in death. The ethically difficult topic of physician-assisted suicide, or even active euthanasia as currently practiced in the Netherlands, is another nascent issue that looms on the moral horizon in the medical management of mortality.

The Netherlands is the only country, as of this writing, that allows physicians, following state-prescribed guidelines, to comply with patient wishes for active euthanasia. General practitioners, who administer euthanasia most often, have a protocol to follow that "enhances scrupulous decision-making with regard to the patient's request for euthanasia" (Ministry of Welfare Report, The Netherlands). Data on the practice in the Netherlands include official government estimates of less than 2 percent of all deaths to an estimated 10 percent as reported by Gomez in his 1991 book, *Regulating Death: Euthanasia and the Case of the Netherlands.*

The public debate over euthanasia continues in the Netherlands, with many physicians preferring to administer "comfort care" as their patients are dying. In the United States and elsewhere, palliative care is the only ethical option to aggressive medical treatment of hospitalized dying patients, although a Michigan physician, Dr. Jack Kevorkian, has challenged this practice by assisting several terminal patients to die. Social researchers have yet to determine whether the strong negative stance of the medical community in the United States toward euthanasia is related to the small number of general physicians compared to the large number of medical specialists who practice in American communities.

The first chapter in this section by Bernard J. Hammes and Robert Bendiksen, "Prolonging Life—Choosing Death: A Clinical Sociological Perspective in Medical-Ethical Decision-making," focuses attention on ethical values of patient autonomy, beneficence and justice as they are addressed by two types of hospital-based committees. These are institutional review boards (IRBs) that monitor the ethics of biomedical and behavioral research, and institutional ethics committees (IECs) that educate and advise physicians who have difficult ethical cases. Hammes and Bendiksen present a representative case study from clinical practice to show how these two committees impact patient care.

"Death-Related Issues in Biomedicine: Euthanasia and AIDS," by Robert Blank, is an introduction on how to conceptualize central questions of biomedical policy regarding death. Blank's typology, which distinguishes dimensions of "voluntariness" and "passive-activeness," points to the confusion surrounding the concept of euthanasia. Many professionals and citizens who express positions or opinions about euthanasia tend to refer only to "active, voluntary" euthanasia, thereby neglecting the common practice of "passive" medical options not to intervene aggressively at the behest of a patient or of a close relative or friend whom the patient has designated as possessing the "durable power of attorney for health care."

Blank provides a sketch of the evolution of court decisions regarding euthanasia, as well as raising questions about cases of Alzheimer's disease. He discusses the role of state legislatures in their attempts to "catch up" with medical science by redefining death as "brain death," and the burgeoning role of the biomedical community in establishing a more responsible policy in rationing of health care services.

The chapter by Judith A. Levy, "The Hospice in the Context of an Aging Society," presents an institutional analysis of "social forces that evoked the hospice movement" and of the "congruence between hospice services and the needs of an aging society." Hospice is both a contemporary practice and an ancient concept of care. Hospices have comforted critically ill and dying people, as well as their families, since the middle ages. England is credited with the first modern hospice—St. Joseph's Hospice in 1905. St. Christopher's Hospice, well known to Americans through its founding medical director, Dr. Cicely Saunders, has been a model of hospice care since 1967.

The first American hospice began providing care in 1974. Whether part of a hospital program or "freestanding," hospice is an institutional resource for physicians in their medical "management" of disease and illness. Hospice, as Levy reminds us, is an accepted alternative to aggressive medical intervention that incorporates humane treatment guidelines as death draws near. The success of hospice in the United States is an indication of the significant changes in physician-patient interaction that have occurred in recent years but, as one respondent in a hospice study by Greg Owen poignantly asked, "Do you have to die to get that kind of care?"

The challenge voiced by an appeal in the late 1970s for more of "that kind of care" did not anticipate its relevance to HIV and AIDS in the decade that followed. Robert Fulton and Greg Owen, in "AIDS: A Sociological Response," offer their analysis of HIV and AIDS in a discussion of clinical sociological import. The human immunodeficiency virus disease no longer is "back-stage," a disease of an isolated few. Rather, AIDS now is "front-stage" in challenging major players, such as government health agencies and medical insurance providers, to respond more adequately in supporting health care providers in their treatment of HIV and AIDS patients.

Fulton and Owen provide a social and epidemiological update of the disease that currently infects an estimated 2 million Americans. Debates abound about the epidemic. Should FDA guidelines limiting access to experimental drugs be expanded to cover other end-stage diseases? How accurate is the accounting of the reported incidence and prevalence rates of the disease provided by the Centers for Disease Control? In Africa, where estimates of HIV infections are more than double those of the United States, public health officials and medical professionals alike are limited not only by inaccurate statistics, but also by inadequate funds and by cultural beliefs and customs that hamper the effectiveness of prevention programs.

Fulton and Owen's sociological analysis of HIV and AIDS moves from a sociohistorical interpretation of stigma to an empirical assessment of five related AIDS epidemics that challenge us. The five epidemics can be found among (1) homosexual and bisexual men; (2) heterosexual women whose sexual partners are IV drug users or bisexual men infected with the virus; (3) heterosexual IV drug users of both sexes; (4) children infected in utero; and (5) "undetermined" cases of AIDS. Importantly, Fulton and Owen propose that we are at risk for an epidemic among the young adult heterosexual population. They conclude their chapter by itemizing the contributions of clinical and applied sociologists who have been involved in sociological practice activities calculated to bring the AIDS epidemic under control.

Another major contribution to a clinical sociological perspective of death and dying has been made by a collegial group of clinicians, researchers and educators, known as the International Work Group on Death, Dying and Bereavement, who are "dedicated to the development of knowledge, research and practice dealing with death, dying and bereavement and with education about death, dying and bereavement." The IWG meets periodically to facilitate informal interaction among its members, as well as to develop standards of practice in death and dying. The social policy documents written by the Work Group are seen increasingly by the health care community as a resource for health policy planning and evaluations.

The final chapter is a compilation of four IWG Assumptions and Principles documents. Each assumption is "a statement of fact on the basis of commonly observed experience" and its derived principle is "a collective judgment as to the proper response to the assumption." The four documents selected for inclusion are: (1) Assumptions and Principles Underlying Standards for Terminal Care; (2) Assumptions and Principles of Spiritual Care; (3) Assumptions and Principles Regarding Bereavement; and (4) Assumptions and Principles of Care for Those Affected by Human Immunodeficiency Virus Disease.

The clinical sociological perspectives represented in this section on "Public Policies and Private Decisions" support sociological interventions for positive social change in responding to death and dying. Sociological practitioners work at all levels of social life, including individual interaction, groups, organizations and even larger units of society. The sociology of death outlined in this third edition of *Death and Identity* calls for even greater articulation between theory and research on death, grief and bereavement and for more effective efforts on behalf of those who confront the ever-present reality of death and loss.

12

Prolonging Life— Choosing Death: A Clinical Sociological Perspective in Medical-Ethical Decision-Making

Bernard J. Hammes, PhD
Robert Bendiksen, PhD

INTRODUCTION

Tracy is an active 20 year old in her second year of college. She suddenly develops symptoms of fatigue, poor appetite, joint aches and mild fevers. After she is extensively evaluated by a team of physicians, she is found to have acute lymphoblastic leukemia (ALL). This disease is a form of cancer of the blood. Primitive white blood cells (lymphoblasts) multiply rapidly, crowding out normal white and red blood cells. This results in serious problems like the inability of the body to fight infections and decreasing the ability of the blood to deliver oxygen to the body. Not treating the disease would likely lead to death in 4 to 6 months at best. Chemotherapy, however, can be highly successful in many cases.

Tracy is immediately presented with treatment options by her physician. One is entering a research study approved by the hospital's institutional review board. This research participation provides the patient with access to the latest thinking in chemotherapy, but it may also require many additional tests and repeated follow-up. As with much chemotherapy, it can produce not only significant burdens for the patient, but also lead to death or permanent side effects. In this particular case, the research protocol was designed to determine whether a more aggressive, initial drug treatment would result in more lengthy remissions. A second program involved less aggressive treatment. Since the two experimental treatments appeared equal, patients who consented to participate are randomly assigned to one of two initial treatment groups. Would these more aggressive treatments result in longer remissions? Would the toxic side effects of the drugs be tolerable? These are the basic questions the research hoped to answer.

Tracy chose to participate in the research. Her initial chemotherapy was successful. She was in remission, but needed repeated follow-up to test for recurrence. As her strength returned, there was hope that she might be cured. However, one month later she returned to her physician, with increased temperature, loss of appetite and fatigue. Her leukemia was back. Again she needed treatment or else faced death. She chose to try treatment, although she admitted to being weary of the needles, the effects of the drugs, and the inability to carry on with her dreams. A second research protocol was offered and accepted. This protocol was only for those who had a relapse of ALL. The object was to determine whether other new drugs would produce a remission and not be too toxic. The first course of this new chemotherapy seemed to go well for a while; then Tracy started to have respiratory distress and low blood pressure. Despite immediate medical treatment, she continued to have difficulty breathing and maintaining blood pressure. It was discovered that she had an infection in her bloodstream. Ultimately, she was transferred to the intensive care unit because she required mechanical ventilation. In the next days it was determined that she showed neurologic signs of brain injury because of inadequate blood flow to the brain. Her condition continued to worsen to the point that the probability of survival or of neurologic recovery was 10 percent or less. If she survived this episode, she faced more chemotherapy and would probably require a bone marrow transplant with only a small chance of cure.

Tracy's family gathered around. She could no longer make decisions or even interact with her family. An "ethics consult" from the institutional ethics committee was called to help the family sort through the alternatives. The technology was available; it could be used. But should it be? Ultimately, the family had not only to face their grief, but also the responsibility of making a decision about medical treatment for Tracy. They chose to discontinue some medical interventions and maintain others for comfort. Tracy died less than 12 hours later, 11 months after discovering that she had leukemia.

Cases like Tracy's remind us that in the last three decades dramatic changes have occurred in the medical and surgical treatment of human illness and disease. From the first reported use of CPR to restore life in 1964 to the first use of genetic material to treat certain diseases in the late 1980s, the advancement of medical science and technology continues with no end in sight. These changes have brought forth new, complex and frequent decisions that force us to review and reconsider our fundamental ethical and moral values.

In the industrial nations in particular, the current human experience of dying has changed before our eyes. Illnesses or injuries that would have caused death in the past can now often be cured or a person can have vital functions maintained. If death cannot be avoided, there may be a choice of how and when death will happen. Frequently, death is accepted and treatment foregone even when life might be sustained, because of the burdens of the treatment. Never before have patients benefitted so much from the skills of physicians, but never before have physicians had to accept so much responsibility for a patient's dying. The fascination and fear of the power of technology and science have never personally affected so many on a daily basis.

The medical and ethical story of these changes has two parts. One part is the expansion and importance of medical research. Approaching illness and disease through the scientific method, using human subjects, allows medical progress to develop more quickly and more successfully. Developments in medical research also produced new ethical questions about the physician/researcher's ethical responsibility to the patient or subject. Can the benefits of this research be realized without using some humans, even after animal testing, for the good of others? The other part of the story is the actual implementation of the results of medical research in approved treatment regimens for patients. Although research subjects may be carefully selected by predetermined criteria, ultimately technology is put in the hands of physicians who decide about the use of the method for each patient. There is no research protocol that indicates which patients are to be treated in practice. It is not always clear how much the trial intervention will help or be valued. Who should make such decisions? How should they to be made? Special ethical guidance may be indicated in certain difficult cases.

This chapter will review two clinical sociological and public policy intervention strategies that have occurred in the past 30 years. They are the development of institutional review boards (IRBs) to monitor medical and behavioral research on human subjects and of institutional ethics committees (IECs) that provide ethical advice to physicians, patients and families. We will consider how these sociological responses have changed the process of making medical decisions and reflect the evolving perspectives on the ethics of medical care.

THE INSTITUTIONALIZATION OF REVIEW BOARDS

The ethics of experimentation, especially with humans in biomedical research, have become institutionalized in the United States during the past quarter century. In the 1960s, several well-publicized cases of government-sponsored research that challenged ethical principles of patients' rights and welfare raised the level of public and professional awareness about these issues.[1] Organizational problems of social control in medical experimentation were documented in a now-famous study of research on human subjects that included two national surveys, one of research institutions and the other of researchers.[2] The study found that "Research with human subjects has produced advances in medicine, but also some instances of ethical abuse. Studies of the attitudes and practices of investigators suggest that better controls are required."[3]

Ethical problems with the conduct and regulation of clinical research have also been documented by Gray,[4] who conducted a sociological case study of an IRB in a large university hospital in the northeastern United States. Gray examined both the way that a research ethics committee exercises control over the use of human subjects in medical experimentation and the ways that patients are used in two actual medical research protocols. The protocols were a double-blind study of a labor-inducing drug and a study of metabolic effects when women fasted for 3 days before a therapeutic abortion. Gray found that nearly 4 out of 10 of the women in the labor-induction study were unaware they were involved in research, even though all appropriate procedures were apparently followed. Gray concluded that although IRB procedures appear to address important concerns about patient rights and patient welfare, problems remain in areas such as degree of patient awareness in studies and of physician control over patient subjects.

Protection of human subjects in medical experimentation first became a public issue with the Nuremberg Trials after World War II. *The Nuremberg Code*[5] enumerates 10 basic ethical principles, the first of which states that "the voluntary consent of the human subject is absolutely essential." This consent includes the conditions of having the legal capacity to give consent, of being able to exercise freedom of choice, and of having sufficient knowledge and comprehension to make an informed decision. Before a potential subject gives consent, she should have information on the nature, duration and purpose of the research, on the research procedure, and on possible harm or disruptions to the person's life. Responsibility for assuring voluntary consent lies directly with the researcher and cannot be delegated. The remaining nine principles require competent researchers who design scientifically valid protocols that are preceded by earlier nonhuman studies and researchers who guarantee human subjects the opportunity to refuse participation without prejudice.

The National Commission for the Protection of Human Subjects of Biomedical and Behavioral Research was created on July 12, 1974, when the President signed into law the National Research Act (PL 93-348). The Commission was charged with identifying the basic ethical principles that should underlie biomedical and behavioral research and with developing guidelines that researchers should follow to apply these principles. The final document of the ethical principles and guidelines was published in *The Belmont Report.*[6] The report acknowledges *The Nuremberg Code* as a prototype of many other ethical statements, including *The Belmont Report.* The report identifies boundaries between practice and research. "The purpose of medical or behavioral practice is to provide diagnosis, preventative treatment or therapy to particular individuals. By contrast, the term 'research' designates an activity designed to test a hypothesis, permit conclusions to be drawn, and thereby develop or contribute to generalizable knowledge (expressed, for example, in theories, principles and statements of relationships)."[7]

The Belmont Report identifies three basic ethical principles that are generally accepted in our culture and that "are particularly relevant to the ethics or research involving human subjects: the principles of respect for persons, beneficence and justice."[8] The principle of "respect for person" includes acknowledgment of autonomous decision-making and of protection of individuals whose autonomy is diminished for whatever reason. The principle of "beneficence" begins with the Hippocratic maxim of "do no harm" and extends to maximizing possible benefits and minimizing possible harm to subjects. The principle of "justice" includes the expectation that people from all stations in life will be considered as candidates for research subjects and that the results of successful research should be made available to anyone in need, regardless of their resources.

The Commission applied the three ethical principles in developing guidelines that include informed consent, risk/benefit assessment and the selection of research subjects. *Informed consent* means that subjects be given the opportunity to choose what they will undergo in medical treatment and research. For this to happen, the potential research subject must have sufficient information on which to base a decision, comprehension of the meaning of the data, and freedom to voluntarily participate or not participate for whatever reason. *Risk/benefit assessment* is a comparison of "the probabilities and magnitudes of possible harms and anticipated benefits."[9] This assessment includes not only psychological and physical factors, but also legal, social and economic harm and benefits. *Selection of research subjects* should follow the principle of distributive justice, with special protection for people in disadvantageous situations.

The National Research Act of 1974 (PL 93-348) directed that an "Institutional Review Board: Ethics Guidance Program" should be written in order to protect human subjects in research funded by the Department of Health and Human Services (DHHS) and the Federal Drug Administration (FDA). These agencies developed their own regulations based on their grant programs, but an effort has been made to bring the two sets of regulations into agreement. The DHHS regulations on "Protection of Human Subjects" are published by the Office for Protection from Research Risks in the *Code of Federal Regulations* (45 CFS 46, 1983) and the FDA regulations are published in the *Federal Register* (January 27, 1981). Other agencies have their own requirements, but the DHHS and FDA regulations are the ones that most directly affect medical and behavioral research.[10]

The DHHS regulations describe the types of research and basic definitions to which these regulations apply. Particular attention in the regulations is given to the type of assurances organizations must provide regarding their IRB and they describe IRB functions and operations, ordinary and expedited review procedures, criteria for IRB approval of research, review by the institution, suspension or termination of IRB approval, cooperative research, IRB records, requirements for informed consent and other special circumstances. The remainder of the DHHS regulations describe what to do when research subjects are fetuses, pregnant women and human in vitro fertilization, prisoners or children. The FDA regulations include similar descriptions of the IRB and its procedures, but additional attention is given to comments from the public review process and guidelines for research on food, drugs and various types of medical devices.

RESEARCH ETHICS AND THE IRB: DIVERSE RESPONSES TO REGULATION

Institutional review boards are not all alike even though regulations suggest conformity. IRBs are located in hospitals and medical clinics as well as in a variety of other research settings. Stopp[11] conducted a survey of 100 colleges and universities in the U.S. and identified three types of IRB processes: (1) a centralized IRB that reviews all protocols (17 percent of academic institutions); (2) ad hoc IRB subgroups that review protocols and report to a centralized IRB (62 percent); and (3) dispersed independent IRB groups located in departments or other academic units (19 percent). An innovative IRB structure is described by Herman[12] where a noninstitutional IRB in Philadelphia contracts with medical institutions in that region to conduct reviews of research protocols. This IRB meets monthly to review and monitor protocols in many different medical institutions.

McNeill[13] compared IRBs in the U.S., Canada, Europe and Australia where he found important differences in philosophy, structure and functioning of IRBs. England, for example, seeks primarily to facilitate medical research rather than emphasize protection of human subjects. Canada and Australia operate their research enterprises independently of the federal government. Scotland has regional IRBs. IRBs in France, Belgium and the Netherlands review only foreign-funded research and research expected to be published in international journals. Denmark has small IRBs and officially recognizes informal monitoring of researchers. The U.S. appears to be most concerned of all these countries with identifying and elaborating specific ethical principles of research. Bergkamp[14] compared U.S. IRBs and Dutch research ethics committees (RECs) and found that U.S. regulations affect all types of research, while the Dutch RECs review only biomedical research. Hall[15] analyzed research ethics committees in England and Wales regarding research on children and found the same great variety in IRBs as did McNeill[16] in his nonrandom observations in Great Britain.

Institutional review boards consider the scientific merit of research protocols as an important component in determining ethical merit. Most members of IRBs are selected because of their expertise in basic or applied science. Hospital IRBs, not surprisingly, tend to have a majority of physicians, many of whom also participate in medical research. The IRB also may include a dentist, laboratory scientist, social scientist, organizational administrator, attorney, chaplain, nurse and clinical ethicist, among others. The IRB regulations require that there be at least one member who is a nonscientist and one member who is not affiliated with the institution or part of the immediate family of a person who is affiliated. No IRB may be either all men or all women. Porter[17] studied IRB members who were unaffiliated with the institution and are nonscientist members. These lay members perceived themselves taking responsibility for representing community attitudes, reviewing consent documents, being advocates for human subjects, evaluating how consent is obtained, being sensitive to ethical procedures, and expressing opinions in deliberations.[18]

The role of laypersons, according to Porter,[19] includes "requiring accountability of experts to the public." Questions raised by lay members and by scientific members who take the role of "citizen," focus the attention of researchers on universal standards of ethical conduct that might be hard for colleagues to raise regarding community values that may not have been addressed, and values, interests and lifestyles of patients and healthy control group subjects. These IRB members spend much of their time reviewing informed consent documents for clarity, but many are not in a position to actually assess the process of obtaining consent from research subjects. Special attention is often given to vulnerable populations, such as children, prisoners, and even employees, as well as to judging the worth of research in terms of risks to life, health and lifestyle, including management of confidential information. The perspectives of community lay members adds an important dimension to the IRB discussions that medical professionals may overlook.

The perspectives of community lay members on an IRB are seen by DHHS and FDA as valuable, but their voice is often limited. Veatch, in his book *Patients as Partners*,[20] examines the IRB process and the impact of group decision-making on high-risk decisions. He concludes: "[Stoner's] initial work led to the conclusion that committees as a whole reach decisions that permit more risky choices than the average of the individual views of the members of the committee would suggest." This implies to Veatch that IRBs, heavily represented by researchers and physicians, will systematically shift the risks acceptable to the committee so that research proposals will be approved, while at the same time limiting "the most wild, individual risk takers."[21] Veatch worries that IRBs tend to load the committee with physicians or researchers, and not recognize the value of other types of expertise. In his view there is a need for representation from the legal, sociological, psychological and religious professions if a committee is to truly consider issues of consent, risks and benefits, and the rights of subjects. The questions raised by Veatch, then, lead to a central concern: How should the structure and function of an IRB be changed so that a wider expertise is recognized and a systematic bias toward approval of research is minimized?

Addressing this issue is not as simple as adding more lay members or other professional members. One has also to deal with the functioning of the committee process itself. Veatch describes several models for an IRB, the first of which is a *peer review committee.* The primary function of an IRB in this model would be to judge the scientific merit and design of the proposal, as well as its scientific risks and benefits. A second model is that of a *jury.* In this model the main role of the IRB would be for members to reflect the common sense of the ordinary person. In the jury model, members would be chosen for their lack of bias rather than for their professional or general expertise. A third possibility is that of a *representative model.* Here members are picked for their general expertise in understanding and communicating the interests of potential research subjects. This type of IRB would take the role of ombudsman in reviewing the merit of protocols.

Veatch favors a role for professional expertise, but believes that this expertise must extend beyond the physician and researcher. He thinks that the dynamics of the committee must more favorably represent community standards than is typically the case with physician-dominated committees. He suggests that this could be accomplished either if the membership of an IRB were selected for the ability to represent the lay person or if the review process consists of two committees. This two-part evaluation would include a review first by a *scientific committee* determining scientific feasibility and judging ethical issues from this profession's point of view, followed by a review of a *community committee* which would have adequate support to make a judgment of scientific worthiness as well as broader ethical issues.

Veatch first published his suggestions for a two-stage IRB process in the *Hastings Center Report*.[22] This occurred a year after the U.S. Department of Health, Education and Welfare (which later became DHHS) revised its policies and regulations regarding membership of IRBs. His remarks seem to have had little impact on the structure or function of IRBs, as today it appears that IRBs are constituted by single committees largely represented by researchers and physicians.

THE IRB AND THE TREATMENT OF PATIENT TRACY

How did the IRB process affect Tracy's medical treatment? She probably had no awareness that the research protocol was prospectively reviewed. The consent form did indicate who she could contact if she had questions about her rights as a research subject. While Tracy may not have been aware of it, certain protections for her and other patients were definitely considered. Before the research treatment could be offered to Tracy, it had to be reviewed by an IRB. Actually, since this same study was being conducted at several medical facilities, it would be reviewed independently at each institution it was offered. The IRBs considered the merits of the research, the design of the study, the potential risks and benefits to both subjects and society, the completeness of the consent process and fairness of the patient population. It is a basic requirement that a medical research protocol will answer important questions about the treatment of patients. Its design must provide a satisfactory way of determining whether the treatment works and is safe.

Given that there are not good treatments for adults with ALL, trying new approaches with drugs that are known to have more effect than others seems reasonable if the risks are not too great. How does one measure risk of the research when the risk for the patient without treatment is certain death? IRBs seem to accept that if the treatment offers some reasonable hope of prolonged survival, a competent adult should have the opportunity to assess the risks and make a choice. In this case where the existing risks to the patient are clear and the treatment has at least some potential benefit, the IRB will likely concern itself with the consent process used with patients and subjects. Attention must be given to clearly informing the patient of the benefits and burdens, of the purpose of the research, of the procedures, of any alternatives, of the financial responsibilities, and of the freedom of the subject to choose to participate. Attention will be given to who will obtain the consent, where and under what condition it will obtained, how much time the patient might be given to decide, and who will witness the process. The consent form is reviewed by the IRB members to assure that the information is both complete and clear.

Tracy's medical treatment was affected by the existence of the IRB. A group of impartial, informed persons considered whether it was reasonable to ask a patient to participate in such research and improve the chance that the patient voluntarily agreed to participate.

INSTITUTIONAL ETHICS COMMITTEES

Once medical science had developed an impressive array of treatments and interventions, a new set of decisions had to be faced by the whole medical community and the patients they treated. When should life-sustaining programs be started? When might they be stopped? As if the medical and ethical complexity were not enough, courts were quickly involved in these matters, further increasing concerns about legal liability. To address these complex questions, a number of early articles supported the use of institutional ethics committees (IECs).[23] In 1975, Dr. Karen Teel[24] recommended that ethics committees assist in decisions when specific treatment decisions were difficult. Massachusetts General Hospital established a permanent committee by the mid-1970s to advise on treatment decisions for terminally ill patients, and many other large hospitals and clinics soon did the same.[25]

Unlike IRBs, IECs have never been mandated by law or regulation. One of the earliest forces for hospitals to develop an IEC was the New Jersey Supreme Court ruling in the Karen Quinlan case (*In re Karen Quinlan*, 355 A. 2nd 647 [NJ 1976]). This 1976 ruling suggested that a hospital committee review cases like *Quinlan* and concur with the attending physician's prognosis. The Court referred to such a committee as an ethics committee, while in fact its given role was to assess prognosis. Nevertheless the Court's ruling stressed the importance of a hospital committee to review treatment options in specific cases before a decision was made. The idea of IECs gained more attention from three articles published in the *Hastings Center Report* in June 1977.[26] IECs got support in the Report of the President's Commission for the Study of Ethical Problems in Medicine and Biomedical and Behavioral Research, *Deciding to Forego Life-Sustaining Treatment*,[27] published in 1983. The report concluded that ethics committees were one way to resolve ethical issues arising in the clinical setting. In 1984, the American Medical Association House of Delegates overwhelmingly advocated the establishment of IECs.[28]

As of 1983, only a few hospitals had formed an IEC. In one systematic survey, Younger[29] found that in a sample of 602 hospitals none of the 202 hospitals with 200 or fewer beds had an IEC and of the 400 with 200 or more beds only 4.3 percent had one. Most of those who had IECs were teaching institutions. These numbers have dramatically changed later during the 1980s. By 1990 the American Hospital Association estimated that IECs "have been formed at 30 percent of hospitals with fewer than 100 beds, 75 percent to 80 percent of hospitals with 200 or more beds and virtually all teaching institutions and large hospitals."[30]

The IEC has several functions.[31] First, IECs plan educational programs for institutional staff about ethical decision-making, and second, IECs develop policies to guide ethical decisions. Most frequently these programs and policies have focused on ethical issues of foregoing life-sustaining medical treatments like cardiopulmonary resuscitation, ventilator support and parenteral nutrition and hydration. IECs also look at how decisions are made to start, to continue or to stop such treatments. The third function is unique and sets an IEC apart from every other institutional committee, including an IRB, by providing advice to staff, patients and family about a specific treatment decision in a particular case. The decision to refer a case to an IEC is optional and to follow the advice is also optional for the decision-makers. It is agreed that patients, family or the attending physician may request an IEC consult. Whether other staff, like nurses, social workers or chaplains, might request a consult is more controversial, and the practice seems to vary. It does not appear that any institution has required a patient, proxy or physician to follow the advice of an IEC. Nevertheless, a strongly supported and argued opinion of an IEC would be difficult for a physician to ignore.

Membership of IECs can vary. In part, membership is determined by the role of the committee and whether the IEC is form by the medical or administrative staff. Clearly if an IEC is to offer consultation to physicians about medical-ethical decisions it is best that it is formed under medical staff authority and have clear representation from the medical staff. Committees need to have the expertise to deal with the complex issues that might be brought to it, and in some large hospitals, specialized IECs are formed.

IECs have several potential pitfalls.[32] They may not, for example, clearly define their role in the institution, or the IEC may be asked to provide emotional support, confirmation of prognosis, public relations or similar functions. The lack of specificity in the IEC role can create confusion on the committee and for those seeking advice. Another concern is that the major benefit of providing varied expertise and perspective to decision-makers may not be fulfilled because an IEC dominated by health professionals may not truly understand the patient's point of view. IECs under pressure of time or the dominance of a powerful individual may be subject to groupthink.

While IECs can and do organize individual conferences and workshops on health care ethics, the members of the IEC are busy in their primary practices and seldom have the time or ability to organize a comprehensive educational program. Even in its role as ethics consultant, ethics committees are limited. While they have the advantage of bringing together diverse points of view and a wide range of expertise, they also can lose credibility by being distant from the bedside and can be under-utilized because they need time to schedule meetings for deliberation. Moreover, as a committee they cannot always respond to the broader needs of families and health professionals that might involve lengthy discussion to have questions answered and fears addressed.

To address these additional roles, some health care and educational institutions have created a new role, that of a clinical ethicist.[33] Such a role is being filled by persons with a variety of backgrounds. In some cases it is filled by physicians or nurses who have gained additional training in ethics. In other cases it is filled by chaplains, lawyers and academics who have clinical experience. Whatever their backgrounds, these persons are being asked to fill the additional educational and consultative roles that arise and cannot be handled by IECs. Their role includes keeping abreast of the current ethical and legal literature, being able to sort out ethical issues that arise in medical decision-making, and developing and providing educational programs in health care ethics. These specialists, depending on their background, come to the institution through very different routes, and they are assigned to a variety of positions. Some work in the chaplaincy department; others may answer to the hospital CEO; still others may be assigned to medical education, a medical school department, or a department in medicine. So far, a single, well-defined role for these persons in health care institutions has not emerged.

THE IEC AND TRACY'S MEDICAL CARE

Tracy's medical care was clearly influenced by the IEC. This Committee had already developed policies about the use of cardiopulmonary resuscitation that guided Tracy's family and physician in making the decision to withhold this intervention, based on knowledge of the patient's wishes and her medical condition. The Committee previously had also encouraged education for the medical and nursing staff that increased awareness and sensitivity to the ethical issues of withholding and withdrawing care. Finally, a consultant from the committee was asked to speak with the family and help them weigh the decision of whether to continue or discontinue medical treatment. While the physician did not have a specific conflict with the family, he wanted a neutral party to facilitate the difficult process of deciding. The family welcomed the service and time provided to sort out the issues.

During the consultation it became clear that many issues needed to be resolved. Representing the family was the father, a brother and his wife, a maternal aunt and a cousin. The patient's parents were divorced 15 years ago. Tracy had been raised by her mother until her death two years ago. Since then she had been living with her brother and his wife. She had kept in touch with her father, but they have not had a close relationship. However, she did have a close relationship with the aunt and a deep friendship with her cousin who was also 20 years old. The family members talked to each other, but there clearly was tension and a fear of direct communication.

In the early part of the discussion the medical condition, treatments and prognosis were reviewed. It was clear that the family had a good understanding of Tracy's medical condition. Next the group reviewed Tracy's values and wishes about her medical care. Because of her young age, no one had talked with her about the possibility of having her death prolonged by medical technology. Each family member had some insight into Tracy's wishes. As the conversation developed, it became clear that each of the family members thought that Tracy would not want heroic medical treatment to prolong her life. At one point the consultant asked each family member to affirm or reject that conclusion. They all agreed. This consensus relieved the brother who thought there might be disagreement with his father or aunt. There was then a discussion of whether the family was ready to make and accept a decision to withhold or withdraw life-support. Although ready, they were not sure what options existed. An order not to use chest compression in the event of cardiac arrest was already in the chart. Other treatment options included discontinuing the use of the ventilator, of drugs to support cardiac function, and of antibiotics. Perhaps the main question, however, was what goal remained for medical care and how it would best be achieved?

The family agreed that the main goal was comfort and dignity in dying. They were asked to think of the treatment options in terms of these goals. They asked for more time to review the decision in the privacy of the family. This plan was supported. They were told that the treating physician would visit them in a couple of hours to review their decisions.

The family decided on their own to withhold all drugs including those supporting cardiac function and those used to treat her infections. Hydration and respiratory ventilation were continued since these were seen as comfort measures by the family, at least in the short term. Twelve hours later Tracy's blood pressure dropped, her heart stopped and she died. As decided, no effort was made to resuscitate her.

Tracy's medical treatment and ultimate death, while a sad story of personal tragedy, also is a modern tale about the possibilities and ethical weight of medical treatment. It is a tale not only of individuals struggling with personal and moral meaning and decision, but also of the way social policy and institutional planning can shape the ethical parameters. IRBs and IECs are ways that ethical values like patient autonomy and self-determination can find a social voice in a complex environment. Although these sociological structures are important changes in a quickly evolving array of medical treatment, they are also a way of identifying, teaching and applying ethical values that have guided Western physicians for over 2000 years. Clinical sociological interventions like IRBs and IECs utilize and integrate micro-level concerns of patients such as Tracy and her family with macro-level organizational and institutional policies that reflect ethical values of autonomy, beneficence and justice.

NOTES

1. H.K. Beecher. 1966. Ethics and Clinical Research. *New England Journal of Medicine* 274:1354-1360; M.H. Pappworth. 1967. *Human Guinea Pigs: Experimentation on Man.* Boston: Beacon Press; Paul A. Freund, ed. 1970. *Experimentation with Human Subjects.* New York: George Braziller; Nathan Hershey and Robert D. Miller. 1976. *Human Experimentation and the Law.* Germantown, MD: Aspen.
2. Bernard Barber, John J. Lally, Julia Loughlin Makarushka and Daniel Sullivan. 1973. *Research on Human Subjects: Problems of Social Control in Medical Experimentation.* New York: Russell Sage Foundation.
3. Ibid., p. 25.
4. Bradford H. Gray. 1975. *Human Subjects in Medical Experimentation: A Sociological Study of the Conduct and Regulation of Clinical Research.* New York: John Wiley & Sons.
5. Robert J. Levine. 1986. *Ethics and Regulation of Clinical Research, 2nd Ed.* Baltimore: Urban & Schwarzenberg.
6. National Commission for the Protection of Human Subjects of Biomedical and Behavioral Research. 1978. *The Belmont Report: Ethical Principles and Guidelines for the Protection of Human Subjects of Research.* Washington, DC: U.S. Government Printing Office.

7. Ibid., p. 3.
8. Ibid., p. 4.
9. Ibid., p. 7.
10. Levine, loc. cit.
11. G. Harry Stopp, Jr. 1985. The Internal IRB Structure: Models in Academic Settings. *IRB* 7:9-10.
12. Samuel S. Herman. 1989. A Noninstitutional Review Board Comes of Age. *IRB* 11:1-6; Samuel S. Herman. 1984. The Noninstitutional Review Board: A Case History. *IRB* 6:1-3,12.
13. Paul M. McNeill. 1989. Research Ethics Review in Australia, Europe and North America. *IRB* 11:4-7.
14. Lucas Bergkamp. 1988. American IRBs and Dutch Research Ethics Committees: How They Compare. *IRB* 10:1-6.
15. David Hall. 1988. Reviewing Research Involving Children: The Practice of British Research Ethics Committees. *IRB* 10:1-5.
16. McNeill, loc. cit.
17. Joan P. Porter. 1986. What Are the Ideal Characteristics of Unaffiliated/Nonscientist IRB Members? *IRB* 8:1-6; Joan P. Porter. 1987. How Unaffiliated/Nonscientist Members of Institutional Review Boards See Their Roles. *IRB* 9:1-6.
18. Ibid., p. 4.
19. Porter, loc. cit.
20. Robert M. Veatch. 1987. *The Patient as Partner: A Theory of Human Experimentation Ethics.* Bloomington: Indiana University Press.
21. Ibid., pp. 108-123.
22. Robert M. Veatch. 1975. Human Experimentation Committee: Professional or Representative? *Hastings Center Report* 5:31-40.
23. Fred Rosner. 1985. Hospital Medical Ethics Committees: A Review of Their Development. *Journal of the American Medical Association* 253:2693-2696; Pat Milmoe McCarrick and Judith Adams. 1989. *Ethics Committees in Hospitals.* Washington, DC: National Reference Center for Bioethics Literature, Scope Note 3.
24. Karen Teel. 1975. The Physician's Dilemma; a Doctor's View: What the Law Should Be. *Baylor Law Review* 27:6-9.
25. A Report of the Clinical Care Committee of Massachusetts General Hospital. 1976. Optimum Care for Hopelessly Ill Patients. *New England Journal of Medicine* 295:362-364.
26. Robert Veatch. 1977. Hospital Ethics Committees: Is There a Role? *Hastings Center Report* 7:22-25; Carol Levine. 1977. Hospital Ethics Committees: A Guarded Prognosis. *Hastings Center Report* 7:25-27; Thomas Shannon. 1977. What Guidance from the Guidelines? *Hastings Center Report* 7:28-30.
27. President's Commission for the Study of Ethical Problems in Medicine and Biomedical and Behavioral Research. 1983. *Deciding to Forego Life-Sustaining Treatment: A Report on the Ethical, Medical, and Legal Issues in Treatment Decisions.* Washington, DC: U.S. Government Printing Office, p. 169.
28. AMA Delegates Approve Resolution Calling for Hospital Ethics Committees. 1984. *Medical World News* 25:67.
29. S.J. Youngner et al. 1983. A National Survey of Hospital Ethics Committees. *Critical Care Medicine* 11:902-905.
30. Experts Say Ruling Could Mean Increased Decisionmaking Roles for Ethics Committees. 1990. *Modern Healthcare* 29:39.

31. Norman Fost and Ronald Cranford. 1985. Hospital Ethics Committees: Administrative Aspects. *Journal of the American Medical Association* 253:2687-2692; Judicial Council. 1985. Guidelines for Ethics Committees in Health Care Institutions. *Journal of the American Medical Association* 253:2698-2699.
32. Bernard Lo. 1987. Behind Closed Doors: Promises and Pitfall of Ethics Committees. *New England Journal of Medicine* 317:46-49; Bowen Hosford. 1986. *Bioethics Committees: The Health Care Provider's Guide*. Rockville, MD: Aspen.
33. Ruth B. Purtilo. 1984. Ethics Consultation in the Hospital. *New England Journal of Medicine* 311:983-986; John La Puma and Stephen E. Toulmin. 1989. Ethics Consultants and Ethics Committees. *Archives of Internal Medicine* 149:1109-1112; John La Puma and David L. Schiedermayer. 1991. Ethics Consultation: Skills, Roles, and Training. *Annals of Internal Medicine* 114:155-160; Bernard J. Hammes and Robert A. Bendiksen. 1990. From the Ivory Tower to the Hospital Ward: A Role Analysis of a Clinical Ethicist. In E.J. Clark, J.M. Fritz, P.P. Rieker, et al., eds., *Clinical Sociological Perspectives on Illness and Loss: The Linkage of Theory and Practice*. Philadelphia: The Charles Press.

13

Death-Related Issues in Biomedicine: Euthanasia and AIDS

Robert H. Blank, PhD

The tremendous advances in technology's capacity to keep the human body biologically alive have also, ironically, deepened some people's commitment to defend the patient's right to die. As mechanical respirators, artificial organs and invasive life-prolonging treatments permit the almost indefinite extension of biological existence, the medical profession is questioning the ethic of keeping the patient alive at all costs. Increasingly, the use of artificial support systems is quietly rejected, particularly among chronically ill elderly patients. DNR (do not resuscitate) instructions or "no codes," often unwritten, limiting the use of lifesaving treatment are commonplace in hospitals. The general public is displaying a similar disillusion with high-technology life extension. The desire to die with dignity, free from the tubes and machines, reflects a growing disenchantment with technological prolongation of life and raises demands for euthanasia policies.

What role should the government take in decisions to forego life-sustaining treatment? The President's Commission[1] argued that because death today is a much less private matter than it once was, usually occurring in a hospital or nursing home with many people involved, the "resolution of disagreements among them is more likely to require formal rules and means of adjudication." Furthermore, because biomedical developments have made death more a matter of deliberate decision, what once was the province of fate now becomes a matter of human choice. Although the commission's long report concluded that the major responsibility for ensuring "morally justified processes of decision making" lies with physicians, it called for institutional safeguards to protect the best interests of patients.

In addition to clarifying the rights, duties and liabilities of all concerned parties, a process in which the courts and legislatures as well as legal and ethical commentators have become embroiled, the government has been drawn into several other highly sensitive death-related areas. The first of these deals with government-mandated aggressive treatment for severely ill newborns. Baby Doe will not disappear as a critical policy issue. Second, the government, particularly at the state level, is involved in the reinvigorated debate over euthanasia in general. Many states have passed various types of legislation specifying the socially acceptable boundaries of euthanasia, particularly when it entails the withholding of artificial life-support systems. Third, the states are intimately involved in redefining death to correspond to the technological advances of the last decades. The swift movement from respiratory death to brain death as the generally accepted standard reflects both the new demand for transplant organs and the public awareness that life on machines is not always preferable to death.

EUTHANASIA

The dramatic expansion of the capacity to prolong life with an array of artificial support systems has raised severe ethical dilemmas concerning the circumstances under which available lifesaving treatment should be terminated. No single biomedical issue has more implications for public policy than euthanasia. Although considerable attention has been focused on euthanasia in terms of terminally ill elderly patients, the concept encompasses many death-hastening actions—withholding treatment from severely ill newborns, unplugging life-support machines at any age or injecting fatal doses of pain-killing drugs into suffering patients, to name a few.

Although euthanasia is by no means new, recent advances in biomedical technology have complicated its meaning. Defined as "good death" by the Greeks, it applied most clearly to "exposure" of sick newborns[2] or to withholding of the limited medical interventions available for the elderly ill. The Greeks defined euthanasia in terms of the interest of the community more than the individual. According to Plato,[3] for instance, "if a man had a sickly constitution and intemperate habits, his life was worth nothing to himself or to anyone else; medicine was not meant for such people and they should not be treated, though they might be richer than Midas."

The present-day availability of extremely intensive (and expensive)

Table 1.

Categories of Euthanasia

	Passive	**Active**
	(omission of measures to prolong life)	(direct inducement of death)
Voluntary	**Passive Voluntary**	**Active Voluntary**
vith patient's express nd informed consent	conscious, rational patient refuses life-prolonging treatment and request is granted	conscious, rational patient requests and is given lethal injection
Speculative	**Passive Speculative**	**Active Speculative**
vithout patient's exress and informed onsent (e.g., infant, omatose or mentally etarded person)	cessation of life-prolonging treatment for comatose patient, or patient otherwise unable to give consent	lethal injection administered to comatose patient, or patient otherwise unable to give informed consent
Involuntary	**Passive Involuntary**	**Active Involuntary**
gainst patient's exress consent	cessation of life-prolonging treatment to conscious, rational patients against their will	lethal injection administered to conscious, rational patients against their will

interventions designed to extend the life of an individual increases the policy significance of such decisions and most Americans have adopted an individual-rights approach to the value of life that Plato's utilitarian intuitions would not have allowed. As a result, the term euthanasia carries negative connotations and is often linked by its opponents with Nazi Germany and genocide. Colorado Governor Richard Lamm's suggestion, that elderly patients have a duty to younger generations to refuse certain kinds of treatment that would extend their lives at great expense, was roundly criticized by many interest groups, though it received surprisingly strong public support.

Classification of Types of Euthanasia

One reason why euthanasia elicits so much controversy is that it deals with death and with questions of who, if anyone, can make irrevocable decisions to die or let die. Few of us like to deal with the topic of death at all, let alone take responsibility for making a life-death decision. The multiple categories of euthanasia, each with an infinite range of permutations, add further complications and misunderstanding. Critics of euthanasia focus their arguments on the most threatening categories and cases, while supporters emphasize the least threatening types. For this reason it is important to begin by categorizing the applications of euthanasia (see Table 1). Many classification schemes have been introduced in the literature, but they generally involve two key dimensions. The first dimension, represented by either several discrete categories or a continuum, relates to the degree to which the patient has given or refused to give voluntary consent to the action. The second dimension concerns whether euthanasia is carried out in a passive or active form.

Voluntariness

Euthanasia is classified as "voluntary" if it is done with the patient's express consent—that is, if the patient has unambiguously expressed a desire to be either allowed or helped to die. Those opposed to all forms of euthanasia attack its voluntary form on several grounds. Some equate it with suicide and argue on sanctity-of-life grounds that society cannot condone such an act. According to these critics, a person has no right to die and must try to remain alive at all costs. There is always some chance of a miracle cure or remission. Those who wish to end their lives, it is argued, are irrational and should certainly not be encouraged or helped to carry out that desire.

Another, more practically oriented argument against voluntary euthanasia contends that many patients who express a will to die are acting under economic and social pressures or are in the temporary grip of depression or pain. In other words, the context is directing their will so that it is no longer free and unconstrained. For example, patients who feel they have become a burden to their family might convince themselves they really want to die. Although this possibility justifies caution in using euthanasia, it alone should not eliminate access to that choice for all patients. Voluntary euthanasia, though controversial, is the least problem-laden form.

At the other extreme is involuntary euthanasia, conducted over the patient's express opposition. This situation differs drastically from the previous one. Although some opponents of euthanasia argue that there is no difference between voluntary and involuntary applications (i.e., that it is wrong under any circumstances), most observers see voluntariness as a key variable and thus support voluntary decisions while rejecting involuntary euthanasia as akin to murder. Few commentators today are willing to permit involuntary applications within the realm of acceptability.

The most controversial and problematic cases are those which fall somewhere between these two ends of the voluntariness continuum. These involve persons who, for whatever reason, cannot give informed consent. Infants, children and some mentally retarded patients are viewed as unable to consent to euthanasia because they lack the capacity to understand the implications of their decisions. Similarly, comatose patients are unable to communicate their desires at the time the decision must be made. These "speculative" instances are the most difficult because we simply do not know what the person would decide if given the opportunity.

Speculative euthanasia requires a proxy consent, usually by family or friends, similar to the consent given for any medical procedure. Critics of euthanasia reject this surrogate-consent option, arguing that it can easily lead to abuse or subordination of the patient's interest to that of the family or physicians. They also reject the "rational person" argument which defines the patient's desires by what a rational person under the same circumstances would decide.

Passive-Active Dimension

The second dimension of this euthanasia classification scheme describes the type of activity used to carry it out. Although, again, there certainly are many shades of distinction, most cases fall clearly into either passive or active categories. Passive euthanasia, currently the most prominent in public debate, is a decision to withhold or withdraw life-prolonging treatment from the patient. In this era of respirators and other artificial life-support technologies, the decision to forego life-sustaining treatment is becoming commonplace—although, since circumstances vary considerably, one must hope it will never become routine.

The Karen Quinlan case and others to be reviewed in this chapter have pushed passive euthanasia to the forefront of national interest in the last decade, spawning a multitude of state statutes designed to let individuals specify in advance their preference concerning acceptable and non-acceptable treatment if they ever reach the point where artificial life-support technologies are necessary. These natural-death laws have authorized "living wills" which contain legally recognized requests not to be kept alive on machines under specified conditions. As such, if carried out, they represent a form of voluntary passive euthanasia. Some opponents of voluntary passive euthanasia argue that allowing even hopeless patients the option of dying is the beginning of a "slippery slope" which will lead next to involuntary passive euthanasia and then to the killing of nonterminal patients like the mentally retarded or senile. In contrast, supporters argue that human beings have the right to die with dignity and to refuse treatment that would dehumanize them.

Passive euthanasia becomes harder to justify in speculative cases, in which the individual has given no express consent (either prior or immediate) to withhold lifesaving treatment. Baby Doe cases are prime examples of parents and physicians making life-death decisions in the absence of the defective infant's capacity to give consent. Similarly, when life-support systems are withheld from comatose patients, it is usually on the assumption that they would have chosen death over the alternative. Although the third parties in these cases might have the patient's interests at heart, they must rationalize their decision on the grounds that the patients, if able to decide, would have made the same choice. Such grounds are necessarily speculative, since one can never know for sure.

Involuntary passive euthanasia, the cessation of life-prolonging treatment to a conscious person against her will, is very difficult to justify morally or legally. In addition, it is contrary to the American medical tradition, which gives preference to patient autonomy. Despite these ethical difficulties, cost-benefit considerations may in the future place substantial pressure on the government to limit the amount of treatment that an individual can receive at public expense. Involuntary passive euthanasia raises the critical conceptual question of whether health and life are positive rights—that is, whether any individual can demand aggressive treatment and expect to receive it, whatever its cost to society. As the potential of life-prolonging technologies expands to artificial organs and an ever broader array of transplantation and regeneration techniques, this category of euthanasia is likely to become more commonplace.

Passive euthanasia, then, refrains from an action which could keep a person alive. In contrast, active euthanasia involves committing an act that leads directly to the death of the patient. In the medical setting this act is usually, though not always, a lethal injection. In several highly publicized cases, family members often frustrated by the medical profession's unwillingness to effectuate death through lethal injection, have shot their suffering spouse or parent. Recent television movies have sympathetically portrayed active euthanasia or mercy killing of persons in advanced stages of Alzheimer's disease.

As with the passive category, forms of active euthanasia can be distinguished according to the degree of consent by the patient. A woman with terminal cancer who convinces her husband to alleviate her pain by killing her, despite lingering questions of how free her decision really is under such traumatic circumstance, represents a case of active voluntary euthanasia. Opponents insist that this type of euthanasia is equivalent to suicide on the part of the patient and homicide by the person who carries it out. Contrarily, proponents argue that the right to die with dignity demands some degree of choice as to the circumstances of death and they contend that the decision-making system has failed when it does not provide a painless and effective way of honoring a dying patient's wishes. But even if we could agree in principle that active voluntary euthanasia may sometimes be justified, consensus in many specific cases would be impossible (such as a patient who refuses to have a leg amputated and chooses to die instead, or a paraplegic or burn patient who demands the right to die).

Active speculative euthanasia, or the administration of death to a patient who is comatose or otherwise unable to give informed consent, raises the same questions as the passive speculative form, in addition to placing the participant in a position of actually performing the act that causes death. Active involuntary euthanasia raises even more questions of personal privacy and autonomy in life-death situations. This form of euthanasia is currently unthinkable, partly because our legal system is designed primarily to protect against acts of commission, though not omission and thus even those hospitals and other third parties that might consider passive involuntary euthanasia in the future are very unlikely to participate in a direct action, against the express wishes of the patient, resulting in that patient's death. Furthermore, active involuntary applications correctly reinforce allusions to Nazi Germany and raise legitimate concerns of a genocidal abuse of euthanasia. This category and to a lesser extent the related active-speculative type, have no support in the United States. The evident inappropriateness of these two forms, however, should not color the genuine debate over the other four types.

Interestingly, the President's Commission on biomedical ethics consciously avoided the term euthanasia in its report, *Deciding to Forego Life-Sustaining Treatment.* It argued[4] that terms such as euthanasia are "hopelessly blurred" and of little use in clarifying the issues. Presumably, the Commission also felt that the word would bring negative connotations to a procedure it was trying to place in a neutral context. "Foregoing life-sustaining treatment" simply sounds less threatening than "euthanasia" or "letting the patient die." Although the Commission's purposes, I believe, were well served by the exclusion of explicit uses of this word, I feel that the general term "euthanasia" has the heuristic advantage of providing a framework for comparing a broader set of conceptually connected applications. Politically, the Commission did what it had to do—for euthanasia still carries with it substantial emotional and controversial implications. Whatever term is used, the issues of euthanasia are becoming increasingly evident.

Euthanasia Policy

> If we take the view that what is essentially human in the life that we share with the animal and vegetable kingdoms is the capacity for thought and love and aesthetic experience and that this capacity makes us a person in the true sense of the word, we cannot wish to preserve an anonymous individual who has been stripped of personality and reduced by incessant pain or physical deterioration to the animal or vegetative level...yet without the medical assistance that voluntary euthanasia would authorize...it is unlikely that most of us would be able to choose a dignified death.[5]

The clamor for the right to die has become a matter of public policy, inextricably involving the legal system in decisions regarding several categories of euthanasia and taking shape as a political issue of increasing importance. Groups such as the American Civil Liberties Union (ACLU) have argued for individual autonomy in choosing to forego treatment. The pro-euthanasia Hemlock Society and the Society for the Right to Die lobby for legislation that would let an individual die with dignity. On the other hand, religious organizations, right-to-life groups, minority groups who see euthanasia as a threat to their interests and some members of the medical profession oppose any action that legalizes the hastening of death.

Surveys of public opinion demonstrate an ambivalence toward euthanasia in general but considerable support for permitting individuals to discontinue the use of life-support technologies that prolong their life with no hope of recovery. A Gallup poll conducted for *Hospitals* magazine in December 1986 found that 70 percent of the respondents were "very willing" to have life-support systems discontinued and 12 percent were "somewhat willing," while only 18 percent were unwilling. Likewise, in a nonrandom poll by *Ladies Home Journal* in April 1987, 97 percent felt that terminally ill people have the "right to euthanasia." In the Gallup survey, 72 percent said they would be willing (46 percent "very willing") to disconnect artificial support systems on behalf of a relative. The proportion of the population opposed to passive voluntary euthanasia appears relatively small, though many of those opposed are very committed in their opposition.

The first major court case to engender public debate over the withholding of life-support systems was resolved in 1976. In *In re Quinlan*, the New Jersey Supreme Court ruled that Karen Quinlan, a young irreversibly comatose woman, had a right to die with dignity and permitted hospital authorities to remove her from the respirator. This decision ended over a year of efforts by Karen's parents to remove her from the life-support system and let her die in peace. The case was disputed in the media spotlight and served as a verbal battleground for groups on all sides of the issue. Importantly, the *Quinlan* ruling came just as many states were moving toward making brain function the criterion for determining when someone is legally dead. Because of the widespread publicity, *Quinlan* generated a multitude of legal actions to terminate extraordinary treatment.

In June 1987 the New Jersey Supreme Court expanded the guidelines it first handed down in *Quinlan*. In its rulings on three companion cases, the Court supported a person's right to refuse to be kept alive by artificial means. Furthermore, the Court extended the right to the friends and family of incompetent patients. The Court stated, "The fateful decision to withdraw life-supporting treatment is extremely personal. Accordingly, a competent patient's right to make that decision will outweigh any countervailing state interests." Moreover, the incompetent patient who has previously expressed his wishes retains the right to refuse such treatment. The Court granted civil and criminal immunity for close friends, relatives or physicians who remove life-sustaining treatment from a patient who had asked not to be kept alive.

In the case of 31-year-old Nancy Ellen Jobes, the Court voted 6 to 1 that a relative or close friend may exercise the right of a patient in an "irreversibly vegetative state" to refuse life-sustaining medical treatment. Also by a 6-to-1 vote, the Court ruled that the choice of an elderly nursing home patient (Hilda Peter, age 67) in a vegetative state who had left clear evidence of her desire to withhold extraordinary treatment must be respected, regardless of her life expectancy. By ruling that the likelihood of ever returning to "cognitive and sapient life," not life expectancy, is the important issue, the Court expanded on its ruling in a 1985 case (*In re Conroy*) in which it had concluded that life-support apparatus may be removed from nursing-home patients who are in pain and who have a life expectancy of less than one year. The third case heard by the Court in 1987 was that of 37-year-old Kathleen Farrell, who was declared competent (though she died before the Court could rule in her case). In a 7-to-0 vote, the Court said a competent person's interest in her self-determination generally outweighs any countervailing state interest.

Along similar lines, courts in an increasing number of states are ruling in favor of patients who desire to have their feeding tubes removed over the hospital's objections. The saga of Elizabeth Bouvia, a disabled patient whose request, in 1984, to be allowed to starve to death while in the hospital gained international attention, demonstrates the political sensitivity of these issues.[6] This case also illustrates the difficulty of arriving at determinative decisions through the courts. Although the California Supreme Court unanimously rejected her original petition to be allowed to die, premising it on the fact that she was demanding in effect that the hospital directly contribute to her death by discontinuing what is "ordinary" treatment for persons in her condition, in 1986 after two years of legal maneuvering, Bouvia again sought a court order forbidding another hospital to force-feed her.

In a similar case in New York state, the State Supreme Court ruled that a man who was in extremely poor and deteriorating health, did not have to be force-fed. The Court observed one key difference from Bouvia's case, though: G. Ross Henninger was 85 years old and had no chance to regain his health and return to his previous quality of lie. In contrast, Elizabeth Bouvia, although severely disabled, was 27 years old. This distinction leaves open the question of to what extent we should discriminate by age, health or any other characteristic if the person requesting euthanasia is competent.

In June 1987, in a similar case (*Delio v. Westchester County Medical Center*), a New York appellate court found that the patient alone has the right to reach the "ultimate decision" to refuse treatment and that there could be no countervailing interest in prolonging life by force-feeding which the patient would have found "demeaning and degrading to his humanity." What makes this case different is that Daniel Delio was in a permanent vegetative state, not legally competent to make the decision. The action to compel termination of tube feeding was brought by his wife, who argued that her husband (who had been a marathon runner) would not want to continue life in a condition that was the antithesis of all he believed in. Although the trial court questioned its authority to prohibit feeding a young (age 34) and what it termed "nonterminally ill patient," the appeals court ruled that the "panoply of rights associated with a competent person's right to self-determination" is not limited by reason of a person's age or medical condition. The Court concluded: "We support the individual's right to refuse treatment and thereby live out his life in dignity and peace for whatever period of time remains."

Although there is still considerable variation among courts on this issue, the trend in case law clearly supports passive euthanasia in cases where the main decision is whether to initiate, continue or terminate the use of artificial life-support systems. Much less clear is the issue of active euthanasia, as neither the courts nor the public have dealt extensively with mercy killing yet. Economic pressures promise to make active euthanasia a major issue in the coming decade.

Policy-making on death-related issues stands approximately where abortion did in the early 1960s. The underlying need to reconsider society's traditional expectations as to suffering, terminal-illness procedures and related matters brings euthanasia inexorably closer to the surface as a political issue. Sensationalized cases are essential to the process of politicalization, however. In the development of abortion politics, the growing subsurface dilemma of thousands of mothers faced with unwanted pregnancies required stimulation from the rubella and thalidomide tragedies (which led to thousands of malformed fetuses) to shake state legislatures into action. Karen Quinlan's and several other high-profile cases performed this function for euthanasia. Many states have passed natural-death laws since the 1970s, and constitutional considerations of equal protection will increasingly press the federal level of government toward nationwide standardization—much like that which *Roe v. Wade* provided for abortion.

As of 1987, 39 states had living-will laws. Of these, 18 had been enacted in the two previous years. Increasingly, these statutes are becoming standardized along the lines of the "Uniform Rights of the Terminally Ill Act" recommended by the National Conference of Commissioners on Uniform State Laws. Some states have replaced earlier living-will statutes with new, broadened laws. The Arkansas "Rights of the Terminally Ill or Permanently Unconscious Act," for instance, authorizes appointment of a health care proxy to act on the patient's behalf when necessary and expands coverage to include permanently comatose patients as well as the terminally ill.[7]

In a related matter of policy, in light of the new capacities to sustain patients beyond the point where their life has any quality, the Joint Commission on Accreditation of Hospitals required all hospitals in the United States to establish, by January 1988, formal policies regarding resuscitation of terminally ill patients. Although many hospitals have had formal do-not-resuscitate (DNR) policies, many other facilities have instead depended on a confusing array of informal "no-code," "slow code," and "partial code" categories, generally with no provisions for patient consent. The failure by many hospitals to acknowledge their actions, often on grounds of potential liability, has acquired increasing policy importance because of the large number of potential candidates, now estimated at over 1.5 million per year.

The new standard requires consent from the patient or family before any decision to withhold cardiopulmonary resuscitation (CPR), which involves treatment of cardiac arrest by external chest compression and some form of artificial respiration. This requirement should reduce the procedural abuses that resulted from the absence of explicit DNR policy and, though stipulating that written orders be documented in the patient's medical record, it should not divert us from looking rigorously at other more common treatment-nontreatment decisions in the critical care setting. Although CPR is a dramatic intervention, because it in effect brings the patient back to life after the traditional signs of death have appeared, we have seen that the range of life-sustaining technologies extends far beyond artificial resuscitation.

Alzheimer's Disease: A New Cause for Euthanasia?

The recent emphasis on the AIDS "epidemic" has overshadowed a disease category that will have increasing policy ramifications and create even greater economic costs: dementia, or senility. The most common form of dementia is Alzheimer's disease, which accounts for about two-thirds of all cases, although over 70 other disorders can cause dementia. In any form, dementia is a devastating illness and exacts a tremendous toll on the patient, family and health care system. Approximately three to six million Americans suffer from dementia and the Office of Technology Assessment[8] estimates that the cost of dementia to the nation in 1985 was between $24 and $28 billion—and is growing rapidly.

Alzheimer's disease causes progressive deterioration of memory, intellect, language, emotional control and perception. The disease is insidious, gradually progressing from subtle symptoms to almost complete mental deterioration. Victims in the advanced stages may be completely dependent on others for years or even decades, causing serious disruptions to the family and a huge financial burden. The number of persons affected by Alzheimer's disease is expected to double in the next decade, primarily because more and more people are living into their seventies or eighties, the age at which dementia usually strikes. The likelihood of developing dementia of some type is estimated at 20 to 30 percent for persons age 85 and over, as compared to only 1 percent for those between 65 and 74 and 7 percent for those age 75 to 84.[9]

Although the cause of Alzheimer's disease is unknown, recent evidence suggests that at least some cases are inherited. Through the use of DNA probes to mark genes, researchers have linked the heritable form of

Alzheimer's disease to chromosome 21, the same chromosome that causes Down's syndrome. The capacity to identify persons with a genetic predisposition toward Alzheimer's disease will eventually create new problems regarding use of that information. It is very unlikely, however, that we will have the capability to either prevent or cure this disease in the near future. According to Cook-Deegan and Whitehouse,[10] even if the most promising of drugs under consideration prove clinically useful, they will only delay onset of the disability or retard its progression.

Increasingly, patients with Alzheimer's disease and other forms of dementia will become candidates for euthanasia. Already spouses have killed their affected partners after watching them deteriorate to the point where they no longer could tolerate that their loved one had entered into a vegetative state. Soon many living wills may include provisions stating that euthanasia, either passive or active, be carried out at a particular stage of mental deterioration. As with all forms of euthanasia, the gray areas between justifiable and unjustifiable cases are very large.

REDEFINING DEATH

Another issue with roots similar to euthanasia, although it has met less opposition, is the need to redefine death within the context of the new capacities to extend biological existence indefinitely. The President's Commission on Bioethics concluded that "in light of ever increasing powers of biomedical science and practice, a statute is needed to provide a clear and socially accepted basis for making definitions of death."[11] While the Commission acknowledged the linkage of this issue to euthanasia, it concluded that, as matters of public policy, the two can be treated separately—thereby avoiding much of the emotional sensitivity that euthanasia arouses.

The traditional medical definition of death has been the permanent cessation of respiration and circulation. The situation used to be unambiguous, because once these functions ceased they could not be restored. But machine-regulated breathing and heartbeat, even when the capacity to breathe spontaneously is irretrievably lost, have made the traditional determination of death inadequate. Now the emphasis is on brain function as a criterion. Because the brain cannot regenerate neural cells, once the entire brain has been seriously damaged, spontaneous respiration can never return, even though breathing may be sustained by respirators or ventilators. The machines can maintain certain organic processes in the body, but they cannot restore consciousness.

This present situation, in which all bodily functions need not cease when the heart stops pumping, has led to the distinction between human life as a strictly biological existence and human life as an integrated set of social, intellectual and communicative dimensions. Just what, we have had to ask, does it mean to be human? Perhaps surprisingly, a reasonably strong consensus has developed that recognizes the possibility of social or cognitive death even though the human organism is kept alive biologically by artificial means. However, some groups remain opposed to the movement toward recognizing brain death and others who approve of the brain-death definition are uncomfortable with the dilemmas technology has created. Willard Gaylin's article on "Harvesting the Dead"[12] opened a serious ethical debate on the status humanhood bestows even after death, however it is defined, occurs.

The first major step toward redefining death occurred in 1968, when rising concern by medical practitioners over how to treat respirator-supported patients led to creation of the "Harvard Criteria" for brain death.[13] These criteria, developed by a Harvard Medical School committee, focused on (1) unreceptivity and unresponsiveness, (2) lack of spontaneous movements or breathing and (3) lack of reflexes. Moreover, a flat electroencephalogram (EEG) showing no discernible electrical activity in the cerebral cortex was recommended as a confirmatory test, when available. All tests were to be repeated at least 24 hours later without demonstrable change before life-support systems could be terminated. These criteria, with some modifications and revisions due to new knowledge and diagnostic technologies, continue to serve as the medical criteria for determining brain death. Their publication led to the mobilizing of considerable support for legislating policy standards of brain death and eliminating the uncertainties faced by hospitals and physicians.

Another force at work during this period was the emergence of organ transplantation techniques and the growing need for organs. For transplants to be successful, a viable, intact organ is needed. The suitability of organs—especially the heart, lungs and liver—for transplantation diminishes rapidly once the donor's respiration and circulation stop. Therefore, the most desirable donors are otherwise healthy persons who have died following traumatic head injuries and whose breathing and blood flow are artificially maintained until after the removal of the organs.[14] Although advocates of the brain-death criterion downplay the extent to which the demand for organs influenced this movement, transplant surgery did give the effort to define brain death a new urgency.[15] This reluctance to link the two developments is understandable, because the connection would imply that we have accepted the revised definition of death only to facilitate use of the "dead" individual's organs. Certainly, organ-transplant facilities have sought and have benefitted from the legal clarity provided by statutes that define brain death. If the only rationale for this new definition of death was to facilitate successful organ transplants, however, support for brain death would be minuscule. Recent efforts to maximize donation of usable organs notwithstanding, organs are procured for transplants in only a small percentage of the cases in which the brain-death criterion is applied.

Like most matters of public health, the determination of death traditionally has been within the province of each state's common law. This dependence on the courts to determine and apply the criterion for death has resulted in considerable uncertainty and a lack of consistency across jurisdictions. With patients often being transported across state lines for treatment, the lack of consistent policy produced confusion and potential for abuse. Two efforts to increase consistency have resulted: many state legislatures have enacted statutory standards and a national standard has been proposed.

In 1970, the Kansas state legislature became the first to recognize brain-based criteria for determination of death. Within several years, four states passed laws patterned on the Kansas model. The Capron-Kass proposal[16] offered the states a more succinct substitute that eliminated some of the Kansas model's ambiguity. To date, seven states have adopted the Capron-Kass model with minor modifications, while three others have done so with more substantial changes. Two other model statutes[17] have been enacted by five and two states, respectively. The American Medical Association's 1979 proposal, which includes extensive provisions to limit liability for persons taking actions under the proposal, has not been adopted in any state. About 10 states have nonstandard statutes that often include parts of one or more of these models, while about 20 states have no statutory determinations of death.

This proliferation of similar yet variant models and statutes led the President's Commission to propose a "Uniform Definition of Death Act." The Act provides for:

1. *Determination of Death.* An individual who has sustained either (1) irreversible cessation of circulatory and respiratory functions, or (2) irreversible cessation of all functions of the entire brain, including the brainstem, is dead. A determination of death must be made in accordance with accepted medical standards.
2. *Uniformity of Construction and Application.* This act shall be applied and construed to effectuate its general purpose to make uniform the law with respect to the subject of this act among states enacting it.[18]

Before its presentation in the final report, this uniform law was approved by the ABA, the AMA and the Uniform Law Commissioners as a substitute for their original proposals.

The Commission recommended that uniform state statutes address general physiological standards rather than specific medical criteria or tests, since the latter continue to change with advances in biomedical knowledge and refined techniques. It concluded that "death is a unitary phenomenon which can be accurately demonstrated either on traditional grounds of irreversible cessation of heart and lung functions or on the basis of irreversible loss of all functions of the entire brain."[19]

Although the Commission opted for total brain death (including the brainstem), not the cessation of selected functions, as its criterion, some argue that partial brain death is a better choice. Can a person be considered dead even though some parts of the brain remain alive? The brainstem can maintain the respiratory system even if the higher brain is not functioning and the Commission contends that to declare dead a person who is spontaneously breathing yet has no higher brain functions would too radically change our definition of death. If, however, it is our higher brain functions that define us as humans, then partial brain death could be a more appropriate standard. As knowledge about the functioning of the brain increases, this issue may either dissipate or intensify. Currently whole brain death has consensual support among most experts and the public.

Whatever standards for determining death are used, they will remain troublesome for some persons. Despite the widespread policy of brain death across the states, thousands of legally brain-dead persons are kept alive by artificial means, usually at the request or demand of the family. The difficulty of letting go, the false hope for a miracle and the confusion of values resulting from the new technologies cause many persons to refuse to authorize unplugging of the artificial life-support machines.

When such a situation exists, more tough questions arise. Can third-party payers, including Medicare and Medicaid, refuse to pay for care of a person who is legally dead? On what grounds can insurers justify such coverage? Can wills be probated in such a case? How can patients be protected from premature termination of helpful treatment under the guise of declaring death? What mechanisms are needed to maintain proper respect for the dignity of a brain-dead person when the various transplant teams need organs to save other patients who are brain-alive?

Although a few short years have powerfully transformed the meaning of death, many questions remain. Our very conception of what it means to be human are challenged by these rapid advances in medical technology. That these innovations present us with critical ethical policy decisions should not by itself be cause for alarm. It is when decisions of this magnitude become easy and coldly routine that we must all question our humanhood.

THE ROLE OF THE BIOMEDICAL COMMUNITY IN BIOMEDICAL POLICY

Even more critical than the general public's support for resource allocation is the cooperation of the health care profession, which itself is highly fractionalized. No health program can succeed without at least tacit support from physicians, hospitals and other health care providers. Physicians are particularly key decision-makers on the demand side of medicine, since they serve as gatekeepers for access to treatment regimens, technologies and drugs. "Physicians are logical agents of rationing because they appear to have direct control over health care dollars."[20] Mulley[21] argues that physicians' relatively subjective decisions about patients' needs largely determine the demand for expensive intensive care treatment and tend to become institutionalized in the administrative decisions of hospitals and planning agencies. Staff doctors, for instance, encourage the use of intensive care units (ICUs) because they want maximum health care to be readily available for their patients should the need arise—not because they want to maintain a minimal occupancy rate in ICU beds. But as more ICU beds become available, patients with less severe diseases are likely to be admitted, despite questions about the effectiveness of these units.[22] Also, the combined impact of fee-for-service payments and third-party reimbursement gives hospitals a natural incentive to respond aggressively to their patients' perceived needs.

Any government attempt to require physicians to allocate medical care on grounds of society's rather than simply the patient's need is bound to conflict with professional ethics and the traditional patient-physician relationship. Pellegrino[23] argues that any steps taken to make the physician the designated guardian of society's resources are morally unsound and factually suspect. According to Aaron and Schwartz,[24] this approach would require a far-reaching attitude change for those many physicians who believe it is unprofessional, if not immoral, to consider costs in deciding what actions to take on behalf of patients. Loewy[25] concludes that economic considerations as they affect either the patient, the hospital or society are "not germane to ethical medical practice" and that it is "dangerous" to introduce such extraneous factors into medical decisions. Dyer[26] answers "an emphatic no" in answer to the question of whether the physician can be society's agent in reducing health costs. Allocation decisions should not be made by doctors at the bedside, he says, because their primary responsibility is to the patient, not society: "To ask conscientious physicians to bear the responsibility for lowering the cost of medical care is to create a conflict of interest that threatens to alter the nature of the doctor-patient relationship and the nature of the medical profession itself."[27] For these reasons, the medical profession in the United States is unlikely to develop norms that require or actively encourage rationing.[28]

Despite its hesitancy, however, the medical profession increasingly will find itself in the difficult position of responding to government initiatives and, eventually, to public pressures to make difficult allocation and rationing decisions. Physicians have always made such decisions (e.g., who gets an ICU bed if the ICU is full) on a case-by-case basis, at the bedside, or in the hospital administrator's office—not under governmental pressure or in a systematic, institutionalized manner. Their central commitment has been to the patient, not society and the current shift toward public allocation poses a clear threat to traditional medical ethics. Harrison Rogers, in his address as outgoing president of the American Medical Association, warned against this threat as reflected in a "very serious movement" toward maintaining a business ethic in medical practice rather than a professional ethic devoted primarily to protecting patients.

> Almost every force being exerted on doctors today is pushing them away from the professional aspects of what they do and toward the business aspects. Governmental DRG [diagnosis-related group] programs, reductions made in Medicare benefits and payments, restrictions on private plans, preadmission certification, second-opinion requirements, requirements for outpatient and ambulatory care—all of those and many others tend to make the doctor think first about the financial aspects of the needed services and whether the patient or a governmental or private third party will be willing or able to pay for them.[29]

Lundberg[30] rhetorically asks how long physicians can continue to make such difficult policy judgments in response to short-term pressures of the moment. Can this piecemeal rationing process continue to dominate in light of the extensive social investment riding on each decision?

In contrast, Hiatt[31] argues that the medical profession must take responsibility for evaluating expensive new medical technologies and techniques before they are made available to consumers. Because of their crucial role as the point of access to health care, Hiatt asserts, doctors must regulate the supply of medical services as a means of cost control. No longer do health care providers automatically have a claim to all the societal resources they believe might benefit their patients, nor should they be able to make allocation decisions without an awareness of the complex ramifications of those decisions for the health care system as a whole. As uncomfortable as this change may be to the medical profession, it is well underway in American society. Moreover, this shift is beginning to occur despite the lack of significant government involvement in the allocation of medical care. It is most directly evident in trends toward corporate health care, health maintenance organizations and the increased allocation role played by benefits managers for large U.S. employers.

The most scarce resource in the health care system in the future may not be money or expensive equipment, but specialized personnel. Recently, the acute shortage of intensive care nurses has caused sudden decreases in the availability of intensive care beds and some types of surgery. Pinkney[32] cites a federal government prediction of a shortage of 1.2 million registered nurses by the year 2000 as but one example of shortages in many areas of hospital employment, from physical therapists to laboratory technicians. Highly trained personnel for transplant operations, although sufficient in most locales under present surgical loads, will be in short supply if transplantation facilities continue to multiply, as is inevitable under current public policy.

Although the shortage of nurses and other highly specialized support personnel is in part a function of limited budgets reflected in low salaries, it also has roots in the conflict between the traditional role of nursing as primary care and the accelerating movement toward specialized, machine-dependent medicine. Within this allocation context, it often is less difficult to secure initial funding for the purchase of prohibitively expensive medical technologies than to pay for the continuing personnel costs required to use and maintain the equipment. This short-sighted approach to expenditure decisions results in situations where a facility cannot use its most advanced equipment because of staffing shortages. This underuse of existing technology is especially frustrating because it represents a waste of substantial investments that could have been put to more productive use. As long as new equipment expenditures take priority over the more mundane and routine operation of medical facilities, shortages of highly trained and motivated support personnel will intensify. Substantially more attention must be directed toward this problem in allocating medical resources.

THE AIDS PROBLEM: A CASE STUDY

No problem in American health care today illustrates the inseparable tie between medicine and politics more vividly than AIDS. In addition to the arduous allocation decisions that will seriously aggravate the already precarious economic context of health care, AIDS raises critical ethical, political and constitutional questions. The prevalence of homosexuals and intravenous drug users among AIDS victims heightens the controversy surrounding any policies designed to control the spread of this disease. The fact that the primary mode of transmittal is sexual intercourse further introduces a moral dimension not present in many other diseases. Finally, because this disease is always fatal, the stakes are considerably higher than for most other communicable diseases. The importance and sensitivity of AIDS, requires a specific discussion of the unique policy questions raised by this disease.

The AIDS virus, now known by convention as the human immunodeficiency virus (HIV), is transmitted through bodily fluids such as semen and blood. It enters the blood through sexual intercourse, transfusions or contaminated needles. Although other routes of infection (such as exchange of saliva) are theoretically possible, there is no data suggesting that HIV is transmitted via casual contact with an infected person. As we will see, this is a critical factor in framing AIDS policy.

One area of confusion with critical policy ramifications is the distinction between carrying the virus and having AIDS. A person may test positive for HIV antibodies upon being exposed to the virus but still exhibit no symptoms of the disease. It is estimated that there might be as many as 2 million carriers of AIDS (i.e., people who have the virus) in the U.S., but of these only a small percentage have the disease itself. A larger proportion have developed AIDS-related complex (ARC), a less lethal illness caused by the virus.

There continues to be disagreement over what proportion of those persons who test positive for HIV antibodies will contract ARC or AIDS. Part of this controversy stems from the uncertainty of the incubation period for AIDS—that is, how long it takes the virus to give rise to the disease. We do know that most of the adults who have died of AIDS as of 1988 were infected early in the decade, but we do not know how many more who were infected then will die in the future.

Early studies estimated that only 5 to 10 percent of persons with HIV would develop AIDS. However, further data have caused this estimate to be revised upward. The Institute of Medicine[33] suggests that at least 25 to 50 percent of infected persons will progress to AIDS within 5 to 10 years of infection, and "the possibility that the percentage may be higher cannot be ruled out." Based on extrapolations from current data, Harris[34] estimates that 40 percent of infected persons will contract AIDS within 7 years and 53 percent within 15 years, even though only 4 percent have developed AIDS within 3 years. He also suggests that the different affected groups studied (homosexuals, hemophiliacs, transfusion patients) may have a different rate and incubation periods.

The skyrocketing costs of AIDS have become a major issue.[35] In a study conducted in 1985 by the Centers for Disease Control,[36] the lifetime hospital costs of the first 10,000 AIDS patients were estimated as totaling $1.473 billion, or $147,000 per patient and the indirect costs attributable to loss of productivity were set at $4.8 billion. Because AIDS patients are predominantly young males, the indirect cost in lost production and future earnings is unusually high. Scitovsky and Rice[37] estimate that by 1991, the annual cost of personal medical care for AIDS patients in the United States will have reached $8.5 billion, with another $2.3 billion being spent on nonpersonal costs such as screening, education and research. They also predict that the indirect costs of AIDS will jump well over tenfold by 1991, to $55.6 billion.

Actually, due to the comparatively small number of patients so far, the cost of AIDS is still much lower than that of other, more common illnesses such as cancer and heart disease. In 1985, the personal medical costs of AIDS represented only 0.2 percent of the total personal health care expenditures in the United States. Scitovsky and Rice[38] estimated that this percentage would stay below 2 percent in the early 1990s. However, the severe strain AIDS cases have already placed on health care resources in a few urban areas, especially New York and San Francisco, suggests that the tremendous increase in AIDS cases projected over the next 5 years will make this disease a critical economic burden to the nation. The total number of AIDS patients alive at any time during the year rose from 9,368 in 1984 to 18,720 in 1985 and 31,440 in 1986. (It is expected to reach 246,000 by 1994.)

As we have seen, the AIDS crisis comes at a time when monies are scarce even for established health programs. AIDS will further aggravate the economic choices and heighten the political factors involved as affected groups demand more governmental support and services. Because of the high cost per patient, the financial burden on the victims of AIDS and their families is crushing. Those affected will clamor loudly and emotionally for economic and political assistance.

One of the earliest steps in the quest to fight AIDS after it emerged in 1981 was the development of a test to identify persons who had been exposed to the virus. Since all persons infected with HIV develop antibodies to it, this enzyme-linked immunosorbant assay (ELISA), which detects antibodies to HIV, provided the means to test individuals and screen populations. ELISA is a relatively easy and inexpensive test. Although it does not identify HIV directly, it can identify who has been exposed to it.

As with genetic testing, however, the presence of an accurate, inexpensive test creates policy issues concerning its proper use.[39] Because AIDS is concentrated in identifiable high-risk groups, any screening efforts targeted at those groups threaten to cause stigmatization. If insurance companies and employers have access to such information, discrimination is likely.[40] Because there is no AIDS vaccine and no way to protect the health of those who test positive, justification of mandatory screening has to be based on the premise that such testing will lead to modification of their behavior. Opponents of mandatory screening for AIDS, however, point out that it is unlikely to lead to the behavior changes needed to impede the spread of AIDS.[41] Under such circumstances, it is difficult to justify invading the privacy of so many persons.

Proponents of mandatory screening for HIV reply, however, that public health takes precedence over individual privacy, particularly when the disease is fatal. This argument has convinced the U.S. military, the Department of State and the Department of Labor to initiate mandatory screening programs.[42] Furthermore, several states have passed and others are considering, laws that would require premarital testing for AIDS; screening in prisons, hospitals or drug dependence clinics; and surveillance and contact testing. Often these proposals have been advocated (and passed) despite opposition from health professionals.

The economic pressure on insurance companies and employers to identify and exclude people at risk for AIDS is growing and the debate as to whether these organizations should be permitted to use HIV testing for routine screening of applicants is intense. Harris[43] argues that if employers, insurance companies and prospective sex partners are not allowed to use the blood test, they may resort to such crude substitutes as marital status, location of residence, history of hepatitis and low white blood cell counts as ways of identifying those infected. This will deny many unaffected as well as infected persons access to jobs and insurance coverage. "In the end, it will be a choice: use the HIV-antibody test or let these cruder tests prevail."[44] Either way, those who test positive will become an underclass, according to Harris.

Discrimination against persons who test positive for HIV is already very real. The general public has not clearly understood the distinction between testing positive for HIV and having AIDS. Affected children have had to obtain court orders to attend school and in at least one case physical intimidation was used against their parents. This near-hysteria about AIDS among some segments of the population is not surprising in light of the rapid and sensational way in which AIDS became a top media story. The experts' early ambivalence concerning modes of transmission, incubation period and most recently the effectiveness of preventive measures does not instill confidence in a public who has been told that AIDS represents an epidemic rivaling the Black Plague. As Singer and Rogers[45] put it: "Finally, vagueness and contradiction in the advice offered by scientists and public health officials contribute to a climate in which fear flourishes.... And because AIDS is a new disease with many unknowns, the advice that is given has changed over time and at times different authorities offer differing advice. This too contributes to a climate of fear." The emphasis in the mid-1980s on AIDS's spread to the heterosexual community did much to fuel public concern, despite public health officials' insistence that AIDS could not be spread by casual contact.

Because prevention of AIDS and rational, humane treatment of its victims (and HIV carriers) depend so heavily on public cooperation, the way in which the public perceives the threat will have a considerable impact on how health officials respond to AIDS. In 1987 the Surgeon General and public health officials initiated a major effort to educate the public on the facts of AIDS and on prevention. The widespread anxiety fueled by continual uncertainty, skepticism and fear of this deadly disease will not easily abate, however. As a result, many AIDS proposals or policies will elicit public controversy. "Issues presented by the AIDS crisis are not new to medical ethics. Issues such as distributive justice, privacy, duties to third parties, experimentation, or respect for human dignity have been at the center of bioethical and public policy debates. The AIDS crisis has only made them more urgent."[46]

If AIDS were striking the general population indiscriminately, the main policy problems would center on allocation of resources. If AIDS were communicated primarily by casual contact, its victims would receive substantial public sympathy. In contrast, the concentration of AIDS among two groups who enjoy little public support—homosexuals and heroin addicts—intensifies the constitutional issues surrounding efforts to control AIDS. With the homosexual lifestyle already facing condemnation from many in society and with heroin addicts enjoying little sympathy from either the public or health professionals, blaming the AIDS victim for his own problem has been popular. Not surprisingly, the distinction between the "innocent" victims of AIDS (such as blood transfusion recipients or children) and those whose lifestyles led to their infections became ingrained in the public dialogue over AIDS. The attempts by the Centers for Disease Control (CDC) and the Surgeon General to shift emphasis of the threat of AIDS to the heterosexual community despite a lack of clear evidence may represent an effort to defuse the blame-the-victim approach.

Additionally, as new cases of AIDS among intravenous (IV) drug users have begun to outnumber those among homosexuals, another politically explosive pattern of infection is apparent. Although blacks make up 12 percent and Hispanics 6 percent of the U.S. population, they represent, respectively, 25 percent and 12 percent of persons with AIDS. From an economic standpoint, these people are least likely to be able to afford the cost of the disease. From a social standpoint, these minorities, who already suffer from discrimination, are highly vulnerable to further stigmatization and invasion of privacy in the name of public health. Any attempts to screen for AIDS that target these high-risk groups will face constitutional challenges on the basis of due process and equal protection of the law.

In March 1987, the U.S. Supreme Court ruled 7 to 2 that anti-discrimination laws do apply to individuals with contagious diseases (*School Board of Nassau County Florida v. Arline*). Although this case dealt specifically with the dismissal of an employee who had tuberculosis, the ruling that communicable diseases are disabilities included under Section 504 of the Rehabilitation Act of 1973 is also applicable to AIDS patients. Employers cannot fire or otherwise discriminate without putting the burden of legal proof on themselves. Furthermore, if they fail to keep HIV test results confidential, they may be held liable for libel or slander.

Under this court ruling, any exclusion of persons with a contagious disease from the protection of the Rehabilitation Act must be based on sound medical evidence of risk to others, not on irrational fears. In the words of Justice William J. Brennan, Jr., writing for the majority, the law's basic purpose is to "ensure that handicapped individuals are not denied jobs or other benefits because of the prejudiced attitudes or the ignorance of others." Although significant legal action over aspects of these questions will continue, the explicit recognition of AIDS as a handicap under federal law assures some degree of legal protection of persons who test positive for HIV or have AIDS. In no way, however, does it eliminate discrimination against AIDS patients in housing, insurance or personal relationships, nor does it specify how concerns for danger to public health should be balanced with an individual's right to privacy. Related issues of exclusion of children from the public schools, the testing and quarantining of prostitutes and transmission of AIDS to children in utero will provide an expanding array of court cases in the coming decade.

AIDS stymies our technologically oriented society because there is no technological fix for it. Most experts express guarded hope at best for medical breakthroughs in stemming the spread of AIDS within the next decade.[47] This means that, at least for the near future, the only effective measure for reducing the spread of HIV infection is to educate the public, particularly those individuals at higher risk.

The realization that we cannot count upon a technical breakthrough has finally caused us to focus on prevention. Placing the policy emphasis on prevention, however, naturally centers the spotlight on identifiable groups whose members are at high risk—segments of the population who, as noted above, are already the subject of stigmatization. Furthermore, because of the nature of AIDS transmission, prevention efforts must demand drastic changes in these individuals' behavior, thereby escalating invasion-of-privacy problems and the political difficulties of implementing the policy. Finally, stressing prevention too heavily could leave AIDS policy open to the charge of failing to respond adequately to the needs of those who have already contracted the disease.

We urgently need a national AIDS policy that encompasses significant funding for education, research and health services. To date, as with the biomedical applications discussed in earlier chapters, there has developed instead a confusing array of state statutes and administrative regulations, with conflicting policies often apparent even within single jurisdictions. While some states have initiated rigid screening programs of varying categories of persons, from prisoners to marriage license applicants, other states have passed no legislation. In 1987 alone, over 450 bills on AIDS were introduced in state legislatures.[48] Of the laws that passed, seven have premarital screening provisions, five mandate testing of prisoners and twenty specify reporting procedures for HIV. This inconsistent policy framework results in considerable inequity in government efforts to deal with AIDS. To some extent, this fragmented policy is the result of the geographical imbalance of AIDS cases thus far. However, as the acute severity of the problem expands beyond New York, San Francisco and Los Angeles and extends across the country, consistent policy will be essential. The debates over insurance and HIV testing are but two of the issues that demand a credible, national AIDS policy forum.[49]

Although the sensational aspects of AIDS attracted an inordinate amount of early attention to this disease, its continuing spread will make AIDS a central political issue of the 1990s, thus dramatizing the public policy dimensions of all the biomedical issues we have discussed. Unfortunately, even our limited advances in our medical knowledge of AIDS have outdistanced our capacity to deal with its sociopolitical aspects. AIDS is at least as much a policy challenge as a technological one. The media's gripping, still proliferating AIDS reports, like the stories of transplants, test-tube babies and genetic intervention, remind us regularly that biomedicine promises to present American society with some of the most difficult policy choices imaginable. How well we handle them will depend largely on how successful we are in informing and educating our citizens on these critical issues.

FIRM FOUNDATIONS: THE CENTRAL QUESTIONS OF BIOMEDICAL POLICY

As a result of our society's deeply rooted dependence on biomedical technology to cure our ills, biomedicine will continue to progress faster than policy can catch up to it. The most rapid advances are likely to occur in the areas of genetic intervention, organ transplantation, neonatal intensive care and brain intervention. Extensions of current technologies—including brain cell transplants from fetuses, organ transplants from anencephalic newborns and interspecies organ transplants—are bound to raise increasingly complex ethical dilemmas and intensify the policy dimensions of biomedical technology.

As technology progresses, though, four basic types of policy questions will remain crucial. First, what level of technological intervention is appropriate for a given problem? How far should we seek to go in controlling our own destiny, in our quest for technological fixes to extend life? Gene therapy to enhance human capabilities and expanded forms of life-prolonging technological intervention will keep this question in prominence. So will the increasing numbers of people who are unwilling to let technology dictate how they die and are taking action through living wills to limit such intervention at that stage.

Second, who should determine whether a particular technology should be developed, should be funded, or should be applied in a specific case? Pressures for governmental controls, even though they threaten the traditional physician-patient relationship and personal autonomy, will increase due to tightening economic constraints. In this era of scarce resources, in part brought on by the high-cost technologies themselves, we can no longer assume that just because a technology is available we can or should use it. I feel strongly that the government must be intimately involved in setting priorities for use of these technologies.

The role of the government becomes even more crucial regarding the question of how to allocate and distribute biomedicine. Should these technologies be equally available to all persons? The traditional market-oriented, third-party payer system leaves many people out. The debate over whether or not the government has a responsibility to pay for expensive treatments when the individual cannot will intensify even more as the potential interventions increase. The ongoing policy battle over who should pay for liver transplants and the emerging demands for government funding of reproductive technologies illustrate the perplexing nature of this dilemma within our political value system. Can we ever justifiably choose not to save the life of an individual who needs a liver transplant when the technology and the new organ are available? What if that person's abuse of alcohol directly caused the condition? What criteria do we use to determine who gets scarce resources? The direct life-or-death implications of these choices for many individuals makes them qualitatively different from typical allocation and rationing decisions.

The fourth central policy question we must address is the impact on society of the use of each new technology. Once a technology becomes widely used, it is usually too late to place limits on its use. Technology assessment must anticipate negative long-term social consequences of any medical intervention before tempting society with that intervention's short-term benefits. Although the government's assessment efforts have increased substantially in the last decade, they are constrained by a value system that largely favors technological progress. As a result, the difficult choices of rejecting specific technologies because of their negative social consequences are not made.

Our society must begin to set its priorities more objectively and recognize that we cannot afford to proceed full speed ahead on the development and use of all biomedical technologies. We must realize that the rapid advances in biomedicine and the many real benefits that accompany them are inseparable from equally real problems and costs. We can no longer afford to blindly embrace technology for its own sake. Instead we must carefully assess the long-term implications of each application before we use it.

NOTES

1. President's Commission for the Study of Ethical Problems in Medicine and Biomedical and Behavioral Research. 1983. *Deciding to Forego Life-Sustaining Treatment.* Washington, DC: U.S. Government Printing Office.
2. Aristotle. *Politics,* p. 327.
3. Plato. *Republic,* p. 98.
4. President's Commission, op. cit., p. 24.
5. Earl of Listowel. 1986. Foreword. In A.B. Downing and Barbara Smoker, eds., *Voluntary Euthanasia: Experts Debate the Right to Die.* London: Peter Owen.
6. Derek Humphry and Ann Wickett. 1986. *The Right to Die: Understanding Euthanasia.* New York: Harper & Row.
7. Society for the Right to Die. 1987. *Handbook of Living Will Laws.* New York: Society for the Right to Die.
8. Office of Technology Assessment. 1987. *Losing a Million Minds: Confronting the Tragedy of Alzheimer's Disease and Other Dementias.* Washington, DC: National Academy Press.
9. Peter J. Cross and Barry J. Gurland. 1987. The Epidemiology of Dementing Disorders. Contract report prepared for Office of Technology Assessment. Springfield, VA: National Technical Information Service.
10. Robert M. Cook-Deegan and Peter J. Whitehouse. 1987. Alzheimer's Disease and Dementia: The Looming Crisis. *Issues in Science and Technology* 3:55.
11. President's Commission, op. cit.
12. Willard Gaylin. 1974. Harvesting the Dead: The Potential for Recycling Human Bodies. *Harper's* (September): 23-30.
13. Ad Hoc Committee of the Harvard Medical School to Examine the Definition of Brain Death. 1968. A Definition of Irreversible Coma. *Journal of the American Medical Association* 205:337.
14. President's Commission, op. cit., p. 23.
15. Renée C. Fox and Judith P. Swazey. 1987. *The Courage To Fail: A Social View of Transplantation and Dialysis.* Chicago: University of Chicago Press.
16. Alexander M. Capron and Leon R. Kass. 1972. Statutory Definition of the Standards for Determining Human Death: An Appraisal and a Proposal. *University of Pennsylvania Law Review* 121:87-104.

17. American Bar Association. 1975. *American Bar Association Annual Report* 100:221-232; National Conference of Commissioners on Uniform State Laws. 1987. Uniform Brain Death Act. *Uniform Laws Annotated* 12:15.
18. President's Commission, op. cit., p. 73.
19. Ibid., p. 1.
20. Allen R. Dyer. 1986. Patients, Not Costs, Come First. *Hastings Center Report* 16:5.
21. Albert G. Mulley. 1981. The Allocation of Resources for Medical Intensive Care. In President's Commission for the Study of Ethical Problems in Medicine and Biomedical and Behavioral Research, *Securing Access to Health Care.* Washington, DC: U.S. Government Printing Office.
22. J.D. Hill, J.R. Hampton and J.R.A. Mitchell. 1978. A Randomized Trial of Home versus Hospital Management of Patients with Suspected Myocardial Infarction. *The Lancet* 1:289.
23. Edmund D. Pellegrino. 1986. Rationing Health Care: The Ethics of Medical Gatekeeping. *Journal of Contemporary Health Law and Policy* 2:23-46.
24. Henry J. Aaron and William B. Schwartz. 1984. *The Painful Prescription: Rationing Hospital Care.* Washington, DC: The Brookings Institution.
25. Erich H. Loewy. 1980. Cost Should 'Not Be a Factor in Medical Care. *New England Journal of Medicine* 302:697.
26. Allen R. Dyer. 1986. Patients, Not Costs, Come First. *Hastings Center Report* 16:6.
27. Ibid.
28. Peter H. Schuck. 1981. Malpractice Liability and the Rationing of Care. *Texas Law Review* 59:1421-1425.
29. Harrison L. Rogers, Jr. 1986. Resisting Pressure. *American Medical News* (June 27-July 4):4.
30. George D. Lundberg. 1983. Rationing Human Life. *Journal of the American Medical Association* 249:2224.
31. H.H. Hiatt. 1975. Protecting the Medical Commons: Who Is Responsible? *New England Journal of Medicine* 293:235-240.
32. Deborah S. Pinkney. 1987. Manpower Crisis: Growing Labor Shortage in All Areas Crippling Hospitals Across Nations. *American Medical News* 1.
33. Institute of Medicine. 1987. Confronting AIDS: Directions for Public Health, Health Care, and Research. *Issues in Science and Technology* 3:93.
34. Jeffrey E. Harris. 1987. The AIDS Epidemic: Looking into the 1990s. *Technology Review* 90:61.
35. Daniel M. Fox. 1987. The Cost of AIDS from Conjecture to Research. *AIDS and Public Policy* 2:25-27.
36. Ann M. Hardy, Kathryn Racuh, Dean Echenberg, W. Meade Morgan and James W. Curran. 1986. The Economic Impact of the First 10,000 Cases of Acquired Immunodeficiency Syndrome in the United States. *Journal of the American Medical Association* 255:209-215.
37. Ann A. Scitovsky and Dorothy P. Rice. 1987. Estimates of the Direct and Indirect Costs of AIDS in the United States, 1985 and 1991. *Public Health Reports* 102:5-17.
38. Ibid.
39. Jack H. Blaine. 1987. AIDS: Regulatory Issues for Life and Health Insurers. *AIDS and Public Policy Journal* 2:2.

40. Mark Scherzer. 1987. AIDS and Insurance: The Case Against HIV Antibody Testing. *AIDS and Public Policy Journal* 2:19-24.
41. Larry Gostin and William J. Curran. 1987. AIDS Screening, Confidentiality, and the Duty to Warn. *American Journal of Public Health* 77:361.
42. Robert F. Hummel. 1987. AIDS, Public Policy, and Insurance. *AIDS and Public Policy Journal* 2:1.
43. Harris, op. cit., pp. 58-65.
44. Ibid.
45. Eleanor Singer and Theresa F. Rogers. 1986. Public Opinion and AIDS. *AIDS and Public Policy Journal* 1:8-13.
46. Norman Quist. 1987. AIDS and Public Policy: Publisher's Introduction. *AIDS and Public Policy Journal* 1:2.
47. Institute of Medicine, op. cit., p. 99.
48. Hilary Lewis. 1987. Acquired Immunodeficiency Syndrome: State Legislative Activity. *Journal of the American Medical Association* 258:2410.
49. Hummel, op. cit., p. 1.

14

The Hospice in the Context of an Aging Society

Judith A. Levy, PhD

With the declines in mortality and fertility rates of the twentieth century, the demographic profile of the United States emerged as that of an "aging society" where most people survive childhood and the middle years to die in old age.[1] The demands of meeting the needs of an increasingly older population have placed enormous strain on American social institutions and raised serious questions about their ability to adapt.[2] Pressure to reorganize the delivery of medical care and social services to the fatally ill, most of whom are older adults, has become particularly salient because of rising costs and perceived insensitivity to patient and family needs.[3] Terminal care, therefore, provides a useful focus for studying the context and processes of institutional change in response to a growing aged population.

In following such an agenda, this chapter examines how the demographic forces of an aging society contributed to the development of the American hospice movement and institutionalization of the hospice concept as a new form of terminal care. Based on a philosophy that developed in England, the term *hospice* denotes both a social movement and a coordinated system of home and inpatient services designed to alleviate the physical, emotional, social and economic stresses of terminal illness and family bereavement. In examining hospice in terms of both forms of collective action, the following analysis is organized around three questions: What are the social forces of an aging society that led to the emergence of the hospice movement in the United States? How do hospice services coincide with the needs of an aging population? What challenges do the pressures of an increasingly aging society pose for the future of the hospice concept?

SOCIAL FORCES THAT EVOKED THE HOSPICE MOVEMENT

Social movements merge when people's lives are affected by some form of structural change or transformation in society.[4] As C. Wright Mills observes, a person loses a job, a marriage breaks up or someone dies and these circumstances merely reflect the personal troubles of the parties involved.[5] But when unemployment soars, divorce rates drastically climb or death takes place through famine or war, we have the makings of a public issue that can fuel collective action. The hospice movement represents one such instance.

The hospice movement draws its momentum from the demographic transition and technological change that followed the close of the nineteenth century.[6] In 1900, most deaths occurred from infectious disease with pneumonia, influenza, tuberculosis and gastroenteritis heading the list.[7] By the last quarter of the twentieth century, however, the epidemiologic profile had changed. As a result of public health measures, improved nutrition, institution of occupational health standards and the pharmacologic advances of the twenties and thirties, infectious disease yielded to heart disease, cancer and other chronic disorders as the major cause of death. This demographic transition created a new set of societal problems affecting the fatally ill, their families and the network of interlocking institutions that comprise the American health care system. Collective response to the personal and institutional stress of contemporary dying led to the emergence of the hospice movement and pressure to alter existing provisions of terminal care. We can understand this process better by examining the sources of strain in an aging society that led to collective action.

The Modern Terminal Care Consumer

The human life course consists of a series of biosocially defined stages in which dying represents the final phase.[8] Each stage has its own set of expectations, role responsibilities and normative prescriptions for people to follow. In societies where death occurs primarily through infectious disease or catastrophic events such as famine or war, the period of the life course spent in dying typically is short, entered suddenly and comes with little warning. Scant biological time may be available to tie up the loose ends of living or bring one's life to anticipated closure. Investments in the social career of dying tend to be low and the content of the role is restricted by the brief time available for role performance and elaboration.[9]

Change in patterns of mortality and morbidity during the first quarter of the twentieth century altered the existing temporal phasing of the life course by expanding the period in which the average person dies. In contrast to the swift and often sudden death characteristic of infectious disease, chronic disorders often involve a lingering trajectory that may be further prolonged through medical science.[10] Early detection programs and improved diagnostic techniques also can lengthen the dying period by informing people of a fatal illness long before the symptoms are subjectively felt. Following the disclosure of a terminal illness, the individual is thrust into a new phase of living based upon an altered biological and social status that may last for months or even years.

Considerable research points to the enormous strains of confronting impending death.[11] Like members of all cultures, people in an aging society face the difficult problem of finding meaning in personal finitude and death.[12] When compared to death from infectious disease, however, the person dying of a degenerative disorder typically has a longer period to contemplate dying and what it means to be dead.

Because having a foreseeable death is the primary criterion that biosocially locates a person in the final period of the life course, "dying" can become a master status that overrides all other designates through which people are recognized and embedded in their social networks. As a fatal illness progresses, waning strength can force the individual to withdraw from the work force, a primary source of personal identity in industrial societies. Normal family roles may need to be relinquished at the very time when the person is struggling to counter a diminished social self. Meanwhile, family and friends may shun the dying out of discomfort with that person's altered status or to avoid the burden of caregiving.[13] Anticipatory grief over the death can also result in people socially treating the terminally ill as if they already are dead.[14]

Because of the negative properties associated with the social role of dying, the challenge for a person with a terminal illness is to find ways to live out what can be a lengthy period of the life course in a manner that is personally satisfying and which preserves a positive self-image. This need is well illustrated by an anecdote related by a nurse who was caring for a young man dying of cancer.[15] Thinking that he might be anxious about death, she tried to reassure her patient that palliative methods would be used to make his dying more comfortable and that he would have someone with him when the time came. Rather than feeling comforted, the young man turned angrily to her said, "Nobody has to help me die, I can do that for myself. Just help me live until I get to die."

These words offer an example of what Mills meant when he wrote of the individualized experience of personal trouble. Beyond receiving medication and comfort, the young man also wanted to remain socially anchored in everyday life. When others in society also have similar feelings or experiences, personal trouble can give way to public concern and action. It was this collective response that helped fuel the hospice movement.

At the cultural level, evidence of a shared search for meaningful dying can be seen in the recent popularity in the United States of films and books that deal with terminal illness. Death has always been a topic guaranteed to sell newspapers, magazines and movies. Indeed, the staples of primetime television—murder, war, suicide and accidental killings—attest to an audience's appetite for stories of violent and impersonal death.[16] With the prolonged fatal illnesses of an aging society, however, a new market has emerged for media accounts that deal with the social aspects of *dying* in contrast to *death*.[17] Over the last two decades, for example, films have featured the dying of a young woman in both *Love Story* and *Terms of Endearment*, an athlete's demise in *Brian's Song*, and the gentle death of an adolescent with a disfiguring disease in *Mask*. However imperfect or stylized by Hollywood imagery these films may be, they reflect a cultural resource through which the general public learns about and seeks meaning in chronic illness and dying.[18]

Perhaps not by happenstance, at least one of the primary roles in each of these media portrayals involves a friend or family member struggling to cope with the impending death. In an aging society, the increased longevity of the human life course has given rise to a dramatic prolongation of the social linkages between family members.[19] This circumstance has extended both the number and intensity of kinship relations that a person potentially can have.[20] In doing so, it has also increased the number of opportunities in which individuals confront the death of someone with whom they have shared a considerable portion of life.

Hospice emerged out of personal experiences and in partial response to the needs of family members to have their loved ones die more comfortably and to have some relief from the burdens of family care.[21] As we will see shortly, concerned family members were joined in this effort by health care providers with similar concerns. Such advocacy for change led by people other than the terminally ill was necessary for hospice movement formation, as those who are dying typically lack the biological time or physical strength needed to forge or maintain a movement on their own behalf.

In this regard, what has been described so far is a series of societal stresses, brought about by demographic changes in mortality and morbidity, that led to a generalized perception that "something ought to be done." Studies of social movements suggest that social strain is a necessary element for collective action. Nonetheless, Dahrendorf also observes that strain is an inherent and ubiquitous problem within any social structure.[22] Thus, social movement theorists have come to recognize that other factors must also be present for a movement to ignite. One of these elements is an emergent world view or ideology that can unite people together in joint purpose and provide a direction for advocates to follow.[23] Within hospice, the emergence of such a shared vision can be traced to the writings and personal experience of a growing cadre of clinical professionals with an interest in redefining the values and structure of terminal care.

Ideology

Robert Kastenbaum notes that the first collective awareness of the dysfunctions of modern terminal care began in the 1950s.[24] Epidemiologically, this decade corresponds to the period in which the prevalence of heart disease, cancer and stroke began its rapid climb.[25] Although a few health care professionals and other clinicians were aware of their experience with the dying, it wasn't until Herman Feifel published *The Meaning of Death* in 1959 that the professional community began to actively discuss the social circumstances surrounding institutional death and its negative affect on the patient and family.

Death as a social problem gained public awareness approximately 10 years later with the publication in 1969 of *On Death and Dying* by Elisabeth Kübler-Ross. Contained within this volume and the subsequent writings produced by her and others following the same philosophy, are a set of clinically based guidelines for patients, families and providers for managing the problematic and social roles of contemporary death. These prescriptions include methods for maintaining the psychosocial well-being of the dying person and bringing an organized closure to the life that is about to end. The clinical goal, underlying much of this body of literature and research, is to provide a supportive physical and social environment where people can "die with dignity."[26]

Such public and professional concern with bringing greater dignity to contemporary death in the United States found its philosophical counterpart in England where Cicely Saunders, a British physician, instituted a new model of palliative care at St. Christopher's Hospice in London. Here, a homelike environment was created within the structure of an institutional setting and patients were kept largely free of pain through new techniques of palliative care.[27] By reorganizing the mode and setting through which terminal care was delivered, Saunder's methods gave the dying greater control over their daily existence and the opportunity to live more fully before death. Taken together, Kübler-Ross provided the ideology and Saunders provided a set of practical techniques through which a social movement directed toward improving terminal care in the United States could be mobilized.[28] This influence was to support the emergence and growth of the American hospice movement in three ways.[29]

First, the concept of death with dignity provided an ideological base for the movement by specifying a set of values and objectives around which to build collective action. Koff summarizes this ideal by noting:

> Enabling a person to die with dignity includes taking whatever measures reduce or eliminate pain and discomfort and always treating the total person not his symptoms. These practices provide security and build trust by focusing on the patient's needs and treating each person as a special and unique being.... Permitting death with dignity also means enabling the person and those important to him to practice rituals or to behave in ways in keeping with their culture and/or lifestyle.[30]

Second, the death with dignity philosophy also provided leadership and support from occupations and professionals strategically situated within the medical system. Hospice is a reform movement that took place *within* medicine and not from *outside* medicine as is popularly believed. At the start of the movement, it was common in volunteer training sessions and hospice literature to routinely point to organized medicine as an enemy to be changed.[31] This practice served the important function of promoting solidarity by providing a common antagonist against which hospice advocates could rally.[32] Yet, close inspection of movement organizers and supporters show that many of the first hospice programs in the United States were located in hospitals and other medical care institutions.[33] Moreover, many of its earliest advocates were doctors, nurses and other professionals in the health care sector.[34]

The death with dignity philosophy approach also provided a third advantage to hospice growth by linking the movement to existing extra movement networks and institutions sharing a similar philosophy. By building alliances with groups such as Reach for Recovery or Widows Helping Widows, the movement broadened its organizational base to gain added support.[35] Such linkages and overlaps provide access to communication and other resources which otherwise might be unattainable.[36]

Institutional Support

In any social movement, outside interests such as government or special interest groups can facilitate or impede collective actions.[37] Almost from the start, hospice received support from a number of extra movement constituencies including health insurers and government.[38] Concern had grown over the rapidly rising cost of health care, much of which was being spent on older people in the last year of life.[39] Hospice care was seen as a low-cost substitute for traditional life-extending treatment.[40] Its concept of a home death also coincided with a growing health care industry.[41] Moreover, its humane methods attracted financial help from a number of foundations and philanthropies such as the American Cancer Society, the United Way and the Robert Wood Johnson Foundation. Thus, hospice was perceived by many as one of the vehicles through which the medical system could be transformed.[42]

In sum, the hospice movement can be seen as a collective response to strain in the personal and institutional arrangements of an aging society resulting from demographic change. Shifts in patterns of disease produced the necessary ingredients for a movement: a constituency, ideology, resources and tentative support from powerful interests within society. By 1984, over 1500 hospice programs existed in the United States, attesting to the movement's growing popularity and successful mobilization.[43] That hospice has become a growing component of the American health care system raises a salient question: How does the hospice concept ameliorate the societal strains that led to its emergence?

CONGRUENCE BETWEEN HOSPICE SERVICES AND THE NEEDS OF AN AGING SOCIETY

Congruence between the perceived benefits of the hospice philosophy and the needs of an aging society can be assessed by examining its application to meeting the problems of its social institutions. Since exploration of all societal institutions is beyond the scope of a single chapter, the following discussion is limited to one societal institution—that of the family. The family offers a particularly rich opportunity to gain insight as hospice services target the patient and family as a single unit of care.[44] Moreover, the plight of patients and families dealing with an impersonal medical system and the crises associated with death and dying was an important force in sparking the movement.[45] The following discourse focuses on congruency between the hospice service functions and the needs of dying people and families. These functions, which are carried out by both nursing staff and volunteers can be summarized as: constructing supportive networks, mediating interaction, providing a structure of meaning, aiding in biographical work and serving as a "midwife" in the dying process.[46]

Constructing Supportive Networks

As noted earlier, the high prevalence of chronic illness in an aging society creates a great burden of care for the person's family and friends. Hospice attempts to ameliorate this stress by providing volunteers to help the patient and family with simple nursing and homemaking chores.[47] In addition, hospice programs typically admit only those patients for whom there is a family member or close friend willing to serve as caregiver. If no one is available, the hospice may press a neighbor or acquaintance into service. From a hospice survival standpoint, this requirement lowers organization risk by assuring that someone outside the hospice takes final responsibility for the patient's care and legal status.[48] It also has the latent function of creating a caregiver where none might otherwise exist. In creating the social role of "hospice caregiver," the hospice specifies and reinforces a set of role relations and responsibilities that bind the provider and recipient of care.

Mediating Interaction

When a family member is dying, the processes and final outcome typically disrupt the interlocking patterns of responsibility and habit that families establish in their daily lives. Death and dying call for a reassignment of family roles and, eventually, adjustment to life without the person who is dead. Hospice volunteers aid in the coping process by babysitting young children and performing routine chores to give family members time together to make these changes before and after the death. Such mediation of relationships also extends to encouraging successful interaction with the many institutions that intersect with a person's death. For example, volunteers may drive the person to see a lawyer or help the family with funeral arrangements.[49]

Considerable evidence also suggests that many people feel uncomfortable being around someone who is dying, a circumstance that can result in stilted interactions or avoidance.[50] Hospice volunteers help to mediate this discomfort by encouraging frank discussions about death. Most hospice programs stipulate that prospective clients must be told that they are dying as a condition for admission. This rule, which reinforces what Glaser and Strauss refer to as an "open awareness context," forces the person to confront the reality of impending death and clears the way for further talk.[51]

Providing Structures of Meaning

Hospice also addresses the psychological needs of an aging society by providing patients and families with a supportive context in which to search for and, perhaps, find the meanings of life and death.[52] Personal awareness of finitude begins early in life and intensifies as aging brings the specter of death closer.[53] Hospice volunteers aid in the search for meaning by encouraging the person and family to face the inevitability of death and find comfort in one another's support. The "death with dignity" philosophy aids in this work by providing volunteers and staff with a structure of meaning around which to organize their work and which they, in turn, pass on to the patient and family.

Biographical Work

When people experience an alteration of personal identity through serious illness, they or their families many engage in what Gubrium and Lynott refer to as "biographical work" to preserve or construct a satisfying identity despite the stigma associated with dying.[54] Hospice volunteers aid in this process by helping to construct a supportive environment where people can live out the final days of their lives within the context of their former self. For example, volunteers organize birthday parties and other special events so that these experiences remain part of their patient's lives.[55] Great emphasis is placed in hospice services on helping people maintain personal contacts and continue activities they enjoyed before their illness.

Serving as Midwives for the Process of Dying

Death and dying as social phenomena are highly visible in traditional societies where death care and burial preparations typically are located within the family or immediate community and where high mortality rates force repeated confrontations with death.[56] In those societies, death roles are well known and are learned within the context and flow of daily life. Such socialization for death and death care, however, does not have an equal counterpart in industrial societies. Here, death and care for the dying typically takes place in formal settings and family, friends and the individual may have little experience with directly managing the realities of death.

To ameliorate this problem, hospice programs provide volunteers with special training that prepares them to work with the dying person and family in managing the common psychological and physiological problems likely to occur with a home death.[57] In this, hospice volunteers function much like midwives for the dying by overseeing the physical and social properties of a hospice death. Their role can be as technically important and emotionally supportive to the family as the traditional role of midwives in birthing.

In sum, when the various functions of hospice volunteers in relation to the family are considered, we find considerable congruency between hospice goals and the personal and institutional needs of an aging society. Like all forms of emergent culture, however, hospice undoubtedly embodies certain inherent properties that are socially dysfunctional. Within the social sciences, theoretical rebellion against the structural functionalist contention that "what exists must work" has taught us to consider the troublesome and problematic elements of emergent culture in addition to its positive contributions. With the exception of the National Hospice Project, few systematic evaluations of hospice have taken place.[58] Nonetheless, the challenge of hospice's survival and success as a reform movement rests heavily upon discovering both the concept's weaknesses and considerable strengths. Given that hospice operates within the complex and constantly changing environment of an aging society, what are the challenges to the hospice movement that lie ahead?

CHALLENGES FOR THE FUTURE

In predicting the future of social movements, many researchers have turned to a natural history approach to explain the process through which movements emerge and reach their final form. While no two movements are alike, the life cycle approach provides a valuable framework for predicting the success and future of the movement as well as for understanding its internal organization. Mauss summarizes the stage model approach by pointing to five phases that make up the natural history of a social movement: (1) incipiency; (2) coalescence; (3) institutionalization; (4) fragmentation; and (5) demise.[59]

Widespread public and private acceptance of the hospice concept marked the successful movement of hospice into the institutional phase. Hospice programs are a common component of many hospitals and other forms of health care facilities. The U.S. government has underwritten the availability of hospice services through Medicare reimbursement.[60] Other third-party payers have made similar commitments.

With institutionalization, the stresses on a movement change. Pressures for accountability emerge in the wake of the movement having successfully advanced its claim. For hospice, these challenges can be observed by examining three major areas where problems occur: ideology, service and accommodation. Each of these bears closer inspection.

Ideology

Hospice emerged as a service alternative to traditional forms of terminal care that encourage the often futile use of medical measures to prolong life, at considerable pain and loss of human dignity.[61] In contrast to the medical model's emphasis on heroic intervention, the death with dignity philosophy incorporates the concept of a "natural death" without the use of painful life-sustaining measures.[62] Consequently, for ideological reasons, most hospices only admit patients for whom further curative therapies appear useless and who make the decision to forego further extraordinary treatment.

Because of the concept's emphasis on natural death, hospice advocates have been sensitive to the importance of dispelling medical and public opinion that hospices represent death houses. Opposition to the hospice concept is often expressed in the fear that widespread acceptance of hospice principles will lead to reduced measures in fighting disease and forestalling death.[63] Within hospice itself, both lay and professionals frequently struggle with ethical questions of how to support the decision of the dying to forego further treatment while, at the same time, protecting their rights to obtain a full life. These ideological dilemmas offer some of the knottiest challenges for hospice volunteers and staff.[64]

Part of the ambiguity stems from the difficulties of identifying the appropriate level where the potential for medical cure has been exhausted.[65] Spontaneous or therapeutically induced remission, which are common with some forms of cancer, complicate predictions of life expectancy making it difficult to decide when to discontinue treatment.[66] Too early a decision to discontinue treatment shortens a patient's life needlessly.

One solution to the dilemma requires patients to try all curative options before admission into a hospice program.[67] This policy, however, denies potential patients the right to stop treatment at will. Moreover, some patients may prefer death to undergoing successful but highly painful and distressing intervention.

Iatrogenic complications during hospice care pose another set of dilemmas. For example, creating a supportive environment where patients can die with dignity entails the use of analgesics and similar forms of symptom control. Use of these measures raises serious ethical questions of whether or not caregivers are justified in providing palliative treatment if it is relatively certain that the treatment will lead to the patient's death.[68] Such a quandary can arise when the doses of morphine required to ease a patient's pain makes him susceptible to pneumonia or decreased breathing.[69]

Similarly, in the course of treatment, a hospice patient may fall and fracture a hip or react adversely to a drug. Such unexpected treatment complications occurred after the decision was made to forego further active treatment. In such instances, certain questions arise.[70] Should iatrogenic complications be treated to prolong life, while other physical conditions are not? Or do these iatrogenic complications become part of a natural death and the patient allowed to die? Not only is the patient's well-being at stake, but also the caregiver's. Families have a great need to know what they are doing is the right thing and watching a loved one die of a treatable condition can lead to guilt and remorse.[71]

Meanwhile, the line that separates palliative methods from curative treatment is frequently blurred. With antitumor treatment, for example, it is often difficult to decide at what point pain controlled through radiation crosses over into extraordinary measures.[72] In such instances, comfort may dictate using measures considered inappropriate for patients experiencing lesser pain.

In short, the ideological decisions in hospice are complex and require constant vigilance to protect patient rights. Hospice programs are typically sensitive to such problems and much of patient review sessions involve such delicate decision-making.[73] Meanwhile, despite attempts to clarify what hospice entails, many patients and families enter hospice not knowing what is involved.[74] Part of the difficulty of communicating this reality stems from the general lack of consensus with which essential terms are defined.[75] Terms such as "imminent" or "extraordinary" mean different things to different people. Also, the hospice concept is still new to many people and a patient's or family's first encounter with the concept may come as part of the death.

Service

Despite the rapid growth of hospice organizations, hospice programs still serve only a small proportion of the two million people who die in the United States each year.[76] Most of those served are cancer patients.[77] Because of its success in providing emotional support and palliative comfort care, pressure now exists to extend the availability of hospice services to a wider population and to other diseases.

In the United States, hospices are most likely to serve white, middle or working class patients from reasonably intact families where there are sufficient resources for someone to devote considerable time to caregiving.[78] Because most hospices require patients to have a full-time caregiver, individuals without families or other resources are unlikely to qualify for care.[79] Moreover, individuals who request care are often screened for having those psychosocial characteristics that would make them successful patients. These policies tend to exclude a number of potential populations that are not currently served.

AIDS patients constitute one underserved population, even in geographic areas where transmission of the virus is prevalent.[80] Because people with AIDS could benefit greatly from emotional support and palliation, they make good candidates for hospice services.[81] Also, many public health experts perceive that hospice may be a cost-effective mode of treatment—a judgment that may result in pressure on hospice to accept more people with AIDS.

Accepting AIDS patients into a hospice program, however, carries considerable organizational risk.[82] People with AIDS who are close to death have often run out of insurance benefits. Meeting their medical needs can seriously drain a hospice's resources. Moreover, volunteers find that caring for AIDS patients is difficult because of the social stigma and emotional crises that these patients experience. As an infectious disorder, AIDS also carries risk of contagion. A number of hospices have reported community opposition to admitting AIDS patients into the same program that serves individuals with other diseases. Fear exists that the disease may spread to patients already weakened by their conditions and to family members.

Children represent a second large, underserved population. In an aging society where death is associated with the old, death in childhood takes on special sadness. Historically, many hospices have been reluctant to care for dying children because of the added emotional stress and special problems that caring for babies and young people represents.[83] Yet, families need the respite care that hospice offers and, like adults, children benefit from the psychological, spiritual and social aspects of the hospice approach.[84]

A third large underserved population is comprised of society's oldest old, those 75 years of age or older, most of whom in an aging society are likely to be women. A large proportion of these women are likely to be living without a spouse who can serve as a caregiver during terminal illness. Moreover, they are less likely to have been gainfully employed to the same extent as men throughout their life course. Consequently, they tend to have lower retirement benefits and fewer resources in old age than do men of similar social class.[85] The absence of someone to serve as caregiver along with an increase in the number of special problems possibly explain why so few women past their seventies receive hospice care.

Accommodation

Unlike social movements of the past, which were financed solely by contributions from their members, today's successful social movements typically draw upon business, foundations and the government for their resources.[86] As a result, most social movement organizations must accommodate to the rules and regulations of those from whom they seek help. The danger with this mode of movement financing is that it easily leads to organizational goal displacement through programs redefining their goals and objectives to meet funding priorities or reimbursement guidelines. Over time, program values become isomorphic with those of the institutions and organizations from which they gain their resources.[87]

In this regard, Medicare reimbursement is expected to have a strong impact on the structure and quality of the delivery of future hospice services. Already, signs exist that hospice programs may be "creaming" pools of potential patients from those individuals most likely to fit the Medicare reimbursement profile.[88] The best candidates include patients who are unlikely to require extensive resource investments.[89] Estimating prognosis is important since programs cannot discharge patients who become costly or outlive their benefits.[90] Meanwhile, Medicare stipulates that the majority of benefits must be delivered in the home, a condition that encourages early hospital discharge despite the need for further hospitalization.[91]

Medicare and other forms of third-party reimbursement have also had an enormous impact on the organization and philosophy of hospices themselves. Third-party payment requires hospice personnel to supply detailed records, follow complex legal regulations and be ready to defend the treatment they deliver.[92] Qualifying for benefits also requires considerable growth and investment in professional staff, a condition likely to undermine the movement's initial emphasis upon lay participation.[93] At the same time, programs that deviate from the single, expensive model for licensing and hospice certification must forego this form of financial aid.[94] The result has been a movement toward increased homogeneity and less innovation among programs.[95] Incentives for programmatic improvement have been reduced by the establishment of minimum standards of operation and restrictions imposed by licensing and certification.[96]

Hospice reimbursements recognize the dilemmas and irony that third-party reimbursements pose. Under intense pressure to comply or forego the benefit, many hospices were reluctant to qualify for benefits as they perceived that these changes would have undesirable effects.[97] Programs that decline to qualify, however, may find themselves pushed out of the service market by certified hospices carrying the Medicare "stamp of approval."[98]

Such restriction and change in the movement appears inevitable from a social movement perspective. If the hospice movement follows the typical life course of a social movement, the success of the institutional stage will be followed by fragmentation and demise of the movement itself.[99] Buoyed by success, members and the general public will lose interest and turn to other pursuits. Conflict may erupt among remaining members and factions over ideological issues, direction of the movement, power and social control. Cooptation may occur as stronger forces outside the movement assume increasingly greater control over its institutionalized form. References to hospice as a social movement will cease as the term becomes synonymous with a component of the health care industry.

In the 1970s, hospice founders worried keenly about the concept's continued survival. This worry disappeared when institutionalization through Medicare guaranteed hospice programs a position in the American health care system. As hospice matures and responds to the forces of an aging society over the next decade, a new question concerning its future has emerged. Advocates and other interested parties no longer need ask: "Will the hospice concept survive?" The answer clearly is yes, but in what form?

NOTES

1. A. Pifer and L. Bronte. 1986. Introduction: Squaring the Pyramid. *Daedalus* 115:1-11.
2. J.L. Palmer and S.G. Gould. 1986. The Economic Consequences of an Aging Society. *Daedalus* 115:295-323.
3. D.D. Callahan. 1987. *Setting Limits: Medical Goals in an Aging Society.* New York: Simon & Schuster; D.S. Greer, V. Mor, J.N. Morris, S. Sherwood, D. Kidder and H. Birnbaum. 1986. An Alternative in Terminal Care: Results of the National Hospice Study. *Journal of Chronic Disease* 39:9-26.
4. R.A. Garner. 1972. *Social Movements in America.* Chicago: Rand McNally.
5. C.W. Mills. 1959. *The Sociological Imagination.* New York: Oxford University Press.
6. L. Lofland. 1978. *The Craft of Dying.* Beverly Hills, CA: Sage.
7. J.B. McKinlay and S.M. McKinlay. 1977. The Questionable Contribution of Medical Measures to the Decline of Mortality in the United States in the Twentieth Century. *Milbank Memorial Fund Quarterly* 55:405-428.
8. V.W. Marshall. 1980. *A Sociology of Death and Dying.* Belmont, CA: Wadsworth.
9. J.A. Levy. 1982a. The Hospice Movement: Creating New Social Worlds for the Dying. Unpublished Ph.D. dissertation, Northwestern University.
10. B.G. Glaser and A.L. Strauss. 1965. *Awareness of Dying.* Chicago: Aldine.
11. J.W. Riley, Jr. 1983. Dying and the Meanings of Death: Sociological Inquiries. In *Annual Review of Sociology,* Vol. IX. Palo Alto, CA: Annual Reviews Inc.
12. Marshall, loc. cit.
13. K. Charmaz. 1980. *The Social Reality of Death.* Reading, MA: Addison-Wesley.
14. D. Sudnow. 1967. *Passing On: The Social Organization of Dying.* Englewood Cliffs, NJ: Prentice-Hall.
15. Levy, op. cit., p. 47.
16. M.J. Arlen. 1978. The Air. In R. Fulton et al., eds., *Death and Dying: Challenge and Change.* Reading, MA: Addison-Wesley.
17. Levy, loc. cit.
18. R. Kastenbaum. 1979. Healthy Dying: A Paradoxical Quest Continues. *Journal of Social Issues* 35:185-206.
19. M.W. Riley. 1985. Women, Men, and the Lengthening Life Course. In A.S. Rossi, ed., *Gender and the Life Course.* New York: Aldine.
20. G.O. Hagestad. 1986. The Aging Society as a Context for Family Life. *Daedalus* 115:119-139.
21. E.K. Abel. 1986. The Hospice Movement: Institutionalizing Innovation. *International Journal of Health Services* 16:71-85.
22. R. Dahrendorf. 1958. Toward a Theory of Social Conflict. *Journal of Social Conflict* 11:170-183.
23. Garner, loc. cit.

24. Kastenbaum, loc. cit.
25. McKinlay and McKinlay, loc. cit.
26. T.H. Koff. 1980. *Hospice: A Caring Community.* Cambridge, MA: Winthrop.
27. L.F. Paradis and S.B. Cummings. 1986. The Evolution in Hospice in America: Toward Organizational Homogeneity. *Journal of Health and Social Behavior* 27:370-386.
28. P.R. Torrens. 1985. Development of Special Care Programs for the Dying: A Brief History. In P.R. Torrens, ed., *Hospice Programs and Public Policy.* Chicago: American Hospital Publishing.
29. Levy, loc. cit.
30. Koff, op. cit., p. 24.
31. Abel, loc. cit.
32. Levy, 1982, loc. cit.
33. Paradis and Cummings, loc. cit.
34. J.A. Levy. 1982b. The Staging of Negotiations Between Hospice and Medical Institutions. *Urban Life* 11:293-312.
35. Abel, loc. cit.
36. Garner, loc. cit.
37. Garner, loc. cit.
38. Levy, 1982a., loc. cit.; Paradis and Cummings, loc. cit.
39. Callahan, loc. cit.
40. S. Tames. 1987. Medicare, Medicaid Coverage. In *Perspectives* (supplement to *Medicine and Health*). New York: McGraw-Hill.
41. Abel, loc. cit.
42. Paradis and Cummings, loc. cit.
43. B.A. McCann. 1985. *Hospice Project Report.* Chicago: Joint Commission on Accreditation of Hospitals.
44. Koff, loc. cit.
45. Levy, 1982b, loc. cit.; Greer et al., loc. cit.
46. J.A. Levy. 1987. A Life Course Perspective on Hospice and the Family. *Marriage and Family Review* 11:39-64.
47. Abel, loc. cit.
48. J.A. Levy. 1986. Mistakes at Work: Building on the Insights of Everett C. Hughes. Paper presented at the annual meeting of the Society for the Study of Social Problems, New York.
49. Koff, loc. cit.
50. Sudnow, loc. cit.
51. Glaser and Strauss, loc. cit.
52. T. Ingles. 1980. St. Christopher's Hospice. In M. Hamilton and H. Reid, eds., *A Hospice Handbook.* Grand Rapids, MI: William B. Erdmanns.
53. Marshall, loc. cit.
54. J.F. Gubrium and R.J. Lynott. 1985. Alzheimer's Disease as Biographical Work. In W.A. Peterson and J. Quadagno, eds., *Social Bonds in Later Life: Aging and Interdependence.* Beverly Hills, CA: Sage.
55. Koff, loc. cit.; J.M Zimmerman. 1986. *Hospice: Complete Care for the Terminally Ill.* Baltimore: Urban & Schwarzenberg.
56. Marshall, loc. cit.
57. Levy, 1982a, loc. cit.
58. D.S. Greer and V. Mor. 1985. How Medicare is Altering the Hospice Movement. *Hastings Center Report* (October):5-9.

59. A.L. Mauss. 1975. *Social Problems as Social Movements.* Philadelphia: J.B. Lippincott.
60. I. Fraser. 1985. Medicare Reimbursement for Hospice Care: Ethical and Policy Implications of Cost-Containment Strategies. *Journal of Health Politics, Policy and Law* 10:565-578.
61. Levy, 1982, loc. cit.
62. Koff, loc. cit.
63. D.E. Gibson. 1984. Hospice: Morality and Economics. *The Gerontologist* 24:4-8.
64. J.A. Levy and A. Gordon. 1987. Stress and Burn-Out in the Social World of Hospice. *The Hospice Journal* 3:29-51.
65. J. Lynn and M. Osterweis. 1985. Ethical Issues Arising in Hospice Care. In P.R. Torrens, ed., *Hospice Programs and Public Policy.* Chicago: American Hospital Publishing.
66. Zimmerman, loc. cit.
67. J. Lynn. 1985. Ethics in Hospice Care. In L.F. Paradis, ed., *Hospice Handbook: A Guide for Managers and Planners.* Rockville, MD: Aspen.
68. Lynn and Osterweis, loc. cit.
69. Gibson, loc. cit.
70. Lynn and Osterweis, loc. cit.
71. D. Crane. 1975. *The Sanctity of Social Life: Physicians' Treatment of Critically Ill Patients.* New York: Russell Sage Foundation.
72. Zimmerman, loc. cit.
73. Levy and Gordon, loc. cit.
74. Levy, 1982a, loc. cit.
75. Lynn, loc. cit.
76. Lynn and Osterweis, loc. cit.
77. Zimmerman, loc. cit.
78. Lynn, loc. cit.
79. Greer and Mor, loc. cit.
80. Tames, loc. cit.
81. J. Pollatsek. 1987. Hospice for AIDS Patients—Break Down Barriers and Accept AIDS Patients. *American Journal of Hospice Care* 4:9-10.
82. Tames, loc. cit.
83. K.H. Lazarus. 1985. Developing a Pediatric Hospice: Organizational Dynamics. In L.F. Paradis, ed., *Hospice Handbook: A Guide for Managers and Planners.* Rockville, MD: Aspen.
84. C.A. Corr and D.M. Corr. 1985. *Hospice Approaches to Pediatric Care.* New York: Springer.
85. C.F. Longino, Jr. 1989. A Population Profile of Very Old Men and Women in the United States. *Sociological Quarterly* 29:559-564.
86. Garner, loc. cit.
87. P.J. DiMaggio and W. Powell. 1983. The Iron Cage Revisited: Institutional Isomorphism and Collective Rationalization in Organization Fields. *American Sociological Review* 48:147-160.
88. Torrens, loc. cit.
89. C. Tehan. 1985. Has Success Spoiled Hospice? *Hastings Center Report* 15:10-13.
90. E.F. Pitorak. 1985. Establishing a Medicare-Certified Inpatient Unit. *Nursing Clinics of North America* 20:311-326.
91. I.B. Corless. 1985. Implications of the New Hospice Legislation and the Accompanying Regulations. *Nursing Clinics of North America* 20:281-298.

92. E.S. Dorang. 1982. A Record-Keeping Method for Hospice-Related Volunteers. *Rehabilitation Nursing* Sept.-Oct.:17-19.
93. Abel, loc. cit.
94. I. Graser, T. Koontz and W.C. Moran. 1986. Medicare Reimbursement for Hospice Care: An Approach for Analyzing Cost Consequences. *Inquiry* 23:141-153.
95. Paradis and Cummings, loc. cit.
96. Tehan, loc. cit.
97. Fraser et al., loc. cit.
98. Fraser et al., loc. cit.
99. Mauss, loc. cit.

15

AIDS: A Sociological Response

Robert Fulton, PhD and
Greg Owen, PhD

INTRODUCTION

Images of what threatens to be a major human catastrophe were presented to the American public in 1986 in the form of a two-hour PBS *Frontline* documentary entitled "AIDS." It featured a *cinema verité* presentation of the life of an afflicted black, male, homosexual prostitute—Fabian Bridges. The program offered the viewer a microcosm of the world within which Fabian found himself, that is, a medical establishment confronted with a new, lethal disease for which there is no known cure or vaccine; a public health service threatened with being overwhelmed by AIDS patients; legislators pulled in different ways by their constituents to respond to the epidemic; and an embattled homosexual community aware that its members currently represent more than two-thirds of all AIDS patients.

Following the film, a panel of medical experts, a legislator, a public health official and representatives of several gay rights organizations were asked to comment on the scenes of Fabian moving about the city of Houston, making contacts with men and engaging in sexual acts. The general confusion and unpreparedness of civic authorities to deal with the disease or the civil rights issues it raised were highlighted by the inability of public officials to prevent Fabian's behavior or remove him from the street. While the program recognized that the AIDS virus was indifferent to race, sex, income or age and that others (IV drug users and transfused individuals) were also afflicted with the disease, the film footage and the discussion focused primarily on the male homosexual. Some panel members expressed deep concern that the film depicting Fabian's life would merely serve to exacerbate homophobia across the country and intensify the hysteria that has surfaced in reaction to this still largely unknown disease. They objected to what they perceived to be a distorted vision of the behaviors of persons with AIDS and felt the film did not reflect actions typical of gay men in the community.

The authorities' treatment of Fabian following his arrest for simple theft reflects several concerns. He was kept in solitary confinement; the materials that he handled (paper, pen, cutlery, etc.) were destroyed; he was not physically touched by any of the police or court officers; and to make certain that he did not constitute a threat to the local community of Houston, the charges against him were dropped and the police department purchased one-way airfare for him to Cleveland where he had relatives. To ensure Fabian's departure, the presiding judge personally contributed $20 toward the fare.

BACKGROUND

In 1981 the initial report of Pneumocystis carinii pneumonia (PCP) among five male homosexuals in Los Angeles marked the recognition of what has come to be known as AIDS. In 1984 a human retrovirus, HTLV-III/LAV (human T-cell lymphotropic virus type III/lymphadenopathy-associated virus) now called HIV (human immunodeficiency virus) was determined to be the causative agent of AIDS and in 1985 blood tests for antibodies to the virus were developed and made available.[1]

Over this relatively short period of time, AIDS cases have been reported in all 50 states, the District of Columbia and four territories. It is estimated that there are upwards of 2 million Americans infected with HIV and that 20 to 30 percent of them are expected to develop the disease within 5 years. (By the end of 1994 it is projected that the cumulative cases of AIDS in the United States meeting the Centers for Disease Control [CDC] surveillance definition will total more than 420,000 cases. During 1991 alone, more than 150,000 individuals required medical attention for AIDS.) The CDC cautions, however, that the empirical model upon which these estimates are based may underestimate the morbidity and mortality attributable to AIDS by as much as 20 percent.[2]

In the last half decade, AIDS has reached pandemic proportions. More than 85 countries report the presence of the disease, with some European countries such as Belgium and France reporting a threefold increase in the incidence of the disease annually.[3] It is estimated that in Africa about 5 million persons are presently infected with the virus.

SOCIAL RESPONSES

When the mode of transmission was initially identified with the particular sexual practices and reported promiscuity of homosexuals, many persons viewed AIDS as a consequence of immoral and self-destructive behaviors by a socially disreputable group; the same attitude was held with respect to the intravenous drug user. Religious attitudes toward homosexuality and the social and legal disapproval of drugs also helped to define the AIDS epidemic in its early stages as a disease that was essentially self-inflicted. The historical condemnation of homosexuality and its designation as a felony in over 25 states in this country also permitted many persons to disregard the illness and its consequences.

The interpretation of illness as a punishment for immoral behavior, as well as the impulse to blame the victim, has a very long history in Western culture. Susan Sontag, in her book *Illness as Metaphor*, describes illness as the "night side of life."[4] She reminds us that throughout history, disease has frequently been taken as metaphor, that it has often been represented as supernatural punishment or demonic possession. Death among the Greeks, for instance, was often seen as a consequence of personal fault or as a result of an ancestor's wrongdoing. With the ushering in of Christianity, the association of disease with divine judgment became even more specific and illness came to be seen as appropriate and just punishment. This is most vividly illustrated in the general response to the Bubonic Plague of the fourteenth century. Reactions took two separate directions. First, the plague was treated as an act of God, as a judgment upon sinners in the way Sodom and Gomorrah were reported to have been destroyed as a result of God's displeasure. In response to such a belief, groups of flagellants appeared in different parts of Europe and beat themselves and others bloody in acts of propitiation and atonement. Anti-Semitism also flared up and Jews were attacked and killed because of the belief that they were responsible for spreading the pestilence. On the other hand, there were those who reacted to the plague passively. The death and misery associated with the plague were seen as the very quintessence of order and control. The view taken was that while illness was indeed a punishment God inflicted on whom He willed, He granted clemency to the faithful.[5]

In *Shoah*, an acclaimed documentary on the Nazi Holocaust, one hears repeated these ancient ideas that have reverberated down through history. In the film, the annihilation of the Jews is justified by some of those interviewed as a consequence of divine judgment: they were killed as a result of their moral corruption and their adamantine refusal to accept Jesus as the Messiah.

So, too, the idea of God's justice is presently heard in the United States in relation to the AIDS epidemic. Throughout the country, particularly among fundamentalist Christians, the disease called AIDS is presented as God's scourge levied against homosexuals, drug users and prostitutes. Various references to the Old Testament are made to support this view:

> If a man also lie with mankind, as he lieth with a woman, both of them have committed an abomination: they shall surely be put to death; their blood shall be upon them (Leviticus 20:13).[6]

> Neither shalt thou bring an abomination into thine house, lest thou be a cursed thing like it, but thou shalt utterly detest it and thou shalt utterly abhor it; for it is a cursed thing (Deuteronomy 7:26).[7]

Theological judgment with respect to AIDS is also related to the traditional prohibitions against fornication and abortion. From the point of view of certain religious communities, abortion clinics, family planning and sex education programs are essentially all of a piece. They are viewed as a falling away from God's ordinances concerning the sanctity of marriage and procreation. Responsibility for and guidance in, the moral and ethical education of children belongs solely to the parents and not to the government or other agencies. Even educational programs that attempt to check the spread of AIDS are seen not only as an assault on parental rights with respect to the moral education of a child, but also as introducing libertarian views and inducements for immoral behavior.

American society is currently challenged to strike a balance between the community's responsibility to prevent the spread of illness through various educational and public health measures and the rights of parents to decide how and in what form their children will receive sex education. Despite the Surgeon General's recent national television appearance recommending that children from the earliest grades be informed about the risks associated with sexual intercourse and that they be fully instructed to ensure the maximum safety for themselves and their sexual partners, many religious groups in the country not only are failing to respond to the issue of AIDS, but are also attempting to terminate such sex education programs as do exist.[8]

While it is clear that AIDS is a sexually transmitted disease, sex education alone is not sufficient to change the customs and mores associated with sexual behavior or the extent to which various precautions will or will not be observed. Research has shown, for example, that otherwise sexually knowledgeable young women will avoid birth control measures in order not to be perceived as promiscuous by their sexual partners.[9] Moreover, for some men and women, engaging in sex without birth control is a way of both expressing and calling forth commitment.

The struggle to direct the minds and the sexual behavior of the young is fraught with other difficulties as well. Of significance is the fear among some blacks that sex education and family planning programs may constitute a conspiracy on the part of the white community to perpetrate genocide against them. The first author encountered this largely unspoken concern when, as a guest speaker at Dr. Martin Luther King's Alma Mater, Morehouse College, in Atlanta some years ago, he had occasion to address a group of pre-seminary students on the topic of death and dying. He was challenged by several students who questioned him sharply about the white community's efforts to restrict black population growth. In any program dealing with sex education in the schools, this issue must be addressed if black support for AIDS education is to be successful.

While we have observed that there is a fear in the black community that sex education and family planning organizations have hidden agendas, it must also be recognized that this fear is present in a somewhat different form among white groups. There is a concern that blacks, Hispanics and Asians have greater birthrates than whites and that promotion of birth control can only aggravate a situation in which particular white groups see their numbers overwhelmed by growing minority populations.

Containment of the epidemic, however, is not the only challenge that AIDS presents to American society. The role of professional caregivers is also brought into question. Because of the relative newness of the disease, few health care professionals have had prior training or experience in treating AIDS patients. Information and technologies concerning the disease increase at a rapid rate and professional caregivers are often hard-pressed to keep current. Moreover, the psychological, neuropsychiatric and broader psychosocial aspects of AIDS are still emerging. In the face of the fact that over 70 percent of AIDS patients develop psychiatric or neuropsychiatric signs and symptoms, lack of appropriate therapies often diminishes the professional caregiver's sense of efficacy. As a consequence, many are expressing a growing unease about the AIDS epidemic.[10] This has led, in turn, to a refusal in some instances to accept acutely ill AIDS patients, a reluctance to carry out invasive procedures and autopsies, or a refusal to admit a seropositive person for medical treatment.[11]

Studies are also beginning to show that caregivers are becoming less tolerant of AIDS patients, particularly homosexuals. In one study, three-quarters of the respondents felt that special units for AIDS patients would provide better care than that available in ordinary hospitals, but only 11 percent said they would be willing to work in such units.[12]

FEAR OF AIDS

The general public, too, displays increased fear and anxiety in the face of the specter of AIDS. Almost daily the news media report incidents or issues involving the disease. The frequency of these reports is in response to the public's growing awareness and concern. These concerns include: the risk which children afflicted with AIDS pose to their schoolmates; the advertisement of condoms on television; the distribution of free needles to drug addicts; and the legal and civil propriety of identifying seropositive persons in official records. Still other reports and news stories tell of persons with AIDS who have lost their jobs, their homes, their medical insurance, or the support of their families and friends.

Individuals from all groups and classes of people seem to fear the disease. Dr. Elisabeth Kübler-Ross, the noted psychiatrist who is recognized worldwide for her work among the dying, was forced to end a presentation early when her largely sympathetic, middle-class audience in Virginia demonstratively opposed her suggestion that the community establish a hospital for the care of abandoned children afflicted with AIDS.[13]

It is ironic that AIDS has appeared at a time in history when American youth, who are much more sexually aware and liberated than their forebears, are to a great extent insulated from the immediate experience of death. The present cohort of young men and women often referred to as the "baby boom generation" have, for the most part, experienced death at a distance. Life expectancy for these persons is beyond 70 years. This generation has received the maximum benefits of an urbanized and technologically advanced existence, while modern health care institutions have protected them from general exposure to illness and disease. For them death has been invisible and abstract. In fact, this is the first generation in history in which there has been only a 5 percent chance that an immediate family member would die before a family member of the "baby boom generation" reached adulthood.[14] While death today can be said to be an experience of the aged, the advent of AIDS threatens to effect a profound change in the mortality rates of the young.

In contrast to Sontag's thesis that illness has historically been viewed as supernatural punishment, this age group would explain the AIDS epidemic as a result of failure to practice proper hygienic measures with respect to both sex and drug use. As in so many other aspects of our culture, the "baby boom generation" thinks of illness as something that can be controlled by the individual or prevented, if not cured, by medical science. Such an attitude, however, fails to recognize the extent to which our collective well-being is often dependent upon the good will of strangers. Surgical patients, for instance, must rely on the generosity of those who regularly volunteer their blood and, as sociologist Richard Titmuss has pointed out in his prescient monograph, *The Gift Relationship*, they have traditionally been assured the greatest margin of safety when the blood they received was donated rather than purchased.[15]

Recently, however, the American Medical Association (AMA) has come out in favor of a system of private blood banking, that is, the storing of the patient's own previously donated blood, so that persons anticipating the need for surgery may eliminate the risk of receiving contaminated blood from an anonymous donor. While this may be useful in certain cases where a limited amount of blood will be needed and where the scheduling of the operation can be both planned and controlled, it poses serious limitations in other circumstances. Some of these limitations are: the shelf life of whole blood is only 6 to 8 weeks; an individual is limited in the amount of blood that can be safely withdrawn over a 12-month period; blood must be stored within a reasonable proximity to the patient in the event of immediate need; at least one and one-half hours are required for blood to be thawed; and, finally, the cost of such a program may be prohibitive for many.

Over and above these considerations, however, the AMA's recommendation evokes a prospect of a new mind-set for the American people: a world of the future in which one donates only to oneself or to immediate family members, who in turn must show evidence of being AIDS-free in order to reciprocate in kind. The proposal foreshadows a new definition of community, one characterized not by civic responsibility and neighborliness, but by a dramatic shift toward self-preservation and "lifeboat" ethics and measured in terms of blood purity.

Titmuss's study of blood donation reminds us of the importance of the voluntary act, especially the gift of blood. Such donations, he argues, serve not only to bind a society together, but also to identify it. When we recall the blood philosophy and policies of the Nazi regime, as well as the American public's own attitudes toward race and blood (until 1942 the American Red Cross identified and kept separate white and black blood), the prospect of such a program threatens to assault the sense of community, as well as militate against the traditions of altruism and volunteerism.

Community is, at best, a fragile thing. Research shows both its strengths and its weaknesses; its substance and its volatility. Extensive studies have shown that communities will respond quickly, vigorously and sympathetically to victims of accidents, as well as to victims of natural disasters such as floods, hurricanes or earthquakes.[16] Furthermore, people who are sick or injured are not blamed for their illnesses, particularly if they act in ways that indicate their desire to get well. They are described as victims of, or as suffering from, diseases over which they have no control. On the other hand, persons who contract a disease such as AIDS and who are perceived to have brought the illness on themselves by their lifestyles are generally held responsible for contracting the disease not only by the public, but also by health care personnel. This opprobrium is in sharp contrast to the concern manifested for athletes who incur injuries in the course of play. This comparison helps to clarify that it is the taboo sexual behavior or intravenous drug use that are anathema and not solely the involvement in the development of a disease or injury. Were it simply the latter, individuals who develop lung cancer following years of smoking would be treated with the same degree of disrespect. The negative evaluation of AIDS patients not only results in ostracism, but as research has indicated, also threatens abandonment by caregivers.[17]

The challenge of care, given the psychosocial and neurologic aspects of the disease, presents a configuration of problems and tasks that caregivers have difficulty confronting. In addition to the fears and apprehensions caregivers may harbor, the patients themselves can display a spectrum of problems ranging from irritability and noncompliant behavior, to anger and depression. Furthermore, the patient may also manifest such neurologic symptoms as aphasia, seizures, blindness and dementia, symptoms which can create further problems in patient-caregiver relationships.

At a recent meeting of the American Academy of Arts and Sciences, Paul Volberding, director of the AIDS program at San Francisco Hospital, cautioned his audience that the health care system in San Francisco is showing severe signs of stress.[18] While the rest of the nation has come to look upon San Francisco as a model for coping with the AIDS crisis, Volberding is concerned that the burnout of health care workers, the ever-increasing number of AIDS cases, the competing needs of other patients, as well as the lack of coordinated long-range planning, may overwhelm San Francisco's health care system. Part of the problem is the sheer burden of caring for the increasing numbers of patients given the limited resources, as well as the severe emotional stress experienced by caregivers as a result of watching so many young persons die. While he notes that the most pressing current problem is one of chronic care, the situation will inevitably worsen, Volberding predicts, as the number of AIDS patients increases, making both the acute and the chronic care systems "hopelessly inadequate." In the face of these and other considerations, the moral and ethical cement that has traditionally bound caregivers to patients threatens to crumble.

HISTORICAL PERSPECTIVE

History records the challenges that plagues and pestilences have presented to humankind. In his study, *Plagues and People*, William McNeill cites the many instances of death-dealing epidemics among human populations.[19] He notes that one advantage the West had over the East in the face of deadly epidemics was the role of caring for the sick, which among Christians was a recognized religious duty. As he observes, elementary nursing care, even when all normal services broke down, greatly reduced mortality. The simple provision of food and water by the caregivers allowed many persons to survive who would otherwise have perished from starvation. Moreover, the effect of a prolonged epidemic more often than not strengthened the Church when other social institutions were discredited for not providing needed services. McNeill further observes that the teachings of the Christian gospel made life meaningful, even in the face of immediate death: not only could survivors find spiritual consolation in the vision of heavenly reunion with their dead relatives or friends, but God's hand was also seen in the work of the life-risking caregivers.[20]

The United States, too, has had its share of plagues and epidemics, one of the most notable of which was the outbreak of yellow fever in Philadelphia in 1793. During the course of that long summer and fall, thousands of citizens of the capital city perished. William Powell, in his currently relevant book, *Bring Out Your Dead*, written in 1965, vividly describes the scene Philadelphia presented at that time: the dying were abandoned, the dead left unburied, orphaned children and the elderly wandered the streets in search of food and shelter. Nearly all who could fled the city, including the President, leaving the victims of the fever to their fate. Among those who remained, however, were Dr. Benjamin Rush, a co-signer of the Declaration of Independence; the mayor; a handful of medical colleagues and their assistants; and an appreciable number of clergy. With the help of a small but redoubtable group of ordinary laborers and craftsmen, they undertook the enormous task of maintaining law and order, providing medical care, food and shelter for the sick and helpless, as well as gathering up and burying the dead.[21]

From reading Dr. Rush's diary and voluminous correspondence written during the time of the epidemic, Powell was able to report that what kept Dr. Rush and the others at their posts, even though many of them were made ill by the fever and some died, was their overriding sense of professional obligation, along with a conviction inspired by the precepts of the New Testament.[22] Unlike the Old Testament with its stern and unforgiving ordinances which are presently being called upon to validate a punitive or passive reaction to the AIDS epidemic, the New Testament calls forth a different view of illness and a different vision of the sick. For example:

> Blessed are the merciful, for they shall obtain mercy (Matthew 5:9).[23]

> ...Jesus went about all Galilee, teaching in their synagogues and preaching the gospel of the kingdom and healing all manner of sickness and all manner of disease among the people. And his fame went throughout all Syria; and they brought unto him all sick people that were taken with diverse disease and torments and those who were possessed with demons and those who were epileptics and those who had the palsy; and he healed them (Matthew 4:23-24).[24]

But even this vision, shared by Christians for centuries, which distinguished sickness from sin and which, along with a sense of professional commitment, permitted Dr. Rush and his fellow Philadelphians to risk their lives in the care of victims of yellow fever, may not be sufficient to persuade contemporary caregivers to stay at their posts. The "baby boom generation," well-educated, highly secular and self-oriented, has learned to blame AIDS on groups whom the society defines as deviant and on the fringes of the community—homosexuals and drug users. There is a very strong likelihood, therefore, that today's young health care practitioner may turn away from those perceived as undeserving of care, despite the fact that a 1981 Gallup Poll of the religious beliefs and practices of 14 countries shows that the United States leads the world, not only in church membership, but also in voluntary service.[25]

The situation is made problematic by the fact that professional caregivers perform their duties by reason of the ethics and standards of their professions, beyond whatever religious or moral commitments they may embrace. Moreover, as more is understood about the transmission of AIDS, personal health risk to the caregiver and subsequent fear of contracting the disease are reduced. Other considerations, however, conflict with the traditional code of professional conduct. In addition to holding homosexuals and IV drug users responsible for the AIDS epidemic, caregivers are beginning to view them as self-seeking, imprudent and acting without regard for the condition or well-being of others. Concern for the health of one's family members, as well as the anxiety felt by family and friends for the AIDS caregiver, also threaten to diminish the caregiver's commitment to the task of serving persons with AIDS. Finally, enlightened Christian caregivers who subscribe to the ethic of grace and compassion and the distinction between "sickness and the sin" are challenged by the New Testament theology proclaimed by Paul:

> ...and likewise also the men, leaving the natural use of the woman, burned in their lust one toward another, men with men working unseemliness and receiving in themselves that recompense of their error which was due (Romans 1:27).[26]

Given such a perspective, acts of altruism can become strained and may, ultimately, cease to be offered.

A singular problem in this regard is the issue of AIDS among incarcerated populations where homosexual behavior is extensive and where a substantial number of prison inmates fall within identified high risk groups for AIDS. As with society at large, AIDS within a prison is more than a simple health problem. Decisions concerning prevention, education, identification and treatment, as well as legal and ethical issues related to medical care and its costs, are but some of the problems that confront the correctional administrator.[27]

As of January 1987, there have been 646 confirmed cases of AIDS reported in the prisons of New York, New Jersey and Florida alone.[28] A recent *New York Times* article reports that in New York State AIDS is now the leading cause of death among all prisoners.[29] The threat of AIDS has raised a multiplicity of problems that would have been unimaginable just a few years ago. For example, some defendants report being deprived of their civil rights because court officers refuse to go near them or even take them into court, while other defendants are released or the charges against them dismissed, because they are dying of AIDS. In fact, judges and parole boards are beginning to question whether persons with AIDS should even be prosecuted and whether dying inmates should not be released.

At the Rikers Island correctional facility in New York State, it was estimated in 1986 that of the 50,000 inmates who were sentenced or were pending indictment, between 11,000 and 12,000 were infected with the AIDS virus. Nevertheless, despite the call by correctional officers for the screening of all prisoners for AIDS, state and city policies prohibit such testing. The result is that infected inmates with no confirmed diagnosis are housed with the general prison population. The significance of this policy becomes clear when examined in light of the National Institute of Justice Report on AIDS in correctional facilities which estimated that prior to the advent of AIDS, 30 percent of all inmates engaged in homosexual activity, while 10 to 20 percent of the overall prison population are subject to rape or other involuntary sexual acts.[30] Unless these behaviors are modified, the prospect of AIDS continuing to spread among prison populations is great and with it an increase in fear among prison staff and administrators.

General concern, moreover, is heightened by the fact that blacks and Hispanics, who make up 39 percent of all persons identified with AIDS in the United States, are also overrepresented in prison populations. This awareness has sparked some minority leaders to demand greater resources to educate minority communities.

AIDS: AN UPDATE

The AIDS epidemic is showing an alarming growth rate throughout the world. In 1987, 87 countries reported the presence of the disease. Today, over 175 countries acknowledge its existence with the number of AIDS cases worldwide reported on the increase. The president of the World Health Organization recently predicted that the number of persons afflicted with the AIDS virus will reach 40,000,000 by the end of the decade.

But AIDS is not simply a medical matter. Recently, the senior author was with an American medical group that went to China to study the epidemic. What the experience showed was that there are in effect two faces to the epidemic—one medical and the other political. China was a good place to see both faces of this worldwide crisis.

In China, there are an increasing number of persons who are being infected with the AIDS virus. Officially, this is explained as a result of Chinese nationals having sexual relations with foreigners, through receiving contaminated blood from abroad, or through illegal IV drug use. Importantly, there is no transmission of AIDS reported as a result of homosexuality. As far as official China is concerned, homosexuality is nonexistent. Chinese sociologists, on the other hand, know otherwise. Nevertheless, the reality is that in China homophobia is so pronounced that Chinese health officials would rather blind themselves to the full extent of the disease than admit to the existence of homosexuals.

In the United States, ironically, the opposite prevails. Here, AIDS is perceived essentially as an affliction of homosexuals. For the past 10 years, since the first cases of AIDS among gay men were reported, the American media has identified the epidemic as one for which homosexuals are primarily at risk.

A recent Tom Brokaw TV program on AIDS highlighted that perception even after 10 years—even after IV drug users, women, mothers, children, prostitutes and blood-transfused persons have been identified as sick with, or at risk for, the disease—it was in the person of a dying gay man that the disease was presented to the American public. Like a Chinese official, Tom Brokaw guards the "great wall" that separates "them" from "us." The American media—Tom Brokaw is by no means the exception—continues to promote the idea that AIDS is essentially a gay man's disease. The facts are otherwise. Little more than half of the persons who presently have AIDS identify themselves as homosexual. Actually, the percentage of gay men among all persons with AIDS has continued to decrease over the past 10 years, whereas the percentage of persons with AIDS who are reported IV drug users or related to drug users through family, or sexual contact, has continued to increase. Persons who are not identified with either group are also showing an increase in rates of infection. The media, as well as government spokespersons—both here and abroad—continue, nevertheless, to describe the epidemic as if the general population were not at risk.

To be sure, in the beginning of the epidemic in the United States, the disease, as far as we know, afflicted only homosexuals. Since that time, however, the epidemic has taken on an a different profile. Therein lies one of the primary difficulties. For not only do we adults, but our children also, continue to believe that the epidemic of AIDS has nothing to do with the general heterosexual or non-IV-drug-using population. Importantly, recent research has shown that sexually active high school and college students also accept the media's "message."

It is believed by many, as we have observed, that AIDS is the price one pays for immoral or illicit behavior; and, in effect, to contract the AIDS virus means one got only what one deserved. Regrettably a similar idea can be found sometimes among caregivers of patients dying of lung cancer when they express the belief that if the patients had been more intelligent, or taken seriously the government warnings against smoking, they would not be in the fix they are in. One hears that kind of reasoning with respect to the AIDS epidemic. This is a point of view which not only serves to discourage us from taking the epidemic seriously, but it also serves to separate the people of "good" behavior from those of "bad."

So far we have been talking about the social epidemic of AIDS; let us now focus on the disease itself.

First, the virus is unusual in that it destroys a person's immune system. Thus, the body's ability to ward off the different opportunistic diseases that subsequently present themselves is seriously compromised. For instance, many new cases of tuberculosis are being reported in the United States every month and researchers fear that the increase in the number of cases may be associated with undetected cases of HIV. Ironically, only a few years ago the American Medical Association believed tuberculosis would be soon eliminated from the United States and anticipated the day when TB hospitals could be closed.

The second factor that makes the virus so problematic and different from almost any other contagious disease—especially one that can be sexually transmitted (gonorrhea in some women is an exception)—is the fact that the virus is asymptomatic and can remain so for many years. When syphilis first appeared in Europe in the fifteenth century, for example, the afflicted person knew he was infected and so did everyone else. The florid markings on the body left no doubt as to one's condition. As we know, different diseases present different symptoms. Measles, mumps, chicken pox, scarlet fever and so on, readily demonstrate this. The symptoms of fever and malaise associated with many diseases, moreover, generally discourage intimate interaction with others. With the AIDS virus, however, we have a disease that is not only asymptomatic, but can also remain dormant, while still infectious, for a decade or more. Tragically it has demonstrated that it is grievously lethal as well with a mortality rate of more than 90 percent. Add to this the sexual permissiveness of the present generation and the fact that generally few young heterosexual men and women believe that they are at risk for AIDS, and we are confronted with the prospect of an epidemic of unprecedented proportions.

It is important for us to appreciate the fact that HIV is a disease that is associated with sexuality and thus is also a moral issue in American society. Until Dr. Kinsey published his now famous study on American sexual behavior in the 1940s, and *Playboy,* Dr. Ruth, Oprah Winfrey and others came on the scene, the open discussion of sexuality in America was virtually an impossibility. Even today, sex and sexuality—despite blatant commercial exploitation—is still a stigmatizing and taboo-ridden subject for a great portion of the American population.

It is as if Pandora's Box has been flung open releasing all of our sexual fears and taboos. But, as a society, we are not alone. The same evening in Beijing that Chinese health officials addressed our delegation and assured us that there were no homosexuals in China, two members of our group visited a homosexual bar.

Because we have the same kinds of discrepant and discordant views in our own society as they do in China and the same kinds of disagreements as to what is proper behavior, or what is proper to discuss in public, there is even today relatively little "positive" opposition from the general public to the disease. For the most part, few people are "tackling" the disease where it exists, or "confronting it" where possible. One place where we can "confront" the disease, of course, is in our own personal behavior. To the extent to which HIV is sexually transmitted, or transmitted through IV injection, its avoidance is a question of behavior. But there is the rub—how do we as individuals, or as a society, modify or change our behavior or the behavior of others so as to avoid the disease called AIDS?

HIV is not a disease that has to decimate the populations of the world. The disease has the possibility of being brought under control by human action. The disease is not at all infectious the way hepatitis B is, for instance. Indeed, you have to work hard to contract HIV—you have to go out of your way; you have to roll up your sleeve so to speak, or take off your clothes; you have to find a needle and share it with another person; or most often, you have to go to the effort of engaging in unprotected sexual intercourse a considerable number of times.

HIV is a disease that is controllable—once we make up our minds.

The point is, right now the American community has still not decided to address the epidemic where it is most relevant—that is, on the epidemic's own terms. In New York State, for example, it has been reported that sex education programs in the public schools are being challenged and are at risk of being discontinued.

There are, of course, public officials, educators and health care professionals, as well as AIDS activists and volunteers, who are acting vigorously and with dedication to combat the disease. Many citizen and church groups, moreover, are committed to the struggle. But at the same time, in many instances, we fail to acknowledge the sexuality of high school and college students, or provide them with the knowledge and understanding necessary for them to avoid the risk of contracting HIV.

Case in point: Three years ago, the Minnesota State Board of Education conducted a survey of high school students, with respect to their health and social behavior. Included in the survey were questions relating to their knowledge, attitudes and behavior in regard to the AIDS epidemic. Approximately 90,000 students were surveyed—representing more than 90 percent of all high school students in the state. Not all high school students were allowed to participate in the full survey, however. Questions concerning sexual activity were removed from the survey booklet by officials of some school districts. The questions were deleted on the grounds that they would be too offensive to the students, or would invade their privacy, or that parents would be offended by the school board usurping their parental responsibility.

The Report, however, showed the following: 60 percent of the senior girls and 62 percent of the senior boys reported that they were sexually active. Moreover, 29 percent of the 9th graders reported having experienced sexual intercourse at least once. These are many of the same students for whom high school principals and other school officials expressed concern that the subject of sexuality would be too sensitive for them to address.

The Board of Education Report was made available for free distribution on January 1, 1990. There are, however, high school teachers in Minnesota who have never heard of the published report, let alone read it. The Report has never been discussed except once in the *Minneapolis Star.* It has never been commented upon by any television station in Minnesota, as far as is known. Recently the senior author had the occasion to speak to over 120 Minnesota high school teachers and only one in 10 knew the results of the survey.

We need to take a much harder look at this issue than we have so far. It is a small minority of people who, in effect, say, when they oppose sex education in the schools, or surveys of this kind, that they would rather risk the alternative (that is, pregnancy, disease, or possibly death from AIDS) than for their children to be knowledgeable about, or protected from, its threat. Parents, moreover, who claim that sex education belongs in the home, do not necessarily practice what they preach. The Minnesota Study shows, for instance, that only 31 percent of the 12th graders reported that their source of information about sex came from their parents, while 80 percent reported that their information about sex came from friends. (The percentages add up to more than 100 because students were allowed to give more than one answer.) Eighty-four percent of the 12th graders, furthermore, reported that their knowledge about AIDS came from TV and radio, compared to only 22 percent of the students who reported that their information about AIDS came from their parents. Obviously, such discrepancies between words and actions need to be addressed if we are going to confront the epidemic successfully—squeamishness or prudishness is not the way to respond to this life-threatening epidemic.

Research shows that students at primarily white middle-class high schools, colleges and universities engage in behaviors that put them at risk for sexually transmitted diseases—including HIV. The senior author's study of 1000 first-year students at the University of Minnesota shows that 78.6 percent have already experienced sexual intercourse. This figure is comparable to findings at the University of Vermont and to other college studies. Not only do the different studies show that the overwhelming majority of students never discuss their sexual behavior or sexual history with their partners, but the studies also show a lower rate of condom use than among high school students. Significantly, the studies also show that many sexually active students will have more than one sexual partner a year. At the University of Minnesota, for instance, 53 percent of the sexually active students reported two or more partners within the year. This, of course, is significant for the potential spread of any venereal disease—including HIV—especially when so few male students report the regular use of a condom.

What we need to acknowledge is the extent of the sexual revolution that has occurred in the United States over the past three decades. A colleague at an eastern university has been conducting surveys of students with respect to their exposure to sexually transmitted diseases. He began his research before the advent of the AIDS epidemic. What he reports is that over the past ten years, sexual activity on his campus has increased appreciably particularly on the part of first-year students. He reports that first-year students are more sexually active than are seniors. This may strike us as peculiar, but he reports that it has to do with the fact that they are the children of the Vietnam generation. As such, they possess, as well as reflect, the attitudes of their previously rebellious parents regarding such issues as political authority, freedom of expression and personal privacy. Our colleague speculates that these young men and women are acting out their liberal politics, sexually, not unlike what their parents did, politically, a generation earlier. This would also seem to be reflected in the percentage of young women, as well as young men, who become sexually active much earlier than their parents. His studies show, for instance, that while a senior on campus may have two sexual partners a year, a sexually active first-year student may have three partners. And, of course, as has been noted earlier, what is important for the spread of any venereal disease, is the number of partners that one may have—especially when there is unprotected sex.

What we found at the University of Minnesota is that the more sexually active the student, the less likely a condom will be utilized. Our study showed that two-thirds of the students reported using condoms during their first act of sexual intercourse but only one-third reported using a condom during their last act of sexual intercourse. The implications of this finding are quite apparent and are further borne out by the evidence that rates of sexually transmitted diseases among American college students are increasing.

Ironically, the different studies also show that students, for the most part, know all about venereal diseases, including HIV and how these diseases are transmitted sexually. They, in fact, know all they need to know to protect themselves from any sexually transmitted disease. What seems to take precedence over their knowledge, however, is that they believe that they are not at risk. Particularly, there is the strong belief expressed that they are essentially exempt from the AIDS epidemic because it is a gay man's disease, or an IV drug user's disease, or a disease of black men and women who live in the inner city.

What we need to recognize, if we are to understand the attitudes of young people toward the epidemic, is the fact that they have spent the last 10 years in front of a television set, where they have been continually reassured that this is not a disease that concerns them personally. The reason they do not act in a way consistent with their intellectual awareness is simply that they do not believe that, as non-IV-drug-using heterosexuals, they are at risk for HIV.

But there is more to the epidemic that we have to be concerned about than simply the student's sense of invulnerability. Two other factors need to be mentioned that potentially increase the risk that the virus will spread through high school and college populations. The two factors are sexual networking and hypergamy.

The concept of sexual networking refers to the web of interconnecting relationships that is created when the members of a group or community interact. The network will expand or contract depending upon the number of social or physical contacts that are made by each individual over a period of time. For instance, if all students were virgins or if sexually active students were monogamous, that is, restricted their sexual behavior to only one other person, then a sexual network would not exist and the risk of HIV transmission or any other sexually transmitted disease, would be virtually nil. But students who are sexually active with more than two partners make up a sexual network that can facilitate the spread of any disease including HIV.

Sociologists call college campuses semi-bounded populations. In some ways they could be described as captive populations, somewhat like patients in a hospital or inmates in prison. That is, if anything is going around, it will come around because the same people are continually interacting with each other. We see this phenomenon in our prisons where HIV has spread dramatically over the past few years despite all efforts on the part of prison authorities to prohibit both homosexual behavior and/or IV drug use. Last year according to the Justice Department, HIV infection in American prisons increased 86 percent.

In a study done at an eastern university, sexually active students reported having more than three partners over the course of one year. What this means from a sexual network perspective is that literally thousands of students are involved, albeit indirectly, in each sexual act. The implications of this fact for the epidemic are obvious, particularly when couples forego disease protection.

Permit us to interject a comment about disease control and birth control as they relate to this discussion. Probably the majority of single, urban, middle-class women today who are sexually active rely on the birth control pill. Upper-middle-class young women, particularly, rely on the pill. The pill, with rare exception, emancipates them from the risk of pregnancy. Of course, the risk of contracting a sexually transmitted disease is still present, but young people today are confident that penicillin and other antibiotics will take care of that contingency. They have come to believe in the miracle of modern medicine and the efficacy of a "Magic Bullet." Young women from rural areas or small towns, however, are oftentimes not as fortunate to have access to the pill as urban women. Family and religious attitudes and the proscription against premarital sexual intercourse and such factors as greater lack of anonymity, tend to limit their options to a somewhat greater degree then their urban counterparts. Consequently, they rely more frequently on condoms. This is one of the findings from a survey at a prestigious eastern school located in a rural state. It was reported that sexually active women from out-of-state primarily used the pill, while in-state women, on the other hand, relied on the condom. The upshot of this difference in behavior on the part of these young women from different social and geographic backgrounds was shown in their different rates of sexually transmitted diseases. The out-of-state women reported almost twice the rate of infection from venereal disease as did their in-state counterparts—31 percent compared to 17 percent.

This brings us to the second factor—hypergamy. Hypergamy means to marry up. It is an anthropological term that refers to a practice found among East Indian families of arranging a marriage for their daughters to a man of higher status within a particular caste. It is a useful concept for us when we study the sexual behavior of college students because of what we have just described regarding social class differences and the risk of venereal disease. It is also a useful concept in understanding the dating and mating practices of young American men and women. In brief, the presence of urban, upper-middle class men and women on a prestigious college campus located in a rural area in which there are also in-state students means that there will be considerable competition for potential marital partners. And as we have come to learn this will involve both sexual experimentation as well as partner exchange among students of different social backgrounds.

In brief, it can be stated that unless we find a vaccine or cure for the virus, the risk of it being spread among college students continues to increase. And what is important to recognize is that in all likelihood it will be spread by those students who are most socially attractive, affluent and geographically mobile. Consider for a moment Spring Break. At this festive time of the year tens of thousands of young people, mostly college students, will gather at locations such as Daytona Beach, Sanabel Island, Padre Island and Balboa Beach. They will come from Minnesota, Oregon, Texas, Vermont and probably from every other state in the Union. Today, according to the Department of Public Health, the percentage of college students who are suspected of being HIV-positive is higher than in the general population—it is estimated to be around 2.5 per thousand. Some of the young people who arrive at these resort areas, without doubt, will engage in sexual relations—even those who may otherwise be in a monogamous relationship. Such casual sexual behavior is called "off-island" sex by the students. The rationale is that what one does outside of one's own town doesn't count; it is time out of life, as it were.

Sexual casualness is not limited, however, to "off-island" occasions like Spring Break. The Minnesota Survey showed, for instance, that 11 percent of the student respondents had sexual relations with persons whose names they did not know. The same kind of behavior can be expected during Spring Break. And as it has been observed, it will be those students who can afford a vacation and who feel most secure about their health and well-being, as well as their invulnerability to HIV, who will be most involved.

Finally, what needs to be realized is that there is not just one—but six—related AIDS epidemics. First there is the epidemic among gay or homosexual men. While the percentage of gay men among the total number of AIDS cases is less than it was, one should not be misled by newspaper headlines. The epidemic among gay men continues. In 1991 alone, the number of AIDS cases among gay men increased 12 percent.

The second epidemic is among young heterosexual women whose sexual partners are IV-drug-using men infected with the virus and/or bisexual men; AIDS cases among this group increased 29 percent in 1991.

The third epidemic is among heterosexual men who are IV drug users; they reported a 22 percent increase in AIDS cases in 1991.

The fourth epidemic affects young children; it is called pediatric AIDS. These are children born to mothers who are HIV-positive. The number of such children afflicted with AIDS increased almost 30 percent in 1991. It is important to note that a child born of an HIV-infected mother stands a 30 to 50 percent chance of contracting the disease. Of those who do, the majority will not live past their fifth birthday. This last fact is just one more of the many reasons why this disease is so serious. No other disease in human history has threatened to kill the next generation. Syphilis killed children as did measles, but the percentage of such deaths to births was relatively low, perhaps 3 to 5 percent—no more than 10 percent. The AIDS epidemic, on the other hand, has the potential of killing almost one out of every two babies that is born of an HIV-infected mother. Nothing like this disease has ever been seen before in terms of its potential to threaten not only the life of a child but also the very survival of a society.

The fifth epidemic is called the "undetermined" cases of AIDS. There are today almost 6000 AIDS cases in which the source of infection is unknown. It is believed, however, that these cases can be accounted for, in part, through the sexual behavior of covert bisexual men who contract the disease and transmit it to their wives or other sexual partners. This conclusion is based upon a study conducted at the University of Minnesota in 1990, in which the social characteristics of persons with a known mode of transmission were compared with those of the "undetermined" cases. This fifth epidemic is just beginning and the number of persons who have contracted AIDS by this mode, while presently small, is, nevertheless, growing. While the study shows that the majority of persons who constitute the "undetermined" cases are middle-aged men and women who live in non-metropolitan areas, there is good reason to believe that before long this bridging phenomenon will also come to affect younger sexually active men and women—especially those young men and women who are today on our college campuses. There is good reason to say this. Research shows that many bisexuals are also young, well-educated professionals who reside in metropolitan areas and it is reasonable to assume that they maintain college or university connections. They have the potential, therefore, to be part of the sexual network that we have described—a network that can probably be found on every campus across the United States. The sixth epidemic which has yet to materialize, will, we predict, be among this young adult population. The Centers for Disease Control, however, has offered some evidence that this epidemic has already begun.

ROLE OF SOCIAL SCIENCE

In the face of a burgeoning pandemic for which there is currently no vaccine for prevention or medication for cure, the question before us is what can social science contribute to the understanding and mitigation of the wide range of social and psychological, as well as clinical problems associated with AIDS?

If education is one of our major lines of defense against this lethal disease, it is our challenge as professionals and as community members to determine what the major social issues are and to bring to them the knowledge requisite to increased understanding and, hopefully, resolution.

Sociologists have already begun to address the challenge of AIDS, both as educators and as researchers. An organization known as the Sociologist AIDS Network (SAN) has been formed and an agenda drawn up that includes the development of a bibliography on the social dimensions of AIDS, the publication of a newsletter and the compilation of a directory of sociologists working in the area.[31]

Karolynn Siegel directs sociological research on AIDS at Memorial Sloan-Kettering Cancer Center in New York City and is presently studying the sexual behavior of gay men. Siegel and others have also made a content analysis of AIDS information brochures published around the country. It is their judgment that many brochures fail either to inform successfully or to motivate for change. In order to effect a change in behavior, they conclude, anxiety levels must be high enough to promote change, but not so high that they trigger denial.[32]

Albert Chabot, a medical sociologist whose area of specialty is the sociology of death, has established a program called "Wellness" that provides training for volunteers who offer personal attention to individuals with AIDS. The program also provides them with information about relevant medical and social resources in the Detroit community.[33]

Jill Joseph, an epidemiologist, with her colleagues at the University of Michigan School of Public Health, is studying 1000 sexually active gay men from the Chicago area. The study is designed to determine to what extent gay men are changing or modifying their attitudes and behaviors in response to the perceived risk of AIDS. Preliminary findings indicate that about 80 percent of the subjects have changed their behavior in some way to reduce the risk of contracting AIDS.[34]

Levi Kamel, a former director of AIDS services in California, designs AIDS education programs. He works in small towns where gay populations are largely invisible. By drawing upon his skills in qualitative research methods, he is able to estimate the size of the gay community and its level of consciousness about the epidemic.[35] Such ethnographic research makes it possible to design and estimate the costs associated with proposed educational programs.

Samuel Friedman, of Narcotic and Drug Research, Inc., is conducting research on the potential for organizing education and self-help programs among IV drug users. There are several strong inhibitors to self-organization among this population. On the one hand, the illegality of the activity makes organization dangerous, while on the other hand, time, money and attention to the addiction leave few resources for other activities.[36]

Medical and sociological research teams have made significant progress since 1981. Over this brief period of time the etiologic agent of AIDS has been identified, serologic tests to check the blood supply have been developed and recommendations for the prevention of AIDS have been published. Sociologic understanding came first, however. It was the early research of William Darrow, a research sociologist at the Centers for Disease Control and others that enabled the development of sociograms (i.e., a diagrammatic display of social linkages) of sexual contacts which linked AIDS patients in different cities. By questioning these homosexual men, specific behaviors and sexual practices were uncovered which allowed for greater understanding of the manner in which AIDS was transmitted. This information was critical and continues to be of the utmost importance for AIDS education and prevention programs.[37]

Social scientists actively involved in AIDS education and research programs have expressed concern, however, that neither public policy makers nor behavioral scientists are responding appropriately to this social problem, a problem that the National Academy of Sciences recently went on record as describing as the greatest catastrophe of the twentieth century.[38]

In the face of this devastating disease and the absence of an effective cure, our only recourse to limit the spread of AIDS is effective educational programs directed toward prevention of the transmission of the virus. Even if these programs are successful, other programs will be needed which focus on the mitigation of the many social and psychological problems that follow in the wake of an AIDS diagnosis.

NOTES

1. *Public Health Reports.* 1986. 101:341-342.
2. Ibid., p. 342.
3. Michael Serrill. 1987. In the Grip of the Scourge. *Time* (February 16): 58-59.
4. Susan Sontag. 1977. *Illness as Metaphor.* New York: Farrar, Straus & Giroux, p. 3.
5. Ibid.
6. *Holy Bible,* Authorized King James Version, New Scofield Reference Edition. 1967. New York: Oxford University Press, p. 153.
7. Ibid., p. 227.
8. *Minneapolis Star and Tribune,* 1986 (November 28).
9. Arland Thorton and Marlene Studor. 1987. Adolescent Religiosity and Contraceptive Usage. *Journal of Marriage and the Family* 49:117-128.
10. Leon McKusick. 1986. *What To Do About AIDS: Physicians and Mental Health Professionals Discuss the Issues.* Berkeley: University of California Press.
11. Odyssey of AIDS Victims Ends in Death. 1983. *American Medical News,* November 4:3 (See also T.C. Gayle and D.G. Ostrow. 1986. Psychiatric and Ethical Issues Pertinent to the Design and Evaluation of AIDS Health Care Programs. *Quality Review Bulletin* 12(8):286-294).
12. C.J. Douglas and T. Kalam. 1985. Homophobia Among Physicians and Nurses: An Empirical Study. *Hospital and Community Psychiatry* 36:1309-1311.
13. Wayne Engel. 1986. AIDS: Dealing with the Hysteria. *Virginia Medical Journal* 113:222.
14. Robert Fulton and Greg Owen. 1987. Death and Society. *Omega* 18:379-395.
15. Richard Titmuss. 1971. *The Gift Relationship.* New York: Vintage Books, p. 22.
16. K. David Pijawka, Beverly Cuthbertson and Richard S. Olson. 1987. Coping with Extreme Hazard Events: Emerging Themes in Natural and Technological Disaster Research. *Omega* 18:281-297.
17. Gayle and Ostrow, op. cit.
18. Deborah Barnes. 1987. AIDS Stresses Health Care in San Francisco. *Science* 235:964.
19. William H. McNeill. 1976. *Plagues and Peoples.* Garden City: Anchor.
20. Ibid., p. 108.
21. J.H. Powell. 1965. *Bring Out Your Dead.* New York: Times, Inc.
22. Ibid., passim.
23. *Holy Bible,* op. cit., p. 998.
24. Ibid., p. 997.
25. Oxford Analytica. 1986. *America in Perspective.* Boston: Houghton Mifflin, pp. 121-124.
26. *Holy Bible,* op. cit., p. 998.
27. National Institute of Justice. 1986. *AIDS in Correctional Facilities: Issues and Options.* Washington, DC: Department of Justice, U.S. Government Printing Office, pp. 10-13.
28. Loc. cit.
29. *The New York Times.* 1987 (March 5).
30. National Institute of Justice, op. cit., p. 15.
31. Ellen Berg. 1986. Sociological Perspectives on AIDS. *Footnotes* (American Sociological Association) 14:8.
32. Loc. cit.

33. Loc. cit.
34. *ISR Newsletter.* 1986. (Autumn):3.
35. Berg, op. cit., p. 8.
36. Ibid., p. 9.
37. Ibid., p. 8.
38. *The New York Times.* 1986 (November).

16

Social Policy Assumptions and Principles on Terminal Care, Spirituality, Bereavement and AIDS

International Work Group on Death, Dying and Bereavement

ASSUMPTIONS AND PRINCIPLES UNDERLYING STANDARDS FOR TERMINAL CARE*

There is agreement that patients with threatening illnesses, including progressive malignancies, need appropriate therapy and treatment throughout the course of the illness. At one stage, therapy is directed toward investigation and intervention in order to control or cure such illness and alleviate associated symptoms. For some persons, however, the time comes when cure and remission are beyond the capacity of current treatment. It is then

* The IWG Committee on Terminal Care: Florence S. Wald (Chairperson), Ina Ajemian, Donna Bettes, Esther Lucille Brown, Robert Buckingham, Loma Feigenberg, Zelda Foster, Robert Fulton, Alice M. Heath, Barbara Hill, Jeffrey Houpt, Richard Kalish, Bernice Kastenbaum, Robert Kastenbaum, Priscilla Kissick, Sylvia Lack, Ida M. Martinson, Douglas McKell, Balfour Mount, Colin M. Parkes, Cicely Saunders, John Scott, Kenneth Spilman, E. Carleton Sweetser, Richard J. Torpie, Mary L.S. Vachon, Henry J. Wald, Thomas West and J. William Worden.

that the intervention must shift to what is often termed "palliative treatment," which is designed to control pain in the broadest sense and to provide personal support for patients and family during the terminal phase of illness. In general, palliative care requires limited use of apparatus and technology, rather extensive personal care and an ordering of the physical and social environment is seen to be therapeutic in itself.

There are two complementary systems of treatment which may often overlap: one system is concerned with eliminating a curable disease and the other with relieving the symptoms resulting from the relentless progress of an incurable illness. There must be openness, interchange and overlap between the two systems so that the patient receives continuous appropriate care. The patient should not be subjected to aggressive treatment that offers no real hope of being effective in curing or controlling the disease and which may only cause further distress. Obviously, the clinician must be on the alert for any shifts that may occur in the course of a terminal illness, which may make the patient again a candidate for active treatment. Patients suffer not only from inappropriate active care, but also from inept terminal care. This is well documented by studies that only confirm what dying patients and their families know at first hand.

These principles have been prepared as an aid to those who have initiated or are planning programs for the terminally ill in delineating standards of care.

General Considerations

1. *Assumption:* The care of the dying is a process involving needs of the patient, family and caregivers.
   Principle: The interaction of these groups of individuals must constantly be assessed with the aim being the best possible care of the patient. This cannot be accomplished, however, if the needs of family and caregivers are negated.
2. *Assumption:* The problems of the patient and family facing terminal illness include a wide variety of issues: psychologic, legal, social, spiritual, economic and interpersonal.
   Principle: Care requires collaboration of many disciplines working as an integrated clinical team, meeting for frequent discussions and with commonness of purpose.
3. *Assumption:* Dying tends to produce a feeling of isolation.
   Principle: All that counteracts unwanted isolation should be encouraged; social events and shared work, inclusive of all involved, should be arranged so that meaningful relations can be sustained and developed.

4. *Assumption:* It has been the tradition to train caregivers not to become emotionally involved, but in terminal illness the patient and family need to experience the personal concern of those taking care of them.
   Principle: Profound involvement without loss of objectivity should be allowed and fostered; realizing this may present certain risks to the caregiver.
5. *Assumption:* Health care services customarily lack coordination.
   Principle: The organizational structure must provide links with existing health care professionals in the community.
6. *Assumption:* A supportive physical environment contributes to the sense of well being of patients, family and caregivers.
   Principle: The environment should provide adequate space, furnishings that put people at ease, the reassuring presence of personal belongings and symbols of life cycles.

The Patient

1. *Assumption:* There are patients for whom aggressive curative treatment becomes increasingly inappropriate.
   Principle: These patients need highly competent professionals, skilled in terminal care.
2. *Assumption:* The symptoms of terminal disease can be controlled.
   Principle: The patient should be kept as symptom-free as possible. Pain in all its aspects should be controlled. The patient must remain alert and comfortable.
3. *Assumption:* Patients' needs may change over time.
   Principle: Staff must recognize that other services may have to be involved, but that continuity of care should be provided.
4. *Assumption:* Care is most effective when the patient's lifestyle is maintained and life philosophy respected.
   Principle: The terminally ill patient's own framework of values, preferences and life outlook must be taken into account in planning and conducting treatment.
5. *Assumption:* Patients are often treated as if incapable of understanding or of making decisions.
   Principle: Patients' wishes for information about their condition should be respected. They should be allowed full participation in their care and a continuing sense of self-determination and self-control.
6. *Assumption:* Dying patients often suffer through helplessness, weakness, isolation and loneliness.

Principle: The patient should have a sense of security and protection. Involvement of family and friends should be encouraged.

7. *Assumption:* The varied problems and anxieties associated with terminal illness can occur at any time of day or night.
   Principle: Twenty-four-hour care must be available seven days a week for the patient and family where and when it is needed.

The Family

1. *Assumption:* Care is usually directed toward the patient. In terminal illness the family must be the unit of care.
   Principle: Help should be available to all those involved, whether patient, relation or friend, to sustain communication and involvement.
2. *Assumption:* The course of the terminal illness involves a series of clinical and personal decisions.
   Principle: Interchange between patient, family and clinical team is essential to enable an informed decision to be made.
3. *Assumption:* Many people do not know what the dying process involves.
   Principle: The family should be given time and opportunity to discuss all aspects of dying, death and related emotional needs with the staff.
4. *Assumption:* The patient and family need the opportunity for privacy and being together.
   Principle: The patient and family should have time alone and privacy both while the patient is living and after death occurs. A special space may need to be provided.
5. *Assumption:* Complexity of treatment and time-consuming procedures can cause disruption for the patient and the family.
   Principle: Procedures must be so arranged as not to interfere with adequate time for patient, family and friends to be together.
6. *Assumption:* Patients and families facing death frequently experience a search for the meaning of their lives, making the provision of spiritual support essential.
   Principle: The religious, philosophic and emotional components of care are as essential as the medical, nursing and social components and must be available as part of the team approach.
7. *Assumption:* Survivors are at risk emotionally and physically during bereavement.
   Principle: The provision of appropriate care for survivors is the

responsibility of the team who gave care and support to the deceased.

The Staff

1. *Assumption:* The growing body of knowledge in symptom control, patient-and-family-centered care and other aspects of the care of the terminally ill is now readily available.
   Principle: Institutions and organizations providing terminal care must orient and educate new staff and keep all staff informed about developments as they occur.
2. *Assumption:* Good terminal care presupposes emotional investment on the part of the staff.
   Principle: Staff needs time and encouragement to develop and maintain relationships with patients and relatives.
3. *Assumption:* Emotional commitment to good terminal care will often produce emotional exhaustion.
   Principle: Effective staff support systems must be readily available.

ASSUMPTIONS AND PRINCIPLES OF SPIRITUAL CARE*

In those areas of the world where medical care has been shaped by sophisticated technologies and complicated health care delivery systems, efforts to humanize patient care are essential if the integrity of the human being is not to be obscured by the system. This is especially needed for individuals with chronic maladies or those who are in the process of dying.

Dying is more than a biological occurrence. It is a human, social and spiritual event. Too often the spiritual component of patients is neglected. The challenge to the health care provider is to recognize the spiritual dimension of patient care and to make resources available for those individuals who wish them and in the form desired.

Spirituality is concerned with the transcendental, inspirational and existential way to live one's life as well as, in a fundamental and profound sense, with the person as a human being. The search for spirituality may be heightened as one confronts death. This uniquely human concern is expressed in a variety of ways, both formal and informal. Those who provide care for dying persons must respect each person's spiritual beliefs and

---

* The IWG Committee on Spiritual Care: Inge Corless and Florence Wald (Chairpersons), Norman Autton, Sally Bailey, Marjory Cockburn, Roderick Cosh, Barrie DeVeber, Iola DeVeber, David Head, Dorothy C.H. Ley, John Mauritzen, Jane Nichols, Patrice O'Connor, and Takeshi Saito.

preferences and develop the resources necessary to meet the spiritual needs of patients, family members and staff. These resources and associated support should be offered as necessary throughout the bereavement period.

While the modern hospice movement has arisen within Western society with its particular cultural, social and spiritual milieu, the following principles may be applicable in and adapted to other countries and cultures. Ultimately the Assumptions and Principles of Spiritual Care should influence other aspects of health care and be integrated into the larger system. Their need and manner of implementation, however, will be shaped by the spiritual life of a given individual and society.

General Considerations

1. *Assumption:* Each person has a spiritual dimension.
   Principle: In the total care of a person, her spiritual nature must be considered along with the mental, emotional and physical dimensions.
2. *Assumption:* A spiritual orientation influences mental, emotional and physical responses to dying and bereavement.
   Principle: Caregivers working with dying and bereaved persons should be sensitive to this interrelationship.
3. *Assumption:* Although difficult, facing terminal illness, death and bereavement can be a stimulus for spiritual growth.
   Principle: Persons involved in these circumstances may wish to be given spiritual questions, time and attention.
4. *Assumption:* In a multicultural society a person's spiritual nature is expressed in religious and philosophical beliefs and practices which differ widely depending upon one's race, sex, class, religion, ethnic heritage and experience.
   Principle: No single approach to spiritual care is satisfactory for all in a multicultural society; many kinds of resources are needed.
5. *Assumption:* Spirituality has many facets. It is expressed and enhanced in a variety of ways both formal and informal, religious and secular, including, but not limited to: symbols, rituals, practices, patterns and gestures, art forms, prayers and meditation.
   Principle: A broad range of opportunities for expressing and enhancing one's spirituality should be available and accessible.
6. *Assumption:* The environment shapes and can enhance or diminish one's spirituality.
   Principle: Care should be taken to offer settings which will accommodate individual preference as well as communal experience.

7. *Assumption:* Spiritual concerns often have a low priority in health care systems.
   Principle: Health care systems presuming to offer total care should plan for and include spiritual care as reflected in a written statement of philosophy and resources of time, money and staff.
8. *Assumption:* Spiritual needs can arise at any time of the day or night, any day of the week.
   Principle: A caring environment should be in place to enhance and promote spiritual work at any time, not just at designated times.
9. *Assumption:* Joy is part of the human spirit. Humor is a leaven needed even, or especially, in times of adversity of despair.
   Principle: Caregivers, patients and family members should feel free to express humor and to laugh.

The Individual and the Family

1. *Assumption:* Human beings have diverse beliefs, understandings and levels of development in spiritual matters.
   Principle: Caregivers should be encouraged to understand various belief systems and their symbols, as well as to seek to understand an individual's particular interpretation of them.
2. *Assumption:* Individuals and their families may have divergent spiritual insights and beliefs. They may not be aware of these differences.
   Principle: Caregivers should be aware of differences in spirituality within a family or close relationship and be alert to any difficulties which might ensue.
3. *Assumption:* The degree to which the patient and family wish to examine and share spiritual matters is highly individual.
   Principle: Caregivers must be nonintrusive and sensitive to individual desires.
4. *Assumption:* Health care institutions and professionals may presume they understand, or may ignore, the spiritual needs of dying persons.
   Principle: Spiritual needs can only be determined through a thoughtful review of spiritual assumptions, beliefs, practices, experiences, goals and perceived needs with the patient, or family and friends.
5. *Assumption:* People are not always aware of, and may not be able or wish to articulate, spiritual issues.
   Principle: (a) Caregivers should be aware of individual desires and sensitive to unexpressed spiritual issues. (b) Individuals need access to resources and to people who are committed to deepened exploration of and communication about spiritual issues.
6. *Assumption:* Much healing and spiritual growth can occur in an

individual without assistance. Many people do not desire or need professional assistance in their spiritual development.
Principle: Acknowledgment and support, listening to and affirming an individual's beliefs or spiritual concerns should be offered and may be all that is needed.

7. *Assumption:* Patients may have already provided for their spiritual needs in a manner satisfactory to themselves.
   Principle: The patient's chosen way of meeting spiritual needs should be honored by the caregivers.
8. *Assumption:* The spiritual needs of dying persons and their families may vary during the course of the illness and fluctuate with changes in physical symptoms.
   Principle: Caregivers need to be alert to the varying spiritual concerns that may be expressed directly or indirectly during different phases of illness.
9. *Assumption:* Patients and their families are particularly vulnerable at the time of impending death.
   Principle: Caregivers should guard against proselytizing for particular types of beliefs and practices.
10. *Assumption:* As death approaches, spiritual concerns may arise which may be new or still unresolved.
    Principle: (a) Caregivers should be prepared to work with new concerns and insights, as well as those which are long-standing. (b) Caregivers must recognize that not all spiritual problems can be resolved.
11. *Assumption:* The spiritual care of the family may affect the dying person.
    Principle: Spiritual care of family and friends is an essential component of total care for the dying.
12. *Assumption:* The family's need for spiritual care does not end with the death of the patient.
    Principle: Spiritual care may include involvement by caregivers in the funeral and should be available throughout the bereavement period.

The Caregivers

1. *Assumption:* Caregivers, like patients, may have or represent different beliefs as well as different spiritual or religious backgrounds and insights.
   Principle: Caregivers have the right to expect respect for their belief systems.

2. *Assumption:* Many health care workers may be unprepared or have limited personal development in spiritual matters.
   Principle: (a) Staff members should be offered skillfully designed opportunities for exploration of values and attitudes about life and death, their meaning and purpose. (b) Caregivers need to recognize their limitations and make appropriate referrals when the demands for spiritual care exceed their abilities or resources.
3. *Assumption:* The clergy is usually seen as having primary responsibility for the spiritual care of the dying.
   Principle: Caregivers should be aware that they each have the potential for providing spiritual care, as do all human beings and should be encouraged to offer spiritual care to dying patients and their families as needed.
4. *Assumption:* Caregivers may set goals for the patient, the family and themselves which are inflexible and unrealistic. This may inhibit spontaneity and impede the development of a sensitive spiritual relationship.
   Principle: Caregivers and health care institutions should temper spiritual goals with realism.
5. *Assumption:* Ongoing involvement with dying and bereaved persons may cause a severe drain of energy and uncover old and new spiritual issues for the caregiver.
   Principle: Ongoing spiritual education, growth and renewal should be a part of a staff support program, as well as a personal priority for each caregiver.

The Community

1. *Assumption:* Spiritual resources are available within the community and can make a valuable contribution to the care of the dying patient.
   Principle: Spiritual counselors from the community should be integral members of the caregiving team.
2. *Assumption:* No one caregiver can be expected to understand or address all the spiritual concerns of patients and families.
   Principle: Staff members addressing the needs of patients and families should utilize spiritual resources and caregivers available in the community.

Education

1. *Assumption:* Contemporary education for health care professionals often lacks reference to the spiritual dimension of care.

Principle: Health care curricula should foster an awareness of the spiritual dimension in the clinical setting.

2. *Assumption:* Education in spiritual care is impeded by a lack of fundamental research.
   Principle: Research about spiritual care is needed to create a foundation of knowledge which will enhance education and enrich and increase the spiritual aspect of the provision of health care.
3. *Assumption:* Freedom from bias is a problem in the conduct of research into spiritual care.
   Principle: Research should be carried out into the development and application of valid and reliable measures of evaluation.

ASSUMPTIONS AND PRINCIPLES REGARDING BEREAVEMENT*

We are all vulnerable to the profound feelings that accompany loss, whether they be of our own impending death or loss of health, the death or loss of health of someone we love, the loss of relationships, function, dreams, or possessions. Loss can result in a wide range of emotional, physical, intellectual, social, familial, economic and spiritual disruptions.

Grief and bereavement are normal and can be resolved with one's already existing resources. However, depending on a number of factors and circumstances, bereaved people may require the assistance of appropriately trained persons to provide a climate of support and acceptance.

General Considerations

1. *Assumption:* Grief is normal and is often resolved with one's existing resources.
   Principles: Since many grieving persons do not require professional intervention, caregivers may be helpful by simply acknowledging and affirming the normalcy of the process.
2. *Assumption:* Grief is experienced in varying combinations of intensity and duration.
   Principle: At any time in the grieving process, care may be needed and should be accessible.
3. *Assumption:* The problems of the bereaved vary greatly. Grief may

---

* The IWG Committee on Bereavement: Jane Nichols (Chairperson), Elizabeth Berrey, Jerry Coash, William Lamers, Jack Lynch, Joy Rogers and Kenneth Spilman. Contributors: Inge B. Corless, Loma Feigenberg, Margaret Miles, Balfour M. Mount, Colin M. Parkes, Dennis Robbins, Mary L.S. Vachon and Florence Wald.

be accompanied by serious physical, social, emotional, intellectual, spiritual and economic disruption.
Principle: Grieving and bereaved persons may benefit from the assistance of appropriately trained persons, professional or nonprofessional, skilled in bereavement work and well informed concerning other resources that may be helpful in grief work.

4. *Assumption:* Persons experiencing acute grief frequently have difficulty coping with a range of practical, psychosocial, economic and religious matters which may influence their functioning.
Principle: Persons experiencing acute grief may benefit from assistance in contracting and accepting support from specialized services dealing with legal, religious, vocational, economic, sexual and social problems.
5. *Assumption:* Grief can accompany or follow a wide variety of losses, including loss of health, death, divorce, separation and amputation.
Principle: Bereavement care should be considered for a variety of losses.
6. *Assumption:* The experience and expression of grief and the needs that emerge may vary widely from individual to individual. They are subject to many variables, including past experiences, cultural expectations, personal beliefs and relationships.
Principle: When bereavement care is needed, there is no single approach or method that routinely assists the bereaved. Care may include a number of formal and informal methods such as one-to-one or group counseling, discussion groups, practical help, intensive therapy, self-help groups and the use of the arts such as music, art and drama.
7. *Assumption:* Despite the fact that loss is painful, it can be a stimulus for growth.
Principle: In addition to support, bereavement care includes facilitation of personal, psychological, social and spiritual growth.
8. *Assumption:* Bereaved persons may be particularly vulnerable.
Principle: Caregivers seek to recognize this vulnerability and assist in protecting the bereaved, helping them to utilize their own personal strengths and support systems.
9. *Assumption:* Bereaved persons have differing personal philosophies as well as moral and religious values.
Principle: Care for the bereaved respects the individuality of those being supported and incorporates variations in accordance with differing belief systems.
10. *Assumption:* Bereaved persons are often unaware of, or unable to reach out to, community resources which might meet their needs.

Principle: Caregivers should seek to provide continuing opportunities for the bereaved to "make connection." Outreach methods should be included in early bereavement follow-up.

11. *Assumption:* The bereaved may become overreliant on caregivers.
    Principle: Caregivers should minimize the development of undue dependency.
12. *Assumption:* The bereaved may not accept the offer of relationships with individual caregivers.
    Principle: Caregivers must be nonintrusive and sensitive to the individual desires of the bereaved.
13. *Assumption:* Some of the difficulties that arise in bereavement may be predicted prior to, or at the time of, loss.
    Principle: Care for the bereaved should make use of available predictors.
14. *Assumption:* Ritual and ceremonies of leavetaking (e.g., funerals) allow the loss to be acknowledged in a symbolic and formal way. They provide an opportunity for the expression of feelings and personal spiritual, social, ethnic and family belief systems in an appropriate setting.
    Principle: Bereavement care should be compatible with the personal spirituality, religious rituals and social customs of the bereaved.
15. *Assumption:* Bereaved persons often receive fragmented care which may complicate and disrupt the resolution of grief.
    Principle: Continuity of program planning and communication among caregivers is important.
16. *Assumption:* Care of the bereaved is usually assigned a low priority in health care planning.
    Principle: Caregivers must seek concrete ways to develop bereavement care as an integral component of health care through planning, education, training and implementation.
17. *Assumption:* Caregivers can distance themselves from the bereaved by categorizing them.
    Principle: Caregivers must avoid the tendency to be judgmental and to use terms that imply mental illness or aberration.

The Family

1. *Assumption:* As the patient approaches death, it may be difficult for family members to resolve unfinished business, express feelings and participate in the provision of care. Such difficulties may add to the emotional burden of the bereaved.
   Principle: Caregivers should facilitate the participation of family

members in the care of the patient and nurture communication and contact between patient and family members.

2. *Assumption:* At times the needs and ambivalent feelings of individual family members will be in conflict with the needs and desires of others who are emotionally involved.
   Principle: The patient, family and others who are emotionally involved may require assistance if they are to recognize and allow their conflicting needs and ambivalent feelings.
3. *Assumption:* The family system and its usual dynamics may be disrupted and changed by the loss of a family member and the ensuing grief.
   Principle: The caregiver should, when necessary, be ready to assist grieving families as they adapt to the changes in organization and relationships related to the death of their loved one.
4. *Assumption:* The expression of grief by individual family members is an added source of stress within the family and can be disruptive.
   Principle: Families may need help to recognize and tolerate differing grieving patterns of members.
5. *Assumption:* Loss of a key family member often results in change in social or community status and thus deprives the person and the family of support groups and networks to which they are accustomed.
   Principle: Persons or families experiencing loss should have assistance available to make the transition to newly defined roles and to re-enter or develop needed support systems.
6. *Assumption:* When adult family members are struggling with their own acute grief, they are often incapable of providing adequate support to grieving children.
   Principle: Attention must be paid to meeting the needs of children in a grieving family when the surviving parent is temporarily unable to provide the required support.
7. *Assumption:* Latent or active family problems may surface, intensify or continue, and may be further complicated by the death of the family member.
   Principle: Those caring for family members during bereavement need to have a basic understanding of human behavior, family dynamics and the psychology of grief and bereavement in order to identify needs.
8. *Assumption:* Abrupt termination of important relationships with primary health care personnel after the death of a patient may subject the bereaved family members to secondary losses.
   Principle: Post-death follow-up by primary health care personnel is

desirable to provide continuity, although they may not continue as central caregivers.

The Caregivers

1. *Assumption:* All caregivers have experienced losses.
   Principle: As caregivers we are responsible for attending to the continuing task of recognizing and integrating our personal losses.
2. *Assumption:* Working with the bereaved may reawaken feelings associated with former losses and may also engender new loss.
   Principle: Caregivers must be sensitive to interrelationships between their personal lives and their work with the bereaved. Responsibility for perceiving and resolving loss belongs both to the individuals and to their work community.
3. *Assumption:* Ongoing involvement with the bereaved may lead to stress for caregivers and may result in burnout.
   Principle: The issue of staff stress must be addressed with provisions made for emotional support and clinical supervision. This is a joint responsibility of the individual and organization.
4. *Assumption:* Loss and grief are universal experiences which may be manifested differently.
   Principle: Multidisciplinary and cross-cultural interchange should be included in training.
5. *Assumption:* Not all bereaved persons require the services of professional caregivers.
   Principle: The development of programs to select, train and support lay caregivers is a responsibility of the professional.
6. *Assumption:* Caregivers have disparate levels of preparation and endurance and different areas of prejudice.
   Principle: Caregivers need to recognize their limitations and make referrals when the demands of caregiving exceed their expertise and resources.

The Community Program

1. *Assumption:* Important supportive relationships for the bereaved already exist in family, religious and social networks.
   Principle: Professional caregivers are not lone helpers and need to see themselves as part of a larger group of lay and professional providers of support.
2. *Assumption:* In some communities agencies exist which work capably with the bereaved.

Principle: Where effective care exists, services should not be duplicated.

3. *Assumption:* The community at large has limited education regarding bereavement.
   Principle: Effective educational programs should be available to all persons in the community.
4. *Assumption:* Bereavement can be financially expensive.
   Principle: Bereavement care should be delivered as effectively and as economically as possible.
5. *Assumption:* Elements of duality, exclusion, ageism, sexism and racism exist within our society.
   Principle: Regardless of age, race, sex, socioeconomic status, educational level or chosen lifestyle, all persons should have bereavement support readily available.

Research

1. *Assumption:* There is much to learn about grief and bereavement, the needs of those who grieve, and appropriate response.
   Principle: There is a need to increase research, evaluation, analysis and synthesis in this field.

ASSUMPTIONS AND PRINCIPLES OF CARE FOR THOSE AFFECTED BY HIV DISEASE*

Infection with the human immunodeficiency virus (HIV) constitutes a worldwide threat. The virus initiates a chronic disease, the end stage of which is termed acquired immunodeficiency disease syndrome (AIDS). While a terminal illness may occur at any point in the disease, depletion of the immune system increases likelihood after the onset of AIDS. The World Health Organization predicts that by the turn of the century 40 million persons will be infected. Even if a vaccine were to be made available, the problem of HIV infection would not be resolved. Given the number of persons who are currently infected—estimated to be between 5 and 10 million—health care systems will be challenged to the utmost.

The AIDS pandemic has profound implications for both the individual and society. In the future if one is not infected by the virus, one will assuredly be affected by its consequences. The International Work Group

---

* The IWG Committee on AIDS: Inge B. Corless (Chairperson), Robert Bendiksen, Robert Fulton, Unni Harvei, Britt Hysing-Dahl, Elizabeth P. Lamers, Patricia MacElveen-Hoehn, Patrice O'Connor, Tore Schjolberg and Eileen Stevenson.

on Death, Dying and Bereavement takes the following position with regard to the treatment and prevention of human immunodeficiency virus disease.

Basic Premises

1. The public health response to HIV disease has been formed by the political and social response to individuals infected with the virus.
2. Public health officials have attempted to safeguard individual liberties while protecting the health of the public.
3. Given the free flow of individuals within and between societies and the variations of immune response to the virus, quarantine of individuals infected with HIV is both an ineffective and inappropriate response to the epidemic.
4. HIV-1 antibody testing should be voluntary and based on informed consent.
5. Anonymous testing must be an available option.
6. Pre- and post-test counseling is essential for an effective testing program.
7. The individual has the right to privacy and to confidentiality with respect to her medical condition.
8. Individuals who are seropositive have an obligation to inform the person or persons with whom blood or body fluids may be exchanged.
9. Individuals have a right to know the seropositive status of persons with whom blood or bodily fluids are likely to be exchanged.
10. Individuals have a responsibility to protect themselves from HIV infection.
11. Contact tracing of partners potentially at risk for HIV infection should be implemented where feasible and particularly in low prevalence areas.
12. Individuals infected with HIV should have access to appropriate health care and should not be denied such care on the basis of race, creed, sex, sexual orientation or economic status.
13. Treatment provided to HIV-infected individuals should be nonjudgmental and nondiscriminatory.
14. It is the responsibility of all those providing information to the public about the HIV pandemic to be certain that it is accurate, timely and complete information.
15. Educational presentations through the media aimed at preventing the spread of HIV infection should avoid stereotyped wording that fails to distinguish between "high-risk behaviors" and "high-risk groups."

16. Educational materials designed to inform citizens about risks for HIV infection should be sensitive to linguistic, cultural, religious and educational variations in the populations being served.
17. Educational materials for health care workers pertaining to HIV disease should address the caregivers' attitudes, fears, values, beliefs and knowledge about the disease.
18. Appropriate HIV education for health care workers should address the psychosocial and spiritual needs of HIV-infected persons and their families in addition to the treatment of the infection and its manifestations.
19. Health care workers have a responsibility to provide services and compassionate care to individuals infected with HIV, in keeping with the ethical codes that govern their professions.
20. Health care workers must use universal precautions and effective disinfection procedures in fulfilling their professional responsibilities.
21. Health care workers, using *universal* precautions and effective disinfection procedures in fulfilling their professional responsibilities, have not been known to transmit HIV to their patients.
22. HIV-infected health care workers are expected to observe professional standards and safeguards in order to protect their patients from the risk of HIV infection.
23. Hospice and palliative care programs have a responsibility to provide care to individuals who are terminally ill with AIDS.
24. Governments should take appropriate measures to assure the personal safety and civil rights of the HIV infected person.
25. Governments at all levels should take a leadership role in addressing the HIV pandemic in nonjudgmental and nondiscriminatory terms, in committing the resources necessary to caring for those affected and in developing education, prevention and treatment programs.
26. Developed countries have a moral as well as medical obligation to share their knowledge, expertise and resources concerning HIV infection with developing countries.

The Patient

1. *Assumption:* Respect for the patient, regardless of source of infection, is essential for good care.
   Principle: Stigmas and taboos associated with HIV infection should be recognized and challenged both in and by the family, community and society.
2. *Assumption:* Care is most effective when the patient's life philosophy is respected.

Principle: The HIV-infected person's own framework of values, preferences and life outlook must be taken into account in planning and providing treatment that is appropriate for and respectful of that individual.

3. *Assumption:* The care of those ill with HIV disease is a process that involves the needs of patients and their families, as well as those of the caregivers.
   Principle: The interactions of those involved in the care of a patient must be assessed continually to achieve the best possible care of the patient. Optimal care cannot be accomplished, however, if the needs of the family and caregivers are neglected or negated.
4. *Assumption:* It is important to avoid paternalistic interactions with patients. Individual rights to self-determination must be respected.
   Principle: Patients' wishes for information about their condition should be respected. They should be given complete information about their condition, as is desired, encouraged to participate fully in their health care and supported in maintaining their self-determination.
5. *Assumption:* Dying patients often have personal and family issues to resolve.
   Principle: Patients should have support and the opportunity to resolve personal and family conflicts.
6. *Assumption:* Patients with HIV disease often experience weakness, helplessness, loneliness and isolation.
   Principle: The patient should be provided with a sense of protection and security by encouraging the continuing involvement of family and friends. Emotional, social and spiritual, as well as physical needs must be addressed.
7. *Assumption:* The patient's needs will change over time.
   Principle: Staff must be alert to changes in the patient, the need for the inclusion of additional services and for the provision of continuity of care.
8. *Assumption:* There are HIV-infected persons for whom newly available or experimental drugs or treatments may be appropriate.
   Principle: New or experimental drugs or therapies that may provide symptomatic relief and enhance the quality of life of HIV-infected individuals should be incorporated into palliative care, in accordance with the ethical principles of justice, beneficence and respect for persons.
9. *Assumption:* There are patients for whom aggressive, curative treatment becomes increasingly inappropriate.
   Principle: Experimental or aggressive therapies should be discon-

tinued when it results in a decrease of the quality of life, or at the patient's request.

10. *Assumption:* Many of the physical and psychological symptoms secondary to HIV infection can be relieved.
    Principle: The patient should be kept as symptom-free, comfortable and alert as possible. Discomfort in all aspects should be controlled to the extent possible.
11. *Assumption:* The varied problems and anxieties associated with a progressive illness can occur at any time of the day or night.
    Principle: Twenty-four-hour care must be available seven days a week for the patient and family, where and when it is needed.

The Family

1. *Assumption:* In terminal illness the patient and family must be the unit of care.
   Principle: (a) Help should be available to all involved, whether family of origin, family of choice or friend so as to sustain communication and involvement. (b) Potential conflict between family of origin and family of choice needs to be acknowledged and addressed.
2. *Assumption:* The course of a terminal illness involves a series of clinical and personal decisions.
   Principle: Communication among patient, family and clinical team is essential to informed decision-making.
3. *Assumption:* Many people do not know how to manage infectious diseases in the home.
   Principle: In order to provide care at home, families should receive education for infection control.
4. *Assumption:* Many people do not know what the dying process involves.
   Principle: The family members should be given time and opportunity to discuss all aspects of dying, including their emotional needs, with the staff.
5. *Assumption:* The patient and family need opportunities to be together privately.
   Principle: The patient and family should have time alone, while the patient is living and after death occurs. A special area may need to be provided.
6. *Assumption:* Complexity of procedures and time-consuming treatment can interfere with the life of the patient and family.

Principle: Procedures must be arranged in order to provide adequate time for patients, families and friends to be together.

7. *Assumption:* Patients and families facing death frequently experience a search for the meaning of their lives, making the provision of spiritual support essential.
   Principle: Emotional, religious, spiritual and philosophical elements are integral to a comprehensive program of care.
8. *Assumption:* Family members can be at risk physically and emotionally during the course of illness and during bereavement.
   Principle: Appropriate care and support of family members must be made available.

The Program

1. *Assumption:* The problems of the patient and family facing HIV disease and terminal illness encompass a wide variety of issues: physical, psychological, social, spiritual, economic and legal.
   Principle: Care requires the collaboration of individuals from many disciplines working as an integrated clinical team, meeting for frequent discussions with commonness of purpose.
2. *Assumption:* Health care services customarily lack interdisciplinary and interorganizational coordination.
   Principle: The organizational structure must provide links with health care professionals and organizations in the community.
3. *Assumption:* A supportive physical environment contributes to the sense of well-being of families and caregivers.
   Principle: The environment should provide adequate space and furnishings and the reassuring presence of personal belongings, all of which contribute to putting people at ease.
4. *Assumption:* Support for those providing care is crucial in the long-term care of persons with HIV disease and their families.
   Principle: Formal and informal mechanisms for staff support need to be developed.
5. *Assumption:* Home care is often desirable from a personal, social and economic perspective.
   Principle: Expertise about the home care of persons with HIV disease should be promulgated so as to meet the needs of patients and families.
6. *Assumption:* Persons living with HIV disease and their families have developed much hard-won knowledge as a result of their illness experience.
   Principle: It is vital to acknowledge the contribution that persons

with HIV disease and their families can make as educators to health professionals and to society.

7. *Assumption:* Serial or multiple loss of family members or friends may generate different and more problematic reactions than a single loss.
   Principle: The consequences of serial or multiple losses must be more fully studied. In the meantime special attention must be provided to those who have experienced such losses.

The Caregivers

1. *Assumption:* Health care workers may have attitudes, beliefs and prejudices concerning people with HIV disease which impair their ability to provide care.
   Principle: All health care workers attending people with HIV disease must explore their knowledge, attitudes and responses toward the spectrum of HIV-related issues. Individual caregivers' biases must not be allowed to compromise care.
2. *Assumption:* A body of knowledge in symptom control, patient- and family-centered care and other aspects of the care of persons living with HIV disease is available.
   Principle: Institutions and organizations providing care to those infected with HIV disease must orient and educate caregivers and keep everyone informed about developments as they occur.
3. *Assumption:* Effective care of persons living with HIV disease presupposes emotional investment on the part of caregivers.
   Principle: Caregivers require time and encouragement to develop and maintain relationships with patients and their significant others.
4. *Assumption:* Care of persons living with HIV disease can produce emotional exhaustion.
   Principle: Effective staff support systems must be readily available.
5. *Assumption:* Caregivers may sustain punctures of their skin by contaminated needles and sharp instruments as well as other exposures which result in occupationally acquired HIV disease.
   Principle: Organizations and governments have a responsibility to compensate staff members for occupationally acquired HIV disease.
6. *Assumption:* Some health care workers may be unprepared or uncomfortable discussing spiritual matters.
   Principle: (a) Caregivers should be offered opportunities to explore values and attitudes about life and death. (b) Caregivers need to recognize their limitations and make appropriate referrals for pastoral care and counseling when the demands for spiritual care exceed their abilities or resources.

7. *Assumption:* The clergy are usually seen as having primary responsibility for the spiritual care of the dying.
   Principle: Caregivers should be aware that they each have the potential for addressing many of the spiritual needs of their patients and should be encouraged to offer spiritual care, as requested and within the limit of their capabilities, to dying patients and their families.
8. *Assumption:* Ongoing involvement with dying and bereaved persons may cause a severe drain of energy and uncover old and new spiritual issues for the caregiver.
   Principle: Ongoing spiritual education, growth and renewal should be a part of a staff support program, as well as a personal priority for each caregiver.

Bibliography

I. SOCIOLOGICAL PERSPECTIVES ON DEATH

Aiken, L.R. 1985. *Dying, Death, and Bereavement.* Boston: Allyn & Bacon.

Aisenberg, Ruth B. and Rosenthal, Ammon. 1976. Congenital Heart Disease Thanatological Research. *Omega.* 7:335-350.

Axelrod, Charles David. 1986. Reflections on the Fear of Death. *Omega.* 17:51-64.

Badone, Ellen. 1987. Changing Breton Responses to Death. *Omega.* 18:77-83.

Baltes, Margret M. 1977. On the Relationship between Significant Yearly Events and Time of Death: Random or Systematic Distribution? *Omega.* 8:165-172.

Belin, Robert. 1981. Social Functions of Denial of Death. *Omega.* 12:25-35.

Benoliel, Jeanne Quint. 1981. Death Counseling and Human Development Issues and Intricacies. *Death Education.* 4:337-353.

Benoliel, Jeanne Quint (Editor). 1982. Death Education for the Health Professional. *Death Education.* 5:297-408.

Benoliel, Jeanne Quint. 1985. Loss and Adaptation: Circumstances, Contingencies, and Consequences. *Death Studies.* 9:217-233.

Bermann, Sandra and Richardson, Virginia. 1986. Social Change in the Salience of Death among Adults in America: A Projective Assessment. *Omega.* 17:195-207.

Bluebond-Langner, Myra. 1989. Worlds of Dying Children and Their Well Siblings. *Death Studies.* 13:1-16.

Campbell, Thomas W., Abernathy, Virginia, and Waterhouse, Gloria J. 1983. Do Death Attitudes of Nurses and Physicians Differ? *Omega.* 14:43-49.

Candy-Gibbs, Sandra E., Sharp, Kay Colby, and Petrun, Craig J. 1984. The Effects of Age, Object, and Cultural/Religious Background on Children's Concepts of Death. *Omega.* 15:329-346.

Carse, James P. 1980. *Death and Existence: A Conceptual History of Human Mortality.* New York: John Wiley and Sons.

Castles, Mary Reardon and Keith, Patricia M. 1979. Patient Concerns, Emotional Resources, and Perception of Nurse and Patient Roles. *Omega.* 10:27-33.

Charmaz, Kathy. 1980. *The Social Reality of Death: Death in Contemporary America.* Reading, MA: Addison-Wesley Publishing Company.

Chidester, David. 1990. *Patterns of Transcendence: Religion, Death, and Dying.* Belmont, CA: Wadsworth Publishing Company.

Clark, E.J., Fritz, J.M., Rieker, P.P., Kutscher, A.H., and Bendiksen, R.A. (Editors). 1990. *Clinical Sociological Perspectives on Illness and Loss: The Linkage of Theory and Practice.* Philadelphia: The Charles Press.

Cole, Thomas. 1979. The Ideology of Old Age and Death in American History. *American Quarterly.* 31:223-231.

Corless, I.B., Germino, B., Pittman, M. (Editors). 1992. *A Challenge for Living: Dying, Death and Bereavement.* Boston: Jones and Bartlett Publishers.

Corr, Charles A. 1984. A Model Syllabus for Children and Death Courses. *Death Education.* 8:11-28.

Corr, Charles A., Nabe, Clyde M. and Corr, Donna M. 1994. *Death and Dying: Life and Living.* Pacific Grove, CA: Brooks/Cole Publishing Company.

Counts, David. R. 1976. The Good Death in Kaliai: Preparation for Death in Western New Britain. *Omega.* 7:367-372.

Crase, Darrell and Leviton, Dan. 1987. Forum for Death Education and Counseling: Its History, Impact, and Future. *Death Studies.* 11:345-359.

Davidson, Glen W. and Zimmerman, Larry W. (Editors). 1990. Human Remains: Contemporary Issues. *Death Studies.* 14:491-641.

Day, Stacey and Fulton, Robert (Editors). 1986. *Cancer, Stress and Death* (2nd Edition). New York: Plenum.

DeFrain, J. 1986. *Stillborn: The Invisible Death.* Lexington, MA: Lexington Books.

DeSpelder, Lynne Ann and Strickland, Albert Lee. 1992. *The Last Dance: Encountering Death and Dying* (3rd Edition). Mountain View, CA: Mayfield Publishing Company.

Dickinson, George E. and Pearson, Algene A. 1980. Death Education and Physicians' Attitudes toward Dying Patients. *Omega.* 11:167-174.

Dickinson, George E., Sumner, Edward D., and Durand, Ronald P. 1987. Death Education in U.S. Professional Colleges: Medical, Nursing, and Pharmacy. *Death Studies.* 11:57-61.

Dickinson, George E., Sumner, Edward D., and Frederick, Lynn M. 1992. Death Education in Selected Health Professions. *Death Studies.* 16:281-289.

Doebler, Bettie Anne and Warnicke, Retha M. 1986. Sex Discrimination after Death: A Seventeenth-Century English Study. *Omega.* 17:309-320.

Doka, Kenneth J. 1981. The Social Organization of Terminal Care in Two Pediatric Hospitals. *Omega.* 12:345-354.

Doka, Kenneth J. 1989. The Awareness of Mortality in Midlife: Implications for Later Life. *Gerontology Review.* 2:19-28.

Durlak, Joseph A. and Kass, Richard A. 1981. Clarifying the Measurement of Death Attitudes: A Factor Analytic Evaluation of Fifteen Self-Report Death Scales. *Omega.* 12:129-141.

Epley, Rita J. 1977. The Stigma of Dying: Attitudes toward the Terminally Ill. *Omega.* 8:379-393.

Epting, Franz R. and Neimeyer, Robert A. (Editors). 1983. Personal Meanings of Death: Applications of Personal Construct Theory to Clinical Practice. *Death Education.* 7:87-327.

Feifel, Herman (Editor). 1977. *New Meanings of Death.* New York: McGraw-Hill.

Feifel, Herman (Editor). 1982. Death in Contemporary America. *Death Education.* 6:105-174.

Feifel, Herman and Schag, Daniel. 1980. Death Outlook and Social Issues. *Omega.* 11:201-215.

Fox, Renée C. (Editor). 1980. The Social Meaning of Death. *Annals of the Academy of Political and Social Science.* 447:1-99.

Fox, Renée C. 1981. The Sting of Death in American Society. *Social Science Review.* 37:42-59.

Fulton, Robert. 1976. *Death, Grief and Bereavement: A Bibliography, 1945-1975.* New York: Arno.

Fulton, Robert and Bendiksen, Robert (Editors). 1976. *Death and Identity* (2nd Edition). Bowie, MD: Robert J. Brady Company.

Fulton, Robert, Markusen, Eric, Owen, Greg, and Sheiber, Jane (Editors). 1978. *Death and Dying: Challenge and Change.* San Francisco: Boyd and Fraser.

Fulton, Robert, Odenyo, Amos, and Fagerberg, Sonja. 1978. The Luo Way of Death: Rendezvous with Rebellion. *Studia Africana.* 1:127-142.

Fulton, Robert and Reed, Margaret. 1981. *Death, Grief and Bereavement: A Bibliography 1975-1980.* New York: Arno.

Fulton, Robert, Scheiber, Jane, Owen, Greg, and Markusen, Eric. 1978. *Death and Dying: Challenge and Change.* Reading, PA: Addison-Wesley.

Grove, W. 1979. Sex, Marital Status and Mortality. *American Journal of Sociology.* 84:45-67.

Hale, Christiane B. 1990. *Infant Mortality: An American Tragedy.* Washington, DC: Population Reference Bureau.

Hale, R.J., Schmitt, R.J. and Leonard, W.M. II. 1984. Social Value of the Age of the Dying Patient. *Sociological Focus.* 17:157-173.

Harrison, Albert A. and Kroll, Neal E.A. 1985. Variations in Death Rates in the Proximity of Christmas: An Opponent Process Interpretation. *Omega.* 16:181-192.

Haub, Carl and Yanagishita, Machiko. 1992. *World Population Data Sheet.* Washington, DC: Population Reference Bureau.

Hawkins, Anne Hunsaker. 1990. Constructing Death: Three Pathographies about Dying. *Omega.* 22:301-317.

Helgeland, John. 1984. The Symbolism of Death in the Later Middle Ages. *Omega.* 15:145-160.

Hershisen, Marvin R. and Quarantelli, E.L. 1976. The Handling of the Dead in a Disaster. *Omega.* 7:195-208.

Holck, Frederick H. 1978. Life Revisited (Parallels in Death Experiences). *Omega.* 9:1-11.

Holman, E. Alison. 1990. Death and the Health Professional: Organization and Defense in Health Care. *Death Studies.* 14:13-24.

Hood, R.W. Jr. and Morris, R.J. 1983. Toward a Theory of Death Transcendence. *Journal for the Scientific Study of Religion.* 22:353-365.

Hynson, Lawrence M. Jr. 1978. Belief in Life After Death and Societal Integration. *Omega.* 9:13-18.

Irish, D.P., Lundquist, K.F. and Nelson, V.J. (Editors). 1993. *Ethnic Variations in Dying, Death, and Grief: Diversity in Universality.* Washington, DC: Taylor & Francis.

Jackson, Charles O. 1977. Death Shall Have No Dominion: The Passing of the World of the Dead in America. *Omega.* 8:195-203.

Jackson, Charles O. (Editor). 1977. *Passing: The Vision of Death in America.* Westport, CT: Greenwood Press.

Jankofsky, Klaus P. and Stuecker, Ewe. 1983. Altruism: Reflections on a Neglected Aspect in Death Studies. *Omega.* 14:335-353.

Johnston, Ralph C. Jr. 1988. *Confronting Death: Psychoreligious Responses.* Ann Arbor, MI: UMI Research Press.

Kalish, Richard A. and Reynolds, David K. 1976. *Death and Ethnicity: A Psychocultural Study.* Farmingdale, NY: Baywood.

Kamara, J. Lawrence. 1978. The Bio-Social Paradox in the Black Community: Life Gets Longer but Not Healthier. *Omega.* 9:301-312.

Kamerman, J.B. 1988. *Death in the Midst of Life: Social and Cultural Influences on Death, Grief and Mourning.* Englewood Cliffs, NJ: Prentice-Hall.

Kastenbaum, Robert. 1992. *The Psychology of Death* (2nd Edition). New York: Springer Publishing Company.

Kastenbaum, Robert. 1993. Avery D. Weisman, M.D.: An Omega Interview. *Omega.* 27: 97-103.

Kastenbaum, Robert. 1993. Reconstructing Death in Postmodern Society. *Omega.* 27:75-89.

Kastenbaum, R. and Kastenbaum, B. (Editors). *The Encyclopedia of Death.* Phoenix: Oryx Press.

Kearl, Michael C. 1989. *Endings: A Sociology of Death and Dying.* New York: Oxford University Press.

Kearl, Michael C. and Harris, Richard. 1981. Individualism and the Emerging "Modern" Ideology of Death. *Omega.* 12:269-280.

Kellehear, Allan. 1984. Are We a "Death-Denying" Society? A Sociological Review. *Social Science and Medicine.* 18:713-721.

Killilea, Alfred G. 1977. Some Political Origins of the Demand of Death. *Omega.* 8:205-214.

Killilea, Alfred G. 1980. Death Consciousness and Social Consciousness: A Critique of Ernest Becker and Jacques Choron on Denying Death. *Omega.* 11:185-200.

Killilea, Alfred G. 1985. Nuclearism and the Denial of Death. *Death Studies.* 9:253-265.

Klatt, Heinz-Joachim. 1991. In Search of a Mature Concept of Death. *Death Studies.* 15:177-187.

Kunz, Phillip R. and Summers, Jeffrey. 1979. A time to Die: A Study of the Relationship of Birthdays and Time of Death. *Omega* 10:281-289.

Leming, Michael R. and Dickinson, George E. 1990. *Understanding Dying, Death and Bereavement* (2nd Edition). Fort Worth, TX: Holt, Rinehart & Winston.

Lester, David. 1990. The Collett-Lester Fear of Death Scale: The Original Version and a Revision. *Death Studies* 14:451-468.

Lester, David. 1991. The Lester Death Attitude Scale. *Omega.* 23:67-75.

Leviton, Dan. 1986. Thanatological Theory and My Dying Father. *Omega.* 17:127-144.

Lifton, Robert Jay. 1979. *The Broken Connection: On Death and the Continuity of Life.* New York: Simon and Schuster.

Lofland, Lynn H. (Editor). 1976. *Toward a Sociology of Death and Dying.* New York: Russell Sage.

Lonetto, Richard. 1980. *Children's Conceptions of Death.* New York: Springer Publishing Company.

Marshall, Victor W. 1980. *Last Chapters: A Sociology of Aging and Dying.* Belmont, CA: Wadsworth Publishing Company.

Mathews, Robert C. and Mister, Rena D. 1987. Measuring an Individual's Investment in the Future: Symbolic Immortality, Sensation Seeking, and Psychic Numbness. *Omega.* 18:161-173.

McDonald, Gerald W. 1976. Sex, Religion, and Risk-Taking Behavior as Correlates of Death Anxiety. *Omega.* 7:35-44.

McIntosh, John L. 1989. Official U.S. Elderly Suicide Data Bases: Levels, Availability, Omissions. *Omega.* 19:337-350.

Menz, R. 1984. The Denial of Death and the Out-of-the-Body Experience. *Journal of Religion and Health.* 23:317-329.

Meshot, Christopher M. and Leitner, Larry M. 1993. Death Threat, Parental Loss, and Interpersonal Style: A Personal Construct Investigation. *Death Studies.* 17: 319-332.

Michalowski, Jr., Raymond J. 1976. The Social Meanings of Violent Death. *Omega.* 7:83-93.

Minton, Barbara and Spilka, Bernard. 1976. Perspectives on Death in Relation to Powerlessness and Form of Personal Religion. *Omega.* 7:261-268.

Morgan, John D. (Editor). 1988. Cultural and Religious Perspectives of Death. *Death Studies.* 12:85-180.

Mount, Eric Jr. 1983. Individualism and Our Fears of Death. *Death Education.* 7:25-31.

Nagamine, Takahiko. 1988. Attitudes toward Death in Rural Areas of Japan. *Death Studies.* 12:61-68.

Nash, Mary Louise. 1977. Dignity of Persons in the Final Phase of Life — An Exploratory Study. *Omega.* 8:71-80.

Neimeyer, Robert A. and Chapman, Kenneth M. 1980. Self/Ideal Discrepancy and Fear of Death: The Test of an Existential Hypothesis. *Omega.* 11:233-240.

Neimeyer, Robert A. and Krieger, Seth R. 1979. The Threat Index: A Research Report. *Death Education.* 3:245-270.

Nimocks, Mittie J., Webb, Lynn, and Connell, John B. 1987. Communication and the Terminally Ill: A Theoretical Model. *Death Studies.* 11:323-344.

Ordal, Carol C. 1983. Death as Seen in Books Suitable for Young Children. *Omega.* 14:249-277.

Pacholski, Richard A. 1986. Death Themes in Music: Resources and Research Opportunities. *Death Studies.* 10:239-263.

Palmer, Stuart and Humphrey, John A. 1977. Suicide and Homicide: A Test of a Role Theory of Destructive Behavior. *Omega.* 8:45-58.

Papadatou, Danai and Papdatos, C. (Editors). 1991. *Children and Death.* New York: Hemisphere Publishing Corporation.

Parsons, Talcott. 1978. Death in the Western World. Pp. 331-351 in *Action Theory and the Human Condition.* New York: The Free Press.

Peck, Dennis L. 1980. Towards a Theory of Suicide: The Case for Modern Fatalism. *Omega.* 11:1-14.

Perkes, A. Cordell and Schildt, Roberta. 1979. Death-Related Attitudes of Adolescent Males and Females. *Death Education.* 2:359-368.

Pine, Vanderlyn R. 1986. The Age of Maturity for Death Education: A Socio-Historical Portrait of the Era 1976-1985. *Death Studies.* 10:209-231.

Pollack, Jerrold M. 1979. Correlates of Death Anxiety: A Review of Empirical Studies. *Omega.* 10:97-121.

Preston, Samuel H. 1976. *Mortality Patterns in National Populations: With Special Reference to Recorded Causes of Death.* New York: Academic Press.

Pruyser, Paul W. 1984. Existential Impact of Professional Exposure to Life-Threatening or Terminal Illness. *Bulletin of the Menninger Clinic.* 48:357-367.

Rodabough, Tillman. 1981. How We Know about Death: Research Strategies. *Death Education.* 4:315-336.

Rosel, Natalie. 1978. Toward a Social Theory of Dying. *Omega.* 9:49-55.

Ross, Lawrence M. and Pollio, Howard R. 1991. Metaphors of Death: A Thematic Analysis of Personal Meanings. *Omega.* 23:291-307.

Ruby, Jay. 1988. Portraying the Dead. *Omega.* 19:1-20.

Sassower, Raphael and Grodin, Michael A. 1986. Epistemological Questions Concerning Death. *Death Studies.* 10:341-353.

Schmitt, Raymond L. 1982. Symbolic Immortality in Ordinary Contexts: Impediments to the Nuclear Era. *Omega.* 13:95-116.

Schulz, Richard and Aderman, David. 1976. How the Medical Staff Copes with Dying Patients: A Critical Review. *Omega.* 7:11-21.

Simpson, Michael A. 1976. Brought in Dead. *Omega.* 7:243-248.

Simpson, Michael A. 1979. The Lady Vanishes...or Getting Rid of the Body. *Omega.* 10:261-270.

Stannard, David E. (Editor). 1975. *Death in America.* Philadelphia: University of Pennsylvania Press.

Stannard, David E. 1977. *The Puritan Way of Death.* New York: Oxford University Press.

Steinzor, Bernard. 1978. Death and the Construction of Reality: A Revisit to the Literature from 1960. *Omega.* 9:97-124.

Stephen, Donna L. 1991. A Discussion of Avery Weisman's Notion of Appropriate Death. *Omega.* 24:301-308.

Stephenson, John S. 1985. *Death, Grief, and Mourning: Individual and Social Realities.* New York: The Free Press.

Stephenson, Peter H. (Editor). 1983. Dying in Cross-Cultural Perspective. *Omega.* 14:99-154.

Stillion, Judith M. 1984. Perspectives on the Sex Differential in Death. *Death Education.* 8:237-256.

Stillion, Judith M. (Editor). 1984. Suicide: Practical, Developmental, and Speculative Issues. *Death Education.* 8:1-151.

Stillion, Judith M. and McDowell, Eugene E. 1991. Examining Suicide from a Life Span Perspective. *Death Studies.* 15:327-354.

Stillion, Judith M. et al. 1988. Dimensions of the Shadow: Children of Six Nations Respond to the Nuclear Threat. *Death Studies.* 12:227-251.

Swain, Helen L. 1979. Childhood Views of Death. *Death Education.* 2:341-358.

Sweeting, Helen N. and Gilhooly, Mary L. M. 1991. Doctor, Am I Dead? A Review of Social Death in Modern Societies. *Omega.* 24:251-269.

Tate, Frederic B. 1989. Impoverishment of Death Symbolism: The Negative Consequences. *Death Studies.* 13:305-317.

Teitge, J. Smith. 1984. Cryogenics: Producing a State of Suspended Reality. *Death Education.* 8:169-177.

Thompson, Leslie M. and Cozart, William. 1981. Is Life Living? Defining Death in a Technological Age. *Death Education.* 5:205-214.

Thorson, James A. 1985. A Funny Thing Happened on the Way to the Morgue: Some Thoughts on Humor and Death, and a Taxonomy of the Humor Associated with Death. *Death Studies.* 9:201-216.

Thrush, John C., Paulus, George S., and Thrush, Phyllis I. 1979. The Availability of Education on Death and Dying: A Survey of U.S. Nursing Schools. *Death Education.* 3:131-142.

Unruh, David R. 1981. Is There a Sociology of Death? *Contemporary Sociology.* 10:508-512.

U.S. Bureau of the Census. 1992. *Statistical Abstract of the United States* (112th Edition). Washington, DC: Government Printing Office.

Walton, Douglas. 1976. On the Rationality of Fear of Death. *Omega.* 7:1-10.

Wass, Hannelore, Berardo, Felix M., and Neimeyer, Robert A. 1994. *Dying: Facing the Facts* (3rd Edition). New York: Hemisphere Publishing Corporation.

Wass, Hannelore, Guenther, Zenita C., and Towry, Betty J. 1979. United States and Brazilian Children's Concepts of Death. *Death Education.* 3:41-55.

Watson, Wilbur H. 1976. The Aging Sick and the Near Dead: A Study of Some Distinguishing Characteristics and Social Effects. *Omega.* 7:115-123.

Wear, Delese. 1989. Cadaver Talk: Medical Students' Accounts of Their Year-Long Experience. *Death Studies.* 13:379-391.

Weeks, Duane and Johnson, Catherine. 1992. A Second Decade of High School Death Education. *Death Studies.* 16:269-279.

Weir, Robert. 1980. A Realistic Perspective on Death. *Death Education.* 4:77-83.

Welch, Charles E. III. 1982. The Timing of Death in Athens, Georgia, 1974-1980: A Research Note. *Omega.* 13:389-394.

Westin, Robert H. 1980. *Ars Moriendi* Tradition and Visualization of Death in Roman Baroque Sculpture: Death Education in the Seventeenth-Century. *Death Education.* 4:111-123.

Wood, John B. 1986. The Birthday-Deathday Effect: Fact or Artifact? *Omega.* 17:321-326.

Zusne, Leonard. 1986. Some Factors Affecting the Birthday-Deathday Phenomenon. *Omega.* 17:9-26.

II. GRIEF AND THE PSYCHOSOCIAL PROCESS OF MOURNING

Atkinson, Trudie. 1980. Teacher Intervention with Elementary School Children in Death-Related Situations. *Death Education.* 4:149-163.

Atkinson, Trudie L. 1982. Race as a Factor in Teachers' Responses to Children's Grief. *Omega.* 13:243-250.

Attig, Thomas. 1989. Coping with Mortality: An Essay on Self-Mourning. *Death Studies.* 13:361-370.

Attig, Thomas. 1990. Relearning the World: On the Phenomenology of Grieving. *Journal of the British Society for Phenomenology.* 21:53-66.

Attig, Thomas. 1991. The Importance of Conceiving Grief as an Active Process. *Death Studies.* 15:385-393.

Averill, J.R. and Nunley, E.P. 1988. Grief as an Emotion and as a Disease: A Social-Constructionist Perspective. *Journal of Social Issues.* 44:79-95.

Bahr, H.M. and Harvey, C.D. 1980. Correlates of Morale among the Newly Widowed. *Journal of Social Psychology.* 110:219-233.

Ball, Justine F. 1976. Widow's Grief: The Impact of Age and Mode of Death. *Omega.* 7:307-333.

Behnke, Marylou, Reiss, John, and Neimeyer, Greg. 1987. Grief Responses of Pediatric House Officers to a Patient's Death. *Death Studies.* 11:169-176.

Bohannon, Judy Rollins. 1991. Religiosity Related to Grief Levels of Bereaved Mothers and Fathers. *Omega.* 23:153-159.

Bolton, Christopher and Camp, Delpha J. 1986. Funeral Rituals and the Facilitation of Grief Work. *Omega.* 17:343-352.

Bowlby, John. 1980. *Attachment and Loss, Volume III: Loss.* New York: Basic Books.

Brabant, Sarah. 1989. Old Pain or New Pain: A Social Psychological Approach to Recurrent Grief. *Omega.* 20:273-279.

Burke, Mary L., Hainsworth, Margaret A., Eakes, Georgene G., and Lindgren, Carolyn L. 1992. Current Knowledge and Research on Chronic Sorrow: A Foundation for Inquiry. *Death Studies.* 16:231-245.

Campbell, Jane, Swank, Paul, and Vincent, Ken. 1991. The Role of Hardiness in the Resolution of Grief. *Omega.* 23:53-65.

Clark, Duncan B. 1981. A Death in the Family: Providing Consultation to the Police on the Psychological Aspects of Suicide and Accidental Death. *Death Education.* 5:143-155.

Corr, Charles A., Fuller, Helen F., Barnickol, Carol Ann, and Corr, Donna (Editors). 1991. *Sudden Impact Death Syndrome: Who Can Help and How.* New York: Springer Publishing Company.

Cox, Harold. 1980. Mourning Population: Some Considerations of Historically Comparable Assassinations. *Death Education.* 4:125-138.

Davis, B.H. 1987. Disability and Grief. *Social Casework.* 68:352-357.

Demi, Alice S. and Miles, Margaret S. 1987. Parameters of Normal Grief: A Delphi Study. *Death Studies.* 11:397-412.

Demi, Alice Sterner and Miles, Margaret Shandor. 1988. Suicide Bereaved Parents: Emotional Distress and Physical Health Problems. *Death Studies.* 12:297-307.

Detmer, Carol Michler, and Lamberti, Joseph W. 1991. Family Grief. *Death Studies.* 15:363-374.

Doka, Kenneth J. 1984. Expectation of Death, Participation in Funeral Arrangements, and Grief Adjustment. *Omega.* 15:119-129.

Doka, Kenneth J. 1986. Loss upon Loss: The Impact of Death after Divorce. *Death Studies.* 10:441-449.

Doka, Kenneth J. 1987. Silent Sorrow: Grief and the Loss of Significant Others. *Death Studies.* 11:455-469.

Doka, Kenneth J. (Editor). 1989. *Disenfranchised Grief: Recognizing Hidden Sorrow.* Lexington, MA: Lexington Books.

Doka, Kenneth J. 1992. The Monkey's Paw: The Role of Inheritance in the Resolution of Grief. *Death Studies.* 16:45-58.

Dunlop, Richard S. 1980. Training Bereavement Therapists. *Death Education.* 4:165-178.

Dunn, Dana S., Goldbach, Kristen R., Lasker, Judith N., and Toedter, Lori J. 1991. Explaining Pregnancy Loss: Parents' and Physicians' Attributions. *Omega.* 23:13-23.

Engel, George L. 1980. A Group Dynamic Approach to Teaching and Learning about Grief. *Omega.* 11:45-59.

Feeley, Nancy and Gottlieb, Laurie N. 1988. Parents' Coping and Communication following Their Infant's Death. *Omega.* 19:51-67.

Fein, Melvyn L. 1990. *Role Change: A Resocialization Perspective.* New York: Praeger.

Folta, Jeanne R. and Deck, Edith. 1980. Grief, Grief Therapy and Continuing Education. In O. Margolis (Editor). *Acute Grief: Counseling the Bereaved.* New York: Columbia University Press.

Fox, Sandra Sutherland. 1984. Children's Anniversary Reactions to the Death of a Family Member. *Omega.* 15:291-305.

Frederick, Jerome F. 1976. Grief as a Disease Process. *Omega.* 7:297-305.

Frederick, Jerome F. 1982. The Biochemistry of Bereavement: Possible Basis for Chemotherapy? *Omega*. 13:295-303.

Fulton, Robert. 1987. The Many Faces of Grief. *Death Studies*. 11:243-256.

Geis, Sally B., Fuller, Ruth L., and Rush, Julian. 1986. Lovers of AIDS Victims: Psychosocial Stresses and Counseling Needs. *Death Studies*. 10:43-53.

Gilbert, Kathleen R. 1989. Interactive Grief and Coping in the Marital Dyad. *Death Studies*. 13:605-626.

Graham-Pole, John, Wass, Hannelore, Eyberg, Sheila, and Chu, Luis. 1989. Communicating with Dying Children and Their Siblings: A Retrospective Analysis. *Death Studies*. 13:465-483.

Hardt, Dale Vincent. 1978. An Investigation of the Stages of Grief and Bereavement. *Omega*. 9:279-285.

Hoagland, Alice. 1983. Bereavement and Personal Constructs: Old Theories and New Concepts. *Death Education*. 7:175-193.

Horacek, Bruce J. 1991. Toward a More Viable Model of Grieving and Consequences for Older Persons. *Death Studies*. 15:459-472.

Hoyt, Michael F. 1980. Clinical Notes Regarding the Experience of "Presence" in Mourning. *Omega*. 11:105-111.

Hughes, Cornelius and Fleming, Dagmar. 1991. Grief Casualties on Skid Row. *Omega*. 23:109-118.

Hughes, Cynthia Bach, and Page-Lieberman, Judith. 1989. Fathers Experiencing a Perinatal Loss. *Death Studies*. 13:537-556.

Jackson, Edgar N. 1979. Wisely Managing Our Grief: A Pastoral Viewpoint. *Death Education*. 3:143-155.

Jacobs, Selby C., Kosten, Thomas R., Kasl, Stanislav V., Ostfeld, Adrian, M., Berkman, Lisa, and Charpentier, Peter. 1987. Attachment Theory and Multiple Dimensions of Grief. *Omega*. 18:41-52.

Johnson, R.J., Lund, D.A., and Diamond, M.T. 1986. Stress, Self-Esteem, and Coping during Bereavement among the Elderly. *Social Psychology Quarterly*. 49:273-279.

Jones, William H. 1978. Emergency Room Sudden Death: What Can Be Done for the Survivors? *Death Education*. 2:231-245.

Kalish, Richard A. 1985. *Death, Grief, and Caring Relationships*. Monterey, CA: Brooks/Cole.

Kastenbaum, Robert. 1987. Vicarious Grief: An Intergenerational Phenomenon? *Death Studies*. 11:447-453.

Kirkley-Best, Elizabeth, Kellner, Kenneth R., and Ladue, Terry. 1984. Attitudes toward Stillbirth in a Sample of Obstetricians. *Omega*. 15:317-327.

Klass, Dennis. 1981. Elisabeth Kübler-Ross and the Tradition of the Private Sphere: An Analysis of Symbols. *Omega*. 12:241-267.

Klass, Dennis. 1984. Bereaved Parents and the Compassionate Friends: Affiliation and Healing. *Omega*. 15:353-373.

Klass, Dennis. 1987. John Bowlby's Model of Grief and the Problem of Identification. *Omega*. 18:13-32.

Klass, Dennis. 1988. *Parental Grief: Solace and Resolution*. New York: Springer Publishing Company.

Klass, Dennis. 1993. Solace and Immortality: Bereaved Parents' Continuing Bond with Their Children. *Death Studies*. 17: 343-368.

Klass, Dennis and Marwit, Samuel J. 1988. Toward a Model of Parental Grief. *Omega*. 19:31-50.

LaGrand, Louis E. 1981. Loss Reactions of College Students: A Descriptive Analysis. *Death Education.* 5:235-248.

LaGrand, Louis E. 1991. United We Cope: Support Groups for the Dying and Bereaved. *Death Studies.* 15:207-230.

Lattanzi, Marcia and Hale, Mary Ellis. 1984. Giving Grief Words: Writing during Bereavement. *Omega.* 15:45-52.

Leliaert, Richard M. 1989. Spiritual Side of "Good Grief": What Happened to Holy Saturday. *Death Studies.* 13:103-117.

Lofland, Lynn H. 1985. The Social Shape of Emotion: The Case of Grief. *Symbolic Interaction.* 8:171-190.

Lord, Janice Harris. 1987. Survivor Grief following a Drunk-Driving Crash. *Death Studies.* 11:413-435.

Lund, Dale A. et al. 1985. Identifying Elderly with Coping Difficulties after Two Years of Bereavement. *Omega.* 16:213-224.

Lund, D.A., Caserta, M.S., Dimond, M.F., and Gray, R.M. 1986. Impact of Bereavement on the Self-Conceptions of Older Surviving Spouses. *Symbolic Interaction.* 9:235-244.

Marris, Peter. 1974. *Loss and Change.* London: Routledge & Kegan Paul.

Martinson, Ida, Davies, Betty, and McClowry, Sandra. 1991. Parental Depression following the Death of a Child. *Death Studies.* 15:259-267.

Mawson, D., Markes, I.M., Ramm, L., and Stern, R.S. 1981. Guided Mourning for Morbid Grief: A Controlled Study. *British Journal of Psychiatry.* 138:185-193.

May, Harold J. and Breme, Frederick J. 1982. SIDS Family Adjustment Scale: A Method of Assessing Family Adjustment to Sudden Infant Death Syndrome. *Omega.* 13:59-74.

McClowry, S.G., Davies, E.B., May, K.A., Kulenkamp, E., and Martinson, I.M. 1987. The Empty Space Phenomenon: The Process of Grief in the Bereaved Family. *Death Studies.* 11:361-374.

McIntosh, John L. and Wrobleski, Adina. 1988. Grief Reactions among Suicide Survivors: An Exploratory Comparison of Relationships. *Death Studies.* 12:21-39.

Metzger, Anne M. 1979. A Q-Methodological Study of the Kübler-Ross Stage Theory. *Omega.* 10:291-301.

Miles, Margaret Shandor and Demi, Alice Sterner. 1983. Toward the Development of a Theory of Bereavement Guilt: Sources of Guilt in Bereaved Parents. *Omega.* 14:299-314.

Miles, Margaret Shandor, Demi, Alice Sterner, and Mostyn-Aker, Pat. 1984. Rescue Workers Reactions following the Hyatt Hotel Disaster. *Death Education.* 8:315-531.

Moody, Richard A. and Moody, Carol P. 1991. A Family Perspective: Helping Children Acknowledge and Express Grief following the Death of a Parent. *Death Studies.* 15:587-602.

Moss, Miriam S. and Moss, Sidney Z. 1983. The Impact of Parental Death on Middle Aged Children. *Omega.* 14:65-75.

Moss, Miriam S. and Moss, Sidney Z. 1984. Some Aspects of the Elderly Widow(er)'s Persistent Tie with the Deceased Spouse. *Omega.* 15:195-206.

Murphy, Patricia Ann. 1986. Parental Death in Childhood and Loneliness in Young Adults. *Omega.* 17:219-228.

Murphy, Patricia. 1991. Parental Divorce in Children and Loneliness in Young Children. *Omega.* 23:25-35.

Murphy, Shirley A. 1986. Stress, Coping, and Mental Health Outcomes following a Natural Disaster: Bereaved Family Members and Friends Compared. *Death Studies.* 10:411-429.

Nagy, Frank. 1985. A Model for a Donated Body Program in a School of Medicine. *Death Studies.* 9:245-251.

O'Bryant, Shirley L. 1990. Forewarning of a Husband's Death: Does It Make a Difference for Older Widows? *Omega.* 22:227-239.

Parkes, Colin Murray. 1986. The Caregiver's Griefs. *Journal of Palliative Care.* 1:5-7.

Parkes, Colin Murray. 1987. *Bereavement: Studies of Grief in Adult Life.* Madison, CT: International Universities Press.

Parkes, Colin Murray. 1989. Bereavement as a Psycho-Social Transition: Processes of Adaptation to Change. *Journal of Social Issues.* 44:53-66.

Parkes, Colin Murray and Weiss, Robert S. 1983. *Recovery from Bereavement.* New York: Basic Books.

Peach, Mary Rae and Klass, Dennis. 1987. Special Issues in the Grief of Parents of Murdered Children. *Death Studies.* 11:81-88.

Peppers, Larry G. 1987. Grief and Elective Abortion: Breaking the Emotional Bond? *Omega.* 18:1-12.

Peppers, Larry G. and Knapp, Ronald J. 1980. *Motherhood and Mourning: Perinatal Death.* New York: Praeger.

Pfost, Karen S., Stevens, Michael J., et al. 1989. Relationship of Purpose in Life to Grief Experiences in Response to the Death of a Significant Other. *Death Studies.* 13:371-378.

Ponzetti, James J. Jr. and Johnson, Mary A. 1991. The Forgotten Grievers: Grandparents' Reactions to the Death of Grandchildren. *Death Studies.* 115:157-167.

Price, David M. and Murphy, Patrick A. 1984. Staff Burnout in the Perspective of Grief Theory. *Death Education.* 8:47-58.

Reeves, Nancy C. and Boersma, M.J. 1989. The Therapeutic Use of Ritual in Maladaptive Grieving. *Omega.* 20:281-291.

Retsinas, Joan. 1988. A Theoretical Reassessment of the Applicability of Kübler-Ross' Stages of Dying. *Death Studies.* 12:207-216.

Rodabough, Tillman. 1980. Alternatives to the Stages Model of the Dying Process. *Death Education.* 4:1-19.

Rodgers, Beth L. and Cowles, Kathleen, V. 1991. The Concept of Grief: An Analysis of Classical and Contemporary Thought. *Death Studies.* 15:443-458.

Rosen, Elliott J. 1988. Family Therapy in Cases of Interminable Grief for the Loss of a Child. *Omega.* 19:187-202.

Rosen, Helen. 1984. Prohibitions against Mourning in Childhood Sibling Loss. *Omega.* 15:307-316.

Rosen, Helen. 1986. *Unspoken Grief: Coping with Childhood Sibling Loss.* Lexington, MA: Lexington Books.

Rosenblatt, P.C. 1983. *Bitter, Bitter Tears.* Minneapolis, MN: University of Minnesota Press.

Rosenblatt, P.C. 1988. Grief: The Social Context of Private Feelings. *Journal of Social Issues.* 44:67-78.

Rosenblatt, P.C. and Burns, L.H. 1989. Long-term Effects of Perinatal Loss. *Journal of Family Issues.* 7:237-253.

Rosenblatt, P.C. and Elde, C. 1990. Shared Remembrance about a Deceased Parent: Implications for Grief Education and Grief Counseling. *Family Relations.* 39:206-210.

Rosenblatt, P.C., Walsh, P.R. and Jackson, D. 1976. *Grief and Mourning in Cross-Cultural Perspective.* New Haven, CT: Human Relations Area Files Press.

Rubin, Simon Shimshon. 1984. Maternal Attachment and Child Death: On Adjustment, Relationship, and Resolution. *Omega.* 15:347-352.

Sable, Pat. 1991. Attachment, Loss of Spouse, and Grief in Elderly Adults. *Omega.* 23:129-142.

Sanders, Catherine M. 1982. Effects of Sudden vs. Chronic Illness Death on Grief and Bereavement Outcome. *Omega.* 13:227-241.

Sanders, Catherine M. 1984. Therapists, Too, Need to Grieve. *Death Education.* 8:27-35.

Sanders, Catherine M. 1989. *Grief: The Mourning After.* New York: Wiley.

Schwab, Reiko. 1990. Paternal and Maternal Coping with the Death of a Child. *Death Studies.* 14:407-422.

Shanfield, Stephen B. 1981. The Mourning of the Health Care Professional: An Important Element in Education about Death and Loss. *Death Education.* 4:385-395.

Shanfield, Stephen, Swain, Barbara J., and Benjamin, G. Andrew H. 1986. Parents' Responses to the Death of Adult Children from Accidents and Cancer: A Comparison. *Omega.* 17:289-297.

Sherizen, Sanford and Paul, Lester. 1977. Dying in a Hospital Intensive Care Unit: The Social Significance for the Family of the Patient. *Omega.* 8:29-40.

Shuchter, S.R. 1986. *Dimensions of Grief.* San Francisco: Jossey-Bass Publications.

Silverman, Phyllis R. 1981. *Helping Women Cope with Grief.* Beverly Hills, CA: Sage Publications.

Smith, Anne Clarke and Borgers, Sherry B. 1988. Parental Grief Response to Perinatal Death. *Omega.* 19:203-214.

Staubacher, Carol. 1991. *Men & Grief.* New York: New Harbinger Publications, Inc.

Stevenson, Robert G. 1986. The Shuttle Tragedy, "Community Grief," and the Schools. *Death Studies.* 10:507-518.

Stroebe, Margaret S., Stroebe, Wolfgang, Gergen, Kenneth J., and Gergen, Mary. 1981. The Broken Heart: Reality or Myth? *Omega.* 12:87-106.

Stroebe, Wolfgang and Stroebe, Margaret S. 1987. *Bereavement and Health: The Psychological and Physical Consequences.* New York: Cambridge University Press.

Strommen, Merton P. and Strommen, A. Irene. 1993. *Five Cries of Grief: One Family's Journey to Healing After the Tragic Death of a Son.* New York: Harper Collins Publishers.

Thornton, Gordon, Robertson, Donald U., and Mlecko, Mary Lou. 1991. Disenfranchised Grief and Evaluations of Social Support by College Students. *Death Studies.* 15:355-362.

Torrez, Diana J. 1992. Sudden Infant Death Syndrome and the Stress-Buffer Model of Social Support. *Clinical Sociology Review.* 10:170-181.

Viney, Linda L. 1991. The Personal Construct Theory of Death and Loss: Toward a More Individually Oriented Grief Therapy. *Death Studies.* 15:139-155.

Viney, Linda L., Henry, Rachael M., Walker, Beverly M., and Crooks, Levinia. 1991. The Psychosocial Impact of Multiple Deaths from AIDS. *Omega.* 24:151-168.

Wadsworth, John S. and Harper, Dennis C. 1991. Grief and Bereavement in Mental Retardation: A Need for a New Understanding. *Death Studies*. 15:281-292.

Wambach, Julie Ann. 1985. The Grief Process as a Social Contract. *Omega*. 16:201-211.

Weizman, S.G. and Kamm, P. 1985. *About Mourning: Support and Guidance for the Bereaved*. New York: Human Sciences Press.

Widdison, Harold A. and Salisbury, Howard G. 1989. The Delayed Stress Syndrome: A Pathological Delayed Grief Reaction? *Omega*. 20:293-306.

Wilson, Ann L. and Soule, Douglas J. 1981. The Role of a Self-Help Group in Working with Parents of a Stillborn Baby. *Death Education*. 5:175-186.

Wood, Gracie. 1981. Balance as a Key Concept in the Resolution of Grief. *Death Education*. 5:249-265.

Woodfield, Robert L. and Viney, Linda L. 1984. A Personal Construct Approach to the Conjugally Bereaved Woman. *Omega*. 15:1-13.

Worden, J. William. 1991. *Grief Counseling and Grief Therapy: A Handbook for the Mental Health Practitioner* (2nd Edition). New York: Springer.

Wrolleski, Adina. 1984. The Suicide Survivors Grief Group. *Omega*. 15:173-184.

Zambelli, Grace C., Clark, Elizabeth Johns, Barile, Laurel, and deJong, Ann F. 1988. An Interdisciplinary Approach to Clinical Intervention for Childhood Bereavement. *Death Studies*. 12:41-50.

III. BEREAVEMENT AND THE SOCIOLOGICAL RESPONSE TO DEATH

Akiyama, Hiroko, Holtzman, Joseph, and Britz, William E. 1986. Pet Ownership and Health Status During Bereavement. *Omega*. 17:187-193.

Anderson, T.B. 1984. Widowhood as a Life Transition: Its Impact on Kinship Ties. *Journal of Marriage and the Family*. 46:105-114.

Arens, D.A. 1983. Widowhood and Well-Being: An Examination of Sex Differences within a Causal Model. *International Journal of Aging and Human Development*. 15:27-40.

Ariès, P. 1981. *The Hour of Our Death*. New York: Alfred A. Knopf.

Arling, G. 1976. The Elderly Widow and Her Family, Neighbors, and Friends. *Journal of Marriage and the Family*. 38:757-768.

Balk, David E. 1991. Sibling Death, Adolescent Bereavement, and Religion. *Death Studies*. 15:1-20.

Bankoff, E.A. 1983. Social Support and Adaptation to Widowhood. *Journal of Marriage and the Family*. 45:827-839.

Barely, S.R. 1983. The Codes of Death: The Semiotics of Funeral Work. *Urban Life*. 12:3-31.

Barrett, Carol J. and Schneweis, Karen M. 1980. An Empirical Search for Stages of Widowhood. *Omega*. 11:97-104.

Barrett, T.W. and Scott, T.B. 1990. Suicide Bereavement and Recovery Patterns Compared with Nonsuicidal Bereavement Patterns. *Suicide and Life-Threatening Behavior*. 20:1-15.

Bass, David M., Noelker, Linda S., Townsend, Aloen L., and Deimling, Gary T. 1990. Losing an Aged Relative: Perceptual Differences between Spouses and Adult Children. *Omega*. 21:21-40.

Bendiksen, Robert. 1990. Facing Death with Children. Pp. 205-218 in E.J. Clark et al. (Editors). *Clinical Sociological Perspectives on Illness and Loss: The Linkage of Theory and Practice.* Philadelphia: The Charles Press.

Bendiksen, Robert and Berg, Phillip. 1978. Religion and Life Crisis Counseling. *The Clergy Gadfly.* 5:1-3.

Bendiksen, Robert and Fulton, Robert. 1975. Death and the Child: An Anterospective Test of the Childhood Bereavement and Later Behavior Hypothesis. *Omega.* 6:45-59.

Benes, Peter (Editor). 1976. *Puritan Gravestone Art: The Dublin Seminar for New England Folk Life* (Volumes I & II). Boston: Boston University Scholarly Publications.

Benfield, D. Gary and Nichols, Jane A. 1984. Attitudes and Practice of Funeral Directors toward Newborn Death. *Death Education.* 8:155-167.

Berardo, Felix M. (Editor). 1985. Survivorship: The Other Side of Death and Dying. *Death Studies.* 9:1-75.

Bergen, M. Betsy and Williams, Robert R. 1981. Alternative Funerals: An Exploratory Study. *Omega.* 12:71-78.

Borg, S. and Lasker, J.N. 1988. *When Pregnancy Fails: Families Coping with Miscarriage, Ectopic Pregnancy, Stillbirth, and Infant Death* (2nd Edition). New York: Basic Books.

Bowling, Ann. 1988. Who Dies after Widow(er)hood? A Discriminant Analysis. *Omega.* 19:135-153.

Bradfield, C.D. and Myers, A.A. 1980. Clergy and Funeral Directors: An Explication in Role Conflict. *Review of Religious Research.* 21:343-350.

Bryer, K.B. 1979. The Amish Way of Death. *American Psychologist.* 34:255-261.

Burks, Valerie K., Lund, Dale A., Gregg, Charles H., and Bluhm, Harry P. 1988. Bereavement and Remarriage for Older Adults. *Death Studies.* 12:51-60.

Calhoun, L.G., Abernathy, C.B., and Selby, J.W. 1986. The Rules of Bereavement: Are Suicidal Deaths Different? *Journal of Community Psychology.* 14:213-218.

Calhoun, Lawrence and Allen, Breon G. 1991. Social Reactions to the Survivor of a Suicide in the Family: A Review of the Literature. *Omega.* 23:95-107.

Calhoun, Lawrence G., Selby, James W., and Steelman, Jonathan K. 1988. A Collation of Funeral Directors' Impressions of Suicidal Deaths. *Omega.* 19:365-373.

Carey, Raymond G. 1979. Weathering Widowhood: Problems and Adjustment of the Widowed during the First Year. *Omega.* 10:163-174.

Carlson, Lisa. 1987. *Caring for Your Own Dead.* Hinesburg, VT: Upper Access Publishers.

Caserta, Michael S. and Lund, Dale A. 1992. Bereaved Older Adults Who Seek Early Professional Help. *Death Studies.* 16:17-30.

Cleiren, Marc. 1993. *Bereavement and Adaptation: A Comparative Study of the Aftermath of Death.* Washington, DC: Hemisphere Publishing Corporation.

Consumers Union. 1977. *Funerals: Consumers' Last Rights.* Mount Vernon, NY: Consumers Union.

Conway, Shoshanna E. Williams, Hayship, Bert, and Tandy, Ruth E. 1991. Similarity of Perceptions of Bereavement Experiences between Widows and Professionals. *Omega.* 23:37-51.

Cowell, Daniel David. 1985. Funerals, Family, and Forefathers: A View of Italian-American Funeral Practices. *Omega.* 16:69-85.

Davidowitz, Mitchell and Myrick, Robert D. 1984. Responding to the Bereaved: An Analysis of "Helpful" Statements. *Death Education.* 8:1-10.

Davies, Elizabeth M.B. 1987. The Family Environment in Bereaved Families and Its Relationship to Surviving Sibling Behavior. *Children's Health Care.* 17:22-32.

Dawson, Grace D., Santos, John F., and Burdick, David C. 1990. Differences in Final Arrangements between Burial and Cremation as the Method of Body Disposition. *Omega.* 21:129-146.

Demi, Alice S. 1984. Social Adjustment of Widows after a Sudden Death: Suicide and Non-Suicide Survivors Compared. *Death Education.* 8:91-111.

Diamond, M.F., Lund, D.A., and Caserta, M.S. 1987. The Role of Social Support in the First Two Years of Bereavement in an Elderly Sample. *Gerontologist.* 27:599-604.

Doka, Kenneth J. 1981. Recent Bereavement and Registration for Death Studies Courses. *Omega.* 12:51-60.

Dunn, Robert G. and Morrish-Vidners, Donna. 1987. The Psychological and Social Experience of Suicide Survivors. *Omega.* 18:175-215.

Euster, Gerald L. 1991. Memorial Contributions: Remembering the Elderly Deceased and Supporting the Bereaved. *Omega.* 23:169-179.

Farrell, James J. 1980. *Inventing the American Way of Death: 1830-1920.* Philadelphia: Temple University Press.

Ferraro, K.F., Mutran, E., and Barresi, C.M. 1984. Widowhood, Health and Friendship Support in Later Life. *Journal of Health and Social Behavior.* 25:246-259.

Folta, Jeanne R. and Deck, Edith. 1987. Elderly Black Widows in Rural Zimbabwe. *Journal of Cross-Cultural Gerontology.* 2:321-342.

French, Hal W. 1985. The Clergy and the Funeral Director: Complementary or Contrasting Perspectives? *Death Studies.* 9:143-153.

Fulton, Robert. 1982. The Role of the Funeral Director in Contemporary America. In C. Lesnoff-Caravaglia (Editor). *Aging and the Human Condition.* New York: Human Sciences Press.

Fulton, Robert. 1990. Cremation. In *World Book Encyclopedia.* Chicago: Field Education Corporation.

Garrity, Thomas F. and Wyss, James. 1976. Death, Funeral and Bereavement Practices in Appalachian and Non-Appalachian Kentucky. *Omega.* 7:209-228.

Glick, I.O. Weiss, R.S., and Parkes, C.M. 1976. *The First Year of Bereavement.* Bowie, MD: The Charles Press.

Goldberg, Helene S. 1981. Funeral and Bereavement Rituals of Kota Indians and Orthodox Jews. *Omega.* 12:117-128.

Gray, Ross E. 1988. Meaning of Death: Implications for Bereavement Theory. *Death Studies.* 12:309-317.

Habenstein, Robert and Lamers, William. 1981. *The History of American Funeral Directing.* Milwaukee: Bulfin.

Hansson, R.O. and Remondet, J.H. 1988. Old Age and Widowhood: Issues of Personal Control and Independence. *Journal of Social Issues.* 44:159-174.

Haraldsson, Erlandur. 1988. Survey of Claimed Encounters with the Dead. *Omega.* 19:103-113.

Hayes, Christopher L. and Kalish, Richard A. 1987. Death-Related Experiences and Funerary Practices of the Hmong Refugee in the United States. *Omega.* 18:63-70.

Henley, S.H.A. 1984. Bereavement following Suicide: A Review of the Literature. *Current Psychological Research and Reviews.* 3:53-61.

Hershberger, Paul J. and Walsh, W. Bruce. 1990. Multiple Role Involvements and the Adjustment to Conjugal Bereavement: An Exploratory Study. *Omega.* 21:91-102.

Hill, Arthur C. 1983. The Impact of Urbanism on Death and Dying among Black People in a Rural Community in Middle Tennessee. *Omega.* 14:171-186.

Hiltz, S.R. 1978. Widowhood: A Roleless Role. *Marriage and Family Review.* 1:1-10.

Huntington, R. and Metcalf, B. 1979. *Celebrations of Death: The Anthropology of Mortuary Rituals.* Cambridge: Cambridge University Press.

Irion, Paul E. 1990. Changing Patterns of Ritual Response to Death. *Omega.* 22:159-172.

Jordan, John R. 1991. Cumulative Loss, Current Stress, and the Family: A Pilot Investigation of Individual and Systemic Effects. *Omega.* 23:309-332.

Kalekin-Fishman, Devorah and Klingman, Avigdor. 1988. Bereavement and Mourning in Nonreligious Kibbutzim. *Death Studies.* 12:253-270.

Kalish, Richard A. and Goldberg, Helene. 1978. Clergy Attitudes toward Funeral Directors. *Death Education.* 2:247-260.

Kalish, Richard A. and Goldberg, Helene. 1979. Community Attitudes toward Funeral Directors. *Omega.* 10:335-346.

Kallenberg, Kjell. 1992. View of Life in Bereavement and Loss. In Cox, G.R. and Fundis, R.J. (Editors). *Spiritual, Ethical and Pastoral Aspects of Bereavement.* Amityville, NY: Baywood.

Kaprio, J., Koskenvuo, M., and Rita, H. 1987. Mortality after Bereavement: A Prospective Study of 95,647 Widowed Persons. *American Journal of Public Health.* 77:283-287.

Kastenbaum, Robert, Peyton, Sara, and Kastenbaum, Beatrice. 1976. Sex Discrimination after Death. *Omega.* 7:351-359.

Kearl, Michael C. 1986. Death as a Measure of Life: A Research Note on the Kastenbaum-Spilka Strategy of Obituary Analysis. *Omega.* 17:65-78.

Klass, Dennis. 1982. Self-Help Groups for the Bereaved: Theory, Theology, and Practice. *Journal of Religion and Health.* 21:307-324.

Klass, Dennis. 1986. Marriage and Divorce among Bereaved Parents in a Self-Help Group. *Omega.* 17:237-249.

Klass, Dennis and Shinners, Beth. 1982. Professional Roles in a Self-help Group for the Bereaved. *Omega.* 13:361-375.

Krell, R. and Rabkin, L. 1991. The Effects of Sibling Death on the Surviving Child: A Family Perspective. *Family Process.* 18:471-477.

Leming, Michael R. 1979. Religion and Death: A Test of Homans' Thesis. *Omega.* 10:347-364.

Levak, Milena Maselli. 1979. Motherhood by Death among the Borro Indians of Brazil. *Omega.* 10:323-334.

Lopata, H.Z. 1979. *Women as Widows: Support Systems.* New York: Elsevier.

Lund, D.A. (Editor). 1989. *Older Bereaved Spouses: Research with Practical Applications.* New York: Taylor and Francis/Hemisphere.

Lund, D.A., Caserta, M.S., and Diamond, M.F. 1988. A Comparison of Bereavement Adjustments between Mormon and Non-Mormon Older Adults. *Journal of Religion and Aging.* 5:75-92.

Lund, Dale A., Caserta, Michael S., Van Pelt, Jan, and Gass, Kathleen A. 1990. Stability of Social Support Networks after Later-Life Spousal Bereavement. *Death Studies.* 14:53-73.

Maris, Robert W. 1981. *Pathways to Suicide: A Survey of Self-Destructive Behavior.* Baltimore: Johns Hopkins University Press.

Masamba, Jean and Kalish, Richard. 1976. Death and Bereavement: The Role of the Black Church. *Omega.* 7:23-34.

Mauritzen, John. 1988. Pastoral Care for the Dying and the Bereaved. *Death Studies.* 12:111-122.

McCown, Darlene E. 1984. Funeral Attendance, Cremation, and Young Siblings. *Death Education.* 8:349-363.

McGee, Marsha. 1980. Faith, Fantasy, and Flowers: A Content Analysis of the American Sympathy Card. *Omega.* 11:25-35.

McNiel, D.E., Hatcher, C., and Reubin, R. 1988. Family Survivors of Suicide and Accidental Death: Consequences for Widows. *Suicide and Life-Threatening Behavior.* 18:137-148.

Metress, Eileen. 1990. The American Wake of Ireland: Symbolic Death Ritual. *Omega.* 21:147-153.

Meyer, Richard E. (Editor). 1989. *Cemeteries and Gravemarkers: Voices of American Culture.* Ann Arbor: University of Michigan Press.

Morgan, D.L. 1989. Adjustment to Widowhood: Do Social Networks Really Make It Easier? *The Gerontologist.* 29:101-107.

Moss, Miriam S., Lesher, Emerson L., and Moss, Sidney Z. 1986. Impact of the Death of an Adult Child on Elderly Parents: Some Observations. *Omega.* 17:209-218.

Osterweiss, M., Solomon, F., and Green, M. (Editors). 1984. *Bereavement: Reactions, Consequences and Care.* Washington, DC: National Academy Press.

Parkes, Colin Murray. 1987. Models of Bereavement Care. *Death Studies.* 11:257-261.

Peterson, Steven A. and Greil, Arthur L. 1990. Death Experience and Religion. *Omega.* 21:75-82.

Petrillo, Gay. 1989. The Distant Mourner: An Examination of the American Gravedigger. *Omega.* 20:139-148.

Pine, Vanderlyn R. 1979. *Caretaker of the Dead: The American Funeral Director.* New York: John Wiley and Sons.

Prichard, Shawn and Epting, Franz. 1991. Children and Death: New Horizons in Theory and Measurement. *Omega.* 24:271-288.

Range, Lillian M. and Calhoun, Lawrence G. 1990. Responses following Suicide and Other Types of Death: The Perspective of the Bereaved. *Omega.* 21:311-320.

Range, Lillian M. and Martin, Stephen K. 1990. How Knowledge of Extenuating Circumstances Influences Community Reactions toward Suicide Victims and Their Bereaved Families. *Omega.* 21:191-198.

Range, Lillian M. and Niss, Nathan M. 1990. Long-Term Bereavement from Suicide, Homicide, Accidents, and Natural Deaths. *Death Studies.* 14:423-433.

Raphael, B. 1983. *The Anatomy of Bereavement.* New York: Basic Books.

Rodabough, Tillman. 1981. Funeral Roles: Ritualized Expectations. *Omega.* 12:227-240.

Rosenblatt, Paul C., Spoentgen, Patricia, Karis, Terri A., Dahl, Carla, Kaiser, Tamara, and Elde, Carol. 1991. Difficulties in Supporting the Bereaved. *Omega.* 23:119-128.

Rowles, Graham D. and Comeaux, Malcolm L. 1986. Returning Home: The Interstate Transportation of Human Remains. *Omega.* 17:103-113.

Rubin, Nissan. 1985. Unofficial Memorial Rites in an Army Unit. *Social Forces.* 63:795-809.

Rubin, Nissan. 1986. Death Customs in a Non-Religious Kibbutz: The Use of Sacred Symbols in a Secular Society. *Journal for the Scientific Study of Religion.* 25:292-303.

Rubin, Nissan. 1990. Social Networks and Mourning: A Comparative Approach. *Omega.* 21:113-127.

Sanders, Catherine M. 1979. A Comparison of Adult Bereavement in the Death of a Spouse, Child, and Parent. *Omega.* 10:303-322.

Sanders, Catherine M. 1980. Comparison of Younger and Older Spouses in Bereavement Outcome. *Omega.* 11:217-232.

Schachter, Sherry. 1991. Adolescent Experiences with the Death of a Peer. *Omega.* 24:1-11.

Schorer, C.E. 1989. Two Centuries of Miami Indian Death Customs. *Omega.* 20:75-79.

Schotzinger, Kathleen A. and Best, Elizabeth Kirkley. 1987. Closure and the Cadaver Experience: A Memorial Service for Deeded Bodies. *Omega.* 18:217-227.

Sheskin, Arlene. 1979. *Cryonics: A Sociology of Death and Bereavement.* New York: Irvington Publishers, Inc.

Sheskin, Arlene and Wallace, Samuel E. 1976. Differing Bereavements: Suicidal, Natural, and Accidental Death. *Omega.* 7:229-242.

Silverman, Phyllis. 1986. *Widow-to-Widow.* 1986. New York: Springer.

Silverman, Sam M. and Silverman, Phyllis R. 1979. Parent-Child Communication in Widowed Families. *American Journal of Psychoanalysis.* 33:428-441.

Sklar, Fred. 1991. Grief as a Family Affair: Property Rights, Grief Rights, and the Exclusion of Close Friends as Survivors. *Omega.* 24:109-121.

Sklar, Fred and Hartley, Shirley F. 1990. Close Friends as Survivors: Bereavement Patterns in a "Hidden" Population. *Omega.* 21:103-112.

Sklar, Fred and Huneke, Kathleen D. 1987. Bereavement, Ministerial Attitudes, and the Future of Church-Sponsored Bereavement Support Groups. *Omega.* 18:89-102.

Sloane, David Charles. 1991. *The Last Great Necessity: Cemeteries in American History.* Baltimore: The Johns Hopkins University Press.

Smith, K.R. and Zick, C.D. 1986. Incidence of Poverty among the Recently Widowed: Mediating Factors in the Life Course. *Journal of Marriage and the Family.* 48:619-630.

Solomon, Mark I. 1982. The Bereaved and the Stigma of Suicide. *Omega.* 13:377-387.

Souter, Susan J. and Moore, Timothy E. 1989. A Bereavement Support Program for Survivors of Cancer Deaths: A Description and Evaluation. *Omega.* 20:31-43.

Spiegelman, Vivian and Kastenbaum, Robert. 1990. Pet Rest Memorial: Is Eternity Running Out of Time? *Omega.* 21:1-13.

Spilka, Bernard, Lacey, Gerald, and Gelb, Barbara. 1979. Sex Discrimination after Death: A Replication, Extension and a Difference. *Omega.* 10:227-233.

Stroebe, Margaret S. and Stroebe, Wolfgang. 1989. Who Participates in Bereavement Research? A Review and Empirical Study. *Omega.* 20:1-19.

Stroebe, M.S., Stroebe, W., and Hansson, R.O. 1988. Bereavement Research: An Historical Introduction. *Journal of Social Issues.* 44:1-18.

Stroebe, W., Stroebe, M.S., and Domittner, G. 1988. Individual and Situational Differences in Recovery from Bereavement: A Risk Group Identified. *Journal of Social Issues.* 44:143-158.

Swanson, Elizabeth A. and Bennett, Teresa F. 1982. Degree of Closeness: Does It Affect the Bereaved's Attitudes toward Selected Funeral Practices? *Omega.* 13:43-50.

Taylor, Deborah A. 1983. Views of Death from Sufferers of Early Loss. *Omega.* 14:77-82.

Tokunaga, Howard T. 1985. The Effect of Bereavement upon Death-Related Attitudes and Fears. *Omega.* 16:267-280.

U.S. Federal Trade Commission. 1984. *Consumer Guide to the FTC Funeral Rule.* Washington, DC: Federal Trade Commission.

Ulmer, Ann, Range, Lillian M., and Smith Peggy C. 1991. Purpose in Life: A Moderator of Recovery from Bereavement. *Omega.* 23:279-289.

Unruh, David R. 1976. The Funeralization Process: Toward A Model of Social Time. *Mid-American Review of Sociology.* 1:9-25.

Van Arsdale, Peter W. and Radetsky, Carol L. 1983. Life and Death in New Guinea. *Omega.* 14:155-169.

Vess, James, Moreland, John, and Schwebel, Andrew I. 1985. Understanding Family Role Reallocation following a Death: A Theoretical Framework. *Omega.* 16:115-126.

Wagner, Katherine G. and Calhoun, Lawrence. G. 1991. Perceptions of Social Support by Suicide Survivors and Their Social Networks. *Omega.* 24:61-73.

Walker, K.N., MacBride, A., and Vachon, M. 1977. Social Support Networks and the Crisis of Bereavement. *Social Science and Medicine.* 11:35-41.

Weisman, Avery D. 1990. Bereavement and Companion Animals. *Omega.* 22:241-248.

Weiss, R.S. 1988. Loss and Recovery. *Journal of Social Issues.* 44:37-52.

IV. PUBLIC POLICIES AND PRIVATE DECISIONS

Adams, David W. 1982. Ethical Dilemmas in the Dying Patient. In S. Yelaga (Editor). *Ethical Issues in Social Work.* Springfield, IL: Charles C Thomas.

Aggleton, Peter, Davies, Peter, and Hart, Graham (Editors). 1990. *AIDS: Individual, Cultural and Policy Dimensions.* New York: The Falmer Press.

Akerlund, Britt Mari and Norberg, Astrid. 1990. Powerlessness in Terminal Care of Demented Patients: An Exploratory Study. *Omega.* 21:15-19.

Annas, G. 1991. The Health Care Proxy and the Living Will. *New England Journal of Medicine.* 324:1210-1213.

Anspach, R.R. 1987. Prognostic Conflict in Life and Death Decisions: The Organization as an Ecology of Knowledge. *Journal of Health and Social Behavior.* 28:215-231.

Bass, David M. 1982. Response Bias in Studying Hospice Clients' Needs. *Omega.* 13:305-318.

Bass, David M. 1985. Characteristics of Hospice Patients and Their Caregivers. *Omega.* 16:51-68.

Bass, David M., Pestello, Fred P., and Garland, T. Neal. 1984. Experiences with Home Hospice Care: Determinants of Place of Death. *Death Education.* 8:199-222.

Beauchamp, Tom and Childress, James F. 1979. *Principles of Biomedical Ethics.* New York: Oxford University Press.

Bendiksen, Robert. 1989. Hospice: Do You Have to Die to Get That Kind of Care? Pp. vii-ix in M. McElligot and G.R. Kreibich. *A Training Manual for Hospice Volunteers*. La Crosse, WI: Lutheran Hospital Learning Systems.

Benrubi, B. 1992. Euthanasia: The Need for Procedural Guidelines. *New England Journal of Medicine*. 326:197-198.

Bergerson, James P. and Handley, Paul R. 1992. Bibliography on AIDS-Related Bereavement and Grief. *Death Studies*. 16:247-267.

Blanchet, Kevin D. (Editor). 1988. *AIDS: A Health Care Management Response*. Rockville, MD: Aspen Publishers, Inc.

Blank, Robert H. 1988. *Life, Death, and Public Policy*. DeKalb, IL: Northern Illinois University Press.

Blendon, Robert J., Szalay, Ulrike S., and Knox, Richard A. 1992. Should Physicians Aid Their Patients in Dying? *Journal of the American Medical Association*. 267:2658-2662.

Blumenfield, Michael, Levy, Norman B., and Kaufman, Diane. 1978. The Wish to be Informed of a Fatal Illness. *Omega*. 9:323-326.

Brescia, Frank J., Sadof, Matthew, and Barstow, Janice. 1984. Retrospective Analysis of a Home Care Hospice Program. *Omega*. 15:37-44.

Buckingham, Robert W. 1982. Hospice Care in the United States: The Process Begins. *Omega*. 13:159-171.

Burnell, George M. 1993. *Final Choices: To Live or To Die in an Age of Medical Technology*. New York: Insight Books.

Callahan, Daniel. 1990. *What Kind of Life: The Limits of Medical Progress*. New York: Simon and Schuster.

Carey, Raymond G. and Posavac, Emil J. 1978. Attitudes of Physicians on Disclosing Information to and Maintaining Life for Terminal Patients. *Omega*. 9:67-77.

Celo Cruz, Maria T. 1992. Aid-in-Dying: Should We Decriminalize Physician-Assisted Suicide and Physician-Committed Euthanasia? *American Journal of Law & Medicine*. 18: 369-394.

Ching, Chwee Lye and Ramsey, Michael Kirby. 1984. Volunteers and the Care of the Terminal Patient. *Omega*. 15:237-244.

Clark, R.E. and LaBeff, E.E. 1982. Death Telling: Managing the Delivery of Bad News. *Journal of Health and Social Behavior*. 23:366-380.

Cole, John J. 1989. Moral Dilemma: To Kill or Allow to Die? *Death Studies*. 13:393-406.

Connelly, R.J. 1989. The Sentiment Argument for Artificial Feeding of the Dying. *Omega*. 20:229-237.

Corless, Inge B. 1983. Models of Hospice Care. Pp. 540-550 in Chaska, N. (Editor). *The Nursing Profession: A Time to Speak*. New York: McGraw-Hill Book Company.

Corless, Inge B., Germino, Barbara and Pittman-Lindeman, Mary (Editors). 1993. *A Challenge for Living: Dying, Death, and Bereavement*. Boston: Jones and Bartlett Publishers.

Corless, Inge B. and Pittman-Lindeman, Mary A. (Editors). 1988. AIDS: Principles, Practices and Politics. *Death Studies*. 12:371-607.

Corless, Inge B. and Pittman-Lindeman, Mary A. (Editors). 1989. *AIDS: Principles, Practices and Policies*. New York: Hemisphere Publishing Corporation.

Corr, Charles A. 1991. A Task-Based Approach to Coping with Dying. *Omega*. 24:81-94.

Corr, Charles A. and Corr, Donna M. 1983. *Hospice Care: Principles and Practice.* New York: Springer.

Corr, Charles A. and Corr, Donna M. (Editors). 1985. *Hospice Approaches to Pediatric Care.* New York: Springer.

Corr, Charles A. and Corr, Donna M. 1992. Adult Hospice Day Care. *Death Studies.* 16:155-171.

Council on Ethical and Judicial Affairs of the AMA. 1991. Guidelines for the Appropriate Use of Do-Not-Resuscitate Orders. *Journal of the American Medical Association.* 265:1874-1875.

Crane, Diana. 1975. *The Sanctity of Social Life: Physician's Treatment of Critically Ill Patients.* New York: Russell Sage.

Cranford, R.E. and Douder, A.E. (Editors). 1984. *Institutional Ethics Committees and Health Care Decision-Making.* Ann Arbor, MI: Health Administration Press.

Culver, Charles M. and Gert, Bernard. 1990. Beyond the Living Will: Making Advance Directives More Useful. *Omega.* 21:253-258.

Dannis, M., Sutherland, L., et al. 1991. A Prospective Study of Advanced Directives for Life-Sustaining Care. *New England Journal of Medicine.* 324:883-888.

Davis, Gary and Jassen, Arne. 1980. An Experiment in Death Education in the Medical Curriculum: Medical Students and Clergy "On-Call" Together. *Omega.* 11:157-166.

Devins, Gerald M. 1980. Contributions of Health and Demographic Status to Death Anxiety and Attitudes toward Voluntary Euthanasia. *Omega.* 11:293-302.

Devins, Gerald M. and Diamond, Robert T. 1976. The Determination of Death. *Omega.* 7:277-296.

Doyle, Derek. 1991. Palliative Care Education and Training in the United Kingdom: A Review. *Death Studies.* 15:95-103.

Feigenberg, Loma. 1980. *Terminal Care: Friendship Contracts with Dying Patients.* (Translated by Patrick Hort) New York: Brunner/Mazel.

Feigenberg, Loma and Fulton, Robert. 1977. Care for the Dying: A Swedish Perspective. *Omega.* 8:215-228.

Feigenberg, Loma and Schneidman, Edwin S. 1979. Clinical Thanatology and Psychotherapy: Some Reflections on Caring for the Dying Person. *Omega.* 10:1-8.

Feigenberg, Loma et al. 1980. The Role of the Psychiatrist in the Care of the Dying. *Omega.* 11:279-280.

Fieweger, Margaret and Smilowitz, Michael. 1984. Relational Conclusion through Interaction with the Dying. *Omega.* 15:161-172.

Fox, Renée C. and Swazey, Judith P. 1978. *The Courage to Fail: A Social View of Organ Transplants and Dialysis* (2nd Edition). Chicago: University of Chicago Press.

Freidson, Eliot. 1985. The Reorganization of the Medical Profession. *Medical Care Review.* 42:11-35.

Fuller, Ruth L., Geis, Sally B., and Rush, Julian. 1988. Lovers of AIDS Victims: A Minority Group Experience. *Death Studies.* 12:1-7.

Fulton, Robert and Owen, Greg. 1981. Hospice in America: From Principle to Practice. In C. Saunders (Editor). *Hospice: The Living Idea.* London: Edward Arnold.

Garfield, Charles A., Larson, Dale G., and Schuldberg, David. 1982. Mental Health Training and the Hospice Community: A National Survey. *Death Education.* 6:189-204.

Gert, B. and Culver, C.M. 1986. Distinguishing between Active and Passive Euthanasia. *Geriatric Medicine and Social Policy.* 2:29-36.

Gomez, Carlos F. 1991. *Regulating Death: Euthanasia and the Case of The Netherlands.* New York: The Free Press.

Gostin, Lawrence O. (Editor). 1990. *AIDS and the Health Care System.* New Haven, CT: Yale University Press.

Gostin, Lawrence O. 1992. Ethics Committees and Medical Futility. *Law, Medicine & Health Care.* 20: 277-405.

Gray, Bradford. 1975. *Human Subjects in Medical Experimentation.* New York: Wiley Interscience.

Gray-Toft, Pamela A. and Anderson, James G. 1986. Sources of Stress in Nursing Home Terminal Patients in a Hospice. *Omega.* 17:27-39.

Gruman, Gerald J. 1978. Ethics of Death and Dying: Historical Perspective. *Omega.* 9:203-237.

Hammes, Bernard J. and Bendiksen, Robert. 1990. From the Ivory Tower to the Hospital Ward: A Role Analysis of a Clinical Ethicist. Pp. 135-147 in E.J. Clark et al. (Editors). *Clinical Sociological Perspectives on Illness and Loss: The Linkage of Theory and Practice.* Philadelphia: The Charles Press.

Hansen, Leslie C. and McAlear, Charles A. 1983. Terminal Cancer and Suicide: The Health Care Professional's Dilemma. *Omega.* 14:241-248.

Hatfield, C.B. et al. 1983. Attitudes about Death, Dying, and Terminal Care: Differences among Groups at a University Teaching Hospital. *Omega.* 14:51-63.

Haug, M. 1978. Aging and the Right to Terminate Medical Treatment. *Journal of Gerontology.* 33:586-591.

Hayslip, Bert, Hoffman, Josephine, and Weatherly, Doris. 1990. Response Bias in Hospice Evaluation. *Omega.* 22:63-74.

Heller, D. Brian and Schneider, Carl D. 1977. Interpersonal Methods for Coping with Stress: Helping Families of Dying Children. *Omega.* 8:319-331.

Hessing, Dick J. and Elffers, Henk. 1986. Attitude toward Death, Fear of Being Declared Dead Too Soon, and Donation of Organs after Death. *Omega.* 17:115-126.

Hine, Virginia H. 1979. Dying at Home: Can Families Cope? *Omega.* 10:175-187.

Hoggatt, Loretta and Spilka, Bernard. 1978. The Nurse and the Terminally Ill Patient: Some Perspectives and Projected Actions. *Omega.* 9:255-266.

Homer, Louise E. 1984. Organizational Defenses against the Anxiety of Terminal Illness: A Case Study. *Death Education.* 8:137-154.

Hosford, Bowen. 1986. *Bioethics Committees: The Health Care Providers Guide.* Rockville, MD: Aspen Systems Corporation.

Hoy, Andrew M. 1985. Breaking Bad News to Patients. *British Journal of Hospital Medicine.* 34:96-99.

Humphrey, Derek and Wickett, Ann. 1986. *The Right to Die: Understanding Euthanasia.* Eugene, OR: The Hemlock Society.

Husebo, Stein. 1988. Is Euthanasia a Caring Thing to Do? *Journal of Palliative Care.* 4:115-118.

Ingram, Ellen and Ellis, Jon B. 1992. Attitudes toward Suicidal Behavior: A Review of the Literature. *Death Studies.* 16:31-43.

Johnson, D., Fitsch, J.P., and McIntosh, W.A. 1980. Acceptance of Conditional Suicide and Euthanasia among Adult Americans. *Suicide and Life-Threatening Behavior.* 10:157-166.

Jorgenson, David E. and Neubecker, Ron C. 1980. Euthanasia: A National Survey of Attitudes toward Voluntary Termination of Life. *Omega.* 11:281-291.

Kamerman, Jack. 1991. Corrections Officers and AIDS: Balancing Professional Distance and Personal Involvement. *Death Studies.* 15:375-384.

Kapusinski, Anthony, Sutterlin, Teri, Hobbins, Katie Lou, Wright, Ronald, and Bendiksen, Robert. 1989. Problem Solving Sociology and AIDS: Learning Creative Problem Solving in an Undergraduate Sociology Seminar. *Clinical Sociology Review.* 7:178-197.

Kastenbaum, Robert. 1976. Towards Standards of Care for the Terminally Ill: A Few Guiding Principles. *Omega.* 7:191-193.

Kay, W. et al. 1988. *Euthanasia of the Companion Animal.* Philadelphia: The Charles Press.

Kilburn, Linda H. 1988. *The Hospice Operations Manual.* Arlington, VA: National Hospice Organization.

Kincade, Jean E. 1982. Attitudes of Physicians, Housestaff, and Nurses on Care for the Terminally Ill. *Omega.* 13:333-344.

Kirp, David L. and Bayer, Ronald (Editors). 1992. *AIDS in the Industrialized Democracies: Passions, Politics, and Policies.* Montreal: McGill-Queen's University Press.

Klenow, Daniel J. and Youngs, George A. Jr. 1987. Changes in Doctor/Patient Communication of a Terminal Prognosis: A Selective Review and Critique. *Death Studies.* 11:263-277.

Klopfer, Frederick J. and Price, William F. 1978. Euthanasia Acceptance as Related to Afterlife Belief and Other Attitudes. *Omega.* 9:245-253.

Kotch, Jonathan B. and Cohen, Susan R. 1985. SIDS Counselors' Reports of Own and Parents' Reactions to Reviewing the Autopsy Report. *Omega.* 16:129-139.

Kutner, N.G. 1987. Issues in the Application of High Cost Medical Technology: The Case of Organ Transplantation. *Journal of Health and Social Behavior.* 28:23-26.

Labus, Janet G. and Dambrot, Faye H. 1985. A Comparative Study of Terminally Ill Hospice and Hospital Patients. *Omega.* 16:225-232.

Lamb, David. 1985. *Death, Brain Death and Ethics.* Albany, NY: State University of New York Press.

Lamers, William M. 1988. Hospice Research: Some Reflections. *The Hospice Journal.* 4:3-11.

Lamers, William M. 1989. Hospital Ethics Committees: Converting Conflict to Consensus. *Orthopedic Surgeon's Legal Letter.* 12:3-8.

Latimer, Elizabeth J. 1991. Caring for Seriously Ill and Dying Patients: Philosophy and Ethics. *Canadian Medical Association Journal.* 144:859-864.

Latimer, Elizabeth J. 1991. Ethical Decision-Making in the Care of the Dying and Its Application to Clinical Practice. *Journal of Pain and Symptom Management.* 6:329-336.

Latimer, Elizabeth J. 1991. Euthanasia: A Physician's Reflections. *Journal of Pain and Symptom Management.* 6:487-491.

Lauter, H. and Meyer, J.E. 1984. Active Euthanasia without Consent: Historical Comments on a Current Debate. *Death Education.* 8:89-98.

Levine, Robert J. 1986. *Ethics and the Regulation of Clinical Research* (2nd Edition). Baltimore: Urban and Schwarzenberg.

Ley, Dorothy C.H. 1985. Palliative Care in Canada: The First Decade and Beyond. *Journal of Palliative Care.* 1:32-35.

Light, Donald Jr. 1976. Professional Problems in Treating Suicidal Persons. *Omega.* 7:59-68.

Linehan, Elizabeth A. 1981. Neocortical Tests and Personal Death: A Reply to Robert Veatch. *Omega.* 12:329-337.

Logue, Barbara J. 1993. *Last Rights: Death Control and the Elderly in America.* New York: Lexington Books.

Lynn, Joanne (Editor). 1989. *By No Extraordinary Means: The Choice to Forgo Life-Sustaining Food and Water.* Bloomington, IN: Indiana University Press.

Mann, Jonathan, Tarantola, Daniel J. M. and Netter, Thomas W. (Editors). 1992. *AIDS in the World: A Global Report.* Cambridge, MA: Harvard University Press.

Manuel, C., Enel, P., Reviron, D., et al. 1990. The Ethical Approaches to AIDS: A Bibliographical Review. *Journal of Medical Ethics.* 16:14-17.

Markusen, Eric, Owen, Greg, Fulton, Robert, and Bendiksen, Robert. 1977. SIDS: The Survivor as Victim. *Omega.* 8:277-284.

McCartney, James J. and Trau, Jane Mary. 1990. Cessation of the Artificial Delivery of Food and Fluids: Defining Terminal Illness and Care. *Death Studies.* 14:435-444.

McKitrick, Daniel. 1981. Counseling Dying Clients. *Omega.* 12:165-187.

Miller, Heather G., Turner, Charles F. and Moses, Lincoln E. (Editors). 1990. *AIDS: The Second Decade.* Washington, DC: National Academy Press.

Moore, W.R. 1983. Perceptions of Terminal Illness by Family Physicians and Relatives. *Omega.* 14:369-376.

Mor, V., Greer, D.S., and Kastenbaum, R. 1988. *The Hospice Experiment: Report of the National Hospice Study.* Baltimore: Johns Hopkins University Press.

Mor, V. and Masterson-Allen, S. 1987. *Hospice Care Systems: Structure, Process, Costs, and Outcome.* New York: Springer.

Mumma, Christina M. and Benoliel, Jeanne Quint. 1984. Care, Cure, and Hospital Dying Trajectories. *Omega.* 15:275-268.

Nagi, Mostafa H., Pugh, M.D., and Lazerine, Neil G. 1977. Attitudes of Catholic and Protestant Clergy toward Euthanasia. *Omega.* 8:153-164.

National Commission for the Protection of Human Subjects of Biomedical and Behavioral Research. 1978. *The Belmont Report.* Washington, DC: U.S. Department of Health, Education, and Welfare.

Nelkin, Dorothy, Willis, David P. and Parris, Scott V. (Editors). 1991. *A Disease of Society: Cultural and Institutional Responses to AIDS.* Cambridge: Cambridge University Press.

Ostheimer, J.M. 1980. The Polls: Changing Attitudes toward Euthanasia. *Public Opinion Quarterly.* 44:123-128.

Paradis, Lenora Finn. 1984. Hospice Program Integration: An Issue for Policymakers. *Death Education.* 8:383-398.

Pellegrino, Edmund and Thomasma, David C. 1990. *For the Patient's Good: The Restoration of Beneficence in Health Care.* New York: Oxford University Press.

Piel, Jonathan (Editor). 1989. *The Science of AIDS: A Scientific American Reader.* New York: W.H. Freeman and Company.

Portnoy, Russell K. (Editor). 1991. Special Issue on Medical Ethics: Physician-Assisted Suicide and Euthanasia. *Journal of Pain and Symptom Management.* 6:279-328.

Prakasa, R.V., Staten, F., and Nandini, R. 1988. Racial Differences in Attitudes toward Euthanasia. *Euthanasia Review.* 2:260-277.

Price, Trevor R. and Bergen, Bernard J. 1977. The Relationship to Death as a Source of Stress for Nurses on a Coronary Care Unit. *Omega.* 8:229-238.

Quenneville, Yves, Falardeau, Maurice, and Rochette, Dennis. 1981. Evaluation of Staff Support System in a Palliative Care Unit. *Omega.* 12:355-358.

Quill, Timothy E. 1993. *Death and Dignity: Making Choices and Taking Charge.* New York: W.W. Norton & Company.

Raphael, Beverly. 1979. A Primary Prevention Action Programme: Psychiatric Involvement following a Major Rail Disaster. *Omega.* 10:211-226.

Rebok, George W. and Hoyer, William J. 1979. Clients Nearing Death: Behavioral Treatment Perspectives. *Omega.* 10:191-201.

Riley, Matilda White, Ory, Marcia O., and Zablotsky, Diane. 1989. *AIDS in an Aging Society: What We Need to Know.* New York: Springer Publishing Company.

Rinaldi, Anoel and Kearl, Michael C. 1990. The Hospice Farewell: Ideological Perspectives of Its Professional Practitioners. *Omega.* 21:283-300.

Root-Bernstein, Robert. 1993. *Rethinking AIDS: The Tragic Cost of Premature Consensus.* New York: The Free Press.

Ruark, J.E., Raffin, T.A., et al. 1988. Initiating and Withdrawing Life Support: Principles and Practices in Adult Medicine. *New England Journal of Medicine.* 318:25-30.

Salladay, Susan A. 1982. The Administrative Role in Hospice Planning and Organization. *Death Education.* 6:227-248.

Salloway, Jeffrey Colman and Volek, Paul J. 1987. Professions, Families, and Control in the Management of the Cadaver Organ Donor. *Death Studies.* 11:35-55.

Sankar, Andrea. 1991. *Dying at Home: A Family Guide for Caregiving.* Baltimore: The Johns Hopkins University Press.

Saul, Shura and Saul, Sidney R. 1977. Old People Talk about the Right to Die. *Omega.* 8:129-139.

Schroeder-Sheker, Therese. 1993. Music for the Dying: A Personal Account of the New Field of Music Thanatology — History, Theories, and Clinical Narratives. *Advances: The Journal of Mind-Body Health.* 9:36-48.

Shuman, Carolyn R., Fournet, Glenn P., Zelhart, Paul F., Roland, Billy C., and Estes, Robert E. 1992. Attitudes of Registered Nurses toward Euthanasia. *Death Studies.* 16:1-15.

Siegel, Karolynn and Tuckel, Peter. 1984. Rational Suicide and the Terminally Ill Cancer Patient. *Omega.* 15:263-269.

Simmons, Roberta G., Klein, Susan D., and Simmons, Richard L. 1977. *The Gift of Life: The Social and Psychological Impact of Organ Transplantation.* New York: John Wiley.

Simmons, Roberta G. 1991. Altruism and Sociology. *The Sociological Quarterly.* 32:1-22.

Smith, George P. and Hall, Clare. 1986. Cryonic Suspension and the Law. *Omega.* 17:1-7.

Sociological Practice Association. 1990. Ethical Standards of Sociological Practitioners. Pp. 181-191 in E.J. Clark et al. (Editors). *Clinical Sociological Perspectives on Illness and Loss: The Linkage of Theory and Practice.* Philadelphia: The Charles Press.

Starr, Paul. 1982. *The Social Transformation of American Medicine.* New York: Basic Books.

Steininger, Marion and Colsher, Sandra. 1978. Correlates of Attitudes about "The Right to Die" among 1973 and 1976 High School and College Students. *Omega.* 9:355-368.

Stine, Gerald J. 1993. *Acquired Immune Deficiency Syndrome: Biological, Medical, Social, and Legal Issues.* Englewood Cliffs, NJ: Prentice-Hall, Inc.

Stoddard, Sandol 1991. *The Hospice Movement: A Better Way of Caring for the Dying* (Revised Edition). New York: Vintage Books.

Stoller, Eleanor Palo. 1980. The Impact of Death-Related Fears on Attitudes of Nurses in a Hospital Work Setting. *Omega.* 11:85-96.

Swyter, Jai. 1978. When is Life Without Value? A Study of Life-Death Decisions on a Hemodialysis Unit. *Omega.* 9:369-380.

Thomasma, David C. 1987. The Context as a Moral Rule in Medical Ethics. Pp. 142-156 in R.A. Wright (Editor). *Human Values in Health Care: The Practice of Ethics.* New York: McGraw-Hill Book Company.

Thompson, Edward H. 1985. Palliative and Curative Care Nurses' Attitudes toward Dying and Death in the Hospital Setting. *Omega.* 16:233-242.

van der Maas, P.J., van Delden, J.J.M. and Pijnenborg, L. 1992. *Euthanasia and Other Medical Decisions Concerning the End of Life: An Investigation Performed upon Request of the Commission of Inquiry into the Medical Practice Concerning Euthanasia.* Amsterdam: Elsevier.

Veatch, Robert M. 1987. *The Patient as Partner: A Theory of Human Experimentation Ethics.* Bloomington, IN: Indiana University Press.

Walton, Douglas N. 1981. Neocortical versus Whole-brain Conceptions of Personal Death. *Omega.* 12:339-344.

Wanzer, Sidney H. et al. 1984. The Physician's Responsibility toward Hopelessly Ill Patients. *New England Journal of Medicine.* 310:955-959.

Wanzer, Sidney H. et al. 1989. The Physician's Responsibility toward Hopelessly Ill Patients: A Second Look. *New England Journal of Medicine.* 320:844-849.

Wass, Hannelore (Editor). 1978. The Hospice: Development and Administration. *Death Education.* 2:1-230.

Wass, Hannelore, Christian, Milton, Myers, Jane, and Murphy, Milledge Jr. 1978. Similarities and Dissimilarities in Attitudes toward Death in a Population of Older Persons. *Omega.* 9:337-354.

Weir, Robert F. (Editor). 1986. *Ethical Issues in Death and Dying* (2nd Edition). New York: Columbia University Press.

Wrenn, Robert L. 1991. College Management of Student Death: A Survey. *Death Studies.* 15:395-402.

Zinner, Ellen S. 1992. Setting Standards: Certification Efforts and Considerations in the Field of Death and Dying. *Death Studies.* 16:67-77.

Zusman, Marty E. and Tschetter, Paul. 1984. Selecting Whether to Die at Home or in a Hospital Setting. *Death Education.* 8:365-381.

Zussman, Robert. 1992. *Intensive Care: Medical Ethics and the Medical Profession.* Chicago: The University of Chicago Press.

Index